T0138853

Robust and Error-Free Geometric Computing

Robust and Error-Free
Geometric Computing

Dave Eberly

CRC Press
Taylor & Francis Group
Boca Raton London New York

CRC Press is an imprint of the
Taylor & Francis Group, an **informa** business

CRC Press
Taylor & Francis Group
6000 Broken Sound Parkway NW, Suite 300
Boca Raton, FL 33487-2742

© 2020 by Taylor & Francis Group, LLC
CRC Press is an imprint of Taylor & Francis Group, an Informa business

No claim to original U.S. Government works

Printed on acid-free paper
International Standard Book Number-13: 978-0-3673-5294-3 (Hardback)

Visit the Taylor & Francis Web site at
http://www.taylorandfrancis.com

and the CRC Press Web site at
http://www.crcpress.com

CV 07.10.2020 0250

Contents

Preface   xi

Trademarks   xv

List of Figures   xvii

List of Tables   xix

Listings   xxi

1   Introduction   1
   1.1   Eigendecomposition for 3×3 Symmetric Matrices   6
      1.1.1   Computing the Eigenvalues   7
      1.1.2   Computing the Eigenvectors   7
      1.1.3   A Nonrobust Floating-Point Implementation   8
      1.1.4   A Robust Floating-Point Implementation   16
         1.1.4.1   Computing the Eigenvalues   17
         1.1.4.2   Computing the Eigenvectors   19
      1.1.5   An Error-Free Implementation   22
   1.2   Distance between Line Segments   22
      1.2.1   Nonparallel Segments   23
      1.2.2   Parallel Segments   26
      1.2.3   A Nonrobust Floating-Point Implementation   26
      1.2.4   A Robust Floating-Point Implementation   29
         1.2.4.1   Conjugate Gradient Method   29
         1.2.4.2   Constrained Conjugate Gradient Method . .   30
      1.2.5   An Error-Free Implementation   33

2   Floating-Point Arithmetic   35
   2.1   Binary Encodings   36
   2.2   Binary Encoding of 32-bit Floating-Point Numbers   36
   2.3   Binary Encoding of 64-bit Floating-Point Numbers   39
   2.4   Rounding of Floating-Point Numbers   41
      2.4.1   Round to Nearest with Ties to Even   42
      2.4.2   Round to Nearest with Ties to Away   42
      2.4.3   Round toward Zero   43
      2.4.4   Round toward Positive   44

| | 2.4.5 | Round toward Negative | 44 |
| | 2.4.6 | Rounding Support in C++ | 44 |

3 Arbitrary-Precision Arithmetic   **47**
	3.1	Binary Scientific Notation	47
	3.2	Binary Scientific Numbers	48
		3.2.1 Addition	49
		3.2.2 Subtraction	50
		3.2.3 Multiplication	50
	3.3	Binary Scientific Rationals	51
		3.3.1 Addition and Subtraction	52
		3.3.2 Multiplication and Division	52
	3.4	Conversions	52
		3.4.1 Floating-Point Number to BSNumber	53
		3.4.2 BSNumber to Floating-Point Number	54
		3.4.3 BSRational to BSNumber of Specified Precision	57
		3.4.4 BSNumber to BSNumber of Specified Precision	60
	3.5	Performance Considerations	62
		3.5.1 Static Computation of Maximum Precision	62
		3.5.1.1 Addition and Subtraction	63
		3.5.1.2 Multiplication	64
		3.5.2 Dynamic Computation of Maximum Precision	68
		3.5.3 Memory Management	68

4 Interval Arithmetic   **71**
	4.1	Arithmetic Operations	72
	4.2	Signs of Determinants	79
	4.3	Primal Queries	81
		4.3.1 Queries in 2D	81
		4.3.2 Queries in 3D	85

5 Quadratic-Field Arithmetic   **89**
	5.1	Sources of Rounding Errors	90
		5.1.1 Rounding Errors when Normalizing Vectors	90
		5.1.2 Errors in Roots to Quadratic Equations	91
		5.1.3 Intersection of Line and Cone Frustum	91
	5.2	Real Quadratic Fields	94
		5.2.1 Arithmetic Operations	95
		5.2.2 Allowing for Non-Square-Free d	96
		5.2.3 Allowing for Rational d	97
	5.3	Comparisons of Quadratic Field Numbers	98
	5.4	Quadratic Fields with Multiple Square Roots	101
		5.4.1 Arithmetic Operations	101
		5.4.2 Composition of Quadratic Fields	102
	5.5	Estimating a Quadratic Field Number	103

5.5.1   Estimating a Rational Number 103
5.5.2   Estimating the Square Root of a Rational Number . . 104
5.5.3   Estimating a 1-Root Quadratic Field Number 107
5.5.4   Estimating a 2-Root Quadratic Field Number 110
      5.5.4.1   Two Nonzero Radical Coefficients 111
      5.5.4.2   Three Nonzero Radical Coefficients 120

6   Numerical Methods   **127**
6.1   Root Finding 127
   6.1.1   Function Evaluation 128
   6.1.2   Bisection 131
   6.1.3   Newton's Method 135
   6.1.4   Hybrid Newton-Bisection Method 138
   6.1.5   Arbitrary-Precision Newton's Method 139
6.2   Polynomial Root Finding 141
   6.2.1   Discriminants 142
   6.2.2   Preprocessing the Polynomials 144
   6.2.3   Quadratic Polynomial 145
   6.2.4   Cubic Polynomial 147
      6.2.4.1   Nonsimple Real Roots 147
      6.2.4.2   One Simple Real Root 148
      6.2.4.3   Three Simple Real Roots 149
   6.2.5   Quartic Polynomial 152
      6.2.5.1   Processing the Root Zero 153
      6.2.5.2   The Biquadratic Case 153
      6.2.5.3   Multiplicity Vector $(3,1,0,0)$ 154
      6.2.5.4   Multiplicity Vector $(2,2,0,0)$ 154
      6.2.5.5   Multiplicity Vector $(2,1,1,0)$ 154
      6.2.5.6   Multiplicity Vector $(1,1,1,1)$ 155
   6.2.6   High-Degree Polynomials 160
      6.2.6.1   Bounding Root Sequences by Derivatives . . 161
      6.2.6.2   Bounding Roots by Sturm Sequences 162
      6.2.6.3   Root Counting by Descartes' Rule of Signs . 164
      6.2.6.4   Real-Root Isolation 164
6.3   Linear Algebra 165
   6.3.1   Systems of Linear Equations 165
   6.3.2   Eigendecomposition for 2×2 Symmetric Matrices . . 169
   6.3.3   Eigendecomposition for 3×3 Symmetric Matrices . . 170
   6.3.4   3D Rotation Matrices with Rational Elements 172

7   Distance Queries   **175**
7.1   Introduction 175
   7.1.1   The Quadratic Programming Problem 176
   7.1.2   The Linear Complementarity Problem 176
   7.1.3   The Convex Quadratic Programming Problem 177

		7.1.3.1	Eliminating Unconstrained Variables	177
		7.1.3.2	Reduction for Equality Constraints	178
7.2	Lemke's Method			179
	7.2.1	Terms and Framework		180
	7.2.2	LCP with a Unique Solution		181
	7.2.3	LCP with Infinitely Many Solutions		183
	7.2.4	LCP with No Solution		185
	7.2.5	LCP with a Cycle		186
	7.2.6	Avoiding Cycles when Constant Terms are Zero		187
7.3	Formulating a Geometric Query as a CQP			190
	7.3.1	Distance Between Oriented Boxes		190
	7.3.2	Test-Intersection of Triangle and Cylinder		191
7.4	Implementation Details			193
	7.4.1	The LCP Solver		193
	7.4.2	Distance Between Oriented Boxes in 3D		195
	7.4.3	Test-Intersection of Triangle and Cylinder in 3D		197
	7.4.4	Accuracy Problems with Floating-Point Arithmetic		199
	7.4.5	Dealing with Vector Normalization		201

8 Intersection Queries — **209**

8.1	Method of Separating Axes			210
	8.1.1	Separation by Projection onto a Line		210
	8.1.2	Separation of Convex Polygons in 2D		211
	8.1.3	Separation of Convex Polyhedra in 3D		214
	8.1.4	Separation of Convex Polygons in 3D		215
	8.1.5	Separation of Moving Convex Objects		218
	8.1.6	Contact Set for Moving Convex Objects		222
8.2	Triangles Moving with Constant Linear Velocity			222
	8.2.1	Two Moving Triangles in 2D		223
	8.2.2	Two Moving Triangles in 3D		229
8.3	Linear Component and Sphere			233
	8.3.1	Test-Intersection Queries		234
		8.3.1.1	Line and Sphere	234
		8.3.1.2	Ray and Sphere	235
		8.3.1.3	Segment and Sphere	236
	8.3.2	Find-Intersection Queries		237
		8.3.2.1	Line and Sphere	237
		8.3.2.2	Ray and Sphere	237
		8.3.2.3	Segment and Sphere	238
8.4	Linear Component and Box			239
	8.4.1	Test-Intersection Queries		240
		8.4.1.1	Lines and Boxes	240
		8.4.1.2	Rays and Boxes	243
		8.4.1.3	Segments and Boxes	246
	8.4.2	Find-Intersection Queries		249

	8.4.2.1	Liang–Barsky Clipping	250
	8.4.2.2	Lines and Boxes	254
	8.4.2.3	Rays and Boxes	255
	8.4.2.4	Segments and Boxes	257
8.5	Line and Cone		259
	8.5.1	Definition of Cones	259
	8.5.2	Practical Matters for Representing Infinity	261
	8.5.3	Definition of a Line, Ray and Segment	261
	8.5.4	Intersection with a Line	262
	8.5.4.1	Case $c_2 \neq 0$	262
	8.5.4.2	Case $c_2 = 0$ and $c_1 \neq 0$	263
	8.5.4.3	Case $c_2 = 0$ and $c_1 = 0$	264
	8.5.5	Clamping to the Cone Height Range	264
	8.5.6	Pseudocode for Error-Free Arithmetic	265
	8.5.6.1	Intersection of Intervals	265
	8.5.6.2	Line-Cone Query	266
	8.5.7	Intersection with a Ray	273
	8.5.8	Intersection with a Segment	274
	8.5.9	Implementation using Quadratic-Field Arithmetic	276
8.6	Intersection of Ellipses		277
	8.6.1	Ellipse Representations	277
	8.6.1.1	The Standard Form for an Ellipse	278
	8.6.1.2	Conversion to a Quadratic Equation	278
	8.6.2	Test-Intersection Query for Ellipses	279
	8.6.3	Find-Intersection Query for Ellipses	282
	8.6.3.1	Case $d_4 \neq 0$ and $e(\bar{x}) \neq 0$	284
	8.6.3.2	Case $d_4 \neq 0$ and $e(\bar{x}) = 0$	285
	8.6.3.3	Case $d_4 = 0$, $d_2 \neq 0$ and $e_2 \neq 0$	287
	8.6.3.4	Case $d_4 = 0$, $d_2 \neq 0$ and $e_2 = 0$	288
	8.6.3.5	Case $d_4 = 0$ and $d_2 = 0$	288
8.7	Intersection of Ellipsoids		293
	8.7.1	Ellipsoid Representations	293
	8.7.1.1	The Standard Form for an Ellipsoid	293
	8.7.1.2	Conversion to a Quadratic Equation	294
	8.7.2	Test-Intersection Query for Ellipsoids	294
	8.7.3	Find-Intersection Query for Ellipsoids	294
	8.7.3.1	Two Spheres	295
	8.7.3.2	Sphere-Ellipsoid: 3-Zero Center	295
	8.7.3.3	Sphere-Ellipsoid: 2-Zero Center	296
	8.7.3.4	Sphere-Ellipsoid: 1-Zero Center	298
	8.7.3.5	Sphere-Ellipsoid: No-Zero Center	298
	8.7.3.6	Reduction to a Sphere-Ellipsoid Query	299

9 Computational Geometry Algorithms   **301**
    9.1   Convex Hull of Points in 2D   301
          9.1.1   Incremental Construction   302
          9.1.2   Divide-and-Conquer Method   309
    9.2   Convex Hull of Points in 3D   315
          9.2.1   Incremental Construction   315
          9.2.2   Divide-and-Conquer Method   318
    9.3   Delaunay Triangulation   321
          9.3.1   Incremental Construction   322
                  9.3.1.1   Inserting Points   323
                  9.3.1.2   Linear Walks and Intrinsic Dimension   323
                  9.3.1.3   The Insertion Step   325
          9.3.2   Construction by Convex Hull   327
    9.4   Minimum-Area Circle of Points   329
    9.5   Minimum-Volume Sphere of Points   333
    9.6   Minimum-Area Rectangle of Points   335
          9.6.1   The Exhaustive Search Algorithm   335
          9.6.2   The Rotating Calipers Algorithm   337
                  9.6.2.1   Computing the Initial Rectangle   339
                  9.6.2.2   Updating the Rectangle   340
                  9.6.2.3   Distinct Supporting Vertices   341
                  9.6.2.4   Duplicate Supporting Vertices   341
                  9.6.2.5   Multiple Polygon Edges of Minimum Angle .   343
                  9.6.2.6   The General Update Step   345
          9.6.3   A Robust Implementation   345
                  9.6.3.1   Avoiding Normalization   346
                  9.6.3.2   Indirect Comparisons of Angles   347
                  9.6.3.3   Updating the Support Information   347
                  9.6.3.4   Conversion to a Floating-Point Rectangle . .   348
    9.7   Minimum-Volume Box of Points   349
          9.7.1   Processing Hull Faces   350
                  9.7.1.1   Comparing Areas   351
                  9.7.1.2   Comparing Volumes   351
                  9.7.1.3   Comparing Angles   352
          9.7.2   Processing Hull Edges   352
          9.7.3   Conversion to a Floating-Point Box   353

Bibliography   **355**

Index   **359**

Preface

Computer programming has always been of interest to me as a mechanism to study mathematics and geometry. My mathematics graduate study was at the University of Colorado, completed in 1984. The topic was the qualitative behavior of solutions to a simplified model of solid fuel combustion formulated as a nonlinear parabolic partial differential equation. I was able to obtain some insight into the behavior by programming a numerical differential equation solver, using the Crank–Nicholson method and Gauss–Seidel iteration, and visualizing the results using computer graphics. The desktop computer I used had an Intel 80486 CPU, an Intel 80487 floating-point coprocessor and an enhanced graphics adapter (EGA). These days you might find such hardware in a museum about ancient computing devices.

In 2011, I had the opportunity to revisit the topic for a paper in the Rocky Mountain Journal of Mathematics that was dedicated to the advisor of my mathematics advisor. I implemented the numerical differential equation solver using pixel shaders on an NVIDIA GeForce 9800 GT. Yes, the hardware had evolved signicantly, but even so the idea of compute shaders and GPGPU was in its infancy. The numerical solutions for the combustion models were computed in a reasonable amount of time, allowing for saving the data to disk and creating video clips of the simulation. The experiments consisted of solving the model numerically for dimensions 1, 2 and 3 on rectangular lattice domains of sizes 256, 256^2 and 256^3, respectively. An experiment generated the fuel temperature values on the lattice at 2^{20} time steps. For each time step, the Gauss–Seidel iteration was applied 8 times. The execution times, including memory bandwidth costs between CPU and GPU, were 44 milliseconds, 79 milliseconds and 12879 milliseconds, respectively for the dimensions.

Now in 2019, the numerical computing and visual display using GPGPU and compute shaders or NVIDIA's CUDA occur in real time. A much more complicated fluid dynamics simulation using Navier–Stokes equations is available as part of the downloadable source code at the Geometric Tools website, `https://www.geometrictools.com`. This simulation runs at 60 frames per second on a Microsoft Windows 10 desktop computer with an NVIDIA GeForce GTX 1080. It runs at 120 frames on an Ubuntu Linux 18.04 desktop computer with an NVIDIA GeForce GTX 1070.

Early in my career, I participated in the video game industry. The computers we worked on had Intel Pentium processors (the pre-core era) and 3dfx cards (hardware rasterization). I was impressed with the computation power of the graphics accelerators, but computing graphics, physics and mathematics on a CPU was relatively slow. Video games required realism at real-time rates, so accuracy and robustness were typically sacrificed for speed. Physical simulations suffered badly in this tradeoff. Over the years of graphics hardware evolution, and with the introduction of CPU cores and GPGPU, I could see that as computing power increased, the tradeoff could be revisited with the anticipation of obtaining better robustness and accuracy without sacrificing speed.

Later in my career I was exposed to enough applications having a geometric flavor that I drifted towards geometric computing. This type of computing has haunted me to the point of wanting to obtain exact results despite the costs. I had to wait until retirement in order to spend full time on the endeavor. This book and its accompanying source code are the outcome of the effort for obtaining robust or exact computing for geometric algorithms. Many of the ideas are not unique and have been used for years. In particular, computing with arbitrary-precision (rational) arithmetic or with interval arithmetic is necessary for correct implementations of standard computational geometry algorithms such as generating a convex hull or Delaunay triangulation. Some of the ideas might be new to you. In particular, much of this book involves the topic of quadratic-field arithmetic, which is a mixture of rational and symbolic arithmetic that is typically found in packages such as Mathematica. However, one of the design goals of the C++ source code involves template programming to encapsulate the implementations in a manner that allows the user simply to choose the arithmetic type as a template parameter rather than have to use separate implementations per type. This gives the quadratic-field arithmetic a flavor different from that of commercial computer algebra software.

As with all my books, source code can be found at the Geometric Tools website. I had hoped to make the book an encyclopedic reference with applications of the ideas to a large collection of geometric algorithms, but that would have made the book significantly more expensive than it should be. Moreover, I would still be writing for the next several years. Instead, as geometric algorithms are implemented based on the concepts in the book, I will post them to the website with PDF documentation describing the implementations. One topic that I did not include in this book is an arithmetic system based on algebraic numbers. Several sections on eigendecomposition actually use arithmetic operations for such systems, but there is a need for additional infrastructure; specifically, comparisons of numbers in an algebraic-number-based arithmetic system must be supported. As a bonus feature for this book, the Geometric Tools website has a PDF that describes the full infrastructure for algebraic-number-based arithmetic systems, and source code is provided.

I wish to thank the reviewers of the book proposal: Dennis Wenzel, Alan McIntyre and Dinesh Manocha. They all had great comments about how to structure the book, what to include and what not to include. Another big thanks go to Justin Hunt, a friend in the United Kingdom, who once again agreed to redraw my badly drawn line art. Thanks to my editor Rick Adams for supporting me in publishing this book and encouraging me to think smaller than 1000 pages. Finally, thanks to the production team at Taylor & Francis and CRC Press for its usual superior job of finalizing all the details necessary to publish the book.

Trademarks

- Microsoft Windows, Microsoft DirectX and Microsoft Visual Studio are trademarks of Microsoft Corporation.

- Intel is a registered trademark and Intel Core is a trademark of Intel Corporation.

- Mathematica is a registered trademark of Wolfram Research, Inc.

- IEEE Standard 754-2008 is a trademark of IEEE.

- NVIDIA GeForce and CUDA are trademarks of NVIDIA Corporation.

- 3dfx is a trademark of 3dfx Interactive. (The company was acquired by NVIDIA in 2000.)

List of Figures

1.1   The graph of $g(\beta) = \beta^3 - 3\beta - 1$ where $\det(B) = 1$.   18
1.2   Partitioning of the st-plane by the unit square $[0, 1]^2$.   24
1.3   Various level curves $R(s, t) = L$.   25

2.1   IEEE Binary32 encoding.   37
2.2   IEEE Binary64 encoding.   39
2.3   Round to nearest with ties to even.   42
2.4   Round to nearest with ties to away.   43
2.5   Round toward zero.   43
2.6   Round toward positive.   44
2.7   Round toward negative.   45

3.1   Numbers of type float on the real line.   55

4.1   An expression tree.   75

5.1   Specific geometric configuration for line and cone frustum. . .   92
5.2   Geometric configuration for Newton's method.   105
5.3   Graph of $f(t)$ for $a > b$ and $c = 0$.   112
5.4   Graph of $f(t)$ for $a = \sqrt{20}$ and $b = \sqrt{6}$.   115
5.5   Graph of $f(t)$ for $a = \sqrt{24}$ and $b = \sqrt{3}$.   116
5.6   Graph of $f(t)$ for $a > b > c > 0$.   120

6.1   Graph of $G(t) = (1 - \cos t)/t^2$ for $t \in [0, 6\pi]$.   129
6.2   Graph of the implementation of $G(t)$ for small t-values. . . .   130
6.3   Mathematica graph of $G(t)$ for small t-values.   130

7.1   An LCP with a unique solution.   181
7.2   An LCP with infinitely many solutions.   184

8.1   Separated or overlapping polygons.   211
8.2   Feature contact of polygons.   212
8.3   Testing whether moving boxes will intersect.   221
8.4   Some triangle configurations for the first time of contact. . .   228
8.5   The Minkowski sum of an oriented box and a line.   240
8.6   The Minkowski sum of an oriented box and a ray.   244

8.7   Projections of an oriented box and a ray onto a line.   244
8.8   The Minkowski sum of an oriented box and a segment.   247
8.9   Projections of an oriented box and a segment onto a line. . .   247
8.10 Line clipping against the x-faces of the box.   251
8.11 2D view of a single-sided cone.   260
8.12 Geometric configurations when $c_2 \neq 0$.   263
8.13 Geometric configurations when $c_2 = 0$ and $c_1 \neq 0$.   264
8.14 Geometric configuration when $c_0 = c_1 = c_2 = 0$.   264
8.15 Graph of ellipse $w^2 + c(x) = 0$ and polynomial $c(x)$.   283
8.16 Graph when $c_4 \neq 0$ and $\bar{e} \neq 0$.   284
8.17 Configurations for two spheres in find-intersection query. . . .   296

9.1   A point set and its convex hull.   302
9.2   A point and convex hull with upper and lower tangents. . . .   303
9.3   Relationships of a point to a line segment.   306
9.4   Two convex hulls and their upper and lower tangents.   311
9.5   Two convex hulls and the search for the lower tangent.   311
9.6   Extreme points to initialize search are on same vertical line. .   314
9.7   Merging a point and a convex hull.   316
9.8   Divide-and-conquer for 3D convex hulls.   319
9.9   A nonsimple terminator when merging hulls.   320
9.10 Triangulations of finite point sets.   321
9.11 The two triangulations for a convex quadrilateral.   322
9.12 Two circumcircles for triangles.   322
9.13 Linear walk through a mesh.   324
9.14 Retriangulating when point inside current triangulation. . . .   326
9.15 Retriangulating when point outside current triangulation. . .   328
9.16 Delaunay triangulation in 2D from convex hull in 3D.   328
9.17 Growing a candidate for minimum-area circle of points. . . .   330
9.18 Bounding rectangle containing polygon edge.   338
9.19 Two polygon edges are parallel to rectangle edges.   341
9.20 Duplicate supporting vertices.   342
9.21 Multiple polygon edges that attain the minimum angle. . . .   344

List of Tables

1.1   Bounds on the roots of $g(\beta)$.   19

2.1   Quantities of interest for binary32.   38
2.2   Quantities of interest for binary64.   41

4.1   Endpoints of the multiplication interval.   73

5.1   Estimating a 2-root quadratic field number.   111

6.1   Classification of roots for a depressed quartic polynomial. ...   152
6.2   Signs of the Sturm polynomials for $t^3 + 3t^2 - 1$.   163
6.3   Signs of the Sturm polynomials for $(t-1)^3$ at various t-values.   163

Listings

1.1   DXMath interfaces for computing a bounding box of points. .   8

1.2   Function CalculateEigenVectorsFromCovarianceMatrix.   8

1.3   Function SolveCubic.   9

1.4   Evaluate DXMath bounding box code.   10

1.5   Function CalculateEigenVector.   11

1.6   Function CalculateEigenVectors.   14

1.7   Robust computing eigenvector for multiplicity-1 eigenvalue. .   19

1.8   Robust computing orthogonal complement of vector.   20

1.9   Robust computing eigenvector for multiplicity-2 eigenvalue. .   21

1.10   Final eigenvector as cross product of other eigenvectors. . . .   22

1.11   Nonrobust computing distance between line segments.   26

1.12   Incorrect interior minimum point due to rounding errors. . .   28

1.13   Minimum point classified as interior rather than boundary. .   28

1.14   Robust computing distance between line segments.   31

1.15   Comparison of distance from different implementations. . . .   32

2.1   Union to access floating-point number or its bit pattern. . . .   36

2.2   Decoding a number of type float.   37

2.3   Decoding a number of type double.   39

2.4   Setting the rounding mode of the FPU.   45

3.1   Convert a subnormal float to a BSNumber.   53

3.2   Convert a normal float to a BSNumber.   53

3.3   Convert an infinity or NaN float to a BSNumber.   54

3.4   Convert a BSNumber in $(0, 2^{-149})$ to a subnormal float.   55

3.5   Convert a BSNumber in $[2^{-149}, 2^{-126})$ to a subnormal float. . . .   56

3.6   Convert a BSNumber in $[2^{-126}, 2^{128})$ to a normal float.   56

3.7   Convert a BSRational to a floating-point number.   58

3.8   Convert a BSNumber to a BSNumber with specified precision. .   60

3.9   Determine number of bits for arbitrary-precision operators. .   65

3.10   Determine number of bits for determinants.   66

3.11   Determine number of bits for specific input data set.   68

4.1   Compute intervals at leaf nodes of expression tree.   75

4.2   Compute intervals at interior nodes of expression tree.   76

4.3   Functions used to compute intervals of expression tree.   76

4.4   Interval arithmetic for $x * y + z * w - 2/(3 + t * u * v)$.   78

4.5   C++ interval arithmetic for $x * y + z * w - 2/(3 + t * u * v)$. .   78

4.6   Compute exact sign of determinant.   79

4.7   The wrapper class for primal queries.   81
4.8   Query for point location relative to a line.   82
4.9   Query for point location relative to a triangle.   83
4.10 Query for point location relative to a circumcircle.   84
4.11 Query for point location relative to a plane.   85
4.12 Query for point location relative to a triangle.   86
4.13 Query for point location relative to a circumsphere.   87
5.1   Approximation errors when normalizing a vector.   90
5.2   Comparison operators in C++.   98
5.3   Testing whether $w = x + y\sqrt{d}$ is equal to 0.   98
5.4   Testing whether $w = x + y\sqrt{d}$ is less than 0.   99
5.5   Estimate $\sqrt{a^2}$ to p bits of precision where a^2 is rational. . . .   105
5.6   Estimate a quadratic field number $z = x + y\sqrt{d}$.   107
5.7   Verify estimates of quadratic field numbers.   108
5.8   Estimate $a + b$ where a^2 and b^2 are rational.   113
5.9   Estimate $a - b$ where a^2 and b^2 are rational.   116
5.10 Verify $\nabla h \neq (0,0,0)$ on $\mathcal{D}$.   123
6.1   Naive floating-point implementation for $(1 - \cos(t))/t^2$. . . .   128
6.2   Robust floating-point implementation for $(1 - \cos(t))/t^2$. . . .   131
6.3   Floating-point bisection of a function.   132
6.4   Rational bisection of a function.   133
6.5   Fixed-precision rational bisection of a function.   133
6.6   Naive floating-point Newton's method.   135
6.7   More robust floating-point Newton's method.   136
6.8   Robust floating-point Newton's method.   136
6.9   Hybrid Newton-bisection root finding.   138
6.10 Fixed-precision rational Newton's method.   139
6.11 Floating-point quadratic roots.   145
6.12 Mixed rational floating-point quadratic roots.   146
6.13 Mixed rational floating-point cubic roots.   150
6.14 Mixed rational floating-point quartic roots.   156
6.15 Rational Gaussian elimination.   165
6.16 Rational Gauss-Seidel iteration.   166
6.17 Fixed-precision rational Gauss-Seidel iteration.   168
7.1   Polynomial less-than comparison.   188
7.2   LCPSolverShared base class.   193
7.3   Distance between two oriented boxes.   195
7.4   Test-intersection for triangle and finite cylinder.   197
7.5   Nonrobust floating-point negativity test in LCP solver.   199
7.6   Inaccurate distance because of rounding errors.   199
7.7   Rounding errors when normalizing cylinder axis direction. . .   201
7.8   Double-precision test-intersection for triangle and cylinder. .   202
7.9   Rational test-intersection for triangle and cylinder.   203
7.10 Quadratic-field test-intersection for triangle and cylinder. . .   204
7.11 Comparison of test-intersections for triangle and cylinder. . .   206

7.12 Triangle-cylinder intersection on cylinder cap. 207
8.1 Separating axis tests for 2D convex polygons. 212
8.2 Separating axis tests for 3D convex polyhedra. 214
8.3 Separating axis tests for 3D convex polygons. 216
8.4 Determine first contact time by separating axis tests. 218
8.5 Data structures to compute contact points for 2D triangles. . 223
8.6 Modified projection-sorting algorithm. 224
8.7 Modified update-times algorithm. 225
8.8 Determine contact between moving 2D triangles. 226
8.9 Determine contact set between moving 2D triangles. 228
8.10 Data structures to compute contact points for 3D triangles. . 230
8.11 Compute the configuration of a 3D triangle. 230
8.12 Determine contact set between moving 3D triangles. 231
8.13 Test-intersection for line and sphere. 234
8.14 Test-intersection for ray and sphere. 235
8.15 Test-intersection for segment and sphere. 236
8.16 Find-intersection for line and sphere. 237
8.17 Find-intersection for ray and sphere. 238
8.18 Find-intersection for segment and sphere. 238
8.19 Test-intersection for line and 3D oriented box. 241
8.20 Test-intersection for line and 3D aligned box. 242
8.21 Test-intersection for line and 3D aligned box. 243
8.22 Test-intersection for ray and 3D oriented box. 245
8.23 Test-intersection for ray and 3D aligned box. 246
8.24 Test-intersection for segment and 3D oriented box. 248
8.25 Test-intersection for segment and 3D aligned box. 248
8.26 Clipping code against $x = e_0$ when $x_d > 0$. 250
8.27 Clipping code against $x = e_0$ when $x_d < 0$. 252
8.28 Clipping code against $x = e_0$ when $x_d = 0$. 252
8.29 Clipping code against $x = -e_0$ when $x_d > 0$. 252
8.30 Clipping code against $x = -e_0$ when $x_d < 0$. 252
8.31 Clipping code against $x = -e_0$ when $x_d = 0$. 253
8.32 Liang–Barsky clipping of line to box face. 253
8.33 Clipping of line against 3D box. 254
8.34 Clipping of ray against 3D box. 255
8.35 Clipping of segment against 3D box. 257
8.36 Find-intersection for finite intervals. 265
8.37 Find-intersection for finite interval and semiinfinite interval. . 266
8.38 Find-intersection for line and cone. 267
8.39 Find-intersection for ray and cone. 273
8.40 Find-intersection for segment and cone. 274
8.41 Find-intersection for ellipses: $d_4 \neq 0$ and $e(\bar{x}) \neq 0$. 284
8.42 Find-intersection for ellipses: $d_4 \neq 0$ and $e(\bar{x}) = 0$. 286
8.43 Find-intersection for ellipses: $d_4 = 0$, $d_2 \neq 0$ and $e_2 \neq 0$. . . . 287
8.44 Find-intersection for ellipses: $d_4 = 0$, $d_2 \neq 0$ and $e_2 = 0$. . . . 288

8.45 Find-intersection for ellipses: $d_4 = 0$, $d_2 = 0$ and $e_2 = 0$. . . . 289
8.46 Find-intersection for ellipses: $d_4 = 0$, $d_2 = 0$ and $e_2 \neq 0$. . . . 290
9.1 Incremental construction of 2D convex hull. 302
9.2 Robust incremental construction of 2D convex hull. 304
9.3 Robust collinearity test for three points. 305
9.4 Merge operation when current hull is a line segment. 307
9.5 Merge operation when current hull is a convex polygon. . . . 307
9.6 Update convex hull for incoming point and tangent points. . 308
9.7 Divide-and-conquer algorithm: 2D convex hull. 309
9.8 Divide-and-conquer algorithm: recursive hull finding. 310
9.9 Divide-and-conquer algorithm: merge. 312
9.10 Divide-and-conquer algorithm: computing hull tangents. . . . 313
9.11 Incremental construction of 3D convex hull. 316
9.12 Recursive algorithm for minimum-area circle. 331
9.13 Nonrecursive algorithm for minimum-area circle. 332
9.14 Robust support update for minimum-area circle of points. . . 333
9.15 Recursive algorithm for minimum-volume sphere. 334
9.16 Nonrecursive algorithm for minimum-volume sphere. 334
9.17 $O(n^2)$ algorithm for minimum-area rectangle. 336
9.18 Smallest rectangle with edge coincident with polygon edge. . 339
9.19 Rectangle data structure for minimum-area rectangle. 348
9.20 Computing center and extents for minimum-area rectangle. . 348
9.21 Conversion of rectangle from rational to floating-point. . . . 349
9.22 Mutually orthogonal edge search for minimum-volume box. . 352
9.23 Box data structure for minimum-volume box. 353
9.24 Conversion of box from rational to floating-point. 354

Chapter 1

Introduction

Geometric algorithms are prevalent in a variety of fields including among others CAD-CAM, robotics, physical simulations and video games. If a field involves anything 3D, there is invariably a geometric component to it. Some of the algorithms might be relatively simple to formulate mathematically and then implement. In video games, given a 3D scene populated with a set of polyhedral objects, one might want to know what is visible along the line of sight. The abstract query is one of line-object intersection. Some of the algorithms might be more complicated to formulate. In robotics, a robot navigates through a 3D scene populated with objects and is required not to collide with any of those objects. A conservative approach in a simulation is to create convex polyhedra as bounding volumes for the objects and for the robot itself and then choose a path for the robot so that the robot's polyhedron bound does not intersect the other polyhedron bounds. The abstract query for computing the bounds involves determining the convex hull of point sets. And some of the algorithms might be quite complicated to formulate and implement. In CAD-CAM, a common operation is to compute the union or intersection of two closed 2-manifold triangle meshes, each representing the boundary of a complex object. Developing Boolean operations on meshes sounds simple enough, but the bookkeeping details and the underlying geometry and topology make implementing such algorithms tedious and challenging.

The mathematical formulations for geometric algorithms are only one part of the process. Another part is implementing the algorithms on a computer using IEEE Standard 754™-2008 floating-point arithmetic. In standard programming languages, the two choices for floating-point types are float, which is a 32-bit type with 24 bits of precision, or double, which is a 64-bit type with 53 bits of precision. The general rule of thumb for programmers is to use float when speed is preferred or double when accuracy is preferred. Graphics and physics engines for video games tend to use float. Scientific computing packages tend to use double. Regardless of which type used, rounding errors in the floating-point arithmetic can be a source of pain when implementing geometric algorithms.

This book is about ways to make the implementations of algorithms robust or error free. By *robust*, I mean that if floating-point arithmetic is chosen, the implementation of the algorithm is designed knowing where the sensitive portions are that are prone to rounding errors and then handling those portions in a manner that minimizes the impact of the errors on the output. By *error free*,

I mean that the implementation of the algorithm supports arbitrary-precision arithmetic and symbolic manipulation that leads to an exact mathematical representation of the output. Only at that time are estimates made, if necessary, to obtain floating-point results. The estimates allow for the user to specify the number of bits of precision.

One of the main problems with geometric algorithms involves branching that is based on signs of expressions computed using floating-point arithmetic. When you believe you have a nonrobust algorithm, it is necessary to analyze that algorithm and understand what happens if a sign misclassification steers the execution into a block of code that does not match the geometric configuration that is expected. Three expectations are presented next when redesigning an algorithm to be robust or error free:

1. It is necessary to understand the mathematical framework of the geometric or numeric problem. Are the presumably incorrect outputs of your unit testing due to rounding errors and lack of robustness? Or is the implementation itself incorrect?

2. It is necessary to understand that floating-point arithmetic is not the same as real-valued arithmetic. A mathematical algorithm that is correct for real-valued arithmetic might not be robust when computed using floating-point arithmetic. Naturally, your code has to be tied to the mathematics in some manner, but always keep in the back of your mind to be aware of each code block you write and how it might or might not be sensitive to floating-point rounding errors.

3. Select test examples that are nearly at the cutoff for switching between an if-block and an else-block. For example, if part of your code computes the length of a vector and then branches based on whether the length is positive or zero, select a test case where the length is nearly zero. Execute the code until you reach the if-test (length is positive) where the length is small. Continue the execution until you compute the final output. Now repeat the experiment to get to the if-test. Set the program counter to the else-block (length is zero) and continue the execution until you compute the final output. If the results are greatly different, you should think about whether or not the length test is appropriate. Perhaps the algorithm can be formulated differently so that it does not have an if-test that is so sensitive to a sign misclassification.

The source code that accompanies this book is the Geometric Tools Library (GTL). Many of the examples here use the GTL to illustrate the concepts of the book. The code is available online at https://www.geometrictools.com and contains much more than what is described here. The code is written using C++ and template programming so that the template parameters are chosen to be floating-point types or arbitrary-precision types. In cases where this cannot happen, a type-trait framework is provided to switch on whether the type is floating point or arbitrary precision.

A couple of examples are presented in this chapter as motivation for the topics discussed in the book. Each example includes a basic analysis of the algorithm followed by a nonrobust floating-point implementation and reasons why that is the case. A robust floating-point implementation is also provided, the design based on an analysis of why the nonrobust implementation can fail. Error-free implementations are mentioned, but the actual discussion is postponed until later in the book after all the computational framework is explained.

Section 1.1 contains a detailed analysis of the DirectX Mathematics library code for computing the eigenvalues and eigenvectors of 3×3 symmetric matrices. That code is used internally for supporting the construction of oriented bounding boxes for a set of points. The cubic polynomial whose roots are the eigenvalues is solved using a standard algorithm that is correct mathematically but suffers from rounding errors when using floating-point arithmetic. The eigenvector construction is mathematically flawed, but has some code that attempts to make the construction robust not realizing the implementation is incorrect.

Section 1.2 contains a detailed discussion about computing the distance between two line segments in any dimension. A straightforward implementation of the mathematical details works for most cases when computing with floating-point arithmetic, but when the segments are nearly parallel, rounding errors can cause the computed distances to be significantly different from the theoretical distances. The heart of the problem is the code for solving a system of two equations in two unknowns. The nearly parallel segments cause the matrix of the system to be nearly singular, leading to subtractive cancellation in numerators of some fractions followed by division with numbers nearly zero. The numerators are effectively noise and the division magnifies the noise greatly. A different mathematical approach is used instead for robustness. It uses a conjugate gradient algorithm to locate the minimum of a quadratic function of two variables.

Chapter 2 is a summary of basic properties of IEEE Standard 754™-2008 floating-point numbers and arithmetic. The bit patterns for the representations are important for implementing an arbitrary-precision arithmetic library. Of equal importance is the concept of rounding. IEEE floating-point arithmetic defines several rounding modes that can be selected by the programmer as needed. Two of these rounding modes—round toward positive and round toward negative—are necessary to support interval arithmetic. The rounding modes are also supported in the GTL arbitrary-precision arithmetic code.

Chapter 3 describes the mathematics for arbitrary-precision arithmetic as implemented in the GTL. However, it is possible to wrap any arbitrary-precision arithmetic library in order to use it for the concepts described in this book. The examples presented here use the GTL classes BSNumber (binary scientific numbers) and BSRational (binary scientific rationals) to illustrate the ideas and to execute the experiments listed here.

For many geometric algorithms, branching statements are based on testing the signs of arithmetic expressions to steer the execution into the correct block of code to handle the corresponding geometric configuration. This is particularly the case for compuational geometry algorithms such as convex hull construction and Delaunay triangulation. Other types of code have similar sign tests; for example, the classification of the roots and the determination of the root multiplicities of a polynomial involve sign testing of various expressions, so it is important to compute the signs correctly. Chapter 4 covers the topic of interval arithmetic for which the inputs and outputs of arithmetic expressions are intervals of floating-point numbers. The initial intervals are based on guarantees by the IEEE Standard 754™-2008 floating-point arithmetic regarding how the outputs of an arithmetic operation are related to the theoretical results. An addition can be performed so that the output is rounded up, becoming an upper bound for the sum. The addition can also be performed so that the output is rounded down, becoming a lower bound for the sum. The resulting interval becomes the input to arithmetic operations occurring downstream. For sign testing, the final interval of numbers is analyzed for whether or not it contains 0. If it does not, the theoretical value of the sign is known. If it does, the expressions are computed again using arbitrary-precision arithmetic. The hope is that the number of such restarts is small, so the amortized cost of using interval arithmetic is within the requirements for performance of the application. Even though interval arithmetic is most commonly used with floating-point arithmetic, there are applications where interval arithmetic of arbitrary-precision numbers is useful. Some of these occur in the examples presented in the book.

The most important chapter in the book regarding error-free computations is Chapter 5 on the topic of quadratic-field arithmetic. When implemented on a computer, this concept becomes a mixture of arbitrary-precision arithmetic and symbolic arithmetic that allows exact representations of outputs to geometric algorithms when those outputs involve square roots. Many algorithms involve square root computations, especially those used for normalizing vectors. The mathematics of quadratic fields is discussed, including the relaxation of constraints one typically encounters in an abstract algebra presentation of the topic. Arithmetic expressions are allowed that have multiple square roots, which is common in 3D algorithms that involve an orthogonal basis of vectors for which normalization is avoided to prevent rounding errors from entering the calculations. A detailed discussion is provided for how one estimates quadratic-field numbers to a user-specified number of bits of precision. At this time, the results are no longer error-free, but the only errors that occur in the entire implementation are those in estimating, which is fully under the user's control by specifying the precision.

The remaining four chapters are about specific topics where arbitrary-precision arithmetic and quadratic-field arithmetic are useful. Chapter 6 covers some standard topics in numerical methods. Most of the discussion is about root finding, and in particular for polynomial functions. A section on systems of linear equations shows that error-free results are not possible for very large systems because the cost of multiplication of arbitrary-precision arithmetic is enormous for numbers having many bits. However, arbitrary-precision libraries can be designed to allow the user to round the results using one of the IEEE rounding modes, effectively leading to a fixed-precision arithmetic library where the user may specify the precision itself. Such a library can be used to solve linear systems in a reasonable time with precision greater than offered by float or double. A final pair of sections describes error-free algorithms for computing an eigendecomposition of a 2×2 matrix or a 3×3 matrix. The eigendecomposition for 3×3 matrices uses a limited arithmetic system involving algebraic numbers and modular polynomial operations. The final outputs are a mixture of rational numbers and symbolic expressions for the eigenvalues, and only at that time is it necessary to estimate the results by floating-point numbers.

Chapter 7 is about computing distance between two geometric objects, usually both of convex polygonal type (linear component, convex polygon, convex polyhedron). The main topic is minimization of convex quadratic functions with linear inequality constraints, called convex quadratic programming. Such a problem can be converted to a linear complementarity problem (LCP), which can be solved iteratively to obtain an exact result when using arbitrary-precision arithmetic. The number of iterations is finite, although it is not always clear what the maximum number of iterations is. If the LCP is executed with floating-point arithmetic, sign misclassifications can lead to distances that are significantly incorrect, especially when the geometric objects have some type of parallelism relative to each other; for example, parallel segments or two boxes with a pair of parallel axes with one from each box. Some discussion is provided about avoiding vector normalization. Typically in a distance query, a unit-length vector is provided, say, for a line direction. If that vector was obtained by floating-point normalization, then it might not be unit length because of rounding errors. Many geometric algorithms can avoid this if the mathematical details lead to the squared length of the vector appearing in the computations or by using quadratic-field numbers where the square root expression represents the vector length.

Chapter 8 is about intersection queries between two geometric objects. A useful paradigm called the method of separating axes is discussed. It is easy to use for stationary objects, but it also applies to objects moving with constant linear velocities. In the motion case, the first time of contact can be computed. Three sections in this chapter are about the intersection of linear components with a sphere, a box or a cone. The first two are relatively simple and can be computed using arbitrary-precision arithmetic. The line-cone example is quite detailed, having a lot of code blocks, and requires a 2-root quadratic-field arithmetic system to produce error-free results. The final two sections in that chapter are about intersection queries for ellipses and ellipsoids. The test-intersection query is coordinate free and applies both to ellipses and ellipsoids. The algorithm is to create a function that has a unique root for positive real numbers. The function coefficients are computed exactly using arbitrary-precision arithmetic. The unique root is then found using iterative root-finding methods, so at that time the solution is no longer exact; however, the user specifies the precision for the root finding and thereby controlling the only source of rounding errors. The find-intersection query for ellipses is quite detailed and supports arbitrary-precision arithmetic. The find-intersection query for ellipsoids requires an eigendecomposition of a symmetric 3×3 matrix, which is implemented using a mixture of rational arithmetic and symbolic arithmetic. The latter involves a limited arithmetic system for algebraic numbers. The intersection set consists of points and/or curves. Numerical methods must be used to compute points on the curve, but each point can be computed to a user-specified precision.

Chapter 9 presents several standard computational geometry problems and shows how to solve them in an error-free manner using arbitrary-precision arithmetic and quadratic-field arithmetic. Two algorithms are described for computing the convex hull of points in 2D, namely, an incremental insertion algorithm and a divide-and-conquer algorithm. The convex hull of points in 3D is implemented using incremental insertion. The minimum-area circle of points in 2D and the minimum-volume sphere of points in 3D are implemented using Welzl's randomized algorithm. The minimum-area rectangle of points in 2D uses the method of rotating calipers. The minimum-volume box of points in 3D uses O'Rourke's theorem. The convex hull of the points is computed. The theorem says the minimum-volume box is supported by a face of the convex hull or by three mutually perpendicular edges of the convex hull. This algorithm is tedious to implement using error-free computation.

1.1   Eigendecomposition for 3×3 Symmetric Matrices

Let A be an $n \times n$ symmetric matrix with real-valued elements. Such matrices have only real-valued eigenvalues, and there must be n eigenvectors that form an orthonormal basis for $\mathbb{R}^n$. The matrix has an eigendecomposition $A = RDR^\mathsf{T}$, where R is an orthogonal matrix whose columns are eigenvectors and where D is a diagonal matrix whose diagonal entries are eigenvalues.

A standard mathematics course on linear algebra formulates the eigendecomposition as follows. If $A\mathbf{V} = t\mathbf{V}$ for some nonzero vector $\mathbf{V}$ and a scalar t, then t is said to be an eigenvalue of A with corresponding eigenvector $\mathbf{V}$. The vector equation can be rewritten as $(A - tI)\mathbf{V} = \mathbf{0}$, where I is the $n \times n$ identity matrix and $\mathbf{0}$ is the $n \times 1$ zero vector. In order for a nonzero vector to be the solution to a homogeneous linear system, the matrix $A - tI$ must be singular; that is, $\det(A - tI) = 0$. The determinant is a polynomial, say, $p(t) = \det(A - tI)$, which is called the *characteristic polynomial* for A. The roots of $p(t)$ are the eigenvalues of A. For a root t, the solutions to $(A - tI)\mathbf{V} = \mathbf{0}$ are found by row-reducing $A - tI$, identifying the free variables and solving for the basic variables in terms of the free variables. The number of free variables is the dimension of the vector subspace of $\mathbb{R}^n$ consisting of eigenvectors corresponding to t; this subspace is called the eigenspace of t. The number of free variables is also the multiplicity of the root t.

For $n = 2$, the algorithm described in the previous paragraph is reasonable to use when computing with floating-point arithmetic. However, for $n = 3$, various problems can arise. The remainder of this section assumes that $n = 3$.

1.1.1 Computing the Eigenvalues

The roots of a cubic polynomial can be computed using closed-form equations. Let $c(t) = t^3 + et^2 + ft + g$. The polynomial can be converted to the depressed cubic polynomial $\bar{c}(s) = s^3 + ps + q$, where $t = s - e/3$, $p = f - e^2/3$ and $q = g - ef/3 + 2e^3/27$. Define $h = q^2/4 + p^3/27$. If $h > 0$, $\bar{c}(s)$ has one real-valued root and a pair of roots that are complex conjugates. If $h < 0$, $\bar{c}(s)$ has three distinct roots. If $h = 0$ and $q = 0$, then $p = 0$ is forced and $\bar{c}(s)$ has the root 0 of multiplicity 3. If $h = 0$ and $p \neq 0$, then $\bar{c}(s)$ has one root $3q/p$ of multiplicity 1 and another root $-3q/(2p)$ of multiplicity 2. Otherwise, $\bar{c}(s)$ has three distinct roots,

$$
\begin{aligned}
s_0 &= 2\sqrt{-p/3}\,(\cos\theta) \\
s_1 &= -\sqrt{-p/3}\,(\cos\theta + \sqrt{3}\sin\theta) \\
s_2 &= -\sqrt{-p/3}\,(\cos\theta - \sqrt{3}\sin\theta)
\end{aligned}
\tag{1.1}
$$

where $\theta = \mathrm{acos}(-q/(2\sqrt{-p^3/27}))/3$. To convert back to the t-variable for the roots of $c(t)$, add $e/3$ to any computed root of $\bar{c}(s)$.

1.1.2 Computing the Eigenvectors

If $p(t) = (t - t_0)^3$, the root t_0 has multiplicity 3 and $A - t_0I$ is the zero matrix (rank 0). The eigenspace is 3-dimensional with an eigenvector basis $\{(1,0,0),(0,1,0),(0,0,1)\}$.

If $p(t) = (t - t_0)(t - t_1)(t - t_2)$ with distinct roots, each matrix $A - t_iI$ has rank 2. A search must be made for two linearly independent rows; there are three pairs to test. Once a pair is found, the cross product is an eigenvector for t_i. It suffices to compute an eigenvector for t_0 and an eigenvector for t_1. Eigenspaces are orthogonal to each other, so an eigenvector for t_2 is the cross product of an eigenvector for t_0 with an eigenvector for t_1.

If $p(t) = (t - t_0)^2(t - t_1)$, the root t_0 has multiplicity 2 with a 2-dimensional eigenspace and the matrix $A - t_0I$ has rank 1. Locate a nonzero row of $A - t_0I$, call it $\mathbf{U}$ and compute two vectors $\mathbf{V}_0$ and $\mathbf{V}_1$ that are orthogonal to $\mathbf{U}$ and are themselves orthogonal. The eigenspace for t_0 has basis $\{\mathbf{V}_0, \mathbf{V}_1\}$. For symmetric matrices, eigenvectors for distinct eigenvalues must be orthogonal, so it turns out that $\mathbf{U}$ is an eigenvector for t_1.

1.1.3   A Nonrobust Floating-Point Implementation

This section contains code excerpts from the DirectX Mathematics code that is available to developers; the version is DIRECTX_MATH_VERSION 313. I will refer to this code as the DXMath code. It uses the MIT License. In all code listings provided here, the license preamble found in the DXMath files is included to satisfy the copyright-notice condition of that license.

The direct implementation of the eigendecomposition algorithm described in this section for 3×3 symmetric matrices is typically ill conditioned. It can be found in the files DirectXCollision.h and DirectXCollision.inl and is used to support the construction of a bounding box that contains an array of points. Listing 1.1 shows the relevant interfaces.

```
//------------------------------------------------------------
// DirectXCollision.h - C++ Collision Math library
//
// Copyright (c) Microsoft Corporation. All rights reserved.
// Licensed under the MIT License.
//
// http://go.microsoft.com/fwlink/?LinkID=615560
//------------------------------------------------------------

struct BoundingOrientedBox
{
    // Other class members and functions are defined here.

    static void CreateFromPoints(BoundingOrientedBox& Out, size_t Count,
        const XMFLOAT3* pPoints, size_t Stride);
};

// Compute the roots to x^3 + e x^2 + f x + g and return them as t, u and v.
bool SolveCubic(float e, float f, float g, float* t, float* u, float* v);

// Compute an eigenvector for eigenvalue e of the covariance matrix.
XMVECTOR CalculateEigenVector(float m11, float m12, float m13, float m22,
    float m23, float m33, float e);

// Compute eigenvectors for the eigenvalues of the covariance matrix. Includes some
// postprocessing to ensure orthogonality.
bool CalculateEigenVectors(float m11, float m12, float m13, float m22,
    float m23, float m33, float e1, float e2, float e3, XMVECTOR* pV1,
    XMVECTOR* pV2, XMVECTOR* pV3);

// Compute eigenvectors for the eigenvalues of the covariance matrix.
bool CalculateEigenVectorsFromCovarianceMatrix(float Cxx, float Cyy,
    float Czz, float Cxy, float Cxz, float Cyz, XMVECTOR* pV1,
    XMVECTOR* pV2, XMVECTOR* pV3);
```

Listing 1.1: Interfaces for computing a bounding box for an array of points. The covariance matrix of the points is computed and its linearly independent eigenvectors are used as the box axis directions. The points are projected onto the axes to form three intervals, one per axis. The center of the box has components, one per interval midpoint.

The function CreateFromPoints calls CalculateEigenVectorsFromCovarianceMatrix, the latter shown in Listing 1.2.

```
//---
```

```
// DirectXCollision.inl — C++ Collision Math library
//
// Copyright (c) Microsoft Corporation. All rights reserved.
// Licensed under the MIT License.
//
// http://go.microsoft.com/fwlink/?LinkID=615560
//
bool CalculateEigenVectorsFromCovarianceMatrix(float Cxx, float Cyy,
    float Czz, float Cxy, float Cxz, float Cyz, XMVECTOR* pV1,
    XMVECTOR* pV2, XMVECTOR* pV3)
{
    // Calculate the eigenvalues by solving a cubic equation.
    float e = -(Cxx+Cyy+Czz);
    float f = Cxx*Cyy+Cyy*Czz+Czz*Cxx-Cxy*Cxy-Cxz*Cxz-Cyz*Cyz;
    float g = Cxy*Cxy*Czz+Cxz*Cxz*Cyy+Cyz*Cyz*Cxx-Cxy*Cyz*Cxz*2.0f
              -Cxx*Cyy*Czz;

    float ev1, ev2, ev3;
    if( !DirectX::Internal::SolveCubic(e,f,g,&ev1,&ev2,&ev3) )
    {
        // set them to arbitrary orthonormal basis set
        *pV1 = g_XMIdentityR0.v;
        *pV2 = g_XMIdentityR1.v;
        *pV3 = g_XMIdentityR2.v;
        return false;
    }

    return DirectX::Internal::CalculateEigenVectors(Cxx,Cxy,Cxz,Cyy,Cyz,
        Czz,ev1,ev2,ev3,pV1,pV2,pV3);
}
```

Listing 1.2: The CalculateEigenVectorsFromCovarianceMatrix function in the DX-Math code.

I was asked a technical support question about the minimum-volume box code at my website as an alternative to the DirectX Mathematics code. The client said that the DirectX Mathematics code was not producing acceptable bounding boxes for their point sets. They provided me with a data set that was built from a cube in the first octant with corner $(0,0,0)$ and side length 100 which was then rotated and translated. I determined the problem was numerical rounding errors in the SolveCubic code that is shown in Listing 1.3.

```
//
// DirectXCollision.inl — C++ Collision Math library
//
// Copyright (c) Microsoft Corporation. All rights reserved.
// Licensed under the MIT License.
//
// http://go.microsoft.com/fwlink/?LinkID=615560
//
bool SolveCubic(float e, float f, float g, float* t, float* u, float* v)
{
    float p, q, h, rc, d, theta, costh3, sinth3;

    // deberly: Compute coefficients for the depressed cubic t^3 + pt + q.
    p = f - e * e / 3.0f;
    q = g - e * f / 3.0f + e * e * e * 2.0f / 27.0f;

    // deberly: Compute the discriminant whose sign is used for root classification.
    h = q * q / 4.0f + p * p * p / 27.0f;
```

```
if( h > 0 )
{
    // deberly: This block cannot be reached theoretically for the characteristic
    // polynomial of a symmetric matrix.
    *t = *u = *v = 0.f;
    return false;  // only one real root
}

if( ( h == 0 ) && ( q == 0 ) )  // all the same root
{
    *t = - e / 3;
    *u = - e / 3;
    *v = - e / 3;

    return true;
}

// deberly: The special case handling of h = 0 and p ≠ 0 does not occur here.

// deberly: At this point it is guaranteed that h ≤ 0 and p ≤ 0. Moreover, if p = 0
// and q ≠ 0, then h > 0 and the code would have exited in the block testing h > 0.
// Consequently, p < 0.

// deberly: The argument of the sqrtf function is actually −p³/27 > 0, so the sqrtf is
// valid and the output is d ≥ 0. It is not clear why there is a test for d < 0. It is
// possible that rounding errors can cause q²/4 − h to be slightly negative, in which
// case the sqrtf function will return a NaN.
d = sqrtf( q * q / 4.0f − h );
if( d < 0 )
    rc = −powf( −d, 1.0f / 3.0f );
else
    rc = powf( d, 1.0f / 3.0f );

theta = XMScalarACos( −q / ( 2.0f * d ) );
costh3 = XMScalarCos( theta / 3.0f );
sinth3 = sqrtf( 3.0f ) * XMScalarSin( theta / 3.0f );
*t = 2.0f * rc * costh3 − e / 3.0f;
*u = −rc * ( costh3 + sinth3 ) − e / 3.0f;
*v = −rc * ( costh3 − sinth3 ) − e / 3.0f;

    return true;
}
```

Listing 1.3: The SolveCubic function in the DXMath code. I added comments
(tagged with deberly) to help describe what the function is doing.

The test program to evaluate the BoundingOrientedBox::CreateFromPoints function is in Listing 1.4.

```
int main()
{
    // The rotated and translated cube.
    std::vector<Vector3<float>> vertices =
    {
        Vector3<float>{−59.372719f,  26.978844f,  39.425350f},
        Vector3<float>{−29.475891f, 116.858276f,   7.364998f},
        Vector3<float>{1.924920f,  −16.858200f, −26.308300f},
        Vector3<float>{13.762627f,  26.978811f, 107.625198f},
        Vector3<float>{31.821747f,  73.021233f, −58.368652f,},
        Vector3<float>{43.659454f, 116.858246f,  75.564850f},
        Vector3<float>{75.060265f, −16.858232f,  41.891552f},
        Vector3<float>{104.957092f, 73.021202f,   9.831200f}
    };
```

```
DirectX :: BoundingOrientedBox  box;
DirectX :: BoundingOrientedBox :: CreateFromPoints (box,   vertices . size (),
    (DirectX :: XMFLOAT3 const*) vertices . data (),   sizeof (Vector3<float >));
// box.Center = (22.7921867, 50.0000229, 24.6282730)
// box.Extents = (82.1649017, 66.8582535, 82.9969254)
// box.Orientation = (-0.000000000, 0.000000000, -0.000000000, 1.00000000)

// Internally, the parameters of SolveCubic are
// e = -59999.9922, f = 1.19999974e+9, g = -7.99999787e+12
// p = 128.000000, q = 1048576.00, h = 2.74877972e+11
// Because h > 0, values t, u and v are all set to zero and the function returns false.
// The eigenvectors are then set to the default (1,0,0), (0,1,0) and (0,0,1).

// I executed the solver using exact rational arithmetic for e, f, g, p, q and h. The
// estimates below are those numbers rounded to double precision.
// re = -59999.994140625000, rf = 1199999765.6250050, rg = -7999997656250.1006
// rp = -6.4158812e-6, rq = 1.973604e-9, rh = -8.807716e-18
// The values h and rh have opposite signs and are orders of magnitude different.
// Rounding errors can have a very large bite to them. The eigenvalues were computed
// as 20000.0, 19999.9961 and 19999.9980.

// Executing my own eigensolver.
SymmetricEigensolver3x3<float > es;
std :: array<float , 3> eval;
std :: array<std :: array<float , 3>, 3> evec;
es (covar00 ,  covar01 ,  covar02 ,  covar11 ,  covar12 ,  covar22 ,  false ,  +1,
    eval ,  evec );
// eval =  19999.9941, 19999.9961, 19999.9980
// evec[0] =  0.0722742379, 0.997384787, 0.000000000
// evec[1] = -0.913869500, 0.0662224069, -0.400571018
// evec[2] = -0.399523437, 0.0289509650, 0.916265726
return  0;
}
```

Listing 1.4: A test program to evaluate the DXMath code for computing an oriented bounding box for a set of points.

The differences between SolveCubic p, q and h computed using floating-point arithmetic and the values computed using rational arithmetic are enormous. The class SymmetricEigensolver3x3 uses an iterative algorithm that is robust as recommended by the bible of matrix computations [14].

It turns out that the code for computing eigenvectors is also problematic; in fact, the output can be completely wrong. An attempt is made to infer the rank of $A - tI$ from numerical computations, which is known to be ill conditioned. Using rational arithmetic, the rank can be determined from an exact classification of the real-valued roots, a topic covered in Section 6.2. Listing 1.5 contains the DXMath source code for CalculateEigenVector.

```
//-----------------------------------------------------
// DirectXCollision.inl – C++ Collision Math library
//
// Copyright (c) Microsoft Corporation. All rights reserved.
// Licensed under the MIT License.
//
// http://go.microsoft.com/fwlink/?LinkID=615560
//-----------------------------------------------------
```

```
XMVECTOR CalculateEigenVector(float m11, float m12, float m13, float m22,
    float m23, float m33, float e)
{
```

// deberly: Compute the cross product of the first two rows of $M - eI$. This is an attempt
// to find two linearly independent rows whose cross product is an eigenvector, which
// implicitly assumes that e has multiplicity 1 so that the rank of $M - eI$ is 2.

```
    float fTmp[3];
    fTmp[0] = m12 * m23 - m13 * ( m22 - e );
    fTmp[1] = m13 * m12 - m23 * ( m11 - e );
    fTmp[2] = ( m11 - e ) * ( m22 - e ) - m12 * m12;

    XMVECTOR vTmp = XMLoadFloat3(reinterpret_cast<const XMFLOAT3*>(fTmp));
```

// deberly: The next statement is an exact comparison of vTmp to $(0,0,0)$.
// Floating-point rounding errors can lead to a nonzero vector with very small
// components, so there can be a misclassification here.

```
    if( XMVector3Equal( vTmp, XMVectorZero() ) ) // planar or linear
    {
```

// deberly: The first two rows of $M - eI$ are linearly dependent. This code appears
// to assume that the rank of $M - eI$ is 1 and searches only for a nonzero row.
// However, it is possible that (row1,row3) or (row2,row3) is a linearly independent
// pair, in which case the rank of $M - eI$ is 2 and we should not be in this block
// of code.
//
// The next block of code attempts to find a nonzero row of $M - eI$, which
// assumes the rank is 1, equivalent to e having multiplicity 2. Such a row is an
// eigenvector for the other eigenvalue e' that has multiplicity 1. The conditionals
// use exact comparison to find a row that is exactly $(0,0,0)$. Floating-point rounding
// errors can lead to a nonzero vector with very small components, so there can be a
// misclassification here. It is better to find the nonzero row of largest length.

```
        float f1, f2, f3;
```

// we only have one equation - find a valid one

```
        if( ( m11 - e != 0 ) || ( m12 != 0 ) || ( m13 != 0 ) )
        {
            f1 = m11 - e; f2 = m12; f3 = m13;
        }
        else if( ( m12 != 0 ) || ( m22 - e != 0 ) || ( m23 != 0 ) )
        {
            f1 = m12; f2 = m22 - e; f3 = m23;
        }
        else if( ( m13 != 0 ) || ( m23 != 0 ) || ( m33 - e != 0 ) )
        {
            f1 = m13; f2 = m23; f3 = m33 - e;
        }
        else
        {
```

// deberly: To get here, all three rows of $M - eI$ are zero, which implies M is
// diagonal with eigenvalue e of multiplicity 3. In this situation, $(1,0,0)$ is an
// eigenvector of M as are $(0,1,0)$ and $(0,0,1)$. The problem is that
// CalculateEigenVector is called for each of the three eigenvalues. When the
// eigenvalues are all the same, $(1,0,0)$ is returned every time, which does not
// produce an orthonormal basis of three eigenvectors.

// error, we'll just make something up - we have NO context

```
            f1 = 1.0f; f2 = 0.0f; f3 = 0.0f;
        }
```

// deberly: This code does not always produce an eigenvector. See the example
// provided later. Instead, if (f_1, f_2, f_3) is the nonzero row, then the eigenvectors
// are perpendicular to it. Construct two such vectors, themselves perpendicular.

```
// But this only works when you know e has multiplicity 2, which is not known
// within the outermost if-block.
if( f1 == 0 )
    vTmp = XMVectorSetX( vTmp, 0.0f );
else
    vTmp = XMVectorSetX( vTmp, 1.0f );

if( f2 == 0 )
    vTmp = XMVectorSetY( vTmp, 0.0f );
else
    vTmp = XMVectorSetY( vTmp, 1.0f );

if( f3 == 0 )
{
    vTmp = XMVectorSetZ( vTmp, 0.0f );
    // recalculate y to make equation work
    if( m12 != 0 )
        vTmp = XMVectorSetY( vTmp, -f1 / f2 );
}
else
{
    vTmp = XMVectorSetZ( vTmp, ( f2 - f1 ) / f3 );
}
}
// deberly: else V is an eigenvector for e

// deberly: 1e-5f and 1e5f are magic numbers. This is a hack that is not justified
// mathematically. If V is nearly zero, its components might have had all their most
// significant bits subtracted away, in which case multiplying by 1e5f just magnifies
// the noise.
if( XMVectorGetX( XMVector3LengthSq( vTmp ) ) > 1e-5f )
{
    return XMVector3Normalize( vTmp );
}
else
{
    // Multiply by a value large enough to make the vector nonzero.
    vTmp = XMVectorScale( vTmp, 1e5f );
    return XMVector3Normalize( vTmp );
}
}
```

Listing 1.5: The CalculateEigenVector function in the DXMath code. I added comments (tagged with deberly) to help describe what the function is doing.

As an example where the eigenvector construction does not produce the expected results, consider the matrix

$$C = \begin{bmatrix} 2 & 1 & 1 \\ 1 & 2 & 1 \\ 1 & 1 & 3 \end{bmatrix} \tag{1.2}$$

The eigenvalues of C are 1, $3 + \sqrt{2} \doteq 4.41421$ and $3 - \sqrt{2} \doteq 1.58579$, which are all distinct numbers. The corresponding eigenspaces are 1-dimensional. Unit-length eigenvectors are $(-1, 1, 0)/\sqrt{2}$ for eigenvalue 1, $(1, 1, \sqrt{2})/\sqrt{6}$ for eigenvalue $3 + \sqrt{2}$ and $(-1, -1, \sqrt{2})/\sqrt{6}$ for eigenvalue $3 - \sqrt{2}$. The internal call to SolveCubic by CalculateEigenVectorsFromCovarianceMatrix produces the eigenvalues 4.41421318, 0.999999285 and 1.58578694, in that order. Notice that the theoretical eigenvalue 1 is estimated by 0.999999285 because of floating-point rounding errors. The internal call to CalculateEigenVector for this eigen-value produces vTmp $= (-7.15255737e-07, -7.15255737e-07, 1.43051147e-06)$. The theoretical value is $(0,0,0)$ because the first two rows of $C - I$ are both $(1,1,1)$, which implies their cross product is the zero vector. The comparison of vTmp to $(0,0,0)$ fails, after which the squared length is computed. It is smaller than (the magic number) 10^{-5}, so the vec-tor is multiplied by (the magic number) 10^5 and normalized to obtain $(-0.408248276, -0.408248276, 0.816496551)$. This is not an eigenvector for eigenvalue 1, because all such correct eigenvectors have last component 0. Had the code computed the cross product of the first and third rows, it would have returned $(0.707106233, -0.707107246, 5.05761477e-7)$, which is an accu-rate estimate.

Another example is when $C = I$, the identity matrix. As predicted, the CalculateEigenVector calls also return $(1,0,0)$. The parent function that calls these is CalculateEigenVectors and is shown in Listing 1.6.

```
//────────────────────────────────────────────
// DirectXCollision.inl – C++ Collision Math library
//
// Copyright (c) Microsoft Corporation. All rights reserved.
// Licensed under the MIT License.
//
// http://go.microsoft.com/fwlink/?LinkID=615560
//────────────────────────────────────────────
bool CalculateEigenVectors(float m11, float m12, float m13, float m22,
    float m23, float m33, float e1, float e2, float e3, XMVECTOR* pV1,
    XMVECTOR* pV2, XMVECTOR* pV3)
{
    *pV1 = DirectX::Internal::CalculateEigenVector(
        m11, m12, m13, m22, m23, m33, e1 );
    *pV2 = DirectX::Internal::CalculateEigenVector(
        m11, m12, m13, m22, m23, m33, e2 );
    *pV3 = DirectX::Internal::CalculateEigenVector(
        m11, m12, m13, m22, m23, m33, e3 );

    bool v1z = false;
    bool v2z = false;
    bool v3z = false;

    XMVECTOR Zero = XMVectorZero();

    if ( XMVector3Equal( *pV1, Zero ) )
        v1z = true;

    if ( XMVector3Equal( *pV2, Zero ) )
        v2z = true;

    if ( XMVector3Equal( *pV3, Zero ))
        v3z = true;

    // check for non-orthogonal vectors
    bool e12 = (fabsf(XMVectorGetX(XMVector3Dot(*pV1,*pV2)))>0.1f);
    bool e13 = (fabsf(XMVectorGetX(XMVector3Dot(*pV1,*pV3)))>0.1f);
    bool e23 = (fabsf(XMVectorGetX(XMVector3Dot(*pV2,*pV3)))>0.1f);

    // deberly: This code is an acknowledgement that CalculateEigenvector is not
    // correctly implemented. Eigenvectors cannot be zero (by definition) and
    // eigenvectors for different eigenspaces must be orthogonal.
```

```
if ((v1z && v2z && v3z)   // deberly: all Vi are zero
  || (e12 && e13 && e23)  // deberly: all pairs (Vi,Vj) not perpendicular
  || (e12 && v3z)         // deberly: V3 zero, (V1,V2) not perpendicular
  || (e13 && v2z)         // deberly: V2 zero, (V1,V3) not perpendicular
  || (e23 && v1z))        // deberly: V1 zero, (V2,V3) not perpendicular
{
    // all eigenvectors are 0- any basis set
    *pV1 = g_XMIdentityR0.v;
    *pV2 = g_XMIdentityR1.v;
    *pV3 = g_XMIdentityR2.v;
    return true;
}

// deberly: V3 is not zero here. The goal is to construct two vectors V1 and V2
// that are orthogonal to V3. Nothing in the construction guarantees that V1 and
// V2 will be eigenvectors.
if ( v1z && v2z )
{
    XMVECTOR vTmp = XMVector3Cross( g_XMIdentityR1, *pV3 );
    if ( XMVectorGetX( XMVector3LengthSq( vTmp ) ) < 1e-5f )
    {
        vTmp = XMVector3Cross( g_XMIdentityR0, *pV3 );
    }
    *pV1 = XMVector3Normalize( vTmp );
    *pV2 = XMVector3Cross( *pV3, *pV1 );
    return true;
}

// deberly: similar comment as last block
if ( v3z && v1z )
{
    XMVECTOR vTmp = XMVector3Cross( g_XMIdentityR1, *pV2 );
    if ( XMVectorGetX( XMVector3LengthSq( vTmp ) ) < 1e-5f )
    {
        vTmp = XMVector3Cross( g_XMIdentityR0, *pV2 );
    }
    *pV3 = XMVector3Normalize( vTmp );
    *pV1 = XMVector3Cross( *pV2, *pV3 );
    return true;
}

// deberly: similar comment as last block
if ( v2z && v3z )
{
    XMVECTOR vTmp = XMVector3Cross( g_XMIdentityR1, *pV1 );
    if ( XMVectorGetX( XMVector3LengthSq( vTmp ) ) < 1e-5f )
    {
        vTmp = XMVector3Cross( g_XMIdentityR0, *pV1 );
    }
    *pV2 = XMVector3Normalize( vTmp );
    *pV3 = XMVector3Cross( *pV1, *pV2 );
    return true;
}

// deberly: At this point, at most one of the Vi is zero.

// deberly: V1 is zero or (V1,V2) are not perpendicular. V2 and V3 are not zero.
// Construct V1 perpendicular to V2 and V3.
if ( ( v1z ) || e12 )
{
    *pV1 = XMVector3Cross( *pV2, *pV3 );
    return true;
}

// deberly: similar comment as last block
```

```
if ( ( v2z ) || e23 )
{
    *pV2 = XMVector3Cross( *pV3, *pV1 );
    return true;
}

// deberly: similar comment as last block
if ( ( v3z ) || e13 )
{
    *pV3 = XMVector3Cross( *pV1, *pV2 );
    return true;
}

    return true;
}
```

Listing 1.6: The CalculateEigenVectors function in the DXMath code. I added comments (tagged with deberly) to help describe what the function is doing.

For $C = I$, the three eigenvectors computed by CalculateEigenVector are all $(1, 0, 0)$, so e12, e13 and e23 are all false. This causes the function to set the eigenvectors to the standard basis $(1, 0, 0)$, $(0, 1, 0)$, $(0, 0, 1)$, which luckily happens to be correct for this example. Generally, the incorrectness of CalculateEigenvector is what needs to be fixed. The CalculateEigenVectors function is a hack that attempts to postprocess the incorrect vectors and produce an orthogonal set. The resulting set might not consist of eigenvectors.

A word of warning: When an eigenvalue has multiplicity 2, an eigendecomposition algorithm can compute any pair of orthogonal eigenvectors in the 2-dimensional eigenspace. When an eigenvalue has multiplicity 3, the algorithm can compute any triple of orthogonal eigenvectors. Such is the curse of multiplicity. When using the covariance-matrix approach to computing oriented bounding boxes, repeated (or numerically nearly repeated) eigenvalues can lead to boxes that are not a good fit. In the example discussed previously, the 8 points are the vertices of a cube, so theoretically the covariance matrix has a single eigenvalue of multiplicity 3. The numerical solvers can return any 3 orthogonal vectors, including in worst case those vectors that lead to the maximum-area box containing the points.

1.1.4   A Robust Floating-Point Implementation

An algorithm that is robust in practice is provided at the Wikipedia page [36] in the section entitled **3 × 3 matrices**. The eigenvalue construction is similar to that of the DXMath code, where the depressed cubic polynomial is generated first. However, an additional step is used to scale the polynomial so that the roots are in the interval $[-2, 2]$. The same trigonometric identity for cosine is used to provide closed-form equations for the eigenvalues.

The Wikipedia discussion includes pseudocode and a reference to a 1961 paper in the Communications of the ACM entitled *Eigenvalues of a symmetric 3 × 3 matrix*. Some important details are omitted from the Wikipedia page. In particular, it is helpful to visualize the graph of the cubic polynomial $\det(\beta I - B) = \beta^3 - 3\beta - \det(B)$ in order to understand the location of the polynomial roots. This information is essential to compute eigenvectors for a repeated root. The Wikipedia page mentions briefly the mathematical details for generating the eigenvectors, but the discussion does not make it clear how to do so robustly in a computer program.

Let A be a real-valued symmetric 3×3 matrix,

$$A = \begin{bmatrix} a_{00} & a_{01} & a_{02} \\ a_{01} & a_{11} & a_{12} \\ a_{02} & a_{12} & a_{22} \end{bmatrix} \tag{1.3}$$

The *trace* of a matrix A, denoted $\text{trace}(A)$, is the sum of the diagonal entries of A. The determinant of A is denoted $\det(A)$. The characteristic polynomial for A is

$$f(\alpha) = \det(\alpha I - A) = \alpha^3 - c_2 \alpha^2 + c_1 \alpha - c_0 \tag{1.4}$$

where I is the 3×3 identity matrix and where

$$c_2 = \text{trace}(A), \quad c_1 = \left(\text{trace}^2(A) - \text{trace}(A^2)\right)/2, \quad c_0 = \det(A) \tag{1.5}$$

Given scalars $p > 0$ and q, define the matrix B by $A = pB + qI$. It is the case that A and B have the same eigenvectors. If $\mathbf{v}$ is an eigenvector of A, then by definition, $A\mathbf{v} = \alpha\mathbf{v}$ where α is an eigenvalue of A; moreover,

$$\alpha\mathbf{v} = A\mathbf{v} = pB\mathbf{v} + q\mathbf{v} \tag{1.6}$$

which implies $B\mathbf{v} = ((\alpha - q)/p)\mathbf{v}$. Therefore, $\mathbf{v}$ is an eigenvector of B with corresponding eigenvalue $\beta = (\alpha - q)/p$, or equivalently $\alpha = p\beta + q$. If the eigenvalues and eigenvectors of B are computed, these equations allow converting them to the eigenvalues and eigenvectors of A.

1.1.4.1 Computing the Eigenvalues

Define $q = \text{trace}(A)/3$ and $p = \sqrt{\text{trace}\left((A - qI)^2\right)/6}$ so that $B = (A - qI)/p$. The Wikipedia discussion does not point out that B is defined only when $p \neq 0$. If A is a scalar multiple of the identity, then $p = 0$. On the other hand, the pseudocode at the Wikipedia page has special handling for a diagonal matrix A, which happens to include the case $p = 0$. The remainder of the construction here assumes $p \neq 0$. Some algebraic manipulation will show that $\text{trace}(B) = 0$ and the characteristic polynomial is

$$g(\beta) = \det(\beta I - B) = \beta^3 - 3\beta - \det(B) \tag{1.7}$$

Choosing $\beta = 2\cos(\theta)$, the characteristic polynomial becomes

$$g(\theta) = 2\left(4\cos^3(\theta) - 3\cos(\theta)\right) - \det(B) \tag{1.8}$$

Using the trigonometric identity $\cos(3\theta) = 4\cos^3(\theta) - 3\cos(\theta)$ produces

$$g(\theta) = 2\cos(3\theta) - \det(B) \tag{1.9}$$

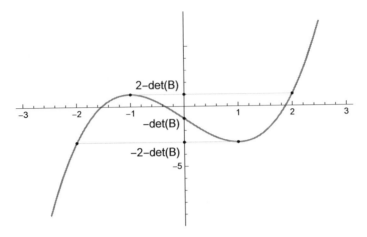

FIGURE 1.1: The graph of $g(\beta) = \beta^3 - 3\beta - 1$ where $\det(B) = 1$. The graph was drawn using [44].

The roots of g are obtained by solving for θ in the equation $\cos(3\theta) = \det(B)/2$. Knowing that B has only real-valued roots, it must be that θ is real-valued which implies $|\cos(3\theta)| \leq 1$. This additionally implies that $|\det(B)| \leq 2$. The real-valued roots of $g(\theta)$ are

$$\beta = 2\cos\left(\theta + \frac{2\pi k}{3}\right), \quad k = 0, 1, 2 \tag{1.10}$$

where $\theta = \arccos(\det(B)/2)/3$, and all roots are in the interval $[-2, 2]$.

The function $g(\beta)$ can be examined in greater detail. The first derivative is $g'(\beta) = 3\beta^2 - 3$, which is zero when $\beta = \pm 1$. The second derivative is $g''(\beta) = 3\beta$, which is not zero when $g'(\beta) = 0$. Therefore, $\beta = -1$ produces a local maximum of g and $\beta = +1$ produces a local minimum of g. The graph of g has an inflection point at $\beta = 0$ because $g''(0) = 0$. A typical graph is shown in Figure 1.1. The roots of $g(\beta)$ are indeed in the interval $[-2, 2]$. Generally, $g(-2) = g(1) = -2 - \det(B)$, $g(-1) = g(2) = 2 - \det(B)$ and $g(0) = -\det(B)$. The roots are named so that $\beta_0 \leq \beta_1 \leq \beta_2$. It is known that $\beta_0 + \beta_1 + \beta_2 = 0$ because $\mathrm{trace}(B) = 0$. Define $\phi_0 = \theta + 2\pi/3$, $\phi_1 = \theta + 4\pi/3$ and $\phi_2 = \theta$. Table 1.1 shows bounds for the roots. It is also known that $\beta_0 + \beta_1 + \beta_2 = 0$ because $\mathrm{trace}(B) = 0$.

As mentioned previously, the case of diagonal A is handled separately, so the polynomial $g(\beta)$ has roots in one of two categories. The first category is that there is a root of multiplicity 2 and a root of multiplicity 1. This occurs when $\det(B) = \pm 2$; the roots are ± 1. The eigenvector construction can be handled as a special case. The second is that all three roots are simple, in which case the eigenspaces are 1-dimensional.

Computing the eigenvectors for distinct and *well-separated* eigenvalues

TABLE 1.1: Bounds on the roots of $g(\beta)$.

$\det(B) > 0$	$\phi_0 \in (2\pi/3, 5\pi/6)$	$\cos(\phi_0) \in (-\sqrt{3}/2, -1/2)$	$\beta_0 \in (-\sqrt{3}, -1)$
	$\phi_1 \in (4\pi/3, 3\pi/2)$	$\cos(\phi_1) \in (-1/2, 0)$	$\beta_1 \in (-1, 0)$
	$\phi_2 \in (0, \pi/6)$	$\cos(\phi_2) \in (\sqrt{3}/2, 1)$	$\beta_2 \in (\sqrt{3}, 2)$
$\det(B) < 0$	$\phi_0 \in (5\pi/6, \pi)$	$\cos(\phi_0) \in (-1, -\sqrt{3}/2)$	$\beta_0 \in (-2, -\sqrt{3})$
	$\phi_1 \in (3\pi/2, 5\pi/3)$	$\cos(\phi_1) \in (0, 1/2)$	$\beta_1 \in (0, 1)$
	$\phi_2 \in (\pi/6, \pi/3)$	$\cos(\phi_2) \in (1/2, \sqrt{3}/2)$	$\beta_2 \in (1, \sqrt{3})$
$\det(B) = 0$	$\phi_0 = 5\pi/6$	$\cos(\phi_0) = -\sqrt{3}/2$	$\beta_0 = -\sqrt{3}$
	$\phi_1 = 3\pi/2$	$\cos(\phi_1) = 0$	$\beta_1 = 0$
	$\phi_2 = \pi/6$	$\cos(\phi_2) = \sqrt{3}/2$	$\beta_2 = \sqrt{3}$

is generally robust. However, if a root is repeated (or two roots are nearly the same numerically), issues can occur when computing the 2-dimensional eigenspace. Fortunately, the special form of $g(\beta)$ leads to a robust algorithm.

1.1.4.2 Computing the Eigenvectors

The discussion is based on constructing an eigenvector for β_0 when $\beta_0 < 0 < \beta_1 \leq \beta_2$. The implementation must also handle the construction of an eigenvector for β_2 when $\beta_0 \leq \beta_1 < 0 < \beta_2$. The corresponding eigenvalues of A are α_0, α_1, and α_2, ordered as $\alpha_0 \leq \alpha_1 \leq \alpha_2$. The eigenvectors for α_0 are solutions to $(A - \alpha_0 I)\mathbf{v} = \mathbf{0}$. The matrix $A - \alpha_0 I$ is singular (by definition of eigenvalue) and in this case has rank 2; that is, two rows are linearly independent. Write the system of equations as shown next,

$$\begin{bmatrix} 0 \\ 0 \\ 0 \end{bmatrix} = \mathbf{0} = (A - \alpha_0 I)\mathbf{v} = \begin{bmatrix} \mathbf{r}_0^\mathsf{T} \\ \mathbf{r}_1^\mathsf{T} \\ \mathbf{r}_2^\mathsf{T} \end{bmatrix} \mathbf{v} = \begin{bmatrix} \mathbf{r}_0 \cdot \mathbf{v} \\ \mathbf{r}_1 \cdot \mathbf{v} \\ \mathbf{r}_2 \cdot \mathbf{v} \end{bmatrix} \qquad (1.11)$$

where $\mathbf{r}_i$ are the 3×1 vectors whose transposes are the rows of the matrix $A - \alpha_0 I$. Assuming the first two rows are linearly independent, the conditions $\mathbf{r}_0 \cdot \mathbf{v} = 0$ and $\mathbf{r}_1 \cdot \mathbf{v} = 0$ imply $\mathbf{v}$ is perpendicular to both rows. Consequently, $\mathbf{v}$ is parallel to the cross product $\mathbf{r}_0 \times \mathbf{r}_1$. Normalize the cross product to obtain a unit-length eigenvector.

It is unknown which two rows of the matrix are linearly independent, so all pairs of rows must be processed. If two rows are nearly parallel, the cross product will have length nearly zero. For numerical robustness, this suggests looking at the three possible cross products of rows and choose the pair of rows for which the cross product has largest length. Alternatively, elementary row and column operations could be applied to reduce the matrix so that the last row is (numerically) the zero vector; this effectively is the algorithm of using Gaussian elimination with full pivoting. In the pseudocode shown in Listing 1.7, the cross product approach is used.

```
void ComputeEigenvector0(Matrix3x3 A, Real eigenvalue0,
    Vector3& eigenvector0)
{
```

```
Vector3 row0(A(0,0) - eigenvalue0, A(0,1), A(0,2));
Vector3 row1(A(0,1), A(1,1) - eigenvalue0, A(1,2));
Vector3 row2(A(0,2), A(1,2), A(2,2) - eigenvalue0);
Vector3 r0xr1 = Cross(row0, row1);
Vector3 r0xr2 = Cross(row0, row2);
Vector3 r1xr2 = Cross(row1, row2);
Real d0 = Dot(r0xr1, r0xr1);
Real d1 = Dot(r0xr2, r0xr2);
Real d2 = Dot(r1xr2, r1xr2);
Real dmax = d0;
int imax = 0;
if (d1 > dmax) { dmax = d1; imax = 1; }
if (d2 > dmax) { imax = 2; }
if (imax == 0)
{
    eigenvector0 = r0xr1 / sqrt(d0);
}
else if (imax == 1)
{
    eigenvector0 = r0xr2 / sqrt(d1);
}
else
{
    eigenvector0 = r1xr2 / sqrt(d2);
}
}
```

Listing 1.7: Pseudocode for computing the eigenvector corresponding to the eigenvalue α_0 of A that was generated from the root β_0 of the cubic polynomial for B that has multiplicity 1.

If the other two eigenvalues are well separated, the algorithm of Listing 1.7 may be used for each eigenvalue. However, if the two eigenvalues are nearly equal, Listing 1.7 can have numerical issues. The problem is that theoretically when the eigenvalue is repeated $(\alpha_1 = \alpha_2)$, the rank of $A - \alpha_1 I$ is 1. The cross products of any pair of rows is the zero vector. Determining the rank of a matrix numerically is ill conditioned.

A different approach is used to compute an eigenvector of $A - \alpha_1 I$. The eigenvectors corresponding to α_1 and α_2 are perpendicular to the eigenvector **W** of α_0. Compute unit-length vectors **U** and **V** such that $\{\mathbf{U}, \mathbf{V}, \mathbf{W}\}$ is a right-handed orthonormal set; that is, the vectors are all unit length, mutually perpendicular and $\mathbf{W} = \mathbf{U} \times \mathbf{V}$. The computations can be done robustly using floating-point arithmetic, as shown in Listing 1.8.

```
void ComputeOrthogonalComplement(Vector3 W, Vector3& U, Vector3& V)
{
    Real invLength;
    if (fabs(W[0]) > fabs(W[1]))
    {
        // The component of maximum absolute value is either W[0] or W[2].
        invLength = 1 / sqrt(W[0] * W[0] + W[2] * W[2]);
        U = Vector3(-W[2] * invLength, 0, +W[0] * invLength);
    }
    else
    {
        // The component of maximum absolute value is either W[1] or W[2].
        invLength = 1 / sqrt(W[1] * W[1] + W[2] * W[2]);
        U = Vector3(0, +W[2] * invLength, -W[1] * invLength);
    }
    V = Cross(W, U);
```

}

Listing 1.8: Robust computation of **U** and **V** for a specified **W**.

A unit-length eigenvector **E** of $A - \alpha_1 I$ must be a circular combination of **U** and **V**; that is, $\mathbf{E} = x_0 \mathbf{U} + x_1 \mathbf{V}$ for some choice of x_0 and x_1 with $x_0^2 + x_1^2 = 1$. There are exactly two such unit-length eigenvectors when $\alpha_1 \neq \alpha_2$ but infinitely many when $\alpha_1 = \alpha_2$.

Define the 3×2 matrix $J = [\mathbf{U} \, \mathbf{V}]$ whose columns are the specified vectors. Define the 2×2 symmetric matrix $M = J^\mathsf{T}(A - \alpha_1 I)J$. Define the 2×1 vector $\mathbf{X} = J\mathbf{E}$ whose rows are x_0 and x_1. The 3×3 linear system $(A - \alpha_1 I)\mathbf{E} = \mathbf{0}$ reduces to the 2×2 linear system $M\mathbf{X} = \mathbf{0}$. M has rank 1 when $\alpha_1 \neq \alpha_2$, in which case M is not the zero matrix, or rank 0 when $\alpha_1 = \alpha_2$, in which case M is the zero matrix. Numerically, the cases must be detected and handled properly.

In the event M is not the zero matrix, select the row of M that has largest length and normalize it. A solution **X** is perpendicular to the normalized row, so choose **X** with unit length. The normalization first factors out the largest component of the row and discards it to avoid floating-point underflow or overflow when computing the length of the row. If M is the zero matrix, then any choice of unit-length **X** suffices. Listing 1.9 contains pseudocode for computing a unit-length eigenvector corresponding to α_1.

```
void ComputeEigenvector1(Matrix3x3 A, Vector3 eigenvector0,
    Real eigenvalue1, Vector3& eigenvector1)
{
    Vector3 AU = A*U, AV = A*V;
    Real m00 = Dot(U, AU) - eigenvalue1;
    Real m01 = Dot(U, AV);
    Real m11 = Dot(V, AV) - eigenvalue1;
    Real absM00 = fabs(m00), absM01 = fabs(m01), absM11 = fabs(m11);
    if (absM00 >= absM11)
    {
        Real maxAbsComp = max(absM00, absM01);
        if (maxAbsComp > 0)
        {
            if (absM00 >= absM01)
            {
                m01 /= m00;  m00 = 1 / sqrt(1 + m01 * m01);  m01 *= m00;
            }
            else
            {
                m00 /= m01;  m01 = 1 / sqrt(1 + m00 * m00);  m00 *= m01;
            }
            eigenvector1 = m01 * U - m00 * V;
        }
        else
        {
            eigenvector1 = U;
        }
    }
    else
    {
        Real maxAbsComp = max(absM11, absM01);
        if (maxAbsComp > 0)
        {
            if (absM11 >= absM01)
            {
                m01 /= m11;  m11 = 1 / sqrt(1 + m01 * m01);  m01 *= m11;
```

```
        }
        else
        {
            m11 /= m01;   m01 = 1 / sqrt(1 + m11 * m11);   m11 *= m01;
        }
        eigenvector1 = m11 * U - m01 * V;
    }
    else
    {
        eigenvector1 = U;
    }
  }
}
```

Listing 1.9: Pseudocode for computing the eigenvector corresponding to the eigenvalue α_1 of A that was generated from the root β_1 of the cubic polynomial for B that potentially has multiplicity 2.

The remaining eigenvector must be perpendicular to the first two computed eigenvectors as shown in Listing 1.10.

```
ComputeEigenvector0(A, eigenvalue0, eigenvector0);
ComputeEigenvector1(A, eigenvector0, eigenvalue1, eigenvector1);
eigenvector2 = Cross(eigenvector0, eigenvector1);
```

Listing 1.10: The remaining eigenvector is simply a cross product of the first two computed eigenvectors, and it is guaranteed to be unit length (within numerical tolerance).

1.1.5   An Error-Free Implementation

A robust algorithm that uses exact arithmetic to obtain a correct result symbolically and can then be estimated with floating-point arithmetic is found in Section 6.3.3. The algorithm is based on manipulating symbolically the eigenvalues when constructing the eigenvectors, using modular polynomial operations so that the symbolic expressions involve only linear and quadratic polynomials of the eigenvalue.

1.2   Distance between Line Segments

The algorithm applies to segments in any dimension. Let the endpoints of the first segment be $\mathbf{P}_0$ and $\mathbf{P}_1$ and the endpoints of the second segment be $\mathbf{Q}_0$ and $\mathbf{Q}_1$. The segments can be parameterized by $\mathbf{P}(s) = (1-s)\mathbf{P}_0 + s\mathbf{P}_1$ for $s \in [0,1]$ and $\mathbf{Q}(t) = (1-t)\mathbf{Q}_0 + t\mathbf{Q}_1$ for $t \in [0,1]$.

The squared distance between two points on the segments is the quadratic function

$$R(s,t) = |\mathbf{P}(s) - \mathbf{Q}(t)|^2 = as^2 - 2bst + ct^2 + 2ds - 2et + f \qquad (1.12)$$

where

$$a = (\mathbf{P}_1 - \mathbf{P}_0) \cdot (\mathbf{P}_1 - \mathbf{P}_0), \quad b = (\mathbf{P}_1 - \mathbf{P}_0) \cdot (\mathbf{Q}_1 - \mathbf{Q}_0)$$
$$c = (\mathbf{Q}_1 - \mathbf{Q}_0) \cdot (\mathbf{Q}_1 - \mathbf{Q}_0), \quad d = (\mathbf{P}_1 - \mathbf{P}_0) \cdot (\mathbf{P}_0 - \mathbf{Q}_0), \quad (1.13)$$
$$e = (\mathbf{Q}_1 - \mathbf{Q}_0) \cdot (\mathbf{P}_0 - \mathbf{Q}_0), \quad f = (\mathbf{P}_0 - \mathbf{Q}_0) \cdot (\mathbf{P}_0 - \mathbf{Q}_0)$$

For nondegenerate segments, $a > 0$ and $c > 0$, but the implementation will allow degenerate segments and handle them correctly. In the degenerate cases, there is either a point-segment pair or a point-point pair. Observe that

$$ac - b^2 = |(\mathbf{P}_1 - \mathbf{P}_0) \times (\mathbf{Q}_1 - \mathbf{Q}_0)|^2 \geq 0 \quad (1.14)$$

The segments are not parallel when their direction vectors are linearly independent, in which case the cross product of directions is not zero and $ac - b^2 > 0$. In this case, the graph of $R(s,t)$ is a paraboloid and the level sets $R(s,t) = L$ for constants L are ellipses. The segments are parallel when $ac - b^2 = 0$, in which case the graph of $R(s,t)$ is a parabolic cylinder and the level sets are lines. Define $\Delta = ac - b^2$.

The goal is to minimize $R(s,t)$ over the unit square $[0,1]^2$. Because R is a continuously differentiable function, the minimum occurs either at an interior point of the square where the gradient $\nabla R = 2(as - bt + d, -bs + ct - e) = (0,0)$ or at a point on the boundary of the square. Define $F(s,t) = as - bt + d$ and $G(s,t) = -bs + ct - e$. The candidates for the minimum are the four corners $(0,0)$, $(1,0)$, $(0,1)$, and $(1,1)$; the four edge points $(\hat{s}_0, 0)$, $(\hat{s}_1, 1)$, $(0, \hat{t}_0)$ and $(1, \hat{t}_1)$, where $F(\hat{s}_0, 0) = 0$, $F(\hat{s}_1, 1) = 0$, $G(0, \hat{t}_0) = 0$ and $G(1, \hat{t}_1) = 0$; and $(\bar{s}, \bar{t})$ when $\Delta > 0$, where $F(\bar{s}, \bar{t}) = 0$ and $G(\bar{s}, \bar{t}) = 0$. Some computations will show that $\hat{s}_0 = -d/a$, $\hat{s}_1 = (b-d)/a$, $\hat{t}_0 = e/c$, $\hat{t}_1 = (b+e)/c$, $\bar{s} = (be - cd)/\Delta$ and $\bar{t} = (ae - bd)/\Delta$.

A simple algorithm is to compute all 9 critical points, the last one only when $\Delta > 0$, evaluate R at those points and then select the one that produces the minimum squared distance. However, this is a slow algorithm. A smarter search for the correct critical point is called for.

1.2.1   Nonparallel Segments

When $\Delta > 0$ the line segments are not parallel. The gradient of R is zero only when $\bar{s} = (be - cd)/\Delta$ and $\bar{t} = (bd - ae)/\Delta$. If $(\bar{s}, \bar{t}) \in [0,1]^2$, then it is the minimum of R; otherwise, the minimum must occur on the boundary of the square. To find the correct boundary, consider Figure 1.2, The central square labeled region 0 is the domain of R, $(s,t) \in [0,1]^2$. If $(\bar{s}, \bar{t})$ is in the interior of region 0, then the two closest points on the line segments are interior points of those segments.

Suppose $(\bar{s}, \bar{t})$ is in region 1. The level curves of R are ellipses. At the point where $\nabla R = (0,0)$, the level curve degenerates to a single point $(\bar{s}, \bar{t})$. The global minimum of R occurs there, call it $L_{\min}$. As the level values L increase from $L_{\min}$, the corresponding ellipses are increasingly farther away from $(\bar{s}, \bar{t})$.

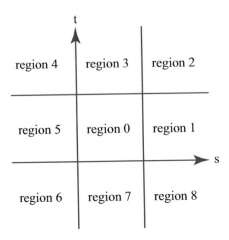

FIGURE 1.2: Partitioning of the st-plane by the unit square $[0,1]^2$.

There is a smallest level value L_0 for which the corresponding ellipse just touches the domain edge $s = 1$ at a value $\hat{t}_1 \in [0,1]$. For level values $L < L_0$, the corresponding ellipses do not intersect the domain. For level values $L > L_0$, portions of the domain lie inside the corresponding ellipses. In particular any points of intersection of such an ellipse with the edge must have a level value $L > L_0$. Therefore, $R(1,t) > R(1,\hat{t}_1)$ for $t \in [0,1]$ and $t \neq \hat{t}_1$. The point $(1,\hat{t}_1)$ provides the minimum squared-distance between two points on the line segments. The point on the first line segment is an endpoint and the point on the second line segment is interior to that segment. Figure 1.3 illustrates the idea by showing various level curves.

An alternate way of visualizing where the minimum distance point occurs on the boundary is to intersect the graph of R with the plane $s = 1$. The curve of intersection is a parabola and is the graph of $\phi(t) = R(1,t)$ for $t \in [0,1]$. Now the problem has been reduced by one dimension to minimizing a function $\phi(t)$ for $t \in [0,1]$. The minimum of $\phi(t)$ occurs either at an interior point of $[0,1]$, in which case $\phi'(t) = 0$ at that point, or at an endpoint $t = 0$ or $t = 1$. Figure 1.3 shows the case when the minimum occurs at an interior point. At that point the ellipse is tangent to the line $s = 1$. In the endpoint cases, the ellipse might touch just one of the corners of the domain but not necessarily tangentially.

To distinguish between the interior point and endpoint cases, the same partitioning idea applies in the one-dimensional case. The interval $[0,1]$ partitions the real line into three intervals, $t < 0$, $t \in [0,1]$ and $t > 1$. Let $\phi'(\tilde{t}) = 0$. If $\tilde{t} < 0$, then $\phi(t)$ is an increasing function for $t \in [0,1]$. The minimum restricted to $[0,1]$ must occur at $t = 0$, in which case R attains its minimum at $(s,t) = (1,0)$. If $\tilde{t} > 1$, then $\phi(t)$ is a decreasing function for $t \in [0,1]$. The minimum for ϕ occurs at $t = 1$ and the minimum for R occurs

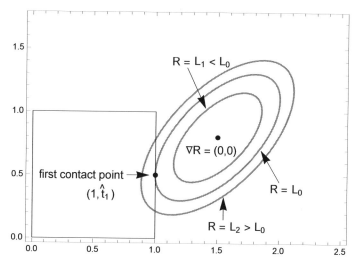

FIGURE 1.3: Various level curves $R(s,t) = L$. The plot was generated using [44].

at $(s,t) = (1,1)$. Otherwise, $\tilde{t} = \hat{t}_1 \in [0,1]$, ϕ attains its minimum at $\hat{t}_1$ and R attains its minimum at $(s,t) = (1,\hat{t}_1)$.

The occurrence of $(\bar{s},\bar{t})$ in region 3, 5 or 7 is handled in the same way as when the global minimum is in region 1. If $(\bar{s},\bar{t})$ is in region 3, then the minimum occurs at $(\hat{s}_1, 1)$ for some $\hat{s}_1 \in [0,1]$. If $(\bar{s},\bar{t})$ is in region 5, then the minimum occurs at $(0,\hat{t}_0)$ for some $t \in [0,1]$. Finally, if $(\bar{s},\bar{t})$ is in region 7, then the minimum occurs at $(\hat{s}_0, 0)$ for some $\hat{s}_0 \in [0,1]$. Determining whether the first contact point is at an interior or endpoint of the appropriate interval is handled in the same way discussed earlier.

If $(\bar{s},\bar{t})$ is in region 2, it is possible the level curve of R that provides first contact with the domain touches either edge $s = 1$ or edge $t = 1$. Let $\nabla R = (R_s, R_t)$ where R_s and R_t are the first-order partial derivatives of R. Because the global minimum occurs in region 2, it must be that the partial derivatives cannot both be positive. The choice is made for edge $s = 1$ or $t = 1$ based on the signs of $R_s(1,1)$ and $R_t(1,1)$. If $R_s(1,1) > 0$, then $R_t(1,1) \leq 0$. As the edge $s = 1$ is traversed towards $(1,1)$, $R(1,t)$ must decrease to $R(1,1)$. The directional derivative $(-1,0) \cdot (R_s(1,1), R_t(1,1)) = -R_s(1,1) < 0$, which means R must decrease from $R(1,1)$ as the edge $t = 1$ is traversed towards $(0,1)$. Therefore, the minimum must occur on the edge $t = 1$. Similarly, if $R_t(1,1) > 0$, then $R_s(1,1) \leq 0$. As the edge $t = 1$ is traversed towards $(1,1)$, $R(s,1)$ must decrease to $R(1,1)$. The directional derivative $(0,-1) \cdot (R_s(1,1), R_t(1,1)) = -R_t(1,1) < 0$, which means R must decrease from $R(1,1)$ as the edge $s = 1$ is traversed towards $(1,0)$. Therefore, the minimum must occur on the edge $s = 1$. In the final case that $R_s(1,1) \leq 0$ and

$R_t(1,1) \leq 0$, the minimum occurs at $(1,1)$. Determining whether the minimum is interior to the edge or an endpoint is handled similarly to the case of region 1. The occurence of $(\bar{s}, \bar{t})$ in regions 4, 6 or 8 is handled similarly.

1.2.2 Parallel Segments

When $\Delta = 0$, the segments are parallel and the gradient of R is zero on an entire st-line, $as - bt + d = 0$ for all real-valued t. If this line intersects the domain in a segment, then all points on that segment attain the minimum squared distance. Geometrically, this means that the projection of one segment onto the line containing the other segment is an entire interval of points. If the line $as - bt + 0$ does not intersect the domain, then only a pair of endpoints attains minimum squared distance, one endpoint per segment. In parameter space, the minimum is attained at a corner of the domain. In either case, it is sufficient to search the boundary of the domain for the critical point that leads to a minimum.

The quadratic factors to $R(s,t) = a(s - bt/a)^2 + 2d(s - bt/a) + f$, where $ac = b^2$, $e = bd/a$ and $b \neq 0$. R is constant along lines of the form $s - bt/a = k$ for constants k, and the minimum of R occurs on the line $as - bt + d = 0$. This line must intersect both the s-axis and the t-axis because a and b are not zero. Because of parallelism, the line is also represented by $-bs + ct - e = 0$.

1.2.3 A Nonrobust Floating-Point Implementation

The implementation of the algorithm was designed so that at most one floating-point division occurs when computing the minimum distance and corresponding closest points. Moreover, the division was deferred until needed—in some cases no division was needed.

The logic for computing parameters for closest points on segments is shown in the Listing 1.11. The design goal was to minimize division operations for speed. The cost of divisions is not as big an issue as it was many years ago, unless an application must call the distance query at real-time rates for a large number of segment pairs.

```
// Code goes here for computing a, b, c, d, e with dot products.
det = a*c - b*b;
if (det > 0) // nonparallel segments
{
    bte = b*e, ctd = c*d;
    if (bte <= ctd)  // s <= 0
    {
        if (e <= zero)  // t <= 0 (region 6)
        {
            s = (-d >= a ? 1 : (-d > 0 ? -d/a : 0));
            t = 0;
        }
        else if (e < c)  // 0 < t < 1 (region 5)
        {
            s = 0;
            t = e/c;
        }
```

```
            else   // t ≥ 1 (region 4)
            {
                s = (b−d >= a ? 1 : (b−d > 0 ? (b−d)/a : 0));
                t = 1;
            }
        }
    else   // s > 0
    {
        s = bte − ctd;
        if (s >= det)   // s ≥ 1
        {
            if (b+e <= 0)   // t ≤ 0 (region 8)
            {
                s = (−d <= 0 ? 0 : (−d < a ? −d/a : 1));
                t = 0;
            }
            else if (b+e < c)   // 0 < t < 1 (region 1)
            {
                s = 1;
                t = (b+e)/c;
            }
            else   // t ≥ 1 (region 2)
            {
                s = (b−d <= 0 ? 0 : (b−d < a ? (b−d)/a : 1));
                t = 1;
            }
        }
        else   // 0 < s < 1
        {
            ate = a*e, btd = b*d;
            if (ate <= btd)   // t ≤ 0 (region 7)
            {
                s = (−d <= 0 ? 0 : (−d >= a ? 1 : −d/a));
                t = 0;
            }
            else   // t > 0
            {
                t = ate − btd;
                if (t >= det)   // t ≤ 1 (region 3)
                {
                    s = (b−d <= 0 ? 0 : (b−d >= a ? 1 : (b−d)/a));
                    t = 1;
                }
                else   // 0 < t < 1 (region 0)
                {
                    s /= det;
                    t /= det;
                }
            }
        }
    }
}
else // parallel segments
{
    if (e <= 0)
    {
        s = (−d <= 0 ? 0 : (−d >= a ? 1 : −d/a));
        t = 0;
    }
    else if (e >= c)
    {
        s = (b−d <= 0 ? 0 : (b−d >= a ? 1 : (b−d)/a));
        t = 1;
    }
    else
```

```
    {
        s = 0;
        t = e/c;
    }
}
```

Listing 1.11: Pseudocode for the nonrobust algorithm for computing closest points between two segments and the corresponding distance.

The code block for region 0 is shown in Listing 1.11. To arrive at this block, the presumption is that the minimum of $R(s,t)$ occurs at an interior point of the domain. The divisions by Δ were deferred until actually needed. The code conforms to the mathematics of the problem, but unfortunately when computing with floating-point arithmetic, the (s,t) value might not be accurate due to rounding errors in the division. Two problems can occur in the division. First, the numerators and denominator are both small, which can lead to inaccurate floating-point results. Listing 1.12 illustrates this using double-precision numbers.

```
// The input segments.
P0 = (-1.0264718499965966,    9.6163341007195407e-7, 0.0)
P1 = ( 0.91950808032415809, -1.0094441192690283e-6, 0.0)
Q0 = (-1.0629447383806110,    9.2709540082141753e-7, 0.0)
Q1 = ( 1.0811583868227901, -1.0670017179567367e-6, 0.0)

// Computations that lead to region 0.
a = 3.7868378892150543
b = 4.1723816501877566
c = 4.5971782115109665
d = 0.070975508796052952
e = 0.078201633969291237
det = 1.2079226507921703e-13
s = 5.0737192225369654e-14   // numerator before division by det
t = 4.8072656966269278e-14   // numerator before division by det
s = 0.42003676470588236      // after division by det
t = 0.39797794117647056      // after division by det

// The distance |((1 - s)P0 + sP1) - ((1 - t)Q0 + tQ1)|.
distance = 0.00055025506003679664

// The parameters using exact rational arithmetic with conversion back to double
// precision at the end. The conversion can lose some precision.
sTrue = 0.42457281934252261
tTrue = 0.40235148377129676

// The true distance is zero; there is no precision loss on conversion to double.
distanceTrue = 0
```

Listing 1.12: An example where the minimum point is interior but some numerical rounding errors lead to an inaccurate result.

Second, subtractive cancellation occurs when computing the numerators in the first place, leading to a misclassification; that is, the numerical computations steer the execution of the block for region 0, but theoretically the minimum occurs on the domain boundary. Listing 1.13 illustrates this.

```
// The input segments.
P0 = (-1.0896217473782599,    9.7236145595088601e-7, 0.0)
P1 = ( 0.91220578597858548, -9.4369829432107506e-7, 0.0)
```

```
Q0 = (-0.9001044750213623 7,    9.0671446351334441e-7,  0.0)
Q1 = ( 1.0730877178721130,     -9.8185787633992740e-7,  0.0)

// Computations that lead to region 0.
a = 4.0073134733092228
b = 3.9499904603425491
c = 3.8934874300993294
d = -0.37938089385085144
e = -0.37395400223322062
det = 1.7763568394002505e-15
s = 2.2204460492503131e-16   // numerator before division by det
t = 4.4408920985006262e-16   // numerator before division by det
s = 0.125     // after division by det
t = 0.25      // after division by det

// The distance |((1 - s)P₀ + sP₁) - ((1 - t)Q₀ + tQ₁)|.
distance = 0.43258687891076358

// The divisions are accurate but the numerators are not because of subtractive
// cancellation. The algorithm using exact arithmetic produces
// sTrue = 0.094672127942504153
// tTrue = 0
// distanceTrue = 1.1575046138574105e-7
```

Listing 1.13: An example where the minimum point is classified as interior but the theoretically correct point is on the domain boundary.

The exact value for the s-numerator $be - cd$ is of the form $1.u * 2^{-54}$, where u has 197 bits. The conversion to double produces -3.6091745045569584e-17, so in fact s is negative and the algorithm never gets into the region-0 block. The error due to the misclassification is enormous!

1.2.4   A Robust Floating-Point Implementation

The primary failure of the nonrobust implementation is when the computation of numerator $be - cd$ for s or numerator $ae - bd$ for t has subtractive cancellation. The division by a nearly zero Δ amplifies the error so that the computed (s, t) is a really bad estimate of the location of the minimum. It is not tractable to try refining the estimate because it is not clear in which direction to search for a better estimate.

1.2.4.1   Conjugate Gradient Method

Instead, use a *constrained conjugate gradient* approach, one that is robust numerically. To motivate this, note that the quadratic function to minimize is

$$R(s,t) = \begin{bmatrix} s & t \end{bmatrix} \begin{bmatrix} a & -b \\ -b & c \end{bmatrix} \begin{bmatrix} s \\ t \end{bmatrix} + 2 \begin{bmatrix} d & -e \end{bmatrix} \begin{bmatrix} s \\ t \end{bmatrix} + f \tag{1.15}$$

$$= \mathbf{p}^{\mathsf{T}} M \mathbf{p} + 2\mathbf{k}^{\mathsf{T}} \mathbf{p} + f$$

where $\mathbf{p}$ is the 2-tuple of s and t, and M and $\mathbf{k}$ are clear from context. The minimum of R occurs when its gradient is the zero vector,

$$\nabla R = 2M\mathbf{p} + 2\mathbf{k} = \mathbf{0} \tag{1.16}$$

The solution is

$$\mathbf{p} = -M^{-1}\mathbf{k} = \frac{-1}{ac - b^2} \begin{bmatrix} c & b \\ b & a \end{bmatrix} \begin{bmatrix} d \\ -e \end{bmatrix} = \frac{1}{ac - b^2} \begin{bmatrix} be - cd \\ ae - bd \end{bmatrix} \tag{1.17}$$

This solution is what needs to be computed numerically.

With no constraints on $\mathbf{p}$, the conjugate gradient method for minimization may be used to compute the minimum of R in two steps. The first step starts at any point $\mathbf{p}_0$ and computes the minimum of R along the line $\mathbf{p}_0 + u(1, 0)$. Let that point be named $\mathbf{p}_1$. The second step starts at the point and computes the minimum of R along the line $\mathbf{p}_1 + v\mathbf{D}$, where $\mathbf{D} = (D_0, D_1)$ is a *conjugate direction* corresponding to $(1, 0)$ relative to the matrix M. Such a direction has the property

$$0 = (1, 0) \cdot M\mathbf{D} = aD_0 - bD_1 \tag{1.18}$$

One such choice is $\mathbf{D} = (b, a)$. With constraints, the second step requires slightly more attention.

1.2.4.2   Constrained Conjugate Gradient Method

First, compute the parameter point $(\hat{s}_0, 0)$ that minimizes R along the line $t = 0$. The solution is $\hat{s}_0 = -d/a$. Second, compute the parameter point $(\hat{s}_1, 1)$ that minimizes R along the line $t = 1$. The solution is $\hat{s}_1 = (b - d)/a$. The difference of these points is

$$(\hat{s}_1, 1) - (\hat{s}_0, 0) = (b/a, 1) \tag{1.19}$$

which happens to be a conjugate direction for $(1, 0)$. Compute the intersection of the parameter domain and the line through these two points. If there is no intersection or the intersection is a single point, the minimum of R occurs at a corner of the domain. If there is a segment of intersection, the minimum of R must occur on that segment.

When there is a segment of intersection, let its endpoints be $\mathbf{E}_0$ and $\mathbf{E}_1$. Define $\phi(z) = R((1 - z)\mathbf{E}_0 + z\mathbf{E}_1)$ and $H(z) = \phi'(z)$ for $z \in [0, 1]$. The minimization is now a 1D problem. The minimum must occur when $H(z) = 0$ or at an endpoint of the interval, $z = 0$ or $z = 1$. The function $H(z)$ is linear, so a simple equation must be solved when $H(0)$ and $H(1)$ have opposite signs. If either of $H(0)$ and $H(1)$ is zero, then the corresponding (s, t) point is the location of where the gradient of R is $(0, 0)$. If $H(0)$ and $H(1)$ are both positive or both negative, the minimum of H occurs at the endpoint corresponding to the minimum absolute value of those derivatives.

The beauty of the approach is that when $H(z) = 0$ has a solution for $z \in (0, 1)$, then that solution is $\bar{z} = H(0)/(H(0) - H(1))$. If $H(0)$ is nearly zero and suffers from subtractive cancellation, then $H(0) - H(1)$ has the same sign and is nearly zero. If the numerical errors cause the computed $\bar{z}$ to be outside $[0, 1]$, simply clamp the result to the interval. $H(z)$ is nearly zero on the entire segment, so $\phi(z)$ (R on the segment) is nearly constant. The clamping will not significantly affect the accuracy of the distance, although it can affect the accuracy of the location of the minimum. Because the situation is 1D, the subtractive cancellation cannot steer the execution away from the line segment that contains the minimum. This is much better than in the 2D situation where the subtractive cancellation steers the execution away from the true minimum in an unknown direction.

The implementation is provided in the GTL code. In addition to the robustness for two nondegenerate segments, code was added to handle degenerate segments. Those cases are easy to understand, so focus on the nondegenerate segments. Consider the code shown in the Listing 1.14.

```
// Code goes here for computing a, b, c, d, e with dot products.
f00 = d, f10 = d + a, f01 = d - b, f11 = d + a - b;  // dR/ds at corners
g00 = -e, g10 = -e - b, g01 = -e + c, g11 = -e -b + c;  // dR/dt at corners
hatS[0] = GetClampedRoot(a, f00, f10);
hatS[1] = GetClampedRoot(a, f01, f11);
classify[0] = (hatS[0] <= 0 ? -1 : (hatS[0] >= 1 ? 1 : 0));
classify[1] = (hatS[1] <= 0 ? -1 : (hatS[1] >= 1 ? 1 : 0));
if (classify[0] == -1 && classify[1] == -1)
{
    // minimum occurs on s = 0 for 0 <= t <= 1
    parameter[0] = 0;
    parameter[1] = GetClampedRoot(c, g00, g01);
}
else if (classify[0] == +1 && classify[1] == +1)
{
    // minimum occurs on s = 1 for 0 <= t <= 1
    parameter[0] = 1;
    parameter[1] = GetClampedRoot(c, g10, g11);
}
else
{
    // The line dR/ds = 0 intersects domain [0, 1]^2 in a nondegenerate segment.
    // The edge[i] flags store which domain edge contains the endpoint end[i].
    int edge[2];
    Real end[2][2];
    ComputeIntersection(hatS, classify, end);

    // Analyze the function H(z) = dR/dt((1 - z) * end[0] + z * end[1]) for z ∈ [0, 1].
    ComputeMinimumParameters(hatS, edge, end, parameter);
}

Real GetClampedRoot(Real sigma, Real h0, Real h1)
{
    if (h0 >= 0) { return 0; }
    if (h1 <= 0) { return 1; }
    Real root = -h0 / sigma;
    if (root > 1) { root = 0.5; }
    return root;
}
```

Listing 1.14: Pseudocode for a robust implementation of distance between segments.

The function GetClampedRoot returns the root of the linear function $h(z) =$

$h_0 + \sigma z$ on the interval $[0, 1]$, or if the root is outside the interval, it is clamped to the interval. It is required that h_0 and $h_1 = h_0 + \sigma$ have opposite signs, in which case there is a root on the real line. The code has a guard against the numerical division generating a number larger than one (it cannot be negative). In this case, h_0 and h_1 are both nearly zero, so choosing a root of 0.5 does not significantly affect the accuracy of downstream computations. For an ultimate guard, replace the assignment to 0.5 by a (slower) bisection routine applied to $h(z)$.

The domain and the segments with endpoints $(\hat{s}_0, 0)$ and $(\hat{s}_1, 1)$ can be intersected. However, $\hat{s}_i$ might be unreliable numerically when either of a or c is nearly zero and the $\hat{s}_i$ values are large-magnitude floating-point numbers. To avoid this numerical problem, the function ComputeIntersection computes the intersection points directly on the domain edges. The classify[] values allow determining which domain edges are intersected. For example, if classify[0] is -1 and classify[1] is 0, then the initial segment must intersect the domain edge $s = 0$ for some $t \in [0, 1]$. The computation of t itself involves a division by b, but to be in this situation it is known that $b \neq 0$. It can be close to zero, but then so is the numerator. The same idea can be used as in GetClampedRoot— test the numerical result of the division and, if outside $[0, 1]$, use 0.5 as the value. Again, for an ultimate guard, use bisection applied to a linear function.

Once the endpoints are computed, evaluate $H(z)$ at those points, which is the job of GetMinimumParameters. If $H(0)$ is zero, the function returns the (s, t) parameters at the corresponding endpoint. If $H(1)$ is zero, the function returns the (s, t) parameters at the corresponding endpoint. If $H(0)$ and $H(1)$ have opposite signs, then solve $H(z)$ for its unique root. Once again, test the numerical result of a division and choose 0.5 if that result is outside $[0, 1]$. The final cases are when $H(0)$ and $H(1)$ have the same sign. The endpoint with minimum H-value is not the (s, t) that minimizes the function. Apply GetClampedRoot on the edge containing that endpoint, which is why the edge[] flags can be computed.

The segments of Listings 1.12 and 1.13 discussed previously were also tested using exact rational arithmetic and using the robust algorithm. The results are in Listing 1.15.

```
//The segments of Listing 1.12.
// nonrobust algorithm
s = 0.42003676470588236
t = 0.39797794117647056
distance = 0.00055025506003679664
// exact arithmetic
sTrue = 0.42457281934252261
tTrue = 0.40235148377129676
distanceTrue = 0.0
// robust algorithm
sRobust = 0.41853798375537504
tRobust = 0.39687428969544680
distanceRobust = 9.7307189345304538e−10

// The segments of Listing 1.13.
// nonrobust algorithm
s = 0.125
```

```
t = 0.25
distance = 0.43258687891076358
// exact arithmetic
sTrue = 0.094672127942504153
tTrue = 0.0
distanceTrue = 1.1575046138574105e−7
// robust algorithm
sRobust = 1.0
tRobust = 0.91846616235720013
distanceRobust = 1.1575046138574101e−7
```

Listing 1.15: The segments of Listings 1.12 and 1.13 tested in the nonrobust algorithm were tested also using exact rational arithmetic and using the robust algorithm.

In Listing 1.13, $\hat{s}_0$ = 0.094672127942504153, $\hat{s}_1 > 1$, so compute the t-intersection on $s = 1$, which is $\tilde{t}$ = 0.91846616235720013. The endpoints of the segment defining $H(z)$ are $\mathbf{E}_0 = (\hat{s}_0, 0)$ and $\mathbf{E}_1 = (1, \tilde{t})$. The values of H are $H(0)$ = -5.5511151231257827e-17 and $H(1) = 0$. There is numerical error in these computations which lead to selection of $\mathbf{E}_1$ rather than $\mathbf{E}_0$ as the minimum point. However, R does not vary much on the segment, so there is not much error in the distance computation. What this does say, though, is that reasonable continuity can be expected in the distance computations, but closest points are not expected to have continuity. Even theoretically, the continuity of closest points is not guaranteed as the segments vary from nonparallel to nonparallel, passing through a parallel configuration along the way.

1.2.5 An Error-Free Implementation

As it turns out, the nonrobust implementation Listing 1.11 for floating-point numbers produces theoretically correct (error-free) results when using arbitrary-precision rational arithmetic.

Chapter 2

Floating-Point Arithmetic

The standard approach to mathematical computing uses floating-point numbers and their associated floating-point arithmetic. The assumption throughout the book is that you are familiar with the basics of such computing. At a high level, it is sufficient to understand how floating-point numbers are represented in memory and to be familiar with the arithmetic operations of addition, subtraction, multiplication, division and square roots. Considering floating-point inputs to these operations as real numbers, the theoretical outputs are not necessarily representable exactly as floating-point numbers, but they must be rounded to floating-point numbers.

The semantics of floating-point arithmetic, the binary encodings of floating-point numbers and the rounding modes are described in the IEEE Standard 754™-2008 [3], which contains much more than what is usually covered in a numerical computing class in a Computer Science program. Floating-point arithmetic is commonly supported in hardware as a *floating-point unit* (FPU) associated with a central processing unit (CPU) or graphics processing unit (GPU). The focus of the IEEE Standard 754™-2008 document is mainly for hardware implementers. In addition to the basic floating-point framework, it includes requirements such as how to deal with arithmetic underflow (flush-to-zero semantics) and overflow (representations of infinities), indeterminate expressions (ratios involving zeros and infinities), and generation and propagation of exceptions for unexpected conditions (special representations for not-a-number [NaN] with payload, quiet NaNs, signaling NaNs).

Although the IEEE Standard 754™-2008 document describes floating-point number systems in terms of how many bits of precision are desired, the basic floating-point types used in practice are the 32-bit floating-point type float (24 bits of precision) and the 64-bit floating-point type double (53 bits of precision). For the purpose of this book, it is sufficient to understand the binary encodings of float and double and to understand the rounding algorithms used to obtain floating-point numbers from other numbers. The main goals are to support conversion from floating-point inputs to arbitrary-precision inputs, to support conversion from arbitrary-precision outputs to floating-point outputs and to produce intervals with rational endpoints that bound the theoretical outputs from operations on floating-point or arbitrary-precision numbers.

2.1 Binary Encodings

The IEEE Standard 754™-2008 defines *binary interchange formats* for floating-point numbers. In each format, a floating-point number has a unique encoding. The formats supported by most hardware are 32-bit (C++ type float), referred to as Binary32, and 64-bit (C++ type double), referred to as Binary64. The type name BinaryN is used to represent the N-bit floating-point number. The type will be treated as a C or C++ union; see Listing 2.1.

```
typedef union
{
    UIntegerN encoding;     // the N-bit encoding
    FloatN number;          // the floating-point number
}
BinaryN;
```

Listing 2.1: A union is used to access a floating-point number or manipulate its bits via an unsigned integer.

For the two standard floating-point types, UInteger32 is uint32_t, Float32 is float, UInteger64 is uint64_t and Float64 is double.

The encoding for BinaryN has *signed zeros*, $+0$ and -0. At first glance, having two representations for zero might be considered unnecessary, but there are numerical applications where it is important to support this. The encoding also has *signed infinities*, $+\infty$ and $-\infty$. Infinities have special rules applied to them during arithmetic operations. Finally, the encoding has special values, each called *Not-a-Number* (NaN). Some of these are called *quiet NaNs* that are used to provide diagnostic information when unexpected conditions occur during floating-point computations. The others are called *signaling NaNs* and also provide diagnostic information while supporting the needs of specialized applications. Signaling NaNs are used for exception handling; most compilers provide support for hooking up handlers to specific exceptions during floating-point computations. A NaN has an associated *payload* whose meaning is at the discretion of the implementer. The IEEE Standard 754™-2008 has many requirements regarding the handling of NaNs in numerical computations.

2.2 Binary Encoding of 32-bit Floating-Point Numbers

The encoding of float is shown in Figure 2.1. The *sign* of the number is stored in bit 31. A 0-valued bit is used for a nonnegative number and a 1-valued bit is used for a negative number. The exponent is stored in bits 23 through 30, but is represented using a bias. If the *biased exponent* stored in the eight bits is b, then the actual exponent is $e = b - 127$. The *trailing*

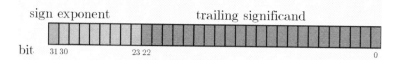

FIGURE 2.1: The encoding of the 32-bit floating-point type float.

significand is stored in bits 0 through 22. A *normal* number has an additional 1-valued bit prepended to the trailing significand to form the *significand* of the number; this bit is considered to be hidden in the sense it is not explicitly stored in the 32-bit encoding. A *subnormal* number has an additional 0-valued bit prepended to the trailing significand. To be precise, the 32-bit quantity is interpreted as follows. Let s be the 1-bit sign, let b be the 8-bit biased exponent and let t be the 23-bit trailing significand. Listing 2.2 shows how the binary encoding represents 32-bit floating-point numbers.

```
float  x = <some 32−bit floating−point number>;
uint32_t  s = (0x80000000 & x.encoding) >> 31;   // sign
uint32_t  b = (0x7f800000 & x.encoding) >> 23;   // biased exponent
uint32_t  t = (0x007fffff & x.encoding);   // trailing significand

if (b == 0)
{
    if (t == 0)   // zeros
    {   // x = (−1)^s * 0 [allows for +0 and −0]
    }
    else   // subnormal numbers
    {   // x = (−1)^s * 0.t * 2^−126
    }
}
else if (b < 255)   // normal numbers
{   // x = (−1)^s * 1.t * 2^(b−127)
}
else   // special numbers
{
    if (t == 0)
    {   // x = (−1)^s * ∞
    }
    else
    {
        if (t & 0x00400000)
        {   // x = quiet NaN
        }
        else
        {   // x = signaling NaN
        }
        // payload = t & 0x003fffff
    }
}
```

Listing 2.2: Decoding a number of type float.

The maximum unbiased exponent is $e_{\max} = 127$. The minimum unbiased exponent is $e_{\min} = 1 - e_{\max} = -126$. The relationship between the minimum

TABLE 2.1:   Quantities of interest for binary32.

name	value	name	value
F32_NUM_ENCODING_BITS	32	F32_MAX_TRAILING	0x007fffff
F32_NUM_EXPONENT_BITS	8	F32_SUP_TRAILING	0x00800000
F32_NUM_SIGNIFICAND_BITS	24	F32_POS_ZERO	0x00000000
F32_NUM_TRAILING_BITS	23	F32_NEG_ZERO	0x80000000
F32_EXPONENT_BIAS	127	F32_MIN_SUBNORMAL	0x00000001
F32_MAX_BIASED_EXPONENT	255	F32_MAX_SUBNORMAL	0x007fffff
F32_SIGN_MASK	0x80000000	F32_MIN_NORMAL	0x00800000
F32_NOT_SIGN_MASK	0x7fffffff	F32_MAX_NORMAL	0x7f7fffff
F32_BIASED_EXPONENT_MASK	0x7f800000	F32_INFINITY	0x7f800000
F32_TRAILING_MASK	0x007fffff		
F32_NAN_QUIET_MASK	0x00400000		
F32_NAN_PAYLOAD_MASK	0x003fffff		

and maximum exponents is required by the IEEE Standard 754™-2008. The number of bits in the significand is $p = 24$, which includes the 23 bits of the trailing significand and the leading 1-valued bit for normal numbers. The subnormal numbers have a leading 0-valued bit, so the number of significant bits for subnormals is always smaller than p.

The encoding has signed zeros, $+0$ (encoding 0x00000000) and -0 (encoding 0x80000000), and signed infinities, $+\infty$ (encoding 0x7f800000) and $-\infty$ (encoding 0xff800000).

The smallest positive subnormal number occurs when $b = 0$ and $t = 1$, which is $2^{e_{\min}+1-p} = 2^{-149}$. All finite floating-point numbers are integral multiples of this number. The largest positive subnormal number occurs when $b = 0$ and t has all 1-valued bits, which is $2^{e_{\min}}(1 - 2^{1-p}) = 2^{-126}(1 - 2^{-23})$. The smallest positive normal number occurs when $b = 1$ and $t = 0$, which is $2^{e_{\min}} = 2^{-126}$. The largest positive normal number occurs when $b = 254$ and t has all 1-valued bits, which is $2^{e_{\max}}(2 - 2^{1-p}) = 2^{127}(2 - 2^{-23})$.

The subnormals are in the interval $(0, 2^{-126})$. Zero, the subnormals, and the normals in $[0, 2^{-125}]$ are uniformly distributed. Just as for the 8-bit floating-point numbers, for each unbiased exponent $\lambda > 1$, the numbers with that exponent are uniformly distributed in the interval $[2^{\lambda}, 2^{\lambda+1}]$ but at half the frequency for the numbers in the interval $[2^{\lambda-1}, 2^{\lambda}]$.

When implementing floating-point arithmetic in software, it is convenient to define some quantities of interest as listed in Table 2.1. The enumerate F32_INFINITY is assigned to a number that corresponds to the encoding 2^{128}, but this is not to be considered the value of $+\infty$. Infinities are handled differently from finite floating-point numbers. The enumerate is for bit-pattern testing in the software implementation.

In the GTL, IEEEBinary32 is a class whose data member is a union of a float member named number and a uint32_t member named encoding. The encoding

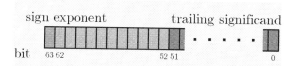

FIGURE 2.2: The encoding of the 64-bit floating-point type double.

is the bit pattern of the 32-bit binary representation of the floating-point number. Various information and operations are available through this class.

2.3 Binary Encoding of 64-bit Floating-Point Numbers

The encoding of double is shown in Figure 2.2. The *sign* of the number is stored in bit 63. A 0-valued bit is used for a nonnegative number and a 1-valued bit is used for a negative number. The exponent is stored in bits 52 through 62, but is represented using a bias. If the *biased exponent* stored in the eleven bits is b, then the actual exponent is $e = b - 1023$. The *trailing significand* is stored in bits 0 through 51. A *normal* number has an additional 1-valued bit prepended to the trailing significand to form the *significand* of the number; this bit is considered to be hidden in the sense it is not explicitly stored in the 32-bit encoding. A *subnormal* number has an additional 0-valued bit prepended to the trailing significand. To be precise, the 64-bit quantity is interpreted as follows. Let s be the 1-bit sign, let b be the 11-bit biased exponent and let t be the 52-bit trailing significand. Listing 2.3 shows how the binary encoding represents 64-bit floating-point numbers.

```
double x = <some 64-bit floating-point number>;
uint64_t s = (0x8000000000000000 & x.encoding) >> 63;  // sign
uint64_t b = (0x7ff0000000000000 & x.encoding) >> 52;  // biased exponent
uint64_t t = (0x000fffffffffffff & x.encoding);  // trailing significand

if (b == 0)
{
    if (t == 0)  // zeros
    {
        // x = (-1)^s * 0 [allows for +0 and -0]
    }
    else  // subnormal numbers
    {
        // x = (-1)^s * 0.t * 2^-1022
    }
}
else if (b < 2047)  // normal numbers
{
    // x = (-1)^s * 1.t * 2^b-1023
}
```

```
else  // special numbers
{
    if  (t == 0)
    {
        // x = (−1)ˢ * ∞
    }
    else
    {
        if  (t & 0x0008000000000000)
        {
            // x = quiet NaN
        }
        else
        {
            // x = signaling NaN
        }
        // payload = t & 0x0007ffffffffffff
    }
}
```

Listing 2.3: Decoding a number of type double.

The maximum unbiased exponent is $e_{\max} = 1023$. The minimum unbiased exponent is $e_{\min} = 1 - e_{\max} = -1022$. The relationship between the minimum and maximum exponents is required by the IEEE Standard 754™-2008. The number of bits in the significand is $p = 53$, which includes the 52 bits of the trailing significand and the leading 1-valued bit for normal numbers. The subnormal numbers have a leading 0-valued bit, so the number of significant bits for subnormals is always smaller than p.

The encoding has signed zeros, $+0$ (encoding 0x0000000000000000) and -0 (encoding 0x8000000000000000), and signed infinities, $+\infty$ (encoding 0x7ff0000000000000) and $-\infty$ (encoding 0xfff0000000000000).

The smallest positive subnormal number occurs when $b = 0$ and $t = 1$, which is $2^{e_{\min}+1-p} = 2^{-1074}$. All finite floating-point numbers are integral multiples of this number. The largest positive subnormal number occurs when $b = 0$ and t has all 1-valued bits, which is $2^{e_{\min}}(1 - 2^{1-p}) = 2^{-1022}(1 - 2^{-52})$. The smallest positive normal number occurs when $b = 1$ and $t = 0$, which is $2^{e_{\min}} = 2^{-1022}$. The largest positive normal number occurs when $b = 2046$ and t has all 1-valued bits, which is $2^{e_{\max}}(2 - 2^{1-p}) = 2^{1023}(2 - 2^{-52})$.

The subnormals are in the interval $(0, 2^{-1022})$. Zero, the subnormals, and the normals in $[0, 2^{-1021}]$ are uniformly distributed. Just as for the 8-bit floating-point numbers, for each unbiased exponent $\lambda > 1$, the numbers with that exponent are uniformly distributed in the interval $[2^{\lambda}, 2^{\lambda+1}]$ but at half the frequency for the numbers in the interval $[2^{\lambda-1}, 2^{\lambda}]$.

When implementing floating-point arithmetic in software, it is convenient to define some quantities of interest as listed in Table 2.2. The enumerate F64_INFINITY is assigned to a number that corresponds to the encoding 2^{1024}, but this is not to be considered the value of $+\infty$. Infinities are handled differently from finite floating-point numbers. The enumerate is for bit-pattern testing in the software implementation.

In the GTL, IEEEBinary64 is a class whose data member is a union of a double member named number and a uint64_t member named encoding. The

TABLE 2.2: Quantities of interest for binary64.

name	value	name	value
F64_NUM_ENCODING_BITS	64	F64_MAX_TRAILING	0x000fffffffffffff
F64_NUM_EXPONENT_BITS	11	F64_SUP_TRAILING	0x0010000000000000
F64_NUM_SIGNIFICAND_BITS	53	F64_POS_ZERO	0x0000000000000000
F64_NUM_TRAILING_BITS	52	F64_NEG_ZERO	0x8000000000000000
F64_EXPONENT_BIAS	1023	F64_MIN_SUBNORMAL	0x0000000000000001
F64_MAX_BIASED_EXPONENT	2047	F64_MAX_SUBNORMAL	0x000fffffffffffff
F64_SIGN_MASK	0x8000000000000000	F64_MIN_NORMAL	0x0010000000000000
F64_NOT_SIGN_MASK	0x7fffffffffffffff	F64_MAX_NORMAL	0x7fefffffffffffff
F64_BIASED_EXPONENT_MASK	0x7ff0000000000000	F64_INFINITY	0x7ff0000000000000
F64_TRAILING_MASK	0x000fffffffffffff		
F64_NAN_QUIET_MASK	0x0008000000000000		
F64_NAN_PAYLOAD_MASK	0x0007ffffffffffff		

encoding is the bit pattern of the 64-bit binary representation of the floating-point number. Various information and operations are available through this class.

2.4   Rounding of Floating-Point Numbers

Floating-point numbers have a fixed precision, 24 bits for type float and 53 bits for type double. Consequently, arithmetic operations applied to floating-point numbers can produce numbers that theoretically require more bits of precision than is available by the underlying type. These results must be *rounded* to floating-point numbers. The FPU has registers that have more bits of precision than the underlying type. These store an intermediate value that can then be rounded to a floating-point number of the underlying type.

The IEEE Standard 754™-2008 specifies five different rounding modes: *round-to-nearest-ties-to-even* (default), *round-to-nearest-ties-to-away*, *round-toward-zero*, *round-toward-positive* and *round-toward-negative*. These are defined next with application to a number of the form $\sigma d.r$, where σ is $+1$ or -1 (the sign of the number), where d is a nonnegative integer (the integer part of the number) and where r is a nonnegative integer (the fractional part of the number). Although the discussion and figures refer to integers, they are a simplification of the actual situation. The rounding occurs based on the bits that occur after the trailing significand. Think of the discussion and figures as applying to floating-point numbers with their bit patterns shifted.

The selection of the rounding mode is controlled by a function call that configures the FPU accordingly. When an arithmetic operation such as assignment, addition, subtraction, multiplication, division or square root occurs and

FIGURE 2.3: An illustration of round to nearest with ties to even.

the result rounded based on the currently active rounding mode, the result is said to be *correctly rounded*. The result is the floating-point number (of the underlying type) closest to the theoretical result.

Rounding errors are inherent in nearly all mathematical code that uses floating-point arithmetic. In many cases the errors generated by a sequence of operations do not accumulate enough to cause a significant difference between the floating-point result and the theoretical result. In some cases, though, the floating-point result is drastically different. This is typical in many implementations of geometric algorithms. It is important to understand how floating-point rounding errors occur in any such algorithm you choose to implement.

2.4.1   Round to Nearest with Ties to Even

This rounding mode is the default. If the fractional part is smaller than half, the number is rounded down, and if the fractional part is larger than half, the number is rounded up. When the fractional part is exactly half, to avoid bias the number is rounded down when the integer part is even but rounded up when the integer part is odd. This rounding mode is considered to be the best for general computing as it is unbiased. The mathematical summary is

$$\text{round}_e(\sigma d.r) = \begin{cases} \sigma d, & 0.r < 1/2 \text{ or } (0.r = 1/2 \text{ and } d \text{ is even}) \\ \sigma(d+1), & 0.r > 1/2 \text{ or } (0.r = 1/2 \text{ and } d \text{ is odd}) \end{cases} \quad (2.1)$$

Figure 2.3 illustrates this on the number line for several intervals. The use of parentheses and brackets in the figure is consistent with their use in interval notation: parenthesis means exclude the point and bracket means include the point. Examples are $\text{round}_e(1.1) = 1$, $\text{round}_e(1.9) = 2$, $\text{round}_e(1.5) = 2$, $\text{round}_e(2.5) = 2$, $\text{round}_e(-1.1) = -1$, $\text{round}_e(-1.5) = -2$ and $\text{round}_e(-2.5) = -2$.

2.4.2   Round to Nearest with Ties to Away

If the fractional part is smaller than half, the number is rounded down, and if the fractional part is larger than half, the number is rounded up. When the fraction is half, the rounding is away from zero, meaning that the rounding is to the largest magnitude integer neighbor. This rounding mode is biased, so use it only when it makes sense in your floating-point computing. The standard

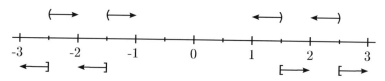

FIGURE 2.4: An illustration of round to nearest with ties to away.

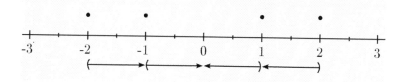

FIGURE 2.5: An illustration of round toward zero.

mathematics library rounding functions std::round, std::lround and std::llround are unaffected by changes in the FPU rounding mode. Moreover, they all use round to nearest with ties to away. The mathematical summary is

$$\text{round}_a(\sigma d.r) = \begin{cases} \sigma d, & 0.r < 1/2 \\ \sigma(d+1), & 0.r \geq 1/2 \end{cases} \quad (2.2)$$

Figure 2.4 illustrates this on the number line for several intervals. Examples are $\text{round}_a(1.1) = 1$, $\text{round}_a(1.9) = 2$, $\text{round}_a(1.5) = 2$, $\text{round}_a(2.5) = 3$, $\text{round}_a(-1.1) = -1$, $\text{round}_a(-1.5) = -2$ and $\text{round}_a(-2.5) = -3$.

This rounding mode is not required by the IEEE Standard 754™-2008 for a binary format implementation of floating-point numbers. It is required for a decimal format implementation.

2.4.3 Round toward Zero

This mode rounds the floating point number to the integer neighbor that is smallest in magnitude, which amounts to truncation of the fractional part. The standard mathematics library function std::trunc is unaffected by changes in the FPU rounding mode, and it implements rounding toward zero. The mathematical summary is

$$\text{round}_z(\sigma d.r) = \sigma d \quad (2.3)$$

Figure 2.5 illustrates this on the number line for several intervals. Some examples are $\text{round}_z(1) = 1$, $\text{round}_z(1.1) = 1$, $\text{round}_z(-1.1) = -1$, $\text{round}_z(-2) = -2$, $\text{round}_z(0.1) = +0$ and $\text{round}_z(-0.1) = -0$. The last two examples emphasize that in floating-point arithmetic, the rounding can produce a signed zero.

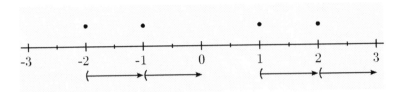

FIGURE 2.6: An illustration of round toward positive.

2.4.4　Round toward Positive

When a number is not exactly an integer, the rounding is in the direction of the positive axis. If i is an integer and $x \in (i, i+1)$, the rounded value is $\text{round}_p(x) = i + 1$. The equation is more complicated when the number is formulated as $x = \sigma d.r$, but this is necessary to understand the implementation for floating-point numbers. In this mode, the rounded value is d in all cases but one: the number is positive, the fractional part is positive and the rounded value is $d + 1$. The mathematical summary is

$$\text{round}_p(\sigma d.r) = \begin{cases} \sigma d, & r = 0 \text{ or } (r > 0 \text{ and } \sigma < 0) \\ \sigma d + 1, & r > 0 \text{ and } \sigma > 0 \end{cases} \qquad (2.4)$$

Figure 2.6 illustrates this on the number line for several intervals. Some examples are $\text{round}_p(1) = 1$, $\text{round}_p(1.1) = 2$, $\text{round}_p(-1.1) = -1$, $\text{round}_p(-2) = -2$ and $\text{round}_p(-0.7) = -0$. The last example emphasizes that in floating-point arithmetic, the rounding can produce negative zero.

2.4.5　Round toward Negative

Rounding toward negative is similar to that of rounding toward positive. If i is an integer and $x \in (i, i+1)$, the rounded value is $\text{round}_n(x) = i$. In terms of $x = \sigma d.r$ for floating-point rounding, the rounded value is d in all cases but one: the number is negative, the fractional part is positive and the rounded value is $d - 1$. The mathematical summary is

$$\text{round}_n(\sigma d.r) = \begin{cases} \sigma d, & r = 0 \text{ or } (r > 0 \text{ and } \sigma > 0) \\ \sigma d - 1, & r > 0 \text{ and } \sigma < 0 \end{cases} \qquad (2.5)$$

Figure 2.7 illustrates this on the number line for several intervals. Some examples are $\text{round}_n(1) = 1$, $\text{round}_n(1.1) = 1$, $\text{round}_n(-1.1) = -2$, $\text{round}_n(-2) = -2$ and $\text{round}_n(0.7) = +0$. The last example emphasizes that in floating-point arithmetic, the rounding can produce positive zero.

2.4.6　Rounding Support in C++

The floating-point environment consists of floating-point status flags and control modes. The status flags are modified by floating-point operations and

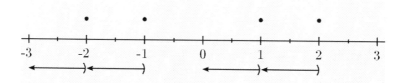

FIGURE 2.7: An illustration of round toward negative.

are accessed by a program to determine information about the operations. For example, if a division by zero occurs, the appropriate status flag is set to indicate this state. Underflow and overflow in arithmetic operations are also reported via status flags. The control modes give the program the ability to specify the rounding mode for a sequence of operations and to specify the types of exceptions that should be trapped for a sequence of operations.

A standardized environment for accessing the floating-point environment is provided by C++ 11 and later [24]. The rounding mode control is of most importance and will be used in the source code that accompanies this book. Listing 2.4 contains code for specifying the rounding modes.

```cpp
#include <Mathematics/IEEEBinary.h>
#include <cfenv>
#include <iostream>

void RoundingSupportCPP(double x)
{
    auto currentMode = std::fegetround();   // = FE_TONEAREST
    IEEEBinary32 y;

    // round to nearest ties to even
    std::fesetround(FE_TONEAREST);
    y.number = (float)x;
    std::cout << "round x to nearest = "
        << y.number << " , " << std::hex << y.encoding << std::endl;

    // round towards negative
    std::fesetround(FE_DOWNWARD);
    y.number = (float)x;
    std::cout << "round x downward = "
        << y.number << " , " << std::hex << y.encoding << std::endl;

    // round towards positive
    std::fesetround(FE_UPWARD);
    y.number = (float)x;
    std::cout << "round x upward = "
        << y.number << " , " << std::hex << y.encoding << std::endl;

    // round towards zero
    std::fesetround(FE_TOWARDZERO);
    y.number = (float)x;
    std::cout << "round x toward zero = "
        << y.number << " , " << std::hex << y.encoding << std::endl;

    std::fesetround(currentMode);
}
```

```
int main()
{
    double x;

    x = 0.123456789123456789;
    RoundingSupportCPP(x);
    // FE_TONEAREST: y.number = 0.123456791, y.encoding = 0x3dfcd6ea
    // FE_DOWNWARD: y.number = 0.123456784, y.encoding = 0x3dfcd6e9
    // FE_UPWARD: y.number = 0.123456791, y.encoding = 0x3dfcd6ea
    // FE_TOWARDZERO: y.number = 0.123456784, y.encoding = 0x3dfcd6e9

    x = 1.0 + std::ldexp(1.0, -24) + std::ldexp(1.0, -25);
    // x = 1.0000000894069672
    RoundingSupportCPP(x);
    // FE_TONEAREST: y.number = 1.00000012, y.encoding = 0x3f800001
    // FE_DOWNWARD: y.number = 1.00000000, y.encoding = 0x3f800000
    // FE_UPWARD: y.number = 1.00000012, y.encoding = 0x3f800001
    // FE_TOWARDZERO: y.number = 1.00000000, y.encoding = 0x3f800000

    x = 1.0 + std::ldexp(1.0, -24);
    // x = 1.0000000596046448
    RoundingSupportCPP(x);
    // FE_TONEAREST: y.number = 1.00000000, y.encoding = 0x3f800000
    // FE_DOWNWARD: y.number = 1.00000000, y.encoding = 0x3f800000
    // FE_UPWARD: y.number = 1.00000012, y.encoding = 0x3f800001
    // FE_TOWARDZERO: y.number = 1.00000000, y.encoding = 0x3f800000

    x = +(1.0 + std::ldexp(1.0, -23) + std::ldexp(1.0, -24));
    // x = 1.0000001788139343
    RoundingSupportCPP(x);
    // FE_TONEAREST: y.number = 1.00000024, y.encoding = 0x3f800002
    // FE_DOWNWARD: y.number = 1.00000012, y.encoding = 0x3f800001
    // FE_UPWARD: y.number = 1.00000024, y.encoding = 0x3f800002
    // FE_TOWARDZERO: y.number = 1.00000012, y.encoding = 0x3f800001

    x = -(1.0 + std::ldexp(1.0, -23) + std::ldexp(1.0, -24));
    // x = -1.0000001788139343
    RoundingSupportCPP(x);
    // FE_TONEAREST: y.number = -1.00000024, y.encoding = 0xbf800002
    // FE_DOWNWARD: y.number = -1.00000024, y.encoding = 0xbf800002
    // FE_UPWARD: y.number = -1.00000012, y.encoding = 0xbf800001
    // FE_TOWARDZERO: y.number = -1.00000012, y.encoding = 0xbf800001
    return 0;
}
```

Listing 2.4: Code for setting the rounding mode of the FPU. The class IEEE-Binary32 is a union of a float named number and a uint32_t named encoding. The class IEEEBinary64 is a union of a double named number and a uint64_t named encoding.

The function std::fegetround allows one to query what the current rounding mode is. The function std::fesetround allows one to specify the desired rounding mode. The supported rounding modes do not include rounding to nearest with ties to away, but a floating-point hardware implementation could include this, in which case the rounding mode name is provided as an extension to the C++ support.

Chapter 3

Arbitrary-Precision Arithmetic

The IEEE Standard 754™-2008 is usually implemented in hardware for 32-bit floating-point numbers of type float and 64-bit floating-point numbers of type double. Type float has 24 bits of precision and type double has 53 bits of precision. For most geometric algorithms, the number of bits of precision provided by these types is insufficient to guarantee exact results. In many cases, it is desirable to obtain exact results, in which case there is a need for an arbitrary-precision number system. This chapter describes the ideas for arbitrary-precision arithmetic based on binary encodings of numbers.

A specific implementation of the ideas is found in the GTL. One practical matter involves the number of bits required to represent an exact result in an expression tree that has large depth. In practice this leads to consuming large amounts of memory and reduced computing time due to the overhead of managing that memory in the global heap. The computing time can be reduced by using multithreading on the CPU so that the memory management costs are amortized across multiple cores. However, if the number of bits required for an exact result is known at development time, the heap storage can be replaced by stack storage, leading to reduced costs in memory management. The stack objects are themselves large, so the compiler used for this approach must be configured to allocate a sufficiently large stack for the program. With this approach it is also possible to implement the arithmetic on a GPU for increased speed, but the memory management of arbitrary-precision objects is the programmer's responsibility.

3.1 Binary Scientific Notation

A real number r may be written exactly in base-two scientific notation, which is referred to as *binary scientific notation*,

$$r = \sigma \left(1 + \sum_{i=0}^{\infty} c_i \, 2^{-(i+1)}\right) 2^p = \sigma(1.c) * 2^p \tag{3.1}$$

where c_i are the bits, each having a value either zero or one. The term $1.c$ is a shorthand notation for 1 plus the infinite summation with $c = c_0 c_1 \cdots$ the sequence of bits. The power p is an integer. The sign is $\sigma \in \{-1, 0, 1\}$. The number zero is represented simply by 0; it is sufficient to choose $c = 0$ and $p = 0$ in the representation.

Allowing an infinite sum, the representation for a rational number is not unique. For example, the number one has a representation $1.0*2^0$, which means the power is $p = 0$ and coefficients are $c_i = 0$ for all i. Another representation is $1.\bar{1}^\infty * 2^{-1} = 0.111\cdots$, where the power is $p = -1$ and coefficients are $c_i = 1$ for all i. The notation $\bar{1}^\infty$ indicates that the number 1 is repeated an infinite number of times. Uniqueness can be obtained in one of two ways, by choosing a finite sum (if there is one) or by choosing the representation with the smallest power p. Not all numbers have finite representations; for example, $1/3 = 1.\overline{01}^\infty * 2^{-2}$, where $\overline{01}^\infty$ indicates that the number pair 01 is repeated *ad infinitum*.

3.2   Binary Scientific Numbers

For computing with numbers in binary scientific notation, only finite sums are allowed,

$$r = \sigma \left(1 + \sum_{i=0}^{n} c_i \, 2^{-(i+1)} \right) 2^p = \sigma(1.c) * 2^p \qquad (3.2)$$

where $n \geq 0$. The set B of all such finite sums is referred to as *binary scientific numbers* and is a strict subset of the rational numbers $\mathbb{Q}$. More details about binary scientific numbers are provided next.

Let B be the set of binary scientific numbers, which consists of numbers of the form in equation (3.2). Addition, subtraction and multiplication of numbers in B are naturally defined based on the arithmetic of rational numbers. If x and y are in B, then so are $x + y$, $x - y$ and $x * y$. Division is not allowed, because the ratio x/y does not necessarily have a finite representation. If not, x/y is not a binary scientific number. However, it is possible to define the set of ratios of binary scientific numbers for which addition, subtraction, multiplication and division are well defined. The implementation of arithmetic operations involves modifying the binary scientific notation to obtain a representation that is a product of an integer and a power of two.

Specifically, consider $1.u * 2^p$. If $1.u = 1$, then $u = 0$ and define $\hat{u} = 1$. If $1.u > 0$ and u has n bits, then the last bit is a 1-bit. Define $\hat{u} = 1u_0 \cdots u_{n-1} = \hat{u}_n \hat{u}_{n-1} \cdots \hat{u}_1 \hat{u}_0$, where $u_{n-1} = 1$ and $\hat{u}_n = \hat{u}_0 = 1$. In either case, $\hat{u}$ is an $(n+1)$-bit odd integer with $n \geq 0$ and $1.u * 2^p = \hat{u} * 2^{p-n}$. It is important to note that the indexing of $\mathbf{u}$ and the indexing of $\hat{\mathbf{u}}$ are different. Equation (3.3) summarizes this for future reference,

$$x = 1.u * 2^p = 1u_0 \cdots u_{n-1} * 2^p = \hat{u} * 2^{p-n} = \hat{u}_n \cdots \hat{u}_0 * 2^{p-n} \qquad (3.3)$$

Generally, $\hat{u}_k = u_{n-1-k}$ for $0 \le k \le n-1$, $\hat{u}_n = 1$, and $\hat{u}_n = u_{n-1} = 1$.

The number $1.u * 2^p$ is represented as the triple $(\hat{u}, p, n)$. In the discussion of binary operations, variable names x and y are used for the inputs and variable name z is used for the output. Let $x = 1.u * 2^p$, where u has n bits; then $\hat{u} = 1u$ and x is represented by the triple $(\hat{u}, p, n)$. Let $y = 1.v * 2^q$, where v has m bits; then $\hat{v} = 1v$ and y is represented by the triple $(\hat{v}, q, m)$. Let $z = 1.w * 2^r$, where w has ℓ bits; then $\hat{w} = 1w$ and z is represented by the triple $(\hat{w}, r, k)$. The goal is to compute $(\hat{w}, r, k)$ from $(\hat{u}, p, n)$ and $(\hat{v}, q, m)$.

The next several sections provide the arithmetic details for binary scientific numbers. The implementation depends on an abstraction for unsigned integer arithmetic named UInteger. The GTL provides support for B via the class BSNumber.

3.2.1 Addition

Let $x > 0$ and $y > 0$. The sum is

$$x + y = 1.u * 2^p + 1.v * 2^q = \hat{u} * 2^{p-n} + \hat{v} * 2^{q-m} \tag{3.4}$$

If $p - n \ge q - m$,

$$\hat{u} * 2^{p-n} + \hat{v} * 2^{q-m} = \left(\hat{u} * 2^{(p-n)-(q-m)} + \hat{v} \right) * 2^{q-m} = \tilde{w} * 2^{q-m} \tag{3.5}$$

where $\tilde{w} = \hat{u} * 2^{(p-n)-(q-m)} + \hat{v}$, a positive integer. The leading 1-bit of $\tilde{w}$ occurs at index ℓ and the trailing 1-bit occurs at index t with $\ell \ge t$.

If $p - n > q - m$, then $\tilde{w}$ is odd, $t = 0$ and $\hat{w} = \tilde{w}$ with $k = \ell$ and $r = k + q - m$. If $p - n = q - m$, then $\tilde{w}$ is even. The integer $\tilde{w}$ is shifted right by t places to obtain $\hat{w}$, a $(k+1)$-bit number with $k = \ell - t$. In either case,

$$x + y = \tilde{w} * 2^{q-m} = \hat{w} * 2^{q-m+t} = 1.w * 2^{q-m+t+k} = 1.w * 2^{q-m+\ell} \tag{3.6}$$

which implies $r = q - m + \ell$.

If $p - n < q - m$, a similar construction is applied but now $\tilde{w} = \hat{u} + \hat{v} * 2^{(q-m)-(p-n)}$. The leading 1-bit of $\tilde{w}$ occurs at index ℓ and the trailing 1-bit occurs at index t. Shift right $\tilde{w}$ by t bits to obtain $\hat{w}$ and set $k = \ell - t$ to obtain

$$x + y = \tilde{w} * 2^{p-n} = \hat{w} * 2^{p-n+t} = 1.w * 2^{p-n+t+k} = 1.w * 2^{p-n+\ell} \tag{3.7}$$

which implies $r = p - n + \ell$.

If $x = 0$ (or $y = 0$), the addition is trivial and $z = y$ (or $z = x$). An implementation can quickly test the signs of the representations for the inputs and provide the branching logic to perform the addition. In all cases, the implementation requires addition of arbitrary-precision integers that are positive.

3.2.2   Subtraction

Let $x > y > 0$. The difference $x - y$ is computed similarly to the sum $x + y$ except that the $\tilde{w}$ integer is a difference of positive integers rather than a sum. The difference is

$$x - y = 1.u * 2^p - 1.v * 2^q = \hat{u} * 2^{p-n} - \hat{v} * 2^{q-m} \tag{3.8}$$

If $p - n \geq q - m$,

$$\hat{u} * 2^{p-n} - \hat{v} * 2^{q-m} = \left(\hat{u} * 2^{(p-n)-(q-m)} - \hat{v} \right) * 2^{q-m} = \tilde{w} * 2^{q-m} \tag{3.9}$$

where $\tilde{w} = \hat{u} * 2^{(p-n)-(q-m)} - \hat{v}$, a positive integer. Equation (3.6) is still valid with the understanding that $\tilde{w}$ is computed as a difference of integers rather than a sum.

If $p - n < q - m$, then $\tilde{w} = \hat{u} - \hat{v} * 2^{(q-m)-(p-n)}$, which is also a positive integer. Equation (3.7) is still valid with the understanding that $\tilde{w}$ is computed as a difference of integers rather than a sum.

For the case that $y > x > 0$, it is sufficient to compute $y - x$ using the aforementioned algorithm and then set the sign σ to -1. If $x = 0$ (or $y = 0$), the subtraction is trivial with only bookkeeping required for the sign σ of the result. In all cases, the implementation requires subtraction of arbitrary-precision integers that are positive.

For the cases when $x < 0$ or $y < 0$, the addition might transform to one of subtraction or vice versa. For example, if $x > 0$ and $y < 0$, the addition is $x + y = x - (-y)$, which requires the subtraction algorithm. Similarly, the subtraction is $x - y = x + (-y)$, which requires the addition algorithm. The GTL implementation of BSNumber provides the special case operations that are called by the arithmetic operator functions for addition and subtraction depending on the signs of the inputs.

3.2.3   Multiplication

The product of $x = 1.u * 2^p$ and $y = 1.v * 2^q$ is $z = 1.w * 2^r$, where w and r must be determined. Both $1.u$ and $1.v$ are in the half-open interval $[1, 2)$, so their product is in the half-open interval $[1, 4)$; that is, $1.u * 1.v = b_1 b_0.f$ where $b_1 b_0 \in 1, 2, 3$ and $0.f$ is the fractional part in $[0, 1)$. If $b_1 = 0$, then $b_0 = 1$, $0.w = 0.f$ and $r = p + q$. If $b_1 = 1$, then $0.w = 0.b_0 f$ and $r = p + q + 1$.

If $u = 0$, then $x * y = 1.v * 2^{p+q}$. If $v = 0$, then $x * y = 1.u * 2^{p+q}$; otherwise, $u > 0$ and $v > 0$, so at least one bit of u is nonzero and at least one bit of v is not zero. Using the notation introduced previously, the product $x * y$ is written as

$$x * y = 1.u * 2^p * 1.v * 2^q = \hat{u} * \hat{v} * 2^{p-n+q-m} = \hat{w} * 2^{p+q-n-m} \tag{3.10}$$

where $\hat{w} = \hat{u} * \hat{v}$ is the product of integers. The product of an $(n+1)$-bit odd integer and an $(m+1)$-bit odd integer is an odd integer with either $n+m+1$ or $n+m+2$ bits. For example, consider the case $n=4$ and $m=3$. The product of the two smallest odd integers with the specified number of bits is (in binary) $10001 * 1001 = 10011001$, which has $n+m+1 = 8$ bits. The product of the two largest odd integers with the specified number of bits is $11111 * 1111 = 111010001$, which has $n+m+2 = 9$ bits.

The right-hand side of equation (3.10) must be converted to standard form. Define $c=0$ when the leading bit of $\hat{w}$ is at index $n+m$ or $c=1$ when the leading bit is at index $n+m+1$, and define $k=n+m+c$. Therefore, $\hat{w}$ is an $(k+1)$-bit odd integer of the form $\hat{w} = 1w_0 \cdots w_{k-1} = 1.w_0 \cdots w_{k-1} * 2^k = 1.w * 2^k$, where $w_{k-1} = 1$ and the last equality defines w. The product $x*y$ is therefore

$$x*y = 1.w * 2^{p+q-n-m+k} = 1.w * 2^{p+q+c} = 1.w * 2^r \qquad (3.11)$$

The implementation of multiplication in the GTL class BSNumber multiplies $\hat{w} = \hat{u} * \hat{v}$, sets c by examining the location of the leading bit of $\hat{w}$, say, ℓ, and computes $r = p + q + c$, finally representing $z = x*y$ as the triple $(\hat{w}, r, k)$.

3.3 Binary Scientific Rationals

The ratio of two binary scientific numbers, $x/y = 1.u * 2^p / 1.v * 2^q$, is not necessarily a binary scientific number because the representation in binary scientific notation might have an infinite number of 1-bits. The number $1/3$ was one such number, where $1 = 1*2^0$, $3 = 1.1*2^1$ but $1/3 = 1.\overline{01}^\infty *2^{-2}$, where $\overline{01}^\infty$ indicates that the number pair 01 is repeated *ad infinitum*. In abstract algebraic terms, the set B of binary scientific numbers is not closed under division. This section describes another set of numbers for which division is defined.

Let B be the set of binary scientific numbers. For $x \in B$ and $y \in B$, define the ratio as x/y where $y \neq 0$. Although this suggests a division operation, it is only notational. The ratios are defined as the set of 2-tuples $R = \{(x,y) : x \in B, y \in B \setminus \{0\}\}$. The set $B \setminus \{0\}$ is the set B but with 0 discarded.

As with rational numbers, a single abstract ratio can have multiple representations. For example, $1/3$ and $2/6$ represent the same number. Also, $0/1$ and $0/2$ are both representations for zero. It is possible to obtain a unique representation by computing the greatest common divisor of the numerator and denominator and then cancel that factor from both. That is, let $r = n/d$ be a rational number with $n > 0$ and $d > 0$. Let g be the greatest common divisor of n and m, say, $n = g * n'$ and $d = g * d'$, where n' and d' have no common divisors other than 1. The rational number r is then represented uniquely by n'/d'. The number 0 is uniquely represented by choosing the ratio

0/1. When computing numerically, the unique representation is not necessary although it might be desirable in helping to reduce the number of bits of precision required to represent both numerators and denominators.

The next several sections provide the arithmetic details for binary scientific rational numbers. The GTL implementation of ratios of the set R and its arithmetic operations is class BSRational. The members of the class include the numerator and denominator as BSNumber objects.

3.3.1   Addition and Subtraction

Given ratios $r_0 = (x_0, y_0)$ and $r_1 = (x_1, y_1)$ in R, *addition* and *subtraction* are defined by

$$r_0 \pm r_1 = (x_0 * y_1 \pm x_1 * y_0, y_0 * y_1) \tag{3.12}$$

This definition is consistent with the notation using fractions,

$$r_0 \pm r_1 = \frac{x_0}{y_0} \pm \frac{x_1}{y_1} = \frac{x_0 y_1 \pm x_1 y_0}{y_0 y_1} \tag{3.13}$$

where the result is computed by constructing the common denominator of the two fractions. The components of the 2-tuple are computed using multiplication and addition of binary scientific numbers.

3.3.2   Multiplication and Division

Multiplication of two ratios is defined by

$$r_0 * r_1 = (x_0 * x_1, y_0 * y_1) \tag{3.14}$$

where in fraction notation,

$$r_0 r_1 = \frac{x_0}{y_0} \frac{x_1}{y_1} = \frac{x_0 x_1}{y_0 y_1} \tag{3.15}$$

Division is defined similarly as long as the denominator is not zero,

$$r_0 / r_1 = (x_0 * y_1, x_1 * y_0) \tag{3.16}$$

where in fraction notation,

$$\frac{r_0}{r_1} = \frac{\frac{x_0}{y_0}}{\frac{x_1}{y_1}} = \frac{x_0 y_1}{x_1 y_0} \tag{3.17}$$

3.4   Conversions

All finite floating-point numbers are rational numbers. In order to support arbitrary-precision arithmetic for a sequence of computations with floating-point inputs and outputs, conversions between floating-point numbers and binary scientific numbers and binary scientific rationals are required. This section describes several conversions that are commonly encountered.

3.4.1 Floating-Point Number to BSNumber

The conversion algorithm is described for type float. The algorithm for type double is similar. In fact, the GTL implementation uses a template function that handles either type by using the GTL template class IEEEBinary that defines the various parameters associated with the floating-point type.

Listing 2.2 contains the abstract branching logic that determines the category for the input float number. The zeros $+0$ and -0 both map to the same BSNumber, the one whose sign is zero, whose biased exponent is zero and whose unsigned integer is zero.

The float positive subnormals are of the form $0.u * 2^{-126}$, where $u = u_{22} \cdots u_0 > 0$ is the trailing significand with 23 bits. Let the leading 1-bit of u occur at index ℓ and let the trailing 1-bit occur at index t with $0 \leq t \leq \ell \leq 22$; then $0.u * 2^{-126} = u_\ell \cdots u_t * 2^{-126-(23-t)} = u_\ell \cdots u_t * 2^{t-149}$. The right-shift of u to obtain an odd integer is $u \gg t$. Pseudocode is shown in Listing 3.1.

```
float subnormal = <some number>;
uint32_t s = GetSign(subnormal);   // 0x00000000 or 0x80000000
uint32_t b = GetBiasedExponent(subnormal);   // b = 0 for subnormals
uint32_t u = GetTrailingSignificand(subnormal);   // trailing 23 bits
int32_t t = GetTrailingBit(u);   // index of trailing 1-bit of u
BSNumber bsn;
bsn.sign = (s > 0 ? -1 : 1);
bsn.biasedExponent = t - 149;
bsn.uinteger = (u >> t);
```

Listing 3.1: Conversion of a subnormal float to a BSNumber.

The float positive normals are of the form $1.u * 2^{b-127} = 1.u_{22} \cdots u_0 * 2^{b-127}$, where $u \geq 0$ is the trailing significand with 23 bits and b is the biased exponent with $1 \leq b \leq 254$. If $u = 0$, the number is $1 * 2^{b-127}$ where $\hat{u} = 1$. If $u > 0$, let the trailing 1-bit of u occur at index t; then $1.u * 2^{b-127} = 1u_{22} \cdots u_t * 2^{b-127-(23-t)} = 1u_{22} \cdots u_t * 2^{b+t-150}$. The unsigned integer for the BSNumber is obtained by prepending u with 1 and then shifting right by t to obtain the odd integer $\hat{u}$. Pseudocode is shown in Listing 3.2.

```
float normal = <some number>;
uint32_t s = GetSign(normal);   // 0x00000000 or 0x80000000
uint32_t b = GetBiasedExponent(normal);   // 1 <= b <= 254 for normals
uint32_t u = GetTrailingSignificand(normal);   // trailing 23 bits
BSNumber bsn;
if (u > 0)
{
    int32_t t = GetTrailingBit(u);   // index of trailing 1-bit of u
    bsn.sign = (s > 0 ? -1 : 1);
    bsn.biasedExponent = b + t - 150;
    bsn.uinteger = ((u | (1 << 23)) >> t);
}
else
{
    bsn.sign = (s > 0 ? -1 : 1);
```

```
bsn.biasedExponent = b - 127;
bsn.uinteger = 1;
}
```

Listing 3.2: Conversion of a normal float to a BSNumber.

In practice, BSNumber is used only for finite floating-point numbers, so ensure that your inputs are not infinities or NaNs. In the GTL implementation, if the floating-point number is an infinity or NaN, an exception is thrown. However, this behavior can be turned off via a preprocessor macro. An infinity is then converted to $\pm 2^{128}$ and a NaN is converted to ± 0. Pseudocode is shown in Listing 3.3.

```
float special = <infinity or NaN>;
uint32_t s = GetSign(special);    // 0x00000000 or 0x80000000
uint32_t b = GetBiasedExponent(special);    // b = 255 for specials
uint32_t u = GetTrailingSignificand(special);    // trailing 23 bits
BSNumber bsn;
if (u == 0)
{
    // Error: Input is an infinity. Throw an exception or ...
    bsn.sign = (s > 0 ? -1 : 1);
    bsn.biasedExponent = 128;
    bsn.uinteger = 1;
}
else
{
    // Error: Input is a NaN (quiet or silent). Throw an exception or ...
    bsn.sign = (s > 0 ? -1 : 1);
    bsn.biasedExponent = 0;
    bsn.uinteger = 0;
}
```

Listing 3.3: Conversion of an infinity or NaN float to a BSNumber.

3.4.2 BSNumber to Floating-Point Number

The conversion algorithm is described for type float. The algorithm for type double is similar.

The conversion from a BSNumber to a float is generally not exact. Typically, a sequence of operations with binary scientific numbers will produce a result with more than 24 bits of precision. In this case, a rounding algorithm must be used to obtain only 24 bits of precision. The pseudocode uses round-to-nearest-ties-to-even just for illustration.

Figure 3.1 illustrates the real number line and the location of floating-point numbers on it. Underflow occurs in the interval of real numbers $(0, 2^{-149})$, which cannot be represented by float numbers. Subnormals occur in the interval of real numbers $[2^{-149}, 2^{-126})$. Normals occur in the interval of real numbers $[2^{-126}, 2^{128})$. Overflow occurs in the interval of real numbers $[2^{128}, \infty)$, which cannot be represented by float numbers. The floating-point number $0.\overline{0}^{22}1 * 2^{-126} = 2^{-149}$ is the smallest subnormal, where the notation $\overline{0}^{22}$ means that 0 is repeated 22 times. The largest subnormal is $0.\overline{1}^{23} * 2^{-126}$. The smallest normal is 2^{-126} and the largest normal is $1.\overline{1}^{23} * 2^{127}$.

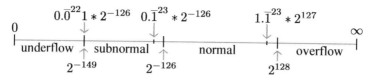

FIGURE 3.1: The real number line and locations of some float numbers.

Let $x \in (0, 2^{-149})$ be a BSNumber. The two float numbers closest to x are the interval endpoints. The midpoint of the interval is 2^{-150}. If $x \leq 2^{-150}$, it is rounded to zero. If $x > 2^{-150}$, it is rounded to 2^{-149}. Pseudocode is shown in Listing 3.4.

```
BSNumber bsn = <a nonzero number>;
uint32_t s = (bsn.sign < 0 ? 1 : 0);
uint32_t b;   // biased exponent for float
uint32_t u;   // trailing significand for float
int32_t p = bsn.GetExponent();   // biasedExponent + numBits - 1
if (p < -149)
{
    if (p < -150 || bsn.uinteger == 1)
    {
        // round to 0 (bsn.uinteger is 1, this is a tie, so round to even)
        b = 0;
        u = 0;
    }
    else
    {
        // round to 2^-149
        b = 0;
        u = 1;
    }
}
// else: other cases discussed later

union { float number; uint32_t encoding; } result;
result.encoding = (s << 31) | (b << 23) | u;
```

Listing 3.4: Conversion of a BSNumber in $(0, 2^{-149})$ to 0 or the minimum subnormal float.

Let $x = 1.u * 2^p = \hat{u} * 2^{p-n}$ be a BSNumber in the interval $[2^{-149}, 2^{-126})$, so $-149 \leq p < -126$. The number of bits of $\hat{u} = 1u$ is $n+1$, where it is possible that $n+1 > 24$ which exceeds the precision of float. The number may be written as

$$x = \left(0.1u * 2^{-q}\right) * 2^{-126} = 0.\overline{0}^q \hat{u} * 2^{-126} = 0.\tilde{t} * 2^{-126} \qquad (3.18)$$

where $q = -(p + 127)$ with $0 \leq q \leq 22$ and $\tilde{t} = \overline{0}^q \hat{u}$ is a bit pattern starting with q 0-bits and ending with the bits of $\hat{u}$.

A 23-bit trailing significand t must be generated from $\tilde{t}$ in order to create a float subnormal $y = 0.t * 2^{-126}$. The number of bits of $\tilde{t}$ is $m = n + 1 + q$. If $m \leq 23$, then $t = \tilde{t}$. If $m \geq 24$, then choose the indexing scheme $\tilde{t} = \tilde{t}_{22} \cdots \tilde{t}_0 \tilde{w}$, where $\tilde{w}$ are the trailing bits of the pattern. There is at least one trailing bit, call it w_0. If $w_0 = 0$, round down to obtain $t = \tilde{t}_{22} \cdots \tilde{t}_0$. Otherwise $w_0 = 1$; if $\hat{u} = 1$, then $0.\tilde{t} = 1/2$ which leads to rounding up, but if $\hat{u} > 1$, then $0.\tilde{t} > 1/2$ because $\hat{u}$ is an odd integer (by design of binary scientific numbers). In either case, round up by computing $t' = t + 1$. If no carry-out occurs in the summation, then $y = 0.t' * 2^{-126}$. If carry-out occurs, then t consists of all 1-bits and $y = 1.0 * 2^{-126}$ which is the minimum normal float number.

Pseudocode is shown in Listing 3.5. The algorithm of the previous paragraph is encapsulated in GetSubnormalTrailing.

```
BSNumber bsn = <a nonzero number>;
uint32_t s = (bsn.sign < 0 ? 1 : 0);
uint32_t b;   // biased exponent for float
uint32_t t;   // trailing significand for float
int32_t p = bsn.GetExponent();   // biasedExponent + numBits − 1
if (−149 <= p && p < −126)
{
    int32_t q = −(p + 127);
    t = bsn.GetSubnormalTrailing(q);
    if (t & (1 << 23))
    {
        // The first 23 bits of û were all 1 and the remaining bits led to rounding up,
        // so round up to the minimum normal.
        b = 1;
        t = 0;
    }
    else
    {
        b = 0;
    }
}
// else: other cases discussed later

union { float number; uint32_t encoding; } result;
result.encoding = (s << 31) | (b << 23) | u;
```

Listing 3.5: Conversion of a BSNumber in $[2^{-149}, 2^{-126})$ to a subnormal float.

Let $x = 1.u * 2^p = \hat{u} * 2^{p-n}$ be a BSNumber in the interval $[2^{-126}, 2^{128})$, so $-126 \leq p < 128$. The number of bits of $\hat{u} = 1u$ is $n + 1$, where it is possible that $n + 1 > 24$ which exceeds the precision of float.

A 23-bit trailing significand t must be generated so that $y = 1.t * 2^p = \hat{t} * 2^{p-k}$, where t has k bits (to be determined), is the floating-point number closest to x. The number of bits of $\hat{u}$ is $m = n + 1$. If $m \leq 24$, then $\hat{t} = \hat{u}$. If $m \geq 25$, then choose the indexing scheme $\hat{t} = 1hatt_{22} \cdots \hat{t}_0\hat{w}$, where $\hat{w}$ are the trailing bits. There is at least one trailing bit, call it w_0. If $w_0 = 0$, round down to obtain $\hat{t} = 1\hat{t}_{22} \cdots \hat{t}_0$; otherwise, $w_0 = 1$ and $\hat{u}$ being an odd integer require rounding up. To round up, compute $\hat{t}' = \hat{t} + 1$. If no carry-out occurs in the summation, then $y = \hat{t}' * 2^p$. If carry-out occurs, the $\hat{t}$ consists of all 1-bits and $y = 1.0 * 2^{p+1}$. Moreover, with carry-out and $p = 127$, overflow occurs and y becomes the float positive infinity.

Pseudocode is shown in Listing 3.6.

```
BSNumber bsn = <a nonzero number>;
uint32_t s = (bsn.sign < 0 ? 1 : 0);
uint32_t b;   // biased exponent for float
uint32_t t;   // trailing significand for float
```

```
int32_t p = bsn.GetExponent();    // biasedExponent + numBits - 1
if (-126 <= p && p < 128)
{
    t = bsn.GetNormalTrailing();
    if (t & (1 << 24))
    {
        // The first 24 bits of û were all 1 and the remaining bits led to rounding up,
        // so round up to the closest normal that is larger.
        ++b;
        t >>= 1;
    }
    // Eliminate the leading 1 (implied for IEEE normal floats)
    t &= ~(1 << 24);
}
// else p < -127 and cases were discussed previously or p >= 128 and all such binary
// scientific numbers are converted to positive infinity.

union { float number; uint32_t encoding; } result;
result.encoding = (s << 31) | (b << 23) | u;
```

Listing 3.6: Conversion of a BSNumber in $[2^{-126}, 2^{128})$ to a normal float.

The block of code that increments b and shifts-right t is not intuitive. To get to this block, note that $x = 1.\overline{1}^{23} f * 2^p$, where the first bit of f is 1. The float biased exponent is $b = p + 127$ and the t returned from GetNormalTrailing is 2^{24}. To round up, add 1 to $1.\overline{2}^{23}$ to obtain $10.0 * 2^p = 1.0 * 2^{p+1}$. To obtain the equivalent for the float result, the biased exponent must be incremented and the trailing significand must be zero. The shift-right produces $t = 2^{23}$, but regardless of rounding the returned t had an explicit 1 stored at index 23 because of the conversion to normal form. That bit is cleared so that $t = 0$.

3.4.3 BSRational to BSNumber of Specified Precision

Let the binary scientific rational have numerator $n = 1.u * 2^p$ and denominator $d = 1.v * 2^q \neq 0$. The ratio is

$$\frac{n}{d} = \begin{cases} (1.u)/(1.v) * 2^{p-q}, & 1.u \geq 1.v \\ 2(1.u)/(1.v) * 2^{p-q-1}, & 1.u < 1.v \end{cases} \tag{3.19}$$

The ratios on the right-hand side are rational numbers in the interval $[1, 2)$ and so represent the right-hand side as $1.w * 2^r$ with the understanding that w is potentially an infinite sequence of bits.

To compute the exponent e for the result, use the comparison operator for binary scientific numbers. Compute $e = p - q$ and modify $n = 1.u$ and $d = 1.v$. If $n < d$, subtract 1 from e (it is now $p - q - 1$) and add 1 to the exponent for n (it is now $2 * (1.u)$ with $n \geq d$). At this time $n/d = 1.w$. Compute enough bits of w to obtain the floating-point number closest to n/d using one of the rounding algorithms discussed in Section 2.4.

The conversion algorithm uses binary scientific rational arithmetic. Starting with $n/d = 1.w_0 w_1 \cdots$, subtract 1 and multiply by 2 to obtain $2(n-d)/d = w_0.w_1 \cdots$. The new numerator is $n_0 = 2(n-d)$, so $n_0/d = w_0.w_1 \cdots$. If $n_0 \geq d$, then $w_0 = 1$ and repeat the algorithm to move w_1 before the binary point.

If $n_0 < d$, then $w_0 = 0$; the next numerator is simply $n_1 = 2n_0$ because no subtraction by 1 is necessary. The algorithm is repeated until the specified precision (number of bits) has been computed. As the bits are discovered, they are OR-ed into an unsigned integer to be used as the significand of the floating-point number, say, $w_0 w_1 \cdots w_{p-1}$ where $w_0 = 1$.

The remaining bits of w must be examined to determine in which direction to round. At this time in the algorithm, $n/d = r_0.r_1 \cdots \in [0, 2)$. The specified rounding mode is applied to the r-bits. For the mode round-to-nearest-ties-to-even, $v = n/d - 1 \in [-1, 1)$ and rounding up occurs when $v > 0$ (the remainder $0.r > 1/2$) or when $v = 0$ and $w_{p-1} = 1$ (the remainder $0.r == 1/2$ and the last bit of the integer part is odd). For the mode round-toward-positive, rounding up occurs when $n/d > 0$ and the original number to be converted is positive. For the mode round-toward-negative, rounding down occurs when $n/d > 0$ and the original number to be converted is negative. For round-toward-zero, only truncation occurs, so the integer part of computed previously is used as-is.

The round-up operation amounts to adding 1 to $w_0 w_1 \cdots w_{p-1}$. The constraint on nonzero binary scientific numbers is that the unsigned integer representing the bits is a positive integer. The sum is not necessarily positive. If it is even, it must be right-shifted by some number s of bits. The power e ($p - q$ or $p - q - 1$) is updated by adding s to it. The biased exponent for the binary scientific number is then set to $e - (p - 1)$.

Pseudocode is shown in Listing 3.7.

```
BSNumber Convert(BSRational input, int precision, int roundingMode)
{
    if (input.sign == 0)
    {
        return 0;
    }

    // The ratio is abstractly of the form n/d = (1.u * 2^p)/(1.v * 2^q). Convert to the form
    // (1.u/1.v) * 2^(p-q) if 1.u ≥ 1.v, or 2 * (1.u/1.v) * 2^(p-q-1) if 1.u < 1.v, which are in
    // the interval [1, 2).
    BSNumber n = input.numerator, d = input.denominator;
    int sign = n.sign * d.sign;
    n.sign = 1;
    d.sign = 1;

    // The native member of BSNumber is the biased exponent. The exponent is computed
    // from it and the number of bits in the unsigned integer container, so get/set functions
    // are used here.
    int pmq = n.GetExponent() - d.GetExponent();
    n.SetExponent(0);
    d.SetExponent(0);
    if (n < d)
    {
        n.SetExponent(n.GetExponent() + 1);
        --pmq;
    }

    // Prepare the output to have its bits set. The size is the number of uint words in the
    // unsigned integer array container for output.
    int precisionM1 = precision - 1;
    BSNumber output;
```

```
output . uinteger . SetNumBits ( precision );
output . uinteger . SetAllBitsToZero ();
output . sign = sign ;
output . biasedExponent = pmq − precisionM1 ;
int size = output . uinteger . GetSize ();
int current = size − 1;
int lastBit = −1;
uint∗ bits = output . uinteger . GetBits ();
uint mask = (1 << ( precisionM1 % 32));
```

```
// Let p be the precision. At this time, n/d = 1.c ∈ [1, 2). Define the sequence of bits
// w = 1c = w_{p−1}w_{p−2} . . . w_0 r, where w_{p−1} = 1. The bits r after w_0 are used for
// rounding based on the user-specified rounding mode. Compute p bits for w, the
// leading bit guaranteed to be 1 and occurring at index (1 ≪ (precision-1)).
for (int i = precisionM1 ; i >= 0; −−i )
{
    if (n < d)
    {
        n = 2 ∗ n;
        lastBit = 0;
    }
    else
    {
        n = 2 ∗ ( n − d );
        bits [ current ] |= mask ;
        lastBit = 1;
    }

    if ( mask == 0x00000001u )
    {
        −−current ;
        mask = 0x80000000u ;
    }
    else
    {
        mask >>= 1;
    }
}
```

```
// At this point as a sequence of bits, r = n/d = r_0 r_1 . . . . The function call
// output.uinteger.RoundUp() adds 1 to output.uinteger and then right-shifts the
// result to an odd integer. The return value is the number s of bits shifted.
if ( roundingMode == FE_TONEAREST )
{
    n = n − d;
    if ( n . sign > 0 || ( n . sign == 0 && lastBit == 1))
    {
        // round up
        output . biasedExponent += output . uinteger . RoundUp ();
    }
    // else round down, equivalent to truncating the r bits.
}
else if ( roundingMode == FE_UPWARD )
{
    if ( n . sign > 0 && sign > 0)
    {
        // round up
        output . biasedExponent += output . uinteger . RoundUp ();
    }
    // else round down, equivalent to truncating the r bits.
}
else if ( roundingMode == FE_DOWNWARD )
{
    if ( n . sign > 0 && sign < 0)
    {
```

```
        // Round down. This is the round-up operation applied to output.uinteger,
        // but the final sign is negative which amounts to rounding down.
        output.biasedExponent += output.uinteger.RoundUp();
    }
    // else round down, equivalent to truncating the r bits.
}
// else roundingMode == FE_TOWARDZERO. Truncate the r bits, which requires no
// additional work.

return output;
}
```

Listing 3.7: Conversion of a BSRational to a floating-point number. The precision must be positive and not exceed the maximum number of bits of the arbitrary-precision type. The rounding mode is one of the four supported by C++ in <cfenv>.

3.4.4   BSNumber to BSNumber of Specified Precision

Another useful operation involves converting a high-precision binary scientific number to a low-precision binary scientific number. Let the input be $x = 1.u * 2^e$ with $\hat{u} = 1u$ an odd integer with $n+1$ bits. Let $p \geq 1$ be the user-specified number of bits of precision of the output. That output is $y = 1.v * 2^e$ with $\hat{v} = 1v$ an odd integer with p bits.

If the input is 0, the output is 0. Or if $p \geq n+1$, the input already has at most the specified precision, so the output is the input. In both cases, $y = x$.

Let $p < n+1$. The simplest algorithm for computing the output uses a bit-by-bit copy of the first $p-1$ bits of $\hat{u}$ to $\hat{v}$ followed by rounding the remaining bits based on the user-specified rounding mode. Naturally, the algorithm can be optimized to process blocks of bits at a time. Pseudocode is shown in Listing 3.8.

```
BSNumber Convert(BSNumber input, int precision, int roundingMode)
{
    // The BSNumber zero has no precision, so set the output to the input.
    if (input == 0)
    {
        return input;
    }

    // Let p be the precision and n+1 be the number of bits of the input. Compute n+1-p.
    // If it is nonpositive, then the requested precision is already satisfied by the input.
    int np1mp = input.uinteger.GetNumBits() - precision;
    if (np1mp <= 0)
    {
        return input;
    }

    // At this point, the requested number of bits is smaller than the number of bits in the
    // input. Round the input to the smaller number of bits using the specified rounding mode.
    BSNumber output;
    output.uinteger.SetNumBits(precision);
    output.uinteger.SetAllBitsToZero();
    int const outSize = output.uinteger.GetSize();
    int const precisionM1 = precision - 1;
    int const outLeading = precisionM1 % 32;
```

```
uint outMask = (1 << outLeading);
uint* outBits = output.uinteger.GetBits();
int outCurrent = outSize - 1;

int inSize = input.uinteger.GetSize();
int inLeading = (input.uinteger.GetNumBits() - 1) % 32;
uint inMask = (1 << inLeading);
uint* inBits = input.uinteger.GetBits();
int inCurrent = inSize - 1;

int lastBit = -1;
for (int i = precisionM1; i >= 0; --i)
{
    if (inBits[inCurrent] & inMask)
    {
        outBits[outCurrent] |= outMask;
        lastBit = 1;
    }
    else
    {
        lastBit = 0;
    }

    if (inMask == 0x00000001u)
    {
        --inCurrent;
        inMask = 0x80000000u;
    }
    else
    {
        inMask >>= 1;
    }

    if (outMask == 0x00000001u)
    {
        --outCurrent;
        outMask = 0x80000000u;
    }
    else
    {
        outMask >>= 1;
    }
}
```

```
// At this point as a sequence of bits, the remainder is r = u_{n-p} ... u_0.
int inSign = input.GetSign();
int outExponent = input.GetExponent();
if (roundingMode == FE_TONEAREST)
{
    // Determine whether u_{n-p} is positive.
    uint positive = (inBits[inCurrent] & inMask) != 0u;
    if (positive && (np1mp > 1 || lastBit == 1))
    {
        // round up
        outExponent += output.uinteger.RoundUp();
    }
    // else round down, equivalent to truncating the r bits.
}
else if (roundingMode == FE_UPWARD)
{
    // The remainder r must be positive because n - p >= 0 and u_0 == 1.
    if (sign > 0)
    {
        // round up
        outExponent += output.uinteger.RoundUp();
    }
```

```
      // else round down, equivalent to truncating the r bits.
  }
  else if (roundingMode == FE_DOWNWARD)
  {
      // The remainder r must be positive because n − p ≥ 0 and u₀ = 1.
      if (inSign < 0)
      {
          // Round down. This is the round-up operation applied to output.uinteger,
          // but the final sign is negative which amounts to rounding down.
          outExponent += output.uinteger.RoundUp();
      }
      // else round down, equivalent to truncating the r bits.
  }
  // else roundingMode == FE_TOWARDZERO. Truncate the r bits, which requires no
  // additional work.

  output.SetSign(inSign);
  output.SetBiasedExponent(outExponent − precisionM1);
}
```

Listing 3.8: Conversion of a BSNumber to a BSNumber with a user-specified precision p. The precision must be positive and not exceed the maximum number of bits of the arbitrary-precision type. The rounding mode is one of the four supported by C++ in <cfenv>.

3.5   Performance Considerations

The GTL provides a class UIntegerAP32 that supports the unsigned integer storage and logic for arbitrary precision arithmetic. The storage is of type std::vector<uint32_t>. For a large number of computations and for a large required number of bits of precision to produce an exact result, the two main runtime bottlenecks are allocation and deallocation of the std::vector arrays together and copying of arrays. To remedy this, a template class UIntegerFP32<N> is provided that allows the user to specify the maximum number N of 32-bit words required to store the exact final result in a sequence of computations. The storage is of type std::array<uint32_t>. Moreover, the code has been optimized to compute quantities in-place and to use move semantics whenever possible in order to reduce the time for copying.

3.5.1   Static Computation of Maximum Precision

The technical challenge for using UIntegerFP32<int N> is to determine how large N must be for a sequence of computations. Let x and y be arbitrary-precision numbers and let $z = x \circ y$, where $\circ$ is one of $+$, $-$, $*$ or $/$. The exact result z is also an arbitrary-precision number, which generally will require more bits of precision than its inputs.

A set A of arbitrary-precision numbers has parameters associated with it. Define $b_{\max}(A)$ to be the maximum number of bits of precision, define $e_{\min}(A)$ to be the minimum exponent and define $e_{\max}(A)$ to be the maximum exponent. For the set of finite float numbers F: $b_{\max}(F) = 24$, $e_{\min}(F) = -149$ and $e_{\max}(F) = 127$. For the set of finite double numbers D: $b_{\max}(D) = 53$, $e_{\min}(D) = -1074$ and $e_{\max}(D) = 1023$. When computing a binary operation $z = x \circ y$, define X, Y and Z to be the sets of arbitrary-precision numbers that contain numbers x, y and z, respectively. The parameters for the output set Z are necessarily dependent on the parameters for the input sets X and Y. The relationships are explored in this section.

Let $a \in A$ be of the form $a = 1.u * 2^p = \hat{u} * 2^{p-n}$, where $\hat{u}$ is an $(n+1)$-bit odd integer with $1 \le n+1 \le b_{\max}(A)$. The exponent p satisfies $e_{\min}(A) \le p \le e_{\max}(A)$. In A, the smallest positive number is $a_{\min}$ and the largest positive number is $a_{\max}$ with representations

$$
\begin{aligned}
a_{\min} &= 1 * 2^{e_{\min}(A)} \\
a_{\max} &= 1.\overline{1}^{b_{\max}(A)} * 2^{e_{\max}(A)} = \overline{1}^{b_{\max}(A)+1} * 2^{e_{\max}(A)-b_{\max}(A)}
\end{aligned}
\tag{3.20}
$$

The maximum number of bits is constrained by

$$
b_{\max}(A) \le e_{\max}(A) - e_{\min}(A)
\tag{3.21}
$$

which ensures that each positive number of A is an integer multiple of $a_{\min}$.

3.5.1.1 Addition and Subtraction

The addition of positive numbers potentially leads to an increase in the number of bits of precision and an increase in the maximum exponent. On the other hand, subtraction of positive numbers leads to a reduction of these parameters. However, when determining the parameters for expressions such as $x+y$ and $x-y$, at compile time the signs of x and y are usually not known. To be conservative, the parameters are computed for the addition operator and then used for the subtraction operator.

The minimum exponent is attained by the smaller of $x_{\min}$ and $y_{\min}$, where the minimum values are defined by equation (3.20); therefore $e_{\min}(Z) = \min\{e_{\min}(X), e_{\min}(Y)\}$.

The maximum exponent is attained by $z_{\max} = x_{\max} + y_{\max}$, where the maximum values of the inputs are defined by equation (3.20). Consider the case $e_{\max}(X) \ge e_{\max}(Y)$. If no carry-out occurs in the sum, then $e_{\max}(X)$ is the maximum exponent. If there is a carry-out, then $e_{\max}(X) + 1$ is the maximum exponent. A carry-out occurs when a 1-bit of $x_{\max}$ overlaps with a 1-bit of $y_{\max}$; this happens when $e_{\max}(X) - b_{\max}(X) + 1 \le e_{\max}(Y)$. Similarly, if $e_{\max}(Y) \ge e_{\max}(X)$, the maximum exponent is $e_{\max}(Y)$ when there is no carry-out or $e_{\max}(Y) + 1$ when there is a carry-out. The carry-out occurs when $e_{\max}(Y) - b_{\max}(Y) + 1 \le e_{\max}(X)$.

The maximum number of bits is attained by adding the largest number of one input set with the smallest number of the other input that also has the most 1-bits possible. Consider the case $e_{\max}(X) \geq e_{\max}(Y)$. The sum that leads to the maximum number of bits is

$$x_{\max} + \bar{y} = \overline{1}^{b_{\max}(X)} * 2^{e_{\max}(X)-b_{\max}(X)+1} + \overline{1}^{b_{\max}(Y)} * 2^{e_{\min}(Y)} \qquad (3.22)$$

If no carry-out occurs in the sum, then $e_{\max}(X) - e_{\min}(Y) + 1$ is the maximum number of bits. If there is a carry-out, then $e_{\max}(X) - e_{\min}(Y) + 2$ is the maximum number of bits. A carry-out occurs when a 1-bit of $x_{\max}$ overlaps with a 1-bit of $\bar{y}$; this happens when $e_{\max}(X) - b_{\max}(X) + 1 \leq e_{\min}(Y) + b_{\max}(Y) - 1$. If $e_{\max}(Y) \geq e_{\max}(X)$, the sum that leads to the maximum number of bits is

$$\bar{x} + y_{\max} = \overline{1}^{b_{\max}(X)} * 2^{e_{\min}(X)} + \overline{1}^{b_{\max}(Y)} * 2^{e_{\max}(Y)-b_{\max}(Y)+1} \qquad (3.23)$$

If no carry-out occurs in the sum, then $e_{\max}(Y) - e_{\min}(X) + 1$ is the maximum number of bits. If there is a carry-out, then $e_{\max}(Y) - e_{\min}(X) + 2$ is the maximum number of bits. A carry-out occurs when a 1-bit of $\bar{x}$ overlaps with a 1-bit of $y_{\max}$; this happens when $e_{\max}(Y) - b_{\max}(Y) + 1 \leq e_{\min}(X) + b_{\max}(X) - 1$.

Equation (3.24) summarizes the relationships of the parameters for addition,

$$e_{\min}(Z) = \min\{e_{\min}(X), e_{\min}(Y)\}$$

$$e_{\max}(Z) = \begin{cases} e_{\max}(X) + c_0(X,Y), & e_{\max}(X) \geq e_{\max}(Y) \\ e_{\max}(Y) + c_0(Y,X), & e_{\max}(Y) \geq e_{\max}(X) \end{cases}$$

$$b_{\max}(Z) = \begin{cases} e_{\max}(X) - e_{\min}(Y) + 1 + c_1(X,Y), & e_{\max}(X) \geq e_{\max}(Y) \\ e_{\max}(Y) - e_{\min}(X) + 1 + c_1(Y,X), & e_{\max}(Y) \geq e_{\max}(X) \end{cases} \qquad (3.24)$$

$$c_0(U,V) = \begin{cases} 1, & e_{\max}(U) - b_{\max}(U) + 1 \leq e_{\max}(V) \\ 0, & e_{\max}(U) - b_{\max}(U) + 1 > e_{\max}(V) \end{cases}$$

$$c_1(U,V) = \begin{cases} 1, & e_{\max}(U) - e_{\min}(V) + 1 \leq b_{\max}(U) + b_{\max}(V) - 1 \\ 0, & e_{\max}(U) - e_{\min}(V) + 1 > b_{\max}(U) + b_{\max}(V) - 1 \end{cases}$$

3.5.1.2   Multiplication

Multiplication is $z = x * y = (1.u * 2^p) * (1.v * 2^q) = (\hat{u} * \hat{v}) * 2^{(p-n)+(q-m)} = \hat{w} * 2^{(p-n)+(q-m)}$. As mentioned in Section 3.2.3, the maximum number of bits required for computing the integer $\hat{w}$ is $(n+1) + (m+1)$; therefore, $b_{\max}(Z) = b_{\max}(X) + b_{\max}(Y)$.

The minimum exponent occurs by multiplying the smallest numbers to which x and y can be subject to their precision and minimum-exponent constraints. The numbers are $1 * 2^{p_{\min}}$ and $1 * 2^{q_{\min}}$. The product is $1 * 2^{p_{\min}+q_{\min}}$; therefore, $e_{\min}(Z) = e_{\min}(X) + e_{\min}(Y)$.

The maximum exponent occurs by multiplying the largest numbers to which x and y can be subject to their precision and maximum-exponent constraints,

$$
\begin{aligned}
x_{\max} * y_{\max} &= \overline{1}^{b_{\max}(X)} * 2^{e_{\max}(X)-b_{\max}(X)+1} * \\
&\quad \overline{1}^{b_{\max}(Y)} * 2^{e_{\max}(Y)-b_{\max}(Y)+1} \\
&= \hat{w} * 2^{(e_{\max}(X)-b_{\max}(X)+1)+(e_{\max}(Y)-b_{\max}(Y)+1)} \\
&= 1.w * 2^{e_{\max}(X)+e_{\max}(Y)+1}
\end{aligned}
\tag{3.25}
$$

where $\hat{w}$ has $b_{\max}(X) + b_{\max}(Y)$ bits and w has $b_{\max}(X) + b_{\max}(Y) + 1$ bits; therefore, $e_{\max}(Z) = e_{\max}(X) + e_{\max}(Y) + 1$.

Equation (3.26) summarizes the relationships of the parameters for multiplication,

$$
\begin{aligned}
b_{\max}(Z) &= b_{\max}(X) + b_{\max}(Y) \\
e_{\min}(Z) &= e_{\min}(X) + e_{\min}(Y) \\
e_{\max}(Z) &= e_{\max}(X) + e_{\max}(Y) + 1
\end{aligned}
\tag{3.26}
$$

The GTL provides a class named BSPrecision that allows a user to specify expressions and then compute N for the fixed-precision UIntegerFP32<N>. Listing 3.9 shows how to determine the number of bits required to compute sums, products and ratios of arbitrary-precision numbers. The number of words for an expression is what is used for the template parameter N.

```
BSPrecision  fx(BSPrecision::IS_FLOAT),  fy(BSPrecision::IS_FLOAT);
// emin = -149, emax = 127, b = 24, w = 1
BSPrecision  dx(BSPrecision::IS_DOUBLE),  dy(BSPrecision::IS_DOUBLE);
// emin = -1074, emax = 1023, b = 53, w = 2
BSPrecision  ix(BSPrecision::IS_INT32),  iy(BSPrecision::IS_INT32);
// emin = 0, emax = 30, b = 31, w = 1
BSPrecision  sum,  product,  ratio;

// sum and product of 'float' type
sum = fx + fy;
// bsn: emin = -149, emax = 128, b = 277, w = 9
// bsr: emin = -298, emax = 256, b = 554, w = 18
product = fx * fy;
// bsn: emin = -298, emax = 255, b = 48, w = 2
// bsr: emin = -298, emax = 255, b = 48, w = 2

// sum and product of 'double' type
sum = dx + dy;
// bsn: emin = -1074, emax = 1024, b = 2098, w = 66
// bsr: emin = -2148, emax = 2048, b = 4196, w = 132
product = dx * dy;
// bsn: emin = -2148, emax = 2047, b = 106, w = 4
// bsr: emin = -2148, emax = 2047, b = 106, w = 4

// sum and product of 'int' type
sum = ix + iy;
// bsn: emin = 0, emax = 31, b = 32, w = 1
// bsr: emin = 0, emax = 62, b = 63, w = 2
product = ix * iy;
// bsn: emin = 0, emax = 61, b = 62, w = 2
// bsr: emin = 0, emax = 61, b = 62, w = 2

// sum and product of mixed types 'float' and 'double'
```

```
sum = dx + fy;   // same for fx + dy
// bsn: emin = -1074, emax = 1023, b = 1173, w = 37
// bsr: emin = -1223, emax = 1152, b = 2375, w = 75
product = dx * fy;   // same for fx * dy
// bsn: emin = -1223, emax = 1151, b = 77, w = 3
// bsr: emin = -1223, emax = 1151, b = 77, w = 3

// sum and product of mixed types 'int' and 'float'
sum = ix + fy;   // same for fx + iy
// bsn: emin = -149, emax = 127, b = 128, w = 4
// bsr: emin = -149, emax = 159, b = 308, w = 10
product = ix * fy;   // same for fx * iy
// bsn: emin = -149, emax = 158, b = 55, w = 2
// bsr: emin = -149, emax = 158, b = 55, w = 2

// ratio of various types (valid only for BSRational)
ratio = fx / fy;
// bsr: emin = -298, emax = 255, b = 48, w = 2
ratio = dx / dy;
// bsr: emin = -2148, emax = 2047, b = 106, w = 4
ratio = ix / iy;
// bsr: emin = 0, emax = 61, b = 62, w = 2
ratio = fx / iy;   // same for ix / fy
// bsr: emin = -149, emax = 158, b = 55, w = 2
```

Listing 3.9: Code for determining the number of bits required to compute sums, products and ratios of arbitrary-precision numbers. The reported numbers are the minimum exponent emin, the maximum exponent emax, the maximum number of bits b and the number of 32-bit words required to store the maximum number of bits. The comments with bsn are the values for BSNumber and the comments with bsr are the values for BSRational.

Listing 3.10 shows how to compute the number of bits required to compute determinants for square matrices of size 2, 3 and 4.

```
// It is not necessary to have distinct BSPrecision inputs, because all inputs have the same
// precision parameters. The code computes the parameters for the output, not the actual
// determinant. In the comments, the matrix is A = [a_ij] with entry a_ij in row i and column j.
BSPrecision fx(BSPrecision::IS_FLOAT), dx(BSPrecision::IS_DOUBLE);

// The determinant is a_00 a_11 − a_01 a_10.
BSPrecision fd2 = fx*fx−fx*fx;
// bsn: emin = -298, emax = 256, b = 554, w = 18
// bsr: emin = -596, emax = 512, b = 1108, w = 35
BSPrecision dd2 = dx*dx−dx*dx;
// bsn: emin = -2148, emax = 2048, b = 4196, w = 132
// bsr: emin = -4296, emax = 4096, b = 8392, w = 263

// The determinant is a_00(a_11 a_22 − a_12 a_21) − a_01(a_10 a_22 − a_12 a_20) + a_02(a_10 a_21 − a_11 a_20).
// The parameters of the three 2 × 2 determinants in the expression are all the same, so fdet2
// and ddet2 can be used for multiple inputs.
BSPrecision fd3 = fx*fd2−fx*fd2+fx*fd2;
// bsn: emin = -447, emax = 386, b = 834, w = 27
// bsr: emin = -1341, emax = 1156, b = 2498, w = 79
BSPrecision dd3 = dx*dd2−dx*dd2+dx*dd2;
// bsn: emin = -3222, emax = 3074, b = 6297, w = 197
// bsr: emin = -9666, emax = 9220, b = 18887, w = 591

// The determinant is computed using a cofactor expansion of the first row,
```

```
// a₀₀ det(M₀₀) − a₀₁ det(M₀₁) + a₀₂ det(M₀₂) − a₀₃ det(M₀₃), where Mᵢⱼ is the 3 × 3
// matrix obtained from A by removing row i and column j.
BSPrecision fd4 = fx*fd3−fx*fd3+fx*fd3−fx*fd3;
// bsn: emin = -596, emax = 517, b = 1114, w = 35
// bsr: emin = -2384, emax = 2062, b = 4447, w = 139
BSPrecision dd4 = dx*dd3−dx*dd3+dx*dd3−dx*dd3;
// bsn: emin = -4296, emax = 4101, b = 8398, w = 263
// bsr: emin = -17184, emax = 16398, b = 33583, w = 1050
```

```
// The determinant is computed using the Laplace expansion theorem.
// u₀ = a₀₀a₁₁ − a₀₁a₁₀, v₀ = a₂₀a₃₁ − a₂₁a₃₀
// u₁ = a₀₀a₁₂ − a₀₂a₁₀, v₁ = a₂₀a₃₂ − a₂₂a₃₀
// u₂ = a₀₀a₁₃ − a₀₂a₁₀, v₂ = a₂₀a₃₃ − a₂₃a₃₀
// u₃ = a₀₁a₁₂ − a₀₂a₁₁, v₃ = a₂₁a₃₂ − a₂₂a₃₁
// u₄ = a₀₁a₁₃ − a₀₃a₁₁, v₄ = a₂₁a₃₃ − a₂₃a₃₁
// u₅ = a₀₂a₁₃ − a₀₃a₁₂, v₅ = a₂₂a₃₃ − a₂₃a₃₂
// d = u₀v₅ − u₁v₄ + u₂v₃u₃v₂ − u₄v₁ + u₅v₀
fd4 = fd2*fd2−fd2*fd2+fd2*fd2+fd2*fd2−fd2*fd2+fd2*fd2;
// bsn: emin = -596, emax = 518, b = 1115, w = 35
// bsr: emin = -3576, emax = 3088, b = 6665, w = 209
dd4 = dd2*dd2−dd2*dd2+dd2*dd2+dd2*dd2−dd2*dd2+dd2*dd2;
// bsn: emin = -4296, emax = 4102, b = 8399, w = 263
// bsr: emin = -25776, emax = 24592, b = 50369, w = 1575
```

Listing 3.10: Code for determining the number of bits required to compute determinants for squared matrices of size 2, 3 and 4.

The determinant for a 4×4 matrix has two results based on different expressions for that quantity. The first tree uses a cofactor expansion by a row or a column of the matrix, which reduces the computation to a sum of determinants of 3×3 matrices. The second tree uses the Laplace expansion theorem [8], which reduces the computation to a sum of products of determinants of 2×2 matrices. The outputs of the two trees have different precision parameters, even though the trees evaluate to the same rational number for a given input matrix. Remember that the precision parameter equations are worst-case estimates. The BSRational estimates are influenced greatly by the number of additions and subtractions because the sum of rationals is $n_0/d_0 + n_1/d_1 = (n_0d_1 + n_1d_0)/(d_0d_1)$ and requires an increase in precision parameters due to the multiplications and sum in the numerator of the output. However, for the determinant computations with float or double inputs, all BSRational denominators are 1, which implies that the numerator is a sum of BSNumber objects—it has no multiplications. If an expression has no division operations, it is better to use BSNumber inputs rather than BSRational.

The BSPrecision class computes the worst-case precision parameters for an expression. However, the magnitudes of these numbers might not be indicative of the cost of evaluating the expression for given inputs. To compute the determinant of a 4×4 matrix, the cofactor expansion requires 40 multiplications and 23 additions, whereas the Laplace expansion formula requires 30 multiplications and 17 additions. The computation time is smaller for the Laplace expansion than for the cofactor expansion, despite BSPrecision reporting that the precision parameters are larger for the Laplace expansion than for the cofactor expansion.

3.5.2   Dynamic Computation of Maximum Precision

The preprocessor symbol GTL_COLLECT_UINTEGERAP32_STATISTICS is disabled in the UIntegerAP32 header file. Enable the flag to expose a static class member in UIntegerAP32 that is used to count the maximum number of bits used in a sequence of computations. This number is a rough estimate for N for the specific input data. Whether or not this is large enough no matter what your inputs must be determined by the user. Enabling the flag also requires the user to define a global object in the executable unit, namely, std::atomic<size_t> gsUIntegerAP32MaxSize. It is atomic in case the executable unit uses multithreading. Listing 3.11 shows how to measure N assuming the aforementioned flag is enabled.

```
float x, y, z;  // all initialized to finite floating-point numbers
UIntegerAP32 :: SetMaxSizeToZero ();
BSNumber<UIntegerAP32> nx(x), ny(y), nz(z);
BSNumber<UIntegerAP32> temp0 = nx + ny * nz;
BSNumber<UIntegreAP32> temp1 = nx * ny + nz;
BSNumber<UIntegerAP32> result = temp0 * temp1;
size_t maxWords = UIntegerAP32 :: GetMaxSize ();
```

Listing 3.11: Counting the maximum number of bits required for a specific input data set.

A similar system exists for UIntegerFP32, even though the storage is of fixed size (template parameter N). The system tracks mSize, the number of array elements used, to determine whether a smaller N will work.

3.5.3   Memory Management

The class UIntegerAP32 uses std::vector for dynamically resizable storage. Once these objects become sufficiently large, memory allocation, memory deallocation and memory copies become a noticeable bottleneck. UIntegerAP32 is designed to compute arithmetic operations in-place to minimize creation of new objects and copies. However, they are not entirely unavoidable in application code. In order to avoid copies, the classes UIntegerAP32, BSNumber, and BSRational have support for C++ move semantics in the form of a move construct and a move operator. When creating temporary BSNumber or BSRational objects that are assigned to other objects, one should consider whether to replace an assignment x = y by a move x = std::move(y).

Although std::move may be passed a std::array, there are no pointers to steal, so the operation becomes a copy. The class UIntegerFP32 uses std::array for fixed-size storage, but its move operator does not apply a move to the array. The reason is that the array has the maximum storage required for the computations, but member mSize keeps track of the number of array elements that are used. Typically, this is smaller than the template parameter N, so both the assignment and move operators for UIntegerFP32 copy only mSize elements, which minimizes copy time.

If a large N is chosen for UIntegerFP32<N>, the default stack size (typically 1 MB) is usually not sufficiently large. The compiler settings for a project should be increased significantly. How this is accomplished depends on the compiler. In Microsoft Visual Studio, this is accomplished by modifying the *stack reserve size*.

Assuming N is chosen large enough to allow any finite floating-point input, the memory of a std::array<uint32_t,N> container is never fully utilized. In most applications, speed is the most important goal, so the memory usage is a necessary evil. That said, the arbitrary precision library is structured so that a user can design and implement the UIntegerType interface, presumably to be more efficient about memory consumption. Such an implementation could also use the same std::array storage but include a memory manager that manages a heap of array objects. Each UIntegerType object can have a pointer member to a std::array rather than its own array, and the memory manager assigns pointers to the members during the arithmetic operations. The memory manager might even partition its heap into subheaps of various maximum sizes, assigning pointers to available blocks that do not waste too much space.

Chapter 4

Interval Arithmetic

Many computational geometry algorithms have common subproblems that involve correctly determining the sign of arithmetic expressions. When computing with floating-point arithmetic, rounding errors can lead to a misclassification of the sign. Arbitrary-precision arithmetic can be used to avoid this problem. In practice when the number of inputs to an algorithm is large enough that the cost of correct sign classification is noticeable, interval arithmetic can be used first to decide (if possible) that an expression evaluates to a positive or a negative number. In some cases, interval arithmetic does not provide enough information to conclude that an expression does not evaluate to zero. The expression must then be computed using arbitrary-precision arithmetic. The goal is that the re-evaluations occur infrequently, leading to an amortized cost that is significantly less than that using only arbitrary-precision arithmetic.

Let the real numbers be denoted $\mathbb{R}$. The discussion uses interval notation for the *extended real numbers*, $\overline{\mathbb{R}}$, which includes $\mathbb{R}$ and representations for positive infinity (∞) and negative infinity ($-\infty$). For any $x \in \mathbb{R}$, the comparisons $-\infty < x$ and $x < +\infty$ are always true. Let a and b be extended real numbers with $a < b$. The *closed interval* is $[a, b] = \{x \in \overline{\mathbb{R}} : a \leq x \leq b\}$. The *open interval* is $(a, b) = \{x \in \overline{\mathbb{R}} : a < x < b\}$. The *half-open (half-closed) intervals* are $[a, b) = \{x \in \overline{\mathbb{R}} : a \leq x < b\}$ and $(a, b] = \{x \in \overline{\mathbb{R}} : a < x \leq b\}$. Degenerate intervals are allowed; for example, the single value c is represented by the degenerate interval $[c, c]$. In the context of interval arithmetic, this allows binary operations when the operands are either single numbers or nondegenerate intervals.

The abstract problem is to evaluate a real-valued function of a real-valued variable, say $y = f(x)$, where $x \in \text{domain}(f)$ and $y \in \text{range}(f)$. In practice, the representation of x as a floating-point number is usually an approximation to x. Floating-point rounding errors occur during the evaluation of the function. In the end, neither x nor y are the real numbers in the abstract problem.

Using mathematical conventions, the function can be evaluated on a set D contained in its domain. The output is a set R contained in its range; that is,

$$f(D) = \{f(x) : x \in D \subseteq \text{domain}(f)\} \subseteq \text{range}(f) \tag{4.1}$$

The set $f(D)$ is all the possible y-values obtained by evaluating f at all the possible x-values in D. The notation is convenient in that when D is a (small) interval whose endpoints are floating-point numbers and that is known to contain the real number x, the theoretical value y is in the set $f(D)$. One example is $f(x) = x^2$ with $f([2,3]) = [4,9]$ and $f([-2,1]) = [0,4]$. Another example is $f(x) = 1/x$ with $f([2,3]) = [1/3,1/2]$ and $f([-3,2]) = (-\infty, -1/3] \cup [1/2, +\infty)$.

When f represents an arithmetic expression with addition, subtraction, multiplication and division operations, interval arithmetic is the process of accepting a floating-point input x and computing bounding intervals as operations are applied. The end result is an interval (or intervals) that contain the true value y. For the application to geometric algorithms, the goal is to correctly classify the sign of the true value y. If D is an interval bound on the true value x, the classification succeeds when $f(D)$ contains only positive numbers, which implies y must be positive even though its true value is not known. Similarly, if $f(D)$ contains only negative numbers, then y must be negative. If $f(D)$ contains zero, the outcome is inconclusive: y might or might not be zero. In this case, arbitrary-precision arithmetic must be used to compute the true value of y to know its sign.

4.1 Arithmetic Operations

The input intervals are $[u_0, u_1]$ and $[v_0, v_1]$ with $u_0 \le u_1$ and $v_0 \le v_1$. Given a binary operation $\circ$ that is one of addition, subtraction, multiplication or division, the output set obtained by applying the operation to the input intervals is

$$[u_0, u_1] \circ [v_0, v_1] = \{u \circ v : u \in [u_0, u_1], v \in [v_0, v_1]\} \qquad (4.2)$$

The interval operations are summarized in equation (4.3).

$$\begin{aligned}
[u_0, u_1] + [v_0, v_1] &= [u_0 + v_0, u_1 + v_1] \\
[u_0, u_1] - [v_0, v_1] &= [u_0 - v_1, u_1 - v_0] \\
[u_0, u_1] * [v_0, v_1] &= [\min_{i,j}\{u_i v_j\}, \max_{i,j}\{u_i v_j\}] \\
[u_0, u_1] / [v_0, v_1] &= [u_0, u_1] * (1/[v_0, v_1])
\end{aligned}$$

$$\qquad (4.3)$$

$$1/[v_0, v_1] = \begin{cases}
[1/v_1, 1/v_0], & 0 \notin [v_0, v_1] \\
[1/v_1, +\infty], & v_0 = 0 \\
[-\infty, 1/v_0], & v_1 = 0 \\
[-\infty, 1/v_0] \cup [1/v_1, +\infty], & 0 \in (v_0, v_1)
\end{cases}$$

The multiplication operation involves minima and maxima of sets of numbers. Although all four products can be computed directly followed by minimum and maximum operations, an analysis of signs of the endpoints leads to the cases presented in Table 4.1. The output interval is $[w_0, w_1]$, where $w_0 = \min_{i,j}\{u_i v_j\}$ and $w_1 = \max_{i,j}\{u_i v_j\}$.

TABLE 4.1: Endpoints of the multiplication interval.

conditions	w_0	w_1
$u_0 \geq 0$ and $v_0 \geq 0$	$u_0 v_0$	$u_1 v_1$
$u_0 \geq 0$ and $v_1 \leq 0$	$u_1 v_0$	$u_0 v_1$
$u_0 \geq 0$ and $v_0 < 0 < v_1$	$u_1 v_0$	$u_1 v_1$
$u_1 \leq 0$ and $v_0 \geq 0$	$u_0 v_1$	$u_1 v_0$
$u_1 \leq 0$ and $v_1 \leq 0$	$u_1 v_1$	$u_0 v_0$
$u_1 \leq 0$ and $v_0 < 0 < v_1$	$u_0 v_1$	$u_0 v_0$
$u_0 < 0 < u_1$ and $v_0 \geq 0$	$u_0 v_1$	$u_1 v_1$
$u_0 < 0 < u_1$ and $v_1 \leq 0$	$u_1 v_0$	$u_0 v_0$
$u_0 < 0 < u_1$ and $v_0 < 0 < v_1$	$\min\{u_0 v_1, u_1 v_0\}$	$\max\{u_0 v_0, u_1 v_1\}$

The interval operations are stated in terms of the arithmetic of real numbers. They may also be used directly when using arbitrary-precision arithmetic. The GTL code has a class APInterval that implements interval arithmetic for an arbitrary-precision type, either BSNumber (no division supported) or BSRational (all operations supported). The GTL code also has a class FPInterval that implements interval arithmetic for types float or double. It turns out that interval arithmetic can also be implemented for quadratic-field numbers which are the topic of Chapter 5.

The definitions must be slightly modified to handle floating-point arithmetic. For example, addition has input intervals $[u_0, u_1]$ and $[v_0, v_1]$ whose endpoints are floating-point numbers. The output interval is $[w_0, w_1] = [u_0 + v_0, u_1 + v_1]$, where w_i are real numbers. When computing with floating-point arithmetic, the sums that produce the output endpoints potentially have rounding errors. If $u \in [u_0, u_1]$ and $v \in [v_0, v_1]$ are real numbers, then the theoretically correct sum $w = u + v \in [w_0, w_1]$. Let f_i be the floating-point sums that were obtained from w_i based on the current rounding mode of the FPU; that is, $w_i = f_i + e_i$ where e_i is the rounding error. A program computes the output interval $[f_0, f_1]$. If $e_0 \geq 0$ and $e_1 \leq 0$, then $[w_0, w_1] \subseteq [f_0, f_1]$ and the floating-point interval is a bounding interval for the sum of the input intervals. If $e_0 > 0$, then $w_0 < f_0$ and w might be in the interval $[w_0, f_0]$, which means $[f_0, f_1]$ is not a bounding interval for w. Similarly, if $e_1 < 0$, then $f_1 < w_1$ and w might be in the interval $[f_1, w_1]$, which means $[f_0, f_1]$ is not a bounding interval. The default FPU rounding mode is round-to-nearest-ties-to-even, which can lead to $e_0 > 0$ or $e_1 < 0$. The mode must be set to round-toward-negative when computing w_0, which guarantees that $e_0 \leq 0$. The mode must be set to round-toward-positive when computing w_1, which guarantees that $e_1 \geq 0$. It is then guaranteed that $[w_0, w_1] \subseteq [f_0, f_1]$, so $[f_0, f_1]$ is a bounding interval for w.

Given two floating-point numbers u and v and a binary floating-point operation $\circ$, let $\text{round}_n(u \circ v)$ denote the result of the operation with mode round-toward-negative and let $\text{round}_p(u \circ v)$ denote the result of the operation with mode round-toward-positive. The interval operations are summarized in equation (4.4).

$$[u_0, u_1] + [v_0, v_1] = [\text{round}_n(u_0 + v_0), \text{round}_p(u_1 + v_1)]$$
$$[u_0, u_1] - [v_0, v_1] = [\text{round}_n(u_0 - v_1), \text{round}_p(u_1 - v_0)]$$
$$[u_0, u_1] * [v_0, v_1] = [\min_{i,j}\{\text{round}_n((u_i v_j)\}, \max_{i,j}\{\text{round}_p(u_i v_j)\}]$$
$$[u_0, u_1] / [v_0, v_1] = [u_0, u_1] * (1/[v_0, v_1])$$

$$(4.4)$$

$$1/[v_0, v_1] = \begin{cases} [\text{round}_n(1/v_1), \text{round}_p(1/v_0)], & 0 \notin [v_0, v_1] \\ [\text{round}_n(1/v_1), +\infty], & v_0 = 0 \\ [-\infty, \text{round}_p(1/v_0)], & v_1 = 0 \\ [-\infty, \text{round}_p(1/v_0)] \cup [\text{round}_n(1/v_1), +\infty], & 0 \in (v_0, v_1) \end{cases}$$

In the context of this book, the use of interval arithmetic is restricted to arithmetic expressions involving only addition, subtraction and multiplication. Although the applications are designed to avoid explicit reference to the infinities, ∞ is defined to be the floating-point number F32_INFINITY from Table 2.1 for type float or F64_INFINITY from Table 2.2 for type double. In C++, these are provided by std::numeric_limits<T>::infinity(), where T is either float or double. The symbol $-\infty$ is defined to be the negation of the aforementioned quantites.

The division operator requires special attention when implementing interval arithmetic. The output set for $1/[v_0, v_1]$ when $0 \in (v_0, v_1)$ consists of two intervals. To avoid this case, an application should decompose such an input interval as $[v_0, v_1] = [v_0, 0) \cup \{0\} \cup [0, v_1]$. Branching logic can be applied to each of the subintervals using only the first three cases for division in equation (4.4).

An arithmetic expression can be thought of as a tree, called an *expression tree*, where the leaf nodes represent the floating-point constants and variables of the expression and where the interior nodes represent the intermediate terms during evaluation of the expression. Each interior node represents the number that is the output of a binary operation whose inputs are the child nodes. The tree concept also applies when the inputs and outputs are intervals that represent error bounds. For example, consider the expression

$$e = x * y + z * w - 2/(3 + t * u * v) \qquad (4.5)$$

The expression has the tree shown in Figure 4.1. The order of operations for $t * u * v = (t * u) * v$ is based on the precedence rules for multiplication.

Each pair of leaf nodes that are the operands of a binary operation are used to compute an interval for that operation. In particular, these subexpressions are $x * y$, $z * w$ and $t * u$. Listing 4.1 contains pseudocode for the operations. The default rounding mode of the FPU is round-to-nearest-ties-to-even, which must be restored after modifying the mode. The two modes used in interval arithmetic are round-toward-positive (roundUpward) and round-toward-negative (roundDownward).

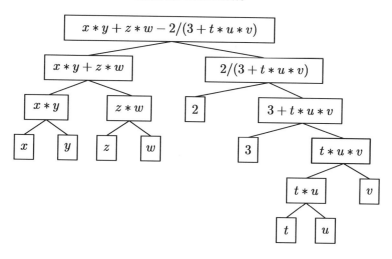

FIGURE 4.1: The expression tree associated with the expression e of equation (4.5).

```
// The function name Operation is one of Add, Sub or Mul with corresponding op of
// +, - or *, respectively.
FPInterval Operation(FPType u, FPType v)
{
    FPInterval w;
    RoundingMode saveMode = GetRoundingMode();
    SetRoundingMode(roundDownward);
    w[0] = u op v;
    SetRoundingMode(roundUpward);
    w[1] = u op v;
    SetRoundingMode(saveMode);
    return w;
}

// Return the interval representing the full set of finite FPType numbers when the
// divisor is zero.
FPInterval Div(FPType u, FPType v)
{
    if (v != 0)
    {
        FPInterval w;
        RoundingMode saveMode = GetRoundingMode();
        SetRoundingMode(roundDownward);
        w[0] = u / v;
        SetRoundingMode(roundUpward);
        w[1] = u / v;
        SetRoundingMode(saveMode);
        return w;
    }
    else { return Reals(); }
}

FPInterval Reals() { return FPInterval(-infinity,+infinity); }
```

Listing 4.1: Pseudocode to compute the initial intervals at the leaf nodes of the expression tree. The type FPType is either float or double.

Pseudocode for supporting functions that provide rounding to compute intervals at interior nodes is shown in Listing 4.2.

```
// The function name Operation is one of Add, Sub or Mul with corresponding op of
// +, - or *, respectively.
FPInterval Operation(FPType u0, FPType u1, FPType v0, FPType v1)
{
    FPInterval w;
    RoundingMode saveMode = GetRoundingMode();
    SetRoundingMode(roundDownward);
    w[0] = u0 op v0;
    SetRoundingMode(roundUpward);
    w[1] = u1 op v1;
    SetRoundingMode(saveMode);
    return w;
}

FPInterval Mul2(FPType u0, FPType u1, FPType v0, FPType v1)
{
    RoundingMode saveMode = GetRoundingMode();
    SetRoundingMode(roundDownward);
    FPType u0mv1 = u0 * v1;
    FPType u1mv0 = u1 * v0;
    SetRoundingMode(roundUpward);
    FPType u0mv0 = u0 * v0;
    FPType u1mv1 = u1 * v1;
    SetRoundingMode(saveMode);
    return FPInterval(min(u0mv1, u1mv0), max(u0mv0, u1mv1));
}

FPInterval Reciprocal(FPType v0, FPType v1)
{
    FPInterval w;
    RoundingMode saveMode = GetRoundingMode();
    SetRoundingMode(roundDownward);
    w[0] = 1 / v1;
    SetRoundingMode(roundUpward);
    w[1] = 1 / v0;
    SetRoundingMode(saveMode);
    return w;
}

FPInterval ReciprocalDown(FPType v)
{
    RoundingMode saveMode = GetRoundingMode();
    SetRoundingMode(roundDownward);
    FPType recpv = 1 / v;
    SetRoundingMode(saveMode);
    return FPInterval(recpv, +infinity);
}

FPInterval ReciprocalUp(FPType v)
{
    RoundingMode saveMode = GetRoundingMode();
    SetRoundingMode(roundUpward);
    FPType recpv = 1 / v;
    SetRoundingMode(saveMode);
    return FPInterval(-infinity, recpv);
}
```

Listing 4.2: Pseudocode for supporting functions used when computing intervals at interior nodes of the expression tree.

Finally, Listing 4.3 contains pseudocode for computing the intervals at interior nodes.

```
FPInterval Add(FPType u,FPInterval v)
{
    return Add(u,u,v[0],v[1]);
}

FPInterval Add(FPInterval u,FPType v)
{
    return Add(u[0],u[1],v,v);
}

FPInterval Add(FPInterval u,FPInterval v)
{
    return Add(u[0],u[1],v[0],v[1]);
}

FPInterval Sub(FPType u,FPInterval v)
{
    return Sub(u,u,v[0],v[1]);
}

FPInterval Sub(FPInterval u,FPType v)
{
    return Sub(u[0],u[1],v,v);
}

FPInterval Sub(FPInterval u,FPInterval v)
{
    return Sub(u[0],u[1],v[0],v[1]);
}

FPInterval Mul(FPType u,FPInterval v)
{
    if (u >= 0) { return Mul(u,u,v[0],v[1]); }
    else        { return Mul(u,u,v[1],v[0]); }
}

FPInterval Mul(FPInterval u,FPType v)
{
    if (v >= 0) { return Mul(u[0],u[1],v,v); }
    else        { return Mul(u[1],u[0],v,v); }
}

FPInterval Mul(FPInterval u,FPInterval<FPType> v)
{
    if (u[0] >= 0)
    {
        if (v[0] >= 0)      { return Mul(u[0],u[1],v[0],v[1]); }
        else if (v[1] <= 0) { return Mul(u[1],u[0],v[0],v[1]); }
        else                { return Mul(u[1],u[1],v[0],v[1]); }
    }
    else if (u[1] <= 0)
    {
        if (v[0] >= 0)      { return Mul(u[0],u[1],v[1],v[0]); }
        else if (v[1] <= 0) { return Mul(u[1],u[0],v[1],v[0]); }
        else                { return Mul(u[0],u[0],v[1],v[0]); }
    }
    else
    {
        if (v[0] >= 0)      { return Mul(u[0],u[1],v[1],v[1]); }
        else if (v[1] <= 0) { return Mul(u[1],u[0],v[0],v[0]); }
        else                { return Mul2(u[0],u[1],v[0],v[1]); }
    }
}

FPInterval Div(FPType u,FPInterval v)
{
    if (v[0] > 0 || v[1] < 0) { return u*Reciprocal(v[0],v[1]); }
```

```
    else
    {
        if  (v[0] == 0)           { return  u*ReciprocalDown(v[1]);  }
        else if  (v[1] == 0)      { return  u*ReciprocalUp(v[0]);    }
        else                      { return  Reals();                 }
    }
}

FPInterval  Div(FPInterval  u,FPType v)
{
    if  (v > 0)        { return  Div(u[0],u[1],v,v);  }
    else if  (v < 0)   { return  Div(u[1],u[0],v,v);  }
    else               { return  Reals();             }
}

FPInterval  Div(FPInterval  u,FPInterval  v)
{
    if  (v[0] > 0 || v[1] < 0) { return  u*Reciprocal(v[0],v[1]);  }
    else
    {
        if  (v[0] == 0)           { return  u*ReciprocalDown(v[1]);  }
        else if  (v[1] == 0)      { return  u*ReciprocalUp(v[0]);    }
        else                      { return  Reals();                 }
    }
}
```

Listing 4.3: Pseudocode for functions used to compute intervals at interior nodes of the expression tree.

The interval arithmetic for the expression of equation (4.5) with the corresponding expression tree of Figure 4.1 is shown in Listing 4.4.

```
FPInterval  leaf0  = Mul(x,y);          // x*y
FPInterval  leaf1  = Mul(z,w);          // z*w
FPInterval  leaf2  = Mul(t,u);          // t*u
FPInterval  intr0  = Add(leaf0, leaf1); // (x*y)+(z*w)
FPInterval  intr1  = Mul(leaf2,v);      // (t*u)*v
FPInterval  intr2  = Add(3,intr1);      // 3+(t*u)*v
FPInterval  intr3  = Div(2,intr2);      // 2/(3+(t*u)*v)
FPInterval  root   = Sub(intr0,intr3);  // ((x*y)+(z*w))-(2/(3+(t*u)*v))
```

Listing 4.4: Interval arithmetic for $x * y + z * w - 2/(3 + t * u * v)$.

In C++, FPInterval can be implemented as a template class, where the template type is float or double. A constructor is provided that takes a single number x to produce interval $[x, x]$ and a constructor that takes two numbers x_0 and x_1 to produce an interval $[x_0, x_1]$. The class uses operator overloading for the Add, Sub, Mul and Div functions described previously. Listing 4.5 shows the interval arithmetic for the example expression using float and then double.

```
template <T>
void Compute(T x,T y,T z,T w,T t,T u,T v,T w,T& e,FPInterval<T>& ie)
{
    FPInterval<T> ix(x), iy(y), iz(z), iw(w), it(t), iu(u), iv(v);
    ie = ix * iy + iz * iw - T(2) / (T(3) + it * iu * iv);
    e = x * y + z * w - T(2) / (T(3) + t * u * v);
}

void Experiment()
{
    // Choose x = 1, y = 2, z = 3, w = 4, t = 5, u = 6 and w = 7. The exact result is
    // 2980/213 = 13.990610328638497652...
```

```
    float fe;
    FPInterval<float> intervalFE;
    Compute(1.0f, 2.0f, 3.0f, 4.0f, 5.0f, 6.0f, 7.0f, fe, intervalFE);
    // fe = 13.9906101
    // intervalFE = [13.9906101, 13.9906111]

    double de;
    FPInterval<double> intervalDE;
    Compute(1.0, 2.0, 3.0, 4.0, 5.0, 6.0, 7.0, de, intervalDE);
    // de = 13.990610328638498
    // intervalDE = [13.990610328638496, 13.990610328638498]
}
```

Listing 4.5: Interval arithmetic for $x*y+z*w-2/(3+t*u*v)$ using C++.

The problem of correct classification of the signs of arithmetic expressions is fundamental in geometric algorithms. When floating-point arithmetic is used to evaluate the expressions, rounding errors can lead to misclassifications of signs. Arbitrary-precision arithmetic can be used to avoid the misclassification. If performance becomes an issue for the sign classifications using only arbitrary-precision arithmetic, interval arithmetic can be used to determine quickly whether the sign is positive or negative if possible. If interval arithmetic is inconclusive, then a re-evaluation is required using arbitrary-precision arithmetic. Some of the common subproblems of geometric algorithms that require correct sign classification are described in the next two sections.

4.2 Signs of Determinants

The classic use of interval arithmetic in computational geometry algorithms is determining the exact signs of determinants. In particular, these occur in *primal queries* that are common low-level queries in the algorithms.

Listing 4.6 contains GTL code for computing the exact sign of the determinant.

```
using BSN = BSNumber<UIntegerAP32>;

template <typename FPType, typename OutputType>
void ComputeDeterminant(Matrix2x2<FPType> const& A, OutputType& det)
{
    OutputType a00(A(0,0)),a01(A(0,1)),a10(A(1,0)),a11(A(1,1));
    det = a00*a11-a01*a10;
}

template <typename FPType, typename OutputType>
void ComputeDeterminant(Matrix3x3<FPType> const& A, OutputType& det)
{
    OutputType a00(A(0,0)),a01(A(0,1)),a02(A(0,2));
    OutputType a10(A(1,0)),a11(A(1,1)),a12(A(1,2));
    OutputType a20(A(2,0)),a21(A(2,1)),a22(A(2,2));
    OutputType c0 = a11*a22-a12*a21;
    OutputType c1 = a10*a22-a12*a20;
    OutputType c2 = a10*a21-a11*a20;
```

```
    det = a00*c0−a01*c1+a02*c2;
}

template <typename FPType, typename OutputType>
void ComputeDeterminant(Matrix4x4<FPType> const& A, OutputType& det)
{
    OutputType a00(A(0, 0)), a01(A(0, 1)), a02(A(0, 2)), a03(A(0, 3));
    OutputType a10(A(1, 0)), a11(A(1, 1)), a12(A(1, 2)), a13(A(1, 3));
    OutputType a20(A(2, 0)), a21(A(2, 1)), a22(A(2, 2)), a23(A(2, 3));
    OutputType a30(A(3, 0)), a31(A(3, 1)), a32(A(3, 2)), a33(A(3, 3));
    OutputType u0 = a00*a11−a01*a10, v0 = a20*a31−a21*a30;
    OutputType u1 = a00*a12−a02*a10, v1 = a20*a32−a22*a30;
    OutputType u2 = a00*a13−a02*a10, v2 = a20*a33−a23*a30;
    OutputType u3 = a01*a12−a02*a11, v3 = a21*a32−a22*a31;
    OutputType u4 = a01*a13−a03*a11, v4 = a21*a33−a23*a31;
    OutputType u5 = a02*a13−a03*a12, v5 = a22*a33−a23*a32;
    det = u0*v5−u1*v4+u2*v3+u3*v2−u4*v1+u5*v0;
}

// MatrixType is one of Matrix2x2<FPType>, Matrix3x3<FPType> or
// Matrix4x4<FPType>. Calls are SignDeterminant<float>(A) or
// SignDeterminant<double>(A).
template <typename FPType, typename MatrixType>
int SignDeterminant(MatrixType const& A)
{
    FPInterval<FPType> idet;
    ComputeDeterminant(A, idet);
    FPType const zero(0);
    if (idet[0] > zero)
    {
        return +1;
    }
    else if (idet[1] < zero)
    {
        return −1;
    }
    else
    {
        // The interval contains 0, so compute the determinant using arbitrary-precision
        // arithmetic.
        BSN rdet;
        ComputeDeterminant(A, rdet);
        return rdet.GetSign();
    }
}
```

Listing 4.6: GTL code for computing the exact sign of the determinant of an $N \times N$ matrix. The type FPType is either float or double.

It is possible to use BSNumber<UIntegerFP32<N>> so that the rational objects live on the stack rather than being dynamically allocated from the heap. See Section 3.5.1 for determining N. For 2×2 matrices, N is 18 for type float or 132 for type double. For 3×3 matrices, N is 27 for type float or 197 for type double. For 4×4 matrices, N is 35 for type float or 263 for type double.

4.3 Primal Queries

Primal queries are common subproblems that arise in many geometric algorithms. The ones presented in this section involve relationships between points and objects. In 2D, the objects are lines, triangles and circles. In 3D, the objects are planes, tetrahedra and spheres. Of course, other common queries can be added to the list, but for the current GTL algorithms, only these are needed.

The queries for 2D and 3D are presented separately here. These can be implemented using only rational arithmetic, but the versions provided here use interval arithmetic to optimize for speed. The wrapper class is structured as shown in Listing 4.7.

```
template <typename FPType, typename APType>
class PrimalQuery
{
public:
    static int Query(query_inputs_of_FPType)
    {
        FPType const zero(0);
        FPInterval<FPType> iresult;
        QueryHelper(query_inputs_of_FPType, iresult);
        if (iresult[0] > zero)
        {
            return +1;
        }
        else if (iresult[1] < zero)
        {
            return -1;
        }
        else
        {
            APType rresult;
            QueryHelper(query_inputs_of_FPType, rresult);
            return Sign(rresult);
        }
    }
private:
    template <typename OutputType>
    static void QueryHelper(query_inputs_of_FPType, OutputType&);
};
```

Listing 4.7: The wrapper class for primal queries. Each query is implemented as a pair of member functions, one public and one private.

This is the same pattern used for computing the exact sign of determinants of matrices. The returned int is the exact sign of the query in $\{-1, 0, 1\}$. In some special cases, the query is formulated in terms of other queries, in which case the associated helper function might not be required.

4.3.1 Queries in 2D

Consider a line containing two points $\mathbf{V}_0$ and $\mathbf{V}_1$ with the direction vector $\mathbf{D} = \mathbf{V}_1 - \mathbf{V}_0 = (d_0, d_1)$. This vector is not required to be unit length.

A normal vector is $\mathbf{N} = \mathbf{D}^{\perp} = (d_1, -d_0)$ and is obtained geometrically by rotating $\mathbf{D}$ clockwise by 90 degrees. In this sense, $\mathbf{N}$ is said to point to the right side of the line. The vector $-\mathbf{N}$ points to the left side of the line. The query is to determine whether a point $\mathbf{P}$ is on the right side of the line, on the left side of the line or on the line itself. To be on the right side, it is required that $\mathbf{N} \cdot (\mathbf{P} - \mathbf{V}_0) > 0$. To be on the left side, it is required that $\mathbf{N} \cdot (\mathbf{P} - \mathbf{V}_0) < 0$. To be on the line, it is required that $\mathbf{N} \cdot (\mathbf{P} - \mathbf{V}_0) = 0$. These tests require determining the sign of a dot product. If floating-point arithmetic is used, rounding errors can lead to misclassification of the sign when the dot product is nearly zero. Rational arithmetic can be used instead to compute the correct sign. Listing 4.8 contains GTL code for the query.

```
// Return +1 for P on right side, -1 for P on left side, 0 for P on line.
template <typename FPType, typename APType>
int PrimalQuery<FPType,APType>::ToLine(Vector2<FPType> const& P,
    Vector2<FPType> const& V0, Vector2<FPType> const& V1)
{
    FPType const zero(0);
    FPInterval<FPType> iresult;
    ToLineHelper(P, V0, V1, iresult);
    if (iresult[0] > zero)
    {
        return +1;
    }
    else if (iresult[1] < zero)
    {
        return -1;
    }
    else
    {
        APType rresult;
        ToLineHelper(P, V0, V1, rresult);
        return rresult.GetSign();
    }
}

template <typename FPType, typename APType>
template <typename OutputType>
void PrimalQuery<FPType,APType>::ToLineHelper(Vector2<FPType> const& P,
    Vector2<FPType> const& V0, Vector2<FPType> const& V1,
    OutputType& result)
{
    OutputType p0(P[0]), p1(P[1]);
    OutputType v00(V0[0]), v01(V0[1]), v10(V1[0]), v11(V1[1]);
    result = (p0 - v00) * (v11 - v01) - (v10 - v00) * (p1 - v01);
}
```

Listing 4.8: GTL code for querying a point location relative to a line.

Typically, APType is BSNumber<UIntegerAP32>, which uses the heap. It is possible to use BSNumber<UIntegerFP32<N>> so that the objects live on the stack rather than in the heap. See Section 3.5.1 for determining N. For ToLine, N is 18 for float or 132 for double. When APType is BSRational<UIntegerFP32<N>>, N is 35 for float or 263 for double.

Consider a triangle with counterclockwise-ordered vertices $\mathbf{V}_0$, $\mathbf{V}_1$ and $\mathbf{V}_2$. The query is to determine whether a point $\mathbf{P}$ is strictly outside, strictly inside or on the triangle. The query is formulated using three ToLine queries, as shown in Listing 4.9. No helper function is required for this query.

```
// Return +1 for P outside triangle, -1 for P inside triangle, 0 for P on triangle.
template <typename FPType, typename APType>
int PrimalQuery<FPType, APType>:: ToTriangle (Vector2<FPType> const& P,
    Vector2<FPType> const& V0, Vector2<FPType> const& V1,
    Vector2<FPType> const& V2)
{
    int sign0 = ToLine(P, V1, V2);
    if (sign0 > 0) // P is strictly outside, right of line of edge ⟨V₁, V₂⟩.
    {
        return +1;
    }

    int sign1 = ToLine(P, V2, V0);
    if (sign1 > 0) // P is strictly outside, right of line of edge ⟨V₂, V₀⟩.
    {
        return +1;
    }

    int sign2 = ToLine(P, V0, V1);
    if (sign2 > 0) // P is strictly outside, right of line of edge ⟨V₀, V₁⟩.
    {
        return +1;
    }

    // If all signs are negative, P is strictly inside the triangle. If at least one sign
    // is zero, P is on an edge of the triangle.
    return ((sign0 && sign1 && sign2) ? -1 : 0);
}
```

Listing 4.9: GTL code for querying a point location relative to a triangle.

To select APType as the type BSNumber<UIntegerFP32<N>> for objects on the stack, the value N is the same as for the query ToLine, which is 8 for float and 132 for double, because the worst-case path has the same computational complexity. When APType is BSRational<UIntegerFP32<N>>, N is 35 for float or 263 for double.

Consider a triangle with counterclockwise-ordered vertices $\mathbf{V}_0$, $\mathbf{V}_1$ and $\mathbf{V}_2$. The query is to determine whether a point $\mathbf{P}$ is strictly outside, strictly inside or on the circumscribing circle of the triangle. This query is used in Delaunay triangulation of a point set. From the study of Delaunay triangulations, if $\mathbf{P}$ is on the circumcircle, then the point and the triangle vertices are said to be cocircular. Projecting the points onto the paraboloid $z = x^2 + y^2$, they must be coplanar, which is equivalent to a tetrahedron with the four points as vertices being degenerate (zero volume). If $\mathbf{P}$ is inside the circle, then the four points project onto the paraboloid and are the vertices of a tetrahedron. The vertex $\mathbf{P}$ is outside the bowl of the paraboloid. If $\mathbf{P}$ is outside the circle, then the tetrahedron of projection has vertex $\mathbf{P}$ inside the bowl of the paraboloid. These tests involve computing the signed volume of a tetrahedron,

$$
\begin{aligned}
S &= \det \begin{bmatrix} \mathbf{P}^\mathsf{T} & |\mathbf{P}|^2 & 1 \\ \mathbf{V}_0^\mathsf{T} & |\mathbf{V}_0|^2 & 1 \\ \mathbf{V}_1^\mathsf{T} & |\mathbf{V}_1|^2 & 1 \\ \mathbf{V}_2^\mathsf{T} & |\mathbf{V}_2|^2 & 1 \end{bmatrix} \\
&= \det \begin{bmatrix} (\mathbf{V}_0 - \mathbf{P})^\mathsf{T} & (\mathbf{V}_0 - \mathbf{P})^\mathsf{T}(\mathbf{V}_0 + \mathbf{P}) \\ (\mathbf{V}_1 - \mathbf{P})^\mathsf{T} & (\mathbf{V}_1 - \mathbf{P})^\mathsf{T}(\mathbf{V}_1 + \mathbf{P}) \\ (\mathbf{V}_2 - \mathbf{P})^\mathsf{T} & (\mathbf{V}_2 - \mathbf{P})^\mathsf{T}(\mathbf{V}_2 + \mathbf{P}) \end{bmatrix}
\end{aligned}
\tag{4.6}
$$

where $\mathbf{V}_i$ and $\mathbf{P}$ are considered to be 2×1 vectors. The point $\mathbf{P}$ is outside the circumcircle when $\mathrm{Sign}(S) = +1$, inside the circumcircle when $\mathrm{Sign}(S) = -1$ or on the circumcircle when $\mathrm{Sign}(S) = 0$. Listing 4.10 contains code for computing the query.

```cpp
// Return +1 for P outside circle, −1 for P inside circle, 0 for P on circle.
template <typename FPType, typename APType>
int PrimalQuery<FPType,APType>::ToCircumcircle(Vector<FPType> const& P,
    Vector2<FPType> const& V0, Vector2<FPType> const& V1,
    Vector2<FPType> const& V2)
{
    FPType const zero(0);
    FPInterval<FPType> iresult;
    ToCircumcircleHelper(P, V0, V1, V2, iresult);
    if (iresult[0] > zero)
    {
        return +1;
    }
    else if (iresult[1] < zero)
    {
        return −1;
    }
    else
    {
        APType rresult;
        ToCircumcircleHelper(P, V0, V1, V2, rresult);
        return rresult.GetSign();
    }
}

template <typename FPType, typename APType>
template <typename OutputType>
void PrimalQuery<FPType,APType>::ToCircumcircleHelper(
    Vector2<FPType> const& P, Vector2<FPType> const& V0,
    Vector2<FPType> const& V1, Vector2<FPType> const& V2,
    OutputType& result)
{
    OutputType p0(P[0]), p0(P[1]), v00(V0[0]), v01(V0[1]);
    OutputType v10(V1[0]), v11(V1[1]), v20(V2[0]), v21(V2[1]);
    OutputType dv00p0 = v00 − p0, difv01p1 = v01 − p1;
    OutputType sv00p0 = v00 + p0, sumv01p1 = v01 + p1;
    OutputType d0 = sv00p0 * dv00p0 + sv01p1 * dv01p1;
    OutputType dv10p0 = v10 − p0, dv11p1 = v11 − p1;
    OutputType sv10p0 = v10 + p0, sv11p1 = v11 + p1;
    OutputType d1 = sv10p0 * dv10p0 + sv11p1 * dv11p1;
    OutputType dv20p0 = v20 − p0, dv21p1 = v21 − p1;
    OutputType sv20p0 = v20 + p0, sv21p1 = v21 + p1;
    OutputType d2 = sv20p0 * dv20p0 + sv21p1 * dv21p1;
    OutputType term0 = dv00p0 * (dv21p1 * d1 − dv11p1 * d2);
    OutputType term1 = dv10p0 * (dv01p1 * d2 − dv21p1 * d0);
    OutputType term2 = dv20p0 * (dv11p1 * d0 − dv01p1 * d1);
    result = term0 + term1 + term2;
}
```

Listing 4.10: GTL code for querying a point location relative to the circumscribed circle of a triangle.

To use BSNumber<UIntegerFP32<N>> for APType to store objects on the stack, N is 35 for type float and 263 for type double. When APType is BSRational<UIntegerFP32<N>>, N is 105 for float or 788 for double.

4.3.2 Queries in 3D

Consider a plane containing three points $\mathbf{V}_0$, $\mathbf{V}_1$ and $\mathbf{V}_2$ with normal vector $\mathbf{N} = (\mathbf{V}_1 - \mathbf{V}_0) \times (\mathbf{V}_2 - \mathbf{V}_0)$. This vector is not required to be unit length. For any point $\mathbf{P}$, compute the dot product $d = \mathbf{N} \cdot (\mathbf{P} - \mathbf{V}_0)$. The point is said to be on the positive side of the plane when $d > 0$, on the negative side of the plane when $d < 0$ or on the plane when $d = 0$. These tests require determining the sign of the dot product. If floating-point arithmetic is used, rounding errors can lead to misclassification of the sign when the dot product is nearly zero. Rational arithmetic can be used instead to compute the correct sign. Listing 4.11 contains GTL code for the query.

```
// Return +1 for P on positive side, −1 for P on negative side, 0 for P on plane.
template <typename FPType, typename APType>
int PrimalQuery<FPType,APType>::ToPlane(Vector3<FPType> const& P,
    Vector3<FPType> const& V0, Vector3<FPType> const& V1)
{
    FPType const zero(0);
    FPInterval<FPType> iresult;
    ToPlaneHelper(P, V0, V1, V2, iresult);
    if (iresult[0] > zero)
    {
        return +1;
    }
    else if (iresult[1] < zero)
    {
        return −1;
    }
    else
    {
        APType rresult;
        ToPlaneHelper(P, V0, V1, V2, rresult);
        return rresult.GetSign();
    }
}


template <typename FPType, typename APType>
template <typename OutputType>
void PrimalQuery<FPType,APType>::ToPlaneHelper(Vector3<FPType> const& P,
    Vector3<FPType> const& V0, Vector3<FPType> const& V1,
    OutputType& result)
{
    OutputType p0(P[0]), p1(P[1]), v00(V0[0]), v01(V0[1]);
    OutputType v10(V1[0]), v11(V1[1]), v20(V2[0]), v21(V2[1]);
    OutputType p0mv00 = p0−v00, p1mv01 = p1−v01, p2mv02 = p2−v02;
    OutputType v10mv00 = v10−v00, v11mv01 = v11−v01, v12mv02 = v12−v02;
    OutputType v20mv00 = v20−v00, v21mv01 = v21−v01, v22mv02 = v22−v02;
    OutputType term0 = p0mv00 * (v11mv01 * v22mv02 − v21mv01 * v12mv02);
    OutputType term1 = v10mv00 * (v21mv01 * p2mv02 − p1mv01 * v22mv02);
    OutputType term2 = v20mv00 * (p1mv01 * v12mv02 − v11mv01 * p2mv02);
    result = term0 + term1 + term2;
}
```

Listing 4.11: GTL code for querying a point location relative to a plane.

Typically, APType is BSNumber<UIntegerAP32>, which uses the heap. It is possible to use BSNumber<UIntegerFP32<N>> so that the objects live on the stack rather than in the heap. See Section 3.5.1 for determining N. For ToLine, N is 27 for type float or 197 for type double. When APType is BSRational<UIntegerFP32<N>>, N is 79 for float or 591 for double.

Consider a tetrahedron with vertices $\mathbf{V}_0$, $\mathbf{V}_1$, $\mathbf{V}_2$ and $\mathbf{V}_3$ that are ordered so that the determinant of a 4×4 matrix is positive. That determinant is

$$d_4 = \det \begin{bmatrix} \mathbf{V}_0 & \mathbf{V}_1 & \mathbf{V}_2 & \mathbf{V}_3 \\ 1 & 1 & 1 & 1 \end{bmatrix} \tag{4.7}$$

where $\mathbf{V}_i$ are considered to be 3×1 vectors. The canonical case is when $\mathbf{V}_0 = (1,0,0)$, $\mathbf{V}_1 = (0,1,0)$, $\mathbf{V}_2 = (0,0,1)$ and $\mathbf{V}_3 = (0,0,0)$. The matrix in the equation (4.7) is the identity and has determinant $d_4 = 1$. This generalizes the ordering for a triangle with vertices $\mathbf{V}_0$, $\mathbf{V}_1$ and $\mathbf{V}_2$ that are considered to be 2×1 vectors. For the triangle, the determinant is computed for a 3×3 matrix,

$$d_3 = \det \begin{bmatrix} \mathbf{V}_0 & \mathbf{V}_1 & \mathbf{V}_2 \\ 1 & 1 & 1 \end{bmatrix} \tag{4.8}$$

If $d_3 > 0$, the triangle is counterclockwise ordered. If $d_3 < 0$, the triangle is clockwise ordered. If $d_3 = 0$, the triangle is degenerate in that its vertices are collinear. The canonical case is when $\mathbf{V}_0 = (1,0)$, $\mathbf{V}_1 = (0,1)$ and $\mathbf{V}_2 = (0,0)$. The use of the terms counterclockwise and clockwise is not meaningful for tetrahedra, so instead a tetrahedron is referred to as positively ordered when $d_4 > 0$, negatively ordered when $d_4 < 0$ or degenerate (coplanar vertices) when $d_4 = 0$.

The query is to determine whether a point $\mathbf{P}$ is strictly outside, strictly inside or on the tetrahedron. The query is formulated using three ToLine queries, as shown in Listing 4.12. No helper function is required for this query.

```
template <typename FPType, typename APType>
int PrimalQuery<FPType,APType>::ToTetrahedron(Vector3<FPType> const& P,
    Vector3<FPType> const& V0, Vector3<FPType> const& V1,
    Vector3<FPType> const& V2, Vector3<FPType> const& V3)
{
    int sign0 = ToPlane(P, V1, V2, V3);
    if (sign0 > 0) // P is strictly outside (positive side of plane of {V1, V2, V3}).
    {
        return +1;
    }

    int sign1 = ToPlane(P, V0, V3, V2);
    if (sign1 > 0) // P is strictly outside (positive side of plane of {V0, V3, V2}).
    {
        return +1;
    }

    int sign2 = ToPlane(P, V0, V1, V3);
    if (sign2 > 0) // P is strictly outside (positive side of plane of {V0, V1, V3}).
    {
        return +1;
    }

    int sign3 = ToPlane(P, V0, V2, V1);
    if (sign3 > 0) // P is strictly outside (positive side of plane of {V0, V2, V1}).
    {
        return +1;
    }

    // If all signs are negative, P is strictly inside the tetrahedron. If at least one sign
    // is zero, P is on a face of the tetrahedron.
    return ((sign0 && sign1 && sign2 && sign3) ? -1 : 0);
```

}

Listing 4.12: GTL code for querying a point location relative to a triangle.

To use BSNumber<UIntegerFP32<N>> for APType to store objects on the stack, N is the same as for the query ToPlane, 27 for type float and 197 for type double, because the worst-case path has the same computational complexity. When APType is BSRational<UIntegerFP32<N>>, N is 79 for float or 591 for double.

Consider a positively oriented tetrahedron with vertices $\mathbf{V}_0$, $\mathbf{V}_1$, $\mathbf{V}_2$ and $\mathbf{V}_3$. The query is to determine whether a point $\mathbf{P}$ is strictly outside, strictly inside or on the circumscribing sphere of the tetrahedron. This query is used in the Delaunay tetrahedralizations of a point set. The determination of $\mathbf{P}$ relative to the circumsphere is similar to that for the point-in-circumcircle analysis. The four vertices and $\mathbf{P}$ are projected onto a hyperparaboloid $w = x^2 + y^2 + z^2$. The resulting simplex (5 vertices in 4-dimensional space) has signed hypervolume, the sign depending on whether the point is strictly outside, strictly inside or on the circumsphere.

The signed hypervolume is

$$
\begin{aligned}
S \;=\; & \det \begin{bmatrix}
\mathbf{P}^\mathsf{T} & |\mathbf{P}|^2 & 1 \\
\mathbf{V}_0^\mathsf{T} & |\mathbf{V}_0|^2 & 1 \\
\mathbf{V}_1^\mathsf{T} & |\mathbf{V}_1|^2 & 1 \\
\mathbf{V}_2^\mathsf{T} & |\mathbf{V}_2|^2 & 1 \\
\mathbf{V}_3^\mathsf{T} & |\mathbf{V}_3|^2 & 1
\end{bmatrix} \\[2mm]
\;=\; & \det \begin{bmatrix}
(\mathbf{V}_0 - \mathbf{P})^\mathsf{T} & (\mathbf{V}_0 - \mathbf{P})^\mathsf{T}(\mathbf{V}_0 + \mathbf{P}) \\
(\mathbf{V}_1 - \mathbf{P})^\mathsf{T} & (\mathbf{V}_1 - \mathbf{P})^\mathsf{T}(\mathbf{V}_1 + \mathbf{P}) \\
(\mathbf{V}_2 - \mathbf{P})^\mathsf{T} & (\mathbf{V}_2 - \mathbf{P})^\mathsf{T}(\mathbf{V}_2 + \mathbf{P}) \\
(\mathbf{V}_3 - \mathbf{P})^\mathsf{T} & (\mathbf{V}_3 - \mathbf{P})^\mathsf{T}(\mathbf{V}_3 + \mathbf{P})
\end{bmatrix}
\end{aligned}
\tag{4.9}
$$

where $\mathbf{V}_i$ and $\mathbf{P}$ are considered to be 3×1 vectors. The point $\mathbf{P}$ is outside the circumsphere when $\mathrm{Sign}(S) = +1$, inside the circumsphere when $\mathrm{Sign}(S) = -1$ or on the circumsphere when $\mathrm{Sign}(S) = 0$. Listing 4.13 contains code for computing the query.

```
// Return +1 for P outside sphere, −1 for P inside sphere, 0 for P on sphere.
template <typename FPType, typename APType>
int PrimalQuery<FPType,APType>::ToCircumsphere(Vector3<FPType> const& P,
    Vector3<FPType> const& V0, Vector3<FPType> const& V1,
    Vector3<FPType> const& V2, Vector3<FPType> const& V3)
{
    FPType const zero(0);
    FPInterval<FPType> iresult;
    ToCircumsphereHelper(P, V0, V1, V2, V3, iresult);
    if (iresult[0] > zero)
    {
        return +1;
    }
    else if (iresult[1] < zero)
    {
        return −1;
    }
    else
    {
        APType rresult;
```

```
            ToCircumsphereHelper(P, V0, V1, V2, V3, rresult);
            return rresult.GetSign();
      }
}

template <typename FPType, typename APType>
template <typename OutputType>
void PrimalQuery<FPType,APType>::ToCircumsphereHelper(
      Vector2<FPType> const& P, Vector2<FPType> const& V0,
      Vector2<FPType> const& V1, Vector2<FPType> const& V2,
      Vector2<FPType> const& V3, OutputType& result)
{
      OutputType p0(P[0]), p1(P[1]), p2(P[2]);
      OutputType v00(V0[0]), v01(V0[1]), v02(V0[2]);
      OutputType v10(V1[0]), v11(V1[1]), v12(V1[2]);
      OutputType v20(V2[0]), v21(V2[1]), v22(V2[2]);
      OutputType v30(V3[0]), v31(V3[1]), v32(V3[2]);
      OutputType dv00p0 = v00 - p0, dv01p1 = v01 - p1, dv02p2 = v02 - p2;
      OutputType sv00p0 = v00 + p0, sv01p1 = v01 + p1, sv02p2 = v02 + p2;
      OutputType d0 = sv00p0 * dv00p0 + sv01p1 * dv01p1 + sv02p2 * dv02p2;
      OutputType dv10p0 = v10 - p0, dv11p1 = v11 - p1, dv12p2 = v12 - p2;
      OutputType sv10p0 = v10 + p0, sv11p1 = v11 + p1, sv12p2 = v12 + p2;
      OutputType d1 = sv10p0 * dv10p0 + sv11p1 * dv11p1 + sv12p2 * dv12p2;
      OutputType dv20p0 = v20 - p0, dv21p1 = v21 - p1, dv22p2 = v22 - p2;
      OutputType sv20p0 = v20 + p0, sv21p1 = v21 + p1, sv22p2 = v22 + p2;
      OutputType d2 = sv20p0 * dv20p0 + sv21p1 * dv21p1 + sv22p2 * dv22p2;
      OutputType dv30p0 = v30 - p0, dv31p1 = v31 - p1, dv32p2 = v32 - p2;
      OutputType sv30p0 = v30 + p0, sv31p1 = v31 + p1, sv32p2 = v32 + p2;
      OutputType d3 = sv30p0 * dv30p0 + sv31p1 * dv31p1 + sv32p2 * dv32p2;
      OutputType a0 = dv00p0 * dv11p1 - dv10p0 * dv01p1;
      OutputType a1 = dv00p0 * dv21p1 - dv20p0 * dv01p1;
      OutputType a2 = dv00p0 * dv31p1 - dv30p0 * dv01p1;
      OutputType a3 = dv10p0 * dv21p1 - dv20p0 * dv11p1;
      OutputType a4 = dv10p0 * dv31p1 - dv30p0 * dv11p1;
      OutputType a5 = dv20p0 * dv31p1 - dv30p0 * dv21p1;
      OutputType b0 = dv02p2 * d1 - dv12p2 * d0;
      OutputType b1 = dv02p2 * d2 - dv22p2 * d0;
      OutputType b2 = dv02p2 * d3 - dv32p2 * d0;
      OutputType b3 = dv12p2 * d2 - dv22p2 * d1;
      OutputType b4 = dv12p2 * d3 - dv32p2 * d1;
      OutputType b5 = dv22p2 * d3 - dv32p2 * d2;
      result = a0 * b5 - a1 * b4 + a2 * b3 + a3 * b2 - a4 * b1;
}
```

Listing 4.13: GTL code for querying a point location relative to the circumscribed sphere of a tetrahedron.

To use BSNumber<UIntegerFP32<N>> for APType to store objects on the stack, N is 44 for type float and 329 for type double. When APType is BSRational<UIntegerFP32<N>>, N is 262 for float or 1969 for double.

Chapter 5

Quadratic-Field Arithmetic

Implementations of geometric algorithms that use floating-point arithmetic are typically not robust because of the rounding errors inherent in the arithmetic. For many applications, modern computers are now fast enough to allow arbitrary-precision implementations, whether on the CPU or GPU. In the GTL, arbitrary-precision support is provided by class BSNumber for algorithms that require only addition, subtraction and multiplication). Class BSRational provides support for the same applications as well as applications that require divisions. The underlying mathematical framework and implementation details can be found in Chapter 3.

Many geometric algorithms require computing expressions that include square root operations. These operations usually occur as a result of normalizing vectors to make them unit length or solving for the real-valued roots of a quadratic polynomial. Even with arbitrary-precision arithmetic, it is generally not possible to compute the square roots without rounding errors. This chapter provides a framework that allows an implementation of geometric algorithms with square root operations but produces results that are a mixture of rational numbers and symbolic representations of the square roots. Once the results are computed, only at that time are the square roots estimated by rational numbers with a user-specified number of bits of precision.

The typical failures in the floating-point implementation of geometric algorithms occur when signs of numerical values are used to control branching. Rounding errors can steer the execution path into a block that does not match the theoretical geometric configuration, which might lead to minor issues or even to catastrophic failure. By deferring the square root operations, the execution path can be steered into the correct blocks of code and avoid the misclassifications.

The mathematical basis for error-free computing when square roots are involved is from abstract algebra, specifically the topic of *real quadratic fields*. Although that topic has some strict constraints that cannot be easily satisfied, the arithmetic operations of the fields may still be used, but rather carefully.

5.1   Sources of Rounding Errors

A couple of common sources of rounding errors that occur in geometric algorithms are discussed next. These include rounding errors from normalizing vectors and rounding errors from computing square roots when solving for roots of a quadratic equation.

5.1.1   Rounding Errors when Normalizing Vectors

A unit-length direction vector is typically provided by specifying a 3-tuple $\mathbf{V}$ and then normalizing it to $\mathbf{U} = \mathbf{V}/|\mathbf{V}|$. When computing with floating-point arithmetic, the square root operation and the division usually have floating-point rounding errors. The computed vector is $\hat{\mathbf{U}}$, but it is an approximation to $\mathbf{U}$ that does not have unit length. Listing 5.1 contains code that illustrates the rounding errors when normalizing a vector.

```
using Rational = BSNumber<UIntegerAP32>;

// Normalize a float-component 3-tuple.
Vector3<float> fV = { 1.0f, 2.0f, 3.0f };
Vector3<float> fU = fV / Length(fV);
// Represent fU as a rational-component 3-tuple.
Vector3<Rational> rU = { fU[0], fU[1], fU[2] };
// Compute the exact squared length of rU.
Rational rSqrLen = Dot(rU, rU);
// = 0x0003FFFF FA4757A5 * 2^-50
// = 1 - ε
// < 1
// = 0x00040000 00000000 * 2^-50
float fSqrLen = (float)rSqrLen;   // 0.999999940

// Normalize a double-component 3-tuple.
Vector3<double> dV = { 1.0, 2.0, 3.0 };
Vector3<double> dU = dV / Length(dV);
// Represent dU as a rational-component 3-tuple.
rU = { dU[0], dU[1], dU[2] };
// Compute the exact squared length of rU.
rSqrLen = Dot(rU, rU);
// = 0x00000200 00000000 000CC8B2 FF10B80F * 2^-106
// = 1 + δ
// > 1
// = 0x00000200 00000000 00000000 00000000 * 2^-106
double dSqrLen = (double)rSqrLen;   // 1.0000000000000000
```

Listing 5.1: Approximation errors when normalizing a vector to obtain a unit-length vector. The code uses the GTL arbitrary-precision class BSNumber.

The float-component vector fV is normalized using floating-point arithmetic, but the result is a floating-point vector that when represented as a rational vector has squared length smaller than 1. The rounding error is within float precision, so fSqrLen shows there is error. The double-component vector dV is normalized using floating-point arithmetic, but the result is a floating-point vector that when represented as a rational vector has squared length larger than 1. The rounding error is smaller than double precision can represent, so dSqrLen makes it appear as if there is no error because the result has been rounded to 1.

5.1.2 Errors in Roots to Quadratic Equations

In many geometric algorithms, a common subproblem is to compute the roots for a quadratic equation $a_2t^2 + a_1t + a_0 = 0$, where $a_2 \neq 0$. The symbolic roots are $t = (-a_1 \pm \sqrt{a_1^2 - 4a_0a_2})/(2a_2)$. The discriminant is $d = a_1^2 - 4a_0a_2$. If $d > 0$, the equation has two distinct real-valued roots. If $d = 0$, the equation has one repeated real-valued root. If $d < 0$, the equation has two distinct complex-valued roots. The correct root classification can be misidentified because of floating-point rounding errors when computing the discriminant.

5.1.3 Intersection of Line and Cone Frustum

As an example, consider an infinite cone that has a vertex $\mathbf{V}$, a unit-length axis direction $\mathbf{D}$ and an angle $\theta \in (0, \pi/2)$ measured from the ray $\mathbf{V} + h\mathbf{D}$. The solid infinite cone contains points $\mathbf{X}$ for which

$$\mathbf{D} \cdot \frac{\mathbf{X} - \mathbf{V}}{|\mathbf{X} - \mathbf{V}|} \geq \cos\theta \tag{5.1}$$

The left-hand side of the inequality involves two unit-length vectors, $\mathbf{D}$ and the normalized vector for $\mathbf{X} - \mathbf{V}$. The dot product is $\cos\phi$ where $\phi \in [0, \pi]$ is the angle between the two unit-length vectors. The inequality is $\cos\phi \geq \cos\theta > 0$, which implies $0 \leq \phi \leq \theta < \pi/2$.

The height of $\mathbf{X}$ relative to the cone is $h = \mathbf{D} \cdot (\mathbf{X} - \mathbf{V})$, which is the signed length of the projection of $\mathbf{X}$ onto the cone axis. A cone frustum is an infinite cone truncated by allowing only heights $h \in [h_{\min}, h_{\max}]$ where $0 \leq h_{\min} < h_{\max} < +\infty$.

A line is defined parametrically by $\mathbf{X}(t) = \mathbf{P} + t\mathbf{U}$, where $\mathbf{P}$ is the line origin, $\mathbf{U}$ is a unit-length line direction and t is any real number.

Consider a cone frustum and line in the geometric configuration shown in Figure 5.1.

The normalization of $\mathbf{X} - \mathbf{V}$ can be avoided by squaring the dot-product inequality,

$$(\mathbf{D} \cdot (\mathbf{X} - \mathbf{V}))^2 - |\mathbf{X} - \mathbf{V}|^2\gamma^2 \geq 0, \quad \mathbf{D} \cdot (\mathbf{X} - \mathbf{V}) \geq 0 \tag{5.2}$$

where $\gamma = \cos\theta$. The intersections of the line and infinite cone are computed by substituting the parametric line equation into the cone equation, which leads to the quadratic equation $c_2t^2 + 2c_1t + c_0 = 0$. The coefficients are

$$\begin{aligned} c_2 &= (\mathbf{D} \cdot \mathbf{U})^2 - \gamma^2(\mathbf{U} \cdot \mathbf{U}) \\ c_1 &= (\mathbf{D} \cdot \mathbf{U})(\mathbf{D} \cdot \boldsymbol{\Delta}) - \gamma^2(\mathbf{U} \cdot \boldsymbol{\Delta}) \\ c_0 &= (\mathbf{D} \cdot \boldsymbol{\Delta})^2 - \gamma^2(\boldsymbol{\Delta} \cdot \boldsymbol{\Delta}) \end{aligned} \tag{5.3}$$

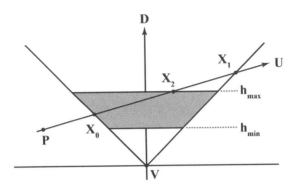

FIGURE 5.1: A specific geometric configuration for a line and a cone frustum. The line intersects the infinite cone at $\mathbf{X}_0$ and $\mathbf{X}_1$, but $\mathbf{X}_1$ is outside the frustum. The segment of intersection of line and frustum is determined by $\mathbf{X}_0$ and by $\mathbf{X}_2$, which is the intersection of the line with the plane of truncation at maximum height.

where $\mathbf{\Delta} = \mathbf{P} - \mathbf{V}$. The geometric configuration of Figure 5.1 indicates that the quadratic equation has two real-valued roots t_0 and t_1 with $t_0 < t_1$,

$$r_0 = \frac{-c_1 - \sqrt{d}}{c_2}, \quad r_1 = \frac{-c_1 + \sqrt{d}}{c_2}, \quad t_0 = \min\{r_0, r_1\}, \quad t_1 = \max\{r_0, r_1\} \quad (5.4)$$

where $d = c_1^2 - c_0 c_2 > 0$. The intersection points are $\mathbf{X}_0 = \mathbf{P} + t_0\mathbf{U}$ and $\mathbf{X}_1 = \mathbf{P} + t_1\mathbf{U}$.

As noted, $\mathbf{X}_1$ is outside the cone frustum. The desired point is instead $\mathbf{X}_2$ which is on the line, so $\mathbf{X}_2 = \mathbf{P} + t_2\mathbf{U}$ for some scalar $t_2 \in (t_0, t_1)$. It has height $h_{\max}$ and corresponding t_2 given by

$$h_{\max} = \mathbf{D} \cdot (\mathbf{X}_2 - \mathbf{V}) = (\mathbf{D} \cdot \mathbf{\Delta}) + t_2(\mathbf{D} \cdot \mathbf{U}), \quad t_2 = \frac{h_{\max} - \mathbf{D} \cdot \mathbf{\Delta}}{\mathbf{D} \cdot \mathbf{U}} \quad (5.5)$$

When using floating-point arithmetic, the computations have various sources of errors. The user specifies the angle θ, but generally $\cos\theta$ can be irrational, so $\cos\theta$ can only be estimated by a rational number to a specified number of bits of precision. In some special cases, though, $\cos^2\theta$ is rational; for example, θ is one of $\pi/6$, $\pi/4$ or $\pi/3$, and the squared cosines γ^2 are $3/4$, $1/2$ or $1/4$, respectively. For now, the assumption is that γ^2 is error free and rational.

The vector $\mathbf{U}$ is assumed to be unit length. If it is computed by normalizing a non-unit-length vector $\widehat{\mathbf{U}}$, the floating-point normalized vector treated as a rational 3-tuple is not necessarily unit length, as shown previously in Listing 5.1. The issue can be resolved easily. The line is also parameterized by $\mathbf{P} + \hat{t}\widehat{\mathbf{U}}$. The relationship between the vectors is $\mathbf{U} = \widehat{\mathbf{U}}/|\widehat{\mathbf{U}}|$ and between the parameters is $t = \hat{t}|\widehat{\mathbf{U}}|$. The intersection points $\mathbf{X}_0$ and $\mathbf{X}_1$ are the same regardless of whether the t-parameterization or the $\hat{t}$-parameterization is used. Normalization of the line direction is not required to compute the segment of intersection. The quadratic coefficients are now

$$
\begin{aligned}
\hat{c}_2 &= (\mathbf{D} \cdot \widehat{\mathbf{U}})^2 - \gamma^2(\widehat{\mathbf{U}} \cdot \widehat{\mathbf{U}}) \\
\hat{c}_1 &= (\mathbf{D} \cdot \widehat{\mathbf{U}})(\mathbf{D} \cdot \boldsymbol{\Delta}) - \gamma^2(\widehat{\mathbf{U}} \cdot \boldsymbol{\Delta}) \\
\hat{c}_0 &= (\mathbf{D} \cdot \boldsymbol{\Delta})^2 - \gamma^2(\boldsymbol{\Delta} \cdot \boldsymbol{\Delta})
\end{aligned}
\tag{5.6}
$$

and the discriminant is $\hat{d} = \hat{c}_1^2 - \hat{c}_0\hat{c}_2$. The quadratic equation has two real-valued roots $\hat{t}_0$ and $\hat{t}_1$ with $\hat{t}_0 < \hat{t}_1$,

$$
\hat{r}_0 = \frac{-\hat{c}_1 - \sqrt{\hat{d}}}{\hat{c}_2}, \quad \hat{r}_1 = \frac{-\hat{c}_1 + \sqrt{\hat{d}}}{\hat{c}_2}, \quad \hat{t}_0 = \min\{\hat{r}_0, \hat{r}_1\}, \quad \hat{t}_1 = \max\{\hat{r}_0, \hat{r}_1\}
\tag{5.7}
$$

The vector $\mathbf{D}$ is also assumed to be unit length. If it was computed using floating-point arithmetic as $\mathbf{D} = \widehat{\mathbf{D}}/|\widehat{\mathbf{D}}|$ for a non-unit-length vector $\widehat{\mathbf{D}}$, rounding errors can cause $\mathbf{D}$ not to be unit length when treated as a rational 3-tuple. This issue can also be resolved easily by substituting $\mathbf{D} = \widehat{\mathbf{D}}/|\widehat{\mathbf{D}}|$ into the coefficients of equation (5.6) and multiplying through by $|\widehat{\mathbf{D}}|^2 = \widehat{\mathbf{D}} \cdot \widehat{\mathbf{D}}$. The multiplication of all quadratic coefficients by the same nonzero scalar does not change the roots of the quadratic polynomial. The new coefficients are

$$
\begin{aligned}
\tilde{c}_2 &= (\widehat{\mathbf{D}} \cdot \widehat{\mathbf{U}})^2 - \gamma^2(\widehat{\mathbf{U}} \cdot \widehat{\mathbf{U}})(\widehat{\mathbf{D}} \cdot \widehat{\mathbf{D}}) \\
\tilde{c}_1 &= (\widehat{\mathbf{D}} \cdot \widehat{\mathbf{U}})(\widehat{\mathbf{D}} \cdot \boldsymbol{\Delta}) - \gamma^2(\widehat{\mathbf{U}} \cdot \boldsymbol{\Delta})(\widehat{\mathbf{D}} \cdot \widehat{\mathbf{D}}) \\
\tilde{c}_0 &= (\widehat{\mathbf{D}} \cdot \boldsymbol{\Delta})^2 - \gamma^2(\boldsymbol{\Delta} \cdot \boldsymbol{\Delta})(\widehat{\mathbf{D}} \cdot \widehat{\mathbf{D}})
\end{aligned}
\tag{5.8}
$$

and the discriminant is $\tilde{d} = \tilde{c}_1^2 - \tilde{c}_0\tilde{c}_2$.

Although the quadratic roots can be computed without normalization, $\mathbf{X}_2$ must be computed using the unnormalized vectors. This involves the expressions of equation (5.5). It is important to note that $h_{\max}$ was chosen by the user to be the maximum height of the cone frustum based on $\mathbf{D}$ being unit length. By using $\widehat{\mathbf{D}}$ instead, the scale of the heights has changed. Using $\widehat{\mathbf{U}}$ and $\hat{t}$ instead of $\mathbf{U}$ and t, equation (5.5) becomes

$$
h_{\max} = (\mathbf{D} \cdot \boldsymbol{\Delta}) + \hat{t}_2(\mathbf{D} \cdot \widehat{\mathbf{U}}), \quad \hat{t}_2 = \frac{h_{\max} - \mathbf{D} \cdot \boldsymbol{\Delta}}{\mathbf{D} \cdot \widehat{\mathbf{U}}}
\tag{5.9}
$$

Using $\widehat{\mathbf{D}}$ instead of $\mathbf{D}$, these equations become

$$
h_{\max}|\widehat{\mathbf{D}}| = (\widehat{\mathbf{D}} \cdot \boldsymbol{\Delta}) + \hat{t}_2(\widehat{\mathbf{D}} \cdot \widehat{\mathbf{U}}), \quad \hat{t}_2 = \frac{h_{\max}|\widehat{\mathbf{D}}| - \widehat{\mathbf{D}} \cdot \boldsymbol{\Delta}}{\widehat{\mathbf{D}} \cdot \widehat{\mathbf{U}}}
\tag{5.10}
$$

In a general-purpose algorithm, it is not known in advance whether $\mathbf{X}_0$

and $\mathbf{X}_1$ are inside the cone frustum. To decide this, compute the heights at these points and compare to the cone height extremes. To determine that $\mathbf{X}_0$ is inside the cone frustum, verify that

$$h_{\min}|\widehat{\mathbf{D}}| \le (\widehat{\mathbf{D}} \cdot \mathbf{\Delta}) + \hat{t}_0(\widehat{\mathbf{D}} \cdot \widehat{\mathbf{U}}) \le h_{\max}|\widehat{\mathbf{D}}| \qquad (5.11)$$

For the sake of argument, suppose $\tilde{c}_2 > 0$, which implies that $\hat{t}_0 = (-\tilde{c}_1 - \sqrt{\tilde{d}})/\tilde{c}_2$. The comparison of heights becomes

$$h_{\min}|\widehat{\mathbf{D}}| \le (\widehat{\mathbf{D}} \cdot \mathbf{\Delta}) + \left(\frac{-\tilde{c}_1 - \sqrt{\tilde{d}}}{\tilde{c}_2} \right) (\widehat{\mathbf{D}} \cdot \widehat{\mathbf{U}}) \le h_{\max}|\widehat{\mathbf{D}}| \qquad (5.12)$$

A similar argument applies for $\hat{t}_1$. A framework for mixing rational and symbolic arithmetic not only requires arithmetic operations, but it requires symbolic comparisons which might involve multiple square roots.

In summary, the computation of $\hat{t}_0$ and $\hat{t}_1$ involves two square roots, so potentially the value $\hat{t}_2$ must be computed. Comparisons must be made in equation (5.12) that involve both square roots. If the square roots are computed at the time they are needed, the rounding errors can propagate downstream and affect the results, potentially in an adverse manner. In particular, a general-purpose find-intersection query between a line and a cone frustum has many branches corresponding to the possible geometric configurations. Rounding errors can steer the execution into a code block that does not correspond to the geometric configuration, and the consequences might or might not be acceptable to the application using such a query. For example, $\tilde{d}$ might be theoretically nonnegative, but rounding errors when computing $\hat{d}$ as a floating-point number can lead to a small negative number. In theory the line intersects the cone, but the rounding errors lead to the conclusion that it does not.

The remainder of the chapter shows how to use a mixture of rational and symbolic arithmetic to defer the square root computations until the very end of the geometric query, only at that time using numerical methods to provide floating-point estimates of the results if needed by the application.

5.2   Real Quadratic Fields

The equations in the geometric queries involve square roots, occurring by themselves for normalized vectors or occurring as numbers of the form $x + y\sqrt{d}$ where $d > 0$. To avoid rounding errors with floating-point addition, subtraction, multiplication and division, the quantities x, y and d are required to be rational numbers. Abstract algebra includes a topic called *real quadratic fields* [39], which provides a model of computation using a mixture of rational and symbolic arithmetic. Such fields have constraints that geometric algorithms generally do not satisfy immediately. Although additional computing can be used to satisfy the constraints, the extra computational cost might not be justified. Whether or not it does is based on the queries and the computational budget.

A real quadratic field consists of numbers of the form $x + y\sqrt{d}$, where x and y are rational numbers and where $d > 1$ is a *square-free integer*. These are integers whose prime factorization involves primes raised only to the first power. The prime numbers themselves are square free. The number 6 is square free because its factorization is $6 = 2^1 3^1$, which has only exponents 1 for the prime factors. The number 18 is not square free because its factorization is $18 = 2^1 3^2$, which has an exponent larger than 1 for the prime factor 3. If d is a square-free integer and $\mathbb{Q}$ is the field of rational numbers, the real quadratic field $\mathbb{Q}(\sqrt{d})$ is the set of numbers $x + y\sqrt{d}$, where $x, y \in \mathbb{Q}$.

A C++ class for quadratic field numbers encapsulates rational numbers x, y and d as class members. The arithmetic operations between class members requires that the two operands have the same d-values. The value d can be shared by class objects, but then the class design becomes more complicated. For now, each class object has its own copy of d. If the memory usage and/or copy expense is an issue for an application, d can be replaced by a constant pointer or constant reference, which implies that the caller maintain a single value for d and ensure that it persists during the lifetime of any class objects using it.

5.2.1 Arithmetic Operations

The addition of two numbers is

$$(x_0 + y_0\sqrt{d}) + (x_1 + y_1\sqrt{d}) = (x_0 + x_1) + (y_0 + y_1)\sqrt{d} \tag{5.13}$$

and the subtraction of two numbers is

$$(x_0 + y_0\sqrt{d}) - (x_1 + y_1\sqrt{d}) = (x_0 - x_1) + (y_0 - y_1)\sqrt{d} \tag{5.14}$$

The additive identity is $0 + 0\sqrt{d}$. The multiplication of two numbers is

$$(x_0 + y_0\sqrt{d}) * (x_1 + y_1\sqrt{d}) = (x_0x_1 + y_0y_1d) + (x_0y_1 + x_1y_0)\sqrt{d} \tag{5.15}$$

The multiplicative identity is $1 + 0\sqrt{d}$. The division of two numbers is the following, where the denominator is not zero,

$$\frac{x_0 + y_0\sqrt{d}}{x_1 + y_1\sqrt{d}} = \frac{x_0 + y_0\sqrt{d}}{x_1 + y_1\sqrt{d}} * \frac{x_1 - y_1\sqrt{d}}{x_1 - y_1\sqrt{d}} = \left(\frac{x_0x_1 - y_0y_1d}{x_1^2 - y_1^2 d}\right) + \left(\frac{x_1y_0 - x_0y_1}{x_1^2 - y_1^2 d}\right)\sqrt{d} \tag{5.16}$$

Although it is assumed that $x_1 + y_1\sqrt{d} \neq 0 + 0\sqrt{d}$, it appears there is a division by zero when $x_1^2 - y_1^2 d = 0$. In fact, this is not possible when x_1 and y_1 are rational numbers and d is square free. The condition $x_1^2 - y_1^2 d = 0$ implies

$d = (x_1/y_1)^2$. The number d is an integer, so y_1 must exactly divide x_1, in which case $k = x_1/y_1$ is an integer with $d = k^2$, which contradicts d being square free because all its prime factors have even powers.

In fact, the same argument shows each quadratic field number $z = x + y\sqrt{d}$ has a unique representation. First, consider the representation of the real number 0. Let $0 = x + y\sqrt{d}$. If $y = 0$, it must be that $x = 0$ and the representation is $0 = 0 + 0\sqrt{d}$. If $y \neq 0$, then $\sqrt{d} = -x/y$ and $d = (x/y)^2$, which contradicts d being square free. Generally, if $z = x_1 + y_1\sqrt{d} = x_2 + y_2\sqrt{d}$ are two representations for z, then subtracting produces $0 = (x_1 - x_2) + (y_1 - y_2)\sqrt{d}$. The unique representation for 0 implies $x_1 = x_2$ and $y_1 = y_2$, so in fact z has only one representation.

5.2.2   Allowing for Non-Square-Free d

Suppose that $d > 1$ is not square free. Factor $d = k^2 d'$, where $k > 1$ is an integer and where $d' \geq 1$ is a square-free integer when it is larger than 1. In practice, only the arithmetic operations and comparisons of numbers in $\mathbb{Q}(\sqrt{d})$ are needed. The comparisons become slightly more costly, but easier to implement than a factorization of $d = k^2 d'$.

The integer d is not the square of an integer when $d' > 1$. The number $z = x + y\sqrt{d}$ with rational x and y can be factored into $z = x + (ky)\sqrt{d'}$, so it is sufficient instead to work with the real quadratic field $\mathbb{Q}(\sqrt{d'})$. The representation of $z \in \mathbb{Q}(\sqrt{d})$ is unique.

The integer d is the square of an integer when $d' = 1$, say $d = k^2$ with $k > 1$. The number $z = x + y\sqrt{d}$ factors into $z = x + yk$. The representation of $z \in \mathbb{Q}(\sqrt{d})$ is not unique. For example, if $d = 4$, then $k = 2$ and $z = x + y\sqrt{4} = x + 2y$. The number $z = 0$ has two representations, $0 + 0 * \sqrt{4}$ and $2 - 1\sqrt{4}$. In fact, zero has infinitely many representations $0 = t(2 - 1\sqrt{4}) = 2t - t\sqrt{4}$ for any rational t. Generally, for $d = k^2$ the number zero has infinitely many representations $0 = t(k - 1\sqrt{d})$ for any rational t. A nonzero number $z = x + y\sqrt{d}$ also has infinitely many representations by adding any of the representations of 0, $z = z + 0 = (x + tk) + (y - t)\sqrt{d}$.

It is possible that $x + y\sqrt{d}$ satisfies the condition $x^2 - y^2 d = 0$. To trap division by zero when d is the square of an integer, it is not sufficient to test that both x and y are zero.

It is possible to determine whether d is the square of an integer using a numerical method for computing its square root. Algorithms for estimating square roots of integers are found at [38]. An estimate for the square root of $d = m * 2^{2n}$ with $1/2 \leq m < 2$ is $x_0 = 2^n$. The iteration scheme $x_{k+1} = (x_k + d/x_k)/2$ converges to $\sqrt{d}$ with quadratic convergence, $\lim_{k \to \infty} x_k = \bar{x}$, so $\bar{x} = (\bar{x} + d/\bar{x})/2$ which implies $\bar{x}^2 = d$. Observe that if x_k underestimates $\sqrt{d}$, then d/x_k overestimates $\sqrt{d}$, and vice versa. Therefore, the iterate $x_{k+1} \in [\min\{x_k, d/x_k\}, \max\{x_k, d/x_k\}]$. Iterate until x_k and d/x_k are in an interval $[j, j+2]$ with integer endpoints j and $j + 2$. If $j^2 = d$ or $(j + 1)^2 = d$ or

$(j + 2)^2 = d$, then d is the square of a rational number; otherwise, $\sqrt{d}$ is irrational and d is not the square of an integer.

5.2.3 Allowing for Rational d

The idea of real quadratic fields can be extended to rational $d > 1$, and the arithmetic operations of equations (5.13) through (5.16) and comparisons of numbers are valid.

Let $d = u/v > 1$, where u and v are positive integers with greatest common divisor of 1. The latter condition means that u and v have no common factors larger than 1. The number d is a *square-free rational number* when u and v are square-free integers. The set $\mathbb{Q}(\sqrt{d})$ of numbers of the form $x + y\sqrt{d}$ is a field.

The number 0 has a unique representation in $\mathbb{Q}(\sqrt{d})$. The proof is by contradiction. Let $0 = x + y\sqrt{d}$. If $y = 0$, then $x = 0$ is forced. If $y \neq 0$, solve for $d = (x/y)^2$, which makes d the square of a rational number, contradicting the assumption that d is square free. Therefore, the only representation of 0 is $0 + 0\sqrt{d}$.

As with integers, in practice the unique representation is not needed, which allows using rational d that is not square free. Moreover, the practical implementation of the concept allows for any nonnegative rational d, including 0 or 1. The comparisons of numbers becomes slightly more costly than when d is square free, but this is generally a minor cost compared to that of arithmetic operations for an implementation of rational numbers.

To avoid the extra cost per comparison when d is the square of a rational number, determine that d is a square in the same manner as that for integers. Factor $d = u'/v'$ for some positive integers u' and v'. Compute the greatest common divisor g of u' and v' and compute $u = u'/g$ and $v = v'/g$. The greatest common divisor of u and v is 1. Now determine whether u and v are squares of integers. If they are, then d is the square of a rational number.

When $d = |\mathbf{V}|^2$ is computed using rational arithmetic for the rational 3-tuple $\mathbf{V}$, the cost of determining whether d is the square of an integer is slightly less expensive. Let $\mathbf{V} = (a_0/b_0, \ldots, a_{n-1}/b_{n-1})$, where a_i and b_i are integers. The squared length is

$$d = \sum_{i=0}^{n-1} \left(\frac{a_i}{b_i}\right)^2 = \frac{\sum_{i=0}^{n-1} \left(a_i^2 \prod_{j=0, j\neq i}^{n-1} b_j^2\right)}{\prod_{j=0}^{n-1} b_j^2} \tag{5.17}$$

The numerator and denominator are integers. The length is

$$\sqrt{d} = \frac{\sqrt{\sum_{i=0}^{n-1} \left(a_i^2 \prod_{j=0, j\neq i}^{n-1} b_j^2\right)}}{\prod_{j=0}^{n-1} |b_j|} = \frac{\sqrt{A}}{B} \tag{5.18}$$

where the last equality defines the positive integers A and B. The length $\sqrt{d}$ is a rational number when the integer A is the square of an integer.

5.3   Comparisons of Quadratic Field Numbers

Given two quadratic field numbers $z_0 = x_0 + y_0\sqrt{d}$ and $z_1 = x_1 + y_1\sqrt{d}$, the branching logic in the geometric algorithms will involve comparisons $z_0 = z_1$, $z_0 \neq z_1$, $z_0 < z_1$, $z_0 \leq z_1$, $z_0 > z_1$ and $z_0 \geq z_1$. When programming the comparisons, only $z_0 = z_1$ and $z_0 < z_1$ contain the mathematical details. The other comparisons are logically based on these: $(z_0 \neq z_1) \Leftrightarrow \neg(z_0 = z_1)$, $(z_0 \leq z_1) \Leftrightarrow \neg(z_1 < z_0)$, $(z_0 > z_1) \Leftrightarrow (z_1 < z_0)$ and $(z_0 \geq z_1) \Leftrightarrow \neg(z_0 < z_1)$. Listing 5.2 shows how to code the comparisons in C++ using comparison operators.

```
bool operator==(Type z0, Type z1) { details_go_here; }
bool operator< (Type z0, Type z1) { details_go_here; }
bool operator!=(Type z0, Type z1) { return !operator==(z0, z1); }
bool operator<=(Type z0, Type z1) { return !operator<(z1, z0); }
bool operator> (Type z0, Type z1) { return operator<(z1, z0); }
bool operator>=(Type z0, Type z1) { return !operator(z0, z1); }
```

Listing 5.2: Comparison operators in C++.

The comparisons between two numbers z_0 and z_1 are also simplified by comparing the difference $w = z_0 - z_1$ to 0. When programming the comparisons, the mathematical details are contained solely in the two comparisons $w = 0$ and $w > 0$. The other comparisons are logically based on equality and less-than comparisons.

Let $w = x + y\sqrt{d} \in Q(\sqrt{d})$, where d is rational but not required to be square free. The comparison $w = 0$ is described next. If $d = 0$ or $y = 0$, it must be that $x = 0$. If $d \neq 0$ and $y \neq 0$, then $x \neq 0$ and $x^2 - y^2 d = 0$ with x and y having opposite sign. Listing 5.3 contains pseudocode for the comparison.

```
struct Rational;   // An implementation of arbitrary-precision arithmetic.
struct QFNumber { Rational x, y, d; };

// The equality comparison w = 0.
bool IsEqualToZero(QFNumber w)
{
    if (w.d == 0 || w.y == 0)
    {
        return w.x == 0;
    }
    else if (w.y > 0)
    {
        if (w.x >= 0)
        {
            return false;
        }
        else // w.x < 0
        {
            return w.x * w.x - w.y * w.y * w.d == 0;
        }
    }
    else // w.y < 0
    {
        if (w.x <= 0)
        {
```

```
                return false;
        }
        else  // w.x > 0
        {
                return w.x * w.x - w.y * w.y * w.d == 0;
        }
    }
}

// The equality comparison z0 == z1.
bool IsEqual(QFNumber z0, QFNumber z1)
{
    if (z0.d == 0 || z0.y == z1.y)
    {
        return z0.x == z1.x;
    }
    else if (z0.y > z1.y)
    {
        if (z0.x >= z1.x)
        {
            return false;
        }
        else  // z0.x < z1.x
        {
            QFNumber w = z0 - z1;
            return w.x * w.x == w.y * w.y * w.d;
        }
    }
    else  // z0.y < z1.y
    {
        if (z0.x <= z1.x)
        {
            return false;
        }
        else  // z0.x > z1.x
        {
            QFNumber w = z0 - z1;
            return w.x * w.x == w.y * w.y * w.d;
        }
    }
}
```

Listing 5.3: Pseudocode for testing whether $w = x + y\sqrt{d}$ is equal to 0.

The function IsEqual is the equality comparison for z_0 and z_1, where $w = z_0 - z_1$. The d-terms of the inputs are required to match, a condition enforced in the C++ implementation. The difference $z_0 - z_1$ is not computed until actually needed. When it is needed, only the terms x^2 and $y^2 d$ are computed but not their difference. In an implementation, the comparisons between rational numbers can be optimized for early-out returns to improve performance, which in this case avoids the cost of the subtraction.

The comparison $w < 0$ is described next. If $d = 0$ or $y = 0$, it must be that $x > 0$. If $d \neq 0$ and $y \neq 0$, some algebraic manipulation is required for the conditions that lead to $x + y\sqrt{d} < 0$. Consider the case $y > 0$. If $x \geq 0$, then $x + y\sqrt{d} > 0$, so $w < 0$ is false. If $x < 0$, then for $w < 0$ it is necessary that $0 < y\sqrt{d} < -x$, which implies $y^2 d < x^2$ and then $x^2 - y^2 d > 0$. Now consider the case $y < 0$. If $x \leq 0$, then $x + y\sqrt{d} < 0$, so $w < 0$ is true. If $x > 0$, then for $w < 0$ it is necessary that $0 < x < -y\sqrt{d}$, which implies $x^2 < y^2 d < 0$ and then $x^2 - y^2 d < 0$. Listing 5.4 contains pseudocode for the comparison.

```
// The less-than comparison w < 0.
bool IsLessThanZero(QFNumber w)
{
    if (w.d == 0 || w.y == 0)
    {
        return w.x < 0;
    }
    else if (w.y > 0)
    {
        if (w.x >= 0)
        {
            return false;
        }
        else // w.x < 0
        {
            return w.x * w.x - w.y * w.y * w.d > 0;
        }
    }
    else // w.y < 0
    {
        if (w.x <= 0)
        {
            return true;
        }
        else // w.x > 0
        {
            return w.x * w.x - w.y * w.y * w.d < 0;
        }
    }
}

// The less-than comparison z0 < z1.
bool IsLessThan(QFNumber z0, QFNumber q1)
{
    if (z0.d == 0 || z0.y == z1.y)
    {
        return z0.x < z1.x;
    }
    else if (z0.y > z1.y)
    {
        if (z0.x >= z1.x)
        {
            return false;
        }
        else // z0.x < z1.x
        {
            QFNumber w = z0 - z1;
            return w.x * w.x > w.y * w.y * w.d;
        }
    }
    else // z0.y < z1.y
    {
        if (z0.x <= z1.x)
        {
            return true;
        }
        else // z0.x > z1.x
        {
            QFNumber w = z0 - z1;
            return w.x * w.x < w.y * w.y * w.d;
        }
    }
}
```

Listing 5.4: Pseudocode for testing whether $w = x + y\sqrt{d}$ is less than 0.

The function IsLessThan is the equality comparison for z_0 and z_1, where $w =$

$z_0 - z_1$. The d-terms of the inputs are required to match, a condition enforced in the C++ implementation. The difference $z_0 - z_1$ is not computed until actually needed. When it is needed, only the terms x^2 and $y^2 d$ are computed but not their difference. In an implementation, the comparisons between rational numbers can be optimized for early-out returns to improve performance, which in this case avoids the cost of the subtraction.

5.4 Quadratic Fields with Multiple Square Roots

Geometric algorithms in 3D typically involve a coordinate system with an orthonormal basis of vectors. For example, a point in 3D can be written as

$$\mathbf{P} = \mathbf{C} + \sum_{i=1}^{3} x_i \mathbf{U}_i \tag{5.19}$$

where $\mathbf{C}$ is the origin of the coordinate system and $\{\mathbf{U}_1, \mathbf{U}_2, \mathbf{U}_3\}$ is a right-handed orthonormal basis. The basis vectors are unit length, mutually perpendicular and $\mathbf{U}_3 = \mathbf{U}_1 \times \mathbf{U}_2$.

As shown in Section 5.1.1, normalization of vectors $\mathbf{V}_i$ can lead to non-unit-length vectors when computing with floating-point arithmetic. Using rational arithmetic, it is possible to create 3 mutually orthogonal vectors starting with the nonzero vector $\mathbf{V}_1 = (v_{11}, v_{12}, v_{13})$. For the sake of argument, let $|v_{13}|$ be the maximum absolute value of the components of $\mathbf{V}_1$. A vector perpendicular to $\mathbf{V}_1$ is $\mathbf{V}_2 = (v_{21}, v_{22}, v_{23}) = (v_{13}, 0, -v_{11})$. A vector perpendicular to $\mathbf{V}_1$ and $\mathbf{V}_2$ is $\mathbf{V}_3 = \mathbf{V}_1 \times \mathbf{V}_2 = (v_{31}, v_{32}, v_{33}) = (-v_{11}v_{12}, v_{11}^2 + v_{13}^2, -v_{12}v_{13})$. Let $\mathbf{U}_i = \mathbf{V}_i / |\mathbf{V}_i|$, which does not necessarily produce unit-length vectors when computing with floating-point arithmetic because of the rounding errors in computing the lengths of $|\mathbf{V}_i|$. Define $d_j = 1/(\mathbf{V}_j \cdot \mathbf{V}_j)$ for $j = 1, 2$ and note that $d_1 d_2 = 1/(\mathbf{V}_3 \cdot \mathbf{V}_3)$. The orthonormal basis vectors are $\mathbf{U}_1 = \mathbf{V}_1 \sqrt{d_1}$, $\mathbf{U}_2 = \mathbf{V}_2 \sqrt{d_2}$ and $\mathbf{U}_3 = \mathbf{V}_1 \times \mathbf{V}_2 \sqrt{d_1 d_2}$.

Referring back to equation (5.19),

$$\mathbf{P} = \mathbf{C} + x_1 \mathbf{V}_1 \sqrt{d_1} + x_1 \mathbf{V}_2 \sqrt{d_2} + x_3 \mathbf{V}_3 \sqrt{d_1 d_2} \tag{5.20}$$

where each component of the point involves a linear combination of $\sqrt{d_1}$, $\sqrt{d_2}$ and $\sqrt{d_1 d_2}$.

5.4.1 Arithmetic Operations

Generally, an arithmetic system can be implemented for a set $\mathbb{Q}(\sqrt{d_1}, \sqrt{d_2})$, where the elements are of the form

$$x_0 + x_1 \sqrt{d_1} + x_2 \sqrt{d_2} + x_3 \sqrt{d_1 d_2} \tag{5.21}$$

The d_i are nonnegative rational numbers and the coefficients x_i are rational numbers. When both d_1 and d_2 are square free, it is possible to prove that the representation of an element is unique.

Addition and subtraction are defined by

$$
\begin{aligned}
&(x_0 + x_1\sqrt{d_1} + x_2\sqrt{d_2} + x_3\sqrt{d_1 d_2}) \pm (y_0 + y_1\sqrt{d_1} + y_2\sqrt{d_2} + y_3\sqrt{d_1 d_2}) \\
&= (x_0 \pm y_0) + (x_1 \pm y_1)\sqrt{d_1} + (x_2 \pm y_2)\sqrt{d_2} + (x_3 \pm y_3)\sqrt{d_1 d_2}
\end{aligned}
\tag{5.22}
$$

Multiplication is defined by

$$
\begin{aligned}
&(x_0 + x_1\sqrt{d_1} + x_2\sqrt{d_2} + x_3\sqrt{d_1 d_2}) * (y_0 + y_1\sqrt{d_1} + y_2\sqrt{d_2} + y_3\sqrt{d_1 d_2}) \\
&= (x_0 y_0 + x_1 y_1 d_1 + x_2 y_2 d_2 + x_3 y_3 d_1 d_2) + \\
&\quad (x_0 y_1 + x_1 y_0 + (x_2 y_3 + x_3 y_2) d_2)\sqrt{d_1} + \\
&\quad (x_0 y_2 + x_2 y_0 + (x_1 y_3 + x_3 y_1) d_1)\sqrt{d_2} + \\
&\quad (x_0 y_3 + x_1 y_2 + x_2 y_1 + x_3 y_0)\sqrt{d_1 d_2}
\end{aligned}
\tag{5.23}
$$

Division is defined by solving $x * y = 1$ for the y_i-components to obtain $y = 1/x = y_0 + y_1\sqrt{d_1} + y_2\sqrt{d_2} + y_3\sqrt{d_1 d_2}$. To show some algebraic patterns in the components, define $d_3 = d_1 d_2$,

$$
\begin{aligned}
y_0 &= (+x_0(x_0^2 - d_1 x_1^2 - d_2 x_2^2 - d_3 x_3^2) + 2d_3 x_1 x_2 x_3)/\Delta \\
y_1 &= (-x_1(x_0^2 - d_1 x_1^2 + d_2 x_2^2 + d_3 x_3^2) + 2d_2 x_0 x_2 x_3)/\Delta \\
y_2 &= (-x_2(x_0^2 + d_1 x_1^2 - d_2 x_2^2 + d_3 x_3^2) + 2d_1 x_0 x_1 x_3)/\Delta \\
y_3 &= (-x_3(x_0^2 + d_1 x_1^2 + d_2 x_2^2 - d_3 x_3^2) + 2x_0 x_1 x_2)/\Delta
\end{aligned}
\tag{5.24}
$$

where

$$
\begin{aligned}
\Delta &= (x_0^2 - (d_1 x_1^2 + d_2 x_2^2 + d_3 x_3^2))^2 \\
&\quad - 4(d_1 x_1^2 d_3 x_3^2 + d_1 x_1^2 d_2 x_2^2 + d_2 x_2^2 d_3 x_3^2) + 8d_3 x_0 x_1 x_2 x_3
\end{aligned}
\tag{5.25}
$$

The complexity of the expressions for the arithmetic operations increases as the number of square root terms increases.

5.4.2   Composition of Quadratic Fields

A convenient and practical way to deal with quadratic fields with multiple square roots is through *composition*. For example, elements of $\mathbb{Q}(\sqrt{d_1}, \sqrt{d_2})$ can be factored as

$$
\begin{aligned}
&x_0 + x_1\sqrt{d_1} + x_2\sqrt{d_2} + x_3\sqrt{d_1 d_2} \\
&= \left(x_0 + x_1\sqrt{d_1}\right) + \left(x_2 + x_3\sqrt{d_1}\right)\sqrt{d_2} = u_0 + u_1\sqrt{d_2}
\end{aligned}
\tag{5.26}
$$

where $u_i \in \mathbb{Q}(\sqrt{d_1})$. When d_1 and d_2 are square free, it is now easy to prove the representations of an element of $\mathbb{Q}(\sqrt{d_1}, \sqrt{d_2})$ unique. For example, to prove that 0 has a unique representation, the argument is the same as that for $\mathbb{Q}(\sqrt{d_1})$. Let $0 = u_0 + u_1\sqrt{d_2}$. If $u_1 = 0$, then $u_0 = 0$ is necessary. If $u_1 \neq 0$, then solve for $d_2 = (u_0/u_1)^2$. Because d_2 is rational, u_0 must be a rational multiple of u_1, say $u_0 = r u_1$ where $r \in \mathbb{Q}$. This implies $d_2 = r^2$, which contradicts d_2 being square free. Therefore, $u_0 = u_1 = 0$ are the only choices for the coefficients.

Arithmetic operations for $\mathbb{Q}(\sqrt{d_1}, \sqrt{d_2})$ are defined by equations (5.13) through (5.16), but now the coefficients are in $\mathbb{Q}(\sqrt{d_1})$ instead of $\mathbb{Q}$.

Comparisons are also defined using the discussion of Section 5.3, except that the internal comparisons of coefficients to the zero of $\mathbb{Q}$ are replaced by comparisons of coefficients to the zero of $\mathbb{Q}(\sqrt{d_1})$.

Effectively, a quadratic field for n square roots is defined recursively by choosing coefficients that are in a quadratic field for $n - 1$ square roots. The base case $n = 1$ involves a real quadratic field. The set $\mathbb{Q}(\sqrt{d_1}, \ldots, \sqrt{d_n})$ has elements $u_0 + u_1\sqrt{d_n}$, where $u_i \in \mathbb{Q}(\sqrt{d_1}, \ldots, \sqrt{d_{n-1}})$.

The GTL implementation is simple and uses recursion with templates. The class name is QFNumber and the code supports any number of square root terms.

5.5 Estimating a Quadratic Field Number

The geometric algorithms will produce quadratic field numbers that are a combination of rational and symbolic quantities. In practice, floating-point approximations to those numbers can be computed for a user-specified number of bits of precision. The approximations in this section use Newton's method with specially designed polynomials whose roots are the quadratic field numbers.

The concepts are illustrated using the GTL classes BSNumber and BSRational, because it makes clear how an initial guess is chosen for Newton's method and how to convert from a rational to a floating-point representation; see Chapter 3 for details about these classes. For another implementation of arbitrary-precision arithmetic, there should be similar support for selecting an initial guess to Newton's method and for converting a rational number to a floating-point number exactly or approximately, depending on the rational number.

5.5.1 Estimating a Rational Number

If BSRational is used for the arbitrary-precision type of the coefficients of the quadratic field number, it is possible that one or more of the coefficients does not have an exact representation as a BSNumber. Examples were provided in Section 3.1.

Section 3.4.3 describes the process of approximating a BSRational by a BSNumber for a user-specified number of bits of precision. The BSNumber can then be converted to a float or double as desired. Typically the number of bits of precision is chosen to be 24 (for float) or 53 (for double), which ensures the conversion from BSNumber to the native floating-point type is exact.

5.5.2   Estimating the Square Root of a Rational Number

Let a^2 be a positive rational number, where $a > 0$ is typically irrational, although the discussion in this section applies even when a is rational. The goal is to approximate $a = \sqrt{a^2}$ to a user-specified precision of p bits. The square root is the positive root of $f(z) = z^2 - a^2$. Given an accurate initial estimate of a, Newton's method can be used to generate iterates that theoretically converge to a. A termination criterion is developed based on the specified precision.

The rational number a^2 can be factored as $a^2 = r^2 2^e$, where $r^2 \in [1/2, 1)$ and where e is an integer. Consequently, $a = \sqrt{r^2 2^e}$. If e is even, then $a = \sqrt{r^2} 2^{e/2}$ with $r^2 \in [1/2, 1)$. If e is odd, then $a = \sqrt{2r^2} 2^{(e-1)/2}$ with $2r^2 \in [1, 2)$. In both cases, the exponent for the factorization of a is an integer. The problem reduces to estimating $s = \sqrt{s^2}$ where $s^2 = r^2 \in [1/2, 1)$ when e is even or $s^2 = 2r^2 \in [1, 2)$ when e is odd.

An initial estimate of s can be obtained by using the floating-point hardware. The rational number s^2 is converted to a double-precision number u with the rounding mode round-toward-positive. The square root of u is computed with the rounding mode round-toward-positive, producing a double-precision number v that is larger than the square root of u. Finally, v is converted to a rational number z_{max} that satisfies the condition $z_{max} > s$.

Define $z_{min} = s^2/z_{max}$. The condition $z_{max} > s$ implies $z_{min} < s$; therefore, $s \in [z_{min}, z_{max}]$. A conservative approach to estimating s uses bisection on the bounding interval, but that algorithm is slow to converge. Instead, Newton's method can be used because the convexity of $f(z)$ guarantees quadratic convergence.

The initial guess for Newton's method is $z_0 = z_{max}$. The iterates are

$$z_{k+1} = z_k - \frac{f(z_k)}{f'(z_k)} = z_k - \frac{z_k^2 - s^2}{2z_k} = (z_k + s^2/z_k)/2 \qquad (5.27)$$

for $k \geq 0$. Notice that $z_{max} = z_0$ and $z_{min} = s^2/z_0$ which implies that $z_1 = (z_{max} + z_{min})/2$, the average of the bounding interval endpoints. The function values satisfy $f(z_0) > 0$ and $f'(z_0) > 0$, which implies $z_1 < z_0$. The geometric configuration for Newton's method for $f(z)$ is shown in Figure 5.2. The iterate z_1 occurs at the intersection of the z-axis and the tangent line to the graph of $f(z)$ at z_0, which makes it clear that $s < z_1 < z_0$. The graph of $f(z)$ was accurately drawn using Mathematica [44], which shows that z_1 is the average of z_0 and s^2/z_0.

The ordering of the relevant quantities on the z-axis and the condition $(z_k + s^2/z_k)/2 > s$ imply $0 < s - s^2/z_k < z_k - s$ for all $k \geq 0$. Each iteration generates a pair z_{max} and z_{min}. These are computed until the difference $z_{max} - z_{min}$ is 0 to p bits of precision, after which z_{min} and z_{max} are estimates of s

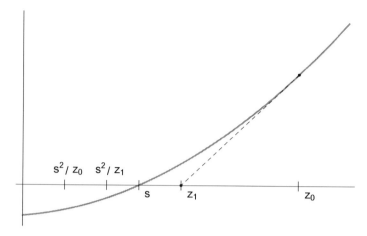

FIGURE 5.2: The geometric configuration for Newton's method that shows the iterates z_k satisfy $s < z_{k+1} < z_k$ for all $k \geq 0$. At each iteration, the square root satisfies $s \in [s^2/z_k, z_k]$ and $s < (z_k + s^2/z_k)/2$.

accurate to p bits of precision. The last step is to multiply these numbers by the proper power of 2 to obtain bounds on $a = \sqrt{a^2}$. That power is $2^{(e-1)/2}$ when e is odd or $2^{e/2}$ when e is even. The modified $z_{\min}$ is guaranteed to be an accurate estimate of a to p bits of precision and is the correctly rounded result when truncating $z_{\min}$ to p bits of precision.

Listing 5.5 contains pseudocode to estimate a bounding interval $[z_{\min}, z_{\max}]$ for $a = \sqrt{a^2}$ with $z_{\min}$ the correctly rounded estimate.

```
void PreprocessSqr(Rational aSqr, Rational& rSqr, int& exponentA)
{
    // Factor a² = r² * 2ᵉ , where r² ∈ [1/2, 1).
    int exponentASqr;
    rSqr = std::frexp(aSqr, &exponentASqr);
    if (exponentASqr & 1) // odd exponent
    {
        // a = √2 * r² * 2^(e-1)/2
        exponentA = (exponentASqr - 1) / 2;
        rSqr = std::ldexp(rSqr, 1);
        // r² ∈ [1, 2)
    }
    else // even exponent
    {
        // a = √r² * 2^e/2
        exponentA = exponentASqr / 2;
        // r² ∈ [1/2, 1)
    }
}

Rational GetMinOfSqrt(Rational rSqr, int exponent)
{
    // Convert the rational number to a double-precision number with round-toward-negative.
    double lowerRSqr;
    Convert(rSqr, FE_DOWNWARD, lowerRSqr);
```

```
        // Compute the square root with round-toward-negative.
        int saveRoundingMode = std :: fegetround ();
        std :: fesetround (FE_DOWNWARD);
        Rational aMin = std :: sqrt (lowerRSqr);
        std :: fesetround (saveRoundingMode);

        // Multiply r by the correct power-of-two to obtain a_min.
        aMin = std :: ldexp (aMin, exponent);
        return aMin;
}

Rational GetMaxOfSqrt(Rational aSqr, int exponent)
{
        // Convert the rational number to a double-precision number with round-toward-positive.
        double upperRSqr;
        Convert (rSqr, FE_UPWARD, upperRSqr);

        // Compute the square root with round-toward-positive.
        int saveRoundingMode = std :: fegetround ();
        std :: fesetround (FE_UPWARD);
        Rational aMax = std :: sqrt (upperASqr);
        std :: fesetround (saveRoundingMode);

        // Multiply r by the correct power-of-two to obtain a_max.
        aMax = std :: ldexp (aMax, exponent);
        return aMax;
}

// Compute a bounding interval for the root, a_min <= a <= a_max, where the endpoints are
// both within the specified precision.
uint32_t EstimateSqrt(Rational aSqr, int p, Rational& aMin, Rational& aMax)
{
        // Factor a^2 = r^2 * 2^e, where r^2 in [1/2, 1). Compute s^2 and the exponent used
        // to generate the estimate of sqrt(a^2).
        Rational sSqr;
        int exponentA;
        PreprocessSqr (aSqr, sSqr, exponentA);

        // Use the FPU to estimate s = sqrt(s^2) to 53 bits of precision with rounding up.
        // Multiply by the appropriate exponent to obtain bound upper a_max > a.
        aMax = GetMaxOfSqrt (sSqr, exponentA);

        // Compute a lower bound a_min < a.
        aMin = aSqr / aMax;

        // Compute Newton iterates until convergence. The estimate closest to a is a_min
        // with a_min <= a <= a_max and a - a_min <= a_max - a. The maximum iterations
        // is specified by the user to guard against an infinite loop.
        Rational threshold = std :: ldexp (Rational(1), -p);
        uint32_t iterate;
        for (iterate = 1; iterate <= maxIterations; ++iterate)
        {
                if (aMax - aMin < threshold)
                {
                        break;
                }
                // Compute the average a_max = (a_min + a_max)/2. Round up to twice the
                // precision to avoid quadratic growth in the number of bits and to ensure
                // that a_min can increase.
                aMax = std :: ldexp (aMin + aMax, -1);
                Convert (aMax, 2*p, FE_UPWARD, aMax);
                aMin = aSqr / aMax;
```

```
    }
    return iterate;
}

// Compute an estimate of the root when you do not need a bounding interval.
uint32_t EstimateSqrt(Rational aSqr, int p, Rational& a)
{
    // Compute a bounding interval a_min ≤ a ≤ a_max.
    Rational aMin, aMax;
    uint32_t numIterates = EstimateSqrt(aSqr, p, aMin, aMax);
    // Use the average of the interval endpoints as the estimate.
    a = std::ldexp(aMin + aMax, -1);
    return numIterates;
}
```

Listing 5.5: Pseudocode for estimating $a = \sqrt{a^2}$ to p bits of precision, where a^2 is a rational number. The returned integer value is the number of iterations of Newton's method used to compute the estimate. The functions std::frexp and std::ldexp are standard mathematics library functions that must be implemented for type Rational.

5.5.3 Estimating a 1-Root Quadratic Field Number

The square root estimation described in the previous section allows estimating a 1-root quadratic field number of the form $x + y\sqrt{d}$ for rational $d \geq 0$. The number $a = \sqrt{y^2 d}$ is estimated to a user-specified p bits of precision followed by the rational addition $x + \mathrm{Sign}(y)a$. The final estimation has at least p bits of precision. Listing 5.6 contains pseudocode for the estimation.

```
// Compute a bounding interval for the root, z_min ≤ z ≤ z_max, where the endpoints are
// both within the specified precision.
uint32_t Estimate(QFNumber z, int p, Rational& zMin, Rational& zMax)
{
    uint32_t numIterates;
    if (z.d != 0 && z.y != 0)
    {
        Rational aSqr = z.y * z.y * z.d;
        numIterates = EstimateSqrt(aSqr, p, zMin, zMax);
        if (z.y > 0)
        {
            zMin = z.x + zMin;
            zMax = z.x + zMax;
        }
        else
        {
            Rational diff = z.x - zMax;
            zMax = z.x - zMin;
            zMin = diff;
        }
    }
    else
    {
        numIterates = 0;
        zMin = z.x;
        zMax = z.x;
    }
    return numIterates;
}

// Compute an estimate of the root when you do not need a bounding interval.
```

```
uint32_t Estimate(Rational x, Rational y, Rational d, int p, Rational& z)
{
    // Compute a bounding interval z_min <= z <= z_max.
    Rational zMin, zMax;
    uint32_t numIterates = Estimate(x, y, d, p, zMin, zMax);
    // Use the average of the interval endpoints as the estimate.
    z = std::ldexp(zMin + zMax, -1);
    return numIterates;
}
```

Listing 5.6: Pseudocode for estimating a quadratic field number $z = x + y\sqrt{d}$. The returned integer value is the number of iterations of Newton's method used to compute the estimate of $\sqrt{y^2 d}$. The sign of y determines whether z_{min} or z_{max} is closest to the true value. If $y > 0$, then z_{min} is closest. If $y < 0$ then z_{max} is closest. If $y = 0$, then $z_{min} = z_{max} = x$, which means there is no error in the estimates.

A GTL program to test the implementation is shown in Listing 5.7. The function Estimate in the actual code uses the QFNumber template implementation.

```
using Rational = BSRational<UIntegerAP32>;

Rational F(QFNumber<Rational, 1> const& z, Rational const& zEstimate)
{
    return zEstimate*(zEstimate-Rational(2)*z.x[0]) +
        (z.x[0]*z.x[0]-z.x[1]*z.x[1]*z.d);
}

int main()
{
    int32_t constexpr precision = std::numeric_limits<double>::digits;
    uint32_t const maxIterations = 8;
    APConversion<BSR> apc(precision, maxIterations);

    QFNumber<BSR, 1> z;
    uint32_t numIterations;
    BSR zMin, zMax, fMin, fMax;
    double dZDbl, dZMin, dZMax, dFMin, dFMax;

    z.x[0] = 0.13547700429678050;
    z.x[1] = 0.83500858999457950;
    z.d = 0.96886777112423139;
    dZDbl = z.x[0] + z.x[1] * std::sqrt(z.d);
    numIterations = apc.Estimate(z, zMin, zMax);
    dZMin = zMin;
    dZMax = zMax;
    fMin = F(z, zMin);
    fMax = F(z, zMax);
    dFMin = fMin;
    dFMax = fMax;
    // numIterations = 2
    // dZDbl = 0.95738498605851619
    // dZMin = 0.95738498605851630
    // dZMax = 0.95738498605851630
    // dFMin = -1.1127184071397530e-32
    // dFMax = +1.1127184071397530e-32

    z.x[0] = 0.13547700429678050;
    z.x[1] = -0.83500858999457950;
    z.d = 0.96886777112423139;
    dZDbl = z.x[0] + z.x[1] * std::sqrt(z.d);
    numIterations = apc.Estimate(z, zMin, zMax);
    dZMin = zMin;
```

```
      dZMax = zMax;
      fMin = F(z, zMin);
      fMax = F(z, zMax);
      dFMin = fMin;
      dFMax = fMax;
      // numIterations = 2
      // dZDbl = -0.68643097746495518
      // dZMin = -0.68643097746495529
      // dZMax = -0.68643097746495529
      // dFMin = +1.1127184071397530e-32
      // dFMax = -1.1127184071397530e-32

      z.x[0] = 0.13547700429678050;
      z.x[1] = 0.83500858999457950;
      z.d = 96886.777112423139;
      dZDbl = z.x[0] + z.x[1] * std::sqrt(z.d);
      numIterations = apc.Estimate(z, zMin, zMax);
      dZMin = zMin;
      dZMax = zMax;
      fMin = F(z, zMin);
      fMax = F(z, zMax);
      dFMin = fMin;
      dFMax = fMax;
      // numIterations = 2
      // dZDbl = 260.04560194821846
      // dZMin = 260.04560194821846
      // dZMax = 260.04560194821846
      // dFMin = -8.1020373233087111e-28
      // dFMax = +8.1020373233087111e-28

      z.x[0] = 0.13547700429678050;
      z.x[1] = -0.83500858999457950;
      z.d = 0.0000096886777112423139;
      dZDbl = z.x[0] + z.x[1] * std::sqrt(z.d);
      numIterations = apc.Estimate(z, zMin, zMax);
      dZMin = zMin;
      dZMax = zMax;
      fMin = F(z, zMin);
      fMax = F(z, zMax);
      dFMin = fMin;
      dFMax = fMax;
      // numIterations = 1
      // dZDbl = 0.13287790304734129
      // dZMin = 0.13287790304734129
      // dZMax = 0.13287790304734129
      // dFMin = +2.0180238788854996e-21
      // dFMax = -2.0180238788854989e-21
      return 0;
}
```

Listing 5.7: A test program for verifying the implementations for estimating square roots of rational numbers and for estimating quadratic field numbers. The estimation code requires a user-specified maximum number of iterations just to guard against infinite loops, which should not theoretically happen.

The returned zMin and zMax numbers are guaranteed to bound the theoretical value of $x + y\sqrt{d}$. The BSRational class has member functions for implicit conversions to float and double. The user-specified precision is that of double and the implicit conversion must lead to dZMin and dZMax being the same number; that is, the rational results when truncated are the correctly rounded double-precision results.

The numbers dZDbl are the evaluation of $x + y\sqrt{d}$ using only double-precision arithmetic. The first two examples have dZDbl different from dZMin (and dZMax), so the double-precision result is not correctly rounded. The last two examples have dZDbl the same as dZMin (and dZMax), so those double-precision evaluations are correctly rounded.

5.5.4   Estimating a 2-Root Quadratic Field Number

A 2-root quadratic field number is of the form $q = (x + y\sqrt{d_1}) + (z + w\sqrt{d_1})\sqrt{d_2} = x + y\sqrt{d_1} + z\sqrt{d_2} + w\sqrt{d_1 d_2}$, where $d_1 \geq 0$, $d_2 \geq 0$ and the coefficients x, y, z and w are rational numbers.

Let $\sigma(v)$ be the sign of v, which is 1 when $v > 0$, 0 when $v = 0$ or -1 when $v < 0$. Each square-root term of q can be written as the product of a sign and an absolute value. The set of absolute-sign pairs is

$$\left\{ (|y|\sqrt{d_1}, \sigma(y)), (|z|\sqrt{d_2}, \sigma(z)), (|w|\sqrt{d_1 d_2}, \sigma(w)) \right\} \tag{5.28}$$

Sort this set by the absolute-value term in nondecreasing order to obtain $\{(a, \sigma_a), (b, \sigma_b), (c, \sigma_c)\}$ with $a \geq b \geq c \geq 0$. Define $\tau_0 = -a - b + c$, $\tau_1 = -a + b - c$, $\tau_2 = a - b - c$ and $\tau_3 = a + b + c$. The ordering of a, b and c implies $\tau_0 \leq \tau_1 \leq \tau_2 \leq \tau_3$. The 2-root number is written as

$$q = x + \sigma_a a + \sigma_b b + \sigma_c c = x + s\tau \tag{5.29}$$

for some $s \in \{-1, 1\}$ and for some $\tau \in \{\tau_0, \tau_1, \tau_2, \tau_3\}$.

The four potential τ_i values are real-valued roots to the polynomial

$$\begin{aligned} f(t) &= (t - \tau_0)(t - \tau_1)(t - \tau_2)(t - \tau_3) \\ &= t^4 - 2(a^2 + b^2 + c^2)t^2 - 8abct \\ &\quad + ((a^2 - b^2)^2 + c^2(c^2 - 2(a^2 + b^2))) \end{aligned} \tag{5.30}$$

For later use, the first-order derivative $f'(t)$ and second-order derivative $f''(t)$ are

$$\begin{aligned} f'(t) &= 4t^3 - 4(a^2 + b^2 + c^2)t - 8abc \\ f''(t) &= 12t^2 - 4(a^2 + b^2 + c^2) \end{aligned} \tag{5.31}$$

The analysis of $f(t)$ depends on which comparison tests occur in $a \geq b \geq c \geq 0$. Each comparison is either a greater-than comparison or an equal-to comparison for a total of 8 possible cases. This section describes the analysis for those cases.

The most complicated cases to analyze are when $a > b > c \geq 0$. The roots of $f(t)$ are distinct, which is equivalent to $f'(\tau_i) \neq 0$ for all i. At its highest level, the algorithm for estimating q is to identify s and τ in equation (5.29) and then estimate τ using Newton's method for $f(t)$ of equation. The function is convex at the root τ if $f''(\tau) > 0$. It is concave at the root when

TABLE 5.1: Estimating a 2-root quadratic field number.

case	$q - x$	sign possibilities	terms
$a = b = c = 0$		no signs	0
$a > b = c = 0$	$\sigma_a a$	$\sigma_a \in \{\pm 1\}$	1
$a = b > c = 0$	$(\sigma_a + \sigma_b)a$	$\sigma_a + \sigma_b \in \{0, \pm 2\}$	0, 1
$a > b > c = 0$	$\sigma_a a + \sigma_b b$	$\sigma_a \in \{\pm 1\}, \sigma_b \in \{\pm 1\}$	2
$a = b = c > 0$	$(\sigma_a + \sigma_b + \sigma_c)a$	$\sigma_a + \sigma_b + \sigma_c \in \{\pm 1, \pm 3\}$	1
$a = b > c > 0$	$(\sigma_a + \sigma_b)a + \sigma_c c$	$\sigma_a + \sigma_b \in \{0, \pm 2\}, \sigma_c \in \{\pm 1\}$	1, 2
$a > b = c > 0$	$\sigma_a a + (\sigma_b + \sigma_c)b$	$\sigma_a \in \{\pm 1\}, \sigma_b + \sigma_b \in \{0, \pm 2\}$	1, 2
$a > b > c > 0$	$\sigma_a a + \sigma_b b + \sigma_c c$	$\sigma_a \in \{\pm 1\}, \sigma_b \in \{\pm 1\}, \sigma_c \in \{\pm 1\}$	3

$f''(\tau) < 0$. In either case, Newton's method converges quadratically given an initial estimate sufficiently close to the root. If $f''(\tau) = 0$, the convergence rate is not easily deduced and the estimation of a root must be handled carefully. Generally, there are functions for which Newton's method does not converge to τ when $f(\tau) = f''(\tau) = 0$ for specific initial estimates. At the maximum root $\tau_3 = a + b + c$, observe that

$$f''(\tau_3)/8 = a^2 + b^2 + c^2 + 3ab + 3ac + 3bc > 0 \qquad (5.32)$$

The function is always convex at this root. At the minimum root $\tau_0 = -a - b + c$, observe that

$$\begin{aligned} f''(\tau_0)/8 &= a^2 + b^2 + c^2 + 3ab - 3ac - 3bc \\ &= (a + b - 2c)(a + b - c) + (ab - c^2) > 0 \end{aligned} \qquad (5.33)$$

The positivity is guaranteed because $(a - b) > 0$, $(a - c) > 0$, $(b - c) > 0$, $(a + b - 2c) = ((a - c) + (b - c)) > 0$, $(a + b - c) = (a + (b - c)) > 0$ and $ab - c^2 > b^2 - c^2 = (b + c)(b - c) > 0$. The function is always convex at this root. It is possible that at the non-extreme roots τ_1 and τ_2, $f''(\tau_1)$ and $f''(\tau_2)$ are positive, negative or zero. Therefore, the estimation is straightforward at the extreme roots but requires more attention at the non-extreme roots.

An implementation of the algorithm is structured to handle cases as shown in Table 5.1. The terms column is the number of nonzero square-root terms in $q - x$. The case of one square-root term in q is covered by Section 5.5.3. The cases of two square-root terms and three square-root terms are described in the remainder of this section.

5.5.4.1 Two Nonzero Radical Coefficients

The ideas are illustrated using the case $a > b > c = 0$ with $q = x + \sigma_a a + \sigma_b b$. The polynomial of equation (5.30) is $f(t) = t^4 - 2(a^2 + b^2)t^2 + (a^2 - b^2)^2 = (t^2 - (a - b)^2)(t^2 - (a + b)^2)$. The graph of $f(t)$ is shown in Figure 5.3. The function is even in its variable t, $f(-t) = f(t)$, so it suffices to estimate roots for which $t > 0$. The other roots are estimated by negations of the estimates for the positive roots.

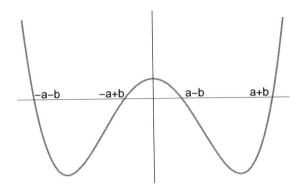

FIGURE 5.3: The graph of $f(t)$ for $a > b$ and $c = 0$.

Given an initial guess t_0, the Newton iterates are

$$t_{k+1} = t_k - f(t_k)/f'(t_k) = (3t_k + g(t_k))/4, \quad k \geq 0 \tag{5.34}$$

where

$$g(t) = \frac{(a^2 + b^2)t^2 - (a^2 - b^2)^2}{t(t^2 - (a^2 + b^2))} \tag{5.35}$$

It can be shown that $g(\tau_i) = \tau_i$ for any root τ_i. The derivative of $g(t)$ is

$$\begin{aligned} g'(t) &= \frac{-(a^2-b^2)^2(a^2+b^2)+2(a^4-4a^2b^2+b^4)t^2-(a^2+b^2)t^4}{t^2(t^2-(a^2+b^2))^2} \\ &= n(t)/d(t) \end{aligned} \tag{5.36}$$

where $g'(t)$ has numerator $n(t)$ and denominator $d(t) \geq 0$. The goal is to prove that $n(t) \leq 0$, which implies $g'(t) \leq 0$. Consequently, if $\tau < 0$ is a root of $f(t)$, an estimate $t_k > \tau$ ensures $g(t_k) < \tau$ and $\tau \in [g(t_k), t_k]$. An estimate $t_k < \tau$ ensures $g(t_k) > \tau$ and $\tau \in [t_k, g(t_k)]$.

Define $u = b/a \in (0, 1)$, $v = t/a > 0$ and $h(u, v) = n(t)/a^6$; then

$$h(u, v) = (-1 + u^2 + u^4 - u^6) + 2(1 - 4u^2 + u^4)v^2 - (1 + u^2)v^4 \tag{5.37}$$

The domain of $h(u, v)$ is $\mathcal{D} = (0, 1) \times (0, +\infty)$, but it is convenient to extend the domain to $\overline{\mathcal{D}} = [0, 1] \times [0, +\infty)$ for determining the maximum value of $h(u, v)$. The maximum must occur for some point $(u, 0)$, some point $(0, v)$, some point $(1, v)$ or at a point $(u, v) \in$ domain where $\nabla h(u, v) = (0, 0)$. On the boundary $v = 0$, $h(u, 0) = -(1 - u^2)(1 - u^4) \leq 0$ for $u \in [0, 1]$. On the boundary $u = 0$, $h(0, v) = -(1 - v^2)^2 \leq 0$ for $v \geq 0$. On the boundary $u = 1$, $h(1, v) = -2v^2(2 + v^2) \leq 0$ for $v \geq 0$. The partial derivatives of $h(u, v)$ are

$$\begin{aligned} h_u(u, v) &= -2u((-1 - 2u^2 + 3u^4) + 4(2 - u^2)v^2 + v^4) \\ h_v(u, v) &= -4v((-1 + 4u^2 - u^4) + (1 + u^2)v^2) \end{aligned} \tag{5.38}$$

The variables u and v are positive in $\mathcal{D}$, so the solution $u = 0$ to $h_u(u, v) = 0$ and the solution $v = 0$ to $h_v(u, v) = 0$ can be discarded. Solving for v^2 in $h_v(u, v) = 0$ produces $v^2 = (u^4 - 4u^2 + 1)/(u^2 + 1)$. Substituting this in $h_u(u, v) = 0$ and multiplying by $(u^2 + 1)^2$ leads to $\delta(u) = 2 - 10u^2 + u^4 + 4u^6 = 0$, where $\delta(u)$ is a cubic polynomial in u^2. It has a single real-valued root $\bar{u} \in (0, 1)$, an estimate given by $\bar{u} \doteq 0.455981$. The corresponding v-value estimate is $\bar{v} \doteq 0.418499$. The corresponding $\bar{h} = h(\bar{u}, \bar{v}) \doteq -0.720787$. It turns out that the graph of $\bar{h}$ at this point is a saddle point. It is also possible to eliminate u from $h_u = 0$ and $h_v = 0$. Compute $p = h_u + 3h_v = (-4 + 11v^2 + v^4) + u^2(10 - v^2)$. Solve $p = 0$ for $u^2 = (v^4 + 11v^2 - 4)/(v^2 - 10)$. Substituting this in $h_v = 0$ and multiplying by $(v^2 - 10)^2$ leads to $\epsilon(v) = -11 + 52v^2 + 61v^4 + 4v^6 = 0$, where $\epsilon(v)$ is a cubic polynomial in v^2. It has a single real-valued root $\bar{v} \in (0, +\infty)$.

The numerical estimates suggest that $h(\mathcal{D}) \leq 0$, but are not in themselves a formal proof of this. It is possible $h(\bar{u}, \bar{v}) > 0$ even though at points nearby $h(u, v) \leq 0$. Interval arithmetic with arbitrary-precision numbers is used to prove that in fact $h(\bar{u}, \bar{v}) < 0$. The theoretical root $\bar{u}$ is in the interval $[u_0, u_1]$, where u_0 and u_1 are double-precision numbers with $u_0 = 0.45598062412214041$ (binary encoding 0x3fdd2ec95b0db677) and $u_1 = 0.45598062412214047$ (binary encoding 0x3fdd2ec95b0db678). The endpoints are consecutive double-precision numbers. The polynomial values are exact rational numbers $\delta(u_0) > 0$ and $\delta(u_1) < 0$; the sign change guarantees $u_0 < \bar{u} < u_1$. The theoretical root $\bar{v}$ is in the interval $[v_0, v_1]$, where v_0 and v_1 are double-precision numbers with $v_0 = 0.41849918836555849$ (binary encoding 0x3fdac8b0d1dbb001) and $v_1 = 0.41849918836555855$ (binary encoding 0x3fdac8b0d1dbb002). The polynomial values are exact rational numbers $\epsilon(v_0) < 0$ and $\epsilon(v_1) > 0$; the sign change guarantees $v_0 < \bar{v} < v_1$. Using arbitrary-precision interval arithmetic, $[h_0, h_1] = h([u_0, u_1, [v_0, v_1]])$, where it turns out that $h_0 < 0$ and $h_1 < 0$; therefore, $h(u, v) < 0$ for $(u, v) \in [u_0, u_1] \times [v_0, v_1]$. In particular, $h(\bar{u}, \bar{v}) < 0$. In summary, $h(u, v) < 0$ for $(u, v) \in (0, 1) \times (0, +\infty)$ which implies $g'(t) < 0$ for $t \neq 0$.

The maximum root is $\tau_3 = a + b$. The graph is convex at that point beecause $f''(\tau_3) = 8(a^2 + 3ab + b^2) > 0$. Choose an initial estimate $t_0 > \tau_3$. The iterates t_k are to the right of the root and $g(t_k)$ are to the left of the root always. The analysis of the sequence of iterates is similar to that of equation (5.27). For each iteration, define $t_{\max} = t_k$ and $t_{\min} = g(t_{\max})$. The root τ_3 is necessarily in the interval $[t_{\min}, t_{\max}]$. The next iterate is $t_{k+1} = t_k - f(t_k)/f'(t_k)$, where $f(t_k) > 0$ and $f'(t_k) > 0$ guarantee that $t_{k+1} < t_k$. Moreover, $t_{k+1} = (3t_{\max} + t_{\min})/4$, which is a weighted average of the interval endpoints and must be larger than τ_3. Listing 5.8 contains pseudocode for estimating τ_3.

```
uint32_t EstimateApB(Rational aSqr, Rational bSqr, int p,
    Rational& tMin, Rational& tMax)
{
    // Factor a^2 = r^2 * 2^e, where r^2 ∈ [1/2, 1). Compute u^2 and the exponent used
    // to generate the estimate of √(a^2).
    Rational uSqr;
```

```
int exponentA;
PreprocessSqr(aSqr, uSqr, exponentA);

// Factor b² = s² * 2ᵉ, where s² ∈ [1/2, 1). Compute v² and the exponent used
// to generate the estimate of √b².
Rational vSqr;
int exponentB;
PreprocessSqr(bSqr, vSqr, exponentB);

// Use the FPU to estimate u = √u² and v = √v² to 53 bits of precision with
// rounding up. Multiply by the appropriate exponents to obtain upper bounds
// a_max > a and b_max > b. This ensures t_max = a_max + b_max > a + b.
Rational aMax = GetMaxOfSqrt(uSqr, exponentA);
Rational bMax = GetMaxOfSqrt(vSqr, exponentB);
tMax = aMax + bMax;

// Compute a lower bound t_min < a + b.
Rational a2pb2 = aSqr + bSqr;
Rational a2mb2 = aSqr - bSqr;
Rational a2mb2Sqr = a2mb2 * a2mb2;
Rational tMaxSqr = tMax * tMax;
tMin = (a2pb2 * tMaxSqr - a2mb2Sqr) / (tMax * (tMaxSqr - a2pb2));

// Compute Newton iterates until convergence. The estimate closest to a + b is t_min
// with t_min < a + b < t_max and (a + b) - t_min < t_max - (a + b). The maximum
// iterations are specified by the user to guard against an infinite loop.
Rational threshold = std::ldexp(Rational(1), -p), three(3);
uint32_t iterate;
for (iterate = 1; iterate <= maxIterations; ++iterate)
{
    if (tMax - tMin < threshold)
    {
        break;
    }
    // Compute the weighted average t_max = (3t_min + t_max)/4. Round up to
    // twice the precision to avoid quadratic growth in the number of bits and
    // to ensure that t_min can increase.
    tMax = std::ldexp(three * tMax + tMin, -2);
    Convert(tMax, 2 * p, FE_UPWARD, tMax);
    tMaxSqr = tMax * tMax;
    tMin = (a2pb2 * tMaxSqr - a2mb2Sqr) / (tMax * (tMaxSqr - a2pb2));
}
return iterate;
}
```

Listing 5.8: Pseudocode for estimating $\tau_3 = a + b$, where $a = p_0\sqrt{e_0}$ and $b = p_1\sqrt{e_1}$ with $p_0 > 0$, $e_0 > 0$, $p_1 > 0$ and $e_1 > 0$. Necessarily a^2 and b^2 are rational numbers. The input p is the user-specified bits of precision for the estimate.

Consider the behavior of the Newton iterates for the root $\tau_2 = a - b$. The analysis of the Newton iterates near the root is similar to that of τ_3 except that now the graph at τ_2 might be convex, concave or have a point of inflection. The second derivative at the root is $f''(\tau_2) = 8(a^2 - 3ab + b^2)$, which can be positive, negative or zero. The sign determines the shape of the graph at τ_2. Generally, the point of inflection occurs at $T = \sqrt{(a^2 + b^2)/3}$ with $f''(T) = 0$.

Figure 5.4 shows the graph of a function with $f''(\tau_2) < 0$. The second derivative $f''(t)$ is negative for $t \in [0, T)$. That basin contains τ_2. To guarantee convergence of the Newton iterates, the initial guess must be a number

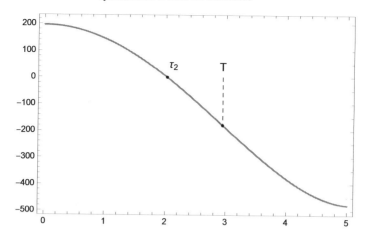

FIGURE 5.4: The graph of the function $f(t)$ for $a = \sqrt{20}$ and $b = \sqrt{6}$. The root is $\tau_2 = \sqrt{20} - \sqrt{6} \doteq 2.022646$, the inflection point is located at $T = \sqrt{26/3} \doteq 2.943920$ and $f''(\tau_2) < 0$.

$t_0 \in [\tau_2, T]$. The tangent lines at points in this interval intersect the t-axis at points in the same interval, and it is guaranteed that $\tau_2 < t_{k+1} < t_k$ for all $k \geq 0$. It is also guaranteed that $g(t_k) < \tau_2$ for all iterates $k \geq 0$. If an initial guess is chosen with $t_0 > T$, then choose a lower bound $\ell < \tau_2$ close to τ_2 and bisect the interval $[t_{\min}, t_{\max}]$ where $t_{\min}$ is initially ℓ and $t_{\max}$ is initially t_0. The bisection proceeds as follows. Compute $t_{\mid} = (t_{\min} + t_{\max})/2$. If $f''(t_{\mid}) > 0$, replace $t_{\max}$ with $t_{\mid}$ and repeat the bisection. If $f''(t_{\mid}) \leq 0$, two cases occur. If $f(t_{\mid}) > 0$, replace $t_{\min}$ with $t_{\mid}$ and repeat the bisection; otherwise, $t_{\mid} \in [\tau_2, T]$, so replace t_0 with $t_{\mid}$ and switch to Newton's method which is now guaranteed to converge.

Figure 5.5 shows the graph of a function with $f''(\tau_2) > 0$. The second derivative $f''(t)$ is positive for $t \in (T, +\infty)$. That basin contains τ_2. To guarantee convergence of the Newton iterates, the initial guess must be a number $t_0 \in [T, \tau_2]$. The tangent lines at points in this interval intersect the t-axis at points in the same interval, and it is guaranteed that $t_k < t_{k+1} < \tau_2$ for all $k \geq 0$. It is also guaranteed that $g(t_k) > \tau_2$ for all iterates $k \geq 0$. If an initial guess is chosen with $t_0 < T$, then choose an upper bound $\mu > \tau_2$ close to τ_2 and bisect the interval $[t_{\min}, t_{\max}]$ where $t_{\min}$ is initially t_0 and $t_{\max}$ is initially μ. The bisection proceeds as follows. Compute $t_{\mid} = (t_{\min} + t_{\max})/2$. If $f''(t_{\mid}) < 0$, replace $t_{\min}$ with $t_{\mid}$ and repeat the bisection. If $f''(t_{\mid}) \geq 0$, two cases occur. If $f(t_{\mid}) < 0$, replace $t_{\max}$ with $t_{\mid}$ and repeat the bisection; otherwise, $t_{\mid} \in [T, \tau_2]$, so replace t_0 with $t_{\mid}$ and switch to Newton's method which is now guaranteed to converge.

It is not possible for $f''(\tau_2) = 0$. Let $a = p_0\sqrt{e_0}$ and $b = p_1\sqrt{e_1}$ where $a > b$, $p_0 > 0$, $p_1 > 0$, $e_0 > 0$ and $e_1 > 0$ are rational numbers. If the second

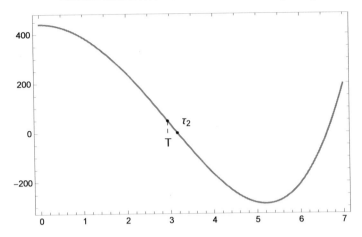

FIGURE 5.5: The graph of the function $f(t)$ for $a = \sqrt{24}$ and $b = \sqrt{3}$. The root is $\tau_2 = \sqrt{24} - \sqrt{3} \doteq 3.166929$, the inflection point is located at $T = \sqrt{25/3} \doteq 2.886751$ and $f''(\tau_2) > 0$.

derivative is zero, then $a^2 - 3ab + b^2 = 0$. Substitute a and b into this equation to obtain $p_0^2 e_0 + p_1^2 e_1 = 3p_0 p_1 \sqrt{e_0 e_1}$. Square the equation and manipulate the terms algebraically to obtain the equation $p_0^4 e_0^2 - 7p_0^2 p_1^2 e_0 e_1 + p_1^4 e_1^2 = 0$. Define the rational number $\lambda = (p_0^2 e_0)/(p_1^2 e_1)$. The previous equation becomes $\lambda^2 - 7\lambda + 1 = 0$ and has roots $\lambda = (7 \pm \sqrt{45})/2$. The roots are irrational, which contradicts the rationality of λ. Therefore, $f''(\tau_2) \neq 0$.

Listing 5.9 contains pseudocode for estimating τ_2.

```
uint32_t EstimateAmB(Rational aSqr, Rational bSqr, int p,
    Rational& tMin, Rational& tMax)
{
    // The return value of the function.
    uint32_t iterate = 0;

    // Compute various quantities that are used later in the code.
    Rational a2tb2 = aSqr * bSqr;   // a² * b²
    Rational a2pb2 = aSqr + bSqr;   // a² + b²
    Rational a2mb2 = aSqr - bSqr;   // a² - b²
    Rational a2mb2Sqr = a2mb2 * a2mb2;   // (a² - b²)²
    Rational twoa2pb2 = std::ldexp(a2pb2, 1);   // 2(a² + b²)
    Rational zero(0), three(3), five(5);

    // Factor a² = r² * 2ᵉ, where r² ∈ [1/2, 1). Compute u² and the exponent used
    // to generate the estimate of √a².
    Rational uSqr;
    int exponentA;
    PreprocessSqr(aSqr, uSqr, exponentA);

    // Factor b² = s² * 2ᵉ, where s² ∈ [1/2, 1). Compute v² and the exponent used
    // to generate the estimate of √b².
    Rational vSqr;
    int exponentB;
```

```
PreprocessSqr(bSqr, vSqr, exponentB);
```

```
// Compute the sign of f''(a − b)/8 = a² − 3ab + b². It can be shown that
// Sign(a² − 3ab + b²) = Sign(a⁴ − 7a²b² + b⁴) = Sign((a² − b²)² − 5a²b²).
Rational signSecDer = a2mb2Sqr − five * a2tb2;
```

```
// Local variables shared by the two main blocks of code.
Rational aMin, aMax, bMin, bMax, tMinSqr, tMaxSqr, tMid, tMidSqr, f;
```

```
if (signSecDer > zero)
{
```

```
    // Choose an initial guess t_min < a − b. Use the FPU to estimate u = √u²
    // and v = √v² to 53 bits of precision with specified rounding. Multiply by
    // the appropriate exponents to obtain t_min = a_min − b_max < a − b.
    aMin = GetMinOfSqrt(uSqr, exponentA);
    bMax = GetMaxOfSqrt(vSqr, exponentB);
    tMin = aMin − bMax;
```

```
    // When a − b is nearly zero, it is possible the lower bound is negative. Clamp
    // t_min to zero to stay on the nonnegative t-axis where the f''-positive basin is.
    if (tMin < zero)
    {
        tMin = zero;
    }
```

```
    // Test whether t_min is in the positive f''(t) basin containing a − b. If it is
    // not, compute a t_min that is in the basis. The sign test is applied to
    // f''(t)/4 = 3t² − (a² + b²).
    tMinSqr = tMin * tMin;
    signSecDer = three * tMinSqr − a2pb2;
    if (signSecDer < zero)
    {
```

```
        // The initial guess satisfies f''(t_min) < 0. Compute an upper bound
        // t_max > a − b and bisect [t_min, t_max] until either the t-value is an
        // estimate of a − b within the specified precision or until f''(t) ≥ 0
        // and f(t) ≥ 0. In the latter case, continue on to Newton's method
        // which is then guaranteed to converge.
        aMax = GetMaxOfSqrt(uSqr, exponentA);
        bMin = GetMinOfSqrt(vSqr, exponentB);
        tMax = aMax − bMin;
        for (iterate = 1; iterate <= maxIterations; ++iterate)
        {
            if (tMax − tMin < mThreshold)
            {
                return iterate;
            }
            tMid = std::ldexp(tMin + tMax, −1);
            tMidSqr = tMid * tMid;
            signSecDer = three * tMidSqr − a2pb2;
            if (signSecDer >= zero)
            {
                f = tMidSqr * (tMidSqr − twoa2pb2) + a2mb2Sqr;
                if (f >= zero)
                {
                    tMin = tMid;
                    tMinSqr = tMidSqr;
                    break;
                }
                else
                {
                    // Round up to twice the precision to avoid quadratic
                    // growth in the number of bits.
                    tMax = tMid;
```

```
                    Convert(tMax, 2*p, FE_UPWARD, tMax);
                }
            }
            else
            {
                // Round down to twice the precision to avoid quadratic
                // growth in the number of bits.
                tMin = tMid;
                Convert(tMin, 2*p, FE_DOWNWARD, tMin);
            }
        }
    }

    // Compute an upper bound tmax > a − b.
    tMax = (a2pb2 * tMinSqr − a2mb2Sqr) / (tMin * (tMinSqr − a2pb2));

    // Compute Newton iterates until convergence. The estimate closest to a − b is
    // tmax with tmin < a − b < tmax and tmax − (a − b) < (a − b) − tmin.
    for (iterate = 1; iterate <= maxIterations; ++iterate)
    {
        if (tMax − tMin < mThreshold)
        {
            break;
        }
        // Compute the weighted average tmin = (3tmin + tmax)/4. Round down
        // to twice the precision to avoid quadratic growth in the number of bits
        // and to ensure that tmax can decrease.
        tMin = std::ldexp(three * tMin + tMax, −2);
        Convert(tMin, 2*p, FE_DOWNWARD, tMin);
        tMinSqr = tMin * tMin;
        tMax = (a2pb2*tMinSqr−a2mb2Sqr)/(tMin*(tMinSqr−a2pb2));
    }
    return iterate;
}

if (signSecDer < zero)
{
    // Choose an initial guess tmax > a − b. Use the FPU to estimate u = √(u²)
    // and v = √(v²) to 53 bits of precision with specified rounding. Multiply by
    // the appropriate exponents to obtain tmax = amax − bmin > a − b.
    aMax = GetMaxOfSqrt(uSqr, exponentA);
    bMin = GetMinOfSqrt(vSqr, exponentB);
    tMax = aMax − bMin;

    // Test whether tmax is in the negative f″(t) basin containing a − b. If it is
    // not, compute a tmax that is in the basis. The sign test is applied to
    // f″(t)/4 = 3t² − (a² + b²).
    tMaxSqr = tMax * tMax;
    signSecDer = three * tMaxSqr − a2pb2;
    if (signSecDer > zero)
    {
        // The initial guess satisfies f″(tmax) < 0. Compute a lower bound
        // tmin < a − b and bisect [tmin, tmax] until either the t-value is an
        // estimate of a − b within the specified precision or until f″(t) ≤ 0
        // and f(t) ≤ 0. In the latter case, continue on to Newton's method
        // which is then guaranteed to converge.
        aMin = GetMinOfSqrt(uSqr, exponentA);
        bMax = GetMaxOfSqrt(vSqr, exponentB);
        tMin = aMin − bMax;
        for (iterate = 1; iterate <= maxIterations; ++iterate)
        {
            if (tMax − tMin < mThreshold)
            {
```

```
        return iterate;
    }
    tMid = std::ldexp(tMin + tMax, -1);
    tMidSqr = tMid * tMid;
    signSecDer = three * tMidSqr - a2pb2;
    if (signSecDer <= zero)
    {
        f = tMidSqr * (tMidSqr - twoa2pb2) + a2mb2Sqr;
        if (f <= zero)
        {
            tMax = tMid;
            tMaxSqr = tMidSqr;
            break;
        }
        else
        {
            // Round down to twice the precision to avoid quadratic
            // growth in the number of bits.
            tMin = tMid;
            Convert(tMin, 2*p, FE_DOWNWARD, tMin);
        }
    }
    else
    {
        // Round up to twice the precision to avoid quadratic
        // growth in the number of bits.
        tMax = tMid;
        Convert(tMax, 2*p, FE_UPWARD, tMax);
    }
    }
}

// Compute a lower bound t_min < a - b.
tMin = (a2pb2 * tMaxSqr - a2mb2Sqr) / (tMax * (tMaxSqr - a2pb2));

// Compute Newton iterates until convergence. The estimate closest to a - b is
// t_min with t_min < a - b < t_max and (a - b) - t_min < t_max - (a - b).
for (iterate = 1; iterate <= maxIterations; ++iterate)
{
    if (tMax - tMin < mThreshold) { break; }
    // Compute the weighted average t_max = (3t_max + t_min)/4. Round up
    // to twice the precision to avoid quadratic growth in the number of bits
    // and to ensure that t_min can decrease.
    tMax = std::ldexp(three * tMax + tMin, -2);
    Convert(tMax, 2*p, FE_UPWARD, tMax);
    tMaxSqr = tMax * tMax;
    tMin = (a2pb2*tMaxSqr-a2mb2Sqr)/(tMax*(tMaxSqr-a2pb2));
}
return iterate;
}

// The sign of the second derivative is Sign(a^4 - 7a^2b^2 + b^4) and cannot be zero.
// Define rational r = a^2/b^2 so that a^4 - 7 * a^2 * b^2 + b^4 = 0. This implies
// r^2 - 7 * r^2 + 1 = 0. The irrational roots are r = (7 ± √45)/2, which is a
// contradiction.
return 0;
}
```

Listing 5.9: Pseudocode for estimating $\tau_2 = a - b$, where $a = p_0\sqrt{e_0}$ and $b = p_1\sqrt{e_1}$ where $a > b$, $p_0 > 0$, $e_0 > 0$, $p_1 > 0$ and $e_1 > 0$. Necessarily a^2 and b^2 are rational numbers. The input p is the user-specified bits of precision for the estimate.

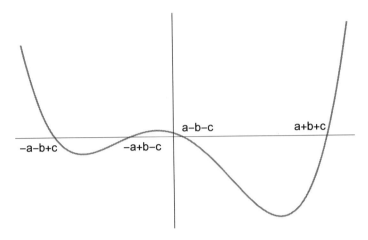

FIGURE 5.6: The graph of $f(t)$ for $a > b > c > 0$.

5.5.4.2   Three Nonzero Radical Coefficients

The ideas are similar to that of two nonzero radical coefficients. The only case of this type is $q = x + \sigma_a a + \sigma_b b + \sigma_c c$, where $a > b > c > 0$. The graph of a typical $f(t)$ is shown in Figure 5.6. The function $f(t)$ is not even as was the case with two nonzero radical coefficients.

The Newton iterates are provided by equation (5.34) where

$$g(t) = \frac{(a^2+b^2+c^2)t^2+6abct-(a^4+b^4+c^4-2(a^2b^2+a^2c^2+b^2c^2))}{t^3-(a^2+b^2+c^2)t-2abc} \qquad (5.39)$$

It can be shown that $g(\tau_i) = \tau_i$ for any root τ_i. The derivative of $g(t)$ is

$$g'(t) = \frac{n(t)}{d(t)} = \frac{n_4 t^4 + n_3 t^3 + n_2 t^2 + n_1 t + n_0}{(t^3 - (a^2 + b^2 + c^2)t - 2abc)^2} \qquad (5.40)$$

where

$$
\begin{aligned}
n_0 &= a^2 b^2(a^2 + b^2) + a^2 c^2(a^2 + c^2) + b^2 c^2(b^2 + c^2) \\
&\quad - (a^6 + b^6 + c^6) - 6a^2 b^2 c^2 \\
n_1 &= -4abc(a^2 + b^2 + c^2) \\
n_2 &= 2(a^4 + b^4 + c^4 - 4(a^2 b^2 + a^2 c^2 + b^2 c^2)) \\
n_3 &= -12abc \\
n_4 &= -(a^2 + b^2 + c^2)
\end{aligned}
\qquad (5.41)
$$

The denominator of $g'(t)$ is $d(t) \geq 0$. The goal is to prove that $n(t) \leq 0$, which implies $g'(t) \leq 0$. Consequently, if $\tau < 0$ is a root of $f(t)$, an estimate $t_k > \tau$ ensures $g(t_k) < \tau$ and $\tau \in [g(t_k), t_k]$. An estimate $t_k < \tau$ ensures $g(t_k) > \tau$ and $\tau \in [t_k, g(t_k)]$. The analysis of the sign of $g'(t)$ is more complicated than the case when $c = 0$, but it is general and applies to n-root quadratic field numbers. The symbolic manipulation was performed with Mathematica [44] but with several steps of human intervention.

Define $u = b/a \in (0,1)$, $v = c/a \in (0,u)$, $w = t/a \in \mathbb{R}$ and $h(u,v,w) = n(t)/a^6$; then

$$
\begin{aligned}
h(u,v,w) = \quad & -1 + u^2 + u^4 - u^6 + u^2v^2 - 6u^4v^2 + u^6v^2 \\
& + u^4v^4 + u^6v^4 - u^6v^6 - 4u^2vw - 4u^4vw - 4u^4v^3w \\
& + 2w^2 - 8u^2w^2 + 2u^4w^2 - 8u^2v^2w^2 - 8u^4v^2w^2 \\
& + 2u^4v^4w^2 - 12u^2vw^3 - w^4 - u^2w^4 - u^2v^2w^4
\end{aligned}
\tag{5.42}
$$

The domain is $\mathcal{D} = \{(u,v,w) : 0 < v < u < 1,\ w \in \mathbb{R}\}$, but it is convenient to extend that domain to $\overline{\mathcal{D}} = \{(u,v,w) : 0 \le v \le u \le 1,\ w \in \mathbb{R}\}$ for determining the maximum value of $h(u,v,w)$. The sign of $g'(t)$ is the sign of $h(u,v,w)$. The boundary $v = 0$ corresponds to $c = 0$, the boundary $u = 1$ corresponds to $a = b$ and the boundary $u = v$ corresponds to $b = c$. All these cases correspond to one or two square root terms and were analyzed previously, and a consequence is that $h(u,0) \le 0$, $h(1,v) \le 0$ and $h(u,u) \le 0$.

It remains to be shown that $h(\mathcal{D}) \le 0$. If the maximum of h occurs in $\mathcal{D}$, then it occurs when $\nabla h = (h_u, h_v, h_w) = (0,0,0)$. Each of these derivatives has a constant factor that is convenient to discard: $p_0 = -h_u/2$, $p_1 = -h_v/2$ and $p_2 = h_w/4$, leading to

$$
\begin{aligned}
p_0 = \quad & -u - 2u^3 + 3u^5 + 6uv^2 - 2u^3v^2 - uv^4 + 2vw + 6u^2vw \\
& + 2v^3w + 8uw^2 - 4u^3w^2 + 8uv^2w^2 + 6vw^3 + uw^4 \\
p_1 = \quad & -v + 6u^2v - u^4v - 2v^3 - 2u^2v^3 + 3v^5 + 2uw + 2u^3w \\
& + 6uv^2w + 8vw^2 + 8u^2vw^2 - 4v^3w^2 + 6uw^3 + vw^4 \\
p_2 = \quad & -uv - u^3v - uv^3 + w - 4u^2w + u^4w - 4v^2w - 4u^2v^2w \\
& + v^4w - 9uvw^2 - w^3 - u^2w^3 - v^2w^3
\end{aligned}
\tag{5.43}
$$

The variable w is eliminated from the equations $p_0 = 0$ and $p_2 = 0$ and from the equations $p_1 = 0$ and $p_2 = 0$ using resultants to obtain

$$
\begin{aligned}
r_0(u,v) &= \text{Resultant}(p_0, p_2, w) \\
&= K_0(1-u^2)(u^2-v^2)(1-v^2)^2 s_0(u,v) \\
r_1(u,v) &= \text{Resultant}(p_1, p_2, w) \\
&= K_1(1-u^2)^2(u^2-v^2)(1-v^2) s_1(u,v)
\end{aligned}
\tag{5.44}
$$

where the polynomials $s_0(u,v)$ and $s_1(u,v)$ have degree 15. The numbers K_0 and K_1 are constants. The polynomials $1-u^2$, $1-v^2$ and u^2-v^2 are not zero in $\mathcal{D}$. They can be cancelled from the resultants, after which only s_0 and s_1 need to be processed further.

The variable v is eliminated from the equations $s_0 = 0$ and $s_1 = 0$ using resultants to obtain

$$
\begin{aligned}
r_2(u) &= \text{Resultant}(s_0, s_1, v) \\
&= K_2 u^{15}(1-u^2)^{50}(1+3u^2)(-5-108u^2+81u^4)^2 \\
&\quad \times (-1+16u^2+9u^4)^2(2-10u^2+u^4+4u^6)^2 \\
&\quad \times (s_2(u))^2
\end{aligned}
\tag{5.45}
$$

where the polynomial $s_2(u)$ has degree 40 and K_2 is a constant. The polynomials u and $1 - u^2$ are not zero on the boundary of the domain, and the polynomials $1 + 3u^2$ and $-5 - 108u^2 + 81u^4$ have no real-valued roots on $[0, 1]$. They can be cancelled from the resultant. The roots on $(0, 1)$ are provided by the remaining polynomials. The polynomial $-1 + 16u^2 + 9u^4$ has root $\bar{u}_0 = \sqrt{-8 + \sqrt{73}}/3 \doteq 0.245855$. The polynomial $2 - 10u^2 + u^4 + 4u^6$ has root $\bar{u}_1 \doteq 0.455981$. The polynomial $s_2(u)$ had root $\bar{u}_2 \doteq 0.280501$. The variable u can be eliminated instead from the equations $s_0 = 0$ and $s_1 = 0$ using resultants, but the final polynomial is $s_2(v)$. This is an implication of the symmetry $h(u, v) = h(v, u)$. The v-roots are the same as the u-roots.

The variable v is eliminated from the equations $p_0 = 0$ and $p_2 = 0$ and from the equations $p_1 = 0$ and $p_2 = 0$ using resultants to obtain

$$
\begin{aligned}
r_3(u, w) &= \text{Resultant}(p_0, p_2, v) \\
&= K_3(1 - u^2)(u^2 - w^2)(1 - w^2)^2 s_3(u, w) \\
r_4(u, w) &= \text{Resultant}(p_1, p_2, w) \\
&= K_4(1 - u^2)^2(u^2 - w^2)(1 - w^2) s_4(u, w)
\end{aligned}
\tag{5.46}
$$

where the polynomial $s_3(u, w)$ has degree 16 and the polynomial $s_4(u, w)$ has degree 17. The numbers K_3 and K_4 are constants. The polynomial $1 - u^2$ is not zero in $\mathcal{D}$. It can be cancelled from the resultants. The polynomial $1 - w^2$ generates w-roots of ± 1. The polynomial $u^2 - w^2$ generates the constraint $u = |w|$. Both resultants have the same simple factors which can be cancelled, after which only s_3 and s_4 need to be processed further.

The variable u is eliminated from the equations $s_3 = 0$ and $s_4 = 0$ using resultants to obtain

$$
\begin{aligned}
r_5(w) &= \text{Resultant}(s_3, s_4, u) \\
&= K_5 w^{22}(1 - w^2)^{50}(5 + 9w^2)(3 + 121w^2)^2 \\
&\quad \times (-3 - 16w^2 + 3w^4)^2(-3 + 16w^2 + 3w^4)^2 \\
&\quad \times (s_5(w))^2
\end{aligned}
\tag{5.47}
$$

where the polynomial $s_5(v)$ has degree 60 and K_5 is a constant. The polynomials $5 + 9w^2$ and $3 + 121w^2$ have no real-valued roots and can be discarded. The polynomial w^2 generates a w-root of 0. The polynomial $1 - w^2$ generates w-roots of ± 1. The polynomial $-3 - 16w^2 + 3w^4$ generates w-roots $(8 \pm \sqrt{73})/3$. The polynomial $-3 + 16w^2 + 3w^4$ generates w-roots $(-8 \pm \sqrt{73})/3$. The polynomial $s_5(w)$ generates w-roots with estimates ± 0.156897, ± 1.294631, ± 4.901538 and ± 23.801729.

If the order of elimination instead were $r_6(v, w) = \text{Resultant}(p_0, p_2, u)$ and $r_7(v, w) = \text{Resultant}(p_1, p_2, w)$, then a common factor is $v^2 - w^2$ for which $v = |w|$ will be included as another constraint. This is also a consequence of the symmetry $h(u, v) = h(v, u)$.

The w-roots 0 and ± 1 and the constraints $u^2 = w^2$ and $v^2 = w^2$ are processed first. The remaining roots are processed last.

Let $w = 0$; then $h_w(u, v, 0) = -uv(1 + u^2 + v^2)$ which is negative in $\mathcal{D}$. This prevents $\nabla h = (0, 0, 0)$ in $\mathcal{D}$.

Let $w = 1$. The polynomials $p_0(u, v, -1)$ and $p_2(u, v, -1)$ have factors $(u-v)$ and $(u-v)^2$, respectively, which are not zero in $\mathcal{D}$ and can be discarded in the sign analysis. Observe that $\text{Resultant}(p_0/(u - v)), p_2/((u - v)^2), v) = (1 - u^2)^2(-324 + 143u^2 + 31u^4)$. The polynomial $-324 + 143u^2 + 31u^4 < 0$ and the polynomial $(1 - u^2)^2 > 0$ in $\mathcal{D}$, which means p_0 and p_2 cannot be zero simultaneously in $\mathcal{D}$. This prevents $\nabla h = (0, 0, 0)$ in $\mathcal{D}$. A similar argument applies when $w = -1$, where p_0 and p_2 have factors $(u - v)$ and $(u - v)^2$, respectively, leading to $\text{Resultant}(p_0/((u - v)), p_2/((u - v)^2)) = (1 - u^2)^2(-324 + 143u^2 + 31u^4) > 0$ in $\mathcal{D}$.

Let $w = u$. The polynomials $p_0(u, v, u)$ and $p_2(u, v, u)$ have common factors $u(1 + v)^2$, which are not zero in $\mathcal{D}$ and can be discarded in the sign analysis. Observe that $\text{Resultant}(p_0/(u(1 + v)^2), p_2/(u(1 + v)^2), v) = (1 - u^2)^2$, which is positive in $\mathcal{D}$, which means p_0 and p_2 cannot be zero simultaneously in $\mathcal{D}$. This prevents $\nabla h = (0, 0, 0)$ in $\mathcal{D}$. A similar argument applies when $w = -u$, where p_0 and p_2 have common factor $u(1-v)^2$ leading to $\text{Resultant}(p_0/(u(1 - v)^2), p_2/(u(1 - v)^2)) = (1 - u^2)^2 > 0$ in $\mathcal{D}$. The same ideas apply to $w = v$ and $w = -v$ with the conclusion that ∇h cannot be $(0, 0, 0)$ in $\mathcal{D}$.

The remaining roots are now handled individually. The goal is to identify the candidate points where ∇h might be $(0, 0, 0)$. For each candidate, a small cuboid is chosen with center at the point and arbitrary-precision interval arithmetic is used to prove that at least one of h_u, h_v or h_w is not zero in that cuboid. If this happens, ∇h cannot be $(0, 0, 0)$ at the candidate.

Define $\alpha(u) = -1 + 16u^2 + 9u^4$ and $\beta(u) = 2 - 10u^2 + u^4 + 4u^6$. The u-roots and v-roots are $\{\bar{u}_0, \bar{u}_1, \bar{u}_2\}$, listed in increasing order, where $\alpha(\bar{u}_0) = 0$, $s_2(\bar{u}_1) = 0$ and $\beta(\bar{u}_2) = 0$. The estimates for the roots, in order, are 0.245855, 0.280501 and 0.455981. Define $\gamma(w) = -3 - 16w + 3w^2$ and $\delta(w) = -3 + 16w + 3w^2$. The w-roots are $\bar{w}_i$ for $0 \le i \le 11$, sorted in increasing order. This set is the union of the roots of $\gamma(w)$, $\delta(w)$ and $s_5(w) = 0$. The estimates of the γ-roots are -0.181335 and 5.514668, the estimates of the δ-roots are -5.514668 and 0.181335, and the esimates of the s_5-roots are ± 0.156897, ± 1.294631, ± 4.901538 and ± 23.801729.

The candidate points for $\nabla h = (0, 0, 0)$ in $\mathcal{D}$ require $u > v$, so the candidates (u, v, w) are $\{(\bar{u}_1, \bar{u}_0, \bar{w}_i)\}_{i=0}^{11}$, $\{(\bar{u}_2, \bar{u}_0, \bar{w}_i)\}_{i=0}^{11}$ and $\{(\bar{u}_2, \bar{u}_1, \bar{w}_i)\}_{i=0}^{11}$. Listing 5.10 shows the GTL code for the interval arithmetic that verifies at least one partial derivative in each cuboid is never zero, proving that $\nabla h \ne (0, 0, 0)$ in $\mathcal{D}$. The bounding intervals for the u-roots have endpoints that are consecutive double-precision numbers. The bounding intervals for the w-roots were chosen manually. A verification was made in other code to prove that the polynomial of each root has opposite signs at the endpoints.

```
using BSN = BSNumber<UIntegerAP32>;     // computations do not involve division
using BSNInterval = APInterval<BSR>;   // arbitrary-precision interval arithmetic

std :: array<double, 2> u0bound =
{
    0.24585536518619394, 0.24585536518619397
};
```

```
std :: array<double, 2> u1bound =
{
    0.28050110590393129, 0.28050110590393135
};

std :: array<double, 2> u2bound =
{
    0.45598062412214041, 0.45598062412214047
};

std :: array<std :: array<double, 2>, 12> wbound =
{{
    { -23.81, -23.80 },
    { -5.515, -5.514 },
    { -4.91, -4.90 },
    { -1.295, -1.294 },
    { -0.1814, -0.1813 },
    { -0.16, -0.15 },
    { 0.15, 0.16 },
    { 0.1813, 0.1814 },
    { 1.294, 1.295 },
    { 4.90, 4.91 },
    { 5.514, 5.515 },
    { 23.80, 23.81 }
}};

BSNInterval iu, iv, iw;
BSNInterval dhdu, dhdv, dhdw;

iu = BSNInterval(u1bound[0], u1bound[1]);
iv = BSNInterval(u0bound[0], u0bound[1]);
for (size_t i = 0; i < 12; ++i)
{
    iw = BSNInterval(wbound[i][0], wbound[i][1]);
    dhdu = DhDu(iu, iv, iw);   // + + + + − − − − + + + +
    dhdv = DhDv(iu, iv, iw);   // − − − − − − + + + + + +
    dhdw = DhDw(iu, iv, iw);   // + + + + − − + + − − − −
}

iu = BSNInterval(u2bound[0], u2bound[1]);
iv = BSNInterval(u0bound[0], u0bound[1]);
for (size_t i = 0; i < 12; ++i)
{
    iw = BSNInterval(wbound[i][0], wbound[i][1]);
    dhdu = DhDu(iu, iv, iw);   // + + + + − − − − + + + +
    dhdv = DhDv(iu, iv, iw);   // − − − − − − + + + + + +
    dhdw = DhDw(iu, iv, iw);   // + + + + − − − − − − − −
}

iu = BSNInterval(u2bound[0], u2bound[1]);
iv = BSNInterval(u1bound[0], u1bound[1]);
for (size_t i = 0; i < 12; ++i)
{
    iw = BSNInterval(wbound[i][0], wbound[i][1]);
    dhdu = DhDu(iu, iv, iw);   // + + + + − − − − + + + +
    dhdv = DhDv(iu, iv, iw);   // + − − − − − + + + + + +
    dhdw = DhDw(iu, iv, iw);   // + + + + − − − − − − − −
}
```

Listing 5.10: Code to verify that $\nabla h \neq (0,0,0)$ on $\mathcal{D}$.

The functions DhDu, DhDv and DhDw are implementations of $h_u(u,v,w)$, $h_v(u,v,w)$ and $h_w(u,v,w)$. The comments after the dhdu, dhdv and dhdw expressions indicate the signs of the partial derivatives on the cuboid. Each comment has 12 signs, one for each selection of the w-root. In fact, none of the partial derivatives can ever be zero on any of the cuboids, but all that is needed is that at least one of the partial derivatives on a cuboid is never zero.

Chapter 6

Numerical Methods

The use of arbitrary-precision arithmetic, interval arithmetic or quadratic-field arithmetic is not a silver bullet for all computing. Many problems involve iterative algorithms and/or a large number of computations that do not produce exact results, require an inordinate number of bits and have performance problems—especially when products of large integers are involved. In the latter case, the straightforward multiplication algorithm for two n-bit integers is $O(n^2)$. The arbitrary-precision arithmetic library must be able to switch from such an algorithm to one, say, that uses fast Fourier transforms for asymptotic order $O(n \log n)$ [16, Chapter 4.3].

Various numerical methods fall into this category, most notably root finding and solving linear systems with large matrices. Certainly floating-point arithmetic can be used for such problems, but the precision is fixed: 24 bits for float and 53 bits for double. An arbitrary-precision library can be designed to allow rounding of computations to p-bits of precision, with rounding modes similar to those of floating-point arithmetic. The GTL implementation of arbitrary-precision arithmetic supports this; see Section 3.4. It is possible to solve numerical methods to a larger precision than what is supported by float or double, but the trade-off is that floating-point arithmetic executes in hardware (on the FPU) and typical arbitrary-precision arithmetic executes in software (on the CPU), so greater precision is obtained at the cost of computation time.

6.1 Root Finding

Given a function $F(t)$ defined on an interval $I \subseteq \mathbb{R}$, the goal is to compute roots $\bar{t} \in I$ for which $F(\bar{t}) = 0$. Floating-point arithmetic and its inherent rounding errors can cause a variety of problems in root finding. One topic of concern that is usually not thought of first is the evaluation of $F(t)$. In many applications the function is implemented based on formulas obtained by a mathematical derivation that is based on real-number arithmetic. It is not always the case that these formulas should be implemented as is. Section 6.1.1 presents a common example in constructiong rotation matrices for small rotation angles.

Two basic root-finding methods are discussed here, bisection and Newton's method. The classical implementations are provided for floating-point arithmetic, but some variations are mentioned that lead to robust root finding. Implementations using arbitrary-precision arithmetic are also included to illustrate the options available when greater precision is allowed.

6.1.1 Function Evaluation

Mathematical derivations are typically used for producing functions in an application, and these derivations are based on real-number arithmetic. The computed results can be unexpected and sometimes catastrophically different from the theoretical resuls. A detailed example is described here regarding construction of 3×3 rotation matrices. A rotation matrix R is parameterized by

$$
\begin{aligned}
R \;=\;& I + F(t)S + G(t)S^2 \\[2mm]
=\;& \begin{bmatrix} 1 & 0 & 0 \\ 0 & 1 & 0 \\ 0 & 0 & 1 \end{bmatrix} + (\sin t)/t \begin{bmatrix} 0 & -c & b \\ c & 0 & -a \\ -b & a & 0 \end{bmatrix} \\[2mm]
& + (1 - \cos t)/t^2 \begin{bmatrix} -(b^2 + c^2) & ab & ac \\ ab & -(a^2 + c^2) & bc \\ ac & bc & -(a^2 + b^2) \end{bmatrix}
\end{aligned} \tag{6.1}
$$

where I is the identity matrix and S is a skew-symmetric matrix. The variable is $t = \sqrt{a^2 + b^2 + c^2}$, $F(t) = (\sin t)/t$ and $G(t) = (1 - \cos t)/t^2$. When $t > 0$, the axis of rotation is the unit-length vector $(a, b, c)/t$. When $t = 0$, $R = I$ in which case there is no axis of rotation. The functions $F(t)$ and $G(t)$ are well defined for $t > 0$. They also have removable singularities at $t = 0$ because $F(0) = \lim_{t \to 0} F(t) = 1$ and $G(0) = \lim_{t \to 0} G(t) = 1/2$. Both functions are continuous for $t \in [0, +\infty)$.

The Taylor series for the function $G(t)$ expanded about $t = 0$ is

$$
G(t) = \sum_{k=0}^{\infty} (-1)^k \frac{t^{2k}}{(2k + 2)!} \tag{6.2}
$$

The graph of $G(t)$ is shown in Figure 6.1. The maximum of $G(t)$ is $1/2$ and the minimum of $G(t)$ is 0 and occurs at $t = 2\pi n$ for $n \geq 1$. The straightforward implementation of $G(t)$ for floating-point type float is shown in Listing 6.1.

```
float G(float t)
{
    return (1.0f - std::cos(t)) / (t * t);
}
```

Listing 6.1: A naive floating-point implementation for $(1 - \cos(t))/t^2$.

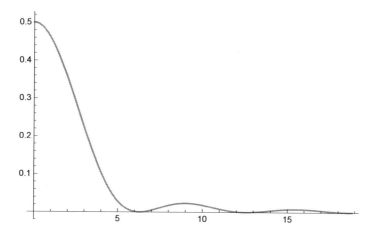

FIGURE 6.1: The graph of $G(t) = (1 - \cos t)/t^2$ for $t \in [0, 6\pi]$. The plot was drawn using Mathematica [44].

The function can be evaluated for all finite and positive float numbers. The experiment was performed using Microsoft Visual Studio 2019 version 16.3.5 in Debug x64 configuration.

For $t \in [0, 2.64697796 * 10^{-23}]$ (encoding [0x00000000, 0x1a000000]), $G(t)$ is not-a-number which is reported by the debugger as -nan(ind). The std::cos function evaluates to 1, and t^2 is smaller than the smallest positive subnormal and is rounded to 0. This leads to an indeterminate of the form 0/0, which is flagged as a NaN.

For $t \in [2.64697828 * 10^{-23}, 2.44140625 * 10^{-4}]$ (encoding [0x1a00000, 0x39800000]), $G(t)$ evaluates to 0 because std::cos evaluates to 1 and t^2 evaluates to a positive number, leading to a number of the form 0/p for $p > 0$.

For $t \in [2.44140654 * 10^{-4}, 4.88281250 * 10^{-4}]$ (encoding [0x39800001, 0x3a000000]), $G(t)$ evaluates to numbers in $[1/3, 1]$, which is certainly not what is expected, because $G(t)$ has a maximum of $1/2$. As t increases, $G(t)$ decreases from 1 to $1/3$. A discontinuity appears where $G(t)$ jumps to $2/3$, after which as t increases, $G(t)$ decreases from $2/3$ to $1/2$. Figure 6.2 shows a graph of $G(t)$ for $t \in [2.44140625 * 10^{-4}, 4.88281250 * 10^{-4}]$ (encoding [0x1a00000, 0x3a000000]). Figure 6.2 shows the discontinuity where $G(t)$ jumps from 0 to 1 and the discontinuity where $G(t)$ jumps from $1/3$ to $2/3$. Regardless, the values of $G(t)$ for $t \in [0, 4.88281250 * 10^{-4}]$ are not accurate except on the specified interval.

Mathematica [44] has its own problems with rounding errors near 0. Figure 6.3 shows the graph of $G(t)$ for small t. The graph is densely drawn because the rounding errors vary with a very small interval centered at $1/2$.

For a function as simple as $G(t)$, the floating-point evaluations are unexpected for t near 0. A reasonable approach to avoiding these problems

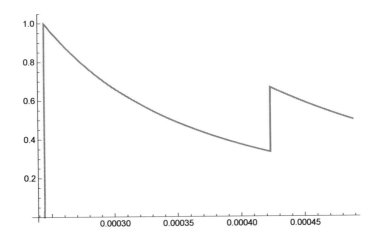

FIGURE 6.2: The graph of the function G(t) of Listing 6.1 for small t-values.

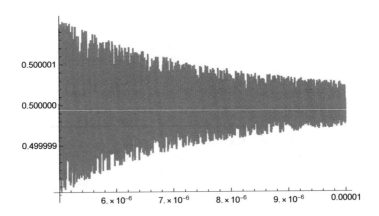

FIGURE 6.3: The Mathematica graph of $G(t) = (1 - \cos t)/t^2$ for small t-values.

is to use an approximation to $G(t)$, whether a Taylor polynomial about $t = 0$ or a minimax polynomial. Both approximations were evaluated for $t \in [0, 4.88281250 * 10^{-4}]$ using type float. The values were 0.5 for this entire interval. That suggests implementing $G(t)$ as shown in Listing 6.2.

```
float G(float t)
{
    if (std::fabs(t) > 4.88281250e-04f)
    {
        return (1.0f - std::cos(t)) / (t * t);
    }
    else
    {
        return 0.5f;
    }
}
```

Listing 6.2: A robust floating-point implementation for $(1 - \cos(t))/t^2$ that is better to use than that of Listing 6.1.

6.1.2 Bisection

Consider a real-valued continuous function $F(t)$ defined on the interval $[t_0, t_1]$ with $F(t_0)F(t_1) < 0$. The function has at least one root on the interval. An estimate of *some* root on the interval is obtained using bisection. The idea is to subdivide the interval to one-half the length and that bounds the root. The subdivision continues until convergence criteria are met. The statement is made that bisection estimates some root. The function might have multiple roots on the interval, but bisection will only locate one of them. In practice, analyses are performed in an attempt to find root-bounding intervals for the function, each interval containing exactly one root. In this case, bisection has no choice but to locate the unique root.

The initial interval length is $L_0 = (t_1 - t_0)$. Compute the midpoint $t_m = (t_0 + t_1)/2$ and evaluate $F(t_m)$. If $F(t_m) = 0$, the midpoint is the root and the algorithm terminates. If $F(t_0)F(t_m) < 0$, then $[t_0, t_m]$ is a root-bounding interval of length $L_1 = L_0/2$; t_1 is assigned t_m and the algorithm is repeated. If $F(t_0)F(t_1) < 0$, then $[t_m, t_1]$ is a root-bounding interval of length $L_1 = L_0/2$; t_0 is assigned t_m and the algorithm is repeated. The termination criterion can be that a user-defined maximum number of iterations n is reached, and the length of the final interval $[\bar{t}_0, \bar{t}_1]$ is $L_n = L_0/2^n$. Either endpoint can be chosen as the estimate of the theoretical root. The maximum absolute error is L_n. Another termination criterion is to iterate until $L_0/2^n < \varepsilon$, where $\varepsilon > 0$ is a small user-specified tolerance. This is equivalent to the previous criterion in the sense that $n = \lceil \log(L_0/\varepsilon)/\log(2) \rceil$.

The algorithm effectively depends on the signs of $F(t_0)$, $F(t_1)$ and $F(t_m)$, including the decision that the initial interval $[t_0, t_1]$ bounds a root. When implementing the algorithm using floating-point arithmetic, rounding errors can lead to misclassifications of signs. An implementation might use a small tolerance parameter $\tau > 0$ for which $F(t)$ is deemed to be zero when $|F(t)| \leq$

τ. Generally, such a parameter depends on the function at hand. Switching to arbitrary-precision arithmetic might not help, because $F(t)$ could very well be defined in terms of elementary functions that cannot be evaluated exactly even for rational inputs; for example, the trigonometric functions fall into this category.

In the implementations provided in this section, the rounding errors when computing $F(t)$ are not taken into consideration. It is assumed that the programmer has chosen an implementation that is suitable for the root-finding problem at hand. In particular, it is desirable for the function to return a value that has the correct sign for each input. A function implementation might very well use interval arithmetic to accomplish this goal.

Also when using floating-point arithmetic, the selection of a maximum number of iterations or a tolerance ε is not necessary. One can take advantage of the set of floating-point numbers being finite. Each bisection step amounts to reducing the interval size by half. Eventually, the interval length is sufficiently small so that the final interval $[\bar{t}_0, \bar{t}_1]$ consists of consecutive floating-point numbers. The termination criterion becomes a test of whether the midpoint of the current interval is equal to an interval endpoint because of rounding errors.

The bisection algorithm is shown in Listing 6.3.

```cpp
// It is assumed that t0 < t1. The returned unsigned integer is the number of iterations used
// in bisection. If it is the maximum unsigned integer, it is unknown whether the interval
// contains a root.
template <typename Real>
uint32_t Bisect(std::function<Real(Real)> const& F, Real t0, Real t1,
    Real& tRoot, Real& fRoot)
{
    // Preamble to the bisection steps.
    Real zero(0);
    Real f0 = F(t0);
    if (f0 == zero) { tRoot = t0; fRoot = f0; return 0; }
    Real f1 = F(t1);
    if (f1 == zero) { tRoot = t1; fRoot = f1; return 0; }
    int sign0 = (f0 > zero ? +1 : -1);
    int sign1 = (f1 > zero ? +1 : -1);
    if (sign0 == sign1)
    {
        // It is unknown whether the interval contains a root.
        tRoot = zero; fRoot = zero;
        return std::numeric_limits<uint32_t>::max();
    }

    // The bisection steps.
    uint32_t iteration;
    for (iteration = 1; /**/; ++iteration)
    {
        tRoot = (Real)0.5 * (t0 + t1);
        fRoot = F(tRoot);
        if (fRoot == zero || tRoot == t0 || tRoot == t1)
        {
            break;
        }

        // Update the correct endpoint to the midpoint.
        int signRoot = (fRoot > zero ? +1 : -1);
        if (signRoot == sign0)
```

```
        {
            t0 = tRoot;
        }
        else   // signRoot === sign1
        {
            t1 = tRoot;
        }
    }
    return iteration;
}
```

Listing 6.3: Bisection of a function on an interval. The algorithm is implemented using Real, which is float or double, and is guaranteed to terminate. Eventually the bisected interval has endpoints that are consecutive floating-point numbers, so the average of these numbers is rounded to one or the other endpoint.

The algorithm does not use division, so the arbitrary-precision type BSNumber may be used as well for type Real. However, there is no longer a guarantee that the loop terminates because no rounding occurs in the averaging of t0 and t1. The code must be modified as shown in Listing 6.4.

```
template <typename Rational>
uint32_t Bisect(std::function<Rational(Rational)> const& F, Rational t0,
    Rational t1, uint32_t maxIterations, Rational& tRoot, Rational& fRoot)
{
    // The preamble is the same as in Listing 6.3 but using Rational instead of Real.
    // :

    // The bisection steps.
    Rational half(0.5);
    uint32_t iteration;
    for (iteration = 0; iteration < maxIterations; ++iteration)
    {
        tRoot = std::ldexp(t0+t1, -1);   // = (t0+t1)/2
        fRoot = F(tRoot);
        if (fRoot == zero)
        {
            break;
        }

        // The endpoint update is the same as in Listing 6.3.
        // :
    }
    return iteration;
}
```

Listing 6.4: Bisection of a function on an interval. The algorithm is implemented using an arbitrary-precision type Rational.

The assumption is that type Rational is an arbitrary-precision type. It is possible to use such a type that also supports rounding to a user-specified number of bits of precision, as shown in Listing 6.5.

```
template <typename Rational>
uint32_t Bisect(std::function<Rational(Rational)> const& F, Rational t0,
    Rational t1, uint32_t maxIterations, uint32_t precision,
    Rational& tRoot, Rational& fRoot)
{
    Convert(t0, precision, FE_TONEAREST, t0);
    Convert(t1, precision, FE_TONEAREST, t1);
```

```
// The preamble is the same as in Listing 6.3 but using Rational instead of Real.
// :

// The bisection steps.
Rational half(0.5);
uint32_t iteration;
for (iteration = 0; iteration < maxIterations; ++iteration)
{
    Rational average = std::ldexp(t0+t1,-1);   // = (t0+t1)/2
    Convert(average, precision, FE_TONEAREST, tRoot);
    fRoot = F(tRoot);
    if (fRoot == zero)
    {
        break;
    }

    // The endpoint update is the same as in Listing 6.3.
    // :
}
return iteration;
}

// or

template <typename Rational>
uint32_t Bisect(std::function<Rational(Rational)> const& F, Rational t0,
    Rational t1, uint32_t precision, Rational& tRoot, Rational& fRoot)
{
    Convert(t0, precision, FE_TONEAREST, t0);
    Convert(t1, precision, FE_TONEAREST, t1);

    // The preamble is the same as in Listing 6.3 but using Rational instead of Real.
    // :

    // The bisection steps.
    Rational half(0.5);
    uint32_t iteration;
    for (iteration = 0; /**/; ++iteration)
    {
        Rational average = std::ldexp(t0+t1,-1);   // = (t0+t1)/2
        Convert(average, precision, FE_TONEAREST, tRoot);
        fRoot = F(tRoot);
        if (fRoot == zero || tRoot == t0 || tRoot == t1)
        {
            break;
        }

        // The endpoint update is the same as in Listing 6.3.
        // :
    }
    return iteration;
}
```

Listing 6.5: Bisection of a function on an interval. The algorithm is implemented using an arbitrary-precision type Rational but with rounding to a user-specified number of bits of precision.

In the code where the maximum number of iterations is not specified and the termination is based on the final interval consisting of two consecutive numbers of the specified precision p, the number of loop iterations will be large when p is large. An application should keep this in mind when implementing bisection.

Also, the midpoint computation is performed as an addition followed by an adjustment of the power of 2 for that number. The idea is to avoid the expense of a multiplication, assuming that the power update is of trivial cost. The increase in the number of bits of precision to compute the average is minor, an increment of 1 based on the analysis of addition of arbitrary-precision numbers. As a result, many bisection steps (using Listing 6.4) can be performed with minimal increase in memory usage but at the expense of a slower algorithm: bisection has linear convergence, but Newton's method has quadratic convergence.

6.1.3 Newton's Method

Consider a real-valued function $F(t)$ defined on an interval $[a, b]$ that is known to have at least one root of F. The function is assumed to have C^1-continuity: $F(t)$ and $F'(t)$ are continuous functions. Let t_0 be an initial estimate for the root. Newton's method consists of computing the iterates

$$t_{k+1} = t_k - \frac{F(t_k)}{F'(t_k)}, \ k \geq 0 \tag{6.3}$$

The geometric motivation was given in Section 5.5.2; see Figure 5.2. Generally, the iterate t_{k+1} is the intersection of the t-axis with the tangent line to the graph of F at $(t_k, F(t_k))$.

The naive implementation is shown in Listing 6.6 and assumes Real is a floating-point type.

```
template <typename Real>
uint32_t Newton(std::function<Real(Real)> const& F,
    std::function<Real(Real)> const& DF, Real tInitial,
    Real& tRoot, Real& fRoot)
{
    tRoot = tInitial;
    fRoot = F(tRoot);
    while (fRoot != (Real)0)
    {
        tRoot = tRoot - fRoot / DF(tRoot);
        fRoot = F(tRoot);
    }
}
```

Listing 6.6: The naive implementation of Newton's method for floating-point arithmetic.

The most glaring problem is the comparison of fRoot to zero. This is a floating-point comparison which is almost never robust. Generally, the probability that the evaluation of F will never be exactly zero, in which case the code has an infinite loop. It is necessary to limit the number of iterations, to provide a termination criterion that gives the caller some assurance that a root (estimate) has been found and to guard against a division by zero when $F'(t)$ is zero at the current root estimate.

An attempt at a more robust algorithm is shown in Listing 6.7.

```
// The number of iterations is the returned unsigned integer. If F'(t) is zero at a root
// estimate, the function returns the maximum unsigned integer. If the iterates fail to
// converge, the function returns maxIterations.
template <typename Real>
uint32_t Newton(std::function<Real(Real)> const& F,
        std::function<Real(Real)> const& DF, Real tInitial,
        uint32_t maxIterations, Real epsilon, Real& tRoot, Real& fRoot)
{
    tRoot = tInitial;
    uint32_t iteration;
    for (iteration = 0; iteration < maxIterations; ++iteration)
    {
        if (std::fabs(fRoot) <= epsilon)
        {
            return iteration;
        }
        Real dfdt = DF(tRoot);
        if (std::fabs(dfdt) == (Real)0)
        {
            return std::numeric_limits<uint32_t>::max();
        }
        tRoot = tRoot - fRoot / dfdt;
        fRoot = F(tRoot);
    }
    return maxIterations;
}
```

Listing 6.7: An attempt at a more robust implementation of Newton's method than that of Listing 6.6. A limit is placed on the number of iterations, a nonnegative tolerance ε is passed for a termination criterion $|F(\bar{t})| \leq \varepsilon$ for which $\bar{t}$ is deemed to be a root estimate and a guard against a division by zero is added.

Generally, Newton's method is effective when estimating a simple root $\bar{t}$. At such a root, $F(\bar{t}) = 0$ but $F'(\bar{t}) \neq 0$. The advice is to obtain as much information about $F(t)$ before blindly using Newton's method in hopes that the root is simple. Roots of odd multiplicity might have a chance of being found, but roots of even multiplicity are difficult to handle.

Listing 6.7 still is not robust enough. The caller has the responsibility to pass ε that is relevant to the function at hand. For example, one might choose $\varepsilon = 10^{-6}$ for type float only to find out that the function values at the iterates are no smaller than 10^{-5}. The loop will execute the maximum number of iterations and the caller will infer that the root was not found, even though the final estimate tRoot might very well be a good estimate. It is the caller's responsibility to choose ε based on an analysis of the function near a root. In practice, the typical behavior is that the root estimates form a cycle of floating-point numbers—the precision of Real is not large enough to force the root estimate to be such that F is sufficiently close to zero. One approach to detecting the cycle is shown in Listing 6.8.

```
// The number of iterations is the returned unsigned integer. If F'(t) is zero at a root
// estimate, the function returns the maximum unsigned integer. If the iterates fail to
// converge, the function returns maxIterations.
template <typename Real>
enum NewtonStatus
{
    CONVERGED,
```

```
        DERIVATIVE_IS_ZERO,
        CYCLE_DETECTED,
        FAILED_TO_CONVERGE
};

template <typename Real>
struct Point
{
    Point(Real inT, Real inF) : t(inT), f(inF) {}

    bool operator<(Point const& other) const { return t < other.t; }

    Real t, f;
};

std::pair<uint32_t, bool> Newton(std::function<Real(Real)> const& F,
    std::function<Real(Real)> const& DF, Real tInitial,
    uint32_t maxIterations, Real epsilon, Real& tRoot, Real& fRoot)
{
    NewtonStatus status = FAILED_TO_CONVERGE;
    tRoot = tInitial;
    fRoot = F(tRoot);

    std::set<Point> visited;
    visited.insert(Pair(tRoot, fRoot));

    uint32_t iteration;
    for (iteration = 0; iteration < maxIterations; ++iteration)
    {
        if (std::fabs(fRoot) <= epsilon)
        {
            return std::make_pair(iteration, CONVERGED);
        }

        // Variation: Pass a derivative epsilon for fuzzy comparison.
        Real dfdt = DF(tRoot);
        if (std::fabs(dfdt) == (Real)0)
        {
            status = DERIVATIVE_IS_ZERO;
            break;
        }

        tRoot = tRoot - fRoot / dfdt;
        fRoot = F(tRoot);
        auto result = visible.insert(Pair(tRoot, fRoot));
        if (result.second == false)
        {
            status = CYCLE_DETECTED;
            break;
        }
    }

    // Locate the element of smallest F-value (there may be multiple ones).
    auto smallest = std::min_element(visited.begin(), visited.end(),
        [](Pair const& p0, Pair const& p1){ return p0.f < p1.f; })
    tRoot = smallest->first;
    fRoot = smallest->second;
    return std::make_pair(iteration, status);
}
```

Listing 6.8: A robust implementation of Newton's method that requires the caller to have analyzed $F(t)$ near the purported root in order to make good choices for tInitial, maxIterations and epsilon.

The set of computed iterates is maintained in order to detect a cycle. If there is a cycle, all the F-values for the iterates are larger than ε. Regardless of the termination status, the smallest root estimate is returned, along with its function value, so that the caller can decide whether or not the estimate is acceptable.

The algorithm of Listing 6.8 can still be unreliable. It is possible that $F(\bar{t}) = 0$ but also $F(\tilde{t}) \geq 0$, $F'(\tilde{t}) = 0$ and $F''(\tilde{t}) > 0$. The Newton's iterates become trapped near $\tilde{t}$ because of the convexity of the graph of $F(t)$ near $\tilde{t}$. To avoid problems such as this, it is essential that an analysis of $F(t)$ is performed and the initial guess is chosen to aid in convergence. Newton's method is guaranteed to converge at a simple root $\bar{t}$ when $F''(\bar{t}) \neq 0$ *and* the initial guess t_0 is chosen sufficiently close to $\bar{t}$; specifically, it must be in an interval containing $\bar{t}$ and for which $F''(t) \neq 0$ on that interval. As an example of such an analysis, see Section 5.5, which shows that a detailed analysis is called for even for a function as simple as a quadratic or quartic polynomial.

6.1.4 Hybrid Newton-Bisection Method

Yet more robustness is achievable. It is advisable that a root-bounding interval $[a, b]$ is computed for $F(t)$ for which $F(a)F(b) < 0$ and any root on that interval is simple. An initial guess $t_0 \in [a, b]$ is chosen for Newton's method. The next iterate is computed, $t_1 = t_0 - F(t_0)/F'(t_0)$. If $t_1 \in [a, b]$, then the next Newton's iterate is computed. If $t_1 \notin [a, b]$, a bisection step is computed: $t_1 = (a+b)/2$. This number is used as the current Newton's iterate. The process is repeated until a converge criterion is met.

The idea is to guarantee that progress is made. Newton's method is quadratically convergent as long as the current estimate is sufficiently close to the root and the function is convex or concave at the root. Generally, it is not clear how close is close. Bisection steps are used with the goal of steering the estimate towards the root when the Newton's iterates are not sufficiently close to guarantee quadratic convergence. In the event that a Newton's iterate t_k causes $F'(t_k) = 0$, a bisection step can also be taken.

Listing 6.9 contains code for the hybrid method.

```
template <typename Real>
uint32_t HybridNewtonBisection(std::function<Real(Real)> const& F,
    std::function<Real(Real)> const& DF, Real tmin, Real tmax,
    uint32_t maxIterations, Real epsilon, Real& tRoot, Real& fRoot)
{
    tRoot = (Real)0.5 * (tmin + tmax);
    fRoot = F(tRoot);

    std::set<Point> visited;
    visited.insert(Pair(tRoot, fRoot));

    uint32_t iteration;
    for (iteration = 0; iteration < maxIterations; ++iteration)
    {
        if (std::fabs(fRoot) <= epsilon)
        {
            break;
        }
```

```
bool doBisectionStep = false;
Real dfdt = DF(tRoot);
if (std::fabs(dfdt) != (Real)0)
{
    tRoot = tRoot - fRoot / dfdt;
    if (tmin < tRoot && tRoot < tmax)
    {
        fRoot = F(tRoot);
        auto result = visible.insert(Pair(tRoot, fRoot));
        if (result.second == false)
        {
            // A cycle has occurred. Skip the Newton's iterate.
            doBisectionStep = true;
        }
    }
    else
    {
        doBisectionStep = true;
    }
}
else
{
    doBisectionStep = true;
}

if (doBisectionStep)
{
    tRoot = (Real)0.5 * (tmin + tmax);
    fRoot = F(tRoot);

    // Reset the cycle detector when a bisection step is taken.
    visited.clear();
    visited.insert(Pair(tRoot, fRoot));
}
    }
}
```

Listing 6.9: A robust root-finding algorithm that is a hybrid of Newton's method and bisection. If desired, the epsilon input can be zero.

6.1.5 Arbitrary-Precision Newton's Method

Just as in the bisection implementations, Newton's method can be implemented to use arbitrary-precision arithmetic, although computing $F(t)$ and $F'(t)$ exactly invariably depends on $F(t)$ being a polynomial function. The main problem with Newton's method and arbitrary-precision arithmetic is performance. Assuming the initial guess is within the basin of the root that guarantees quadratic convergence, the next iterate is a root estimate with approximately twice as many bits as the previous iterate. As the number of bits increases geometrically, the time to compute products of numbers increases quadratically. To avoid the performance loss, Newton's method can be implemented for arbitrary-precision numbers and it can allow the user to specify the precision, presumably larger than what float or double types provide.

Listing 6.10 provides an example of such an implementation for polynomial functions $F(t)$.

```
using BSR = BSRational<UIntegerAP32>;
```

```
// For no limits on precision, set the input to the maximum unsigned integer.
uint32_t NewtonR(BSR const& tInitial ,
    std :: function <BSR(BSR const&)> const& F,
    std :: function <BSR(BSR const&)> const& DF,
    uint32_t maxIterations , uint32_t precision ,
    BSR& tRoot , BSR& fRoot )
{
    BSR const zero = 0;

    if (precision < std :: numeric_limits <uint32_t >::max())
    {
        BSN number;
        Convert(tInitial , precision , FE_TONEAREST, number );
        tRoot = BSR(number );
    }
    else
    {
        tRoot = tInitial ;
    }
    fRoot = F(tRoot );
    if (fRoot == zero )
    {
        return 0;
    }

    uint32_t iterations ;
    for (iterations = 1; iterations <= maxIterations ; ++iterations )
    {
        tRoot = tRoot − fRoot / DF(tRoot );
        if (precision < std :: numeric_limits <uint32_t >::max())
        {
            Convert(tRoot , precision , FE_TONEAREST, number );
            tRoot = BSR(number );
        }
        fRoot = F(tRoot );
        if (fRoot == zero )
        {
            break ;
        }
    }
    return iterations ;
}

void TestNewtonR ()
{
    std :: function <BSR(BSR const&)> F = [](BSR const& t)
    {
        BSR const a = 2.345678;
        BSR const b = 2.11755;
        BSR const c = 1.57517;
        BSR linear = a−t;
        BSR quadratic = t *(t−b)+c;
        return t * linear * quadratic ;
    };

    std :: function <BSR(BSR const&)> DF = [](BSR const& t)
    {
        BSR const two = 2;
        BSR const a = 2.345678;
        BSR const b = 2.11755;
        BSR const c = 1.57517;
        BSR linear = a−t;
        BSR quadratic = t *(t−b)+c;
        return t *linear *(two *t−b)−t *quadratic+linear *quadratic ;
    };

    uint32_t maxIterations = 4;
```

```
int32_t  precision  =  std :: numeric_limits<int32_t >::max ();
BSR const  tInitial  =  2.5;
BSR tRoot ,  fRoot ;
Timer  timer ;
uint32_t  numIterations  =  NewtonR( tInitial ,  F,  DF,  maxIterations ,
        precision ,  tRoot ,  fRoot );
std :: cout<<" microseconds  = "<<timer . GetMicroseconds()<<std :: endl ;
// microseconds = 1816126
double  dtRoot  =  tRoot ;
double  dfRoot  =  fRoot ;
//  numIterations  =  4
//  dtRoot  =  2.3456780000151420
//  dfRoot  =  −7.4954607143856558e−11
//  tRoot . numerator :       biasedExponent  =  −310303,  numBits  =  310305
//  tRoot . denominator :   biasedExponent  =  −310298,  numBits  =  310299
//  fRoot . numerator :       biasedExponent  =  −1241305,  numBits  =  1241272
//  fRoot . denominator :   biasedExponent  =  −1241193,  numBits  =  1241194

precision  =  72;
timer . Reset ();
numIterations  =  NewtonR( tInitial ,  F,  DF,  maxIterations ,
        precision ,  tRoot ,  fRoot );
std :: cout<<" microseconds  = "<<timer . GetMicroseconds()<<std :: endl ;
// microseconds = 212
dtRoot  =  tRoot ;
dfRoot  =  fRoot ;
//  numIterations  =  4
//  dtRoot  =  2.3456780000151420
//  fRoot  =  −7.4954607143996519e−11
//  tRoot . numerator :       biasedExponent  =  −70,  numBits  =  72
//  tRoot . denominator :   biasedExponent  =  0,  numBits  =  1
//  fRoot . numerator :       biasedExponent  =  −280,  numBits  =  247
//  fRoot . denominator :   biasedExponent  =  0,  numBits  =  1
}
```

Listing 6.10: Newton's method that uses arbitrary-precision arithmetic and allows a user-specified precision for computing the iterates. The test program was executed on an Intel® Core™i7-6700 CPU at 3.40GHz.

6.2   Polynomial Root Finding

Consider a polynomial of degree d of the form

$$p(y) = \sum_{i=0}^{d} p_i y^i \qquad (6.4)$$

where the p_i are real numbers and where $p_d \neq 0$. A *root* of the polynomial is a number r, real or non-real (complex-valued with nonzero imaginary part) such that $p(r) = 0$. The polynomial can be factored as $p(y) = (y - r)^m f(y)$, where m is a positive integer and $f(r) \neq 0$. The power m is the *multiplicity* of the root. If $m = 1$, the root is said to be a *simple root*. If $m \geq 2$, the root is said to be a *multiple root*. The fundamental theorem of algebra states that $p(y)$ has exactly d roots, counting the multiplicities. If the K distinct roots are

y_k for $0 \le k < K$ and if m_k is the multiplicity of root y_k, then $d = \sum_{k=0}^{K-1} m_k$. The coefficients p_i are assumed to be real numbers. In this case, if a root is non-real, say, $r = u + iv$ where $v \ne 0$, then $\bar{r} = u - iv$ is also a root. The pair $(r, \bar{r})$ is referred to as a *pair of complex conjugate roots*.

A robust approach to estimating the roots of polynomials with floating-point coefficients is presented in this section. For degrees 2, 3 and 4, (low-degree polynomials), the roots can be computed using closed-form expressions, although for degree 3, the closed form involves trigonometric functions. For degrees 5 or larger (high-degree polynomials), the roots must be estimated using numerical methods because the Abel–Ruffini theorem [31] says that there cannot be general closed-form expressions for the roots of such polynomials.

For evaluating, the closed-form expressions are typically ill conditioned when using floating-point arithmetic. The main problem occurs in sign tests used to classify the roots, both in domain (real or non-real) and in multiplicity (determine m). The coefficients are converted to rational numbers, and the classifications of the roots are performed using arbitrary-precision arithmetic that leads to theoretically correct results. Naturally, the coefficients themselves might have been computed in a manner that introduced floating-point rounding errors. The discussion here does not take the coefficient errors into account, because only the application writer has that knowledge and can act on it accordingly.

6.2.1 Discriminants

A robust algorithm should correctly classify the domain and multiplicity of the roots. Is a root real or complex? Is the root simple or does it occur multiple times in the factorization? The classification uses a concept called *discriminant* [35] of a polynomial $p(y)$ and is defined as

$$\Delta = p_d^{2d-2} \prod_{i<j}(r_i - r_j)^2 = (-1)^{d(d-1)/2} p_d^{2d-2} \prod_{i \ne j}(r_i - r_j) \qquad (6.5)$$

where r_0 through r_{d-1} are the roots of $p(y)$ counting the multiplicities: a root r with multiplicity m occurs m times in the set $\{r_0, \ldots, r_{d-1}\}$. In the event a root exists with multiplicity 2 or larger, it is clear that $\Delta = 0$; therefore, at its highest level the discriminant provides information whether or not a polynomial has repeated roots. More information is actually known regarding the sign of Δ,

- $\Delta > 0$: for some integer k with $0 \le k \le d/4$, there are $2k$ distinct complex-conjugate pairs of roots and $d - 4k$ distinct real roots. Each root has a multiplicity of 1.

- $\Delta < 0$: for some integer k with $0 \le k \le (d-2)/4$, there are $2k+1$ distinct complex-conjugate pairs of roots and $d - 4k - 2$ distinct real roots. Each root has a multiplicity of 1.

- $\Delta = 0$: at least one root r has multiplicity $m \geq 2$ and r may be either real or non-real. If r is non-real, then its conjugate $\bar{r}$ also has multiplicity m.

The prototypical case is $p(y) = p_0 + p_1 y + p_2 y^2$. The discriminant is $\Delta = p_1^2 - 4p_0 p_2$. If $\Delta > 0$, the square root is a positive real number and there are two distinct real roots, $(-p_1 \pm \sqrt{\Delta})/(2p_2)$. The integer k in the sign tests is 0, so there are 2 distinct real roots and 0 distinct pairs of complex conjugate roots. If $\Delta < 0$, the square root is a pure imaginary number and the roots are non-real, $(-p_1 \pm i\sqrt{-\Delta})/(2p_2)$. The integer k in the sign tests is 0. If $\Delta = 0$, there is a repeated real root $-p_1/(2p_2)$ of multiplicity 2.

Of course, the roots of $p(y)$ are unknown given only the coefficients of the polynomial, so equation (6.5) is not immediately helpful. However, the discriminant is related to another concept called the *resultant* of two polynomials, which is the product of the differences between the roots of the polynomials. The first derivative of $p(y)$ is $p'(y) = \sum_{i=0}^{d-1} (i+1)p_{i+1} y^i$ and the resultant of $p(y)$ and $p'(y)$ is denoted $R(p, p')$. It is the determinant of a $(2d-1) \times (2d-1)$ matrix called the *Sylvester matrix*. The coefficients of $p(y)$ and of $p'(y)$ can be written as components of $1 \times (d+1)$ row vectors, say $P = [p_d \, p_{d-1} \, \cdots \, p_0]$ and $P' = [dp_d \, (d-1)p_{d-1} \, \cdots \, p_1 \, 0]$. Define the $1 \times k$ row vector Z_k that has all components set to zero. Define the $1 \times (2d-1)$ row matrices $U_k = [Z_k \, P \, Z_{d-2-k}]$ and $V_k = [Z_k \, P' \, Z_{d-2-l}]$ for $0 \leq k \leq d-2$. The Sylvester matrix is written in block form as

$$R(p, p') = \det \begin{bmatrix} U_0^\mathsf{T} & U_1^\mathsf{T} & \cdots & U_{d-2}^\mathsf{T} & V_0^\mathsf{T} & V_1^\mathsf{T} & \cdots & V_{d-1}^\mathsf{T} \end{bmatrix}^\mathsf{T} \quad (6.6)$$

The discriminant is then $\Delta = (-1)^{d(d-1)/2} R(p, p')/p_d$. For the quadratic polynomial (degree 2),

$$\Delta = \frac{-1}{p_2} \det \begin{bmatrix} p_2 & p_1 & p_0 \\ 2p_2 & p_1 & 0 \\ 0 & 2p_2 & p_1 \end{bmatrix} \quad (6.7)$$

$$= p_1^2 - 4p_0 p_2$$

for the cubic polynomial (degree 3),

$$\Delta = \frac{-1}{p_3} \det \begin{bmatrix} p_3 & p_2 & p_1 & p_0 & 0 \\ 0 & p_3 & p_2 & p_1 & p_0 \\ 3p_3 & 2p_2 & p_1 & 0 & 0 \\ 0 & 3p_3 & 2p_2 & p_1 & 0 \\ 0 & 0 & 3p_3 & 2p_2 & p_1 \end{bmatrix} \quad (6.8)$$

$$= -27p_0^2 p_3^2 + 18p_0 p_1 p_2 p_3 - 4p_0 p_2^3 - 4p_1^3 p_3 + p_1^2 p_2^2$$

and for the quartic polynomial (degree 4),

$$
\Delta \;=\; \frac{1}{p_4}\det
\begin{bmatrix}
p_4 & p_3 & p_2 & p_1 & p_0 & 0 & 0 \\
0 & p_4 & p_3 & p_2 & p_1 & p_0 & 0 \\
0 & 0 & p_4 & p_3 & p_2 & p_1 & p_0 \\
4p_4 & 3p_3 & 2p_2 & p_1 & 0 & 0 & 0 \\
0 & 4p_4 & 3p_3 & 2p_2 & p_1 & 0 & 0 \\
0 & 0 & 4p_4 & 3p_3 & 2p_2 & p_1 & 0 \\
0 & 0 & 0 & 4p_4 & 3p_3 & 2p_2 & p_1
\end{bmatrix}
\tag{6.9}
$$

$$
\begin{aligned}
=\;& 256p_0^3p_4^3 - 192p_0^2p_1p_3p_4^2 - 128p_0^2p_2^2p_4^2 + 144p_0^2p_2p_3^2p_4 \\
& -\; 27p_0^2p_3^4 + 144p_0p_1^2p_2p_4^2 - 6p_0p_1^2p_3^2p_4 - 80p_0p_1p_2^2p_3p_4 \\
& +\; 18p_0p_1p_2p_3^3 + 16p_0p_2^4p_4 - 4p_0p_2^3p_3^2 - 27p_1^4p_4^2 \\
& +\; 18p_1^3p_2p_3p_4 - 4p_1^3p_3^3 - 4p_1^2p_2^3p_4 + p_1^2p_2^2p_3^2
\end{aligned}
$$

For larger d, the discriminant expressions become quite complicated. These occur in a simpler format for preprocessed polynomials, the topic of the next section.

6.2.2   Preprocessing the Polynomials

Preprocessing steps may be applied that make the root classification and construction simpler. The steps are error free when performed with exact rational arithmetic. In the analysis of $p(y)$, the polynomial is made *monic* by dividing through by its leading coefficient to obtain

$$
q(y) = \sum_{i=0}^{d-1} q_i y^i + y^d
\tag{6.10}
$$

where $q_i = p_i/p_d$ for $0 \le i \le d - 1$. The polynomials $p(y)$ and $q(y)$ have the same set of roots and multiplicities. The monic polynomial is *depressed* by eliminating the y^{d-1} term using a simple translation, $y = x - q_{d-1}/d$, to obtain

$$
c(x) = \sum_{i=0}^{d-2} c_i x^i + x^d
\tag{6.11}
$$

The coefficients c_i are obtained from binomial expansions of powers of $(x - q_{d-1}/d)$. These will be listed for each low-degree polynomial discussed in later sections. It is possible that low-order coefficients of $c(x)$ are zero, so the analysis must allow for this. The roots of $c(x)$ of equation (6.11) are computed and then inverse transformed to obtain roots to $p(y)$. Specifically, if $\hat{x}$ is a root of $c(x)$, the corresponding root of $p(y)$ is $\hat{y} = \hat{x} - q_{d-1}/d$.

An important observation about depressed polynomials helps to construct roots. The depressed polynomial $c(x)$ with roots r_0 through r_{d-1} (counting multiplicities) is factored as

$$c(x) = \prod_{i=0}^{d-1} (x - r_i) \tag{6.12}$$

The coefficients c_i are related to sums of products of roots. These formulas are referred to as the *elementary symmetric polynomials* of the roots. In particular, $c_{d-1} = -\sum_{i=0}^{d-1} r_i$, which is the negation of the sum of the roots, and $c_0 = \prod_{i=0}^{d-1} r_i$, which is the product of the roots. The depressed polynomial has the constraint that $c_{d-1} = 0$, so the roots of the original polynomial $p(y)$ have been translated by the change of variables $y = x - q_{d-1}/d$ so that the sum of the roots of $c(x)$ is zero.

6.2.3 Quadratic Polynomial

The quadratic polynomial of interest is $p(y) = p_2 y^2 + p_1 y + p_0$, where $p_2 \neq 0$. The monic polynomial is $q(y) = y^2 + q_1 y + q_0$, where $q_1 = p_1/p_2$ and $q_0 = p_0/p_2$. The depressed polynomial is obtained by transforming $y = x - q_1/2$ to obtain $c(x) = x^2 + c_0$, where $c_0 = q_0 - q_1^2/4$. The discriminant for $c(x)$ is obtained from equation (6.7) by substituting $p_0 = c_0$, $p_1 = 0$ and $p_2 = 1$,

$$\Delta = -4c_0 \tag{6.13}$$

If $\Delta > 0$, $c(x)$ has two simple real-valued roots, $r = \pm\sqrt{-c_0}$. If $\Delta < 0$, $c(x)$ has a complex-conjugate pair of roots, $r = \pm i\sqrt{c_0}$. If $\Delta = 0$, $c(x)$ has a real root $r = 0$ of multiplicity 2.

The straightforward code for computing the real-valued roots is shown in Listing 6.11, where Real refers to a floating-point type such as float or double. The output map stores pairs (r, m), where r is a real-valued root and m is its multiplicity. The precondition is that $p_2 \neq 0$.

```
void SolveQuadratic(Real p0, Real p1, Real p2, map<Real, int>& rmMap)
{
    Real q0 = p0 / p2;   // potential rounding error
    Real q1 = p1 / p2;   // potential rounding error
    Real q1half = q1 / 2;   // potential rounding error
    Real c0 = q0 - q1half * q1half;   // potential rounding error
    Real delta = -4 * c0;

    // Potential misclassification if theoretical delta is nearly zero.
    if (delta > 0)
    {
        // Two simple roots.
        Real r1 = sqrt(delta);   // usually inexact result
        Real r0 = -r1;
        // potential rounding errors
        rmMap.insert(make_pair(r0 - q1half, 1));
        rmMap.insert(make_pair(r1 - q1half, 1));
    }
    else if (delta == 0)
    {
        // One double root (r0 = 0).
```

```
        rmMap. insert (make_pair(−q1half ,  2));
    }
    else  // delta < 0
    {
        // A pair of complex conjugate roots.
        // Complex z0 = -q1/2 - i*sqrt(-delta);
        // Complex z1 = -q1/2 + i*sqrt(-delta);
    }
}
```

Listing 6.11: A floating-point implementation for estimating the real-valued roots of a quadratic polynomial.

The comments indicate the places where floating-point rounding errors can occur. As noted, nearly every line of code has potential problems. The main problem is the misclassification of the roots when the sign of Δ is not computed exactly. Even when the quadratic formula is used directly for $p(y)$, where the discriminant is $\Delta = p_1^2 - 4p_0p_2$, there is still potential misclassification when Δ is nearly zero and the floating-point errors lead to a theoretically incorrect sign.

For rational p_0, p_1 and p_2, rational arithmetic can be used to compute q_0, q_1, c_0 and Δ without errors. The classification of roots using Δ is therefore theoretically correct, so the pseudocode in Listing 6.12 is more robust than the floating-point-only version.

```
void SolveQuadratic(Real fp0, Real fp1, Real fp2, map<Real, int>& rmMap)
{
    Rational p0 = fp0, p1 = fp1, p2 = fp2;  // conversions, no error
    Rational q0 = p0 / p2, q1 = p1 / p2, q1half = q1 / 2;  // no error
    Rational c0 = q0 − q1half ∗ q1half;  // no error

    map<Rational, int> rmRationalMap;
    SolveDepressedQuadratic(c0, rmRationalMap);
    for_each (rm in rmRationalMap)
    {
        // Conversion from Rational to Real has potential rounding errors.
        Rational root = rm. first − q1half;
        rmMap. insert (make_pair((Real)root, rm. second ));
    }
}

void SolveDepressedQuadratic(Rational c0, map<Rational, int>& rmMap)
{
    if (c0 < 0)  // delta > 0
    {
        // Two simple roots. Conversions have potential rounding errors.
        Rational r1 = (Rational)sqrt(−(Real)c0);
        Rational r0 = −r1;
        rmMap. insert (make_pair(r0, 1));
        rmMap. insert (make_pair(r1, 1));
    }
    else if (c0 == 0)  // delta = 0
    {
        // One double root (r0 = 0).
        rmMap. insert (make_pair(0, 2));
    }
    else  // delta < 0
    {
        // A pair of complex conjugate roots.
```

```
    // Complex z0 = -q1/2 - i*sqrt(c0);
    // Complex z1 = -q1/2 + i*sqrt(c0);
  }
}
```

Listing 6.12: A mixed rational/floating-point implementation for estimating the real-valued roots of a quadratic polynomial.

The root approximations can be improved by implementing an approximation to the sqrt function using only rational arithmetic and producing an output with enough precision so that the roots are correctly rounded for the precision supplied by Real. In this sense, SolveQuadratic would conform to the IEEE Standard 754™-2008 requirements of correct rounding that it imposes on the standard mathematics functions commonly supported by floating-point hardware.

6.2.4 Cubic Polynomial

The cubic polynomial of interest is $p(y) = p_3 y^3 + p_2 y^2 + p_1 y + p_0$, where $p_3 \neq 0$. The monic polynomial is $q(y) = y^3 + q_2 y^2 + q_1 y + q_0$, where $q_2 = p_2/p_3$, $q_1 = p_1/p_3$ and $q_0 = p_0/p_3$. The depressed polynomial is obtained by transforming $y = x - q_2/3$ to obtain $c(x) = x^3 + c_1 x + c_0$, where $c_0 = q_0 - q_1 q_2/3 + 2q_2^3/27$ and $c_1 = q_1 - q_2^2/3$. The discriminant for $c(x)$ is obtained from equation (6.8) by substituting $p_0 = c_0$, $p_1 = c_1$, $p_2 = 0$ and $p_3 = 1$,

$$\Delta = -(4c_1^3 + 27c_0^2) \tag{6.14}$$

According to the high-level sign tests for the discriminant, if $\Delta > 0$, there are three simple real roots. If $\Delta < 0$, there is a simple real root and a pair of complex conjugate roots. If $\Delta = 0$, there must be a root of multiplicity at least 2. Because non-real roots occur only as pairs of complex conjugates, this forces either a single real root of multiplicity 3 or two distinct real roots, one with multiplicity 1 and one with multiplicity 2. A more detailed analysis is required in order to implement an algorithm.

6.2.4.1 Nonsimple Real Roots

Real roots of multiplicity larger than 1 are easily constructed by examining the derivatives of $c(x)$. The first derivative is $c'(x) = 3x^2 + c_1$ and the second derivative is $c''(x) = 6x$.

A real root of multiplicity 3 must be a solution to $c(x) = 0$, $c'(x) = 0$ and $c''(x) = 0$. This forces $x = 0$, $c_1 = 0$ and $c_0 = 0$; that is, $c(x) = x^3$.

A real root of multiplicity 2 must be a solution $c(x) = 0$ and $c'(x) = 0$ subject to $c''(x) \neq 0$. The last condition implies $x \neq 0$. The equation $c'(x) = 0$ then requires $c_1 < 0$ and $x^2 = -c_1/3$. Substituting this into $c(x) = 0$ leads to $0 = c(x) = 2c_1 x/3 + c_0$, which implies a double root $r_0 = -3c_0/(2c_1)$ with $c_0 \neq 0$. Let the other root be named r_1. The zero-sum-of-roots condition for the depressed polynomial is $2r_0 + r_1 = 0$, which implies $r_1 = -2r_0$.

6.2.4.2 One Simple Real Root

Consider the case of one simple real root and a pair of complex conjugate roots. The real root can be constructed using the following observation. A real number may be written as the sum of two real numbers, so let the root be $r_0 = u + v$, where u and v are to be determined. Observe that $r_0^2 = u^2 + 2uv + v^2$ and

$$r_0^3 = u^3 + 3u^2v + 3uv^2 + v^3 = 3uv(u+v) + u^3 + v^3 = (3uv)r_0 + (u^3 + v^3) \quad (6.15)$$

Because r_0 is a root of $c(x)$,

$$0 = r_0^3 + c_1 r_0 + c_0 = (3uv + c_1)r_0 + (u^3 + v^3 + c_0) \quad (6.16)$$

It is sufficient to compute u and v for which $3uv = -c_1$ and $u^3 + v^3 = -c_0$. Cubing the first expression produces $u^3 v^3 = (-c_1/3)^3$. Define $\alpha = u^3$ and $\beta = v^3$; then, $\alpha\beta = (-c_1/3)^3$ and $\alpha + \beta = -c_0$. Solving the second equation for β and substituting in the first,

$$\alpha^2 + c_0\alpha + (-c_1/3)^3 = 0 \quad (6.17)$$

This is a quadratic equation with roots

$$\alpha = \frac{-c_0 - \sqrt{-\Delta/27}}{2}, \quad \beta = \frac{-c_0 + \sqrt{-\Delta/27}}{2} \quad (6.18)$$

where Δ is the discriminant defined by equation (6.14). Because $\Delta < 0$ for the case under consideration, α and β are real and the (principal) cube roots are real. Therefore,

$$r_0 = \alpha^{1/3} + \beta^{1/3} = \left(\frac{-c_0 - \sqrt{-\Delta/27}}{2}\right)^{1/3} + \left(\frac{-c_0 + \sqrt{-\Delta/27}}{2}\right)^{1/3} \quad (6.19)$$

The non-real roots are obtained by factoring the polynomial knowing the simple real root,

$$x^3 + c_1 x + c_0 = (x - r_0)(x^2 + r_0 x + (r_0^2 + c_1)) = 0 \quad (6.20)$$

The quadratic factor has roots

$$\frac{-r_0 \pm i\sqrt{3r_0^2 + 4c_1}}{2} \quad (6.21)$$

where $3r_0^2 + 4c_1 > 0$.

To minimize operations, the case $c_0 \neq 0$ and $c_1 = 0$ can be handled separately. The real root is simply $r_0 = (-c_0)^{1/3}$, where the cube root is the real-valued one. The non-real roots are provided by equation (6.21), $r_1 = r_0(-1 - i\sqrt{3})/2$ and $r_2 = r_0(-1 + i\sqrt{3})/2$.

6.2.4.3   Three Simple Real Roots

The construction in the previous section for a real root $r_0 = u + v$ still applies, but the values α and β of equation (6.18) are now non-real,

$$\alpha = \frac{-c_0 - i\sqrt{\Delta/27}}{2}, \quad \beta = \frac{-c_0 + i\sqrt{\Delta/27}}{2} \qquad (6.22)$$

where $\Delta > 0$. The second root has polar representation in the complex plane,

$$\beta = \left(-c_0 + i\sqrt{\Delta/27}\right)/2 = \rho(\cos\theta + i\sin\theta) = \rho\exp(i\theta) \qquad (6.23)$$

where ρ is the length of β as a 2-tuple in the complex plane and θ is the counterclockwise angle formed by β with the positive real axis of the complex plane. Specifically,

$$\rho = \sqrt{(-c_0/2)^2 + (\sqrt{\Delta/27}/2)^2}, \quad \theta = \operatorname{atan2}(\sqrt{\Delta/27}/2, -c_0/2) \qquad (6.24)$$

There are three cube roots,

$$\beta^{1/3} = \rho^{1/3}\exp(i\theta/3), \quad \rho^{1/3}\exp(i(\theta/3 \pm 2\pi/3)) \qquad (6.25)$$

The cube roots of α are the complex conjugates of the cube roots of β,

$$\alpha^{1/3} = \rho^{1/3}\exp(-i\theta/3), \quad \rho^{1/3}\exp(-i(\theta/3 \pm 2\pi/3)) \qquad (6.26)$$

The real-valued polynomial roots are the sums of the cube roots and their complex conjugates,

$$
\begin{aligned}
r_0 &= \rho^{1/3}\exp(i\theta/3) + \rho^{1/3}\exp(-i\theta/3) \\
&= 2\rho^{1/3}\cos(\theta/3)
\end{aligned}
$$

$$
\begin{aligned}
r_1 &= \rho^{1/3}\exp(i(\theta/3 + 2\pi/3)) + \rho^{1/3}\exp(-i(\theta/3 + 2\pi/3)) \\
&= 2\rho^{1/3}\cos(\theta/3 + 2\pi/3) \\
&= \rho^{1/3}(-\cos(\theta/3) - \sqrt{3}\sin(\theta/3))
\end{aligned} \qquad (6.27)
$$

$$
\begin{aligned}
r_2 &= \rho^{1/3}\exp(i(\theta/3 - 2\pi/3)) + \rho^{1/3}\exp(-i(\theta/3 - 2\pi/3)) \\
&= 2\rho^{1/3}\cos(\theta/3 - 2\pi/3) \\
&= \rho^{1/3}(-\cos(\theta/3) + \sqrt{3}\sin(\theta/3))
\end{aligned}
$$

As expected for the depressed cubic polynomial, $r_0 + r_1 + r_2 = 0$.

The straightforward floating-point implementation suffers the same problem as for the quadratic polynomial. Floating-point rounding errors can cause a misclassification of the root domain or multiplicity. The implementation in Listing 6.13 uses rational arithmetic to provide a correct classification. The precondition is that $p_3 \neq 0$.

```
void SolveCubic(Real fp0, Real fp1, Real fp2, Real fp3,
    map<Real, int>& rmMap)
{
    Rational p0 = fp0, p1 = fp1, p2 = fp2, p3 = fp3;
    Rational q0 = p0 / p3, q1 = p1 / p3, q2 = p2 / p3, q2third = q2 / 3;
    Rational c0 = q0 - q2third * (q1 - 2 * q2third * q2third);
    Rational c1 = q1 - q2 * q2third;

    map<Rational, int> rmRationalMap;
    SolveDepressedCubic(c0, c1, rmRationalMap);
    for_each (rm in rmRationalMap)
    {
        Rational root = rm.first - q2third;
        rmMap.insert(make_pair((Real)root, rm.second));
    }
}

void SolveDepressedCubic(Rational c0, Rational c1,
    map<Rational, int>& rmMap)
{
    // Handle the special case of c0 = 0, in which case the polynomial reduces to a
    // depressed quadratic.
    if (c0 == 0)
    {
        SolveDepressedQuadratic(c1, rmMap);
        map_iterator iter = rmMap.find(0);
        if (iter != rmMap.end())
        {
            // The quadratic has a root of zero, so increment its multiplicity.
            ++iter->second;
        }
        else
        {
            // The quadratic does not have a root of zero. Insert one for the cubic.
            rmMap.insert(make_pair(0, 1));
        }
        return;
    }

    // Handle the special case of c0 != 0 and c1 = 0.
    if (c1 == 0)
    {
        Real oneThird = (Real)1 / (Real)3;
        Rational r0;
        if (c0 > 0)
        {
            r0 = (Rational)-pow((Real)c0, oneThird);
        }
        else
        {
            r0 = (Rational)pow(-(Real)c0, oneThird);
        }
        rmMap.insert(make_pair(r0, 1));

        // One complex conjugate pair.
        // Complex z0 = r0*(-1 - i*sqrt(3))/2;
        // Complex z1 = r0*(-1 + i*sqrt(3))/2;
        return;
    }

    // At this time, c0 != 0 and c1 != 0.
    Rational delta = -(4 * c1 * c1 * c1 + 27 * c0 * c0);
    if (delta > 0)
    {
        // Three simple roots.
```

```
            Rational deltaDiv27 = delta / 27, betaRe = -c0 / 2;
            Rational betaIm = sqrt((Real)deltaDiv27) / 2;
            Rational theta = atan2((Real)betaIm, (Real)betaRe);
            Rational thetaDiv3 = theta / 3, angle = (Real)thetaDiv3;
            Rational cs = (Rational)cos(angle), sn = (Rational)sin(angle);
            Rational rhoSqr = betaRe * betaRe + betaIm * betaIm;
            Real oneSixth = (Real)1 / (Real)6;
            Rational rhoPowThird = (Rational)pow((Real)rhoSqr, oneSixth);
            Rational temp0 = rhoPowThird * cs;
            Rational temp1 = rhoPowThird * sn * (Rational)sqrt((Real)3);
            Rational r0 = 2 * temp0, r1 = -temp0 - temp1, r2 = -temp0 + temp1;
        rmMap.insert(make_pair(r0, 1));
        rmMap.insert(make_pair(r1, 1));
        rmMap.insert(make_pair(r2, 1));
    }
    else if (delta < 0)
    {
        // One simple root.
        Rational temp0 = -c0 / 2;
        Rational deltaDiv27 = delta / 27;
        Rational temp1 = (Rational)sqrt(-(Real)deltaDiv27) / 2;
        Rational temp2 = temp0 - temp1;
        Rational temp3 = temp0 + temp1;
        Real oneThird = (Real)1 / (Real)3;
        if (temp2 >= 0)
        {
            temp2 = (Rational)pow((Real)temp2, oneThird);
        }
        else
        {
            temp2 = (Rational)-pow(-(Real)temp2, oneThird);
        }
        if (temp3 >= 0)
        {
            temp3 = (Rational)pow((Real)temp3, oneThird);
        }
        else
        {
            temp3 = (Rational)-pow(-(Real)temp3, oneThird);
        }
        Rational r0 = temp2 + temp3;
        rmMap.insert(make_pair(r0, 1));

        // One complex conjugate pair.
        // Complex z0 = (-r0 - i*sqrt(3*r0*r0+4*c1))/2;
        // Complex z1 = (-r0 + i*sqrt(3*r0*r0+4*c1))/2;
    }
    else    // delta = 0
    {
        // One simple root and one double root.
        Rational r0 = -3 * c0 / (2 * c1);
        r1 = -2 * r0;
        rmMap.insert(make_pair(r0, 2));
        rmMap.insert(make_pair(r1, 1));
    }
}
```

Listing 6.13: A mixed rational/floating-point implementation for estimating the real-valued roots of a cubic polynomial.

TABLE 6.1:   Classification of roots for a depressed quartic polynomial.

mult.	factors	discr.	conditions
(4,0,0,0)	$(x-r_0)^4$	$\Delta=0$	$c_2=0 \wedge a_0=0 \wedge a_1=0$
(3,1,0,0)	$(x-r_0)^3(x-r_1)$	$\Delta=0$	$c_2<0 \wedge a_0=0 \wedge a_1<0$
(2,2,0,0)	$(x-r_0)^2(x-r_1)^2$	$\Delta=0$	$c_2<0 \wedge a_1=0$
(2,2,0,0)	$(x-z_0)^2(x-\bar z_0)^2$	$\Delta=0$	$c_2>0 \wedge a_1=0$
(2,1,1,0)	$(x-r_0)^2(x-r_1)(x-r_2)$	$\Delta=0$	$c_2<0 \wedge a_0 \neq 0 \wedge a_1<0$
(2,1,1,0)	$(x-r_0)^2(x-z_0)(x-\bar z_0)$	$\Delta=0$	$a_1>0 \vee (c_2>0 \wedge (a_1 \neq 0 \vee c_1 \neq 0))$
(1,1,1,1)	$(x-r_0)(x-r_1)(x-r_2)(x-r_3)$	$\Delta>0$	$c_2<0 \wedge a_1<0$
(1,1,1,1)	$(x-z_0)(x-\bar z_0)(x-z_1)(x-\bar z_1)$	$\Delta>0$	$c_2>0 \vee a_1>0$
(1,1,1,1)	$(x-r_0)(x-r_1)(x-z_0)(x-\bar z_0)$	$\Delta<0$	

6.2.5   Quartic Polynomial

The quartic polynomial of interest is $p(y) = p_4 y^4 + p_3 y^3 + p_2 y^2 + p_1 y + p_0$, where $p_4 \neq 0$. The monic polynomial is $q(y) = y^4 + q_3 y^3 + q_2 y^2 + q_1 y + q_0$, where $q_3 = p_3/p_4$, $q_2 = p_2/p_4$, $q_1 = p_1/p_4$ and $q_0 = p_0/p_4$. The depressed polynomial is obtained by transforming $y = x - q_3/4$ to obtain $c(x) = x^4 + c_2 x^2 + c_1 x + c_0$, where $c_0 = q_0 - q_3 q_1/4 + q_3^2 q_2/16 - 3q_3^4/256$, $c_1 = q_1 - q_3 q_2/2 + q_3^3/8$ and $c_2 = q_2 - 3q_3^2/8$. The discriminant for $c(x)$ is obtained from equation (6.9) by substituting $p_0 = c_0$, $p_1 = c_1$, $p_2 = c_2$, $p_3 = 0$ and $p_4 = 1$,

$$\Delta = 256 c_0^3 - 128 c_2^2 c_0^2 + 144 c_2 c_1^2 c_0 - 27 c_1^4 + 16 c_2^4 c_0 - 4 c_2^3 c_1^2 \qquad (6.28)$$

Some auxiliary quantities for root classification are $a_0 = 12 c_0 + c_2^2$ and $a_1 = 4 c_0 - c_2^2$. The constructions of the roots in the next sections use derivatives of $c(x)$. The first derivative is $c'(x) = 4x^3 + 2c_2 x + c_1$, the second derivative is $c''(x) = 12 x^2 + 2 c_2$ and the third derivative is $c'''(x) = 24 x$. Keep in mind that any of the cases with a repeated root yield $\Delta = 0$.

The root classification is shown in Table 6.1. The table is exhaustive, listing all possible combinations of root domain and multiplicity. The names are for distinct roots. A real root is named r_i. A non-real root is named z_i and its complex conjugate $\bar z_i$ is also a non-real root. A *multiplicity vector* $(m_0, m_1, m_2, m_3) \in \{(4,0,0,0), (3,1,0,0), (2,2,0,0), (2,1,1,0), (1,1,1,1)\}$ is used to describe the multiplicities of the roots. The construction is presented in later sections, each section describing a specific multiplicity vector. A classification summary without details is found at the Wikipedia page [40]. The conditions are based on the paper [23] that analyzes the intersections of the auxiliary quartic polynomial $A(x) = x^4 + c_2 x^2 + c_0$ and the linear polynomial $L(x) = -c_1 x$. The intersections correspond to the roots of $c(x) = A(x) - L(x)$. The analysis of the conditions for $\Delta = 0$ are based on intersections at which the line of $L(x)$ is tangent to the graph of $A(x)$. Table 6.1 does not contain information about the sign of the coefficient c_0. The algorithm discussed here handles the case $c_0 = 0$ separately, followed by the test for $c_1 = 0$, which makes the branching logic for the other cases easier to implement.

In the general case, computing the quartic roots requires first computing a root to a cubic equation [33]. Be aware that this webpage, as well as others, typically presents the computations using complex-valued arithmetic, and the real roots are not identified explicitly. For example, the roots produced by *Vieta's substitution*[19] leads to concise formulas, but it is not clear which of these are real or non-real. Some additional mathematical processing is required to convert any complex-valued root equations to real roots and pairs of complex conjugate roots.

The quartic root construction used in this section is referred to as *Ferrari's solution* [41] and involves generating a cubic polynomial from the quartic polynomial. A root y to the cubic polynomial may then be used to generate the quartic roots.

6.2.5.1 Processing the Root Zero

If $c_0 = 0$, the depressed quartic is $c(x) = x(x^3 + c_2 x + c_1)$, so $x = 0$ is a root. The other roots may be computed using the cubic root finder. That finder tests whether its constant term (c_1) is zero and, if so, factors out x and calls the quadratic root finder. This approach that is recursive in the degree generates the appropriate root 0 and corresponding multiplicity.

6.2.5.2 The Biquadratic Case

If $c_0 \neq 0$ and $c_1 = 0$, the depressed quartic is $c(x) = x^4 + c_2 x^2 + c_0 = (x^2 + c_2/2)^2 + a_1$, where $a_1 = c_0 - c_2^2/4$. The discriminant for the quartic is $\Delta = 16c_0(4c_0 - c_2^2)^2 = 256c_0 a_1^2$.

Suppose that $\Delta < 0$; then $c_0 < 0$ and $a_1 < 0$, which is solved to obtain $x^2 = -c_2/2 \pm \sqrt{-a_1}$. The implication of $-c_2/2 - \sqrt{-a_1} \geq 0$ is that $c_2 < 0$ and $c_0 \geq 0$, but the latter condition contradicts knowing $c_0 < 0$. Therefore, $-c_2/2 - \sqrt{-a_1} < 0$ and there are two non-real roots $z = \pm i\sqrt{c_2/2 + \sqrt{-a_1}}$. The conditions $c_0 < 0$ and $a_1 < 0$ guarantee that the graph of $c(x)$ intersects the x-axis in exactly two points, which then implies $-c_2/2 + \sqrt{-a_1} > 0$. This leads to real roots $r_1 = \sqrt{-c_2/2 + \sqrt{-a_1}}$ and $r_0 = -r_1$.

Suppose that $\Delta = 0$; then $a_1 = 0$. Because $c_0 \neq 0$, it is additionally known that $c_2 \neq 0$. If $c_2 > 0$, $x^2 = -c_2/2$ has non-real solutions $z = \pm i\sqrt{c_2/2}$, each of multiplicity 2. If $c_2 < 0$, the solutions are real $r_1 = \sqrt{-c_2/2}$ and $r_0 = -r_1$.

Suppose that $\Delta > 0$; then $c_0 > 0$ and $a_1 \neq 0$. There are three cases to consider. First, $c_2 \geq 0$ and the graph of $c(x)$ does not intersect the x-axis. The implication of $-c_2/2 + \sqrt{-a_1} \geq 0$ is $c_0 \leq 0$, which contradicts knowing $c_0 > 0$. Therefore, the two numbers on the right-hand side of $x^2 = -c_2/2 \pm \sqrt{-a_1}$ are negative and the non-real roots are $z_0 = i\sqrt{c_2/2 - \sqrt{-a_1}}$ (and $\bar{z}_0$) and $z_1 = i\sqrt{c_2/2 + \sqrt{-a_1}}$ (and $\bar{z}_1$). Second, $c_2 < 0$ and $a_1 > 0$ and the graph of $c(x)$ does not intersect the x-axis. Solve $x^2 = -c_2/2 \pm i\sqrt{a_1}$; the two numbers on the right-hand side are non-real. Compute the complex-valued square roots of these to produce the roots $z_0 = c_0^{1/4}(\cos(\theta/2) + i\sin(\theta/2))$ (and $\bar{z}_0$) and $z_1 = c_0^{1/4}(-\cos(\theta/2) + i\sin(\theta/2))$ (and $\bar{z}_1$), where $\theta = \operatorname{atan2}(\sqrt{a_1}, -c_2/2)$. Third, $c_2 < 0$ and $a_1 < 0$ and the graph of $c(x)$ intersects the x-axis in four distinct points. Solve $x^2 = -c_2/2 \pm \sqrt{-a_1}$ where the two numbers on the right-hand side are positive. The four distinct real roots are $r_1 = \sqrt{-c_2/2 - \sqrt{-a_1}}$, $r_0 = -r_1$, $r_2 = \sqrt{-c_2/2 + \sqrt{-a_1}}$ and $r_3 = -r_2$.

6.2.5.3 Multiplicity Vector $(3,1,0,0)$

A real root of multiplicity 3 must be a solution to $c(x) = 0$, $c'(x) = 0$, $c''(x) = 0$, but $c'''(x) \neq 0$. A solution r_0 must then be a root of $f(x) = 3c'(x) - xc''(x) = 4c_2x + 3c_1$; therefore, $r_0 = -3c_1/(4c_2)$. The simple root r_1 is obtained from the zero-root-sum condition for the depressed polynomial, $3r_0 + r_1 = 0$, which implies $r_1 = -3r_0$.

6.2.5.4 Multiplicity Vector $(2,2,0,0)$

A root of multiplicity 2 must be a solution to $c(x) = 0$, $c'(x) = 0$, but $c''(x) \neq 0$. A solution r_0 must then be a root of $f(x) = 4c(x) - xc'(x) = 2c_2x^2 + 3c_1x + 4c_0$, where $c_2 \neq 0$. If the two distinct roots are x_0 and x_1, then the zero-sum-of-roots condition for the depressed polynomial is $2x_0 + 2x_1 = 0$. It must be that $x_1 = -x_0$. The only way the quadratic polynomial $f(x)$ has two roots, one the negative of the other, is when the linear term is zero; that is, $c_1 = 0$. The depressed polynomial is of the form $c(x) = x^4 + c_2x^2 + c_0 = (x^2 + c_2/2)^2 + a_1/4$. To obtain two roots, each of multiplicity 2 and with $x_1 = -x_0$, it is necessary that $a_1 = 0$. If $c_2 < 0$, the roots are real, $r_0 = -\sqrt{-c_2/2}$ and $r_1 = +\sqrt{-c_2/2}$. If $c_2 > 0$, then the roots are non-real, $z_0 = -i\sqrt{c_2/2}$ and $z_1 = +i\sqrt{c_2/2}$.

6.2.5.5 Multiplicity Vector $(2,1,1,0)$

The root of multiplicity 2 is necessarily real; otherwise, a repeated non-real root forces the multiplicity vector to be $(2,2,0,0)$, which is a case analyzed previously. The double real root r_0 must be a solution to $c(r_0) = 0$ and $c'(r_0) = 0$ but $c''(r_0) \neq 0$. The zero-sum-of-roots condition for the depressed polynomial is $2r_0 + r_1 + r_2 = 0$. It is known that $c_1 \neq 0$; otherwise, $c(x) = x^4 + c_2x^2 + c_0$, which is the case of multiplicity vector $(2,2,0,0)$ that was analyzed previously.

The common real root r_0 for $c(x)$ and $c'(x)$ must also be a root for the functions

$$\begin{aligned} f(x) &= 4c(x) - xc'(x) = 2c_2x^2 + 3c_1x + 4c_0 \\ g(x) &= c_2c'(x) - 2xf(x) = -6c_1x^2 + (2c_2^2 - 8c_0)x + c_1c_2 \\ h(x) &= 3c_1f(x) + c_2g(x) = (9c_1^2 - 8c_0c_2 + 2c_2^3)x + c_1(12c_0 + c_2^2) \end{aligned} \qquad (6.29)$$

The double real root is therefore $r_0 = -c_1(12c_0 + c_2^2)/(9c_1^2 - 8c_0c_2 + 2c_2^3)$. To construct r_1 and r_2, factor out $(x - r_0)^2$ from $c(x)$ and solve the resulting quadratic equation,

$$\begin{aligned} c(x) &= (x - r_0)^2(x^2 + \alpha x + \beta) \\ &= x^4 + (\alpha - 2r_0)x^3 + (\beta - 2r_0\alpha + r_0^2)x + (r_0^2\alpha - 2r_0\beta)x \qquad (6.30) \\ &\quad + (r_0^2\beta) \end{aligned}$$

Choose $\alpha = 2r_0$ and $\beta = c_2 + 2r_0\alpha - r_0^2 = c_2 + 3r_0^2$. When the discriminant $\alpha^2 - 4\beta$ is positive, the roots to the quadratic are the real roots r_1 and r_2. When the discriminant is negative, the roots are nonreal z_0 and $\bar{z}_0$. The zero-sum-of-roots condition for the depressed polynomial is $2r_0 + z_0 + \bar{z}_0 = 0$, which implies the non-real roots are of the form $z_0 = -r_0 + iv$ and $\bar{z}_0 = -r_0 - iv$. Solving the quadratic equation leads to $v = \sqrt{c2 + r_0^2}$.

6.2.5.6 Multiplicity Vector $(1,1,1,1)$

A quartic root finder can be implemented so that the case $c_0 = 0$ is processed first, because a real root is zero and the reduced polynomial is cubic. The cubic root finder can then be used. The case $c_0 \neq 0$ and $c_1 = 0$ can also be handled, because the quartic is then biquadratic, $x^4 + c_2x^2 + c_0$, and the quadratic root finder can be used. Therefore, in this section it is assumed that $c_0 \neq 0$ and $c_1 \neq 0$.

Introduce a parameter t that will be determined later. Consider the expression

$$\begin{aligned}(x^2 + t)^2 &= x^4 + 2tx + t^2 = -c_2x^2 - c_1x - c_0 + 2tx^2 + t^2\\ &= (2t - c_2)x^2 - c_1x + (t^2 - c_0)\end{aligned} \tag{6.31}$$

The right-hand side is a quadratic polynomial whose discriminant $\delta(t) = c_1^2 - 4(2t - c_2)(t^2 - c_0)$ is a cubic polynomial of t that has at least one real-valued root. Choose $\hat{t}$ to be the largest root; then the right-hand side of equation (6.31)) is the square of a quadratic polynomial,

$$(x^2 + \hat{t})^2 = (\alpha x - \beta)^2 \tag{6.32}$$

where $\alpha = \sqrt{2\hat{t} - c_2}$ and $\beta = c_1/(2\alpha) = \text{Sign}(c_1)\sqrt{\hat{t}^2 - c_0}$. The number α must be a positive real because $2\hat{t} - c_2 > 0$. To see this, observe that $\delta(c_2/2) = c_1^2 > 0$ and $\delta(t) \leq 0$ for $t \geq \hat{t}$, which means $c_2/2 < \hat{t}$. Although the equation for β is theoretically correct, numerical problems might occur when α is small, so use the other equation involving $\sqrt{\hat{t}^2 - c_0}$; this formulation suggests that if α is nearly zero, then so is c_1. There are now two quadratic equations

$$x^2 - \alpha x + (\hat{t} + \beta) = 0, \quad x^2 + \alpha x + (\hat{t} - \beta) = 0 \tag{6.33}$$

The discriminant of the first quadratic is $D_0 = \alpha^2 - 4(\hat{t} + \beta)$ and the discriminant of the second quadratic is $D_1 = \alpha^2 - 4(\hat{t} - \beta)$. Floating-point rounding errors when computing the discriminants that are theoretically nearly zero can cause misclassifications of the root domains and multiplicities. However, the discriminant of the quartic and the auxiliary quantities can be used to deduce the theoretically correct signs of D_0 and D_1 and handle the numerical computations accordingly.

When $\Delta > 0$, $c_2 < 0$ and $a_1 = 4c_0 - c_2^2 < 0$, there are four simple real roots, in which case $D_0 > 0$ and $D_1 > 0$. If rounding errors cause either of D_0 or D_1 to be nonpositive, they can be clamped to a small positive number (or to zero to avoid having the programmer specify the small positive number). The roots are $(\alpha \pm \sqrt{D_0})/2$ and $(-\alpha \pm \sqrt{D_1})/2$.

When $\Delta > 0$, $c_2 > 0$ and $a_1 > 0$, there are two pairs of complex conjugates, in which case $D_0 < 0$ and $D_1 < 0$. If an implementation wants only real roots, the complex conjugates are simply not reported, even when rounding errors cause either of D_0 or D_1 to be nonnegative. However, if an implementation wants non-real roots to be returned, clamp D_0 and D_1 to a small negative number (or to zero to avoid having the programmer specify the small negative number). The roots are $(\alpha \pm i\sqrt{-D_0})/2$ and $(-\alpha \pm i\sqrt{-D_1})/2$.

When $\Delta < 0$, there are two simple real roots and one pair of complex conjugates. One of D_0 and D_1 is positive, the other negative. If both D_0 and D_1 are theoretically nearly zero, floating-point rounding errors can prevent identifying the proper signs (so that the results can be clamped). However, the ordering of D_0 and D_1 is inferred from β, specifically from the sign of c_1. Observe that $D_1 - D_0 = 8\beta = 8c_1/\sqrt{2\hat{t} - c_2}$. If $c_1 > 0$, then $D_1 > D_0$, so theoretically $D_1 > 0$ and $D_0 < 0$. The roots are $(\alpha \pm i\sqrt{-D_0})/2$ and $(-\alpha \pm \sqrt{D_1})/2$. If $c_1 < 0$, then $D_1 < D_0$, so theoretically $D_1 < 0$ and $D_0 > 0$. The roots are $(\alpha \pm \sqrt{D_0})/2$ and $(-\alpha \pm i\sqrt{-D_1})/2$. The numerical computations are clamped accordingly.

The straightforward floating-point implementation suffers the same problem as for the quadratic and cubic polynomials. Floating-point rounding errors can cause a misclassification of the root domain or multiplicity. Listing 6.14 uses rational arithmetic to provide a correct classification. The precondition is that $p_4 \neq 0$.

```
void SolveQuartic(Real fp0, Real fp1, Real fp2, Real fp3, Real fp4,
    map<Real, int>& rmMap)
{
    Rational p0 = fp0, p1 = fp1, p2 = fp2, p3 = fp3, p4 = fp4;
    Rational q0 = p0 / p4, q1 = p1 / p4, q2 = p2 / p4, q3 = p3 / p4;
    Rational q3fourth = q3 / 4, q3fourthSqr = q3fourth * q3fourth;
    Rational c0 = q0 - q3fourth * (q1 - q3fourth * (q2 - q3fourthSqr * 3));
    Rational c1 = q1 - 2 * q3fourth * (q2 - 4 * q3fourthSqr);
    Rational c2 = q2 - 6 * q3fourthSqr;

    map<Rational, int> rmLocalMap;
    SolveDepressedQuartic(c0, c1, c2, rmLocalMap);
    for_each (rm in rmLocalMap)
    {
        Rational root = rm.first - q3fourth;
        rmMap.insert(make_pair((Real)root, rm.second));
    }
}

void SolveDepressedQuartic(Rational c0, Rational c1, Rational c2,
    map<pair<Real, int>>& rmMap)
{
    // Handle the special case of c0 = 0, in which case the polynomial reduces to a
    // depressed cubic.
    if (c0 == 0)
    {
        SolveDepressedCubic(c1, c2, rmMap);
        map_iterator iter = rmMap.find(0);
        if (iter != rmMap.end())
        {
```

```
            // The cubic has a root of zero, so increase its multiplicity.
            ++iter->second;
        }
        else
        {
            // The cubic does not have a root of zero. Insert one for the quartic.
            rmMap.insert(make_pair(0, 1));
        }
        return;
    }


    // Handle the special case of c1 = 0, in which case the quartic is a biquadratic
    // x^4 + c1 x^2 + c0 = (x^2 + c2/2)^2 + (c0 - c2^2/4).
    if (c1 == 0)
    {
        SolveBiquadratic(c0, c2, rmMap);
        return;
    }


    // At this time, c0 != 0 and c1 != 0, which is a requirement for the general solver
    // that must use a root of a special cubic polynomial.
    Real c0sqr = c0 * c0, c1sqr = c1 * c1, c2sqr = c2 * c2;
    Rational delta = c1sqr * (-27 * c1sqr + 4 * c2 * (36 * c0 - c2sqr))
        + 16 * c0 * (c2sqr * (c2sqr - 8 * c0) + 16 * c0sqr);
    Rational a0 = 12 * c0 + c2sqr;
    Rational a1 = 4 * c0 - c2sqr;


    // Correct classification of the sign of delta.
    if (delta > 0)
    {
        if (c2 < 0 && a1 < 0)
        {
            // Four simple real roots.
            map<Real,int> rmCubicMap;
            SolveCubic(c1sqr-4*c0*c2,8*c0,4*c2,-8,rmCubicMap);
            Rational t = (Rational)GetMaxRoot(rmCubicMap);
            Rational alphaSqr = 2 * t - c2;
            Rational alpha = (Rational)sqrt((Real)alphaSqr);
            Real sgnC1 = (c1 > 0 ? 1 : -1);
            Rational arg = t * t - c0;
            Rational beta = (Rational)(sgnC1 * sqrt(max((Real)arg, 0)));
            Rational D0 = alphaSqr - 4 * (t + beta);
            Rational sqrtD0 = (Rational)sqrt(max((Real)D0, 0));
            Rational D1 = alphaSqr - 4 * (t - beta);
            Rational sqrtD1 = (Rational)sqrt(max((Real)D1, 0));
            Rational r0 = (+alpha - sqrtD0) / 2;
            Rational r1 = (+alpha + sqrtD0) / 2;
            Rational r2 = (-alpha - sqrtD1) / 2;
            Rational r3 = (-alpha + sqrtD1) / 2;
            rmMap.insert(make_pair(r0, 1));
            rmMap.insert(make_pair(r1, 1));
            rmMap.insert(make_pair(r2, 1));
            rmMap.insert(make_pair(r3, 1));
        }
        else // c2 >= 0 or a1 >= 0
        {
            // Two complex-conjugate pairs. The values alpha, D0 and
            // D1 are those of the if-block.
            // Complex z0 = (alpha - i*sqrt(-D0))/2;
            // Complex z0conj = (alpha + i*sqrt(-D0))/2;
            // Complex z1 = (-alpha - i*sqrt(-D1))/2;
            // Complex z1conj = (-alpha + i*sqrt(-D1))/2;
        }
    }
```

```
else  if  (delta < 0)
{
      // Two simple real roots, one complex-conjugate pair.
      map<Real , int> rmCubicMap;
      SolveCubic(c1sqr−4∗c0∗c2,8∗c0,4∗c2,−8,rmCubicMap);
      Rational  t = (Rational)GetMaxRoot(rmCubicMap);
      Rational  alphaSqr = 2 ∗ t − c2;
      Rational  alpha = (Rational)sqrt((Real)alphaSqr);
      Real  sgnC1 = (c1 > 0 ? 1 :  −1);
      Rational  arg = t ∗ t − c0;
      Rational  beta = (Rational)(sgnC1 ∗ sqrt(max((Real)arg , 0)));
      Rational  r0 , r1;
      if  (sgnC1 > 0.0)
      {
            Rational  D1 = alphaSqr − 4 ∗ (t − beta);
            Rational  sqrtD1 = (Rational)sqrt(max((Real)D1, 0));
            r0 = (−alpha − sqrtD1) / 2;
            r1 = (−alpha + sqrtD1) / 2;

            // One complex conjugate pair.
            // Complex z0 = (alpha - i*sqrt(-D0))/2;
            // Complex z0conj = (alpha + i*sqrt(-D0))/2;
      }
      else
      {
            Rational  D0 = alphaSqr − 4 ∗ (t + beta);
            Rational  sqrtD0 = (Rational)sqrt(max((Real)D0, 0));
            r0 = (+alpha − sqrtD0) / 2;
            r1 = (+alpha + sqrtD0) / 2;

            // One complex conjugate pair.
            // Complex z0 = (-alpha - i*sqrt(-D1))/2;
            // Complex z0conj = (-alpha + i*sqrt(-D1))/2;
      }
      rmMap.insert(make_pair(r0 , 1));
      rmMap.insert(make_pair(r1 , 1));
}
else    // delta = 0
{
      if  (a1 > 0 ||  (c2 > 0 && (a1 != 0 ||  c1 != 0)))
      {
            // One double real root, one complex-conjugate pair.
            Rational  r0 = −c1 ∗ a0 / (9 ∗ c1sqr − 2 ∗ c2 ∗ a1);
            rmMap.insert(make_pair(r0 , 2));

            // One complex conjugate pair.
            // Complex z0 = -root0 - i*sqrt(c2 + root0*root0);
            // Complex z0conj = -root0 + i*sqrt(c2 + root0*root0);
      }
      else
      {
            if  (a0 != 0)
            {
                  // One double real root, two simple real roots.
                  Rational  r0 = −c1 ∗ a0 / (9 ∗ c1sqr − 2 ∗ c2 ∗ a1);
                  Rational  alpha = 2 ∗ r0;
                  Rational  beta = c2 + 3 ∗ r0 ∗ r0;
                  Rational  discr = alpha ∗ alpha − 4 ∗ beta;
                  Rational  temp1 = (Rational)sqrt((Real)discr);
                  Rational  r1 = (−alpha − temp1) / 2;
                  Rational  r2 = (−alpha + temp1) / 2;
                  rmMap.insert(make_pair(r0 , 2));
                  rmMap.insert(make_pair(r1 , 1));
                  rmMap.insert(make_pair(r2 , 1));
            }
```

```
            else
            {
                    // One triple real root, one simple real root.
                    Rational r0 = -3 * c1 / (4 * c2);
                    Rational r1 = -3 * r0;
                    rmMap.insert(make_pair(r0, 3));
                    rmMap.insert(make_pair(r1, 1));
            }
        }
    }
}

void SolveBiquadratic(Rational const& c0, Rational const& c2,
    map<Rational, int>& rmMap)
{
```

// Solve $0 = x^4 + c_2 x^2 + c_0 = (x^2 + c_2/2)^2 + a_1$, where $a_1 = c_0 - c_2^2/2$. We know
// that $c_0 \neq 0$ at the time of the function call, so $x = 0$ is not a root. The condition
// $c_1 = 0$ implies the quartic $\Delta = 256 c_0 a_1^2$.

```
    Rational c2Half = c2 / 2;
    Rational a1 = c0 - c2Half * c2Half;
    Rational delta = 256 * c0 * a1 * a1;
    if (delta > 0)
    {
        if (c2 < 0)
        {
            if (a1 < 0)
            {
                    // Four simple roots.
                    Rational temp0 = (Rational)sqrt(-(Real)a1);
                    Rational temp1 = -c2Half - temp0;
                    Rational temp2 = -c2Half + temp0;
                    Rational r1 = (Rational)sqrt((Real)temp1);
                    Rational r0 = -r1;
                    Rational r2 = (Rational)sqrt((Real)temp2);
                    Rational r3 = -r2;
                    rmMap.insert(make_pair(r0, 1));
                    rmMap.insert(make_pair(r1, 1));
                    rmMap.insert(make_pair(r2, 1));
                    rmMap.insert(make_pair(r3, 1));
            }
            else   // a_1 > 0
            {
                    // Two simple complex conjugate pairs.
                    // double thetaDiv2 = atan2(sqrt(a1), -c2/2) / 2;
                    // double cs = cos(thetaDiv2), sn = sin(thetaDiv2);
                    // double length = pow(c0, 1/4);
                    // Complex z0 = length*(cs + i*sn);
                    // Complex z0conj = length*(cs - i*sn);
                    // Complex z1 = length*(-cs + i*sn);
                    // Complex z1conj = length*(-cs - i*sn);
            }
        }
        else   // c2 >= 0
        {
            // Two simple complex conjugate pairs.
            // Complex z0 = -i*sqrt(c2/2 - sqrt(-a1));
            // Complex z0conj = +i*sqrt(c2/2 - sqrt(-a1));
            // Complex z1 = -i*sqrt(c2/2 + sqrt(-a1));
            // Complex z1conj = +i*sqrt(c2/2 + sqrt(-a1));
        }
    }
    else if (delta < 0)
```

```
{
    // Two simple real roots.
    Rational temp0 = (Rational)sqrt(-(Real)a1);
    Rational temp1 = -c2Half + temp0;
    Rational r1 = (Rational)sqrt((Real)temp1);
    Rational r0 = -r1;
    rmMap.insert(make_pair(r0, 1));
    rmMap.insert(make_pair(r1, 1));

    // One complex conjugate pair.
    // Complex z0 = -i*sqrt(c2/2 + sqrt(-a1));
    // Complex z0conj = +i*sqrt(c2/2 + sqrt(-a1));
}
else    // delta = 0
{
    if (c2 < 0)
    {
        // Two double real roots.
        Rational r1 = (Rational)sqrt(-(Real)c2Half);
        Rational r0 = -r1;
        rmMap.insert(make_pair(r0, 2));
        rmMap.insert(make_pair(r1, 2));
    }
    else    // c2 > 0
    {
        // Two double complex conjugate pairs.
        // Complex z0 = -i*sqrt(c2/2); // multiplicity 2
        // Complex z0conj = +i*sqrt(c2/2); // multiplicity 2
    }
}
}
```

Listing 6.14: A mixed rational/floating-point implementation for estimating the real-valued roots of a quartic polynomial.

6.2.6 High-Degree Polynomials

The Abel–Ruffini theorem [31] states that for polynomials of degree 5 or larger with arbitrary real-valued coefficients, there are no closed-form solutions for the roots. Consequently, roots to such polynomials must be computed using iterative methods. The first step in the process is to compute *bounding intervals for the roots*, where each bounding interval contains a unique root. Bisection or Newton's method can then be used to estimate the root to a desired accuracy. A typical part of the process is *root counting*, which determines the number of roots on a specified interval. If there are multiple roots in the interval, the interval is subdivided to obtain subintervals, each containing a unique root.

The polynomial of degree n is $f(t) = \sum_{i=0}^{n} a_i t^n$, where $a_n \neq 0$. When computing, the assumption is that the coefficients are floating-point numbers. These can be converted exactly to rational numbers. The hope is that the root counting and root bounding can be implemented using arbitrary-precision arithmetic or quadratic-field arithmetic.

The roots can be any real number, so the unboundedness of $\mathbb{R}$ is problematic. A simple reduction for root counting and bounding is the following.

The root counting for $f(t)$ can be performed on the interval $[-1,1]$. Define $s = 1/t$ and $g(s) = s^n f(1/s) = \sum_{i=0}^{n} a_{n-i} s^i$. The roots of $f(t)$ for $|t| > 1$ are the reciprocal roots of $g(s)$ for $s \in (-1,1)$. It suffices to develop root counting and root bounding methods on $[-1,1]$.

Given an interval $[a,b]$ that bounds multiple roots, a simple algorithm for subdividing is to bisect to $[a,(a+b)/2]$ and $[(a+b)/2]$ and to apply the root counting algorithm to each subinterval. Repeat the bisection until the subinterval has a unique root. Naturally, subintervals with no roots need not be processed further.

For testing whether an interval with roots has at least one root with multiplicity 2 or larger, resultants can be used. If $f(t)$ is known to have a root $\bar{t}$ on $[a,b]$, that root has multiplicity 2 or larger when $f'(\bar{t}) = 0$. The resultant of $f(t)$ and $f'(t)$ can be computed. If it is zero, there is a real-valued root of multiplicity 2 or larger. The elimination steps obtained to compute the resultant can be analyzed to determine what are the corresponding repeated roots.

6.2.6.1 Bounding Root Sequences by Derivatives

A simple approach to the root-bounding problem is to partition $\mathbb{R}$ into intervals with the polynomial $f(t)$ monotone on each interval. If it can be determined where the derivative of the polynomial is zero, this set provides the partition. If d_i and d_{i+1} are consecutive values for which $f'(d_i) = f'(d_{i+1}) = 0$, then either $f'(t) > 0$ on (d_i, d_{i+1}) or $f'(t) < 0$ on (d_i, d_{i+1}). In either case, f has at most one root on the interval. The existence of this root is guaranteed by the condition $f(d_i)f(d_{i+1}) < 0$ or $f(d_i) = 0$ or $f(d_{i+1}) = 0$.

Solving $f'(t) = 0$ requires the same techniques as solving $f(t) = 0$. The difference is that $\text{degree}(f') = \text{degree}(f) - 1$. A recursive implementation is warranted for this problem; the base case is the constant polynomial that is either never zero or identically zero on the real line.

If $f'(t) \neq 0$ for $t \in (-\infty, d_0)$, it is possible that f has a root on the semi-infinite interval $(-\infty, d_0]$. Bisection does not help locate a root, because the interval is unbounded. However, it is possible to determine the largest finite interval that contains the roots of a polynomial. The construction relies on the concepts of *spectral radius* and *norm of a matrix* [15]. Given a square matrix A, the spectral radius, denoted $\rho(A)$, is the maximum of the absolute values of the eigenvalues for the matrix. A matrix norm of A, denoted $\|A\|$, is a scalar-valued function that must satisfy the five conditions: $\|A\| \geq 0$, $\|A\| = 0$ if and only if $A = 0$, $\|cA\| = |c|\|A\|$ for any scalar c, $\|A + B\| \leq \|A\| + \|B\|$ and $\|AB\| \leq \|A\|\|B\|$. The relationship between the spectral radius and any matrix norm is $\rho(A) \leq \|A\|$. Given $f(t) = \sum_{i=0}^{n} a_i t^i$, where $a_n = 1$, the companion matrix is

$$
A = \begin{bmatrix}
-a_{n-1} & -a_{n-2} & \cdots & -a_1 & -a_0 \\
1 & 0 & \cdots & 0 & 0 \\
0 & 1 & \cdots & 0 & 0 \\
\vdots & \vdots & \ddots & \vdots & \vdots \\
0 & 0 & \cdots & 1 & 0
\end{bmatrix} \tag{6.34}
$$

The characteristic polynomial is $f(t) = \det(A - tI)$, so the roots of f are the eigenvalues of A. The spectral norm therefore provides a bound for the roots. Because there are many matrix norms to choose from, there are many possible bounds. One such bound is Cauchy's bound,

$$
|t| \le \max\{|a_0|, 1 + |a_1|, \dots, 1 + |a_{n-1}|\} = 1 + \max\{|a_0|, \dots, |a_{n-1}|\} \tag{6.35}
$$

Another bound that can be obtained is the Carmichael and Mason bound,

$$
|t| \le \sqrt{1 + \sum_{i=0}^{n-1} |a_i|^2} \tag{6.36}
$$

If $a_0 \ne 0$, then $f(0) \ne 0$ and the roots of f are bounded away from zero. It is possible to construct lower bounds by using $g(t) = [t^n f(1/t)]/a_0$. The roots of $g(t)$ are the reciprocal roots of $f(t)$. Cauchy's bound applied to $g(t)$ and then taking reciprocals is

$$
|t| \ge \frac{|a_0|}{1 + \max\{1, |a_1|, \dots, |a_{n-1}|\}} \tag{6.37}
$$

The Carmichael and Mason bound is

$$
|t| \ge \frac{|a_0|}{\sqrt{1 + \sum_{i=0}^{n-1} |a_i|^2}} \tag{6.38}
$$

These bounds are used in the recursive call to determine where $f(t)$ is monotone. The polynomial can be factored $f(t) = t^p g(t)$, where $p \ge 0$ and g is a polynomial for which $g(0) \ne 0$. If $p = 0$, then $f = g$ and f is processed for $0 < a \le |t| \le b$, where a and b are bounds computed from the previously mentioned inequalities. If $p > 0$, then g is processed on the intervals obtained by using the bounds from the same inequalities. Other types of root bounds are found at [37].

6.2.6.2 Bounding Roots by Sturm Sequences

The classical approach to root bounding uses Sturm's theorem [43]. Consider a polynomial $f(t)$ defined on the interval $[a, b]$. A Sturm sequence for f is a set of polynomials $f_i(t)$, $0 \le i \le m$, such that $\text{degree}(f_{i+1}) > \text{degree}(f_i)$

TABLE 6.2: Signs of the Sturm polynomials for $t^3 + 3t^2 - 1$.

t	Sign $f_0(t)$	Sign $f_1(t)$	Sign $f_2(t)$	Sign $f_3(t)$	Sign Changes
$-\infty$	-	+	-	+	3
-3	-	+	-	+	3
-2	+	0	-	+	2
-1	+	-	-	+	2
0	-	0	+	+	1
+1	+	+	+	+	0
$+\infty$	+	+	+	+	0

TABLE 6.3: Signs of the Sturm polynomials for $(t-1)^3$ at various t-values.

t	Sign $f_0(t)$	Sign $f_1(t)$	Sign $f_2(t)$	Sign Changes
$-\infty$	-	+	0	1
0	-	+	0	1
$+\infty$	+	+	0	0

and the number of distinct real roots for f in $(a, b]$ is $N(a, b) = s(a) - s(b)$, where $s(a)$ is the number of sign changes of $f_0(a), \ldots, f_m(a)$ and $s(b)$ is the number of sign changes of $f_1(b), \ldots, f_m(b)$. The total number of real-valued roots of f on $\mathbb{R}$ is $s(-\infty) - s(\infty)$. It is not always the case that $m = \text{degree}(f)$.

The classic Sturm sequence is $f_0(t) = f(t)$, $f_1(t) = f'(t)$ and $f_i(t) = -\text{remainder}(f_{i-2}/f_{i-1})$ for $i \geq 2$. The polynomials are generated by this method until the remainder term is a constant. The remainder is computed using Euclidean division. As an example, consider $f(t) = t^3 + 3t^2 - 1$. The Sturm sequence is $f_0(t) = t^3 + 3t^2 - 1$, $f_1(t) = 3t^2 + 6t$, $f_2(t) = 2t + 1$ and $f_3 = 9/4$. Table 6.2 lists the signs of the Sturm polynomials for various t-values and shows that $N(-\infty, -3) = 0$, $N(-3, -2) = 1$, $N(-2, -1) = 0$, $N(-1, 0) = 1$, $N(0, 1) = 1$ and $N(1, \infty) = 0$. Moreover, the number of negative real roots is $N(-\infty, 0) = 2$, the number of positive real roots is $N(0, \infty) = 1$ and the total number of real roots is $N(-\infty, \infty) = 3$.

The next example shows that the number of polynomials in the Sturm sequence is not necessarily $\text{degree}(f) + 1$. The function $f(t) = (t-1)^3$ has a Sturm sequence $f_0(t) = (t-1)^3$, $f_1(t) = 3(t-1)^2$ and $f_2(t) \equiv 0$ because f_1 exactly divides f_0 with no remainder. Table 6.3 lists sign changes for f at various t-values. The total number of real roots is $N(-\infty, \infty) = 1$.

The Wikipedia article for Sturm's theorem [43] points out that in the computer algebra of polynomials with integer coefficients, the Sturm polynomials will have rational coefficients. To avoid rational arithmetic, the article suggests using a pseudodivision for computing the polynomial greatest common divisors.

6.2.6.3   Root Counting by Descartes' Rule of Signs

The approach with Sturm's theorem is considered to be inefficient given the capabilities of current computer CPUs. Instead, Descarte's rule of signs is recommended [34].

Given a polynomial $f(t)$ with terms ordered by decreasing power, the number of positive roots is either equal to the number of sign changes between consecutive nonzero coefficients or is less than that number by an even number. The reduction by an even number accounts for non-real roots that occur as pairs of complex conjugates. A root of multiplicity k is counted as k roots. The number of negative roots of $f(t)$ is the number of positive roots of $f(-t)$.

Let $f(t)$ have degree d. The fundamental theorem of algebra states that the number of roots in the complex plane is d, where a root of multiplicity k is counted as k roots. A root $t = 0$ is easily detected when the constant term is a_0. The polynomial factors as $f(t) = t^k g(t)$, where k is the multiplicity of root 0 and where $g(0) \neq 0$. In this situation, $g(t)$ has degree $d - k$ and that same number of roots in the complex plane. When $f(0) \neq 0$, the minimum number of nonreal roots is $d - (p + n)$ where p is the maximum number of positive roots and n is the maximum number of negative roots.

6.2.6.4   Real-Root Isolation

Generalizations and more recent results for root counting and root bounding are found at [42].

Budan's theorem generalizes Descartes' rule of signs to apply to a polynomial on a specified interval $(a, b]$ rather than the entire set of real numbers.

Vincent's theorem is a real-root-isolation method that is based on the concept of continued fractions. Extensions of the ideas are theorems by Obreschkoff and Ostrowski and by Uspensky.

Bisection algorithms to find bounding intervals are also discussed, including one by Akritas and Collins.

References to the research literature are provided at the Wikipedia page. Pseudocode is provided for some of the algorithms. C++ implementations are somewhat tedious to write. For applications with small degree polynomials, it might very well be simple enough to implement the derivative sequence algorithm or Sturm sequences with rational arithmetic. Bisection of intervals can be used to isolate the real-valued roots. For a general-purpose commercial numerical-symbolic package, the efficiency of the more sophisticated algorithms is required.

6.3 Linear Algebra

In this section, several standard problems in linear algebra are discussed in the context of arbitrary-precision arithmetic.

6.3.1 Systems of Linear Equations

At first glance, solving systems of linear equations $A\mathbf{x} = \mathbf{b}$ using Gaussian elimination is an ideal type of problem for using arbitrary-precision arithmetic to obtain exact solutions. As it turns out, this is not the case when A and $\mathbf{b}$ have a large number of elements. The issue at hand is the amount of time it takes to compute products of two numbers that have a large number of bits.

Listing 6.15 contains an example that shows how long the computation times are for solving linear systems of sizes 6 through 10. The Gaussian elimination implementation is single threaded.

```
void SolveLinearSystem ()
{
    bool success;
    Timer timer;
    int64_t msec;

    Matrix <6, 6, BSR> A6;
    Vector <6, BSR> B6, X6;
    GenerateRandomSystem (A6, B6);
    timer.Reset ();
    success = LinearSystem<BSR>::Solve (6, &A6[0], &B6[0], &X6[0]);
    msec = timer.GetMilliseconds ();
    // 27 milliseconds

    Matrix <7, 7, BSR> A7;
    Vector <7, BSR> B7, X7;
    GenerateRandomSystem (A7, B7);
    timer.Reset ();
    success = LinearSystem<BSR>::Solve (7, &A7[0], &B7[0], &X7[0]);
    msec = timer.GetMilliseconds ();
    // 616 milliseconds

    Matrix <8, 8, BSR> A8;
    Vector <8, BSR> B8, X8;
    GenerateRandomSystem (A8, B8);
    timer.Reset ();
    success = LinearSystem<BSR>::Solve (8, &A8[0], &B8[0], &X8[0]);
    msec = timer.GetMilliseconds ();
    // 14435 milliseconds

    Matrix <9, 9, BSR> A9;
    Vector <9, BSR> B9, X9;
    GenerateRandomSystem (A9, B9);
    timer.Reset ();
    success = LinearSystem<BSR>::Solve (9, &A9[0], &B9[0], &X9[0]);
    msec = timer.GetMilliseconds ();
    // 2624676 milliseconds

    Matrix <10, 10, BSR> A10;
    Vector <10, BSR> B10, X10;
    GenerateRandomSystem (A10, B10);
```

```
    timer.Reset();
    success = LinearSystem<BSR>::Solve(10, &A10[0], &B10[0], &X10[0]);
    msec = timer.GetMilliseconds();
    // 6069147 milliseconds, approximately 1.7 hours
}
```

Listing 6.15: Code for solving linear systems using arbitrary-precision arithmetic with single-threaded Gaussian elimination. The test program was executed on an Intel® Core™i7-6700 CPU at 3.40GHz.

The 10×10 case makes it clear that the performance is unacceptable for large systems. To obtain some improvement in performance, the Gaussian elimination can be implemented to use multithreading, presumably one thread per row-elimination step. If an implementation of multiplication is available that uses fast Fourier transforms [16, Chapter 4.3], the performance can be improved; otherwise, the practical approach is to use arbitrary-precision arithmetic with a user-specified precision applied at various times in the computations.

Alternatively, an iterative algorithm can be used to compute an estimate to the solution. For example, the Gauss-Seidel method is a splitting method where $A = L + D + U$ with L the lower-triangular entries of A, U the upper-triangular entries of A and D the diagonal entries of A. The linear system is written as $(L + D)\mathbf{x} = \mathbf{b} - U\mathbf{x}$. The iteration scheme is

$$\mathbf{x}^{(k+1)} = (L + D)^{-1} \left(\mathbf{b} - U\mathbf{x}^{(k)} \right), \ k \geq 0 \qquad (6.39)$$

for an initial guess $\mathbf{x}^{(0)}$. The matrix $L + D$ is not inverted explicitly; rather, it is computed by forward elimination. The iterative scheme is the following and specifies the components i of the current iterate,

$$\mathbf{x}_i^{(k+1)} = \frac{1}{a_{ii}} \left(b_i - \sum_{j>i} a_{ij} x_j^{(k)} - \sum_{j<i} a_{ij} x_j^{(k+1)}, \right), \ 0 \leq i < n \qquad (6.40)$$

The method might or might not converge. It does converge for matrices that are strictly diagonally dominant; that is, $|a_{ii}| > \sum_{j \neq i} |a_{ij}|$. There are other classes of matrices for which convergence is guaranteed. Listing 6.16 contains an example of using the Gauss-Seidel method with arbitrary-precision arithmetic.

```
void SolveLinearSystemGaussSeidel()
{
    int const size = 10;
    Matrix<size, size, BSR> A;
    Vector<size, BSR> B, X0, X1;
    GenerateRandomStrictlyDiagonallyDominant(A, B);

    // Estimate a solution using Gauss-Seidel iteration.
    Timer timer;
    X0.MakeZero();
    int const maxIterations = 8;
    for (int k = 0; k < maxIterations; ++k)
```

```
{
    for (int i = 0; i < size; ++i)
    {
        X1[i] = B[i];
        for (int j = 0; j < i; ++j)
        {
            X1[i] -= A(i, j) * X0[j];
        }
        for (int j = i + 1; j < size; ++j)
        {
            X1[i] -= A(i, j) * X1[j];
        }
        X1[i] /= A(i, i);
    }
    std::swap(X0, X1);
}
int64_t msec = timer.GetMilliseconds();
// 27251 milliseconds

// Compute the residual to determine error.
timer.Reset();
Vector<size, BSR> residual = A * X0 - B;
msec = timer.GetMilliseconds();
// 2174110 milliseconds, approximately 37 minutes

// Compute the maximum component error.
timer.Reset();
BSR maxError(0);
for (int r = 0; r < size; ++r)
{
    BSR rabs = std::fabs(residual[r]);
    if (rabs > maxError)
    {
        maxError = rabs;
    }
}
msec = timer.GetMilliseconds();
// 2956458 milliseconds, approximately 50 minutes
// maxError = 0.0000733768
}
```

Listing 6.16: Code for estimating the solution to a linear system using the Gauss-Seidel method with arbitrary-precision arithmetic. The test program was executed on an Intel® Core™ i7-6700 CPU at 3.40GHz.

Even using an iterative method, the number of bits increases significantly to make the performance unacceptable. Intuitively, there is no reason to have a full-precision result for iterates that are not yet near the true solution.

In the GTL, BSRational is implemented so that the arithmetic operations use full precision. It is possible to implement a templated class for which one of the template parameters is the integer-valued precision. The arithmetic can be written to perform rounding after each operation, making the class represent a fixed-precision floating-point arithmetic system. However, the geometric and numeric algorithms themselves might benefit by not forcing such a restriction. For example, the expression $x * y + z$, when computed using two floating-point operations, has two sources of rounding errors. The first rounding error occurs in the product $x * y$. The second rounding error occurs in the sum $(x * y) + z$. Current floating-point hardware supports a *fused multiply-add* instruction that computes $x * y + z$ and guarantees that (using the current rounding mode) the result is the floating-point number closest to the theoretical result. The same instruction can be emulated using BSRational by computing $x*y+z$ using the full precision (exact result) and then converting to a p-bit precision number using the Convert function. Instead, the programmer can analyze the algorithm at hand to determine where the computations are sensitive to rounding errors, use full precision in those places where there is sensitivity and round to p-bit precision in those places where there is not. Listing 6.17 provides an example of this approach for the Gauss-Seidel example of Listing 6.16.

```
void SolveLinearSystemGaussSeidelFixedPrecision ()
{
    int const size = 10;
    Matrix<size, size, BSR> A;
    Vector<size, BSR> B, X0, X1;
    GenerateRandomStrictlyDiagonallyDominant(A, B);

    // Estimate a solution using Gauss-Seidel iteration. Use full precision for each iteration
    // but then round the components before the next iteration.
    int32_t const precision = 72;
    Timer timer;
    X0.MakeZero();
    int const maxIterations = 16;
    for (int k = 0; k < maxIterations; ++k)
    {
        for (int i = 0; i < size; ++i)
        {
            X1[i] = B[i];
            for (int j = 0; j < i; ++j)
            {
                X1[i] -= A(i, j) * X0[j];
            }
            for (int j = i + 1; j < size; ++j)
            {
                X1[i] -= A(i, j) * X1[j];
            }
            X1[i] /= A(i, i);
        }
        BSN numerator;
        for (int i = 0; i < size; ++i)
        {
            Convert(X1[i], precision, FE_TONEAREST, numerator);
            X0[i] = BSR(numerator);
        }
        std::cout << "k = " << k << " done" << std::endl;
    }
    int64_t msec = timer.GetMilliseconds();
    // 15869 microseconds

    timer.Reset();
    Vector<size, BSR> residual = A * X0 - B;
    msec = timer.GetMilliseconds();
    // 147 microseconds

    timer.Reset();
    BSR maxError(0);
    for (int r = 0; r < size; ++r)
    {
        BSR rabs = std::fabs(residual[r]);
        if (rabs > maxError)
        {
            maxError = rabs;
        }
    }
```

```
msec = timer.GetMilliseconds();
// 6 microseconds
// maxError = 4.54488e-09
}
```

Listing 6.17: Code for estimating the solution to a linear system using the Gauss-Seidel method with arbitrary-precision arithmetic but with a user-specified precision of 72 bits. The test program was executed on an Intel® Core™i7-6700 CPU at 3.40GHz.

In the example of Listing 6.17, the number of iterations is 16 which is twice that of the full-precision approach of Listing 6.16. The maximum component error is much smaller when rounding to a user-specified precision. The most important aspect, though, is the greatly reduced computation time. Please note that the fixed-precision example times are in *microseconds*, whereas the full-precision example times are in *milliseconds*.

Other iterative algorithms in linear algebra can be solved using arbitrary-precision arithmetic with a user-specified precision. These include eigendecomposition and singular value decomposition. As this section shows, the user-specified precision is greatly desired to obtain speed rather than an exact result. For many applications, especially ones involving engineering in a physical system (for example, CAD-CAM), the exact results are neither necessary nor perhaps even physically meaningful.

6.3.2 Eigendecomposition for 2×2 Symmetric Matrices

Let A be a nonzero 2×2 symmetric matrix with rational elements. The eigenvalues of the matrix must be real-valued and are the roots to the characteristic polynomial

$$p(t) = \det(tI - A) = t^2 - (a_{00} + a_{11})t + (a_{00}a_{11} - a_{01}^2) = t^2 + p_1 t + p_0 \quad (6.41)$$

where the last equality defines the coefficients p_0 and p_1. The eigenvalues are $r = (-p_1 \pm \sqrt{p_1 - 4p_0})/2$, where $p_1 - 4p_0 \geq 0$. Eigenvectors are computed by solving $(rI - A)\mathbf{V} = \mathbf{0}$ for each distinct root r.

If $a_{01} = 0$, then $A = \text{Diag}(a_{00}, a_{11})$ and the eigenvalues are a_{00} and a_{11} with corresponding eigenvectors $(1,0)$ and $(0,1)$, respectively. All quantities are rational, so the eigendecomposition is exact.

Now assume $a_{01} \neq 0$. If the eigenvalues are distinct, each eigenvalue has an associated 1-dimensional eigenspace. If r is an eigenvalue, A has rank 1 and an eigenvector for the eigenvalue is a nonzero row of $rI - A$. The two candidates are $(r - a_{00}, -a_{01})$ and $(-a_{01}, r - a_{11})$. Each candidate must be examined to determine whether or not it is the zero vector. Consider the first row $\mathbf{V} = (r - a_{00}, -a_{01})$ that has squared length

$$|\mathbf{V}|^2 = r^2 - 2a_{00}r + (a_{00}^2 + a_{01}^2)^2 \quad (6.42)$$

For $|\mathbf{V}|^2 = 0$ and $p(t) = 0$ simultaneously, elimination theory leads to

$$b = -a_{01}^2((a_{00} - a_{11})^2 + 4a_{01}^2) = 0 \quad (6.43)$$

For b to be zero, either $a_{01} = 0$ or $(a_{00} - a_{11})^2 + 4a_{01}^2 = 0$ the latter condition also implying $a_{01} = 0$. The active assumption is that $a_{01} \neq 0$, so b cannot be zero and the two polynomials cannot be simultaneously zero at the root r. Therefore, $\mathbf{V}$ is not the zero vector.

The eigenvalues and eigenvectors have elements in the quadratic field $\mathbb{Q}(r)$. Any further computations in an algorithm that use the eigendecomposition can be computed using quadratic-field arithmetic. Estimates of the quadratic-field numbers, when needed, can be computed using the techniques of Section 5.5.3.

6.3.3   Eigendecomposition for 3×3 Symmetric Matrices

Let A be a nonzero 3×3 symmetric matrix with rational elements. The eigenvalues of the matrix must be real-valued and are the roots to the characteristic polynomial

$$
\begin{aligned}
p(t) \;=\; & \det(tI - A) \\
=\; & t^3 - (a_{00} + a_{11} + a_{22})t^2 \\
& + ((a_{00}a_{11} - a_{01}^2) + (a_{00}a_{22} - a_{02}^2) + (a_{11}a_{22} - a_{11}^2))t \qquad (6.44) \\
& - (a_{00}a_{11}a_{22} + 2a_{01}a_{02}a_{12} - a_{00}a_{12}^2 - a_{01}^2 a_{22} - a_{02}^2 a_{11}) \\
=\; & t^3 + p_2 t^2 + p_1 t + p_0
\end{aligned}
$$

where the last equality defines the coefficients p_0, p_1 and p_2. The polynomial has three real-valued roots, not necessarily distinct. Eigenvectors are computed by solving $(rI - A)\mathbf{V} = \mathbf{0}$ for each distinct root r. An analysis of the rows of $rI - A$ is used to compute eigenvectors. The computations are symbolic in the sense that they use algebraic numbers that are roots to polynomials with rational coefficients. Modular operations of polynomials and elimination theory are used to compute eigenvectors corresponding to the eigenvalues. After all symbolic computations are completed, the eigenvalues are estimated—as roots to a polynomial—and the values are used to estimate the components of the eigenvectors.

A zero-valued row of $rI - A$ is easy to detect. The two entries of the row that do not contain r must be zero: $(r - a_{00}, 0, 0)$, $(0, r - a_{11}, 0)$ or $(0, 0, r - a_{22})$. The eigenvector construction is effectively the same as for the 2×2 matrices. For example, if the last row is $(0, 0, r - a_{22})$, for it to be zero it is necessary that $r = a_{22}$ with a corresponding eigenvector of $(0, 0, 1)$. The matrix A is block diagonal with upper-left 2×2 block and lower-right 1×1 block. The 2×2 block is processed as in the 2-dimensional case of the previous section. From this point on, assume that $rI - A$ has no zero-valued rows.

If A has three distinct eigenvalues, then $tI - A$ has rank 2 for each eigenvalue r. The goal is to determine two rows that are linearly independent. The cross product of those rows is an eigenvector corresponding to r. There are three pairs of rows to process. The first two rows are $(t - a_{00}, -a_{01}, -a_{02})$ and

$(-a_{01}, r - a_{11}, -a_{12})$ and have cross product $\mathbf{V} = (v_0, v_1, v_2)$ where

$$
\begin{aligned}
v_0 &= (a_{01}a_{12} - a_{02}a_{11}) + a_{02}t \\
v_1 &= (a_{01}a_{02} - a_{00}a_{12}) + a_{12}t \\
v_2 &= (a_{00}a_{11} - a_{01}^2) - (a_{00} + a_{11})t + t^2
\end{aligned}
\tag{6.45}
$$

If the first two rows are linearly dependent, then $0 = |\mathbf{V}|^2 = q_0 + q_1 t + q_2 t^2 + q_3 t^3 + t^4 = q(t)$, where the last equality defines the polynomial $q(t)$ and the q_i depend only on the elements of A. The value t is a root of $p(t)$, so it is also known that $p_0 + p_1 t + p_2 t^2 + t^3 = 0$. Using elimination theory, the equation $q(t)$ can be reduced modulo $p(t)$,

$$
\begin{aligned}
0 &= q(t) - (q_3 - p_2 - t)p(t) \\
&= (p_0(p_2 - q_3) + q_0) + (p_1(p_2 - q_3) + (q_1 - p_0))t \\
&\quad + (p_2(p_2 - q_3) + (q_2 - p_1))t^2 \\
&= f_0 + f_1 t + f_2 t^2 \\
&= f(t)
\end{aligned}
\tag{6.46}
$$

where the last two equalities define the quadratic polynomial $r(t)$. The equations $p(t) = 0$ and $f(t) = 0$ can be used to eliminate another power of t,

$$
\begin{aligned}
0 &= f_2^2 p(t) - (p_2 f_2 - f_1 + f_2 t)f(t) \\
&= (f_2(p_0 f_2 - p_2 f_0) + f_0 f_1) + (f_2(p_1 f_2 - p_2 f_1) + (f_1^2 - f_0 f_2))t \\
&= g_0 + g_1 t \\
&= g(t)
\end{aligned}
\tag{6.47}
$$

where the last two equalities define the linear polynomial $g(t)$. The equations $f(t) = 0$ and $g(t) = 0$ can be used to eliminate another power of t, thereby producing a constant,

$$
\begin{aligned}
0 &= g_1^2 f(t) - (f_1 g_1 - f_2 g_0 + f_2 g_1 t)g(t) \\
&= f_2 g_0^2 - f_1 g_0 g_1 + f_0 g_1^2
\end{aligned}
\tag{6.48}
$$

If this constant is not zero, then $p(t)$ and $q(t)$ have no roots in common, in which case $|\mathbf{V}|^2 > 0$ and $\mathbf{V}$ is an eigenvector. But if the constant is zero, $p(t)$ and $q(t)$ have a root in common. That root is the solution to $g(t) = 0$, namely, $t = -g_0/g_1$. Regardless, $\mathbf{V} = \mathbf{0}$, so another pair of rows must be tested for linear independence. Of the three possible pairs, one pair must be linearly independent, in which case the cross product is an eigenvector.

If $tI - A$ has an eigenvalue of multiplicity 2, the rank is 1 and only one row of the matrix is linearly independent. Choose the first row $(t - a_{00}, -a_{01}, -a_{02})$, which is not zero by the active assumption for this section. If $a_{01} \neq 0$ or $a_{02} \neq 0$, one vector perpendicular to the row is $(0, a_{02}, -a_{01})$. Another vector perpendicular to the row is obtained by a cross product

$$
\begin{aligned}
&(t - a_{00}, -a_{01}, -a_{02}) \times (0, a_{02}, -a_{01}) \\
&= (a_{01}^2 + a_{02}^2, a_{01}(t - a_{00}), a_{02}(t - a_{00}))
\end{aligned}
\tag{6.49}
$$

If $a_{01} = a_{02} = 0$, the active assumption of the nonzero row implies $t - a_{00} \neq 0$. Two perpendicular vectors are $(0, 1, 0)$ and $(0, 0, 1)$.

If $tI - A$ has an eigenvalue of multiplicity 3, A is diagonal. This case will be found when searching for a row of zeros. Alternatively, it is simple enough to test that $a_{01} = a_{02} = a_{12} = 0$.

In practice, the ranks of $tI - A$ are not known ahead of time for each eigenvalue t. The $p(t) = \det(tI - A)$ has rational coefficients, so the exact classification of root multiplicities of Section 6.2.4 can be used to determine the ranks. However, it is not possible to assign these ranks to a symbolic selection of a root. Instead, pairs of rows are tested for linear independence. If there is a pair, the rank of $tI - A$ is 2. If there is not a pair, the rank of $tI - A$ is 1.

6.3.4   3D Rotation Matrices with Rational Elements

A 3×3 rotation matrix is $[\mathbf{U}_0\ \mathbf{U}_1\ \mathbf{U}_2]$, where the columns form a right-handed orthonormal basis; that is, $|\mathbf{U}_i| = 1$ for all i, $\mathbf{U}_i \cdot \mathbf{U}_j = 0$ for all $i \neq j$ and $\mathbf{U}_i = \mathbf{U}_j \times \mathbf{U}_k$ where (i, j, k) is a cyclic permutation of $(0, 1, 2)$.

The vectors might have been computed using floating-point arithmetic; call these vectors $\mathbf{V}_i$ for $i \in \{0, 1, 2\}$. Rounding errors can destroy the orthonormal-basis condition. Treating the $\mathbf{V}_i$ as 3-tuples of rational numbers, it might be that $|\mathbf{V}| \neq 1$ for one or more i-values. It is also possible that $\mathbf{V}_i \cdot \mathbf{V}_j \neq 0$ for one or more pairs (i, j) with $i \neq j$. Finally, it is possible that $\mathbf{V}_i \neq \mathbf{V}_j \times \mathbf{k}$ for one or more triples (i, j, k) where (i, j, k) is a cyclic permutation of $(0, 1, 2)$.

An orthogonal basis $\{\mathbf{V}_0, \mathbf{V}_1, \mathbf{V}_2\}$ can be computed from the theoretical directions $\mathbf{U}_i$ using rational arithmetic and projections,

$$
\begin{aligned}
\mathbf{V}_0 &= \mathbf{U}_0 \\
\mathbf{V}_1 &= \mathbf{U}_1 - \left(\mathbf{U}_1 \cdot \mathbf{U}_0 / |\mathbf{U}_0|^2\right) \mathbf{U}_0 \\
\mathbf{V}_2 &= \mathbf{V}_0 \times \mathbf{V}_1
\end{aligned}
\tag{6.50}
$$

This approach is a mathematical approximation in the sense that $\mathbf{V}_1$ generally is not parallel to $\mathbf{U}_1$ and $\mathbf{V}_2$ generally is not parallel to $\mathbf{U}_2$. Consequently, an application that requires a numerically computed orthonormal basis—created using the projection approach—will not be exact; for example, see Section 8.4.1 for the test-intersection query of a line and an oriented box.

It is possible to finesse this problem by representing the $\mathbf{U}$-basis as a quaternion that is not necessarily unit length. A unit-length quaternion $q = w_0 + x_0 i + y_0 j + z_0 k$ represents a rotation matrix R that acts on vectors as $R\mathbf{V}$. The matrix is

$$
R = \begin{bmatrix}
w_0^2 + x_0^2 - y_0^2 - z_0^2 & 2(x_0 y_0 - w_0 z_0) & 2(x_0 z_0 + w_0 y_0) \\
2(x_0 y_0 + w_0 z_0) & w_0^2 - x_0^2 + y_0^2 - z_0^2 & 2(y_0 z_0 - w_0 x_0) \\
2(x_0 z_0 - w_0 y_0) & 2(y_0 z_0 + w_0 x_0) & w_0^2 - x_0^2 - y_0^2 + z_0^2
\end{bmatrix}
\tag{6.51}
$$

All product terms involve two quaternion coefficients, which suggests that a non-unit-length quaternion can also be used. If $p = w_1 + x_1 i + y_1 j + z_1 k$ is such a quaternion, then $q = p/\sqrt{w_1^2 + x_1^2 + y_1^2 + z_1^2}$ is a unit-length quaternion. Substituting q into equation (6.51) leads to

$$R = \frac{\begin{bmatrix} w_1^2 + x_1^2 - y_1^2 - z_1^2 & 2(x_1 y_1 - w_1 z_1) & 2(x_1 z_1 + w_1 y_1) \\ 2(x_1 y_1 + w_1 z_1) & w_1^2 - x_1^2 + y_1^2 - z_1^2 & 2(y_1 z_1 - w_1 x_1) \\ 2(x_1 z_1 - w_1 y_1) & 2(y_1 z_1 + w_1 x_1) & w_1^2 - x_1^2 - y_1^2 + z_1^2 \end{bmatrix}}{w_1^2 + x_1^2 + y_1^2 + z_1^2} \tag{6.52}$$

The matrix depending on p clearly has only rational elements when the coefficients of p are rational. For example, if $p = 1i + 2j + 3k + 4$, then

$$R = \frac{1}{30} \begin{bmatrix} 4 & -20 & 22 \\ 28 & 10 & 4 \\ -10 & 20 & 20 \end{bmatrix} \tag{6.53}$$

It is easily verified that $R^\mathsf{T} R = R R^\mathsf{T} = I$ and $\det(R) = 1$, which implies R is a rotation matrix.

The idea of using rational-coefficient quaternions is also useful for exact multiplication of rotation matrices and for exact multiplication of a rotation matrix and a vector. Let q_0 and q_1 be unit-length quaternions that correspond to rotation matrices R_0 and R_1. The quaternion product $q_0 q_1$ corresponds to the rotation matrix product $R_0 R_1$. Now if p_0 and p_1 are quaternions with rational coefficients, are not necessarily unit length and $q_i = p_i/|p_i|$, then $R_0 R_1$ is obtained from $p_0 p_1$ using equation (6.52).

The matrix-vector product of a rotation matrix R and a vector $\mathbf{V} = (v_0, v_1, v_2)$ is $(u_0, u_1, u_2) = \mathbf{U} = R\mathbf{V}$, where the vectors are considered to be 3×1 vectors even though their components are displayed as 3-tuples. If q is a unit-length quaternion corresponding to R, $v = v_0 i + v_1 j + v_2 k$ and $u = u_0 i + u_1 j + u_2 k$, then the matrix-vector product is generated by the quaternion product $u = qvq^*$, where q^* is the conjugate of q. Now if p is a quaternion with rational coefficients, not necessarily unit length and $q = p/|p|$, then $u = (pvp^*)/|p|^2$.

The previous two paragraphs show that rigid motions (rotation and translation) can be computed exactly using rational-coefficient quaternions. Keep in mind that the quaternions themselves might be generated in a simulation that introduces rounding errors. However, any geometric query that supports computing an exact result can use the current rational-coefficient quaternions, but the exact result will be an approximation because of the inherent rounding errors in producing the input quaternions.

Chapter 7

Distance Queries

Algorithms for computing the distance between pairs of standard geometric objects are relatively straightforward to derive mathematically. However, when computing with floating-point arithmetic, parallelism (or near parallelism) of object features can lead to incorrect determination of a pair of points (one per object) that produces the distance between the objects.

This section describes a class of distance algorithms that are based on convex quadratic programming, where the squared distance is a convex quadratic function of parameters used in defining the geometric objects. Convex quadratic programming (CCP) problems can be formulated as linear complementarity problems (LCP) which are an extension of linear programming. The LCP solver is iterative, but it is guaranteed to terminate in a finite number of iterations. The solver is implemented using arbitrary-precision arithmetic to produce exact results.

Several examples for reducing a distance query to an LCP are provided, but a large number of common queries can be reduced using the same process.

7.1 Introduction

This section briefly describes the quadratic programming (QP) problem, a minimization of a quadratic polynomial on a domain defined by linear inequality constraints. The focus is on the convex quadratic programming (CQP) problem, where the matrix of the quadratic polynomial is positive semidefinite. Many geometric algorithms can be formulated as CQPs. A CQP is converted to a linear complementarity problem (LCP) that can be solved using Lemke's Method. The most authoritative book on LCP is [6].

The general framework for QP is presented first, showing how to convert a QP to an LCP. Lemke's method is presented together with several illustrative examples. An implementation for solving an LCP is discussed with attention given to accuracy of the results when using floating-point arithmetic. The LCP solver uses only addition, subtraction, multiplication and division, so assuming the inputs are finite floating-point numbers, such numbers are rational and the solver can use arbitrary-precision floating-point arithmetic to produce exact results.

Some CQPs involve geometric primitives whose parameterizations use unit-length vectors. If these vectors are computed using fixed-precision floating-point arithmetic, numerical rounding errors lead to vectors that are not unit length when interpreted as exact rational inputs. In this situation, the LCP solver will not produce the correct theoretical result that is based on real-valued arithmetic. In many cases, however, quadratic-field arithmetic can be used to solve the LCP exactly. If a distance query is required within this framework, the distance itself is computed only at the very end of the algorithm by approximating the exact quadratic field result by a fixed-precision floating-point number.

For the sake of notation, the set of $n \times 1$ column vectors with real-valued entries is denoted $\mathbb{R}^n$. The set of $r \times c$ matrices with r rows, c columns and real-valued entries is denoted $\mathbb{R}^{r \times c}$.

7.1.1   The Quadratic Programming Problem

Quadratic programming (QP) is concisely stated as follows. Given constants $A \in \mathbb{R}^{n \times n}$, $\mathbf{b} \in \mathbb{R}^n$, $c \in \mathbb{R}$, $D \in \mathbb{R}^{m \times n}$, $\mathbf{e} \in \mathbb{R}^m$ and variable $\mathbf{x} \in \mathbb{R}^n$, minimize $f(\mathbf{x}) = \frac{1}{2}\mathbf{x}^\mathsf{T} A \mathbf{x} + \mathbf{b}^\mathsf{T}\mathbf{x} + c$ subject to the linear inequality constraints $\mathbf{x} \geq \mathbf{0}$ and $D\mathbf{x} \geq \mathbf{e}$. The number of linear inequality constraints is $n + m$.

The linear inequalities define an intersection of half spaces. The intersection can be empty, in which case the QP does not have a solution. For a nonempty intersection that is unbounded and with no additional constraints on A, it is possible the QP has no solution. If the nonempty intersection is a bounded set, that set is necessarily convex. The polynomial f is continuous and defined on a closed bounded set, which guarantees that f attains both a minimum and a maximum on the set.

If $\mathbf{x} \in \mathbb{R}^n$ is a local extremum of the QP, then there exists $\mathbf{y} \in \mathbb{R}^m$ such that $(\mathbf{x}, \mathbf{y})$ satisfies the Karesh-Kuhn-Tucker (KKT) conditions

$$\begin{aligned} \mathbf{u} = \mathbf{b} + A\mathbf{x} - D^\mathsf{T}\mathbf{y} \geq \mathbf{0}, \quad &\mathbf{x} \geq \mathbf{0}, \quad \mathbf{x}^\mathsf{T}\mathbf{u} = 0, \\ \mathbf{v} = -\mathbf{e} + D\mathbf{x} \geq \mathbf{0}, \quad &\mathbf{y} \geq \mathbf{0}, \quad \mathbf{y}^\mathsf{T}\mathbf{v} = 0 \end{aligned} \tag{7.1}$$

The KKT conditions are necessary for the existence of a local extremum. When A is positive semidefinite, the KKT conditions are also sufficient for the existence of a local extremum.

7.1.2   The Linear Complementarity Problem

The *linear complementarity problem (LCP)* is concisely stated as "Given constants $\mathbf{q} \in \mathbb{R}^k$ and $M \in \mathbb{R}^{k \times k}$, find $\mathbf{z} \in \mathbb{R}^k$ such that $\mathbf{z} \geq \mathbf{0}$, $\mathbf{q} + M\mathbf{z} \geq \mathbf{0}$ and $\mathbf{z}^\mathsf{T}(\mathbf{q} + M\mathbf{z}) = \mathbf{0}$. Define $\mathbf{w} = \mathbf{q} + M\mathbf{z}$. Choose $\mathbf{z} \geq \mathbf{0}$ such that $\mathbf{w} \geq \mathbf{0}$ and $\mathbf{z}^\mathsf{T}\mathbf{w} = 0$."

Lemke's method allows computing an LCP solution $\mathbf{z}$ if there exists one or to determine that there is no solution.

7.1.3 The Convex Quadratic Programming Problem

In quadratic programming, when A is positive semidefinite the problem is a *convex quadratic programming (CQP)* problem. The CQP can be converted to an LCP by defining

$$\mathbf{q} = \begin{bmatrix} \mathbf{b} \\ -\mathbf{e} \end{bmatrix}, \quad M = \begin{bmatrix} A & -D^\mathsf{T} \\ D & 0 \end{bmatrix}, \quad \mathbf{z} = \begin{bmatrix} \mathbf{x} \\ \mathbf{y} \end{bmatrix}, \quad \mathbf{w} = \begin{bmatrix} \mathbf{u} \\ \mathbf{v} \end{bmatrix} \tag{7.2}$$

where $k = n + m$. The variable names come from the CQP and the KKT conditions. The matrix M is not symmetric, but it is positive semidefinite because $\mathbf{z}^\mathsf{T} M \mathbf{z} \geq 0$ for all $\mathbf{z}$. The inequality is guaranteed because A is positive semidefinite.

Once formulated as an LCP, solve the problem using Lemke's method to extract the location $\mathbf{x}$ and value f of the local minimum. Observe that the *linear programming* (LP) problem is a special case of CQP when A is the zero matrix, which is positive semidefinite.

7.1.3.1 Eliminating Unconstrained Variables

The CQP problem has the inequality contraint $\mathbf{x} \geq \mathbf{0}$ that says all independent variables must be nonnegative. Some geometric queries involve variables that are unconstrained; that is, they can be any real number. The corresponding CQP must be modified to eliminate such variables.

For example, consider a CQP in 3D with $\mathbf{x} = (x_0, x_1, x_2)$ and whose inequality constraints depend only on x_0 and x_1,

$$x_0 \geq 0, \; x_1 \geq 0, \; D \begin{bmatrix} x_0 \\ x_1 \end{bmatrix} \geq \mathbf{e} \tag{7.3}$$

where D is $m \times 2$ and $\mathbf{e}$ is $m \times 1$. The variable x_2 is unconstrained.

For a fixed pair (x_0, x_1), the function $f(\mathbf{x}) = \mathbf{x}^\mathsf{T} A \mathbf{x}/2 + \mathbf{b}^\mathsf{T}\mathbf{x} + c$ is quadratic in x_2. The minimum with respect to x_2 must occur when the derivative with respect to x_2 is zero. Let $A = [a_{ij}]$ and $\mathbf{b} = [b_j]$; then $0 = \partial f / \partial x_2 = a_{20}x_0 + a_{21}x_1 + a_{22}x_2 + b_2$ and has solution $x_2 = -(a_{20}x_0 + a_{21}x_1 + b_2)/a_{22}$. The function to minimize is $g(x_0, x_1) = f(x_0, x_1, -(a_{20}x_0 + a_{21}x_1 + b_2)/a_{22})$ subject to the constraints of equation (7.3). Using

$$\mathbf{x} = x_0 \mathbf{u}_0 + x_1 \mathbf{u}_1 + \mathbf{u}_2 \tag{7.4}$$

where the $\mathbf{u}$-column vectors written as 3-tuples $\mathbf{u}_0 = (1, 0, -a_{20}/a_{22})$, $\mathbf{u}_1 = (0, 1, -a_{21}/a_{22})$ and $\mathbf{u}_2 = (0, 0, -b_2/a_{22})$, some algebra will show that $g(s, t) = \tilde{\mathbf{x}}^\mathsf{T} \tilde{A} \tilde{\mathbf{x}}/2 + \tilde{\mathbf{b}}^\mathsf{T} \tilde{\mathbf{x}} + \tilde{c}$, where

$$\tilde{A} = \begin{bmatrix} \mathbf{u}_0^\mathsf{T} A \mathbf{u}_0 & \mathbf{u}_0^\mathsf{T} A \mathbf{u}_1 \\ \mathbf{u}_1^\mathsf{T} A \mathbf{u}_0 & \mathbf{u}_q^\mathsf{T} A \mathbf{u}_q \end{bmatrix}, \quad \tilde{\mathbf{b}} = \begin{bmatrix} \mathbf{u}_0^\mathsf{T} A \mathbf{u}_2 \\ \mathbf{u}_1^\mathsf{T} A \mathbf{u}_2 \end{bmatrix}, \quad \tilde{c} = \tfrac{1}{2}\mathbf{u}_2^\mathsf{T} A \mathbf{u}_2 + \mathbf{b}^\mathsf{T}\mathbf{u}_2 + c \tag{7.5}$$

In general, let $\mathbf{x}_c$ be the constrained variables and let $\mathbf{x}_u$ be the unconstrained variables. Partition the various quantities by

$$\mathbf{x} = \begin{bmatrix} \mathbf{x}_c \\ \mathbf{x}_u \end{bmatrix}, \quad A = \begin{bmatrix} A_{cc} & A_{cu} \\ A_{uc} & A_{uu} \end{bmatrix}, \quad \mathbf{b} = \begin{bmatrix} \mathbf{b}_c \\ \mathbf{b}_u \end{bmatrix} \tag{7.6}$$

where the block elements are of the appropriate sizes. The matrix A is symmetric, so $A_{uc} = A_{cu}^{\mathsf{T}}$. The matrix A is also positive definite, so A_{cc} and A_{uu} are positive definite. The quadratic function is

$$f(\mathbf{x}_c, \mathbf{x}_u) = \tfrac{1}{2} \begin{bmatrix} \mathbf{x}_c^{\mathsf{T}} & \mathbf{x}_u^{\mathsf{T}} \end{bmatrix} \begin{bmatrix} A_{cc} & A_{cu} \\ A_{uc} & A_{uu} \end{bmatrix} \begin{bmatrix} \mathbf{x}_c \\ \mathbf{x}_u \end{bmatrix} + \begin{bmatrix} \mathbf{b}_c^{\mathsf{T}} \\ \mathbf{b}_u^{\mathsf{T}} \end{bmatrix} \begin{bmatrix} \mathbf{x}_c \\ \mathbf{x}_u \end{bmatrix} + c \tag{7.7}$$

$$= \tfrac{1}{2}\mathbf{x}_c^{\mathsf{T}} A_{cc}\mathbf{x}_c + \left(\mathbf{x}_u^{\mathsf{T}} A_{uc} + \mathbf{b}_c^{\mathsf{T}}\right)\mathbf{x}_c + \left(\tfrac{1}{2}\mathbf{x}_u^{\mathsf{T}} A_{uu}\mathbf{x}_u + \mathbf{b}_u^{\mathsf{T}}\mathbf{x}_u + c\right)$$

The derivative with respect to the unconstrained variables must be zero,

$$\mathbf{0} = \frac{\partial f}{\partial \mathbf{x}_u} = A_{uc}\mathbf{x}_c + A_{uu}\mathbf{x}_u + \mathbf{b}_u \tag{7.8}$$

The solution is

$$\mathbf{x}_u = -A_{uu}^{-1}\left(A_{uc}\mathbf{x}_c + \mathbf{b}_u\right) \tag{7.9}$$

Substituting this back into the quadratic function produces $g(\mathbf{x}_c) = f(\mathbf{x}_c, \mathbf{x}_u)$ and

$$g(\mathbf{x}_c) = \frac{1}{2}\mathbf{x}_c^{\mathsf{T}} \tilde{A}\mathbf{x}_c + \tilde{\mathbf{b}}^{\mathsf{T}}\mathbf{x}_c + \tilde{c} \tag{7.10}$$

where

$$\begin{aligned} \tilde{A} &= A_{cc} - A_{cu}A_{uu}^{-1}A_{uc} \\ \tilde{b} &= \mathbf{b}_c - A_{cu}A_{uu}^{-1}\mathbf{b}_u \\ \tilde{c} &= \tfrac{1}{2}\mathbf{x}_u^{\mathsf{T}} A_{uu}\mathbf{x}_u + \mathbf{b}_u^{\mathsf{T}}\mathbf{x}_u + c \end{aligned} \tag{7.11}$$

Solve the CQP to minimize $g = \mathbf{x}_c^{\mathsf{T}}\tilde{A}\mathbf{x}_c + \tilde{\mathbf{b}}^{\mathsf{T}}\mathbf{x}_c + \tilde{c}$ subject to $\mathbf{x}_c \geq 0$ and the problem-specific constraints $\tilde{D}\mathbf{x}_c \geq \tilde{\mathbf{e}}$. The solution $\mathbf{x}_c$ is then substituted into equation (7.9) to obtain $\mathbf{x}_u$.

7.1.3.2 Reduction for Equality Constraints

Sometimes the CQP in an n-dimensional setting involves equality constraints. The dimension of the CQP can be reduced by eliminating such constraints. For example, consider a CQP in 3D with $\mathbf{x} = (x_0, x_1, x_2)$ with constraints

$$x_0 \geq 0, \quad x_1 \geq 0, \quad D\mathbf{x} \geq \mathbf{e}, \quad \mathbf{n} \cdot \mathbf{x} + d = 0 \tag{7.12}$$

where D is $m \times 3$, $\mathbf{e}$ is $m \times 1$ and $\mathbf{n} = (n_0, n_1, n_2)$ with $n_2 \neq 0$.

Solve the equality constraint for $x_2 = -(n_0 x_0 + n_1 x_1 + d)/n_2$ and substitute it into both the function $f(\mathbf{x})$ and the inequality constraints $D\mathbf{x} \geq \mathbf{e}$. The reduction $g(x_0, x_1) = f(x_0, x_1, -(n_0 x_0 + n_1 x_1 + d)/n_2)$ uses the same approach that led to equations (7.4) and (7.5), except that $\mathbf{u}_0 = (1, 0, -n_0/n_2)$, $\mathbf{u}_1 = (0, 1, -n_1/n_2)$ and $\mathbf{u}_2 = (0, 0, -d/n_2)$.

The reduction of the inequality constraint $D\mathbf{x} \geq \mathbf{e}$ is as follows. For $D = [D_{ij}]$ and $\mathbf{e} = [e_i]$, each inequality constraint is of the form

$$\begin{aligned} e_i &\leq D_{i0}x_0 + D_{i1}x_1 + D_{i2}x_2 \\ &= D_{i0}x_0 + D_{i1}x_1 - D_{i2}(n_0 x_0 + n_1 x_1 + d)/n_2 \end{aligned} \tag{7.13}$$

Grouping similar terms,

$$(D_{i0} - D_{i2}\, n_0/n_2)x_0 + (D_{i1} - D_{i2}\, n_1/n_2)x_1 \geq e_i + D_{i2}\, d/n_2 \qquad (7.14)$$

Using linear algebra terminology for solving the equality constraint, x_2 is a basic variable and x_0 and x_1 are free variables.

In general, let the ℓ equality constraints for the CQP be $F\mathbf{x} + \mathbf{v} = \mathbf{0}$ where F is $\ell \times n$ and $\mathbf{v}$ is $\ell \times 1$. For a nontrivial problem, it must be that $\ell < n$. Apply row reductions to the linear system of equality constraints to obtain a coefficient matrix that is in reduced row echelon form. Once in this form it is easy to identify the basic variables and the free variables of the linear system. If $\mathbf{x}_b$ is the tuple of basic variables and $\mathbf{x}_f$ is the tuple of free variables, then the reduced row echelon form can be solved for $\mathbf{x}_b = H\mathbf{x}_f + \mathbf{w}$ for some matrix H and vector $\mathbf{w}$.

For simplicity, reorder the components of $\mathbf{x}$ so that $\mathbf{x} = (\mathbf{x}_f, \mathbf{x}_b)$. The general construction for unconstrained variables starting with equation (7.6) can be duplicated with renamed quantities $\mathbf{x}_f$ for $\mathbf{x}_c$, $\mathbf{x}_b$ for $\mathbf{x}_u$, A_{ff} for A_{uu}, A_{fb} for A_{cu}, A_{bb} for A_{uu}, $\mathbf{b}_f$ for $\mathbf{b}_c$ and $\mathbf{b}_b$ for $\mathbf{b}_u$. The resulting $\tilde{A}$, $\tilde{\mathbf{b}}$ and $\tilde{c}$ are used for the function to be minimized, $g(\mathbf{x}_f) = \mathbf{x}_f^\mathsf{T} \tilde{A} \mathbf{x}_f / 2 + \tilde{\mathbf{b}}^\mathsf{T} \mathbf{x}_f + \tilde{c}$.

Partition $D = [D_f \ D_b]$ such that the number of columns of D_f is the number of components of $\mathbf{x}_f$ and the number of columns of D_b is the number of components of $\mathbf{x}_b$. The inequality constraints are

$$
\begin{aligned}
\mathbf{e} \ \leq \ & D\mathbf{x} \\
= \ & \begin{bmatrix} D_f & D_b \end{bmatrix} \begin{bmatrix} \mathbf{x}_f \\ \mathbf{x}_b \end{bmatrix} \\
= \ & D_f \mathbf{x}_f + D_b \mathbf{x}_b \\
= \ & D_f \mathbf{x}_f + D_b (H\mathbf{x}_f + \mathbf{w})
\end{aligned}
\qquad (7.15)
$$

Grouping similar terms,

$$\tilde{D}\mathbf{x}_f = (D_f + D_b H)\mathbf{x}_f \geq \mathbf{e} - D_b \mathbf{w} = \tilde{\mathbf{e}} \qquad (7.16)$$

where the first equality defines $\tilde{D}$ and the last equality defines $\tilde{\mathbf{e}}$.

The reduction in dimension leads to minimizing $g(\mathbf{x}_f) = \mathbf{x}_f^\mathsf{T} \tilde{A} \mathbf{x}_f / 2 + \tilde{\mathbf{b}}^\mathsf{T} \mathbf{x}_f + \tilde{c}$ subject to $\mathbf{x}_f \geq 0$ and $\tilde{D}\mathbf{x}_f \geq \tilde{\mathbf{e}}$.

7.2 Lemke's Method

The standard approach for solving LP is the simplex algorithm using the tableau method. This may also be used to solve an LCP, but an approach that uses different terminology is Lemke's method. The presentation here follows that of [13].

7.2.1   Terms and Framework

The equation $\mathbf{w} = \mathbf{q} + M\mathbf{z}$ is considered to be a *dictionary* for the *basic variables* $\mathbf{w}$ defined in terms of the *nonbasic variables* $\mathbf{z}$. The analogy to a dictionary is that the basic variables are words in the dictionary defined in terms of the nonbasic variables that are other words in the dictionary. If $\mathbf{q} \geq \mathbf{0}$, the dictionary is said to be *feasible*, in which case the LCP has the trivial solution $\mathbf{z} = \mathbf{0}$ and $\mathbf{w} = \mathbf{q}$.

If the dictionary is not feasible, Lemke's method is applied. Assuming that $\mathbf{z} = (z_0, \ldots, z_{n-1})$, the first phase of the algorithm adds an auxiliary variable $z_n \geq 0$ by modifying the dictionary to $\mathbf{w} = \mathbf{q} + M\mathbf{z} + z_n\mathbf{1}$, where $\mathbf{1}$ is the n-tuple whose components are all 1. The i-th equation is selected according to some criterion (described later) that exchanges z_n and w_i by solving the equation for z_n, which now becomes a basic variable. The right-hand side of the equation contains a w_i term, so w_i now becomes a nonbasic variable. The equation for the now-basic z_n is substituted into the other equations to eliminate the right-hand side occurrences of z_n. The equation to solve for z_n is selected so that after the substitutions in the other equations, the modified dictionary is feasible.

The second phase of the algorithm is designed to obtain a dictionary such that the following two conditions are true. First, z_n is nonbasic. Second, for each i, either z_i or w_i is nonbasic. A dictionary for which both conditions are true is said to be a *terminal dictionary*. If the dictionary satisfies only the second condition, it is said to be a *balanced dictionary*. The first phase produces a balanced dictionary, but z_n is in the dictionary (it is a basic variable), so the dictionary is not terminal. The procedure to reach a terminal dictionary is iterative. Each iteration is designed so that a nonbasic variable enters the dictionary and a basic variable leaves the dictionary. The invariant after each iteration is that the dictionary remain feasible and balanced. To ensure this happens and hopefully to avoid producing the same dictionary twice, if a variable has just left the dictionary, then its *complementary variable* must enter the dictionary on the next iterations: A variable cannot leave/enter on one iteration and enter/leave on the next iteration. Once z_n leaves the dictionary, the dictionary is terminal. The condition that z_i or w_i is nonbasic for each $i < n$ means that either $z_i = 0$ or $w_i = 0$; that is, $\mathbf{w}^{\mathsf{T}}\mathbf{z} = 0$ and the LCP is solved.

Two problems can occur during the iterations. First, the variable complementary to the leaving variable cannot enter the dictionary. In this case, the LCP does not have a solution. Second, it is possible to encounter a cycle in the dictionaries, which prevents the algorithm from converging to a solution. When this happens, one of the components of $\mathbf{q}$ in the dictionary has become zero. This is referred to as a *degeneracy*. The algorithm can be modified by introducing symbolic perturbations of the components of $\mathbf{q}$ to avoid the cycles.

Several examples are presented here to illustrate the algorithm.

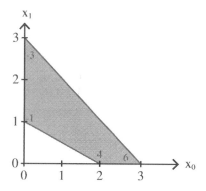

FIGURE 7.1: An LCP with a unique solution.

7.2.2 LCP with a Unique Solution

A linear programming problem with a unique solution provides an example of how to select the variables to exchange in order to obtain a feasible dictionary.

Minimize $f(x_0, x_1) = 2x_0 - x_1$ subject to the constraints $x_0 \geq 0$, $x_1 \geq 0$, $x_0 + x_1 \leq 3$ and $x_0 + 2x_1 \geq 0$. Figure 7.1 shows the domain of f that is defined by the inequality constraints. The function values at the vertices of the domain are shown in medium gray. Visually, the minimum must occur at $(x_0, x_1) = (0, 3)$. The dimension of the LCP is $n = 4$. The LCP quantities of interest are

$$\mathbf{q} = \begin{bmatrix} 2 \\ -1 \\ \hline 3 \\ -2 \end{bmatrix}, \quad M = \left[\begin{array}{cc|cc} 0 & 0 & 1 & -1 \\ 0 & 0 & 1 & -2 \\ \hline -1 & -1 & 0 & 0 \\ 1 & 2 & 0 & 0 \end{array} \right],$$

$$\mathbf{z} = \begin{bmatrix} x_0 \\ x_1 \\ \hline y_0 \\ y_1 \end{bmatrix}, \quad \mathbf{w} = \begin{bmatrix} u_0 \\ u_1 \\ \hline v_0 \\ v_1 \end{bmatrix}$$

(7.17)

The initial dictionary with auxiliary variable z_4 is

$$\begin{aligned} w_0 &= 2 + z_2 - z_3 + z_4 \\ w_1 &= -1 + z_2 - 2z_3 + z_4 \\ w_2 &= 3 - z_0 - z_1 + z_4 \\ w_3 &= -2 + z_0 + 2z_1 + z_4 \end{aligned}$$

(7.18)

Exchange z_4 with one of the w_i and then substitute that equation into the others to obtain a feasible dictionary; that is, choose the exchange equation so that the resulting constants for $\mathbf{q}$ are nonnegative. The coefficients of z_4 are positive, so only the two equations with negative constants need to be examined. The second equation, $z_4 = 1 - z_2 + 2z_3 + w_1$ could be solved, but substituting it in the fourth equation produces $w_3 = -1 + z_0 + 2z_1 - z_2 + 2z_3 + w_1$, which has a negative constant. The resulting dictionary is not feasible. Therefore, the exchange equation is the fourth equation in which case $z_4 = 2 - z_0 - 2z_1 + w_3$. The nonbasic variable z_4 becomes basic (enters the dictionary) and the basic variable w_3 becomes nonbasic (leaves the dictionary). Substituting in the other equations,

$$
\begin{aligned}
w_0 &= 4 - z_0 - 2z_1 + z_2 - z_3 + w_3 \\
w_1 &= 1 - z_0 - 2z_1 + z_2 - 2z_3 + w_3 \\
w_2 &= 5 - 2z_0 - 3z_1 + w_3 \\
z_4 &= 2 - z_0 - 2z_1 + w_3
\end{aligned}
\tag{7.19}
$$

For the initial dictionary, the exchange equation is the one with the minimum $\mathbf{q}$-component.

For the remaining iterations, if v_j is the nonbasic variable that is required to enter the dictionary and become basic (v_j is either z_j or w_j), the exchange equation is the one for which the coefficient of v_j is negative and the nonnegative ratio $-q_i/(m_{ij}v_j)$ is minimum for all i. This is called the *minimum-ratio rule*.

The variable w_3 left the dictionary, so z_3 must now enter the dictionary. Choose the equation that minimizes the quantity mentioned in the previous paragraph. The first and second equations have negative coefficients for z_3. The ratio for the first equation is $4/1$ and the ratio for the second equation is $1/2$, so the second equation is the one to exchange. Solve for z_3 and substitute this into the other equations,

$$
\begin{aligned}
w_0 &= (7/2) - (1/2)z_0 - z_1 + (1/2)z_2 + (1/2)w_1 + (1/2)w_3 \\
z_3 &= (1/2) - (1/2)z_0 - z_1 + (1/2)z_2 - (1/2)w_1 + (1/2)w_3 \\
w_2 &= 5 - 2z_0 - 3z_1 + w_3 \\
z_4 &= 2 - z_0 - 2z_1 + w_3
\end{aligned}
\tag{7.20}
$$

The variable w_1 left the dictionary, so z_1 must now enter the dictionary. All four equations have negative coefficients for z_1 and the ratios are $7/2$, $1/2$, $5/3$ and 1, in order of listing of the equations. The minimum ratio is $1/2$, generated by the second equation. Solve for z_1 and substitute this into the other equations,

$$
\begin{aligned}
w_0 &= 3 + z_3 + w_1 \\
z_1 &= (1/2) - (1/2)z_0 - z_3 + (1/2)z_2 - (1/2)w_1 + (1/2)w_3 \\
w_2 &= (7/2) - (1/2)z_0 + 3z_3 - (3/2)z_2 + (3/2)w_1 - (1/2)w_3 \\
z_4 &= 1 + 2z_3 - z_2 + w_1
\end{aligned}
\tag{7.21}
$$

The variable z_3 left the dictionary, so w_3 must now enter the dictionary.

Only the third equation has a negative coefficient for w_3. Solve for w_3 and substitute this into the other equations,

$$
\begin{aligned}
w_0 &= 3 + z_3 + w_1 \\
z_1 &= 4 - z_0 + 2z_3 - z_2 + w_1 - w_2 \\
w_3 &= 7 - z_0 + 6z_3 - 3z_2 + 3w_1 - 2w_2 \\
z_4 &= 1 + 2z_3 - z_2 + w_1
\end{aligned}
\tag{7.22}
$$

The variable w_2 left the dictionary, so z_2 must now enter the dictionary. The last 3 equations have a negative coefficient for z_2, so the ratios are 4, $7/3$ and 1. The last equation provides the minimum ratio. Solve for z_2 and substitute this into the other equations,

$$
\begin{aligned}
w_0 &= 3 + z_3 + w_1 \\
z_1 &= 3 - z_0 + z_4 - w_2 \\
w_3 &= 4 - z_0 + 3z_4 - 2w_2 \\
z_2 &= 1 + 2z_3 - z_4 + w_1
\end{aligned}
\tag{7.23}
$$

The auxiliary variable z_4 left the dictionary, returning to its initial role as a nonbasic variable. The iterations terminate here and a solution has been found. The variables on the right-hand side of the equation are set to zero: $z_0 = 0$, $z_3 = 0$, $z_4 = 0$, $w_1 = 0$ and $w_2 = 0$. The variables on the left-hand side are then $w_0 = 3$, $z_1 = 3$, $w_3 = 4$ and $z_2 = 0$. The original variables that minimize f are $(x_0, x_1) = (z_0, z_1) = (0, 3)$.

7.2.3 LCP with Infinitely Many Solutions

A linear programming problem with infinitely many solutions provides an example that shows the algorithm will select one of the locations at which the minimum occurs when there are infinitely many such locations.

Minimize $f(x_0, x_1) = x_0 + x_1$ subject to the constraints $0 \le x_0 \le 2$, $0 \le x_1 \le 2$, $x_0 + x_1 \ge 1$ and $x_0 + x_1 \ge 2$. Figure 7.2 shows the domain of f that is defined by the inequality constraints. The constraint $x_0 + x_1 \ge 1$ does not contribute to defining the domain of f; generally, it is not trivial to identify such contraints. The function values at the vertices of the domain are shown in medium gray. The function is constant along the domain edge $x_0 + x_1 = 2$, so any pair (x_0, x_1) on this edge is a minimizer point.

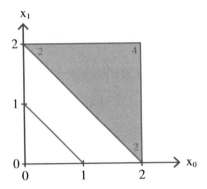

FIGURE 7.2: An LCP with infinitely many solutions.

The dimension of the LCP is $n = 6$. The LCP quantities of interest are

$$\mathbf{q} = \begin{bmatrix} 1 \\ 1 \\ \hline -1 \\ -2 \\ 2 \\ 2 \end{bmatrix}, \quad M = \left[\begin{array}{cc|cccc} 0 & 0 & -1 & -1 & 1 & 0 \\ 0 & 0 & -1 & -1 & 0 & 1 \\ \hline 1 & 1 & 0 & 0 & 0 & 0 \\ 1 & 1 & 0 & 0 & 0 & 0 \\ -1 & 0 & 0 & 0 & 0 & 0 \\ 0 & -1 & 0 & 0 & 0 & 0 \end{array} \right],$$

(7.24)

$$\mathbf{z} = \begin{bmatrix} x_0 \\ x_1 \\ \hline y_0 \\ y_1 \\ y_2 \\ y_3 \end{bmatrix}, \quad \mathbf{w} = \begin{bmatrix} u_0 \\ u_1 \\ \hline v_0 \\ v_1 \\ v_2 \\ v_3 \end{bmatrix}$$

The initial dictionary with auxiliary variable z_6 is

$$\begin{aligned}
w_0 &= 1 - z_2 - z_3 + z_4 + z_6 \\
w_1 &= 1 - z_2 - z_3 + z_5 + z_6 \\
w_2 &= -1 + z_0 + z_1 + z_6 \\
w_3 &= -2 + z_0 + z_1 + z_6 \\
w_4 &= 2 - z_0 + z_6 \\
w_5 &= 2 - z_1 + z_6
\end{aligned}$$

(7.25)

The fourth equation has minimum $\mathbf{q}$-component (-2). Solve for z_6 and substitute this into the other equations,

$$
\begin{aligned}
w_0 &= 3 - z_0 - z_2 - z_3 + z_4 + w_3 \\
w_1 &= 3 - z_0 - z_2 - z_3 + z_5 + w_3 \\
w_2 &= 1 - w_3 \\
z_6 &= 2 - z_0 - z_1 + w_3 \\
w_4 &= 4 - 2z_0 - z_1 + w_3 \\
w_5 &= 4 - z_0 - 2z_1 + w_3
\end{aligned}
\tag{7.26}
$$

The variable w_3 left the dictionary, so z_3 must now enter the dictionary. The first two equations have a negative z_3 coefficient and the same ratio, so either equation can be chosen. Solve the first equation for z_3 and substitute this into the other equations,

$$
\begin{aligned}
z_3 &= 3 - z_0 - z_1 - z_2 - w_0 + z_4 + w_3 \\
w_1 &= 0 + w_0 - z_4 + z_5 \\
w_2 &= 1 - w_3 \\
z_6 &= 2 - z_0 - z_1 + w_3 \\
w_4 &= 4 - 2z_0 - z_1 + w_3 \\
w_5 &= 4 - z_0 - 2z_1 + w_3
\end{aligned}
\tag{7.27}
$$

The variable w_0 left the dictionary, so z_0 must now enter the dictionary. Of the four equations with a negative z_0 coefficient, two of them attain the minimum ratio—the equation with z_6 and the equation with w_4, both having ratio 2. Solve the z_6-equation for z_0 and substitute this into the other equations,

$$
\begin{aligned}
z_3 &= 1 - z_2 - w_0 + z_4 + z_6 \\
w_1 &= 0 + w_0 - z_4 + z_5 \\
w_2 &= 1 - w_3 \\
z_0 &= 2 - z_6 - z_1 + w_3 \\
w_4 &= 0 + z_1 + 2z_6 - w_3 \\
w_5 &= 2 - z_1 + z_6
\end{aligned}
\tag{7.28}
$$

The auxiliary variable z_6 has left the dictionary, so the LCP is solved. The variables on the right-hand side are set to zero: $z_1 = 0$, $z_2 = 0$, $z_4 = 0$, $z_5 = 0$, $z_6 = 0$, $w_0 = 0$ and $w_3 = 0$. The variables on the left-hand side are then $z_3 = 1$, $w_1 = 0$, $w_2 = 1$, $z_0 = 2$, $w_4 = 0$ and $w_5 = 2$. The original variables that minimize f are $(x_0, x_1) = (z_0, z_1) = (2, 0)$. As noted, this is only one of infinitely many minimizers for f.

When w_0 left the dictionary, there were two choices for the equations leading to the minimum ratio. The z_6-equation was chosen for the iteration, which led immediately to a solution $(x_0, x_1) = (2, 0)$. Had the w_4-equation been chosen instead, two additional iterations would be required for z_6 to leave the dictionary. The solution in this case is still $(2, 0)$.

7.2.4 LCP with No Solution

The example in this section is a linear programming problem with no solution. This is demonstrated when a complementary variable cannot enter the dictionary. A general condition is mentioned that ensures there is no solution in this case.

Minimize $f(x_0, x_1) = 2x_0 - x_1$ for $x_0 \geq 0$, $x_1 \geq 0$ and $x_0 + x_1 \geq 0$. The domain of f is an unbounded convex region in the first quadrant. The dimension of the LCP is $n = 3$. The LCP quantities of interest are

$$
\mathbf{q} = \begin{bmatrix} 2 \\ -1 \\ 1 \end{bmatrix}, \quad M = \left[\begin{array}{cc|c} 0 & 0 & -1 \\ 0 & 0 & -1 \\ 1 & 1 & 0 \end{array} \right],
$$

$$
\mathbf{z} = \begin{bmatrix} x_0 \\ x_1 \\ y_0 \end{bmatrix}, \quad \mathbf{w} = \begin{bmatrix} u_0 \\ u_1 \\ v_0 \end{bmatrix}
$$

(7.29)

The initial dictionary with auxiliary variable z_3 is

$$
\begin{aligned}
w_0 &= 2 - z_2 + z_3 \\
w_1 &= -1 - z_2 + z_3 \\
w_2 &= 1 + z_0 + z_1 + z_3
\end{aligned}
$$

(7.30)

The second equation has minimum $\mathbf{q}$-component. Solve for z_3 and substitute this into the other equations,

$$
\begin{aligned}
w_0 &= 3 \\
z_3 &= 1 + z_2 + w_1 \\
w_2 &= 2 + z_0 + z_1 + z_3 + w_1
\end{aligned}
$$

(7.31)

The variable w_1 left the dictionary, so the complementary variable z_1 must now enter the dictionary. However, its coefficient is not negative, so it cannot enter the dictionary. Therefore, the LCP has no solution. This should be intuitively clear because $f(0, x_1) = -x_1$ which has the limit $-\infty$ as $x_1 \to \infty$; that is, f is not bounded below.

7.2.5   LCP with a Cycle

Cycling appears to be a rare occurrence with the minimum-ratio rule. Searching online for such an example has not been fruitful. Other pivoting strategies exist for entering and leaving the dictionary. An example of an LCP with a cycle in the dictionaries is presented in [28]. The cycle example is for a linear programming problem where the objective function is tracked along with the LCP equations. The variable that enters the dictionary is the one in the objective function that has the largest coefficient. The variable that leaves the dictionary is the basic variable with the smallest index, where the z_i variables are assumed to occur before the w_i variables in the indexing. The smallest-index rule is *Bland's rule (smallest-index rule)*.

7.2.6 Avoiding Cycles when Constant Terms are Zero

This section shows how to avoid cycles by perturbing the $\mathbf{q}$-components with powers of a variable ε. The idea is that when the degeneracy occurs the first time because a component of $\mathbf{q}$ becomes zero, add ε to it, making that component a linear polynomial of ε. The arithmetic operations of the LCP iterations now involve a symbolic component—manipulating the polynomial itself using addition and scalar multiplication. If another component of $\mathbf{q}$ becomes zero in a later iteration, then add ε^2 to it, making that component a quadratic polynomial of ε. In the worst case, all components of $\mathbf{q}$ become zero during the iterations and the final component has ε^n added to it for an LCP of dimension n. The polynomials are linearly independent throughout the iterations, so the cycling cannot occur. When the iterations terminate and there is an LCP solution, set ε to zero and report the solution $\mathbf{z}$ and $\mathbf{w}$ in the usual manner.

In the GTL implementation LCPSolver, the code is kept simple by adding the powers of ε to the components of $\mathbf{q}$ even when those components are not zero. The trade-off is that more computations are required to manipulate the polynomials. The code can be optimized to reduce computations by inserting the powers of ε only when needed.

The example presented here illustrates the idea for an LCP where at least one of the $\mathbf{q}$ components becomes zero during the iterations.

Minimize $f(x_0, x_1) = (x_0^2 + 2x_1^2)/2 - (x_0 + x_1)$ subject to the constraints $x_0 \geq 0$, $x_1 \geq 0$ and $2x_0 + x_1 \geq 1$. The LCP formulation is the following, where z_3 is the auxiliary variable,

$$
\begin{aligned}
w_0 &= -1 + z_0 - 2z_2 + z_3 \\
w_1 &= -1 + 2z_1 - z_2 + z_3 \\
w_2 &= -1 + 2z_0 + z_1 + z_3
\end{aligned}
\tag{7.32}
$$

The variable z_3 must enter the dictionary via the equation that has the minimum $\mathbf{q}$-component. All components attain the minimum, so choose the first equation to solve for z_3. The variable w_0 exits the dictionary,

$$
\begin{aligned}
z_3 &= 1 - z_0 + 2z_2 + w_0 \\
w_1 &= 0 - z_0 + 2z_1 + z_2 + w_0 \\
w_2 &= 0 + z_0 + z_1 + 2z_2 + w_0
\end{aligned}
\tag{7.33}
$$

The variable z_0 must enter the dictionary. The minimum-ratio term is generated by the second equation, so w_1 must leave the dictionary,

$$
\begin{aligned}
z_3 &= 1 + w_1 - 2z_1 + z_2 \\
z_0 &= 0 - w_1 + 2z_1 + z_2 + w_0 \\
w_2 &= 0 - w_1 + 3z_1 + 3z_2 + 2w_0
\end{aligned}
\tag{7.34}
$$

The variable z_1 must enter the dictionary. The minimum-ratio term is generated by the first equation, so z_3 must leave the dictionary,

$$
\begin{aligned}
z_1 &= (1/2) + (1/2)w_1 - (1/2)z_3 + (1/2)z_2 \\
z_0 &= 1 - z_3 + 2z_2 + w_0 \\
w_2 &= (3/2) + (1/2)w_1 - (3/2)z_3 + (9/2)z_2 + 2w_0
\end{aligned}
\tag{7.35}
$$

The auxiliary variable z_3 has exited the dictionary and the $\mathbf{q}$ coefficients are nonnegative, so there is a unique solution to the LCP: $\mathbf{w} = (0, 0, 3/2)$ and $\mathbf{z} = (1, 1/2, 0)$. The CQP solution is $(x_0, x_1) = (1, 1/2)$. Observe that $\nabla f(x_0, x_1) = (x_0 - 1, 2x_1 - 1)$ and the global minimum occurs when $(x_0 - 1, 2x_1 - 1) = (0, 0)$, so $x_0 = 1$ and $x_1 = 1/2$. This is the solution found via the LCP. The minimizer point is in the domain defined by the inequality constraints.

Although a cycle was encountered, $\mathbf{q}$ components can still be perturbed by powers of ε. The LCP is

$$
\begin{aligned}
w_0 &= (-1 + \varepsilon) + z_0 - 2z_2 + z_3 \\
w_1 &= (-1 + \varepsilon^2) + 2z_1 - z_2 + z_3 \\
w_2 &= (-1 + \varepsilon^3) + 2z_0 + z_1 + z_3
\end{aligned}
\tag{7.36}
$$

Determining the minimum-ratio now depends on comparisons of polynomials. The less-than operation uses lexicographical ordering. If $\mathbf{a}(x) = \sum_{i=0}^{n} a_i x^i$ and $\mathbf{b}(x) = \sum_{i=0}^{n} b_i x^i$, pseudocode for the less-than operation is in Listing 7.1.

```
bool LessThan(Polynomial a, Polynomial b)
{
    for (int i = 0; i <= n; ++i)
    {
        if (a[i] < b[i])
        {
            return true;
        }
        if (a[i] > b[i])
        {
            return false;
        }
    }
    // At this point, a[i] and b[i] are equal for all i.
    return false;
}
```

Listing 7.1: The polynomial comparison used when perturbing the LCP equations to avoid zero-valued constant terms.

Of the three equations in the LCP, $(-1 + \varepsilon^3) < (-1 + \varepsilon)$ and $(-1 + \varepsilon^3) < (-1 + \varepsilon^2)$, so the last equation has the minimum $\mathbf{q}$ component. The variable z_3 enters the dictionary and the variable w_2 leaves the dictionary,

$$
\begin{aligned}
w_0 &= (\varepsilon - \varepsilon^3) - z_0 - z_1 - 2z_2 + w_2 \\
w_1 &= (\varepsilon^2 - \varepsilon^3) - 2z_0 + z_1 - z_2 + w_2 \\
z_3 &= (1 - \varepsilon^3) - 2z_0 - z_1 + w_2
\end{aligned}
\tag{7.37}
$$

The variable z_2 must enter the dictionary. The first two equations are candidates for the pivoting. The ratios are, in order, $(\varepsilon - \varepsilon^3)/2$ and $(\varepsilon^2 - \varepsilon^3)$. The second ratio is minimum, so w_1 must leave the dictionary,

$$
\begin{aligned}
w_0 &= (\varepsilon - 2\varepsilon^2 + \varepsilon^3) + 3z_0 - 3z_1 + 2w_1 - w_2 \\
z_2 &= (\varepsilon^2 - \varepsilon^3) - 2z_0 + z_1 - w_1 + w_2 \\
z_3 &= (1 - \varepsilon^3) - 2z_0 - z_1 + w_2
\end{aligned}
\tag{7.38}
$$

The variable z_1 must enter the dictionary. The first and last equations are candidates for the pivoting. The ratios are, in order, $(\varepsilon - 2\varepsilon^2 + \varepsilon^3)/3$ and $(1 - \varepsilon^3)$. The first ratio is minimum, so w_0 must leave the dictionary,

$$
\begin{aligned}
z_1 &= ((1/3)\varepsilon - (2/3)\varepsilon^2 + (1/3)\varepsilon^3) \\
&\quad + z_0 - (1/3)w_0 + (2/3)w_1 - (1/3)w_2 \\
z_2 &= ((1/3)\varepsilon + (1/3)\varepsilon^2 - (2/3)\varepsilon^3) \\
&\quad - z_0 - (1/3)w_0 - (1/3)w_1 + (2/3)w_2 \\
z_3 &= (1 - (1/3)\varepsilon + (2/3)\varepsilon^2 - (4/3)\varepsilon^3) \\
&\quad - 3z_0 + (1/3)w_0 - (2/3)w_1 + (4/3)w_2
\end{aligned}
\tag{7.39}
$$

The variable z_0 must enter the dictionary. The second and third equations are candidates for the pivoting. The ratios are, in order, $((1/3)\varepsilon - (2/3)\varepsilon^2 + (1/3)\varepsilon^3)$ and $((1/3) - (1/9)\varepsilon + (2/9)\varepsilon^2 - (4/9)\varepsilon^3)$. The first ratio is minimum, so z_2 must leave the dictionary,

$$
\begin{aligned}
z_1 &= (0 + (2/3)\varepsilon - (1/3)\varepsilon^2 - (1/3)\varepsilon^3) \\
&\quad - z_2 - (2/3)w_0 + (1/3)w_1 + (1/3)w_2 \\
z_0 &= ((1/3)\varepsilon + (1/3)\varepsilon^2 - (2/3)\varepsilon^3) \\
&\quad - z_2 - (1/3)w_0 - (1/3)w_1 + (2/3)w_2 \\
z_3 &= (1 - (4/3)\varepsilon - (1/3)\varepsilon^2 + (2/3)\varepsilon^3) \\
&\quad + 3z_2 + (4/3)w_0 + (1/3)w_1 - (2/3)w_2
\end{aligned}
\tag{7.40}
$$

The variable w_2 must enter the dictionary. The last equation is the only pivoting candidate, so z_3 must leave the dictionary,

$$
\begin{aligned}
z_1 &= ((1/2) - (1/2)\varepsilon^2) \\
&\quad + (1/2)z_2 + (1/2)w_1 - (1/2)z_3 \\
z_0 &= (1 - \varepsilon) \\
&\quad + 2z_2 + w_0 - z_3 \\
w_2 &= ((3/2) - 2\varepsilon - (1/2)\varepsilon^2 + \varepsilon^3) \\
&\quad + (9/2)z_2 + 2w_0 + (1/2)w_1 - (3/2)z_3
\end{aligned}
\tag{7.41}
$$

The auxiliary variable left the dictionary and the $\mathbf{q}$ components with $\varepsilon = 0$ are nonnegative, so the LCP has a unique solution: $\mathbf{w} = (0, 0, 3/2)$ and $\mathbf{z} = (1, 1/2, 0)$. This is the same solution found without the perturbations.

7.3   Formulating a Geometric Query as a CQP

The typical geometric queries that can be formulated as CQPs are distance between objects and test-intersection queries between objects. The latter type of query determines whether or not two objects overlap but does not give information (or gives limited information) about the overlap set.

The first stage for implementing a geometric query is to formulate the corresponding CQP. The second stage is to solve the CQP as an LCP.

7.3.1   Distance Between Oriented Boxes

The following example shows how to set up the convex quadratic programming algorithm for computing the distance between two boxes in any dimension.

A box in n-dimensions can be parameterized by choosing an $n \times 1$ point $\mathbf{k}$ as a box corner, a right-handed orthonormal set of axis directions $\{\mathbf{u}_j\}_{j=0}^{n-1}$ and positive edge lengths $\{\ell_j\}_{j=0}^{n-1}$. A point $\mathbf{p}$ in the box is

$$\mathbf{p}(\xi) = \mathbf{k} + \sum_{j=0}^{n-1} \xi_j \mathbf{u}_j = \mathbf{k} + R\xi, \quad \mathbf{0} \leq \xi \leq \ell \qquad (7.42)$$

where ξ is an $n \times 1$ vector whose components are the ξ_j, R is the $n \times n$ rotation matrix whose columns are the $\mathbf{u}_j$ and ℓ is an $n \times 1$ vector whose components are the ℓ_j.

The goal is to formulate the distance between two boxes as a CQP that can then be solved using an LCP. Let the box centers be $\mathbf{k}_i$, the rotation matrices be R_i and the edge lengths be ℓ_i. The parameterized boxes are

$$\mathbf{p}_i(\xi_i) = \mathbf{k}_i + R_i\xi_i, \quad \mathbf{0} \leq \xi_i \leq \ell_i \qquad (7.43)$$

for $i \in \{0,1\}$. All components are doubly indexed: $\mathbf{p}_i$ has components p_{ij}, $\mathbf{k}_i$ has components k_{ij}, $\mathbf{u}_i$ has components u_{ij}, R_i has columns $\mathbf{u}_i$, ℓ_i has components ℓ_{ij} and ξ_i has components ξ_{ij}.

Define $\boldsymbol{\Delta} = \mathbf{k}_1 - \mathbf{k}_0$. Half the squared distance between two points, one point from each box, is

$$
\begin{aligned}
f(\mathbf{x}) &= |\mathbf{p}_0(\xi_0) - \mathbf{p}_1(\xi_1)|^2 / 2 \\
&= |R_0\xi_0 - R_1\xi_1 - \mathbf{\Delta}|^2 / 2 \\
&= \left(\xi_0^\mathsf{T} R_0^\mathsf{T} R_0 \xi_0 + \xi_1^\mathsf{T} R_1^\mathsf{T} R_1 \xi_1 + \mathbf{\Delta}^\mathsf{T}\mathbf{\Delta} - 2\xi_0^\mathsf{T} R_0^\mathsf{T} R_1 \xi_1 \right. \\
&\qquad \left. - 2\mathbf{\Delta}^\mathsf{T} R_0 \xi_0 + 2\mathbf{\Delta}^\mathsf{T} R_1 \xi_1 \right) / 2 \\
&= \tfrac{1}{2} \left[\, \xi_0^\mathsf{T} \mid \xi_1^\mathsf{T} \,\right]
\left[\begin{array}{c|c} I & -R_0^\mathsf{T} R_1 \\ \hline -R_1^\mathsf{T} R_0 & I \end{array} \right]
\left[\begin{array}{c} \xi_0 \\ \xi_1 \end{array} \right] \\
&\qquad + \left[\, -\mathbf{\Delta}^\mathsf{T} R_0 \mid \mathbf{\Delta}^\mathsf{T} R_1 \,\right]
\left[\begin{array}{c} \xi_0 \\ \xi_1 \end{array} \right] + \tfrac{1}{2}\mathbf{\Delta}^\mathsf{T}\mathbf{\Delta} \\
&= \tfrac{1}{2}\mathbf{x}^\mathsf{T} A \mathbf{x} + \mathbf{b}^\mathsf{T}\mathbf{x} + c
\end{aligned}
\tag{7.44}
$$

where

$$
\mathbf{x} = \left[\begin{array}{c} \xi_0 \\ \xi_1 \end{array} \right], \quad
A = \left[\begin{array}{c|c} I & -R_0^\mathsf{T} R_1 \\ \hline -R_1^\mathsf{T} R_0 & I \end{array} \right], \quad
\mathbf{b} = \left[\begin{array}{c} -R_0^\mathsf{T}\mathbf{\Delta} \\ R_1^\mathsf{T}\mathbf{\Delta} \end{array} \right],
$$

$$
c = \tfrac{1}{2}|\mathbf{\Delta}|^2, \quad \ell = \left[\begin{array}{c} \ell_0 \\ \ell_1 \end{array} \right]
\tag{7.45}
$$

and I is the $n \times n$ identity matrix. Note that $R_0^\mathsf{T} R_0 = R_1^\mathsf{T} R_1 = I$ because R_0 and R_1 are rotation matrices.

The inequality constraints are $\mathbf{0} \le \mathbf{x} \le \ell$. The formal statement of the inequality constraints for the quadratic program is $D\mathbf{x} \ge \mathbf{e}$. For the current example,

$$
D = \left[\begin{array}{c} -I \\ -I \end{array} \right], \quad \mathbf{e} = \left[\begin{array}{c} -\ell_0 \\ -\ell_1 \end{array} \right]
\tag{7.46}
$$

7.3.2   Test-Intersection of Triangle and Cylinder

The following example shows how to set up the convex quadratic programming algorithm for testing for intersection between a triangle and a cylinder in any dimension. The motivation is the 3D problem, but notice that the specialization of a cylinder to 2D is a rectangle, so the intersection query is for a triangle and rectangle.

A nondegenerate (solid) triangle in n-dimensions has vertices $\mathbf{v}_i$ for $i \in \{0, 1, 2\}$ and linearly independent edge directions $\mathbf{d}_j = \mathbf{v}_{j+1} - \mathbf{v}_0$ for $j \in \{0, 1\}$. Define the parameter pair $\mathbf{x} = (x_0, x_1)$. The triangle is parameterized by

$$
\mathbf{p}(\mathbf{x}) = \mathbf{v}_0 + x_0\mathbf{d}_0 + x_1\mathbf{d}_1 = \mathbf{V}_0 + E\mathbf{x}, \quad x_0 \ge 0, \ x_1 \ge 0, \ x_0 + x_1 \le 1 \tag{7.47}
$$

where E is an $n \times 2$ matrix whose columns are the edge directions. A (solid) infinite cylinder is the set of points that are within r units of distance from an axis with origin $\mathbf{k}$ and unit-length direction $\mathbf{u}_0$; r is the radius of the cylinder. A (solid) finite cylinder is the infinite cylinder truncated by two hyperplanes

$\mathbf{u}_0 \cdot (\mathbf{p} - (\mathbf{k} \pm (h/2)\mathbf{u}_0)) = 0$, keeping only those infinite cylinder points between the two hyperplanes; h is the height of the finite cylinder. Let $\{\mathbf{u}_j\}_{j=0}^{n-1}$ be a right-handed orthonormal basis for $\mathbb{R}^n$ for which the first vector in the set is the finite cylinder axis direction. The finite cylinder is parameterized by

$$\mathbf{k} + t_0\mathbf{u}_0 + \sum_{j=1}^{n-1} t_j\mathbf{u}_j = \mathbf{k} + Rt, \quad |t_0| \le h/2, \quad \sum_{j=1}^{n-1} t_j^2 \le r^2 \qquad (7.48)$$

where t is an $n \times 1$ vector whose components are the t_j and R is the $n \times n$ rotation matrix whose columns are the $\mathbf{u}_j$.

The triangle and cylinder intersect when there is at least one triangle point within r units of the cylinder axis and between the two truncating planes. Formulate this using a CQP that minimizes a squared distance. Define $\Delta = \mathbf{v}_0 - \mathbf{k}$. The matrix that projects vectors onto the plane with origin $\mathbf{0}$ and normal $\mathbf{u}_0$ is $P = I - \mathbf{u}_0\mathbf{u}_0^T$. The right-hand side of the third equality in the equation (7.49) uses two properties of a projection matrix: $P^T = P$ and $P^2 = P$. Half the squared distance between a triangle point and a cylinder axis point is

$$\begin{aligned} f(\mathbf{x}) &= \tfrac{1}{2}|P(\mathbf{p}(\mathbf{x}) - \mathbf{k})|^2 \\ &= \tfrac{1}{2}|P(E\mathbf{x} + \Delta)|^2 \\ &= \tfrac{1}{2}(E\mathbf{x} + \Delta)^T P(E\mathbf{x} + \Delta) \\ &= \tfrac{1}{2}\mathbf{x}^T E^T P E\mathbf{x} + \Delta^T P E\mathbf{x} + \tfrac{1}{2}\Delta^T P\mathbf{x} \\ &= \tfrac{1}{2}\mathbf{x}^T A\mathbf{x} + \mathbf{b}^T\mathbf{x} + c \end{aligned} \qquad (7.49)$$

where $A = E^T P E$, $\mathbf{b} = E^T P^T \Delta = E^T P\Delta$ and $c = |\Delta|^2/2$.

The components of x are nonnegative. The other inequality constraints are

$$x_0 + x_1 \le 1, \quad h/2 \ge |t_0| = |\mathbf{u}_0 \cdot (\mathbf{p}(\mathbf{x}) - \mathbf{k})| = |\mathbf{u}_0^T E\mathbf{x} + U_0^T \Delta| \qquad (7.50)$$

In terms of the formal inequality constraints $D\mathbf{x} \ge \mathbf{e}$,

$$D = \begin{bmatrix} -\mathbf{1}^T \\ \mathbf{u}_0^T E \\ -\mathbf{u}_0^T E \end{bmatrix}, \quad \mathbf{e} = \begin{bmatrix} -1 \\ -h/2 - \mathbf{u}_0^T\Delta \\ -h/2 + \mathbf{u}_0^T\Delta \end{bmatrix} \qquad (7.51)$$

where D is a 3×2 matrix where $\mathbf{1}$ is a 2×1 vector whose components are both 1. The vector $\mathbf{e}$ is 3×1.

An LCP solver is used to compute the minimizer $\hat{\mathbf{x}}$ and the corresponding minimum value $\hat{f} = f(\hat{\mathbf{x}})$. The minimum squared distance is $2\hat{f}$. The triangle and cylinder intersect whenever $2\hat{f} \le r^2$.

7.4 Implementation Details

The GTL source code that uses an LCP solver is designed to allow use of fixed-precision floating-point arithmetic (float or double) or arbitrary-precision floating-point arithmetic (via BSRational). See Chapter 3 for details. The latter type allows the LCP solver to produce the exact result under the assumption that the inputs are error free; that is, the inputs are assumed to be finite floating-point numbers that, of course, are rational numbers. Any knowledge about numerical rounding errors in producing the inputs is unknown to the LCP solver, so it cannot take advantage of it.

Various geometric primitives have representations that include unit-length vectors. This is problematic when using arbitrary-precision floating-point arithmetic because typically those vectors are obtained by dividing a floating-point vector by its length. The length involves a square root operation, which generally (as a real number) is irrational and requires a numerical approximation to represent it. A section is included on how to deal with the normalization symbolically, a concept related to the abstract algebraic topic of *real quadratic fields*.

7.4.1 The LCP Solver

The LCP solver in the GTL is a straightforward implementation of the algorithm used in the examples of the previous sections of this chapter. The solver also uses the symbolic perturbation described previously to avoid degeneracy and cycles in the iterations.

Listing 7.2 shows the public interfaces for the classes used to solve LCPs.

```
template <typename Real>
class LCPSolverShared
{
protected:
    // Abstract base class construction. A virtual destructor is not provided because there
    // are no required side effects when destroying objects from the derived classes. The
    //member mMaxIterations is set by this call to the default value of n^2.
    LCPSolverShared(int n);

    // Use this constructor when you need a specific representation of zero and of one to
    // be used when manipulating the polynomials of the base class. In particular, this is
    // needed to select the correct zero and correct one for QFNumber objects.
    LCPSolverShared(int n, Real const& zero, Real const& one);

public:
    // Theoretically, when there is a solution the algorithm must converge in a finite
    // number of iterations. The number of iterations depends on the problem at hand,
    // but we need to guard against an infinite loop by limiting the number. The
    // implementation uses a maximum number of n^2 (chosen arbitrarily). You can set the
    // number yourself. When a call to Solve fails, increase the number of iterations and
    // call Solve again.
    inline void SetMaxIterations(int maxIterations);
    inline int GetMaxIterations() const;
```

```
    // Access the actual number of iterations used in a call to Solve.
    inline int GetNumIterations() const;

    enum Result
    {
        HAS_TRIVIAL_SOLUTION,
        HAS_NONTRIVIAL_SOLUTION,
        NO_SOLUTION,
        FAILED_TO_CONVERGE,
        INVALID_INPUT
    };
};

template <typename Real, int n>
class LCPSolver<Real, n> : public LCPSolverShared<Real>
{
public:
    // Construction. The member mMaxIterations is set by this call to the default value
    // of n².
    LCPSolver();

    // Use this constructor when you need a specific representation of zero and of one to
    // be used when manipulating the polynomials of the base class. In particular, this is
    // needed to select the correct zero and correct one for QFNumber objects.
    LCPSolver(Real const& zero, Real const& one);

    // If you want to know specifically why 'true' or 'false' was returned, pass the address
    // of a Result variable as the last parameter.
    bool Solve(std::array<Real,n> const& q,
        std::array<std::array<Real,n>,n> const& M,
        std::array<Real,n>& w, std::array<Real,n>& z,
        typename LCPSolverShared<Real>::Result* result = nullptr);
};


template <typename Real>
class LCPSolver<Real> : public LCPSolverShared<Real>
{
public:
    // Construction. The member mMaxIterations is set by this call to the default value
    // of n².
    LCPSolver(int n);

    // The input q must have n elements and the input M must be an n × n matrix
    // stored in row-major order. The outputs w and z have n elements. If you want to
    // know specifically why 'true' or 'false' was returned, pass the address of a Result
    // variable as the last parameter.
    bool Solve(std::vector<Real> const& q, std::vector<Real> const& M,
        std::vector<Real>& w, std::vector<Real>& z,
        typename LCPSolverShared<Real>::Result* result = nullptr);
};
```

Listing 7.2: The LCPSolverShared base class encapsulates the support for setting the maximum number of iterations used by the LCP solver and for querying the actual number of iterations used. The Result enumeration is used by derived classes to report the outcome of the solver. The two derived classes include one that uses std::array when the dimension of the LCP is known at compile time and one that uses std::vector when the dimension of the LCP is known only at run time.

7.4.2   Distance Between Oriented Boxes in 3D

Section 7.3.1 showed the construction of the CQP for computing the distance between two oriented boxes in n dimensions. Listing 7.3 shows pseudocode for computing the distance between two oriented boxes in 3 dimensions. The representations of an oriented box in the GTL use a center point and extents (half-lengths), so there is a small adjustment to compute the corners and lengths of the boxes.

```
template <typename Real>
struct Box3
{
    Point3<Real> center;
    Vector3<Real> axis[3];
    Real extent[3];
};

template <typename Real>
struct Box3Box3QueryResult
{
    // Specify the maximum number of LCP iterations. The default in the GTL is N^2 for an
    // LCP with N x 1 vector q and N x N matrix M. The convergence is not guaranteed
    // to occur within N^2 iterations, so a conservative approach in an application is to
    // examine 'status' after the query. If the value is FAILED_TO_CONVERGE, repeat
    // with a larger maxLCPIterations if so desired.
    int maxLCPIterations;

    // The number of iterations used by LCPSolver regardless of whether or not the query
    // is successful.
    int numLCPIterations;

    // The information returned by the LCP solver about what it discovered.
    LCPSolver<Real, 12>::Result status;

    // These members are valid only when queryIsSuccessful is true; otherwise, they are all
    // set to zero.
    Real distance, sqrDistance;
    std::array<Real, 3> box0Parameter;   // the x_i for box0
    std::array<Real, 3> box1Parameter;   // the x_i for box1
    Vector3<Real> closestPoint[2];   // (P0,P1), P0 in box0 and P1 in box1
};

// Set result.maxLCPIterations to the desired value before calling this function.
template <typename Real>
void ComputeDistanceAndClosestPoints(Box3<Real> box0, Box3<Real> box1,
    Box3Box3QueryResult<Real>& result)
{
    // Compute the box corners and difference of corners.
    Point3<Real> K0 = box0.center, K1 = box1.center;
    for (int r = 0; r < 3; ++r)
    {
      K0 -= box0.extent[r] * box0.axis[r];
      K1 -= box1.extent[r] * box1.axis[r];
    }
    Vector3<Real> Delta = K1 - K0;

    // Compute R_0^T Delta and R_1^T Delta.
    Vector3<Real> R0TDelta, R1TDelta;
    for (int r = 0; r < 3; ++r)
    {
        R0TDelta[r] = Dot(box0.axis[r], Delta);
        R1TDelta[r] = Dot(box1.axis[r], Delta);
```

```
}

// Compute R_0^T R_1.
std :: array<std :: array<Real , 3>, 3> ROTR1;
for (int r = 0; r < 3; ++r)
{
    for (int c = 0; c < 3; ++c)
    {
        ROTR1[r][c] = Dot(box0.axis[r], box1.axis[c]);
    }
}

// Compute the lengths from the extents (half-lengths).
std :: array<Real , 3> length0 , length1;
for (int r = 0; r < 3; ++r)
{
    length0 [r] = 2 * box0.extent[r];
    length1 [r] = 2 * box1.extent[r];
}

// The LCP has 6 variables and 6 nontrivial inequality constraints.
std :: array<Real , 12> q =
{
    -ROTDelta [0] , -ROTDelta [1] , -ROTDelta [2] ,
    R1TDelta [0] , R1TDelta [1] , R1TDelta [2] ,   // b
    length0 [0] , length0 [1] , length0 [2] ,
    length1 [0] , length1 [1] , length1 [2]    // -e
};

std :: array<std :: array<Real , 12>, 12> M;   // {{ A, -D^T }, { D, 0 }}
{
    M[ 0] = { 1, 0, 0, -ROTR1[0][0], -ROTR1[0][1], -ROTR1[0][2] ,
              1, 0, 0, 0, 0, 0 };
    M[ 1] = { 0, 1, 0, -ROTR1[1][0], -ROTR1[1][1], -ROTR1[1][2] ,
              0, 1, 0, 0, 0, 0 };
    M[ 2] = { 0, 0, 1, -ROTR1[2][0], -ROTR1[2][1], -ROTR1[2][2] ,
              0, 0, 1, 0, 0, 0 };
    M[ 3] = { -ROTR1[0][0], -ROTR1[1][0], -ROTR1[2][0], 1, 0, 0,
              0, 0, 0, 1, 0, 0 };
    M[ 4] = { -ROTR1[0][1], -ROTR1[1][1], -ROTR1[2][1], 0, 1, 0,
              0, 0, 0, 0, 1, 0 };
    M[ 5] = { -ROTR1[0][2], -ROTR1[1][2], -ROTR1[2][2], 0, 0, 1,
              0, 0, 0, 0, 0, 1 };
    M[ 6] = { -1, 0, 0, 0, 0, 0, 0, 0, 0, 0, 0, 0 };
    M[ 7] = { 0, -1, 0, 0, 0, 0, 0, 0, 0, 0, 0, 0 };
    M[ 8] = { 0, 0, -1, 0, 0, 0, 0, 0, 0, 0, 0, 0 };
    M[ 9] = { 0, 0, 0, -1, 0, 0, 0, 0, 0, 0, 0, 0 };
    M[10] = { 0, 0, 0, 0, -1, 0, 0, 0, 0, 0, 0, 0 };
    M[11] = { 0, 0, 0, 0, 0, -1, 0, 0, 0, 0, 0, 0 };
};

LCPSolver<Real , 12> lcp;
lcp.SetMaxLCPIterations(result.maxLCPIterations);
std :: array<Real , 12> w, z;
if (lcp.Solve(q, M, w, z, &result.status))
{
    result.closestPoint [0] = box0.center;
    for (int i = 0; i < 3; ++i)
    {
        result.box0Parameter[i] = z[i] - box0.extent[i];
        result.closestPoint [0]
            += result.box0Parameter[i] * box0.axis[i];
    }

    result.closestPoint [1] = box1.center;
    for (int i = 0, j = 3; i < 3; ++i, ++j)
```

```
        {
            result.box1Parameter[i] = z[j] − box1.extent[i];
            result.closestPoint[1]
                += result.box1Parameter[i] * box1.axis[i];
        }

        Vector3<Real> diff
            = result.closestPoint[1] − result.closestPoint[0];
        result.sqrDistance = Dot(diff, diff);
        result.distance = sqrt(result.sqrDistance);
    }
    else
    {
        // If you reach this case, the value of 'result' is one of NO_SOLUTION or
        // FAILED_TO_CONVERGE. The value INVALID_INPUT occurs only when the
        // LCPSolver is passed std::vector inputs whose dimensions are not correct.
        for (int i = 0; i < 3; ++i)
        {
            result.box0Parameter[i] = 0;
            result.box1Parameter[i] = 0;
            result.closestPoint[0][i] = 0;
            result.closestPoint[1][i] = 0;
        }
        result.distance = 0;
        result.sqrDistance = 0;
    }

    result.numLCPIterations = lcp.GetNumIterations();
}
```

Listing 7.3: Pseudocode for computing the distance between two oriented boxes in 3 dimensions. A box is parameterized by $\mathbf{p} = \mathbf{c} + \sum_{i=0}^{2} x_i \mathbf{u}_i$ with $|x_i| \leq e_i$. The point $\mathbf{c}$ is the box center and e_i are extents, which are half the edge lengths of the box edges.

7.4.3   Test-Intersection of Triangle and Cylinder in 3D

Section 7.3.2 showed the construction of the CQP for testing for intersection of a triangle and a finite cylinder in n dimensions. Listing 7.4 shows pseudocode for this query in 3 dimensions.

```
template <typename Real>
struct Triangle3
{
    Point3<Real> vertex[3];
};

template <typename Real>
struct Cylinder3
{
    Point3<Real> center;
    Vector3<Real> direction;
    Real radius;
    Real height;
};

template <typename Real>
struct Triangle3Cylinder3QueryResult
{
    // Specify the maximum number of LCP iterations. The default in the GTL is N^2 for an
    // LCP with N x 1 vector q and N x N matrix M. The convergence is not guaranteed
```

```
    // to occur within N²iterations, so a conservative approach in an application is to
    // examine 'status' after the query. If the value is FAILED_TO_CONVERGE, repeat
    // with a larger maxLCPIterations if so desired.
    int maxLCPIterations;

    // The number of iterations used by LCPSolver regardless of whether or not the query
    // is successful.
    int numLCPIterations;

    // The information returned by the LCP solver about what it discovered.
    LCPSolver<Real, 5>::Result status;

    // The test-intersection query returns only a Boolean result.
    bool intersects;
};

// Set result.maxLCPIterations to the desired value before calling this function.
template <typename Real>
void TestIntersection(Triangle3<Real> triangle, Cylinder3<Real> cylinder,
    Triangle3Cylinder3QueryResult<Real>& result)
{
    Vector3<Real> delta = triangle.vertex[0] - cylinder.center;
    Vector3<Real> edge0 = triangle.vertex[1] - triangle.vertex[0];
    Vector3<Real> edge1 = triangle.vertex[2] - triangle.vertex[0];
    Matrix<Real, 3, 2> E;
    E[0][0] = edge0[0];   E[0][1] = edge1[0];
    E[1][0] = edge0[1];   E[1][1] = edge1[1];
    E[2][0] = edge0[2];   E[2][1] = edge1[2];
    Matrix<Real, 3, 3> P = Matrix<Real, 3, 3>::Identity()
        - OuterProduct(cylinder.direction, cylinder.direction);

    Matrix<Real, 2, 3> ETP = Transpose(E) * P;
    Matrix<Real, 2, 2> A = ETP * E;
    Vector2<Real> b = ETP * delta;
    Vector2<Real> U0TE = cylinder.direction * E;
    Real U0Tdelta = Dot(cylinder.direction, delta);
    Matrix<Real, 3, 2> D;
    D[0][0] = -1;          D[0][1] = -1;
    D[1][0] = U0TE[0];     D[1][1] = U0TE[1];
    D[2][0] = -U0TE[0];    D[2][1] = -U0TE[1];
    Vector3<Real> e;
    e[0] = -1.0;
    e[1] = -0.5 * cylinder.height - U0Tdelta;
    e[1] = -0.5 * cylinder.height + U0Tdelta;

    std::array<Real, 5> q = { b[0], b[1], -e[0], -e[1], -e[2] };
    std::array<std::array<Real, 5>, 5> M;
    {
      M[0] = { A[0][0], A[0][1],    -D[0][0], -D[1][0], -D[2][0] },
      M[1] = { A[1][0], A[1][1],    -D[0][1], -D[1][1], -D[2][1] },

      M[2] = { D[0][0], D[0][1],    0, 0, 0 },
      M[3] = { D[1][0], D[1][1],    0, 0, 0 },
      M[4] = { D[2][0], D[2][1],    0, 0, 0 }
    };

    LCPSolver<Real, 5> lcp;
    lcp.SetMaxLCPIterations(result.maxLCPIterations);
    std::array<Real, 5> w, z;
    LCPSolver<Real, 5> lcp;
    if (lcp.Solve(q, M, w, z, &result.status))
    {
        result.intersects = true;
    }
    else
```

```
    {
        // If you reach this case, the value of 'result' is one of NO_SOLUTION or
        // FAILED_TO_CONVERGE. The value INVALID_INPUT occurs only when the
        // LCPSolver is passed std::vector inputs whose dimensions are not correct.
        result.intersects = false;
    }
    result.numLCPIterations = lcp.GetNumIterations;
}
```

Listing 7.4: Pseudocode for testing for the intersection of a triangle and a finite cylinder in 3 dimensions.

7.4.4 Accuracy Problems with Floating-Point Arithmetic

Although the LCP solver allows for fixed-precision or arbitrary-precision floating-point arithmetic, certain geometric configurations can produce inaccurate results when using fixed-precision. The problem is that rounding errors can cause the choices of basic and nonbasic variables in the pivoting of the LCP tableau to be different from those when using arbitrary-precision arithmetic. In particular, the function LCPSolverShared<Real>::Solve contains the code shown in Listing 7.5.

```
if (Augmented(r, driving) < (Real)0)
{
    // Execute when the nonbasic variable coefficient is negative.
}
```

Listing 7.5: The LCP solver test for a negative nonbasic variable coefficient that is not robust when computing with floating-point arithmetic.

Rounding errors can lead to a misclassification. The arbitrary-precision code will enter the conditional block when the coefficient is negative—no matter how small the magnitude—but the fixed-precision code will not when rounding errors cause the computed coefficient to be a small positive number. The opposite can also happen, where the arbitrary-precision code skips the conditional block but the fixed-precision code enters it.

An example for inaccurate results due to rounding error is shown next when computing the distance between a triangle and an oriented box in 3D. The LCP solver code is in the file DistTriangle3AlignedBox3.h. Listing 7.6 shows a test program that computes the distance using fixed precision and using arbitrary precision.

```
int main()
{
    Triangle3<double> triangle;
    triangle.v[0] = { 0.5, 0.5, 1.5 };
    triangle.v[1] = { 0.50000000000000178, 25.5, 1.5 };
    triangle.v[2] = { -0.50000000000000355, 0.5, 1.5 };

    AlignedBox3<double> box;
    box.min =
        {-28.666800635711962,12.285771701019407,-48.666800635711965};
    box.max =
        {-20.476286168365689,20.476286168365682,-40.476286168365689};
```

```
DCPQuery<double, Triangle3<double>,AlignedBox3<double>> query;
auto result = query(triangle, box);
// result.queryIsSuccessful = true
// result.distance = 47.6918933732887069
// result.sqrDistance = 2274.5166935291390473
// result.triangleParameter =
//    (0.0199525116590519,0.4351332588306535,0.5449142295102947)
// result.boxParameter =
//    (-22.6653617332430883,12.2857717010194065,-40.4762861683656610)
// result.closestPoint[0] =
//    (-0.0449142295102958,11.3783314707663372,1.5000000000000000)
// result.closestPoint[1] =
//    (-22.6653617332430883,12.2857717010194065,-40.4762861683656610)
// result.numLCPIterations = 11

typedef BSRational<UIntegerAP32> Rational;
Triangle3<Rational> rtriangle;
rtriangle.v[0] = { 0.5, 0.5, 1.5 };
rtriangle.v[1] = { 0.50000000000000178, 25.5, 1.5 };
rtriangle.v[2] = { -0.50000000000000355, 0.5, 1.5 };

AlignedBox3<Rational> rbox;
rbox.min =
    {-28.666800635711962,12.285771701019407,-48.666800635711965};
rbox.max =
    {-20.476286168365689,20.476286168365682,-40.476286168365689};

DCPQuery<Rational, Triangle3<Rational>,AlignedBox3<Rational>> rquery;
auto rresult = rquery(rtriangle, rbox);
// rresult.queryIsSuccessful = true
// rresult.distance = 46.6845780373756085
// rresult.sqrDistance = 2179.4498265278130020
// rresult.triangleParameter =
//    (0.0000000000000000,0.4387667833180821,0.5612332166819179)
// rresult.boxParameter =
//    (-20.4762861683656894,12.2857717010194065,-40.4762861683656894)
// rresult.closestPoint[0] =
//    (-0.0612332166819192,11.4691695829520519,1.5000000000000000)
// rresult.closestPoint[1] =
//    (-20.4762861683656894,12.2857717010194065,-40.4762861683656894)
// rresult.numLCPIterations = 7
return 0;
}
```

Listing 7.6: Inaccurate distance calculation because of rounding errors when using fixed-precision floating-point arithmetic.

The relative error in the distance is approximately 0.0216. The pairs of closest points are approximately the same in the y- and z-components, but they differ by a significant amount in the x-component.

The geometric issue is that the plane of the triangle is parallel to a face of the box. A very small rotation of the plane of the triangle, say, about the center of the triangle, can cause a large change in the closest points. The closest points can vary greatly with small changes in the triangle vertices.

If fixed-precision floating-point arithmetic must be used, the problems with parallel configurations in the geometric primitives should be handled differently. In the GTL, LCP-based algorithms are provided for the queries, but specialized algorithms using floating-point arithmetic will also be provided that try to resolve the accuracy problems with parallel configurations.

7.4.5 Dealing with Vector Normalization

To motivate the discussion, consider the test-intersection query for a triangle and a cylinder in 3D. The construction of the matrices and vectors in the CQP assumes real-valued arithmetic (error-free computations). In particular, the cylinder axis direction is a unit-length vector $\mathbf{u}_0$.

The problem in an implementation is that if the axis direction is computed by normalizing a vector and then that direction is passed to the query and treated as a 3-tuple of rational numbers, the length is not guaranteed to be 1 (due to rounding errors). For example, suppose the cylinder axis is in the direction of $(1, 2, 3)$. The normalized vector is $(1, 2, 3)/\sqrt{14}$. The normalization code is shown in Listing 7.7.

```
Vector3<double> u0 = { 1.0, 2.0, 3.0 };
double length = sqrt(u0[0]*u0[0]+u0[1]*u0[1]+u0[2]*u0[2]);  // sqrt(14.0)
u0 /= length;
// u0 = (0.26726124191242440, 0.53452248382484879, 0.80178372573727319)

typedef BSRational<UIntegerAP32> Rational;
Vector3<Rational> ru0 = { u0[0], u0[1], u0[2] };
Rational rSqrLength = Dot(ru0, ru0);
// rSqrLength.biasedExponent = -105
// rSqrLength.bits = 0x00000200 0x00000000 0x000cc8b2 0xff10b80f
// Moving the binary point from the right-most bit 105 units to the left,
// rSqrLength = 1.0̄^53 110011001000101100101111111100010000101110000000011111
// where 0̄^53 denotes the occurrence of 53 0-valued bits. Therefore,
// rSqrLength = 1.t where t > 0.
```

Listing 7.7: Rounding errors when normalizing the cylinder axis direction.

Suppose that $\mathbf{u}_0$ was normalized from a vector $\mathbf{v}$; that is, $\mathbf{u}_0 = \mathbf{v}/|\mathbf{v}|$. The vector $\mathbf{v}$ has rational components but its length $|\mathbf{v}|$ is usually irrational. Replace this expression in the CQP for the triangle-cylinder test-intersection query. The projection matrix is $\mathcal{P} = I - \mathbf{v}\mathbf{v}^\mathsf{T}/|\mathbf{v}|^2$ and can be computed exactly using rational arithmetic because of the occurrence of the squared distance. The quadratic matrix is $A = E^\mathsf{T}\mathcal{P}E$ which is also rational because E involves quantities generated by the differences of rational points. The quadratic vector $\mathbf{b} = E^\mathsf{T}\mathcal{P}\Delta$, which is also rational. The quadratic scalar $c = |\Delta|^2/2$ is rational.

Two of the inequality constraints in $D\mathbf{x} \geq \mathbf{e}$ involve the length $|\mathbf{v}|$,

$$(\mathbf{v}/|\mathbf{v}|)^\mathsf{T} E\mathbf{x} \geq -h/2 - (\mathbf{v}/|\mathbf{v}|)^\mathsf{T}\Delta, \quad -(\mathbf{v}/|\mathbf{v}|)^\mathsf{T} E\mathbf{x} \geq -h/2 + (\mathbf{v}/|\mathbf{v}|)^\mathsf{T}\Delta \quad (7.52)$$

Multiplying the inequalites by the length eliminates the division, but the length term itself cannot be eliminated,

$$\mathbf{v}^\mathsf{T} E\mathbf{x} \geq -h|\mathbf{v}|/2 - \mathbf{v}^\mathsf{T}\Delta, \quad -\mathbf{v}^\mathsf{T} E\mathbf{x} \geq -h|\mathbf{v}|/2 + \mathbf{v}^\mathsf{T}\Delta \quad (7.53)$$

If $|\mathbf{v}|$ is irrational, approximate it by a rational number and then execute the

LCP solver using arbitrary-precision floating-point arithmetic. However, the resulting minimizer point $\mathbf{x}$ and corresponding minimum function value $f(\mathbf{x})$ are considered to be approximations.

It is possible to avoid the approximation of the length of a vector that is an input to the LCP solver by using real quadratic fields. The idea is to introduce a symbolic component to the computations that involves the vector length as the square root of a rational number. Details for such an approach can be found in Chapter 3.

To illustrate the use of real quadratic fields, consider the LCP formulation of the convex quadratic program for determining whether a triangle and cylinder intersect. The implementations shown next are for double-precision floating-point arithmetic, for rational arithmetic and for a real quadratic field where d is the rational squared length of the cylinder axis direction.

Listing 7.8 shows the source code for the query when the numeric type is double (64-bit floating-point arithmetic).

```
std :: array<double, 2> TestIntersectionDouble(
    Triangle3<double> const& inTri, Cylinder3<double> const& inCyl)
{
    Vector3<double> delta = inTri.v[0] - inCyl.axis.origin;
    Vector3<double> edge1 = inTri.v[1] - inTri.v[0];
    Vector3<double> edge2 = inTri.v[2] - inTri.v[0];
    Matrix<3, 2, double> E;  E.SetCol(0, edge1);  E.SetCol(1, edge2);
    Matrix<3, 3, double> P = Matrix<3, 3, double>::Identity() -
        OuterProduct(inCyl.axis.direction, inCyl.axis.direction);

    Matrix<2, 3, double> ETP = MultiplyATB(E, P);
    Matrix<2, 2, double> A = ETP * E;
    Vector2<double> b = ETP * delta;
    Vector2<double> u0TE = inCyl.axis.direction * E;
    double u0Tdelta = Dot(inCyl.axis.direction, delta);
    Matrix<3, 2, double> D;
    D(0, 0) = -1.0;   D(0, 1) = -1.0;
    D(1, 0) = u0TE[0];  D(1, 1) = u0TE[1];
    D(2, 0) = -u0TE[0];  D(2, 1) = -u0TE[1];
    Vector3<double> e{ -1.0, -0.5 * inCyl.height - u0Tdelta,
        -0.5 * inCyl.height + u0Tdelta };

    std :: array<double, 5> q = { b[0], b[1], -e[0], -e[1], -e[2] };
    std :: array<std :: array<double, 5>, 5> M;
    {
        M[0] = { A(0, 0), A(0, 1), -D(0, 0), -D(1, 0), -D(2, 0) };
        M[1] = { A(1, 0), A(1, 1), -D(0, 1), -D(1, 1), -D(2, 1) };
        M[2] = { D(0, 0), D(0, 1), 0.0, 0.0, 0.0 };
        M[3] = { D(1, 0), D(1, 1), 0.0, 0.0, 0.0 };
        M[4] = { D(2, 0), D(2, 1), 0.0, 0.0, 0.0 };
    }

    std :: array<double, 5> w, z;
    LCPSolver<double, 5> lcp;
    lcp.Solve(q, M, w, z);
    std :: array<double, 2> result = { z[0], z[1] };
    return result;
}
```

Listing 7.8: Double-precision arithmetic for executing the LCP solver for triangle-cylinder intersection. The computations necessarily have rounding errors.

The returned numbers are the triangle parameters for determining the triangle point closest to the cylinder axis and that is between the two planes of the cylinder caps.

Listing 7.9 shows the source code for the query when the numeric type is BSRational<UIntegerAP32> (arbitrary-precision arithmetic).

```cpp
using Rational = BSRational<UIntegerAP32>;

std :: array<Rational , 2> TestIntersectionRational(
    Triangle3<double> const& inTri , Cylinder3<double> const& inCyl)
{
    Triangle3<Rational> triangle;
    triangle.v[0] = { inTri.v[0][0], inTri.v[0][1], inTri.v[0][2] };
    triangle.v[1] = { inTri.v[1][0], inTri.v[1][1], inTri.v[1][2] };
    triangle.v[2] = { inTri.v[2][0], inTri.v[2][1], inTri.v[2][2] };

    Cylinder3<Rational> cylinder;
    cylinder.axis.origin =
    {
        inCyl.axis.origin[0],
        inCyl.axis.origin[1],
        inCyl.axis.origin[2]
    };
    cylinder.axis.direction =
    {
        inCyl.axis.direction[0],
        inCyl.axis.direction[1],
        inCyl.axis.direction[2]
    };
    cylinder.radius = inCyl.radius;
    cylinder.height = inCyl.height;

    Vector3<Rational> delta = triangle.v[0] - cylinder.axis.origin;
    Vector3<Rational> edge1 = triangle.v[1] - triangle.v[0];
    Vector3<Rational> edge2 = triangle.v[2] - triangle.v[0];
    Matrix<3, 2, Rational> E;
    E.SetCol(0, edge1);
    E.SetCol(1, edge2);
    Matrix<3, 3, Rational> P = Matrix<3, 3, Rational>::Identity() -
        OuterProduct(cylinder.axis.direction, cylinder.axis.direction);

    Matrix<2, 3, Rational> ETP = MultiplyATB(E, P);
    Matrix<2, 2, Rational> A = ETP * E;
    Vector2<Rational> b = ETP * delta;
    Vector2<Rational> u0TE = cylinder.axis.direction * E;
    BSR u0Tdelta = Dot(cylinder.axis.direction, delta);
    Matrix<3, 2, Rational> D;
    Rational rNegOne(-1), rNegHalf(-0.5), rZero(0);
    D(0, 0) = rNegOne;
    D(0, 1) = rNegOne;
    D(1, 0) = u0TE[0];
    D(1, 1) = u0TE[1];
    D(2, 0) = -u0TE[0];
    D(2, 1) = -u0TE[1];
    Vector3<Rational> e;
    e[0] = rNegOne;
    e[1] = rNegHalf * cylinder.height - u0Tdelta;
    e[2] = rNegHalf * cylinder.height + u0Tdelta;

    std::array<Rational, 5> q = { b[0], b[1], -e[0], -e[1], -e[2] };
    std::array<std::array<Rational, 5>, 5> M;
    {
        M[0] = { A(0, 0), A(0, 1), -D(0, 0), -D(1, 0), -D(2, 0) };
        M[1] = { A(1, 0), A(1, 1), -D(0, 1), -D(1, 1), -D(2, 1) };
        M[2] = { D(0, 0), D(0, 1), rZero, rZero, rZero };
```

```
        M[3] = { D(1, 0), D(1, 1), rZero, rZero, rZero };
        M[4] = { D(2, 0), D(2, 1), rZero, rZero, rZero };
    }

    std::array<Rational, 5> w, z;
    LCPSolver<Rational, 5> lcp;
    lcp.Solve(q, M, w, z);

    std::array<Rational, 2> result = { z[0], z[1] };
    return result;
}
```

Listing 7.9: Rational arithmetic for executing the LCP solver for triangle-cylinder intersection. The computations can be inaccurate when the cylinder axis direction is not unit length when computed as the square root of the sum of squares of rational components.

The returned numbers are the triangle parameters for determining the triangle point closest to the cylinder axis and that is between the two planes of the cylinder caps.

Listing 7.10 shows the source code for the query when the numeric type is QFElement for a quadratic field.

```
using Rational = BSRational<UIntegerAP32>;
using QFN1 = QFElement<Rational, 1>;

std::array<QFN1, 2> TestIntersectionQFNumber(
    Triangle3<double> const& inTri, Cylinder3<double> const& inCyl)
{
    Triangle3<Rational> triangle;
    triangle.v[0] = { inTri.v[0][0], inTri.v[0][1], inTri.v[0][2] };
    triangle.v[1] = { inTri.v[1][0], inTri.v[1][1], inTri.v[1][2] };
    triangle.v[2] = { inTri.v[2][0], inTri.v[2][1], inTri.v[2][2] };

    Cylinder3<Rational> cylinder;
    cylinder.axis.origin =
    {
        inCyl.axis.origin[0],
        inCyl.axis.origin[1],
        inCyl.axis.origin[2]
    };
    cylinder.axis.direction =
    {
        inCyl.axis.direction[0],
        inCyl.axis.direction[1],
        inCyl.axis.direction[2]
    };
    cylinder.radius = inCyl.radius;
    cylinder.height = inCyl.height;

    Rational d = Dot(cylinder.axis.direction, cylinder.axis.direction);

    Vector3<Rational> delta = triangle.v[0] - cylinder.axis.origin;
    Vector3<Rational> edge1 = triangle.v[1] - triangle.v[0];
    Vector3<Rational> edge2 = triangle.v[2] - triangle.v[0];
    Matrix<3, 2, Rational> E;
    E.SetCol(0, edge1);
    E.SetCol(1, edge2);
    Matrix<3, 3, Rational> P = Matrix<3, 3, Rational>::Identity() -
        OuterProduct(cylinder.axis.direction, cylinder.axis.direction) / d;

    Matrix<2, 3, Rational> ETP = MultiplyATB(E, P);
    Matrix<2, 2, Rational> A = ETP * E;
    Vector2<Rational> b = ETP * delta;
```

```
Vector2<Rational> u0TE = cylinder.axis.direction * E;
Rational u0Tdelta = Dot(cylinder.axis.direction, delta);
Matrix<3, 2, Rational> D;
Rational rOne(1), rNegOne(-1), rNegHalf(-0.5), rZero(0);
D(0, 0) = rNegOne;
D(0, 1) = rNegOne;
D(1, 0) = u0TE[0];
D(1, 1) = u0TE[1];
D(2, 0) = -u0TE[0];
D(2, 1) = -u0TE[1];
QFN1 const qfnZero(rZero, rZero, d), qfnOne(rOne, rZero, d);
Vector3<QFN1> e;
e[0] = QFN1(rNegOne, rZero, d);
e[1] = QFN1(-u0Tdelta, rNegHalf * cylinder.height, d);
e[2] = QFN1(u0Tdelta, rNegHalf * cylinder.height, d);

std::array<QFN1, 5> q =
{
    QFN1(b[0], rZero, d),
    QFN1(b[1], rZero, d),
    -e[0],
    -e[1],
    -e[2]
};
std::array<std::array<QFN1, 5>, 5> M;
M[0][0] = QFN1(A(0, 0), rZero, d);
M[0][1] = QFN1(A(0, 1), rZero, d);
M[1][0] = M[0][1];
M[1][1] = QFN1(A(1, 1), rZero, d);
M[2][0] = QFN1(D(0, 0), rZero, d);
M[2][1] = QFN1(D(0, 1), rZero, d);
M[3][0] = QFN1(D(1, 0), rZero, d);
M[3][1] = QFN1(D(1, 1), rZero, d);
M[4][0] = QFN1(D(2, 0), rZero, d);
M[4][1] = QFN1(D(2, 1), rZero, d);
M[0][2] = -M[2][0];
M[1][2] = -M[2][1];
M[0][3] = -M[3][0];
M[1][3] = -M[3][1];
M[0][4] = -M[4][0];
M[1][4] = -M[4][1];
for (int r = 2; r < 5; ++r)
{
    for (int c = 2; c < 5; ++c)
    {
        M[r][c] = qfnZero;
    }
}

// The internal code for the LCP solver must create copies of 0 and 1 to assign to
// class members involved in the LCP iterations. These copies must have the d-value
// that matches the input q and M.
LCPSolver<QFN1, 5> lcp(qfnZero, qfnOne);
std::array<QFN1, 5> w, z;
lcp.Solve(q, M, w, z);

std::array<QFN1, 2> result = { z[0], z[1] };
return result;
}
```

Listing 7.10: Quadratic-field arithmetic for a real quadratic field when executing the LCP solver for triangle-cylinder intersection. The computations are exact in the sense of returning parameters of the form $x + y\sqrt{d}$ where x and y are rational numbers and $\sqrt{d}$ is represented symbolically.

The returned numbers are the triangle parameters for determining the triangle point closest to the cylinder axis and that is between the two planes of the cylinder caps.

Notice that most of the quantities in the code are rational numbers. The first introduction of real quadratic field numbers is in the assignment to the 3-tuple **e** in the inequality constraints of equation (7.53); that is, e[1] and e[2] are elements of $\mathbb{Q}(\sqrt{d})$. The call to lcp.Solve will involve arithmetic in the real quadratic field.

Executions of the functions of Listings 7.8, 7.9 and 7.10 are shown in Listing 7.11. In the comments, the rational numbers are listed as odd integers times powers of two, a format described in Chapter 2.

```
int main()
{
    Triangle3<double> triangle;
    triangle.v[0] = { 0.5, -1.0, 0.0 };
    triangle.v[1] = { 3.0, 1.0, 0.0 };
    triangle.v[2] = { 0.5, 2.0, 0.0 };

    Vector3<double> nonUnitDirection{ 1.0, 2.0, 3.0 };
    Cylinder3<double> cylinder;
    cylinder.axis.origin = { 0.0, 0.0, 0.0 };
    cylinder.axis.direction = nonUnitDirection;
    Normalize(cylinder.axis.direction);
    cylinder.radius = 1.0;
    cylinder.height = 2.0;

    // The point on the triangle closest to the cylinder axis is
    // V_0 + (0)(V_1 - V_0) + (11/30)(V_2 - V_0). In the LCP solver, we expect that
    // z = (0, 11/30, .). Note that 11/30 = 0.36‾^∞.

    std::array<double, 2> result;
    result = TestIntersectionDouble(triangle, cylinder);
    // result = (0.00000000000000000, 0.36666666666666670)
    // The second component is an approximation to 11/30.

    std::array<BSR, 2> rresult;
    rresult = TestIntersectionBSRational(triangle, cylinder);
    // rresult[0].numerator = 0
    // rresult[0].denominator = 1
    // rresult[1].numerator = [0x0000096DB6DB6DB6DB5D4719DCA15C7F,-108]
    // rresult[1].denominator = [0x0000066DB6DB6DB6DB5D4719DCA15C7F,-106]
    double temp;
    temp = rresult[0];   // 0.00000000000000000
    temp = rresult[1];   // 0.36666666666666670
    // The second component is an approximation to 11/30.

    cylinder.axis.direction = nonUnitDirection;
    std::array<QFN1, 2> qfresult;
    qfresult = TestIntersectionQFNumber(triangle, cylinder);
    // qfresult[0].x[0].numerator = 0
    // qfresult[0].x[0].denominator = 1
    // qfresult[0].x[1].numerator = 0
    // qfresult[0].x[1].denominator = 1
    // qfresult[0].d.numerator = 14
    // qfresult[0].d.denominator = 1
    // qfresult[0] = 0 + 0 * sqrt(14)
    // qfresult[1].x[0].numerator = [0x0007C5AB,-20] = 11 * 46305 * 2^-20
    // qfresult[1].x[0].denominator = [0x000A992F,-19] = 30 * 46305 * 2^-20
```

```
// qfresult[1].x[1].numerator = 0
// qfresult[1].x[1].denominator = 1
// qfresult[1].d.numerator = 14
// qfresult[1].d.denominator = 1
// qfresult[1] = 11/30 + 0 * sqrt(14)
// The second component is exactly 11/30.
    return 0;
}
```

Listing 7.11: The main function to compare the results of the triangle-cylinder intersection query for various numeric types.

Another slightly more interesting example is shown in Listing 7.12. The triangle intersects the cylinder and the plane of one of the cylinder caps.

```
int main()
{
    Vector3<double> nonUnitDirection{ 1.0, 2.0, 3.0 };
    Vector3<double> perp{ -3.0, 0.0, 1.0 };

    Triangle3<double> triangle;
    triangle.v[0] = 0.125 * perp + 0.5 * nonUnitDirection;
    triangle.v[1] = 0.25 * perp;
    triangle.v[2] = perp;

    Cylinder3<double> cylinder;
    cylinder.axis.origin = { 0.0, 0.0, 0.0 };
    cylinder.axis.direction = nonUnitDirection;
    Normalize(cylinder.axis.direction);
    cylinder.radius = 1.0;
    cylinder.height = 2.0;

    // The point on the triangle inside the planes of the cylinder caps and closest to the
    // cylinder axis is V_0 + (1 - (1/7) * sqrt(14))(V_1 - V_0) + (0)(V_2 - V_0).

    Normalize(cylinder.axis.direction);
    std::array<double, 2> result;
    result = ExecuteDouble(triangle, cylinder);
    // result = (0.46547751617515137, 0.00000000000000000)
    // The first component is an approximation to 1-(1/7)*sqrt(14).

    std::array<Rational, 2> rresult;
    rresult = ExecuteRational(triangle, cylinder);
    // rresult[0].numerator = [0x001bddd422d07e93, -53]
    // rresult[0].denominator = [0x003bddd422d07e93, -53]
    // rresult[1].numerator = 0
    // rresult[1].denominator = 1
    double temp;
    temp = rresult[0];    // 0.46547751617515126
    temp = rresult[1];    // 0.00000000000000000

    cylinder.axis.direction = nonUnitDirection;
    std::array<QFType, 2> qfresult;
    qfresult = ExecuteQFType(triangle, cylinder);
    // qfresult[0].x[0].numerator = [+0x00000031, -5]
    // qfresult[0].x[0].denominator = [+0x00000031, -5]
    // qfresult[0].x[1].numerator = [-0x00000007, -5]
    // qfresult[0].x[1].denominator = [+0x00000031, -5]
    // qfresult[0].d.numerator = 14
    // qfresult[0].d.denominator = 1
    // qfresult[0] = 1 - (1/7) * sqrt(14)
    // qfresult[1].x[0].numerator = 0
```

```
// qfresult[1].x[0].denominator = 1
// qfresult[1].x[1].numerator = 0
// qfresult[1].x[1].denominator = 1
// qfresult[1].d.numerator = 14
// qfresult[1].d.denominator = 1
// qfresult[1] = 0 + 0 * sqrt(14)
// 1 - (1/7)*sqrt(14) is approximately 0.4654775161751512306308930382404
  return 0;
}
```

Listing 7.12: The triangle point inside the cylinder and closest to the cylinder axis is a point on the plane that bounds the top of the cylinder.

Chapter 8

Intersection Queries

Given two geometric objects, a test-intersection query determines whether the objects intersect but not where they intersect. The outcome is a Boolean value (intersect or do-not-intersect). A find-intersection query determines the intersection set between two objects, if it exists.

Similar to distance queries, algorithms for computing the intersection between pairs of standard geometric objects are relatively straightforward to derive mathematically. However, when computing with floating-point arithmetic, parallelism (or near parallelism) of object features can lead to incorrect results for test-intersection queries or to incorrect intersection sets for find-intersection queries.

A popular and powerful test-intersection query involves the method of separating axes, which applies to stationary convex objects. This algorithm is discussed in detail in Section 8.1. The idea extends to objects moving with constant linear velocity. Moreover, when the objects are initially separated but moving towards each other, it is possible to determine the first time of contact, which is useful in the collision detection subsystem of physics engines. Section 8.2 covers this topic.

The term linear components refers to lines, rays and line segments (or segments, for short). Several algorithms for line-object intersection are discussed in the context of arbitrary-precision arithmetic and quadratic-field arithmetic. These include test-intersection and find-intersection queries for linear components with spheres, boxes or cones. Sections 8.3, 8.4 and 8.5 contain the derivations for the queries. The line-cone find-intersection query is particularly complicated, but the intersection set can be computed exactly using 2-root quadratic-field arithmetic.

Sections 8.6 and 8.7 cover the intersection queries for ellipses and ellipsoids. The test-intersection query for ellipses and for ellipsoids are handled with the same mathematical framework. The method of Lagrange multipliers is used for a minimization algorithm that is related to whether the objects overlap, just touch or are separated. The geometric algorithm is formulated to support arbitrary-precision arithmetic. The find-intersection query for ellipses is discussed in great detail. It is a robust method for determining the points of intersection of the two ellipses and is tied to intuitive geometrical features of the ellipses. The find-intersection query for ellipsoids is quite complicated, because the intersection set can contain algebraic curves that are not quadratic. However, exact results are attainable using arithmetic involving algebraic numbers and modular polynomial operations.

8.1 Method of Separating Axes

This section describes the *method of separating axes*, an algorithm for determining whether two stationary convex objects are intersecting. The ideas can be extended to handle moving convex objects and are useful for predicting collisions of the objects and for computing the first time of contact. The current focus of this section is the test-intersection geometric query, which indicates whether an intersection exists or will occur when the objects are moving. The problem of computing the set of intersection is a find-intersection geometric query and is generally more difficult to implement than the test-intersection query. Information from the test-intersection query can help determine the contact set that the find-intersection query must construct when the objects are moving.

8.1.1 Separation by Projection onto a Line

A test for nonintersection of two convex objects is simply stated: If there exists a line for which the intervals of projection of the two objects onto that line do not intersect, then the objects do not intersect. Such a line is called a *separating line* or, more commonly, a *separating axis*.

The translation of a separating line is also a separating line, so mathematically it is sufficient to consider lines that contain the origin. However, in practice, a line is chosen that contains a point of one of the objects. This is helpful to reduce problems caused by rounding errors when computing with floating-point arithmetic.

Given a line containing the origin and with unit-length direction $\mathbf{D}$, the projection of a compact and convex set C onto the line is the interval

$$I = [\lambda_{\min}(\mathbf{D}), \lambda_{\max}(\mathbf{D})] = [\min\{\mathbf{D} \cdot \mathbf{X} : \mathbf{X} \in C\}, \max\{\mathbf{D} \cdot \mathbf{X} : \mathbf{X} \in C\}] \quad (8.1)$$

Two compact convex sets C_0 and C_1 are separated if there exists a direction $\mathbf{D}$ for which the projection intervals I_0 and I_1 do not intersect. Specifically they do not intersect when

$$\lambda_{\min}^{(0)}(\mathbf{D}) > \lambda_{\max}^{(1)}(\mathbf{D}) \text{ or } \lambda_{\max}^{(0)}(\mathbf{D}) < \lambda_{\min}^{(1)}(\mathbf{D}) \quad (8.2)$$

The superscript corresponds to the index of the convex set. Although the comparisons are made where $\mathbf{D}$ is unit length, the comparison results are invariant to changes in length of the vector. This follows from $\lambda_{\min}(t\mathbf{D}) = t\lambda_{\min}(\mathbf{D})$ and $\lambda_{\max}(t\mathbf{D}) = t\lambda_{\max}(\mathbf{D})$ for $t > 0$. The Boolean value of the pair of

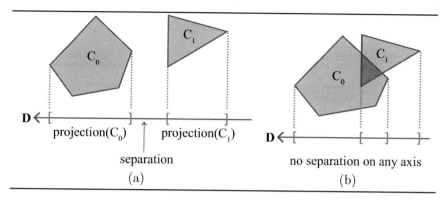

FIGURE 8.1: (a) Nonintersecting convex polygons. (b) Intersecting convex polygons.

comparisons is also invariant when $\mathbf{D}$ is replaced by the opposite direction $-\mathbf{D}$. This follows from $\lambda_{\min}(-\mathbf{D}) = -\lambda_{\max}(\mathbf{D})$ and $\lambda_{\max}(-\mathbf{D}) = -\lambda_{\min}(\mathbf{D})$. When $\mathbf{D}$ is not unit length, the intervals obtained for the separating axis tests are not the projections of the object onto the line; rather they are scaled versions of the projection intervals. No distinction is made between the scaled projection and regular projection. The terminology is also used that the direction vector for a separating axis is called a *separating direction*, which is not necessarily unit length.

The ideas apply to closed convex sets whether bounded or unbounded, but the discussion is restricted to the common case where the sets are convex polygons or convex polyhedra.

8.1.2 Separation of Convex Polygons in 2D

For a pair of convex polygons in 2D, only a finite set of direction vectors needs to be considered for separation tests. That set includes the normal vectors to the edges of the polygons. Figure 8.1(a) shows two nonintersecting polygons that are separated along a direction determined by the normal to an edge of one polygon. Figure 8.1(b) shows two polygons that intersect; there are no separating directions.

The intuition for why only edge normals must be tested is based on having two convex polygons just touching with no interpenetration. Figure 8.2 shows the three possible configurations: edge-edge contact, vertex-edge contact and vertex-vertex contact. The lines between the objects are perpendicular to the separation lines that would occur for the object translated away from the other by an infinitesimal distance.

For $j \in \{0, 1\}$, let C_j be the convex polygons with vertices $\{\mathbf{V}_i^{(j)}\}_{i=0}^{n_j-1}$ that are counterclockwise ordered. The number of vertices for polygon j is n_j. The

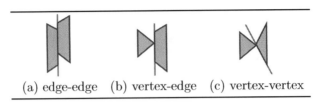

(a) edge-edge   (b) vertex-edge   (c) vertex-vertex

FIGURE 8.2: (a) Edge-edge contact. (b) Vertex-edge contact. (c) Vertex-vertex contact.

direct implementation for a separation test for direction $\mathbf{D}$ involves computing the extreme values of the projection and comparing them. That is, compute $\lambda_{\min}^{(j)}(\mathbf{D}) = \min_{0 \le i < n_0}\{\mathbf{D} \cdot \mathbf{V}_i^{(j)}\}$ and $\lambda_{\max}^{(j)}(\mathbf{D}) = \max_{0 \le i < n_1}\{\mathbf{D} \cdot \mathbf{V}_i^{(j)}\}$ and test the inequalities in equation (8.2). The algorithm is potentially slow because all the vertices are projected onto the line and then sorted to determine the extreme projection values.

Instead, choose the candidate separating axis to be the line with direction $\mathbf{D}$ that passes through a vertex $\mathbf{P}$ of one of the polygons. Moreover, that vertex is an endpoint of an edge that provided the direction $\mathbf{D}$, and $\mathbf{D}$ is chosen to point to the outside of the polygon. The chosen polygon that contains $\mathbf{P}$ is convex, so the projection of that polygon's vertices onto the line $\mathbf{P} + t\mathbf{D}$ is an interval of the form $[T, 0]$ for some $T < 0$. The other polygon's vertices can be projected onto the line one at a time. If a vertex is encountered for which the projection is $t \le 0$, then the line is not a separating axis, but if all the projections have values $t > 0$, the line is separating and the polygons do not intersect.

This algorithm of the previous paragraph is a reasonable modification when the polygons have a large number of nonparallel edges. For triangles or rectangles, the direct implementation is a better choice. In particular, it is a better choice when the rectangles are represented by a center point, two orthonormal axes and two half-width measurements; the projection intervals are trivial to compute with this representation. The assumption is that the polygon vertices are listed in counterclockwise order. Given an edge direction (x_0, x_1), an outward pointing normal is $(x_0, x_1)^{\perp} = (x_1, -x_0)$. Listing 8.1 contains pseudocode for the separating axis tests.

```
struct Vector2 { Real x, y; };

// The vertices are listed in counterclockwise order.
struct ConvexPolygon2 { int numVertices; Vector2 vertex[]; };

Vector2 Perp(Vector2 v) { return Vector2(v.y, -v.x); }

// This function is generic in the sense that the interface ConvexSet<N> has a member
// numVertices and an array vertex[] of N-tuples.
int WhichSide(ConvexSet<N> C, Vector<N> P, Vector<N> D)
{
    // The vertices are projected to the form P + tD. The return value is +1 if all t > 0,
```

```
            // -1 if all t < 0, but 0 otherwise, in which case the line splits the polygon projection.
            int  positive = 0,  negative = 0;
            for (int  i = 0;  i < C.numVertices ++i )
            {
                   // Project a vertex onto the line.
                   Real  t = Dot(D, C.vertex[i] − P);
                   if (t > 0)
                   {
                          ++positive;
                   }
                   else if (t < 0)
                   {
                          ++negative;
                   }
                   if (positive && negative)
                   {
                          // The polygon has vertices on both sides of the line, so the line is not a
                          // separating axis. Time is saved by not having to project the remaining vertices.
                          return 0;
                   }
            }

            // Either positive > 0 or negative > 0 but not both are positive.
            return (positive > 0 ? +1 : −1);
}

// The function returns 'true' when the polygons intersect.
bool TestIntersection (ConvexPolygon2 C0, ConvexPolygon2 C1)
{
            // Test edges of C_0 for separation. Because of the counterclockwise ordering, the
            // projection interval for C_0 is [T,0] where T < 0. Determine whether C_1 is on the
            // positive side of the line.
            for (int  i0=0,  i1=C0.numVertices −1;  i0<C0.numVertices;  i1=i0++)
            {
                   Vector2 P = C0.vertex[i0];
                   Vector2 D = Perp(C0.vertex[i0] − C0.vertex[i1]);   // outward pointing
                   if (WhichSide(C1, P, D) > 0)
                   {
                          // C_1 is entirely on the positive side of the line P + tD.
                          return false;
                   }
            }

            // Test edges of C_1 for separation. Because of the counterclockwise ordering, the
            // projection interval for C_1 is [T,0] where T < 0. Determine whether C_0 is on the
            // positive side of the line.
            for (int  i0=0,  i1=C1.numVertices −1;  i0<C1.numVertices;  i1=i0++)
            {
                   Vector2 P = C1.vertex[i0];
                   Vector2 D = Perp(C0.vertex[i0] − C0.vertex[i1]);   // outward pointing
                   if (WhichSide(C0, P, D) > 0)
                   {
                          // C_0 is entirely on the positive side of the line P + tD.
                          return false;
                   }
            }

            return true;
}
```

Listing 8.1: The separating axis tests for convex polygons in 2 dimensions.

8.1.3 Separation of Convex Polyhedra in 3D

For a pair of convex polyhedra in 3D, only a finite set of direction vectors needs to be considered for separation tests. That set includes the normal vectors to the faces of the polyhedra and vectors generated by a cross product of two edges, one from each polyhedron. The intuition is similar to that of convex polygons in 2D. If the two polyhedra are just touching with no interpenetration, then the contact is one of face-face, face-edge, face-vertex, edge-edge, edge-vertex or vertex-vertex.

For $j \in \{0, 1\}$, let C_j be the convex polyhedra with vertices $\{\mathbf{V}_i^{(j)}\}_{i=0}^{n_j-1}$, edges $\{\mathbf{E}_i^{(j)}\}_{i=0}^{m_j-1}$ and faces $\{\mathbf{F}_i^{(j)}\}_{i=0}^{\ell_j-1}$. Let the faces be planar convex polygons whose vertices are counterclockwise ordered as the face is viewed from outside the polyhedron. Outward pointing normal vectors can be stored with each face as a way of representing the orientation. The pseudocode for 3D that is similar to that in 2D is provided in Listing 8.2. It is assumed that each face has queries which allow access to the face normal and to a vertex on the face. It is also assumed that each edge has a query that allows access to a vertex on the edge.

```
struct Vector3 { Real x, y, z; }
struct Edge3 { Vector3 vertex[2]; };
struct Face3 { int numVertices; Vector3 vertex[]; Vector3 normal; };

struct ConvexPolyhedron3
{
    int numVertices, numEdges, numFaces;
    Vector3 vertex[];
    Edge3 edge[];
    Face3 face[];
};

// The function returns 'true' when the polyhedra intersect.
bool TestIntersection(ConvexPolyhedron C0, ConvexPolyhedron C1)
{
    // Test faces of C_0 for separation. Because of the counterclockwise ordering, the
    // projection interval for C_0 is [T,0] where T < 0. Determine whether C_1 is on the
    // positive side of the line.
    for (int i = 0; i < C0.numFaces; ++i)
    {
        Vector3 P = C0.face[i].vertex[0];
        Vector3 N = C0.face[i].normal;   // outward pointing
        if (WhichSide(C1, P, N) > 0)
        {
            // C_1 is entirely on the positive side of the line P + tN.
            return false;
        }
    }

    // Test faces of C_1 for separation. Because of the counterclockwise ordering, the
    // projection interval for C_1 is [T,0] where T < 0. Determine whether C_0 is on the
    // positive side of the line.
    for (int i = 0; i < C1.numFaces; ++i)
    {
        Vector3 P = C1.face[i].vertex;
        Vector3 N = C1.face[i].normal;   // outward pointing
        if (WhichSide(C0, P, N) > 0)
        {
            // C_0 is entirely on the positive side of the line P + tN.
```

```
                    return false;
            }
    }

    // Test cross products of pairs of edge directions, one edge from each polyhedron.
    for (int i0 = 0; i0 < C0.numEdges; ++i0)
    {
        Vector3 D0 = C0.edge[i0].vertex[1] − C0.edge[i0].vertex[0];
        Vector3 P = C0.edge[i0].vertex[0];
        for (int i1 = 0; i1 < C1.numEdges; ++i1)
        {
            Vector3 D1 = C1.edge[i1].vertex[1] − C1.edge[i1].vertex[0];
            Vector3 N = Cross(D0, D1);

            if (N != Vector3(0, 0, 0))
            {
                int side0 = WhichSide(C0, P, N);
                if (side0 == 0)
                {
                    continue;
                }

                int side1 = WhichSide(C1, P, N);
                if (side1 == 0)
                {
                    continue;
                }

                if (side0 * side1 < 0)
                {
                    // The projections of C_0 and C_1 onto the line P + tN are on
                    // opposite sides of the projection of P.
                    return false;
                }
            }
        }
    }

    return true;
}
```

Listing 8.2: The separating axis tests for convex polyhedra in 3 dimensions. The WhichSide function is the one of Listing 8.1 but for dimension $N = 3$.

The code works correctly for arbitrary-precision arithmetic. If the code is executed instead with floating-point arithmetic, the processing of cross products of edges is not robust. If two edges are parallel (or nearly parallel numerically), the cross product N is nearly zero and its components are effectively noise. The exact comparison to the zero vector is not robust. Typically, a floating-point implementation will test whether the length of N is sufficiently large (via a user-defined epsilon) before entering the block of code that determines which-sidedness.

8.1.4 Separation of Convex Polygons in 3D

For a pair of convex polygons in 3D, again only a finite set of direction vectors needs to be considered for separation tests. For $j = 0$ and $j = 1$, let C_j be the convex polygons with vertices $\{\mathbf{V}_i^{(j)}\}_{i=0}^{m_j-1}$ with the index wrap-around convention $\mathbf{V}_{m_j}^{(j)} = \mathbf{V}_0^{(j)}$. Each set of vertices is necessarily coplanar.

The edges for the polygons are $\mathbf{E}_i^{(j)} = \mathbf{V}_{i+1}^{(j)} - \mathbf{V}_i^{(j)}$ for $0 \le i < m_j$. Let $\mathbf{N}^{(j)}$ be normal vectors for those planes, chosen so that an observer on the side of the plane to which the normal is directed sees the triangle vertices listed in counterclockwise order.

The polygon normals are potential separating directions. If either normal direction separates the polygons, then no intersection occurs. If neither normal direction separates the polygons, then two possibilities exist for the remaining potential separating directions.

The first case is that the polygons are coplanar—effectively the 2D case— and the remaining potential separating directions are those vectors in the common plane and that are perpendicular to the polygon edges, $\mathbf{E}_i^{(j)} \times \mathbf{N}^{(j)}$ for $0 \le j \le 1$ and $0 \le i < m_j$, a total of $2m_j$ vectors. By the convention for choosing the normal vectors, each cross product is in the plane of the polygon and points to the outside of the polygon for its corresponding edge.

The second case is that the polygon planes are not parallel and that each polygon is split by the plane of the other polygon. The remaining potential separating directions are the cross products $\mathbf{E}_i^{(0)} \times \mathbf{E}_j^{(1)}$ for $0 \le i < m_0$ and $0 \le j < m_1$, a total of $m_0 m_1$ vectors.

Listing 8.3 contains pseudocode for the test-intersection query.

```
struct ConvexPolygon3
{
    int numVertices;
    Vector3 vertex [];
    Vector3 normal;    // ... to the plane of the polygon
};

bool TestIntersection(ConvexPolygon3 C0, ConvexPolygon3 C1)
{
    // Test the normal to the plane of C0 for separation. The projection of C0 onto the
    // normal line P + tN produces the degenerate interval [0, 0].
    Vector3 P = C0.vertex[0];
    Vector3 N = C0.normal;
    if (WhichSide(C1, P, N) != 0)
    {
        // C1 is entirely on one side of the plane of C0.
        return false;
    }

    // Test the normal to the plane of C1 for separation. The projection of C1 onto the
    // normal line P + tN produces the degenerate interval [0, 0].
    P = C1.vertex[0];
    N = C1.normal;
    if (WhichSide(C0, P, N) != 0)
    {
        // C0 is entirely on one side of the plane of C1.
        return false;
    }

    // If the planes of the polygons are parallel but separated, the previous code will
    // generate a return (when testing the normal to the plane of C0). Therefore, the
    // remaining cases are that the planes are not parallel or they are the same plane.
    // The distinction is made simply by testing whether the normals are nonparallel or
    // parallel, respectively.
    Vector3 N0xN1 = Cross(C0.normal, C1.normal);
    if (N0xN1 != Vector3(0, 0, 0))    // The planes are not parallel.
```

```
    {
        for (int i0 = 0; i0 < C0.numEdges; ++i0)
        {
            Vector3 D0 = C0.edge[i0].vertex[1] - C0.edge[i0].vertex[0];
            Vector3 P = C0.edge[i0].vertex[0];
            for (int i1 = 0; i1 < C1.numEdges; ++i1)
            {
                Vector3 D1 = C1.edge[i1].vertex[1] - C1.edge[i1].vertex[0];
                Vector3 N = Cross(D0, D1);

                if (N != Vector3(0, 0, 0))
                {
                    int side0 = WhichSide(C0, P, N);
                    if (side0 == 0) { continue; }
                    int side1 = WhichSide(C1, P, N);
                    if (side1 == 0) { continue; }
                    if (side0 * side1 < 0)
                    {
                        // The projections of C_0 and C_1 onto the line P + tN are on
                        // opposite sides of the projection of P.
                        return false;
                    }
                }
            }
        }
    }
    else    // The polygons are coplanar.
    {
        // Test edges of C_0 for separation.
        for (int i0 = 0; i0 < C0.numEdges; ++i0)
        {
            Vector3 P = C0.edge[i0].vertex[0];
            Vector3 D = Cross(C0.edge[i0], C0.normal);   // outward pointing
            if (WhichSide(C1, P, D) > 0)
            {
                // C_1 is entirely on the positive side of the line P + tD.
                return false;
            }
        }

        // Test edges of C1 for separation.
        for (int i1 = 0; i1 < C1.numEdges; ++i1)
        {
            Vector3 P = C1.edge[i1].vertex[0];
            Vector3 D = Cross(C1.edge[i1], C1.normal);   // outward pointing
            if (WhichSide(C0, P, D) > 0)
            {
                // C_0 is entirely on the positive side of the line P + tD.
                return false;
            }
        }
    }

    return true;
}
```

Listing 8.3: The separating axis tests for convex polygons in 3 dimensions. The function WhichSide is the one defined in Listing 8.2.

When using floating-point arithmetic, the same warning about nonrobustness applies as in the convex polyhedron case. The exact comparison of N to the zero vector should be replaced by an epsilon test. However, when computing with arbitrary-precision arithmetic, the code is correct as is.

8.1.5   Separation of Moving Convex Objects

The method of separating axes can be extended to handle convex objects moving with constant linear velocity and no angular velocity. If C_0 and C_1 are convex objects with linear velocities $\mathbf{W}_0$ and $\mathbf{W}_1$, then it can be determined via projections whether the objects will intersect for some time $T \geq 0$. Moreover, if they do, the first time of contact can be computed. Without loss of generality, it is enough to work with a stationary object C_0 and a moving object C_1 with velocity $\mathbf{W}$ because one can always use $\mathbf{W} = \mathbf{W}_1 - \mathbf{W}_0$ to perform the calculations as if C_0 were not moving.

If the C_0 and C_1 are initially intersecting, then the first time of contact is $T = 0$. The set of intersection is itself convex, but computing the set is complicated depending on the nature of the objects themselves. For example, if C_0 and C_1 are convex polygons in 2 dimensions and that overlap initially, the set of intersection is a convex polygon. However, if C_0 is a convex polygon and C_1 is a solid ellipse that overlap in a region of positive area, the set of intersection has a boundary consisting of line segments and elliptical arcs. For many physics simulations, the objects are initially placed so that they are not overlapping.

Let the convex objects be separated initially. The projection of C_1 onto a line with unit-length direction $\mathbf{D}$ is an interval that is moving with speed $s = \mathbf{D} \cdot \mathbf{W}$. If the projection interval of C_1 moves away from the projection interval of C_0, then the two objects will never intersect. The interesting cases are when the projection intervals for C_1 move towards those of C_0.

The intuition for how to predict an intersection is much like that for selecting the potential separating directions in the first place. If the two convex objects intersect at a first time $T_{\text{first}} > 0$, then their projections are not separated along any line. An instant before first contact, the objects are separated. Consequently there must be at least one separating direction for the objects for $T_{\text{first}} - \varepsilon$ for small $\varepsilon > 0$. Similarly, if the two convex objects intersect at a last time $T_{\text{last}} > 0$, then their projections are also not separated at that time along any line, but an instant after last contact, the objects are separated. Consequently there must be at least one separating direction for the objects for $T_{\text{last}} + \varepsilon$ for small $\varepsilon > 0$. Both T_{first} and T_{last} can be tracked as each potential separating axis is processed. After all directions are processed, if $T_{\text{first}} \leq T_{\text{last}}$, then the two objects intersect with first contact time T_{first}. It is also possible that $T_{\text{first}} > T_{\text{last}}$, in which case the two objects cannot intersect. This algorithm is attributed to Ron Levine in a post to the SourceForge game developer algorithms mailing list [17].

Let S_0 and S_1 denote the set of potential separating directions and let $\mathbf{W}_0$ and $\mathbf{W}_1$ denote the velocities for C_0 and C_1, respectively. Listing 8.4 contains pseudocode for testing for intersection of two moving convex objects.

```
bool TestIntersection(Convex C0, Convex C1, Vector W0, Vector W1,
    Real& tFirst, Real& tLast)
{
    Vector W = W1 - W0;   // process as if C0 is stationary, C1 is moving
    tFirst = -infinity;
```

```
        tLast = infinity;

        for (each D0 in C0.S)
        {
            // The potential separating axis is P₀ + sD₀.
            Point P0 = C0.vertices[0]);
            Real speed = Dot(D0,W);    // Assumes D₀ is unit length.

            // Project C₀ onto the separating axis at time 0.
            Real min0, max0;
            ComputeMinMax(P0,D0,C0.numVertices,C0.vertices);

            // Project C₁ onto the separating axis at time 0.
            Real min1, max1;
            ComputeMinMax(P0,D0,C1.numVertices,C1.vertices);

            if (!UpdateTimes(min0,max0,min1,max1,speed,tFirst,tLast))
            {
                return false;
            }
        }

        for (each D1 in C1.S)
        {
            // The potential separating axis is P₁ + sD₁.
            Point P1 = C1.vertices[0]);
            Real speed = Dot(D1,W);    // Assumes D₁ is unit length.

            // Project C₀ onto the separating axis at time 0.
            Real min0, max0;
            ComputeMinMax(P1,D1,C0.numVertices,C0.vertices);

            // Project C₁ onto the separating axis at time 0.
            Real min1, max1;
            ComputeMinMax(P1,D1,C1.numVertices,C1.vertices);

            if (!UpdateTimes(min0,max0,min1,max1,speed,tFirst,tLast))
            {
                return false;
            }
        }

        return true;
}

void ComputeMinMax(Point P, Vector D, int numVertices, Point vertices[],
    Real& min, Real& max)
{
    min = Dot(D, vertices[0] - P), max = min;
    for (int i = 1; i < numVertices; ++i)
    {
        Real dot = Dot(D, vertices[i] - P);
        if (dot < min) { min = dot; } else if (dot > max) { max = dot; }
    }
}

// Update the contact times for the current potential separating axis. If the function returns
// true, the update is successful and you can continue to the next potential separating axis.
// If the function returns false, the convex objects will not intersect.
bool UpdateTimes(Real min0, Real max0, Real min1, Real max1, Real speed,
    Real& tFirst, Real& tLast)
{
    if (max1 < min0)
    {
        // The projection(C₁) is initially on the left of the projection(C₀).
```

```
        if  (!UpdatedSeparated(min0,max0,min1,max1,+speed,tFirst,tLast))
        {
            return  false;
        }
    }
    else  if  (max0 < min1)
    {
        // The projection(C₁) is initially on the right of the projection(C₀).
        if  (!UpdatedSeparated(min1,max1,min0,max0,-speed,tFirst,tLast))
        {
            return  false;
        }
    }
    else
    {
        // The projection(C₀) and projection(C₁) overlap. It is possible that the
        // objects separate at a later time, so the last time of contact potentially
        // needs updating.
        tFirst = 0;
        if  (speed > 0) {  UpdateOverlapping(max0,min1,+speed,tLast); }
        else  if  (speed < 0) {  UpdateOverlapping(max1,min0,-speed,tLast); }
    }

    // Report whether the first and last times of contact are valid.
    return  tFirst <= tLast;
}

bool  UpdateSeparated(Real min0, Real max0, Real min1, Real max1,
    Real speed, Real& tFirst, Real& tLast)
{
    // [min₁,max₁] is initially on the left of [min₀,max₀].
    if  (speed <= 0)
    {
        // The intervals are moving apart.
        return  false;
    }

    Real  t = (min0 - max1) / speed;
    if  (t > tFirst)
    {
        tFirst = t;
    }

    t = (max0 - min1) / speed;
    if  (t < tLast)
    {
        tLast = t;
    }
    return  true;
}

bool  UpdateOverlapping(Real max0, Real min1, Real speed, Real& tLast)
{
    Real  t = (max0 - min1) / speed;
    if  (t < tLast)
    {
        tLast = t;
    }
}
```

Listing 8.4: The separating axis tests to determine first time of contact for convex objects moving with constant linear velocities but no angular velocities. The first time of contact tFirst and the last time of contact tLast are valid only when TestIntersection returns true.

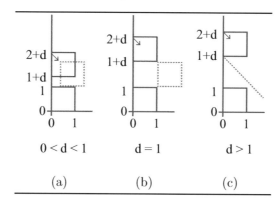

$$0 < d < 1 \qquad\qquad d = 1 \qquad\qquad d > 1$$

(a)   (b)   (c)

FIGURE 8.3: (a) edge-edge intersection predicted. (b) vertex-vertex intersection predicted. (c) no intersection predicted.

The function TestIntersection is written as if the potential separating directions $\mathbf{D}_0$ and $\mathbf{D}_1$ are unit length. However, it turns out that the code is correct even when these directions are not unit length. Portions of the code include sign tests on the speed. The length of $\mathbf{D}$ does not change the outcome of those tests. In the update functions for time, the new time is a ratio whose numerator is a difference of projections and whose denominator is speed. The ratio is structured as $t = (\mathbf{D} \cdot \boldsymbol{\Delta}_0 - \mathbf{D} \cdot \boldsymbol{\Delta}_1)/(\mathbf{D} \cdot \mathbf{W})$. Replacing $\mathbf{D}$ by $\mathbf{U}/|\mathbf{U}|$, where $\mathbf{U}$ is not necessarily unit length, the length $|\mathbf{U}|$ appears multiple times in t-expression, but these terms cancel to obtain $t = (\mathbf{U} \cdot \boldsymbol{\Delta}_0 - \mathbf{U} \cdot \boldsymbol{\Delta}_1)/(\mathbf{U} \cdot \mathbf{W})$. Consequently, the code can be executed with arbitrary-precision arithmetic to obtain an exact result without having to normalize the potential separating directions.

The following example illustrates the ideas. The first box is the unit cube $0 \le x \le 1$ and $0 \le y \le 1$ and is stationary. The second box is initially $0 \le x \le 1$ and $1 + d \le y \le 2 + d$ for some $d > 0$. Let its velocity be $(1, -1)$. Whether or not the second box intersects the first box depends on the value of d. The only potential separating axes are $(1, 0)$ and $(0, 1)$. Figure 8.3 shows the initial configuration for three values of d, one where there will be an edge-edge intersection, one where there will be a vertex-vertex intersection and one where there is no intersection. The black box $[0, 1]^2$ is stationary. The black box with the arrow is moving; the arrow indicates the direction of motion. The dashed dark-gray boxes indicate where the moving box first touches the stationary box. In Figure 8.3(c), the dotted dark-gray line indicates that the moving box will miss the stationary box. For $\mathbf{D} = (1, 0)$, the pseudocode produces min0 $= 0$, max0 $= 1$, min1 $= 0$, max1 $= 1$ and speed $= 1$. The projected intervals are initially overlapping. Because the speed is positive, t $=$ (max0-min1)/speed $= 1 <$ tLast $=$ infinity and tLast is updated to 1. For $\mathbf{D} = (0, 1)$, the pseudocode produces min0 $= 0$, max0 $= 1$, min1 $= 1+$d, max1 $= 2+$d and speed $= $ -1. The moving projected interval is initially on the right of the stationary projected interval. Because the speed is negative, t = (max0-min1)/speed = d > tFirst = 0 and tFirst is updated to d. The next block of code sets t = (min0-max1)/speed = 2+d. The value tLast is not updated because $2 + d < 1$ cannot happen for $d > 0$. On exit from the loop over potential separating directions, $t_{First} = d$ and $t_{last} = 1$. The objects intersect if and only if $t_{first} \leq t_{last}$ or $d \leq 1$. This condition is consistent with the images in Figure 8.3. Figure 8.3(a) has $d < 1$ and Figure 8.3(b) has $d = 1$, intersections occurring in both cases. Figure 8.3(c) has $d > 1$ and no intersection occurs.

8.1.6   Contact Set for Moving Convex Objects

Given two moving convex objects C_0 and C_1 with velocities $\mathbf{W}_0$ and $\mathbf{W}_1$ that are initially not intersecting, the material in the last section showed how to compute the first time of contact T, if it exists. Assuming it does, the sets $C_0 + T\mathbf{W}_0 = \{\mathbf{X} + T\mathbf{W}_0 : \mathbf{X} \in C_0\}$ and $C_1 + T\mathbf{W}_1 = \{\mathbf{X} + T\mathbf{W}_1 : \mathbf{X} \in C_1\}$ are just touching with no interpenetration. Figure 8.2 shows the various configurations for 2D.

The TestIntersection function of Listing 8.4 can be modified to keep track of which vertices, edges and/or faces are projected to the endpoints of the projection interval. At the first time of contact, this information can be used to determine how the two objects are positioned with respect to each other. In 2D, if the contact is vertex-edge or vertex-vertex, the contact set is a single point—a vertex. If the contact is edge-edge, the contact set is a line segment that contains at least one vertex. In 3D, if the contact is vertex-vertex, vertex-edge or vertex-face, then the contact set is a single point—a vertex. If the contact is edge-edge, the contact set is a single point—the intersection of the two lines containing the edges—or a line segment—the edges are on the same line. If the contact is edge-face, then the contact set is a line segment. Otherwise, the contact is face-face and the contact set is the intersection of two planar convex polygons.

8.2   Triangles Moving with Constant Linear Velocity

The method of separating axes can be used to determine the first time and first point of contact between moving convex polygons (2D) or moving convex polyhedron (3D). All the computations in this section are exact when using arbitrary-precision arithmetic. Direction vectors for potentially separating axes do not have to be unit length, so quadratic-field numbers are not required.

8.2.1 Two Moving Triangles in 2D

Consider two triangles, $\langle \mathbf{U}_0, \mathbf{U}_1, \mathbf{U}_2 \rangle$ and $\langle \mathbf{V}_0, \mathbf{V}_1, \mathbf{V}_2 \rangle$, both having counterclockwise ordering. For the sake of indexing notation, define $\mathbf{U}_3 = \mathbf{U}_0$ and $\mathbf{V}_3 = \mathbf{V}_0$. The edge directions are $\mathbf{E}_i = \mathbf{U}_{i+1} - \mathbf{U}_i$ and $\mathbf{F}_i = \mathbf{V}_{i+1} - \mathbf{V}_i$ for $0 \le i \le 2$. Define $(x, y)^\perp = (y, -x)$. Outward pointing normals to the edges are $\mathbf{N}_i = \mathbf{E}_i^\perp$ and $\mathbf{M}_i = \mathbf{F}_i^\perp$ for $0 \le i \le 2$. The six normals are the potential separating directions. Let the triangle velocities be $\mathbf{W}_0$ and $\mathbf{W}_1$.

In Listing 8.4 for testing for intersection of moving convex objects, C_0 and C_1 represent the two triangles. The calculation of the minimum and maximum projections for the triangles can be computed so that additional information is known about how the two triangles are oriented with respect to each other. Three cases occur for the projection: two vertices project to the minimum of the interval and one vertex projects to the maximum; one vertex projects to the minimum of the interval and two vertices project to the maximum; or one vertex projects to the minimum, one vertex projects to the maximum and one vertex projects to an interior point of the interval defined by the minimum and maximum. A flag is associated with each triangle to indicate which of these three cases occurs for a given potential separating direction $\mathbf{D}$; call the flag values M21, M12 and M111. It is also necessary to remember the indices of the vertices that project to the extreme values. Listing 8.5 shows data structures for representing the information.

```
enum ProjectionMap2
{
    M21, M12, M111
};

struct Configuration2
{
    ProjectionMap2 map;
    int index[3];
    Real min, max;
};

enum Side = { NONE, LEFT, RIGHT };
```

Listing 8.5: Data structures to compute contact points for 2D triangles.

The flag Mij refers to i points projecting to the minimum and j points projecting to the maximum; for example, M21 indicates that 2 points project to the minimum and 1 point projects to the maximum. The number index[0] is the index into the array of three triangle vertices for a vertex that maps to the min projection. The number index[2] is the index of that vertex that maps to the max projection. The number index[1] is that of the remaining vertex that can map to the minimum, maximum or some number between them depending on the orientation of the triangle.

When projecting a second triangle onto a potentially separating line determined by the first triangle, it will matter how the projection intervals are ordered. The Side enumeration stores this information. If the side is LEFT, the projection interval of the second triangle is to the left of the projection interval of the first triangle; that is, the maximum of the second projection interval is smaller or equal to the minimum of the first projection interval. If the side is RIGHT, the projection interval of the second triangle is to the right of the projection interval of the first triangle; that is, the minimum of the second projection interval is larger or equal to the maximum of the first projection interval. If the side is NONE, the projection intervals overlap in a subinterval of positive length.

The TestIntersection query of Listing 8.4 can be modified to a FindIntersection query. Two configuration objects are declared, cfg0 for the U-triangle (the C_0 polygon) and cfg1 for the V-triangle (the C_1 polygon). The function ComputeMinMax is modified to the one shown in Listing 8.6.

```
Configuration2 GetConfiguration(Point2 P, Vector2 D, Point2 V[3])
{
    // Compute min and max of interval for triangle. Keep track of vertices that project
    // to min and max.
    Configuration2 cfg;
    Real d[3] = {Dot(D,V[0]-P),Dot(D, V[1]-P),Dot(D,V[2]-P)};
    if (d[0] <= d[1])
    {
        if (d[1] <= d[2])    // d0 ≤ d1 ≤ d2
        {
            if (d[0] != d[1])
            {
                cfg.map = (d[1] != d[2] ? M111 : M12);
            }
            else
            {
                cfg.map = M21;
            }
            cfg.index = {0,1,2};
            cfg.min = d[0];
            cfg.max = d[2];
        }
        else if (d[0] <= d[2])   // d0 ≤ d2 < d1
        {
            if (d[0] != d[2])
            {
                cfg.map = M111;
                cfg.index = {0,2,1};
            }
            else
            {
                cfg.map = M21;
                cfg.index = {2,0,1};
            }
            cfg.min = d[0];
            cfg.max = d[1];
        }
        else   // d2 < d0 ≤ d1
        {
            cfg.map = (d[0] != d[1] ? M12 : M111);
            cfg.index = {2,0,1};
            cfg.min = d[2];
            cfg.max = d[1];
        }
    }
    else
    {
        if (d[2] <= d[1])    // d2 ≤ d1 < d0
        {
            if (d[2] != d[1])
            {
```

```
                cfg.map = M111;
                cfg.index = {2,1,0};
            }
            else
            {
                cfg.map = M21;
                cfg.index = {1,2,0};
            }
            cfg.min = d[2];
            cfg.max = d[0];
        }
        else if (d[2] <= d[0])   // d_1 < d_2 <= d_0
        {
            cfg.map = (d[2] != d[0] ? M111 : M12);
            cfg.index = {1,2,0};
            cfg.min = d[1];
            cfg1.max = d[0];
        }
        else   // d_1 < d_0 < d_2
        {
            cfg.map = M111;
            cfg.index = {1,0,2};
            cfg.min = d[1];
            cfg.max = d[2];
        }
    }
    return cfg;
}
```

Listing 8.6: The modified projection-sorting algorithm of Listing 8.4.

The modified time-updating code of Listing 8.4 is shown in Listing 8.7. The configurations are needed per separating axis, but a pair of global configurations must be maintained to store those configurations associated with the first time of contact (if any).

```
bool UpdateTimes(Configuration2 cfg0, Configuration2 cfg1, Real speed,
    Configuration2& contactCfg0, Configuration2& contactCfg1, Side& side,
    Real& tFirst, Real& tLast)
{
    if (cfg1.max < cfg0.min)
    {
        // The V-interval is initially on the left of the U-interval.
        if (!UpdatedSeparated(cfg0, cfg1,+speed, contactCfg0, contactCfg1,
            tFirst, tLast))
        {
            return false;
        }
        side = LEFT;
    }
    else if (cfg0.max < cfg1.min)
    {
        // The V-interval is initially on the right of the U-interval.
        if (!UpdatedSeparated(cfg1, cfg0,-speed, contactCfg1, contactCg1,
            tFirst, tLast))
        {
            return false;
        }
        side = RIGHT;
    }
    else
    {
        // The U-interval and V-interval overlap. It is possible that the objects
        // separate at a later time, so the last time of contact potentially needs
        // updating.
```

```
    tFirst = 0;
    if (speed > 0)
    {
        UpdateOverlapping(cfg0 , cfg1 ,+speed ,
            contactCfg1 , contactCg1 , tLast );
    }
    else if (speed < 0)
    {
        UpdateOverlapping(cfg1 , cfg0 ,−speed ,
            contactCfg1 , contactCg1 , tLast );
    }
    }

    // Report whether the first and last times of contact are valid.
    return tFirst <= tLast ;
}

bool UpdateSeparated(Configuration2 cfg0 , Configuration2 cfg1 , Real speed ,
    Configuration2& contactCfg0 , Configuration2& contactCfg1 ,
    Real& tFirst , Real& tLast )
{
    // [min1 , max1 ] is initially on the left of [min0 , max0 ].
    if (speed <= 0)
    {
        // The intervals are moving apart.
        return false ;
    }

    Real t = (cfg0 . min − cfg1 . max) / speed ;
    if (t > tFirst )
    {
        tFirst = t ;
        contactCfg0 = cfg0 ;
        contactCfg1 = cfg1 ;
    }

    t = (cfg0 . max − cfg1 . min) / speed ;
    if (t < tLast )
    {
        tLast = t ;
    }
    return true ;
}

bool UpdateOverlapping(Configuration2 cfg0 , Configuration2 cfg1 ,
    Real speed , Real& tLast )
{
    Real t = (cfg0 . max − cfg1 . min) / speed ;
    if (t < tLast )
    {
        tLast = t ;
    }
}
```

Listing 8.7: The modified update-times algorithm of Listing 8.4.

Finally, the modified TestIntersection query to obtain a FindIntersection query is shown in Listing 8.8.

```
struct Triangle2
{
    Point2 vertex [3];
    Vector2 edge [3];
    Vector2 normal [3];
};
```

```
bool FindIntersection (Triangle2 C0, Triangle2 C1, Vector2 W0,
    Vector2 W1, Real& tFirst, Real& tLast, ContactSet& contactSet)
{
    Vector2 W = W1 - W0;    // process as if C₀ is stationary, C₁ is moving
    tFirst = -infinity;
    tLast = infinity;

    Configuration2 contactCfg0, contactCfg1;
    Side side = NONE;

    for (int i = 0; i < 3; ++i)
    {
        // The potential separating axis is P + sN.
        Point2 P = C0.vertex[i];
        Vector2 N = C0.normal[i];
        Real speed = Dot(N,W);

        // Project C₀ onto the separating axis at time 0.
        Configuration2 cfg0 = GetConfiguration(P,N,C0.vertex);

        // Project C₁ onto the separating axis at time 0.
        Configuration2 cfg1 = GetConfiguration(P,N,C1.vertex);

        if (!UpdateTimes(cfg0,cfg1,speed,contactCfg0,contactCfg1,side,
            tFirst,tLast))
        {
            return false;
        }
    }

    for (int i = 0; i < 3; ++i)
    {
        // The potential separating axis is P + sN.
        Point2 P = C1.vertex[i]);
        Vector2 N = C1.normal[i];
        Real speed = Dot(N,W);

        // Project C₀ onto the separating axis at time 0.
        Configuration2 cfg0 = GetConfiguration(P,N,C0.vertex,cfg0);

        // Project C₁ onto the separating axis at time 0.
        Configuration2 cfg1 = GetConfiguration(P,N,C1.vertex,cfg1);

        if (!UpdateTimes(cfg0,cfg1,speed,contactCfg0,contactCfg1,side,
            tFirst,tLast))
        {
            return false;
        }
    }

    contactSet = ComputeContactSet(C0,C1,W0,W1,contactCfg0,contactCfg1,
        side,tFirst);
    return true;
}
```

Listing 8.8: The separating axis tests to determine first time of contact and the contact set for two triangles moving with constant linear velocities but no angular velocities. The first time of contact tFirst and the last time of contact tLast are valid only when FindIntersection returns true.

After the first time of contact (if any) is computed, the triangles are moved by their velocities in order to compute the contact set, say, $\mathbf{U}'_i = \mathbf{U}_i + \mathbf{W}_0$ and $\mathbf{V}'_i = \mathbf{V}_i + \mathbf{W}_1$. Figure 8.4 illustrates the possibilities.

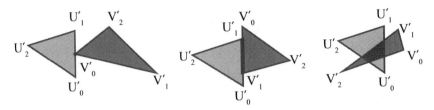

FIGURE 8.4: Some triangle configurations for the first time of contact.

In the left image of Figure 8.4, the U-configuration projection map is M12; one vertex projects to the minimum and two vertices project to the maximum. The V-configuration projection map is M111; one vertex projects to the minimum and one vertex projects to the maximum. The contact set is a single point $\mathbf{V}'_0$.

In the middle image of Figure 8.4, the U-configuration projection map is M12; one vertex projects to the minimum and two vertices project to the maximum. The V-configuraton projection map is M21; two vertices project to the minimum and one vertex projects to the maximum. The contact set is a line segment obtained by sorting the four edge endpoints along the common line of the intersection. In the figure, the line segment is $\langle \mathbf{U}'_1, \mathbf{V}'_1 \rangle$.

In the right image of Figure 8.4, the triangles are already overlapping at time 0. The contact set is more expensive to construct. It can be a single point, a line segment or a convex polygon with at most six sides. This set can be constructed by clipping one triangle against the edges of the other triangle.

Listing 8.9 contains pseudocode for computing the contact set from the contact configurations.

```
ContactSet ComputeContactSet(Triangle2 C0, Triangle2 C1, Vector2 W0,
    Vector2 W1, Configuration2 cfg0, Configuration2 cfg1, Side side,
    Real tFirst)
{
    // Move triangles to first contact.
    Point2 U[3], V[3];
    for (int i = 0; i < 3; ++i)
    {
        U[i] = C0.vertex[i] + tFirst * W0;
        V[i] = C1.vertex[i] + tFirst * W1;
    }

    if (side == RIGHT)    V-interval on right of U-interval
    {
        if (cfg0.map == M21 || cfg0.map == M111)
        {
            // U[cfg0.index[2]] is right-most extreme regardless of cfg1
            return U[cfg0.index[2]];
        }

        // cfg0.map == M12
        if (cfg1.map == M21)
```

```
    {
        // A U-edge and a V-edge are collinear.
        Segment2 seg0(U[cfg0.index[1]],U[cfg0.index[2]]);
        Segment2 seg1(V[cfg1.index[0]],V[cfg1.index[1]]);
        return SegSegIntersection(seg0,seg1);
    }

    // cfg1.map == M12 || cfg1.map == M111
    // V[cfg1.index[0]] is left-most extreme regardless of cfg0
    return V[cfg1.index[0]];
}
else if (side == LEFT)    V-interval on left of U-interval
{
    if (cfg1.map == M21 || cfg1.map == M111)
    {
        // V[cfg1.index[2]] is right-most extreme regardless of cfg0
        return V[cfg1.index[2]];
    }

    // cfg1.map == M12
    if (cfg0.map == M21)
    {
        // A V-edge and a U-edge are collinear.
        Segment2 seg0(U[cfg0.index[0]],U[cfg0.index[1]]);
        Segment2 seg1(V[cfg1.index[1]],V[cfg1.index[2]]);
        return SegSegIntersection(seg0,seg1);
    }

    // cfg0.map == M12 || cfg0.map == M111
    // U[cfg0.index[0]] is left-most extreme regardless of cfg1
    return U[cfg0.index[0]];
}
else // The triangles are initially overlapping.
{
    return TriTriIntersection(U,V);
}
}
```

Listing 8.9: Pseudocode for computing the contact set for two triangles in 2D moving with constant linear velocities.

8.2.2 Two Moving Triangles in 3D

Consider two triangles, $\langle \mathbf{U}_0, \mathbf{U}_1, \mathbf{U}_2 \rangle$ and $\langle \mathbf{V}_0, \mathbf{V}_1, \mathbf{V}_2 \rangle$. For the sake of indexing notation, define $\mathbf{U}_3 = \mathbf{U}_0$ and $\mathbf{V}_3 = \mathbf{V}_0$. The edges are $\mathbf{E}_i = \mathbf{U}_{i+1} - \mathbf{U}_i$ and $\mathbf{F}_i = \mathbf{V}_{i+1} - \mathbf{V}_i$ for $0 \leq i \leq 2$. A normal for the first triangle is $\mathbf{N} = \mathbf{E}_0 \times \mathbf{E}_1$ and a normal for the second triangle is $\mathbf{M} = \mathbf{F}_0 \times \mathbf{F}_1$. If the triangles are not coplanar, then the potential separating directions are $\mathbf{N}$, $\mathbf{M}$ and $\mathbf{E}_i \times \mathbf{F}_j$ for $0 \leq i \leq 2$ and $0 \leq j \leq 2$. If the triangles are parallel, but are not in the same plane, then $\mathbf{N}$ is a separating direction and the other directions need not be tested. Moreover, if $\mathbf{N}$ and $\mathbf{M}$ do not separate non-coplanar triangles, then the vectors $\mathbf{E}_i \times \mathbf{F}_j$ cannot be zero. If the triangles are coplanar, then the potential separating directions are $\mathbf{N} \times \mathbf{E}_i$ and $\mathbf{N} \times \mathbf{F}_i$ for $0 \leq i \leq 2$. This is exactly the 2D situation discussed in Section 8.2.1.

If $\mathbf{D}$ is a potential separating direction, then the block for computing the intervals of projection is more complex than that of its 2D counterpart. Both triangles are projected onto the separating axis. Each projection interval must be sorted to determine the appropriate configuration. The left-right relationship of the two projection intervals must be determined. The set of configurations for the projection of a single triangle consists of the following, each identified by a projection-map enumerate similar to what was provided in 2D. All three vertices project to the same point (M3). This happens when **D** is a normal vector to one of the triangles. Two vertices project to the minimum point of the interval and one vertex projects to the maximum point (M21). One vertex projects to the minimum point of the interval and two vertices project to the maximum point (M12). The three vertices project to distinct points in the interval (M111). Listing 8.10 shows data structures for representing the information.

```
enum ProjectionMap3
{
    M3, M21, M12, M111
};

struct Configuration3
{
    ProjectionMap3 map;
    int index[3];
    Real min, max;
};

enum Side = { NONE, LEFT, RIGHT };
```

Listing 8.10: Data structures to compute contact points for 3D triangles.

The 3D equivalent of GetConfiguration in Listing 8.6 is shown in Listing 8.11.

```
Configuration3 GetConfiguration(Point3 P, Vector3 D, Point3 V[3])
{
    // Compute min and max of interval for triangle. Keep track of vertices that project
    // to min and max.
    Configuration3 cfg;
    Real d[3] = {Dot(D,V[0]-P),Dot(D, V[1]-P),Dot(D,V[2]-P)};
    if (d[0] <= d[1])
    {
        if (d[1] <= d[2])   // d₀ ≤ d₁ ≤ d₂
        {
            cfg.index = {0,1,2};
            cfg.min = d[0];
            cfg.max = d[2];
            if (d[0] != d[1])
            {
                cfg.map = (d[1] != d[2] ? M111 : M12);
            }
            else
            {
                cfg.map = (d[1] != d[2] ? M21 : M3);
            }
        }
        else if (d[0] <= d[2])   // d₀ ≤ d₂ < d₁
        {
            cfg.index = {0,2,1};
            cfg.min = d[0];
            cfg.max = d[1];
            cfg.map = (d[0] != d[2] ? M111 : M21);
        }
```

```
        else    // d₂ < d₀ ≤ d₁
        {
            cfg.index = {2,0,1};
            cfg.min = d[2];
            cfg.max = d[1];
            cfg.map = (d[0] != d[1] ? M12 : M111);
        }
    }
    else
    {
        if (d[2] <= d[1])    // d₂ ≤ d₁ < d₀
        {
            cfg.index = {2,1,0};
            cfg.min = d[2];
            cfg.max = d[0];
            cfg.map = (d[2] != d[1] ? M111 : M21);
        }
        else if (d[2] <= d[0])    // d₁ < d₂ ≤ d₀
        {
            cfg.index = {1,2,0};
            cfg.min = d[1];
            cfg.max = d[0];
            cfg.map = (d[2] != d[0] ? M111 : M12);
        }
        else    // d₁ < d₀ < d₂
        {
            cfg.index = {1,0,2};
            cfg.min = d[1];
            cfg.max = d[2];
            cfg.map = M111;
        }
    }
    return cfg;
}
```

Listing 8.11: Pseudocode to compute the configuration of a triangle in 3D.

The pseudocode for updating the first and last times of contact and for determining the order of the projected intervals is the same as that of Listing 8.7 except that the configurations are now of type Configuration3.

The pseudocode for finding the intersection of two triangles in 3D is similar to that in Listing 8.8, except that the 2D types in the 2D code are replaced by 3D types in the 3D code. The Triangle3 data structure has a 3-tuple normal (to the plane of the triangle), 3-tuple of vertices, a 3-tuple of edges and a 3-tuple of edge normals. Each triangle has 4 potential separating axes, one with triangle-normal direction and three with edge-normal directions. The loop over the 3 potential axes for 2D triangles must be replaced by a loop over the 4 potential axes for 3D triangles.

Finally, there must be a function ComputeContactSet for 3D triangles that uses the configuration information. Listing 8.12 is the extension of Listing 8.9. It is assumed that the following routines exist for use in contact determination: intersection of two line segments (SegSegIntersection), intersection of line segment and triangle that are coplanar (SegTriIntersection), intersection of triangles that are coplanar (CoplanarTriTriIntersection) and intersection of stationary triangles (TriTriIntersection). If the stationary triangles happen to be coplanar, TriTriIntersection contains a call to CoplanarTriTriIntersection.

```
ContactSet GetFirstContact(Triangle3 C0, Triangle3 C1, Vector W0,
```

```
    Vector W1, Configuration3 cfg0 , Configuration3 cfg1 , Side side ,
    Real tFirst)
{
    // Move triangles to first contact.
    Point3 U[3], V[3];
    for (int i = 0; i < 3; ++i)
    {
        U[i] = C0.vertex[i] + tFirst * W0;
        V[i] = C1.vertex[i] + tFirst * W1;
    }

    if (side == RIGHT)    // V-interval on right of U-interval
    {
        if (cfg0.map == M21 || cfg0.map == M111)
        {
            // U[cfg0.index[2]] is right-most extreme regardless of cfg1
            return U[cfg0.index[2]];
        }

        if (cfg1.map == M12 || cfg1.map == M111)
        {
            // V[cfg1.index[0]] is left-most extreme regardless of cfg0
            return U[cfg0.index[2]];
        }

        if (cfg0.map == M12)
        {
            Segment3 seg0(U[cfg0.index[1]],U[cfg0.index[2]]);
            if (cfg1.map == M21)
            {
                Segment3 seg1(V[cfg1.index[0]],V[cfg1.index[1]]);
                return SegSegIntersection(seg0,seg1);
            }
            else   // cfg1.map == M3
            {
                return SegTriIntersection(seg0,V);
            }
        }
        else   // cfg0.map == M3
        {
            if (cfg1.map == M21)
            {
                Segment3 seg1(V[cfg1.index[0]],V[cfg1.index[1]]);
                return SegTriIntersection(seg1,U);
            }
            else   // cfg1.map == M3
            {
                return CoplanarTriTriIntersection(U,V);
            }
        }
    }
    else if (side == LEFT)    // V-interval on left of U-interval
    {
        if (cfg1.map == M21 || cfg1.map == M111)
        {
            // V[cfg1.index[2]] is right-most extreme regardless of cfg0
            return V[cfg1.index[2]];
        }

        if (cfg0.map == M12 || cfg0.map == M111)
        {
            // U[cfg0.index[0]] is left-most extreme regardless of cfg1
            return U[cfg0.index[0]];
        }

        if (cfg1.map == M12)
```

```
{
    {
        Segment3 seg1 (V[cfg1.index[1]],V[cfg1.index[2]]);
        if (cfg0.map == M21)
        {
            Segment3 seg0 (U[cfg0.index[0]],U[cfg0.index[1]]);
            return SegSegIntersection(seg0,seg1);
        }
        else    // cfg0.map == M3
        {
            return SegTriIntersection(seg1,U);
        }
    }
    else    // cfg1.map == M3
    {
        if (cfg0.map == M21)
        {
            Segment3 seg0 (U[cfg0.index[0]],U[cfg0.index[1]]);
            return SegTriIntersection(seg0,V);
        }
        else    // cfg0.map == M3
        {
            return CoplanarTriTriIntersection(UTri,VTri);
        }
    }
}
else    // The triangles are initially intersecting.
{
    return TriTriIntersection(U,V);
}
}
```

Listing 8.12: Pseudocode for computing the contact set for two triangles in 3D moving with constant linear velocities.

8.3   Linear Component and Sphere

Computing the intersection of a line and a sphere, where the sphere is considered to be a solid, is one of the simplest geometric queries that can be computed exactly using quadratic-field numbers. Given a test-intersection query and a find-intersection query involving a line, it is relatively simple to use these to create test-intersection and find-intersection queries involving a ray or segment. The pattern is general given queries for the intersection of a line and a bounded convex object. The intersection set is a point or segment, which can be modified easily using parameterizations for the line, ray and segment.

Consider the general case of intersection between a line and a sphere. A sphere with center $\mathbf{C}$ and radius r is specified by $|\mathbf{X} - \mathbf{C}|^2 - r^2 = 0$. The line is parameterized by $\mathbf{P} + t\mathbf{D}$ for $t \in \mathbb{R}$. The direction vector $\mathbf{D}$ is usually chosen to be unit length; however, this is not necessary for intersection queries for linear components and spheres. In this section, the directions are unnormalized. The ray is parameterized by $t \in [0, +\infty)$ and the segment is parameterized by $t \in [0, 1]$, where the endpoints are $\mathbf{P}$ and $\mathbf{D}$.

Replacing $\mathbf{X}$ by $\mathbf{P} + t\mathbf{D}$ in the sphere equation leads to the quadratic equation

$$
\begin{aligned}
0 &= |t\mathbf{D} + \mathbf{P} - \mathbf{C}|^2 - r^2 \\
&= |\mathbf{D}|^2 t^2 + 2\mathbf{D} \cdot (\mathbf{P} - \mathbf{C})t + |\mathbf{P} - \mathbf{C}|^2 - r^2 \\
&= a_2 t^2 + 2a_1 t + a_0 \\
&= q(t)
\end{aligned}
\tag{8.3}
$$

The quadratic formula may be used to solve the equation formally,

$$
t = \frac{-a_1 \pm \sqrt{a_1^2 - a_0 a_2}}{a_2}
\tag{8.4}
$$

Define $\Delta = a_1^2 - a_0 a_2$. If $\Delta < 0$, the roots are complex-valued, so the line does not intersect the sphere. If $\Delta = 0$, the equation has a repeated real-valued root, so the line intersects the sphere in a single point. Necessarily the line is tangent to the sphere. If $\Delta > 0$, the equation has two distinct real-valued roots, so the line intersects the sphere in two points. The intersections are transverse in the sense that the line passes from outside to inside the sphere and inside to outside the sphere at the two points.

8.3.1 Test-Intersection Queries

The test-intersection queries for linear components and spheres require only a small amount of computation. Exact results can be attained using rational arithmetic as long as $\mathbf{D}$ is not normalized. Quadratic-field arithmetic is not necessary because the square-root calculation of equation (8.4) is avoided. It is also possible to use interval arithmetic with floating-point numbers because the query result depends on signs of computed expressions.

8.3.1.1 Line and Sphere

The test-intersection query avoids the square-root computation of equation (8.3). The sign of $a_0 = |\mathbf{P} - \mathbf{C}|^2 - r^2$ determines whether or not $\mathbf{P}$ is inside the sphere $(a_0 < 0)$, on the sphere $(a_0 = 0)$ or outside the sphere $(a_0 > 0)$. This allows an early exit in the test-intersection query to avoid unnecessary computations: if $a_0 \le 0$, then the line intersects the sphere because $\mathbf{P}$ is inside or on the sphere. Listing 8.13 contains pseudocode for the test-intersection query.

```
bool TestIntersection (Line3<Rational> line , Sphere3<Rational> sphere)
{
    Vector3<Rational> delta = line.P - sphere.C;
    Rational a0 = Dot(delta , delta) - sphere.r * sphere.r;
    Rational zero (0);

    if (a0 <= zero)
    {
        // line.P is inside or on the sphere
```

```
            return true;
    }
    // else line.P is outside the sphere

    Rational a1 = Dot(line.D, delta), a2 = Dot(line.D, line.D);
    Rational discr = a1 * a1 - a0 * a2;
    return discr >= zero;
}
```

Listing 8.13: Pseudocode for the test-intersection query for a line and a sphere.

8.3.1.2 Ray and Sphere

The test-intersection query for a ray and a sphere is similar to the test-intersection query for a line and a sphere except that there is an additional early exit. If the ray origin is inside the sphere ($a_0 \leq 0$), then the ray intersects the sphere; otherwise, the ray origin is outside the sphere. It is possible that the ray is directed away from the sphere, in which case there is no intersection when $t \geq 0$. This geometric condition is equivalent to the squared distance $q(t)$ increasing for all $t \geq 0$. To be increasing, the derivative $q'(t) = 2(t + a_1)$ must satisfy $q'(t) \geq 0$. It is sufficient for $a_1 \geq 0$ to guarantee that this happens. The condition $a_1 \geq 0$ is therefore an early exit for a no-intersection result. Listing 8.14 contains pseudocode for the test-intersection query.

```
bool TestIntersection(Ray3<Rational> ray, Sphere3<Rational> sphere)
{
    Vector3<Rational> delta = ray.P - sphere.C;
    Rational a0 = Dot(delta, delta) - sphere.r * sphere.r;
    Rational zero(0);

    if (a0 <= zero)
    {
        // ray.P is inside or on the sphere
        return true;
    }
    // else ray.P is outside the sphere

    Rational a1 = Dot(ray.D, delta);
    if (a1 >= zero)
    {
        // The ray is directed away from the sphere.
        return false;
    }

    Rational a2 = Dot(ray.D, ray.D);
    Rational discr = a1 * a1 - a0 * a2;
    return discr >= zero;
}
```

Listing 8.14: Pseudocode for the test-intersection query for a ray and a sphere.

8.3.1.3   Segment and Sphere

The test-intersection query for a segment versus sphere is slightly more complicated algebraically than that of ray or line versus sphere, but the end result requires only a minimum of calculation time.

If $q(0) = a_0 \leq 0$, then the segment endpoint $\mathbf{P}$ is inside the sphere and there is an intersection; otherwise, $\mathbf{P}$ is outside the sphere. When it is outside, the segment is directed away from the sphere when $q'(0) = a_1 \geq 0$. In this case, the segment does not intersect the sphere.

If $q(1) = a_0 + 2a_1 + a_2 \leq 0$, then the segment endpoint $\mathbf{P} + \mathbf{D}$ is inside the sphere and there is an intersection; otherwise, $\mathbf{P} + \mathbf{D}$ is outside the sphere. When it is outside, the segment is directed away from the sphere when $q'(1) = 2(a_0 + a_1) \leq 0$. In this case, the segment does not intersect the sphere.

The final case depends on the sign of $\Delta = a_1^2 - a_0 a_2$. The segment intersects the sphere when $\Delta \geq 0$.

Listing 8.15 contains pseudocode for the test-intersection query.

```
bool TestIntersection(Segment3<Rational> segment, Sphere3<Real> sphere)
{
    Vector3<Rational> delta = segment.P - sphere.C;
    Rational a0 = Dot(delta, delta) - sphere.r * sphere.r;
    Rational zero(0);

    if (a0 <= zero)
    {
        // endpoint segment.P is inside or on the sphere.
        return true;
    }
    // else segment.P is outside the sphere

    Rational a1 = Dot(segment.D, delta);
    if (a1 >= zero)
    {
        // The segment is directed away from the sphere.
        return false;
    }

    Rational a2 = Dot(ray.D, ray.D), a0pa1 = a0 + a1, a1pa2 = a1 + a2;
    if (a0pa1 + a1pa2 <= zero)   // q(1) <= 0
    {
        // endpoint segment.P + segment.D is inside or on the sphere.
        return true;
    }
    // else segment.P + segment.D is outside the sphere

    if (a1pa2 <= zero) // q'(1) <= 0
    {
        // The segment is directed away from the sphere.
        return false;
    }

    Real discr = a1 * a1 - a0 * a2;
    return discr >= 0;
}
```

Listing 8.15: Pseudocode for the test-intersection query for a segment and a sphere.

8.3.2 Find-Intersection Queries

The find-intersection queries for linear components and spheres require more computation than that of the test-intersection queries. Exact results can be attained by using quadratic-field arithmetic.

8.3.2.1 Line and Sphere

The find-intersection query is a straightforward implementation of the construction of the quadratic roots of equation (8.4). Exact computation requires use of quadratic-field numbers because of the square-root of the discriminant. Listing 8.16 contains pseudocode for the find-intersection query.

```
bool FindIntersection(Line3<Rational> line, Sphere3<Rational> sphere,
    int& numIntersections, QFNumber<Rational,1> t[2])
{
    Vector3<Rational> delta = line.P - sphere.C;
    Rational a0 = Dot(delta, delta) - sphere.r * sphere.r;
    Rational a1 = Dot(line.D, delta);
    Rational a2 = Dot(line.D, line.D);
    Rational discr = a1 * a1 - a0 * a2;
    Rational zero(0);

    if (discr < zero)
    {
        // two complex-valued roots
        numIntersections = 0;
    }
    else
    {
        Rational one(1), inva2 = one / a2;
        if (discr > zero)
        {
            // two distinct real-valued roots
            t[0] = QFNumber<Rational,1>(-a1, -one, discr) * inva2;
            t[1] = QFNumber<Rational,1>(-a1,+-one, discr) * inva2;
            numIntersections = 2;
        }
        else  // discr == zero
        {
            // one repeated real-valued root
            t[0] = QFNumber<Rational,1>(-a1, zero, zero) * inva2;
            numIntersections = 1;
        }
    }

    return numIntersections > 0;
}
```

Listing 8.16: Pseudocode for the find-intersection query for a line and a sphere.

8.3.2.2 Ray and Sphere

The find-intersection query for a ray and sphere uses the find-intersection query for a line and segment followed by intersecting the t-interval $[t_0, t_1]$ for the segment of intersection with the t-interval $[0, +\infty)$ for the ray. Listing 8.17 contains pseudocode for the find-intersection query.

```
bool FindIntersection (Ray3<Rational> ray, Sphere3<Rational> sphere,
    int& numIntersections, QFNumber<Rational,1> t[2])
{
    Line3<Rational> line (ray.P, ray.D);
    bool intersects = FindIntersection (line, sphere, numIntersections, t);
    if (intersects)
    {
        // The line containing the ray intersects the sphere; the t-interval is [t₀, t₁]. The
        // ray intersects the sphere as long as [t₀, t₁] overlaps the ray t-interval [0, +∞).
        QFNumber<Rational,1> zero (0, 0, t[0].d);   // 0 + 0√d
        if (numIntersections == 2)
        {
            if (t[1] > zero)
            {
                if (t[0] < zero) { t[0] = zero; }
            }
            else if (t[1] < zero)
            {
                numIntersections = 0;
            }
            else   // t[1] == zero
            {
                numIntersections = 1;
            }
        }
        else   // numIntersections == 1
        {
            if (t[0] < zero) { numIntersections = 0; }
        }
    }
    return numIntersections > 0;
}
```

Listing 8.17: Pseudocode for the find-intersection query for a ray and a sphere.

8.3.2.3   Segment and Sphere

The find-intersection query for a segment and sphere uses the find-intersection query for a line and segment followed by intersecting the t-interval $[t_0, t_1]$ for the segment of intersection with the t-interval $[0, 1]$ for the input segment. Listing 8.18 contains pseudocode for the find-intersection query.

```
bool FindIntersection (Segment3<Rational> segment, Sphere3<Rational> sphere,
    int& numIntersections, QFNumber<Rational,1> t[2])
{
    Segment3<Rational> line (segment.P, segment.D);
    bool intersects = FindIntersection (line, sphere, numIntersections, t);
    if (intersects)
    {
        // The line containing the segment intersects the sphere; the t-interval is [t₀, t₁]. The
        // segment intersects the sphere as long as [t₀, t₁] overlaps the input segment
        // t-interval [0, 1].
        QFNumber<Rational,1> zero (0, 0, t[0].d);   // 0 + 0√d
        QFNumber<Rational,1> one (1, 0, t[0].d);   // 1 + 0√d
        if (numIntersections == 2)
        {
            if (t[0] > one || t[1] < zero)
            {
                numIntersections = 0;
            }
```

```
        else if (t[0] == one)
        {
            numIntersections = 1;
        }
        else if (t[1] == zero)
        {
            t[0] = zero;  numIntersections = 1;
        }
        else  // t[0] < 1 && t[1] > 0
        {
            if (t[0] < zero) { t[0] = zero; }
            if (t[1] > one) { t[1] = one; }
        }
    }
    else   // numIntersections == 1
    {
        if (t[0] < zero || t[0] > one) { numIntersections = 0; }
    }
}

return numIntersections > 0;
}
```

Listing 8.18: Pseudocode for the find-intersection query for a segment and a sphere.

8.4   Linear Component and Box

Let the oriented box have center $\mathbf{C}$, orthonormal axis directions $\mathbf{U}_i$ and extents e_i for $0 \leq i \leq 2$. Points in the oriented box are $\mathbf{X} = \mathbf{C} + \sum_{i=0}^{2} y_i \mathbf{U}_i$ where $|y_i| \leq e_i$. The extents can be stored as a 3-tuple $\mathbf{e} = (e_0, e_1, e_2)$. The coefficients of the $\mathbf{U}_i$ can be written as a 3-tuple $\mathbf{Y} = (y_0, y_1, y_2)$. The oriented box points are then $\mathbf{X} = \mathbf{C} + R\mathbf{Y}$, where $R = [\mathbf{U}_0 \ \mathbf{U}_1 \ \mathbf{U}_2]$ is a rotation matrix with the specified columns and where $-\mathbf{e} \leq \mathbf{Y} \leq \mathbf{e}$. The inequality comparisons are componentwise.

An aligned box is defined by a minimum point $\mathbf{a}$ and a maximum point $\mathbf{b}$. A point $\mathbf{X}$ in the box satisfies $\mathbf{a} \leq \mathbf{X} \leq \mathbf{b}$, where the inequality comparisons are componentwise.

An aligned box can be converted to an oriented box by choosing $\mathbf{C} = (\mathbf{b} + \mathbf{a})/2$ and $\mathbf{e} = (\mathbf{b} - \mathbf{a})/2$. An oriented box is an aligned box in its own coordinate system, as described next. In a geometric query, transform points by $\mathbf{Y} = R^\mathsf{T}(\mathbf{X} - \mathbf{C})$. The minimum point is $-\mathbf{e}$ and the maximum point is $\mathbf{e}$. The box axis directions are $(1, 0, 0)$, $(0, 1, 0)$ and $(0, 0, 1)$.

The linear component is $\mathbf{P} + t\mathbf{D}$ where $\mathbf{D}$ is an unnormalized vector in order to support arbitrary-precision arithmetic and quadratic-field arithmetic. The component is a line when $t \in \mathbb{R}$ or a ray when $t \in [0, +\infty)$. A segment has endpoints $\mathbf{P}_0$ and $\mathbf{P}_1$. The center is $\mathbf{P} = (\mathbf{P}_0 + \mathbf{P}_1)/2$ and the t-interval is $-1/2, 1/2]$.

This section discusses test-intersection queries between the box and a lin-

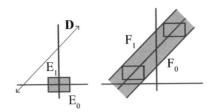

FIGURE 8.5: The Minkowski sum of an oriented box and a line. The oriented box is extruded along the line in the direction **D**. The illustration is based on the oriented box having its center at the origin. If the center were not at the origin, the extruded object would be translated from its current location.

ear component. The algorithm is based on the method of separating axes of Section 8.1, which in turn is based on the Minkowski sums of sets. The section also discusses find-intersection queries, where the intersection set must be computed. The Liang–Barsky clipping algorithm is used. Both types of queries can be implemented using arbitrary-precision arithmetic or quadratic-field arithmetic.

8.4.1 Test-Intersection Queries

This section describes test-intersection queries between boxes and linear components that include lines, rays and segments.

8.4.1.1 Lines and Boxes

The application of the method of separating axes to a line and an oriented box is described here. The Minkowski sum of the oriented box and the line is an infinite convex polyhedron obtained by extruding the oriented box along the line and placing it appropriately in space. Figure 8.5 illustrates this process in two dimensions. Four of the oriented box edges are perpendicular to the plane of the page. Two of those edges are highlighted with points and labeled as E_0 and E_1. The edge E_0 is extruded along the line direction **D**. The resulting face, labeled F_0, is an infinite planar strip with a normal vector $U_0 \times D$, where U_0 is the unit-length normal of the face of the oriented box that is coplanar with the page. The edge E_1 is extruded along the line direction to produce face F_1. Because edges E_0 and E_1 are parallel, face F_1 also has a normal vector U_0. The maximum number of faces that the infinite polyhedron can have is six: project the oriented box onto a plane with normal **D** and obtain a hexagon; one for each of the independent oriented box edge directions. These directions are the same as the oriented box face normal directions, so the six faces are partitioned into three pairs of parallel faces with normal vectors $U_i \times D$.

Now that the potential separating axis directions are known, the separation tests are

$$|\mathbf{D} \times \boldsymbol{\Delta} \cdot \mathbf{U}_0| > e_1|\mathbf{D} \cdot \mathbf{U}_2| + e_2|\mathbf{D} \cdot \mathbf{U}_1|$$
$$|\mathbf{D} \times \boldsymbol{\Delta} \cdot \mathbf{U}_1| > e_0|\mathbf{D} \cdot \mathbf{U}_2| + e_2|\mathbf{D} \cdot \mathbf{U}_0| \qquad (8.5)$$
$$|\mathbf{D} \times \boldsymbol{\Delta} \cdot \mathbf{U}_2| > e_0|\mathbf{D} \cdot \mathbf{U}_1| + e_1|\mathbf{D} \cdot \mathbf{U}_0|$$

where $\boldsymbol{\Delta} = \mathbf{P} - \mathbf{C}$. The term $\mathbf{D} \times \boldsymbol{\Delta} \cdot \mathbf{U}_i$ is used instead of the mathematically equivalent $\mathbf{U}_i \times \mathbf{D} \cdot \boldsymbol{\Delta}$ in order for the implementation to compute $\mathbf{D} \times \boldsymbol{\Delta}$ once, leading to a reduced operation count for all three separation tests. Pseudocode for the test-intersection query of a line and an oriented box in 3 dimensions is shown in Listing 8.21.

```
bool TestIntersection(Line3 line, OrientedBox3 box)
{
    Vector3 PmC = line.P - box.C;
    Vector3 DxPmC = Cross(line.D, PmC);
    Real ADdU[3], ADxPmCdU[3];

    ADdU[1] = abs(Dot(line.D, box.U[1]));
    ADdU[2] = abs(Dot(line.D, box.U[2]));
    ADxPmCdU[0] = abs(Dot(DxPmC, box.U[0]));
    if (ADxPmCdU[0] > box.e[1] * ADdU[2] + box.e[2] * ADdU[1])
    {
        return false;
    }

    ADdU[0] = abs(Dot(line.D, box.U[0]));
    ADxPmCdU[1] = abs(Dot(DxPmC, box.U[1]));
    if (ADxPmCdU[1] > box.e[0] * ADdU[2] + box.e[2] * ADdU[0])
    {
        return false;
    }

    ADxPmCdU[2] = abs(Dot(DxPmC, box.U[2]));
    if (ADxPmCdU[2] > box.e[0] * ADdU[1] + box.e[1] * ADdU[0])
    {
        return false;
    }

    return true;
}
```

Listing 8.19: Pseudocode for the test-intersection query between a line and an oriented box in 3 dimensions. The function abs returns the absolute value of its scalar argument.

The assumption is that $\{\mathbf{U}_0, \mathbf{U}_1, \mathbf{U}_2\}$ is a right-handed orthonormal basis. The vectors are unit length, mutually perpendicular and $\mathbf{U}_i = \mathbf{U}_j \times \mathbf{U}_k$ where (i, j, k) is a cyclic permutation of $(0, 1, 2)$. Equation (8.5) has tests that rely on this assumption. If the box axes were computed numerically, it is possible that one or more of the directions is not unit length. It is also possible that one or more pairs of directions are not perpendicular. This makes it difficult to compute an exact result using arbitrary-precision arithmetic.

An orthogonal basis $\{\mathbf{V}_0, \mathbf{V}_1, \mathbf{V}_2\}$ can be computed from the directions $\mathbf{U}_i$ using rational arithmetic and projections,

$$\begin{aligned} \mathbf{V}_0 &= \mathbf{U}_0 \\ \mathbf{V}_1 &= \mathbf{U}_1 - \left(\mathbf{U}_1 \cdot \mathbf{U}_0/|\mathbf{U}_0|^2\right)\mathbf{U}_0 \qquad (8.6) \\ \mathbf{V}_2 &= \mathbf{V}_0 \times \mathbf{V}_1 \end{aligned}$$

The box parameterization is now $\mathbf{X} = \mathbf{C} + \sum_{i=0}^{2} z_i \mathbf{V}_i$, where $|z_i| \leq f_i = e_i/|\mathbf{V}_i|$. The last equality of the constraints on z_i defines the f_i. The first comparison of equation (8.5) becomes

$$\frac{|\mathbf{D} \times \mathbf{\Delta} \cdot \mathbf{V}_0|}{|\mathbf{V}_0|} > e_1 \frac{|\mathbf{D} \cdot \mathbf{V}_2|}{|\mathbf{V}_2|} + e_2 \frac{|\mathbf{D} \cdot \mathbf{V}_1|}{|\mathbf{V}_1|} \tag{8.7}$$

Using $f_i = e_i/|\mathbf{V}_i|$ and $|\mathbf{V}_2| = |\mathbf{V}_0 \times \mathbf{V}_1| = |\mathbf{V}_0||\mathbf{V}_1|$, the test becomes

$$|\mathbf{D} \times \mathbf{\Delta} \cdot \mathbf{V}_0| > f_1|\mathbf{D} \cdot \mathbf{V}_2| + f_2 \frac{|\mathbf{V}_2|^2 |\mathbf{D} \cdot \mathbf{V}_1|}{|\mathbf{V}_1|^2} \tag{8.8}$$

All quantities are rational except for f_1 and f_2, each of which involves a square root. Now the test can be executed using a comparison of a 2-root quadratic-field number to zero. The other separation tests are similar.

Note that if the box axes are represented as a quaternion, a rational-valued rotation matrix can be computed exactly from the quaternion, after which the columns form a right-handed orthonormal basis with rational-valued components. See Section 6.3.4 for details.

The test-intersection for an aligned box can be formulated by using the center-extent form of the box. Listing 8.20 contains pseudocode for the query.

```
// P is the line origin, D is the unit-length line direction and e contains the box extents. The
// box center has been translated to the origin and the line has been translated accordingly.
bool DoLineQuery(Vector3 P, Vector3 D, Vector3 e)
{
    Vector3 DxP = Cross(D, P);

    if (abs(DxP[0]) > e[1] * abs(D[2]) + e[2] * abs(D[1]))
    {
        return false;
    }

    if (abs(DxP[1]) > e[0] * abs(D[2]) + e[2] * abs(D[0]))
    {
        return false;
    }

    if (abs(DxP[2]) > e[0] * abs(D[1]) + e[1] * abs(D[0]))
    {
        return false;
    }

    return true;
}

bool TestIntersection(Line3 line, AlignedBox3 box)
{
    // Get the centered form of the aligned box.
    Vector3 C = (box.max + box.min) / 2;
    Vector3 e = (box.max - box.min) / 2;

    // Transform the line to the aligned-box coordinate system.
    Vector3 P = line.P - C;
    Vector3 D = line.D;

    return DoLineQuery(P, D, e);
}
```

```
// The query for the line and oriented box but reformulated to use DoLineQuery.
bool TestIntersection(Line3 line , OrientedBox3 box)
{
    // Transform the line to the oriented-box coordinate system.
    Vector3 delta = line.P - box.C;
    Vector3 P, D;
    for (int i = 0; i < 3; ++i)
    {
        P[i] = Dot(delta , box.U[i]);
        D[i] = Dot(line.D, box.U[i]);
    }
    return DoLineQuery(P, D, box.e);
}
```

Listing 8.20: Pseudocode for the test-intersection query between a line and an aligned box in 3 dimensions.

The test-intersection for an oriented box can be formulated by using the center-extent form of the box. Listing 8.21 contains pseudocode for the query.

```
// The query for the line and oriented box but reformulated to use DoLineQuery.
bool TestIntersection(Line3 line , OrientedBox3 box)
{
    // Transform the line to the oriented-box coordinate system.
    Vector3 delta = line.P - box.C;
    Vector3 P, D;
    for (int i = 0; i < 3; ++i)
    {
        P[i] = Dot(delta , box.U[i]);
        D[i] = Dot(line.D, box.U[i]);
    }
    return DoLineQuery(P, D, box.e);
}
```

Listing 8.21: Pseudocode for the test-intersection query between a line and an oriented box in 3 dimensions.

8.4.1.2 Rays and Boxes

The infinite convex polyhedron that corresponds to the Minkowski sum of a line and an oriented box becomes a semi-infinite object in the case of a ray and an oriented box. Figure 8.6 illustrates this process in two dimensions. The semi-infinite convex polyhedron has the same three pairs of parallel faces as for the line, but the polyhedron has the oriented box as an end cap. The oriented box contributes three additional faces and corresponding normal vectors. Therefore, there are six potential separating axes. The separation tests are

$$
\begin{aligned}
|\mathbf{D} \times \mathbf{\Delta} \cdot \mathbf{U}_0| &> e_1|\mathbf{D} \cdot \mathbf{U}_2| + e_2|\mathbf{D} \cdot \mathbf{U}_1| \\
|\mathbf{D} \times \mathbf{\Delta} \cdot \mathbf{U}_1| &> e_0|\mathbf{D} \cdot \mathbf{U}_2| + e_2|\mathbf{D} \cdot \mathbf{U}_0| \\
|\mathbf{D} \times \mathbf{\Delta} \cdot \mathbf{U}_2| &> e_0|\mathbf{D} \cdot \mathbf{U}_1| + e_1|\mathbf{D} \cdot \mathbf{U}_0| \\
|\mathbf{\Delta} \cdot \mathbf{U}_0| &> e_0, \quad (\mathbf{\Delta} \cdot \mathbf{U}_0)(\mathbf{D} \cdot \mathbf{U}_0) \geq 0 \\
|\mathbf{\Delta} \cdot \mathbf{U}_1| &> e_1, \quad (\mathbf{\Delta} \cdot \mathbf{U}_1)(\mathbf{D} \cdot \mathbf{U}_1) \geq 0 \\
|\mathbf{\Delta} \cdot \mathbf{U}_2| &> e_2, \quad (\mathbf{\Delta} \cdot \mathbf{U}_2)(\mathbf{D} \cdot \mathbf{U}_2) \geq 0
\end{aligned}
\tag{8.9}
$$

The first three are the same as for a line. The last three use the oriented box face normals for the separation tests. To illustrate these tests, see Figure 8.7.

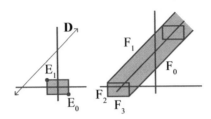

FIGURE 8.6: The Minkowski sum of an oriented box and a ray. The oriented box is extruded along the ray in the direction $\mathbf{D}$. The faces F_0 and F_1 are generated by oriented box edges and $\mathbf{D}$. The faces F_2 and F_3 are contributed from the oriented box.

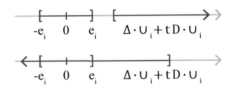

FIGURE 8.7: Projections of an oriented box and a ray onto the line with direction $\mathbf{U}_i$ which is a normal to an oriented box face. The oriented box center $\mathbf{C}$ is subtracted from the oriented box as well as the ray origin $\mathbf{P}$. The translated oriented box projects to the interval $[-e_i, e_i]$, where e_i is the oriented box extent associated with $\mathbf{U}_i$. The translated ray is $\boldsymbol{\Delta} + t\mathbf{D}$, where $\boldsymbol{\Delta} = \mathbf{P} - \mathbf{C}$, and projects to $\mathbf{U}_i \cdot \boldsymbol{\Delta} + t\mathbf{U}_i \cdot \mathbf{D}$.

The projected oriented box is the finite interval $[-e_i, e_i]$. The projected ray is a semi-infinite interval on the t-axis. The origin is $\mathbf{\Delta} \cdot \mathbf{U}_i$ and the direction (a signed scalar) is $\mathbf{D} \cdot \mathbf{U}_i$. The top portion of Figure 8.7 shows a positive signed direction and an origin that satisfies $\mathbf{\Delta} \cdot \mathbf{U}_i > e_i$. The finite interval and the semi-infinite interval are disjoint, in which case the original oriented box and ray are separated. If instead the projected ray direction is negative, $\mathbf{D} \cdot \mathbf{U}_i < 0$, the semi-infinite interval overlaps the finite interval. The original oriented box and ray are not separated by the axis with direction $\mathbf{U}_i$. Two similar configurations exist when $\mathbf{\Delta} \cdot \mathbf{U}_i < -e_i$. The condition $|\mathbf{\Delta} \cdot \mathbf{U}_i| > e_i$ says that the projected ray origin is farther away from zero than the projected box extents. The condition $(\mathbf{\Delta} \cdot \mathbf{U}_i)(\mathbf{D} \cdot \mathbf{U}_i) > 0$ guarantees that the projected ray points away from the projected oriented box.

The implementation of the test-intersection query for a ray and oriented box in 3 dimensions is shown in Listing 8.22.

```
bool TestIntersection(Ray3 ray, OrientedBox3 box)
{
    Vector3 PmC = ray.P - box.C;
    Real DdU[3], ADdU[3], PmCdU[3], APmCdU[3];

    // The ray-specific tests.
    for (int i = 0; i < 3; ++i)
    {
        DdU[i] = Dot(ray.D, box.U[i]);   ADdU[i] = abs(DdU[i]);
        PmCdU[i] = Dot(PmC, box.U[i]);   APmCdU[i] = abs(PmCdU[i]);
        if (APmCdU[i] > box.e[i] and PmCdU[i] * DdU[i] >= 0)
        {
            return false;
        }
    }

    // The line-specific tests.
    Vector3 DxPmC = Cross(ray.D, PmC);
    Real ADxPmCdU[3];

    ADxPmCdU[0] = abs(Dot(DxPmC, box.U[0]));
    if (ADxPmCdU[0] > box.e[1] * ADdU[2] + box.e[2] * ADdU[1])
    {
        return false;
    }

    ADxPmCdU[1] = abs(Dot(DxPmC, box.U[1]));
    if (ADxPmCdU[1] > box.e[0] * ADdU[2] + box.e[2] * ADdU[0])
    {
        return false;
    }

    ADxPmCdU[2] = abs(Dot(DxPmC, box.U[2]));
    if (ADxPmCdU[2] > box.e[0] * ADdU[1] + box.e[1] * ADdU[0])
    {
        return false;
    }

    return true;
}
```

Listing 8.22: Pseudocode for the test-intersection query between a ray and an oriented box in 3 dimensions. The function abs returns the absolute value of its scalar argument.

To use 2-root quadratic-field arithmetic for exact computation, the first three comparisons of equation (8.9) can be processed similarly to what was done for the line-box separation tests using $\mathbf{V}_i$ and f_i. The tests $|\mathbf{\Delta} \cdot \mathbf{U}_i| > e_i$ are processed instead as $|\mathbf{\Delta} \cdot \mathbf{V}_i| > f_i$. The tests $(\mathbf{\Delta} \cdot \mathbf{V}_i)(\mathbf{D} \cdot \mathbf{V}_i) \geq 0$ involve $|\mathbf{V}_i|^2$, which requires only rational arithmetic to compute exactly.

The test-intersection for an aligned box can be formulated by using the center-extent form of the box. Listing 8.23 contains pseudocode for the query.

```
// P is the ray origin, D is the unit-length ray direction and e contains the box extents. The
// box center has been translated to the origin and the ray has been translated accordingly.
bool DoRayQuery(Vector3 P, Vector3 D, Vector3 e)
{
    for (int i = 0; i < 3; ++i)
    {
        if (abs(P[i]) > e[i] && P[i] * D[i] >= 0)
        {
            return false;
        }
    }
    return DoLineQuery(P, D, e);
}

bool TestIntersection(Ray3 ray, AlignedBox3 box)
{
    // Get the centered form of the aligned box.
    Vector3 C = (box.max + box.min) / 2;
    Vector3 e = (box.max - box.min) / 2;

    // Transform the ray to the aligned-box coordinate system.
    Vector3 P = ray.P - C;
    Vector3 D = ray.D;

    return DoRayQuery(P, D, e);
}

// The query for the ray and oriented box is formulated to use DoRayQuery.
bool TestIntersection(Ray3 ray, OrientedBox3 box)
{
    // Transform the ray to the oriented-box coordinate system.
    Vector3 delta = ray.P - box.C;
    Vector3 P, D;
    for (int i = 0; i < 3; ++i)
    {
        P[i] = Dot(delta, box.U[i]);
        D[i] = Dot(ray.D, box.U[i]);
    }
    return DoRayQuery(P, D, box.e);
}
```

Listing 8.23: Pseudocode for the test-intersection query between a ray and an aligned box in 3 dimensions.

8.4.1.3 Segments and Boxes

The segment is represented in center-direction-extent form, $\mathbf{P} + t\mathbf{D}$, where $\mathbf{P}$ is the center of the segment, $\mathbf{D}$ is a unit-length direction vector, ε is the extent (radius) of the segment and $|t| \leq \varepsilon$. The line segment has length 2ε. The semi-infinite convex polyhedron that corresponds to the Minkowski sum of a ray and an oriented box becomes a finite object in the case of a segment

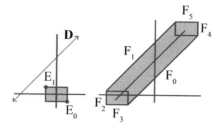

FIGURE 8.8: The Minkowski sum of an oriented box and a segment. The oriented box is extruded along the segment in the direction $\mathbf{D}$. The faces F_0 and F_1 are generated by oriented box edges and $\mathbf{D}$. The faces F_2 and F_3 are contributed from the oriented box at one endpoint. The faces F_4 and F_5 are contributed from the oriented box at the other endpoint.

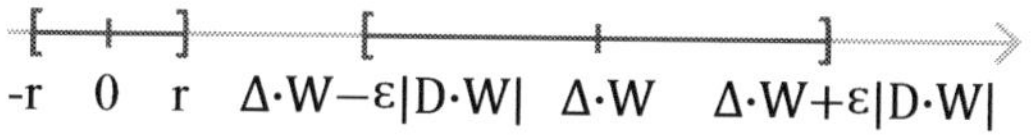

$$-r \quad 0 \quad r \qquad \mathbf{\Delta}\cdot\mathbf{W}-\varepsilon|\mathbf{D}\cdot\mathbf{W}| \qquad \mathbf{\Delta}\cdot\mathbf{W} \qquad \mathbf{\Delta}\cdot\mathbf{W}+\varepsilon|\mathbf{D}\cdot\mathbf{W}|$$

FIGURE 8.9: Projections of an oriented box and a segment onto a line with direction $\mathbf{W}$. The oriented box center $\mathbf{C}$ is subtracted from the oriented box as well as the segment origin $\mathbf{P}$. The translated oriented box projects to an interval $[-r, r]$. The translated segment is $\mathbf{\Delta} + t\mathbf{D}$, where $\mathbf{\Delta} = \mathbf{P} - \mathbf{C}$, and projects to $\mathbf{W} \cdot \mathbf{\Delta} + t\mathbf{W} \cdot \mathbf{D}$.

and an oriented box. Figure 8.8 illustrates the process in two dimensions. The infinite convex polyhedron has the same three pairs of parallel faces as for the ray and line, but the polyhedron has the oriented box as an end cap on both ends of the segment. The oriented box contributes three additional faces and corresponding normal vectors, a total of six potential separating axes. The separation tests are

$$
\begin{aligned}
|\mathbf{D} \times \mathbf{\Delta} \cdot \mathbf{U}_0| &> e_1|\mathbf{D} \cdot \mathbf{U}_2| + e_2|\mathbf{D} \cdot \mathbf{U}_1| \\
|\mathbf{D} \times \mathbf{\Delta} \cdot \mathbf{U}_1| &> e_0|\mathbf{D} \cdot \mathbf{U}_2| + e_2|\mathbf{D} \cdot \mathbf{U}_0| \\
|\mathbf{D} \times \mathbf{\Delta} \cdot \mathbf{U}_2| &> e_0|\mathbf{D} \cdot \mathbf{U}_1| + e_1|\mathbf{D} \cdot \mathbf{U}_0| \\
|\mathbf{\Delta} \cdot \mathbf{U}_0| &> e_0 + \varepsilon|\mathbf{D} \cdot \mathbf{U}_0| \\
|\mathbf{\Delta} \cdot \mathbf{U}_1| &> e_1 + \varepsilon|\mathbf{D} \cdot \mathbf{U}_1| \\
|\mathbf{\Delta} \cdot \mathbf{U}_2| &> e_2 + \varepsilon|\mathbf{D} \cdot \mathbf{U}_1|
\end{aligned}
\tag{8.10}
$$

where ε is the extent of the segment. Figure 8.9 shows a typical separation of the projections on a separating axis with direction $\mathbf{W}$. The intervals are separated when $\mathbf{W} \cdot \mathbf{\Delta} - \varepsilon |\mathbf{W} \cdot \mathbf{D}| > r$ or when $\mathbf{W} \cdot \mathbf{\Delta} + \varepsilon |\mathbf{W} \cdot \mathbf{D}| < -r$. These may be combined into a joint statement: $|\mathbf{W} \cdot \mathbf{\Delta}| > r + \varepsilon |\mathbf{W} \cdot \mathbf{D}|$.

The implementation of the test-intersection query for a segment and oriented box in 3 dimensions is shown in Listing 8.24.

```
bool TestIntersection(Segment3 segment, OrientedBox3 box)
{
    Vector3 PmC = segment.P - box.C;
    Real ADdU[3], PmCdU[3], ADxPmCdU[3];

    // The segment-specific tests.
    for (int i = 0; i < 3; ++i)
    {
        ADdU[i] = abs(Dot(segment.D, box.U[i]));
        PmCdU[i] = abs(Dot(PmC, box.U[i]));
        if (PmCdU[i] > box.e[i] + segment.e * ADdU[i])
        {
            return false;
        }
    }

    // The line-specific tests.
    Vector3 DxPmC = Cross(segment.D, PmC);

    ADxPmCdU[0] = abs(Dot(DxPmC, box.U[0]));
    if (ADxPmCdU[0] > box.e[1] * ADdU[2] + box.e[2] * ADdU[1])
    {
        return false;
    }

    ADxPmCdU[1] = abs(Dot(DxPmC, box.U[1]));
    if (ADxPmCdU[1] > box.e[0] * ADdU[2] + box.e[2] * ADdU[0])
    {
        return false;
    }

    ADxPmCdU[2] = abs(Dot(DxPmC, box.U[2]));
    if (ADxPmCdU[2] > box.e[0] * ADdU[1] + box.e[1] * ADdU[0])
    {
        return false;
    }

    return true;
}
```

Listing 8.24: Pseudocode for the test-intersection query between a segment and an oriented box in 3 dimensions. The function `abs` returns the absolute value of its scalar argument.

To use quadratic-field arithmetic for exact computation, the first three comparisons of equation (8.10) can be processed similarly to what was done for the line-box separation tests using $\mathbf{V}_i$ and f_i. The other tests are of the form $|\mathbf{\Delta} \cdot \mathbf{V}_i| > f_i + \varepsilon |\mathbf{D} \cdot \mathbf{V}_i|$, which also require comparisons of 2-root quadratic-field numbers to zero.

The test-intersection for an aligned box can be formulated by using the center-extent form of the box. Listing 8.25 contains pseudocode for the query.

```
// P is the segment center, D is the unit-length segment direction, segE is the segment extent
// and boxE contains the box extents. The box center has been translated to the origin and
// the segment has been translated accordingly.
bool DoSegmentQuery(Vector3 P, Vector3 D, Real segE, Vector3 boxE)
```

```
{
    for (int i = 0; i < 3; ++i)
    {
        if (abs(P[i]) > segE[i] + r * abs(D[i]))
        {
            return false;
        }
    }
    return DoLineQuery(P, D, boxE);
}


// The query for the segment and aligned box, where the Segment3 object stores segment
//endpoints P0 and P1.
bool TestIntersection(Segment3 segment, AlignedBox3 box)
{
    // Get the centered form of the aligned box.
    Vector3 C = (box.max + box.min) / 2;
    Vector3 boxE = (box.max - box.min) / 2;

    // Transform the segment to the aligned-box coordinate system and convert
    // it to the center-direction-extent form.
    Vector3 P = (segment.P0 + segment.P1) / 2 - C;
    Vector3 D = segment.P1 - segment.P0;

    // Normalize makes D unit length and returns Length(D)/2.
    Real segE = Normalize(D);

    return DoSegmentQuery(P, D, segE, boxE);
}

// The query for the segment and oriented box but reformulated to use DoSegmentQuery.
bool TestIntersection(Segment3 segment, OrientedBox3 box)
{
    // Transform the segment to the oriented-box coordinate system.
    Vector3 P0, P1;
    for (int i = 0; i < 3; ++i)
    {
        P0[i] = Dot(segment.P0, box.U[i]);
        P1[i] = Dot(segment.P1, box.U[i]);
    }
    Vector3 P = (P0 + P1) / 2 - box.C;
    Vector3 D = P1 - P0;

    // Normalize makes D unit length and returns Length(D)/2.
    Real segE = Normalize(D);
    for (int i = 0; i < 3; ++i)
    {
        D[i] = Dot(D, box.U[i]);
    }
    return DoSegmentQuery(P, D, segE, box.e);
}
```

Listing 8.25: Pseudocode for the test-intersection query between a segment and an aligned box in 3 dimensions.

8.4.2 Find-Intersection Queries

The line-box find-intersection query is based on Liang–Barsky clipping [18, 11] of parametric lines against the box faces one at a time. The idea is to start with a t interval $[t_0, t_1]$ representing the current linear component (line, ray or segment). Initially, the interval is infinite: $t_0 = -\infty$ and $t_1 = \infty$. The line is converted to the box coordinate system. The line origin $\mathbf{P}$ is mapped to $\mathbf{P}' = (x_p, y_p, z_p)$ in the box coordinate system via

$$\mathbf{P} = \mathbf{C} + x_p\mathbf{U}_0 + y_p\mathbf{U}_1 + z_p\mathbf{U}_2 \qquad (8.11)$$

Therefore, $x_p = \mathbf{U}_0 \cdot (\mathbf{P} - \mathbf{C})$, $y_p = \mathbf{u}_1 \cdot (\mathbf{P} - \mathbf{C})$ and $z_p = \mathbf{u}_2 \cdot (\mathbf{P} - \mathbf{C})$. The line direction $\mathbf{D}$ is mapped to $\mathbf{D}' = (x_d, y_d, z_d)$ in the box coordinate system via

$$\mathbf{D} = x_d\mathbf{U}_0 + y_d\mathbf{U}_1 + z_d\mathbf{U}_2 \qquad (8.12)$$

Therefore, $x_d = \mathbf{U}_0 \cdot \mathbf{D}$, $y_p = \mathbf{U}_1 \cdot \mathbf{D}$ and $z_d = \mathbf{U}_2 \cdot \mathbf{D}$. In the box coordinate system, the box is naturally axis aligned. If (x, y, z) is a box point, then $|x| \le e_0$, $|y| \le e_1$ and $|z| \le e_2$.

The constructions are based on the box axis directions forming an orthonormal basis. As in the test-intersection queries, quadratic-field arithmetic can be used as long as the numerically computed box axis directions are converted to an orthogonal basis. The arithmetic expressions in the construction are modified as needed to support this.

8.4.2.1 Liang–Barsky Clipping

Figure 8.10 illustrates the clipping of the line $(x_p, y_p, z_p) + t(x_d, y_d, z_d)$ against the x-faces of the box. Figures 8.10(a-c) show clipping against the face $x = -e_0$ and Figures 8.10(d-f) show clipping against the face $x = e_0$. The clipping algorithm depends on the orientation of the line's direction vector relative to the x-axis. For a plane $x = a$, the intersection point of the line and plane is determined by

$$x_p + tx_d = a \qquad (8.13)$$

The value t must be solved for. The three cases are $x_d > 0$, $x_d < 0$ and $x_d = 0$.

Consider $x_d > 0$. In Figure 8.10, the relevant linear components are those with the arrow showing the components pointing generally in the positive x-direction. The t-value for the intersection is $t = (-e_0 - x_p)/x_d$. The decision on clipping is illustrated in the pseudocode of Listing 8.26.

```
if (t > t1) then
{
    cull the linear component;    // Figure 8.10(a)
}
else if (t > t0) then
{
    t0 = t;                       // Figure 8.10(b)
}
else
{
    do nothing;                   // Figure 8.10(c)
}
```

Listing 8.26: Clipping code against $x = e_0$ when $x_d > 0$.

If $x_d < 0$, the relevant linear components in Figure 8.10 are those with the

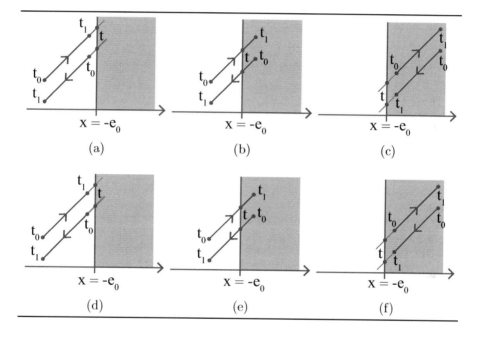

FIGURE 8.10: Line clipping against the x-faces of the box. The cases are referenced in the pseudocode that occurs in this section.

arrow showing the components pointing generally in the negative x direction. The pseudocode is shown in Listing 8.27.

```
if (t < t0) then
{
    cull the linear component;    // Figure 8.10(a)
}
else if (t < t1) then
{
    t1 = t;                       // Figure 8.10(b)
}
else
{
    do nothing;                   // Figure 8.10(c)
}
```

Listing 8.27: Clipping code against $x = e_0$ when $x_d < 0$.

Finally, if $x_d = 0$, the linear component is parallel to the x-faces. The component is either outside the box, in which case it is culled, or inside or on the box, in which case no clipping against the x faces needs to be performed. The pseudocode is shown in Listing 8.28.

```
n = -e0 - xp;
if (n > 0) then
{
    cull the linear component;
}
else
{
    do nothing;
}
```

Listing 8.28: Clipping code against $x = e_0$ when $x_d = 0$.

A similar construction applies for the face $x = e_0$, except that the sense of direction is reversed. The bottom three images of Figure 8.10 apply here. The equation to solve is $x_p + t x_d = e_0$. If $x_d \neq 0$, the solution is $t = (e_0 - x_p)/x_d$. If $x_d > 0$, the pseudocode is shown in Listing 8.29.

```
if (t < t0) then
{
    cull the linear component;    // Figure 8.10(d)
}
else if (t < t1) then
{
    t1 = t;                       // Figure 8.10(e)
}
else
{
    do nothing;                   // Figure 8.10(f)
}
```

Listing 8.29: Clipping code against $x = -e_0$ when $x_d > 0$.

If $x_d < 0$, the pseudocode is shown in Listing 8.30.

```
if (t > t1) then
{
    cull the linear component;    // Figure 8.10(d)
}
else if (t > t0) then
```

```
{
    t0 = t;                        // Figure 8.10(e)
}
else
{
    do nothing;                    // Figure 8.10(f)
}
```

Listing 8.30: Clipping code against $x = -e_0$ when $x_d < 0$.

If $x_d = 0$, the linear component is parallel to the x-faces. The component is either outside the box, in which case it is culled, or inside or on the box, in which case no clipping against the x-faces needs to be performed. The pseudocode is shown in Listing 8.31.

```
n = e0 - xp;
if (n < 0) then
{
    cull the linear component;
}
else
{
    do nothing;
}
```

Listing 8.31: Clipping code against $x = -e_0$ when $x_d = 0$.

A goal of the construction is to keep the clipping code to a minimum. With this in mind, notice that the clipping code for the case $x = e_0$ and $x_d > 0$ is the same as that for the case $x = -e_0$ and $x_d < 0$. The clipping code for the case $x = e_0$ and $x_d < 0$ is the same as that for the case $x = -e_0$ and $x_d > 0$. The cases when $x_d = 0$ differ only by the test of n—in one case tested for positivity, in the other for negativity. Consolidate the six code blocks into three by processing the $x = e_0$ cases using $-x_d$ and $-n = x_p - e_0$. The pseudocode of Listing 8.32 shows the consolidated code. One optimization occurs: a division is performed to compute t only if the linear component is not culled.

```
bool Clip(Real denom, Real numer, Real& t0, Real& t1)
{
    if (denom > 0)
    {
        if (numer > denom * t1)
        {
            return false;
        }
        if (numer > denom * t0)
        {
            t0 = numer / denom;
        }
        return true;
    }
    else if (denom < 0)
    {
        if (numer > denom * t0)
        {
            return false;
        }
        if (numer > denom * t1)
        {
            t1 = numer / denom;
```

```
        }
        return true;
    }
    else
    {
        return numer <= 0;
    }
}
```

Listing 8.32: Liang–Barsky clipping for a linear component against a face of a box.

The return value is false if the current linear component is culled; otherwise, the return value is true, indicating that the linear component was clipped or just kept as is.

8.4.2.2   Lines and Boxes

The clipping against all the faces is encapsulated by the find-intersection queries for a line and a box and is shown in Listing 8.33. As in the test-intersection queries, the code is written for aligned boxes. For oriented boxes, a transformation is applied to convert to a configuration involving aligned boxes after which the query for the aligned box is applied.

```
// P is the line origin, D is the unit-length line direction and e contains the box extents. The
// box center has been translated to the origin and the line has been translated accordingly.
void DoLineQuery(Vector3 P, Vector3 D, Vector3 e, int& numPoints, Real t[2])
{
    // Clip the line against the box faces using the 6 cases mentioned in Figure 8.10.
    Real t0 = -infinity, t1 = +infinity;
    bool notCulled =
        Clip(+D[0], -P[0] - box.e[0], t0, t1) &&
        Clip(-D[0], +P[0] - box.e[0], t0, t1) &&
        Clip(+D[1], -P[1] - box.e[1], t0, t1) &&
        Clip(-D[1], +P[1] - box.e[1], t0, t1) &&
        Clip(+D[2], -P[2] - box.e[2], t0, t1) &&
        Clip(-D[2], +P[2] - box.e[2], t0, t1);

    if (notCulled)
    {
        if (t1 > t0)
        {
            // The intersection is a segment P + t * D with t in [t0,t1].
            numPoints = 2;
            t[0] = t0;
            t[1] = t1;
        }
        else
        {
            // The intersection is a point P + t * D with t = t0.
            numPoints = 1;
            t[0] = t0;
            t[1] = t0;
        }
    }
    else
    {
        // The line does not intersect the box. Return invalid parameters.
        numPoints = 0;
        t[0] = +infinity;
        t[1] = -infinity;
    }
}
```

```
}

// The line-box find-intersection query computes both the parameter interval t[]
// and the corresponding endpoints (if any) of the intersection linear component.
bool FindIntersection(Line3 line, AlignedBox3 box, int& numPoints,
    Real t[2], Vector3 point[2])
{
    // Get the centered form of the aligned box.
    Vector3 C = (box.max + box.min) / 2;
    Vector3 e = (box.max - box.min) / 2;

    // Transform the line to the aligned-box coordinate system.
    Vector3 P = line.P - C;
    Vector3 D = line.D;

    DoLineQuery(P, D, e, numPoints, t);
    for (int i = 0; i < numPoints; ++i)
    {
        point[i] = line.P + t[i] * line.D;
    }

    return numPoints > 0;
}

// The query for the line and oriented box is formulated to use DoLineQuery.
bool FindIntersection(Line3 line, OrientedBox3 box, int& numPoints,
    Real t[2], Vector3 point[2])
{
    // Transform the line to the oriented-box coordinate system.
    Vector3 delta = line.P - box.C;
    Vector3 P, D;
    for (int i = 0; i < 3; ++i)
    {
        P[i] = Dot(delta, box.U[i]);
        D[i] = Dot(line.D, box.U[i]);
    }

    DoLineQuery(P, D, e, numPoints, t);
    for (int i = 0; i < numPoints; ++i)
    {
        point[i] = line.P + t[i] * line.D;
    }

    return numPoints > 0;
}
```

Listing 8.33: Clipping of a line against an aligned box or an oriented box. The returned numPoints is 0 if the line does not intersect the box (entirely clipped), 1 if the line intersects the box in a single point or 2 if the line intersects the box in a segment. The parameter interval is filled with 2 elements regardless of the value of numPoints. This ensures that memory is initialized.

8.4.2.3 Rays and Boxes

The find-intersection query between a ray and a box uses the line-box query to produce an intersection interval $I = [t_0, t_1]$ (possibly empty). The ray-box intersection is generated by the intersection of I with the ray interval $[0, +\infty)$; that is, it is generated by $I \cap [0, +\infty)$. Listing 8.34 contains pseudocode for the query.

```
// P is the ray origin, D is the unit-length ray direction and e contains the box extents. The
// box center has been translated to the origin and the ray has been translated accordingly.
void DoRayQuery(Vector3 P, Vector3 D, Vector3 e, int& numPoints, Real t[2])
{
    DoLineQuery(P, D, e, numPoints, t);
    if (numPoints > 0)
    {
        // The line containing the ray intersects the box in the interval [t0,t1]. Compute
        // the intersection of [t0,t1] and [0,+infinity).
        if (t[1] >= 0)
        {
            if (t[0] < 0)
            {
                t[0] = 0;
            }
        }
        else
        {
            // The line intersects the box but the ray does not.
            numPoints = 0;
        }
    }
}


// The ray-box find-intersection query computes both the parameter interval t[] and the
// corresponding endpoints (if any) of the intersection linear component.
bool FindIntersection(Ray3 ray, AlignedBox3 box, int& numPoints,
    Real t[2], Vector3 point[2])
{
    // Get the centered form of the aligned box.
    Vector3 C = (box.max + box.min) / 2;
    Vector3 e = (box.max - box.min) / 2;

    // Transform the ray to the aligned-box coordinate system.
    Vector3 P = ray.P - C;
    Vector3 D = ray.D;

    DoRayQuery(P, D, e, numPoints, t);
    for (int i = 0; i < numPoints; ++i)
    {
        point[i] = ray.P + t[i] * ray.D;
    }

    return numPoints > 0;
}

// The query for the ray and oriented box is formulated to use DoLineQuery.
bool FindIntersection(Ray3 ray, OrientedBox3 box, int& numPoints,
    Real t[2], Vector3 point[2])
{
    // Transform the ray to the oriented-box coordinate system.
    Vector3 delta = ray.P - box.C;
    Vector3 P, D;
    for (int i = 0; i < 3; ++i)
    {
        P[i] = Dot(delta, box.U[i]);
        D[i] = Dot(ray.D, box.U[i]);
    }

    DoRayQuery(P, D, e, numPoints, t);
    for (int i = 0; i < numPoints; ++i)
    {
        point[i] = ray.P + t[i] * ray.D;
    }
```

```
        return  numPoints > 0;
}
```

Listing 8.34: Clipping of a ray against an aligned box or an oriented box. The
returned numPoints is 0 if the ray does not intersect the box (entirely clipped),
1 if the ray intersects the box in a single point or 2 if the ray intersects the
box in a segment. The parameter interval is filled accordingly with numPoints
elements.

8.4.2.4 Segments and Boxes

The segment is represented in center-direction-extent form, $\mathbf{P}+t\mathbf{D}$, where
$\mathbf{P}$ is the center of the segment, $\mathbf{D}$ is a unit-length direction vector, ε is the
extent (radius) of the segment and $|t| \le \varepsilon$. The line segment has length 2ε.

The find-intersection query between a segment and a box uses the line-
box query to produce an intersection interval $I = [t_0, t_1]$ (possibly empty).
The segment-box intersection is generated by the intersection of I with the
segment interval $[s_0, s_1]$; that is, it is generated by $I \cap [s_0, s_1]$. Listing 8.35
contains pseudocode for the query.

```
// Pseudocode for computing the intersection of two intervals.
bool ComputeIntersection(Real intv0[2], Real intv1[2],
    int& numIntersections, Real overlap[2])
{
    if (intv0[1] < intv1[0] || intv0[0] > intv1[1])
    {
        overlap[0] = +infinity;
        overlap[1] = -infinity;
        numIntersections = 0;
    }
    else if (intv0[1] > intv1[0])
    {
        if (intv0[0] < intv1[1])
        {
            overlap[0] = (intv0[0] < intv1[0] ? intv1[0] : intv0[0]);
            overlap[1] = (intv0[1] > intv1[1] ? intv1[1] : intv0[1]);
            numIntersections = (overlap[0] != overlap[1] ? 2 : 1);
        }
        else  // intv0[0] == intv1[1]
        {
            overlap[0] = intv0[0];
            overlap[1] = overlap[0];
            numIntersections = 1;
        }
    }
    else  // intv0[1] == intv1[0]
    {
        overlap[0] = intv0[1];
        overlap[1] = overlap[0];
        numIntersections = 1;
    }
    return numIntersections > 0;
}

// P is the segment center, D is the unit-length segment direction, segE is the segment extent
// and boxE contains the box extents. The box center has been translated to the origin and
// the segment has been translated accordingly.
void DoSegmentQuery(Vector3 P, Vector3 D, Real segE, Vector3 boxE,
    int& numPoints, Real t[2])
```

```
{
    DoLineQuery(P, D, boxE, numPoints, t);
    if (numPoints > 0)
    {
        // The line containing the segment intersects the box in the interval [t0,t1]. Compute
        // the intersection of [t0,t1] and the segment interval [s0,s1].
        Real s[2] = { -segE, segE }, overlap[2];
        if (ComputeIntersection(t, s, numPoints, overlap)
        {
            for (int i = 0; i < numPoints; ++i)
            {
                t[i] = overlap[i];
            }
        }
    }
}

// The segment-box find-intersection query computes both the parameter interval t[] and the
// corresponding endpoints (if any) of the intersection linear component. The query assumes
// the Segment3 object stores the segment endpoints P0 and P1.
bool FindIntersection(Segment3 segment, AlignedBox3 box, int& numPoints,
    Real t[2], Vector3 point[2])
{
    // Get the centered form of the aligned box.
    Vector3 C = (box.max + box.min) / 2;
    Vector3 boxE = (box.max - box.min) / 2;

    // Transform the segment to the aligned-box coordinate system and convert
    // it to the center-direction-extent form.
    Vector3 P = (segment.P0 + segment.P1) / 2 - C;
    Vector3 D = segment.P1 - segment.P0;

    // Normalize makes D unit length and returns Length(D)/2.
    Real segE = Normalize(D);

    DoSegmentQuery(P, D, segE, boxE, numPoints, t);

    // The segment is in aligned box coordinates, transform back to the original space.
    for (int i = 0; i < numPoints; ++i)
    {
        point[i] = P + C + t[i] * D;
    }

    return numPoints > 0;
}

// The query for the segment and oriented box is formulated to use DoSegmentQuery.
bool FindIntersection(Segment3 segment, OrientedBox3 box, int& numPoints,
    Real t[2], Vector3 point[2])
{
    // Transform the segment to the oriented-box coordinate system.
    Vector3 P0, P1;
    for (int i = 0; i < 3; ++i)
    {
        P0[i] = Dot(segment.P0, box.U[i]);
        P1[i] = Dot(segment.P1, box.U[i]);
    }
    Vector3 P = (P0 + P1) / 2 - box.C;
    Vector3 D = P1 - P0;

    // Normalize makes D unit length and returns Length(D)/2.
    Real segE = Normalize(D);
    D = { Dot(D, box.U[0]), Dot(D, box.U[1]), Dot(D, box.U[2]);

    DoSegmentQuery(P, D, segE, box.e, numPoints, t);
```

```
// The segment is in aligned box coordinates, transform back to the original space.
for (int i = 0; i < numPoints; ++i)
{
    // Compute the intersection point in the oriented-box coordinate system.
    Vector3 Y = P + t[i] * D;

    // Transform the intersection point to the original coordinate system.
    point[i] = box.C+Y[0]*box.U[0]+Y[1]*box.U[1]+Y[2]*box.U[2];
}

return numPoints > 0;
}
```

Listing 8.35: Clipping of a segment against an aligned box or an oriented box. The returned numPoints is 0 if the segment does not intersect the box (entirely clipped), 1 if the segment intersects the box in a single point or 2 if the segment intersects the box in a segment. The parameter interval is filled accordingly with numPoints elements.

8.5 Line and Cone

This section describes an algorithm for computing the set of intersection between a cone and a line, ray or segment. The algorithm is theoretically correct when using real-valued arithmetic. When computing using floating-point arithmetic, rounding errors can cause misclassifications of signs of important expressions, leading to failure of the implementation to produce correct results.

With the exception of the approximation error in computing the cosine of a user-specified cone angle, it is possible to obtain the theoretically correct result by using quadratic-field arithmetic that handles the square root operations to avoid the rounding errors inherent in computing those roots. An implementation of the algorithm is also described in this section. The set of intersection is either empty, a point, a segment, a ray or a line. The final quadratic-field numbers can be converted to floating-point numbers using as many bits of precision as desired.

8.5.1 Definition of Cones

An *infinite single-sided solid cone* has a vertex $\mathbf{V}$, an axis ray whose origin is $\mathbf{V}$ and unit-length direction is $\mathbf{D}$, and an acute cone angle $\theta \in (0, \pi/2)$. A point $\mathbf{X}$ is inside the cone when the angle between $\mathbf{D}$ and $\mathbf{X} - \mathbf{V}$ is in $[0, \theta]$. Algebraically, the containment is defined by

$$\mathbf{D} \cdot \frac{(\mathbf{X} - \mathbf{V})}{|\mathbf{X} - \mathbf{V}|} \geq \cos(\theta) \tag{8.14}$$

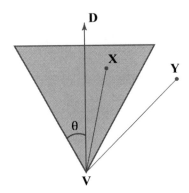

FIGURE 8.11: A 2D view of a single-sided cone. $\mathbf{X}$ is inside the cone and $\mathbf{Y}$ is outside the cone.

when $\mathbf{X} \neq \mathbf{V}$. Equivalently, the containment is defined by

$$\mathbf{D} \cdot (\mathbf{X} - \mathbf{V}) \geq |\mathbf{X} - \mathbf{V}| \cos(\theta) \tag{8.15}$$

which includes the case $\mathbf{X} = \mathbf{V}$. Finally, avoid computing square roots in the implementation by squaring the dot-product equation to obtain a quadratic equation and requiring that only points above the supporting plane of the single-sided cone be considered. The definition is

$$Q(\mathbf{X}) = (\mathbf{X} - \mathbf{V})^{\mathsf{T}} M(\mathbf{X} - \mathbf{V}) \geq 0, \quad \mathbf{D} \cdot (\mathbf{X} - \mathbf{V}) \geq 0 \tag{8.16}$$

where $\gamma = \cos\theta$, $M = \mathbf{D}\mathbf{D}^{\mathsf{T}} - \gamma^2 I$ is a symmetric 3×3 matrix and I the 3×3 identity matrix. Figure 8.11 shows a 2D cone, which is sufficient to illustrate the quantites in 3D. Because of the constraint on θ, both $\cos(\theta) > 0$ and $\sin(\theta) > 0$.

The *height* of a point $\mathbf{X}$ relative to the cone is the length of the projection of $\mathbf{X} - \mathbf{V}$ onto the $\mathbf{D}$-axis, namely, $h = \mathbf{D} \cdot (\mathbf{X} - \mathbf{V})$. The infinite cone can be truncated, either with a minimum height or a maximum height or both. The names and height constraints are as follows. For concise naming, the term single-sided is dropped. Generally, the heights h satisfy $h \in [h_{\min}, h_{\max}]$ with $0 \leq h_{\min} < h_{\max} \leq +\infty$.

- Infinite cone: $h_{\min} = 0$, $h_{\max} = +\infty$.

- Infinite truncated cone: $h_{\min} > 0$, $h_{\max} = +\infty$.

- Finite truncated cone: $h_{\min} = 0$, $h_{\max} < +\infty$.

- Frustum of a cone (or cone frustum): $h_{\min} > 0$, $h_{\max} < +\infty$.

In the discussions here, the term *cone* is used to refer to any one of the four classifications, making clear the specific details of the algorithms for each classification.

8.5.2   Practical Matters for Representing Infinity

A practical matter when defining a cone data structure is how to represent an infinite maximum height, $h_{\max} = +\infty$. With floating-point computations, it is reasonable to choose std::numeric_limits<Real>::infinity() for Real set to float or double. This representation is the special IEEE Standard 754™-2008 floating-point pattern used to represent infinity. If Real will be an arbitrary precision type that does not have a representation for infinity, the next choice could be to use the largest finite floating-point number, std::numeric_limits<Real>::max(). An arbitrary precision type will have code to convert this to a rational representation. However, the semantics for infinity are no longer clear, because the rational representation of the largest finite floating-point number has nothing to do with infinity. For example, if an algorithm required squaring the maximum height, the IEEE Standard 754™-2008 infinity squared still produces infinity. Squaring the largest finite floating-point number represented as a rational number will lead to another rational number, and now comparison semantics no longer work correctly.

In the Cone class of GTL, the setting of minimum and maximum height hides the representation. An infinite height is represented by setting internally the (hidden) class member for maximum height to -1. Internal query code can then test whether a cone is finite or infinite by examining this class member.

If an algorithm requires the concept of infinity, positive or negative, in comparisons, it is generally possible to do so without using the IEEE Standard 754™-2008 infinity representations and without requiring an arbitrary precision arithmetic libray to have infinity representations. Instead, use a *2-point compactification of the real numbers*. Let $x \in (-\infty, +\infty)$ be any real number. Define $y = x/(1 + |x|) \in (-1, 1)$. The function is a bijection and has inverse $x = y/(1 - |y|)$. The compactification occurs when $+1$ is chosen to represent $+\infty$ and -1 is chosen to represent $-\infty$. In this sense, $y = x/(1+|x|)$ maps $[-\infty, +\infty]$ to $[-1, 1]$. To determine whether $x_0 < x_1$, even when either number is an infinity, compute $y_i = x_i/(1+|x_i|)$ and instead compare $y_0 < y_1$. The y-values are always finite. In fact, the bijection maps rational numbers to rational numbers, so the y-comparisons are error free when using arbitrary precision arithmetic. The idea also applies to symbolic arithmetic involving numbers of the form $z = x + y\sqrt{d}$, where x, y and d are rational numbers and $d > 0$; this is the underlying framework for dealing with lengths of vectors symbolically.

8.5.3   Definition of a Line, Ray and Segment

A line is parameterized by $\mathbf{X}(t) = \mathbf{P} + t\mathbf{U}$, where $\mathbf{P}$ is a point on the line (the line origin), $\mathbf{U}$ is typically a unit-length direction vector for the line and t is a real number. A ray has the subset of the line with restriction $t \geq 0$. A segment is a subset of the line with restriction $t \in [0, t_{\max}]$, so the endpoints are $\mathbf{P}$ and $\mathbf{P} + t_{\max}\mathbf{U}$. However, the endpoints are typically specified, say, $\mathbf{E}_0$ and $\mathbf{E}_1$, with $\mathbf{X}(t) = (1-t)\mathbf{E}_0 + t\mathbf{E}_1$ for $t \in [0,1]$.

The line-cone find-intersection query described here does not require $\mathbf{U}$ to be unit length. Sections 8.5.4, 8.5.5 and 8.5.6 assume real-valued arithmetic, which is error-free in the theoretical sense.

In Section 8.5.9, the restriction that $\mathbf{D}$ be unit length is dropped, but then a combination of rational and symbolic arithmetic is needed to compute exact results.

8.5.4   Intersection with a Line

Find the points of intersection with the cone boundary $Q(\mathbf{X}) = 0$, where Q is defined by equation (8.16). Substitute the line equation $\mathbf{X}(t) = \mathbf{P} + t\mathbf{U}$ into the quadratic polynomial of equation (8.14)) to obtain $c_2 t^2 + 2c_1 t + c_0 = 0$, where $\boldsymbol{\Delta} = \mathbf{P} - \mathbf{V}$. The vector $\mathbf{U}$ is not required to be unit length. The coefficients are

$$\begin{aligned}
c_2 &= \mathbf{U}^\mathsf{T} M \mathbf{U} = (\mathbf{D}\cdot\mathbf{U})^2 - \gamma^2(\mathbf{U}\cdot\mathbf{U}) \\
c_1 &= \mathbf{U}^\mathsf{T} M \boldsymbol{\Delta} = (\mathbf{D}\cdot\mathbf{U})(\mathbf{D}\cdot\boldsymbol{\Delta}) - \gamma^2(\mathbf{U}\cdot\boldsymbol{\Delta}) \\
c_0 &= \boldsymbol{\Delta}^\mathsf{T} M \boldsymbol{\Delta} = (\mathbf{D}\cdot\boldsymbol{\Delta})^2 - \gamma^2(\boldsymbol{\Delta}\cdot\boldsymbol{\Delta})
\end{aligned} \qquad (8.17)$$

It is convenient to reduce algorithm branching cases by choosing the line direction $\mathbf{U}$ so that $\mathbf{D}\cdot\mathbf{U} \geq 0$. In practice, the user-specified line direction can be negated to ensure the nonnegative dot product. The t-values at the intersection points are computed, but when reporting this information to the caller, the t-values must be negated to undo the sign change in the line direction. The bounds $h_{\min} \leq \mathbf{D}\cdot(\mathbf{X}(t) - \mathbf{V}) \leq h_{\max}$ become

$$h_{\min} \leq t(\mathbf{D}\cdot\mathbf{U}) + (\mathbf{D}\cdot\boldsymbol{\Delta}) \leq h_{\max} \qquad (8.18)$$

The roots of a quadratic polynomial (possibly degenerate) must be computed subject to linear inequality constraints on t. The roots may be computed as if the cone is infinite. For the infinite truncated cone, the finite cone and the cone frustum, the clamping to finite h-bounds can be applied as a postprocessing step.

8.5.4.1   Case $c_2 \neq 0$

Suppose that $c_2 \neq 0$. The formal roots are $t = (-c_1 \pm \sqrt{\delta})/c_2$, where $\delta = c_1^2 - c_0 c_2$.

If $\delta < 0$, the quadratic polynomial has no real-valued roots, in which case the line does not intersect the double-sided cone, which means it does not intersect cones of any of the 4 classifications.

If $\delta = 0$, the polynomial has a repeated real-value root $t = -c_1/c_2$. This occurs in two different geometric configurations. One configuration is when the line is tangent to the double-sided cone at a single point. The other is when the line contains the cone vertex $\mathbf{V}$, in which case $\mathbf{V} = \mathbf{P} + (-c_1/c_2)\mathbf{U}$.

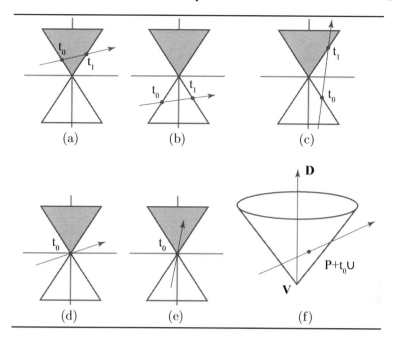

FIGURE 8.12: Geometric configurations when $c_2 \neq 0$. Only the intersections with the positive cone are relevant; that is, where $\mathbf{D} \cdot (\mathbf{X} - \mathbf{V}) \geq 0$. (a) $\delta > 0$ and both points are on the positive cone. (b) $\delta > 0$ and both points are on the negative cone. (c) $\delta > 0$, one point is on the positive cone and one point is on the negative cone. (d) $\delta = 0$, $c_2 < 0$ (**U** is outside the cone), and the line contains the vertex. (e) $\delta = 0$, $c_2 > 0$ (**U** is inside the cone), and the line contains the vertex. (f) $\delta = 0$ and the line is tangent to the cone.

If $\delta > 0$, the polynomial has two distinct real-valued roots, in which case the line intersects the double-sided cone at two points. Figure 8.12 illustrates the various cases. In Figure 8.12, the intersection types with the double-sided cone are as follows: (a) and (b), segments; (c) ray; (d) and (f) point; (e) line. The intersection types with the positive cone are: (a) segment; (b) none; (c) and (e) ray; (d) and (f) point.

8.5.4.2   Case $c_2 = 0$ and $c_1 \neq 0$

If $c_2 = 0$, the vector **U** is a direction vector on the cone boundary because $|\mathbf{D} \cdot \mathbf{U}| = \cos(\theta)$. If $c_1 \neq 0$, the polynomial is in fact linear and has a single root $t = -c_0/(2c_1)$. The line and double-sided cone have a single point of intersection. As before, report the point as an intersection only when it is on the positive cone. If it is, choose the correct t-interval of intersection. Figure 8.13 illustrates a couple of configurations.

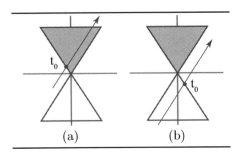

(a)   (b)

FIGURE 8.13: Geometric configurations when $c_2 = 0$ and $c_1 \neq 0$. Only the intersections with the positive cone are relevant; that is, where $\mathbf{D} \cdot (\mathbf{X} - \mathbf{V}) \geq 0$. (a) The line intersects the positive cone in a single point. (b) The line intersects the negative cone in a single point.

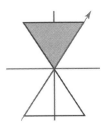

FIGURE 8.14: When $c_0 = c_1 = c_2 = 0$, the line lives on the cone surface and contains the cone vertex.

8.5.4.3   Case $c_2 = 0$ and $c_1 = 0$

The condition $c_2 = 0$ implies the line direction $\mathbf{U}$ is on the cone surface. The condition $c_1 = 0$ is necessary for the line to contain the cone vertex $\mathbf{V}$. Together these conditions and the quadratic equation imply $c_0 = 0$, in which case the line lies on the cone surface. If $c_0 \neq 0$, the line does not intersect the cone. Figure 8.14 illustrates the case $c_0 = c_1 = c_2 = 0$.

8.5.5   Clamping to the Cone Height Range

Generally, various cone types and their corresponding height ranges $[h_{\min}, h_{\max}]$ were defined. The relationship between height h and line parameter t is in equation (8.18). Choose the line direction so that $\mathbf{D} \cdot \mathbf{U} \geq 0$.

For each intersection point of the line and cone, say, occurring at parameter t, compute $h = t(\mathbf{D} \cdot \mathbf{U}) + (\mathbf{D} \cdot \boldsymbol{\Delta})$. When $\mathbf{D} \cdot \mathbf{U} > 0$, given a height h, the value of t can be solved for,

$$t = (h - \mathbf{D} \cdot \boldsymbol{\Delta})/(\mathbf{D} \cdot \mathbf{U}) \tag{8.19}$$

The h-values and t-values increase jointly or decrease jointly. For two intersection points, $t_0 < t_1$ implies $h_0 < h_1$. When $\mathbf{D} \cdot \mathbf{U} = 0$, the line is perpendicular to the cone axis and the heights are the same value $\mathbf{D} \cdot \mathbf{\Delta}$ for all line points.

The idea is to compute the h-interval $[h_0, h_1]$ for the intersection set and intersect it with the h-interval $[h_{\min}, h_{\max}]$ for the cone. If the set is nonempty, the corresponding t-values are computed using equation (8.19) and the linear component quantities are computed from them.

8.5.6 Pseudocode for Error-Free Arithmetic

The algorithm requires find-intersection queries for intervals, where the intervals are finite or semiinfinite. These queries are discussed first.

8.5.6.1 Intersection of Intervals

The find-intersection query requires computing the intersection of finite intervals $[u_0, u_1]$ and $[v_0, v_1]$, where $u_0 \leq u_1$ and $v_0 \leq v_1$. An interval can be degenerate in that its endpoints are the same number. Listing 8.36 contains pseudocode for computing the intersection.

```
int FindIntersection(Real u0, Real u1, Real v0, Real v1, Real overlap[2])
{
    int numValid;
    if (u1 < v0 || v1 < u0)
    {
        numValid = 0;
    }
    else if (v0 < u1)
    {
        if (u0 < v1)
        {
            overlap[0] = (u0 < v0 ? v0 : u0);
            overlap[1] = (u1 > v1 ? v1 : u1);
            if (overlap[0] < overlap[1]) { numValid = 2; }
            else { numValid = 1; }
        }
        else   // u0 == v1
        {
            overlap[0] = u0;
            overlap[1] = u0;
            numValid = 1;
        }
    }
    else   // u1 == v0
    {
        overlap[0] = v0;
        overlap[1] = v0;
        numValid = 1;
    }
    return numValid;
}
```

Listing 8.36: Pseudocode for the find-intersection query of two finite intervals. The function returns an integer value that is the number of valid elements of overlap[]. It is 0 (no intersection), 1 (intervals touch only at an endpoint) or 2 (intervals overlap in an interval).

A semiinfinite interval is of the form $[v, +\infty)$ or $(-\infty, v]$. The first interval contains real numbers t for which $t \geq v$. The second interval contains real numbers t for which $t \leq v$. If the type Real of Listing 8.36 has a representation for infinities, that code applies as well when either input is a semiinfinite interval. Such a representation is not assumed, but additional functions can be implemented with the correct logic for semiinfinite intervals. For the line-cone intersection query, only semiinfinite intervals $[v, +\infty)$ need to be dealt with, so only the query for such an interval is discussed.

Suppose that the first input is the finite interval $[u_0, u_1]$ and the second interval is $[v_0, +\infty]$, where $v_1 = +\infty$ and the closed bracket is suggestive that $+\infty$ is an element of that set. In Listing 8.36, the tests v[1] < u[0] and u[1] > v[1] are always false and the test u[0] < v[1] is always true. The code can be rewritten using these facts, and the input v-interval is passed as the endpoint v_0. Listing 8.37 shows pseudocode for the find-intersection query.

```
int FindIntersection(Real u0, Real u1, Real v, Real overlap[2])
{
    int numValid;
    if (u1 > v)
    {
        numValid = 2;
        overlap[0] = max(u0, v);
        overlap[1] = u1;
    }
    else if (u1 == v)
    {
        numValid = 1;
        overlap[0] = v;
    }
    else // u1 < v
    {
        numValid = 0;
    }
    return numValid;
}
```

Listing 8.37: Pseudocode for the find-intersection query of a finite interval $[u_0, u_1]$ and a semiinfinite interval $[v, +\infty)$. The function returns an integer value that is the number of valid elements of overlap[]. It is 0 (no intersection), 1 (intervals touch only at an endpoint) or 2 (intervals overlap in an interval).

The final find-intersection query involves two semiinfinite intervals $[u, +\infty)$ and $[v, +\infty)$. This query is required when computing the intersection of a ray and a cone with infinite height. It is a simple query that produces the interval $[\max\{u, v\}, +\infty)$.

8.5.6.2 Line-Cone Query

The pseudocode for the line-cone find-intersection query must compute the subset of the line that is contained inside the positive cone. The possible types of subsets are characterized next. The query function returns one of these types. It also returns a 2-tuple Real t[2] that stores the line parameters defining the intersection. The number of valid elements (0, 1 or 2) depends on the type. A corresponding 2-tuple of points is returned, Vector3 P[2]. The type list is

- NONE: There is no intersection. The elements of t[] and P[] are invalid.

- POINT: The intersection consists of a single point. The values t[0] and P[0] are valid, the other pair invalid.

- SEGMENT: The intersection is a segment. All values t[] and P[] are valid. The difference of the two points is necessarily parallel to $\mathbf{U}$.

- RAY_POSITIVE: The intersection is a ray $\mathbf{P} + t\mathbf{U}$ with $t \in [t_0, +\infty)$. The value t[0] stores t_0 and the value P[0] stores $\mathbf{P} + t_0\mathbf{U}$.

- RAY_NEGATIVE: The intersection is a ray $\mathbf{P} + t\mathbf{U}$ with $t \in (-\infty, t_1]$. The value t[1] stores t_1 and the value P[1] stores $\mathbf{P} + t_1\mathbf{U}$.

Listing 8.38 contains pseudocode for the find-intersection query between a line and a cone.

```
struct Line3
{
    Vector3 P;   // origin
    Vector3 U;   // direction, not required to be unit length
};

struct Cone3
{
    Vector3 V;   // vertex
    Vector3 D;   // axis direction, required to be unit length
    Real cosAngleSqr;   // the square of cos(angle) for the cone angle

    // The height range of the cone. The minimum height is hmin ≥ 0. The maximum
    // height is hmax > hmin for a finite cone but −1 for an infinite cone. The Boolean
    // value indicates whether or not hmax is valid (true for a finite cone, false for an
    // infinite cone).
    Real hmin, hmax;
    bool isFinite;
};

// The returned int is one of NONE, POINT, SEGMENT, RAY_POSITIVE
// or RAY_NEGATIVE. The returned t[] and P[] values are as described previously.
int FindIntersection(Line3 line, Cone3 cone, Real t[2], Vector3 P[2])
{
    int intersectionType = DoQuery(line.P, line.U, cone, t);
    ComputePoints(intersectionType, line.P, line.U, t, P);
    return intersectionType;
}

void ComputePoints(int intersectionType, Vector3 origin,
    Vector3 direction, Real t[2], Vector3 P[2])
{
    switch (intersectionType)
    {
        case NONE:
            P[0] = invalid_point;
            P[1] = invalid_point;
            break;
        case POINT:
            P[0] = origin + t[0] * direction;
```

```
            P[1] = invalid_point;
            break;
        case SEGMENT:
            P[0] = origin + t[0] * direction;
            P[1] = origin + t[1] * direction;
            break;
        case RAY_POSITIVE:
            P[0] = origin + t[0] * direction;
            P[1] = invalid_point;
            break;
        case RAY_NEGATIVE:
            P[0] = invalid_point;
            P[1] = origin + t[1] * direction;
            break;
    }
}

int DoQuery(Vector3 P, Vector3 U, Cone3 cone, Real t[2])
{
    // Arrange for an acute angle between the cone direction and line direction. This
    // simplifies the logic later in the code and it supports additional queries involving
    // rays or segments instead of lines.
    int intersectionType;
    Real DdU = Dot(cone.D, U);
    if (DdU >= 0)
    {
        intersectionType = DoQuerySpecial(P, U, cone, t);
    }
    else
    {
        intersectionType = DoQuerySpecial(P, -U, cone, t);
        t[0] = -t[0];
        t[1] = -t[1];
        swap(t[0], t[1]);
        if (intersectionType == RAY_POSITIVE)
        {
            intersectionType = RAY_NEGATIVE;
        }
    }
    return intersectionType;
}

int DoQuerySpecial(Vector3 P, Vector3 U, Cone3 cone, Real t[2])
{
    // Compute the quadratic coefficients.
    Vector3 PmV = P - cone.V;
    Real DdU = Dot(cone.D, U);
    Real UdU = Dot(U, U);
    Real DdPmV = Dot(cone.D, PmV);
    Real UdPmV = Dot(U, PmV);
    Real PmVdPmV = Dot(PmV, PmV);
    Real c2 = DdU * DdU - cone.cosThetaSqr * UdU;
    Real c1 = DdU * DdPmV - cone.cosThetaSqr * UdPmV;
    Real c0 = DdPmV * DdPmV - cone.cosThetaSqr * PmVdPmV;

    if (c2 != 0)
    {
        Real discr = c1 * c1 - c0 * c2;
        if (discr < 0)
        {
            return C2NotZeroDiscrNeg(t);
        }
        else if (discr > 0)
        {
            return C2NotZeroDiscrPos(c1, c2, discr, DdU, DdPmV, cone, t);
        }
```

```
        else
        {
            return C2NotZeroDiscrZero(c1,c2,UdU,UdPmV,DdU,DdPmV,cone,t);
        }
    }
    else if (c1 != 0)
    {
        return C2ZeroC1NotZero(c0,c1,DdU,DdPmV,cone,t);
    }
    else
    {
        return C2ZeroC1Zero(c0,UdU,UdPmV,DdU,DdPmV,cone,t);
    }
}

int C2NotZeroDiscrNeg(Real t[2])
{
    // Block 0. The quadratic polynomial has no real-valued roots. The line does not
    // intersect the double-sided cone.
    return SetEmpty(t);
}

int C2NotZeroDiscrPos(Real c1, Real c2, Real discr, Real DdU,
    Real DdPmV, Cone3 cone, Real t[2])
{
    // The quadratic has two distinct real-valued roots, t0 and t1 with t0 < t1. Also
    // compute the signed heights at the intersection points, h0 and h1 with h0 <= h1.
    // The ordering is guaranteed because the input line satisfies D . U >= 0.
    Real x = -c1 / c2;
    Real y = (c2 > 0 ? 1 / c2 : -1 / c2);
    Real t0 = x - y * sqrt(discr), t1 = x + y * sqrt(discr);
    Real h0 = t0 * DdU + DdPmV, h1 = t1 * DdU + DdPmV;

    if (h0 >= 0)
    {
        // Block 1, Figure 8.12(a). The line intersects the positive cone in two points.
        return SetSegmentClamp(t0, t1, h0, h1, DdU, DdPmV, cone, t);
    }
    else if (h1 <= 0)
    {
        // Block 2, Figure 8.12(b). The line intersects the negative cone in two points.
        return SetEmpty(t);
    }
    else  // h0 < 0 < h1
    {
        // Block 3, Figure 8.12(c). The line intersects the positive cone in a single point
        // and the negative cone in a single point.
        return SetRayClamp(h1, DdU, DdPmV, cone, t);
    }
}

int C2NotZeroDiscrZero(Real c1, Real c2, Real UdU, Real UdPmV,
    Real DdU, Real DdPmV, Cone3 cone, Real t[2])
{
    Real t = -c1 / c2;
    if (t * UdU + UdPmV == 0)
    {
        // To get here, it must be that V = P + (-c1/c2)U, where U is not necessarily
        // a unit-length vector. The line intersects the cone vertex.
        if (c2 < 0)
        {
            // Block 4, Figure 8.12(d). The line is outside the double-sided cone and
            // intersects it only at V.
            Real h = 0;
            return SetPointClamp(t, h, cone, t);
```

```
        }
        else
        {
            // Block 5, Figure 8.12(e). The line is inside the double-sided cone, so the
            // intersection is a ray with origin V.
            Real h = 0;
            return SetRayClamp(h, DdU, DdPmV, cone, t);
        }
    }
    else
    {
        // The line is tangent to the cone at a point different from the vertex.
        Real h = t * DdU + DdPmV;
        if (h >= 0)
        {
            // Block 6, Figure 8.12(f). The line is tangent to the positive cone.
            return SetPointClamp(t, h, cone, t);
        }
        else
        {
            // Block 7. The line is tangent to the negative cone.
            return SetEmpty(t);
        }
    }
}

int C2ZeroC1NotZero(Real c0, Real c1, Real DdU, Real DdPmV,
    Cone3 cone, Real t[2])
{
    // U is a direction vector on the cone boundary. Compute the t-value for the
    // intersection point and compute the corresponding height h to determine whether
    // that point is on the positive cone or negative cone.
    Real t = -c0 / (2 * c1);
    Real h = t * DdU + DdPmV;
    if (h > 0)
    {
        // Block 8, Figure 8.13(a). The line intersects the positive cone and the ray of
        // intersection is interior to the positive cone. The intersection is a ray or segment.
        return SetRayClamp(h, DdU, DdPmV, cone, t);
    }
    else
    {
        // Block 9, Figure 8.13(b). The line intersects the negative cone and the ray
        // of intersection is interior to the negative cone.
        return SetEmpty(t);
    }
}

int C2ZeroC1Zero(Real c0, Real UdU, Real UdPmV, Real DdU, Real DdPmV,
    Cone3 cone, Real t[2])
{
    if (c0 != 0)
    {
        // Block 10. The line does not intersect the double-sided cone.
        return SetEmpty(t);
    }
    else
    {
        // Block 11, Figure 8.14. The line is on the cone boundary. The intersection with
        // the positive cone is a ray that contains the cone vertex. The intersection is
        // either a ray or segment.
        Real t = -UdPmV / UdU;
        Real h = t * DdU + DdPmV;
        return SetRayClamp(h, DdU, DdPmV, cone, t);
```

```
        }
}

int SetEmpty(Real t[2])
{
    t[0] = invalid_real;
    t[1] = invalid_real;
    return NONE;
}

int SetPoint(Real t0, Real t[2])
{
    t[0] = t0;
    t[1] = invalid_real;
    return POINT;
}

int SetSegment(Real t0, Real t1, Real t[2])
{
    t[0] = t0;
    t[1] = t1;
    return SEGMENT;
}

int SetRayPositive(Real t0, Real t[2])
{
    t[0] = t0;
    t[1] = invalid_real;
    return RAY_POSITIVE;
}

int SetRayNegative(Real t1, Real t[2])
{
    t[0] = invalid_real;
    t[1] = t1;
    return RAY_NEGATIVE;
}

int SetPointClamp(Real t0, Real h0, Cone3 cone, Real t[2])
{
    if (cone.HeightInRange(h0))
    {
        // P0.
        return SetPoint(t0, t);
    }
    else
    {
        // P1.
        return SetEmpty(t);
    }
}

void SetSegmentClamp(Real t0, Real t1, Real h0, Real h1, Real DdU,
    Real DdPmV, Cone3 cone, Real t[2])
{
    if (h1 > h0)
    {
        int numValid;
        Real overlap[2];
        if (cone.isFinite)
        {
            numValid = FindIntersection(h0,h1,cone.hmin,cone.hmax,overlap);
        }
        else
        {
            numValid = FindIntersection(h0,h1,cone.hmin,overlap);
        }
```

```
        if (numValid == 2)
        {
            // S0.
            Real t0 = (overlap[0] − DdPmV) / DdU;
            Real t1 = (overlap[1] − DdPmV) / DdU;
            return SetSegment(t0, t1, t);
        }
        else if (numValid == 1)
        {
            // S1.
            Real t0 = (overlap[0] − DdPmV) / DdU;
            return SetPoint(t0, t);
        }
        else    // numValid == 0
        {
            // S2.
            return SetEmpty(t);
        }
    }
    else    // h1 == h0
    {
        if (cone.HeightInRange(h0))
        {
            // S3. D · U > 0 and the line is not perpendicular to the cone axis.
            return SetSegment(t0, t1, t);
        }
        else
        {
            // S4. D · U = 0 and the line is perpendicular to the cone axis.
            return SetEmpty(t);
        }
    }
}

void SetRayClamp(Real h, Real DdU, Real DdPmV, Cone3 cone, Real t[2])
{
    if (cone.isFinite)
    {
        Real overlap[2];
        int numValid = FindIntersection(cone.hmin, cone.hmax, h, overlap);
        if (numValid == 2)
        {   // R0.
            return SetSegment((overlap[0] − DdPmV) / DdU,
                (overlap[1] − DdPmV) / DdU, t);
        }
        else if (numValid == 1)
        {   // R1.
            return SetPoint((overlap[0] − DdPmV) / DdU, t);
        }
        else    // numValid == 0
        {   // R2.
            return SetEmpty(t);
        }
    }
    else
    {   // R3.
        return SetRayPositive((max(cone.hmin, h) − DdPmV) / DdU, t);
    }
}
```

Listing 8.38: Pseudocode for the line-cone find-intersection query.

The code blocks for the find-intersection query are marked with red comments and specify a block number and, if relevant, the figure reference that illustrates the intersection. The Set*Clamp functions also have red comments that label their code blocks. These are actually included in the GTL code and have unit tests associated with each possible combination of block and clamp. The possible combinations are listed next, where B is the block number, S is segment-clamp, R is ray-clamp, P is point-clamp, F is finite cone and I is infinite cone: B0, B1S0F, B1S1F, B1S2F, B1S0I, B1S1I, B1S2I, B1S3, B1S4, B2, B3R0, B3R1, B3R2, B3R3, B4P0, B4P1, B5R0, B5R3, B6P0, B6P1, B7, B8R0, B8R3, B9, B10, B11R0 and B11R3. It is not theoretically possible for a geometric configuration to lead to B5R1, B5R2, B8R1, B8R2, B11R1 or B11R2.

8.5.7 Intersection with a Ray

When the line does not intersect the cone, neither does the ray. When the line intersects the cone (finite or infinite), let the t-interval of intersection be $[t_0, t_1]$ with $t_0 \leq t_1 \leq +\infty$. The ray includes an additional constraint, that $[t_0, t_1]$ overlap with the ray's t-interval $[0, +\infty)$. The final candidate interval for the ray-cone intersection is $[t_0, t_1] \cap [0, +\infty)$, which can be semiinfinite, finite or empty. An implementation must determine which of these is the case and report the appropriate intersection points.

Listing 8.39 contains pseudocode for the find-intersection query between a ray and a cone. It shares several of the functions already mentioned in the line-cone find-intersection query.

```
// The returned 'int' is one of NONE, POINT, SEGMENT, RAY_POSITIVE or RAY_NEGATIVE.
// The returned t[] and P[] values are as described previously.
int FindIntersection(Ray3 ray, Cone3 cone, Real t[2], Vector3 P[2])
{
    // Execute the line-cone query.
    int intersectionType = DoQuery(ray.P, ray.U, cone, t);

    // Clamp the line-cone t-interval of intersection to the ray t-interval [0,+∞).
    switch (intersectionType)
    {
    case NONE:
        break;
    case POINT:
        if (t[0] < 0)
        {
            // Block 12.
            SetEmpty(t);
        }
        // else Block 13.
        break;
    case SEGMENT:
        if (t[1] > 0)
        {
            // Block 14.
            SetSegment(max(t[0], 0), t[1], t);
        }
        else if (t[1] < 0)
        {
            // Block 15.
            SetEmpty(t);
        }
```

```
        else   // t[1] == 0
        {
            // Block 16.
            SetPoint(0, t);
        }
        break;
    case RAY_POSITIVE:
        // Block 17.
        SetRayPositive(max(t[0], 0), t);
        break;
    case RAY_NEGATIVE:
        if (t[1] > 0)
        {
            // Block 18.
            SetSegment(0, t[1], t);
        }
        else if (t[1] < 0)
        {
            // Block 19.
            SetEmpty(t);
        }
        else   // t[1] == 0
        {
            // Block 20.
            SetPoint(0, t);
        }
        break;
    }

    ComputePoints(intersectionType, ray.P, ray.U, t, P);
    return intersectionType;
}
```

Listing 8.39: Pseudocode for the ray-cone find-intersection query. The ray has origin ray.P and direction ray.U, where the direction is not required to be unit length.

The code blocks for the find-intersection query are marked with red comments and specify a block number. These are actually included in the GTL code and have unit tests associated with each block.

8.5.8   Intersection with a Segment

When the line does not intersect the cone, neither does the segment. When the line intersects the cone (finite or infinite), let the t-interval of intersection be $[t_0, t_1]$ with $t_0 \leq t_1$. The segment includes an additional constraint, that $[t_0, t_1]$ overlap with the segment's t-interval $[t_2, t_3]$. The final candidate interval for the segment-cone intersection is $[t_0, t_1] \cap [t_2, t_3]$, which can be finite or empty. An implementation must determine which of these is the case and report the appropriate intersection points.

Listing 8.40 contains pseudocode for the find-intersection query between a ray and a cone. It shares several of the functions already mentioned in the line-cone find-intersection query.

```
// The returned 'int' is one of NONE, POINT, SEGMENT, RAY_POSITIVE or RAY_NEGATIVE.
// The returned t[] and P[] values are as described previously.
int FindIntersection(Segment3 segment, Cone3 cone, Real t[2], Vector3 P[2])
{
```

```
// Execute the line-cone query.
Vector3 U = segment.p[1] - segment.p[0];
int intersectionType = DoQuery(segment.p[0], U, cone, t);

// Clamp the line-cone t-interval of intersection to the segment t-interval [0, 1].
switch (intersectionType)
{
    case NONE:
        break;
    case POINT:
        if (t[0] < 0 || t[0] > 1)
        {
            // Block 21.
            SetEmpty(t);
        }
        // else Block 22.
        break;
    case SEGMENT:
        if (t[1] < 0 || t[0] > 1)
        {
            // Block 23.
            SetEmpty(t);
        }
        else
        {
            Real t0 = max(0, t[0]), t1 = min(1, t[1]);
            if (t0 < t1)
            {
                // Block 24.
                SetSegment(t0, t1, t);
            }
            else
            {
                // Block 25.
                SetPoint(t0, t);
            }
        }
        break;
    case RAY_POSITIVE:
        if (1 < t[0])
        {
            // Block 26.
            SetEmpty(t);
        }
        else if (1 > t[0])
        {
            // Block 27.
            SetSegment(max(0, t[0]), 1, t);
        }
        else
        {
            // Block 28.
            SetPoint(1, t);
        }
        break;
    case RAY_NEGATIVE:
        if (0 > t[1])
        {
            // Block 29.
            SetEmpty(t);
        }
        else if (0 < t[1])
        {
            // Block 30.
            SetSegment(0, min(1, t[1]), t);
```

```
        }
        else
        {
            // Block 31.
            SetPoint(0, t);
        }
        break;
    }

    ComputePoints(intersectionType, segment.p[0], U, t, P);
    return intersectionType;
}
```

Listing 8.40: Pseudocode for the segment-cone find-intersection query. The segment has endpoints segment.p[0] and segment.p[1]. The first endpoint is used as the line origin. The difference of endpoints is used as the line direction, which is not necessarily unit length.

The code blocks for the find-intersection query are marked with red comments and specify a block number. These are actually included in the GTL code and have unit tests associated with each block.

8.5.9   Implementation using Quadratic-Field Arithmetic

The Listings 8.38, 8.39 and 8.40 are written as if Real represents the set of all real numbers. Naturally, this is not possible for a computer implementation. Typically, floating-point types such as 32-bit float or 64-bit double are used. As with any floating-point implementation of a geometric algorithm, rounding errors inherent in floating-point arithmetic can lead to erroneous results. In particular, the code is heavy with floating-point comparisons, so any rounding errors that occur in computing the numbers to be compared can lead to incorrect classifications of the particular geometric configuration of the input data. If the implementation is robust, the computed output and the theoretical output are similar enough that the computed output is an acceptable result for the application at hand.

The goal of this section is to provide an arbitrary precision implementation to avoid the rounding errors yet still have an implementation that is fast enough for an application. The floating-point inputs are rational numbers and can be converted to an arithmetic system that has a data type for such numbers. In GTL, these classes are BSNumber and BSRational. The presence of divisions in the algorithm requires use of BSRational. Arithmetic computations involving addition, subtraction, multiplication and division can be performed without errors.

There are three places in the algorithm where rational arithmetic cannot immediately help.

1. The cone has an angle θ for which $\cos^2 \theta$ must be computed. The value of $\cos \theta$ can be any real number in $[-1, 1]$, and if it is irrational, it cannot be represented exactly. In some special cases, $\cos \theta$ is irrational but $\cos^2 \theta$ is rational; for example, this is the case when $\theta = \pi/4$, whereby

$\cos\theta = 1/\sqrt{2}$ and $\cos^2\theta = 1/2$. Generally, $\cos^2\theta$ must be estimated by a rational number to whatever number of significant digits makes sense for the application. This rational number is then assumed to be an error-free input.

2. Compute the roots to the quadratic polynomial $c_2t^2 + 2c_1t + c_0$. The real-valued roots are $(-c_1 \pm \sqrt{c_1^2 - c_0c_2})/c_2$. The discriminant is $\delta = c_1^2 - c_0c_2$. When $\delta > 0$, the roots are irrational numbers. Floating-point systems provide estimates of the square roots, but these have rounding errors.

3. Although the line direction $\mathbf{U}$ is not required to be unit length, the cone axis direction $\mathbf{D}$ was assumed to be unit length. In an application, one might choose a cone axis direction vector $\mathbf{E}$ that is not unit length and then normalize it to obtain $\mathbf{D} = \mathbf{E}/|\mathbf{E}|$. By doing so, compute the length $|\mathbf{E}|$ which involves yet another square root operation that will have rounding errors. If the squared length $\mathbf{D} \cdot \mathbf{D}$ is computed using rational arithmetic, the result is typically not 1 (although it will be approximately 1).

Item 1 is up to the user of the line-cone find-intersection code to provide as accurate and precise an estimate of $\cos^2\theta$ as is required by the application. Items 2 and 3 are handled by using quadratic-field arithmetic to obtain an exact result. The implemention in the GTL contains the modifications to Listings 8.38, 8.39 and 8.40 that support using 2-root quadratic-field numbers.

8.6 Intersection of Ellipses

Given two ellipses defined implicitly by quadratic polynomial equations, the goal of this section is to describe the algorithms for the test-intersection and find-intersection queries for the ellipses. The test-intersection query considers the ellipses to be solids and determines whether or not they are overlapping, just touching or separated. The find-intersection query considers the ellipses to be hollow and computes the points of intersection if any.

8.6.1 Ellipse Representations

Given an ellipse in a standard form, it can be converted to a quadratic equation of two variables. The conversion in the opposite direction requires slightly more work. The quadratic equation must have solutions, and it must represent an ellipse rather than a parabola or a hyperbola.

8.6.1.1   The Standard Form for an Ellipse

Let the ellipse center be $\mathbf{C}$. Let the ellipse axis directions be $\mathbf{U}_0$ and $\mathbf{U}_1$, a pair of unit-length orthogonal vectors. Let the ellipse extents along those axes be ℓ_0 and ℓ_1, a pair of positive numbers, each measuring the distance from the center to an extreme point along the corresponding axis. An ellipse point $\mathbf{X} = (x, y)$ is represented in the coordinate system $\{\mathbf{C}; \mathbf{U}_0, \mathbf{U}_1\}$ by $\mathbf{X} = \mathbf{C} + \xi_0 \mathbf{U}_0 + \xi_1 \mathbf{U}_1$, where $(\xi_0/\ell_0)^2 + (\xi_1/\ell_1)^2 = 1$. The coordinates can be computed by projection, $\xi_i = \mathbf{U}_i \cdot (\mathbf{X} - \mathbf{C})$, in which case

$$
\begin{aligned}
1 &= \sum_{i=0}^{1} (\xi_i/\ell_i)^2 \\
&= \sum_{i=0}^{1} (\mathbf{U}_i \cdot (\mathbf{X} - \mathbf{C})/\ell_i)^2 \\
&= (\mathbf{X} - \mathbf{C})^\mathsf{T} \left(\sum_{i=0}^{1} \mathbf{U}_i \mathbf{U}_i^\mathsf{T}/\ell_i^2 \right) (\mathbf{X} - \mathbf{C}) \\
&= (\mathbf{X} - \mathbf{C})^\mathsf{T} A (\mathbf{X} - \mathbf{C})
\end{aligned}
\tag{8.20}
$$

where the last equality defines the positive definite matrix A. By definition, such a matrix is symmetric, has positive eigenvalues and is invertible.

In practice, the axis directions might be obtained from vectors $\mathbf{V}_i$ by normalizing, $\mathbf{U}_i = \mathbf{V}_i/|\mathbf{V}_i|$. The normalization generally cannot be performed without rounding errors because of the implied square root when computing the length of $\mathbf{V}_i$. To avoid introducing this error into the inputs of the intersection query, the matrix A can be written as

$$
A = \sum_{i=0}^{1} \frac{\mathbf{V}_i \mathbf{V}_i^\mathsf{T}}{\ell_i^2 |\mathbf{V}_i|^2}
\tag{8.21}
$$

The conversion from this representation to a quadratic equation in two variables involves only rational operations, so no rounding errors are introduced because of normalization.

8.6.1.2   Conversion to a Quadratic Equation

Equation (8.20) expands into a quadratic equation

$$
k_0 + k_1 x + k_2 y + k_3 x^2 + k_4 xy + k_5 y^2 = 0
\tag{8.22}
$$

where the k_i depend on $\mathbf{C}$, $\mathbf{U}_0$, $\mathbf{U}_1$, ℓ_0 and ℓ_1. Conversely, given the coefficients of equation (8.22), factor to the standard form of equation (8.20). The quadratic equation in vector-matrix form is

$$
\begin{aligned}
\mathbf{X}^\mathsf{T} K \mathbf{X} + \mathbf{B}^\mathsf{T} \mathbf{X} + k_0 &= \\
\begin{bmatrix} x & y \end{bmatrix} \begin{bmatrix} k_3 & k_4/2 \\ k_4/2 & k_5 \end{bmatrix} \begin{bmatrix} x \\ y \end{bmatrix} &+ \begin{bmatrix} k_1 & k_2 \end{bmatrix} \begin{bmatrix} x \\ y \end{bmatrix} + k_0 = 0
\end{aligned}
\tag{8.23}
$$

where K and $\mathbf{B}$ are defined by the first equality. To complete the square, observe that

$$
(\mathbf{X} - \mathbf{C})^\mathsf{T} K (\mathbf{X} - \mathbf{C}) = \mathbf{X}^\mathsf{T} K \mathbf{X} - 2\mathbf{C}^\mathsf{T} K \mathbf{X} + \mathbf{C}^\mathsf{T} K \mathbf{C}
\tag{8.24}
$$

To match the linear term of equation (8.23), set $-2K\mathbf{C} = \mathbf{B}$ and $\mathbf{C}^\mathsf{T} K\mathbf{C} = k_0$. To represent an ellipse, K is positive definite which implies it is invertible, so $\mathbf{C} = -K^{-1}\mathbf{B}/2$ which leads to

$$(\mathbf{X} - \mathbf{C})^\mathsf{T} K(\mathbf{X} - \mathbf{C}) = \mathbf{B}^\mathsf{T} K^{-1}\mathbf{B}/4 - k_0 \qquad (8.25)$$

The right-hand side must be nonzero to obtain the standard form of equation (8.20). If so, then divide through by that expression to obtain

$$(\mathbf{X} - \mathbf{C})^\mathsf{T} A(\mathbf{X} - \mathbf{C}) = (\mathbf{X} - \mathbf{C})^\mathsf{T} \frac{K}{\mathbf{B}^\mathsf{T} K^{-1}\mathbf{B}/4 - k_0}(\mathbf{X} - \mathbf{C}) = 1 \qquad (8.26)$$

where the first equality defines the matrix $A = [a_{ij}]$. To represent an ellipse, A must be positive definite, which is equivalent to $a_{00} > 0$, $a_{11} > 0$ and $a_{00}a_{11} - a_{01}^2 > 0$. The matrix can then be factored as shown in equation (8.21). An eigendecomposition is $A = RD^2R^\mathsf{T}$, where $R = [\mathbf{U}_0\ \mathbf{U}_1]$ is an orthonormal matrix whose columns are specified and where $D = \text{Diag}(d_0, d_1)$ is a diagonal matrix with positive diagonal entries. The ellipse axes are the eigenvectors of A and the ellipse axis extents are $\ell_i = 1/d_i$.

Unfortunately, factoring A using an eigensolver cannot be performed with only rational arithmetic. A goal of this section is to avoid floating-point rounding errors until the very end of the process when the root finders must call sqrt, pow, sin or cos. As it turns out, it is possible to determine whether the quadratic equation represents an ellipse using only rational arithmetic. The condition $a_{00}a_{11} - a_{01}^2 > 0$ implies $k_4^2/4 < k_3k_5$, and consequently $k_3 \neq 0$ and $k_5 \neq 0$. Divide the quadratic equation by k_5 and, for simplicity, rename the divided coefficients $k_i \leftarrow k_i/k_5$,

$$\begin{aligned} 0 &= k_0 + k_1x + k_2y + k_3x^2 + k_4xy + y^2 \\ &= (k_0 + k_1x + k_3x^2) + (k_2 + k_4x)y + y^2 \end{aligned} \qquad (8.27)$$

with $k_3 - k_4^2/4 > 0$. The y-term may be eliminated by the transformation $y = w - (k_2 + k_4x)/2$,

$$0 = w^2 + (k_0 - k_2^2/4) + (k_1 - k_2k_4/2)x + (k_3 - k_4^2/4)x^2 \qquad (8.28)$$

The last three terms form a quadratic polynomial in x that must be negative for some interval of x-values in order that the sum with w^2 be zero. Therefore, the polynomial must have two distinct real-valued roots $x_0 < x_1$ and the ellipse points are generated for $x \in [x_0, x_1]$. To have distinct real roots, it is required that $(k_1 - k_2k_4/2)^2 - 4(k_0 - k_2^2/4)(k_3 - k_4^2/4) > 0$.

8.6.2 Test-Intersection Query for Ellipses

The ellipses are defined implicitly by $Q_i(\mathbf{X}) = 0$ for $i \in \{0, 1\}$, where $Q_i(\mathbf{X}) = (\mathbf{X} - \mathbf{C}_i)^\mathsf{T} A_i(\mathbf{X} - \mathbf{C}_i) - 1$, $\mathbf{C}_i$ is the center point and A_i is a positive definite matrix. If $\mathbf{C}_1$ is inside the ellipse $Q_0(\mathbf{X}) = 0$, then the ellipses overlap.

The condition for this case is $\mathbf{\Delta}^\mathsf{T} A_0 \mathbf{\Delta} - 1 \leq 0$, where $\mathbf{\Delta} = \mathbf{C}_1 - \mathbf{C}_0$. Similarly, if $\mathbf{C}_0$ is inside the ellipse $Q_1(\mathbf{X}) = 0$, then the ellipses overlap. The condition for this case is $\mathbf{\Delta}^\mathsf{T} A_1 \mathbf{\Delta} - 1 \leq 0$.

When each center is outside the other ellipse, the overlap or separation depends on a geometric condition. The function $Q_0(\mathbf{X})$ defines a family of level curves, $Q_0(\mathbf{X}) = \ell > -1$, each level curve an ellipse with center $\mathbf{C}_0$. The level set $Q_0(\mathbf{X}) = -1$ contains only $\mathbf{C}_0$. The goal is to compute the point $\mathbf{X}$ on the ellipse $Q_1(\mathbf{X}) = 0$ that minimizes the level value ℓ. If $\ell < 0$, the ellipses overlap. If $\ell = 0$, the ellipses are just touching at a single point. The problem is one of constrained minimization, namely, minimize $Q_0(\mathbf{X})$ subject to $Q_1(\mathbf{X}) = 0$, which can be solved using Lagrange multipliers. Define $H(\mathbf{X}, t) = Q_0(\mathbf{X}) + tQ_1(\mathbf{X})$ and solve $\nabla H(\mathbf{X}, t) = (\mathbf{0}, 0)$. The t-derivative is $\partial H / \partial t = Q_1(\mathbf{X})$ and the spatial derivative is $\partial H / \partial \mathbf{X} = \nabla Q_0(\mathbf{X}) + t\nabla Q_1(\mathbf{X})$. Setting $\partial H / \partial t = 0$ reproduces the constraint $Q_1(\mathbf{X}) = 0$. The equation $\partial H / \partial \mathbf{X} = \mathbf{0}$ is $\nabla Q_0(\mathbf{X}) + t\nabla Q_1(\mathbf{X})$, which implies that the gradient vectors of the quadratic functions are parallel. From the geometry, the level set $Q_1(\mathbf{X}) = 0$ is just touching the level set $Q_0(\mathbf{X}) = \ell_{\min}$, where the level value is the one at which H attains its minimum. The gradients are normal to the level curves and point in opposite directions, which implies $t > 0$.

Using the definitions of the quadratic functions, the parallel-gradient condition is

$$\mathbf{0} = A_0(\mathbf{X} - \mathbf{C}_0) + tA_1(\mathbf{X} - \mathbf{C}_1) = (A_0 + tA_1)(\mathbf{X} - \mathbf{C}_1) + A_0\mathbf{\Delta} \qquad (8.29)$$

The matrix $B(t) = A_0 + tA_1$ is positive definite because A_0 and A_1 are positive definite and $t > 0$; therefore, $B(t)$ is invertible with inverse $J(t) = B(t)^{-1}$. Define $\mathbf{K} = A_0\mathbf{\Delta}$. The parallel-gradient equation can be solved for $\mathbf{X} - \mathbf{C}_1 = -J(t)\mathbf{K}$. Substituting this in the $Q_1(\mathbf{X}) = 0$ ellipse equation leads to $f(t) = 0$, where

$$f(t) = \mathbf{K}^\mathsf{T} J(t) A_1 J(t) \mathbf{K} - 1 \qquad (8.30)$$

By definition, $B(t)J(t) = I$ for all $t > 0$, where I is the identity matrix. Computing the derivative with respect to t, $B(t)J'(t) + B'(t)J(t) = B(t)J'(t) + A_1 J(t) = 0$, where the right-hand side is the zero matrix. This can be solved for $J'(t) = -J(t)A_1 J(t)$. The first-order derivative of $f(t)$ is

$$f'(t) = -2\mathbf{K}^\mathsf{T} J(t) A_1 J(t) A_1 J(t) \mathbf{K} \qquad (8.31)$$

and the second-order derivative of $f(t)$ is

$$f''(t) = 6\mathbf{K}^\mathsf{T} J(t) A_1 J(t) A_1 J(t) A_1 J(t) \mathbf{K} \qquad (8.32)$$

Let the eigendecompositions for the second ellipse matrix be $A_1 = R_1 D_1^2 R_1^\mathsf{T}$, where R_1 is a rotation matrix and where D_1 is a diagonal matrix with positive diagonal entries. The columns of R_1 are the eigenvectors of A_1 and the diagonal entries of D_1^2 are the eigenvalues of A_1. The matrix

$J(t)$ is a similarity transformation of a diagonal matrix as is shown by the following,

$$
\begin{aligned}
B(t) &= A_0 + tA_1 = A_0 + tR_1 D_1^2 R_1^{\mathsf{T}} \\
R_1^{\mathsf{T}} B(t) R_1 &= R_1^{\mathsf{T}} A_0 R_1 + tD_1^2 \\
D_1^{-1} R_1^{\mathsf{T}} B(t) R_1 D_1^{-1} &= D_1^{-1} R_1^{\mathsf{T}} A_0 R_1 D_1^{-1} + tI = P + tI
\end{aligned}
\tag{8.33}
$$

where the last equality defines the positive definite matrix P. This matrix has an eigendecomposition $P = RD^2 R^{\mathsf{T}}$, so

$$
R^{\mathsf{T}} D_1^{-1} R_1^{\mathsf{T}} B(t) R_1 D_1^{-1} R = R^{\mathsf{T}}(P + tI)R = D^2 + tI
\tag{8.34}
$$

The right-hand side is a diagonal matrix $D^2 + tI = \mathrm{Diag}(t + d_0^2, t + d_1^2)$. Define $Q = R_1 D_1^{-1} R$. Equation (8.34) implies $Q^{\mathsf{T}} B(t) Q = D^2 + tI$, $B(t) = Q^{-\mathsf{T}}(D^2 + tI)Q^{-1}$ and

$$
\begin{aligned}
J(t) &= B(t)^{-1} \\
&= Q^{\mathsf{T}}(D^2 + tI)^{-1} Q \\
&= Q\,\mathrm{Diag}\left((t + d_0^2)^{-1}, (t + d_1^2)^{-1}\right) Q^{\mathsf{T}}
\end{aligned}
\tag{8.35}
$$

It can be shown that $Q^{\mathsf{T}} A_1 Q = I$. This relationship and equation (8.35) can be substituted into equations (8.30) through (8.32) to obtain

$$
\begin{aligned}
f(t) &= \mathbf{K}^{\mathsf{T}} Q\,\mathrm{Diag}\left((t + d_0^2)^{-2}, (t + d_1^2)^{-2}\right) Q^{\mathsf{T}}\mathbf{K} - 1 \\
f'(t) &= -2\mathbf{K}^{\mathsf{T}} Q\,\mathrm{Diag}\left((t + d_0^2)^{-3}, (t + d_1^2)^{-3}\right) Q^{\mathsf{T}}\mathbf{K} \\
f''(t) &= 6\mathbf{K}^{\mathsf{T}} Q\,\mathrm{Diag}\left((t + d_0^2)^{-4}, (t + d_1^2)^{-4}\right) Q^{\mathsf{T}}\mathbf{K}
\end{aligned}
\tag{8.36}
$$

It is easily seen that $f'(t) < 0$ and $f''(t) > 0$ for $t > 0$, which means $f(t)$ is strictly decreasing and strictly convex for $t > 0$. Evaluating at $t = 0$, $J(0) = A_0$ and $\mathbf{K} = A_0\Delta$, so equation (8.30) implies $f(0) = \Delta^{\mathsf{T}} A_1 \Delta - 1 > 0$ because the center $\mathbf{C}_1$ is outside the first ellipse. Taking the limit as t becomes unbounded leads to $f(+\infty) = -1$. All these conditions ensure that $f(t)$ has a unique root on $(0, +\infty)$. It is possible to convert $f(t) = 0$ to a quartic polynomial equation in s and compute its roots robustly; see Section 6.2.5. However, knowing that f is strictly decreasing and strictly convex, Newton's method can be used (potentially with a user-defined precision) to locate the root. An initial estimate is $t = 0$, but it is possible to obtain an upper bound on the root and then apply the bisection method for root finding.

Let $\bar{t}$ be the unique root of $f(t)$. Substituting $\mathbf{X}(\bar{t})$ into the first ellipse equation produces $\ell = Q_0(\mathbf{X}(\bar{t}))$. If $\ell < 0$, the ellipses overlap; if $\ell = 0$, the ellipses touch at a point; or if $\ell > 0$, the ellipses are separated.

For an implementation using floating-point arithmetic, the eigendecomposition approach can be used. The eigendecompositions are computed once. The root-finding for $f(t)$ uses the function of equation (8.36). The evaluations of $f(t)$ are relatively inexpensive. For an implementation using rational arithmetic, the eigendecompositions can be avoided, instead using equation (8.30) for the root finding of $f(t)$. Each evaluation of $f(t)$ requires computing $B(t)$ and inverting it to obtain $J(t)$, but rather than doing the full computations for each t, a symbolic formula for $J(t)$ can be derived,

$$J(t) = (A_0 + tA_1)^{-1} = \frac{1}{c(t)} \begin{bmatrix} q_{00}(t) & q_{01}(t) & q_{02}(t) \\ q_{01}(t) & q_{11}(t) & q_{12}(t) \\ q_{02}(t) & q_{12}(t) & q_{22}(t) \end{bmatrix} \tag{8.37}$$

where $c(t) = \sum_{k=0}^{3} c_k t^k$ is a cubic polynomial and $q_{ij}(t) = \sum_{k=0}^{2} q_{ijk} t^k$ are quadratic polynomials. The polynomial coefficients are computed once. Each evaluation of $f(t)$ requires evaluating 7 polynomials for $J(t)$, followed by the same matrix operations that are in common with the floating-point implementation.

8.6.3   Find-Intersection Query for Ellipses

The find-intersection query for ellipses uses the quadratic-equation formulation for ellipses of equation (8.22).

The ellipses may be written as quadratic equations, where it is assumed that $a_5 = b_5 = 1$. In an implementation, the caller can pass a_5 and b_5 and the division by these numbers is performed internally. Let the equations be

$$\begin{aligned} A(x,y) &= a_0 + a_1 x + a_2 y + a_3 x^2 + a_4 xy + y^2 = 0 \\ B(x,y) &= b_0 + b_1 x + b_2 y + b_3 x^2 + b_4 xy + y^2 = 0 \end{aligned} \tag{8.38}$$

According to the last section, these define ellipses when $a_3 - a_4^2/4 > 0$, $b_3 - b_4^2/4 > 0$, $(a_1 - a_2 a_4/2)^2/4 - (a_0 - a_2^2/4)(a_3 - a_4^2/4) > 0$ and $(b_1 - b_2 b_4/2)^2/4 - (b_0 - b_2^2/4)(b_3 - b_4^2/4) > 0$.

Subtract the two equations to obtain the quadratic equation

$$D(x,y) = d_0 + d_1 x + d_2 y + d_3 x^2 + d_4 xy = 0 \tag{8.39}$$

where $d_i = a_i - b_i$ for all i. If $d_i = 0$ for all i, then the two equations are the same and an implementation should report that the ellipses are identical.

Assuming not all $d_i = 0$, define the transformation $y = w - (a_2 + a_4 x)/2$, which eliminates the y-term in $A(x,y) = 0$,

$$\begin{aligned} 0 &= w^2 + (a_0 + a_1 x + a_3 x^2) - (a_2 + a_4 x)^2/4 \\ &= w^2 + (c_0 + c_1 x + c_2 x^2) \\ &= w^2 + c(x) \end{aligned} \tag{8.40}$$

where the last two equalities define $c(x) = c_0 + c_1 x + c_2 x^2$ with $c_0 = a_0 - a_2^2/4$, $c_1 = a_1 - a_2 a_4/2$ and $c_2 = a_3 - a_4^2/4 > 0$. Substituting the change of variables into $D(x,y) = 0$,

$$0 = (d_2 + d_4 x)w + (e_0 + e_1 x + e_2 x^2) = d(x)w + e(x) \tag{8.41}$$

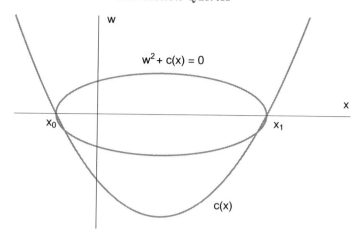

FIGURE 8.15: The graph of the ellipse $w^2 + c(x) = 0$ and the graph of the parabola $c(x)$. The roots of $c(x)$ are x_0 and x_1. The ellipse is defined for $x \in [x_0, x_1]$.

where the last equality defines $d(x) = d_2 + d_4 x$ and $e(x) = e_0 + e_1 x + e_2 x^2$ with $e_0 = d_0 - a_2 d_2/2$, $e_1 = d_1 - (a_2 d_4 + a_4 d_2)/2$ and $e_2 = d_3 - a_4 d_4/2$. The intersection points are pairs (x, w) that solve equations (8.40) and (8.41) simultaneously. The algorithm for solving the equations has several cases that require branching on coefficients d_i; it is helpful to motivate the cases geometrically.

Equation (8.40) can be factored to standard form,

$$\frac{\left(x + \frac{c_1}{2c_2}\right)^2}{\frac{c_1^2 - 4c_0 c_2}{4c_2^2}} + \frac{w^2}{\frac{c_1^2 - 4c_0 c_2}{4c_2}} = 1 \tag{8.42}$$

As mentioned previously, in order for this equation to have solutions it is necessary that $c_2 > 0$ and $c_1^2 - 4c_0 c_2 > 0$. The x-values for which the ellipse is defined is the interval $[x_0, x_1]$, where x_0 and x_1 are the roots of $c(x)$; that is, $c(x) \leq 0$ for $x \in [x_0, x_1]$ in which case $w^2 = -c(x)$ has real-valued solutions for w. Figure 8.15 shows the graph of a typical ellipse and the corresponding graph for $c(x)$.

The analysis of equation (8.41) includes several cases that involve the coefficient $d(x) = d_2 + d_4 x$ of w and whether $e(x)$ is a linear or a quadratic polynomial. In the cases, define $\bar{x} = -d_2/d_4$. Also discussed is whether an intersection is *transverse*, where the graph tangents are not parallel (the graphs cut through each other). If not transverse, the intersection is *tangential*, where the graph tangents are parallel. Equivalently, the graph normals are parallel at the intersection, and the gradients of functions can be used for the normals when the curves are defined implicitly.

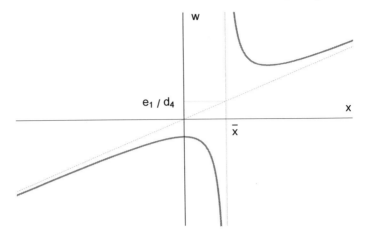

FIGURE 8.16: A typical graph of the hyperbola defined by equation (8.41) when $d_4 \neq 0$ and $e(\bar{x}) \neq 0$. The nonhorizontal asymptote occurs when $e_2 \neq 0$. If $e_2 = 0$, $e(x)$ is linear and the asymptote is horizontal.

8.6.3.1   Case $d_4 \neq 0$ and $e(\bar{x}) \neq 0$

When $d_4 \neq 0$ and $e_2 \neq 0$, equation (8.41) represents a hyperbola with a vertical asymptote $x = \bar{x}$. The other asymptote is $w = (e_2/d_4)x + (e_1d_4 - d_2e_2)/d_4^2$. Figure 8.16 shows a typical graph. In fact, the graph is that of the function $w = -e(x)/d(x)$. Substituting this into equation (8.40), the quartic polynomial $f(x) = c(x)d^2(x) + e^2(x)$ is obtained for which $\bar{x}$ is not a root.

The intersections of the hyperbola and the axis-aligned ellipse correspond to intersections for the original ellipses. It is possible to determine whether the intersection is transverse or tangential. The gradient of the function $w^2 + c(x)$ is $(c'(x), 2w)$ and the gradient of the function $d(x)w + e(x)$ is $(d'(x)w + e'(x), d(x))$. To be parallel, the dot-perp of the gradients must be zero,

$$
\begin{aligned}
0 &= (c'(x), 2w) \cdot (d'(x)w + e'(x), d(x))^{\perp} \\
  &= (c'(x), 2w) \cdot (d(x), -d'(x)w - e'(x)) \\
  &= c'(x)d(x) - 2d'(x)w^2 - 2e'(x)w \\
  &= c'(x)d(x) + 2d'(x)c(x) + 2e(x)e'(x)/d(x) \\
  &= (c'(x)d^2(x) + 2c(x)d(x)d'(x) + 2e(x)e'(x))/d(x) \\
  &= f'(x)/d(x)
\end{aligned}
\tag{8.43}
$$

where w^2 was replaced using equation (8.40) and w was replaced using equation (8.41). If the intersection is tangential for some $\hat{x}$, then $f(\hat{x}) = f'(\hat{x}) = 0$; that is, it is necessary that $\hat{x}$ be a repeated root for $f(x)$. In fact, this is also a sufficient condition based on the geometry of the graphs.

Pseudocode for this case is provided by Listing 8.41.

```
int numPoints = 0;
```

```
Vector2<Real> intersection [4];
bool isTransverse [4];

Real f0 = c0*d2*d2+e0*e0;
Real f1 = c1*d2*d2+2*(c0*d2*d4+e0*e1);
Real f2 = c2*d2*d2+c0*d4*d4+e1*e1+2*(c1*d2*d4+e0*e2);
Real f3 = c1*d4*d4+2*(c2*d2*d4+e1*e2);
Real f4 = c2*d4*d4+e2*e2;  // > 0

map<Real, int> rmMap;  // (root, multiplicity)
SolveQuartic(f0, f1, f2, f3, f4, rmMap);
for_each (rm in rmMap)
{
    Real x = rm.first;
    int multiplicity = rm.second;
    Real w = -(e0 + x * (e1 + x * e2)) / (d2 + d4 * x);
    Real y = w - (a2 + x * a4) / 2;
    intersection [numPoints] = { x, y };
    isTransverse [numPoints] = (multiplicity == 1);
    ++numPoints;
}
```

Listing 8.41: An implementation for the case $d_4 \neq 0$ and $e(\bar{x}) \neq 0$. The graph of $w = -e(x)/d(x)$ is a hyperbola and the points of intersection with the ellipse are generated by roots to the quartic polynomial $f(x)$.

The function SolveQuartic must compute the theoretically correct multiplicity of the root. The GTL quartic root finder satisfies this constraint when Real is a rational arithmetic type.

8.6.3.2   Case $d_4 \neq 0$ and $e(\bar{x}) = 0$

When $e(\bar{x}) = 0$, the hyperbola of the previous section degenerates to a pair of lines. In a sense, the asymptotes of the hyperbola are the limits of the hyperbolic curves as the polynomial coefficients of $e(x)$ vary from a state where $e(\bar{x}) \neq 0$ to a state where $e(\bar{x}) = 0$. The polynomial factors to $e(x) = (d_2 + d_4 x)(h_0 + h_1 x)$, where $h_1 = e_2/d_4$ and $h_0 = (e_1 - d_2 h_1)/d_4$. The lines are $x = \bar{x}$ and $w = -(h_0 + h_1 x)$. Define $h(x) = h_0 + h_1 x$.

An intersection of $x = \bar{x}$ with the ellipse $w^2 + c(x) = 0$ occurs when $c(\bar{x}) \leq 0$, in which case $w = \pm\sqrt{-c(\bar{x})}$. The intersection is transverse when $c(\bar{x}) < 0$ or tangential when $c(\bar{x}) = 0$. These sign tests can be computed accurately when using rational arithmetic.

An intersection of the line $w+h(x) = 0$ with the ellipse $w^2+c(x) = 0$ occurs at roots of the quadratic polynomial $f(x) = h^2(x) + c(x)$. The intersection is tangential when the gradients at the intersection are parallel. The gradient of $w^2 + c(x)$ is $(c'(x), 2w)$ and the gradient of $w + h(x)$ is $(h'(x), 1)$. To be parallel, the dot-perp of the gradients must be zero,

$$\begin{aligned} 0 &= (c'(x), 2w) \cdot (h'(x), 1)^\perp \\ &= (c'(x), 2w) \cdot (1, -h'(x)) \\ &= c'(x) - 2h'(x)w \\ &= c'(x) + 2h(x)h'(x) \\ &= f'(x) \end{aligned} \tag{8.44}$$

The intersection is tangential for some $\hat{x}$ if and only if $f(\hat{x}) = f'(\hat{x}) = 0$; that is, it is necessary that $\hat{x}$ be a repeated root for $f(x)$.

Pseudocode for this case is provided by Listing 8.42.

```
int numPoints = 0;
Vector2<Real> intersection [4];
bool isTransverse [4];
Real translate, w, y;

// Compute intersections of x = x̄ with ellipse.
Real xbar = −d2 / d4, ncbar = −(c0 + xbar ∗ (c1 + xbar ∗ c2));
if (ncbar >= 0)
{
    translate = (a2 + xbar ∗ a4) / 2;
    w = sqrt(ncbar);
    y = w − translate;
    intersection [numPoints] = { xbar, y };
    if (w > 0)
    {
        isTransverse [numPoints++] = true;
        w = −w;
        y = w − translate;
        intersection [numPoints] = { xbar, y };
        isTransverse [numPoints++] = true;
    }
    else
    {
        isTransverse [numPoints++] = false;
    }
}

// Compute intersections of w = −h(x) with ellipse.
Real h1 = e2 / d4;
Real h0 = (e1 − d2 ∗ h1) / d4;
Real f0 = c0 + h0 ∗ h0;
Real f1 = c1 + 2 ∗ h0 ∗ h1;
Real f2 = c2 + h1 ∗ h1;   // > 0

map<Real, int> rmMap;   // (root, multiplicity)
SolveQuadratic(f0, f1, f2, rmMap);
for_each (rm in rmMap)
{
    Real x = rm.first;
    int multiplicity = rm.second;
    translate = (a2 + xbar ∗ a4) / 2;
    w = −(h0 + x ∗ h1);
    y = w − translate;
    intersection [numPoints] = { x, y };
    isTransverse [numPoints++] = (multiplicity == 1);
}
```

Listing 8.42: An implementation for the case $d_4 \neq 0$ and $e(\bar{x}) = 0$. The graph consists of two lines and the points of intersection with the ellipse are generated by roots to the quadratic polynomial $f(x)$.

The function SolveQuadratic must compute the theoretically correct multiplicity of the root. The GTL quadratic root finder satisfies this constraint when Real is a rational arithmetic type.

8.6.3.3 **Case $d_4 = 0$, $d_2 \neq 0$ and $e_2 \neq 0$**

Solve for w directly in equation (8.41), $w = -e(x)/d_2$, where $e(x)$ is a quadratic polynomial ($e_2 \neq 0$). The graph of this equation is a parabola, and the intersections of the parabola with the ellipse need to be computed. Substitute into equation (8.40) and multiply by d_2^2 to obtain the quartic polynomial $f(x) = d_2^2 c(x) + e^2(x)$. The roots of $f(x)$ lead to intersections of the parabola and ellipse.

An intersection is tangential when the gradients at the intersection are parallel. The gradient of $w^2 + c(x)$ is $(c'(x), 2w)$ and the gradient of $d_2 w + e(x)$ is $(e'(x), d_2)$. To be parallel, the dot-perp of the gradients must be zero,

$$
\begin{aligned}
0 &= (c'(x), 2w) \cdot (e'(x), d_2)^{\perp} \\
&= (c'(x), 2w) \cdot (d_2, -e'(x)) \\
&= d_2 c'(x) - 2e'(x)w \\
&= d_2 c'(x) + 2e(x)e'(x)/d_2 \\
&= f'(x)/d_2^2
\end{aligned}
\tag{8.45}
$$

The intersection is tangential for some $\hat{x}$ if and only if $f(\hat{x}) = f'(\hat{x}) = 0$; that is, it is necessary that $\hat{x}$ be a repeated root for $f(x)$.

Pseudocode for this case is provided by Listing 8.43.

```
int numPoints = 0;
Vector2<Real> intersection[4];
bool isTransverse[4];

Real f0 = c0 * d2 * d2 + e0 * e0;
Real f1 = c1 * d2 * d2 + 2 * e0 * e1;
Real f2 = c2 * d2 * d2 + e1 * e1 + 2 * e0 * e2;
Real f3 = 2 * e1 * e2;
Real f4 = e2 * e2;  // > 0

map<Real, int> rmMap;  // (root, multiplicity)
SolveQuartic(f0, f1, f2, f3, f4, rmMap);
for_each (rm in rmMap)
{
    Real x = rm.first;
    int multiplicity = rm.second;
    Real w = -(e0 + x * (e1 + x * e2)) / d2;
    Real y = w - (a2 + x * a4) / 2;
    intersection[numPoints] = { x, y };
    isTransverse[numPoints] = (multiplicity == 1);
    ++numPoints;
}
```

Listing 8.43: An implementation for the case $d_4 = 0$, $d_2 \neq 0$ and $e_2 \neq 0$. The graph of $w = -e(x)/d_2$ is a parabola and the points of intersection with the ellipse are generated by roots to the quartic polynomial $f(x)$.

The function SolveQuartic must compute the theoretically correct multiplicity of the root. The GTL quartic root finder satisfies this constraint when Real is a rational arithmetic type.

8.6.3.4   Case $d_4 = 0$, $d_2 \neq 0$ and $e_2 = 0$

The analysis in the previous section applies equally well here, except that $e(x)$ now is a linear polynomial and the graph of $w = -e(x)/d_2$ is a line. The function whose roots lead to line-ellipse intersections is $f(x) = d_2 c(x) + e^2(x)$, which is a quadratic polynomial. Tangential intersections occur at repeated roots of $f(x)$.

Pseudocode for this case is provided by Listing 8.44.

```
int numPoints = 0;
Vector2<Real> intersection [4];
bool isTransverse [4];

Real f0 = c0 * d2 * d2 + e0 * e0;
Real f1 = c1 * d2 * d2 + 2 * e0 * e1;
Real f2 = c2 * d2 * d2 + e1 * e1;   // ¿ 0

map<Real, int> rmMap;   // (root, multiplicity)
SolveQuadratic(f0, f1, f2, rmMap);
for_each (rm in rmMap)
{
    Real x = rm.first;
    int multiplicity = rm.second;
    Real w = -(e0 + x * e1) / d2;
    Real y = w - (a2 + x * a4) / 2;
    intersection[numPoints] = { x, y };
    isTransverse[numPoints] = (multiplicity == 1);
    ++numPoints;
}
```

Listing 8.44: An implementation for the case $d_4 = 0$, $d_2 \neq 0$ and $e_2 = 0$. The graph of $w = -e(x)/d_2$ is a line and the points of intersection with the ellipse are generated by roots to the quadratic polynomial $f(x)$.

The function SolveQuadratic must compute the theoretically correct multiplicity of the root. The GTL quadratic root finder satisfies this constraint when Real is a rational arithmetic type.

8.6.3.5   Case $d_4 = 0$ and $d_2 = 0$

Equation (8.41) is $e(x) = 0$, where $e(x)$ can be either quadratic or linear, and equation (8.40) is $w^2 + c(x) = 0$. For each root $\hat{x}$ of $e(x)$, if $c(\hat{x}) \leq 0$, there are corresponding solutions $\hat{w} = \pm\sqrt{-c(\hat{x})}$. The technical challenge is to determine the sign of $c(\hat{x})$ accurately without misclassifications due to floating-point arithmetic.

The subcase when $e(x)$ is linear ($e_2 = 0$) is easy to solve. Suppose that $e_1 \neq 0$; then the only root is $\hat{x} = -e_0/e_1$. If $c(\hat{x}) < 0$, there are two transverse intersection points with $\hat{w} = \pm\sqrt{c(\hat{x})}$. If $c(\hat{x}) = 0$, there is one tangential intersection point with $\hat{w} = 0$. For the transverse intersections, when rational arithmetic is used, compute $\hat{x}$ without numerical errors. The computation $c(\hat{x})$ also has no numerical errors, so the sign of $c(\hat{x})$ is known exactly. This allows determining that the intersections are transverse. However, numerical error is (usually) introduced when computing the square root function. Therefore,

$\hat{x}$ is exact but $\hat{w}$ is approximate, even though the intersection is transverse. Pseudocode for this case is provided by Listing 8.45.

```
int numPoints = 0;
Vector2<Real> intersection [4];
bool isTransverse [4];
Real w, y;

Real xhat = -e0 / e1;
Real nchat = -(c0 + xhat * (c1 + xhat * c2));
if (nchat > 0)
{
    Real translate = (a2 + xhat * a4) / 2;
    w = sqrt(nchat);
    y = w - translate;
    intersection [numPoints] = { xhat, y };
    isTransverse [numPoints++] = true;
    w = -w;
    y = w - translate;
    intersection [numPoints] = { xhat, y };
    isTransverse [numPoints++] = true;
}
else if (nchat == 0)
{
    y = -(a2 + xhat * a4) / 2;  // w = 0
    intersection [numPoints] = { xhat, y };
    isTransverse [numPoints++] = false;
}
```

Listing 8.45: An implementation for the case $d_4 = 0$, $d_2 = 0$ and $e_2 = 0$.

When $e_1 = 0$, $e(x) = e_0$ is a constant polynomial. It cannot be zero, because if it were, all $d_i = 0$. However, an implementation can determine this condition early and exit immediately, reporting that the ellipses are the same.

The subcase when $e(x)$ is quadratic ($e_2 \neq 0$) is not as easy to solve. The main problem is computing the correct sign of $c(\hat{x})$ when $\hat{x}$ is a non-rational root of $e(x)$. Let's first make $e(x)$ monic by dividing through by e_2; define $f(x) = f_0 + f_1 x + x^2$, where $f_0 = e_0/e_2$ and $f_1 = e_1/e_2$. The roots are $\hat{x} = -f_1/2 \pm \sqrt{\Delta}$, where $\Delta = f_1^2/4 - f_0$. If $\Delta < 0$, there is nothing to do because there are no real-valued roots. If $\Delta = 0$, the root is repeated and rational, so the exact sign of $c(\hat{x})$ can be computed.

If $\Delta > 0$, there are two distinct roots. Generally, it is not expected that Δ is a squared rational, so the analysis must be conservative and assume that $\sqrt{\Delta}$ will involve numerical rounding errors. A sequence of algebraic manipulations involving inequalities, however, can determine the correct sign of $c(\hat{x})$.

The condition to test is $c(\hat{x}) = c_0 + c_1 \hat{x} + c_2 \hat{x}^2 \leq 0$. Regardless of which root is to be tested, substitute $\hat{x}^2 = -(f_0 + f_1 \hat{x})$ into the inequality to obtain $g_0 + g_1 \hat{x} \leq 0$, where $g_0 = c_0 - c_2 f_0$ and $g_1 = c_1 - c_2 f_1$. Finally, analyze $g_1 \hat{x} \leq -g_0$, which depends on the sign of g_1.

If $g_1 = 0$, the parabolas defined by $c(x)$ and $e(x)$ are the same shape; one is a vertical translation of the other. If $g_0 < 0$, the graph of $e(x)$ is above that of $c(x)$, so both roots $\hat{x}$ of $e(x)$ are in the interval whose endpoints are the roots of $c(x)$; that is, $c(\hat{x}) < 0$ for both roots. Moreover, the generated intersections are transverse. If $g_0 > 0$, the graph of $e(x)$ is below that of $e(x)$, so $c(\hat{x}) > 0$ for both roots and there are no real-valued solutions to $w^2 + c(x) = 0$, which implies there are no ellipse-ellipse intersections. If $g_0 = 0$, the graphs of $e(x)$ and $c(x)$ are the same, so $c(\hat{x}) = 0$ for both roots. The corresponding intersections are both tangential.

Suppose that $g_1 > 0$; $\hat{x} \le -g_0/g_1$ must be analyzed for a root $\hat{x}$ of $e(x)$. For the root $\hat{x} = -f_1/2 + \sqrt{\Delta}$, $\sqrt{\Delta} \le -g_0/g_1 + f_1/2 = r$ is needed, where the last equality defines r. The statement is true when $r \ge 0$ and $\Delta \le r^2$. These conditions may all be computed using rational arithmetic without generating rounding errors. For the root $\hat{x} = -f_1/2 - \sqrt{\Delta}$, $\sqrt{\Delta} \ge -r$ is needed. The statement is true when $r > 0$ or when $r \le 0$ and $\Delta \ge r^2$. The choice of strict inequality versus nonstrict inequality is made to support the determination of transverse or tangential intersection.

Suppose that $g_1 < 0$; $\hat{x} \ge -g_0/g_1$ must be analyzed. For the root $\hat{x} = -f_1/2 - \sqrt{\Delta}$, $\sqrt{\Delta} \le -r$ is needed. The statement is true when $r \le 0$ and $\Delta \le r^2$. For the root $\hat{x} = -f_1/2 + \sqrt{\Delta}$, $\sqrt{\Delta} \ge r$ is needed. The statement is true when $r < 0$ or when $r \ge 0$ and $\Delta \ge r^2$.

Pseudocode for this case is provided by Listing 8.46. The function SpecialIntersection is used to compute y from $\hat{x}$ and to set the condition about transversality.

```
struct Result
{
    int numPoints;
    Vector2<Real> intersection [4];
    bool isTransverse [4];
};

Result result;
result.numPoints = 0;

Real f0 = e0 / e2, f1 = e1 / e2;
Real mid = -f1 / 2;
Real discr = mid * mid - f0;
if (discr > 0)
{
    // The roots are x̂ = -f₁/2 + s√(f₁²/4 - f₀) for s ∈ {-1,1}.
    Real sqrtDiscr = sqrt(discr);
    Real g0 = c0 - c2 * f0, g1 = c1 - c2 * f1;
    if (g1 > 0)
    {
        // It is required that s√(f₁²/4 - f₀) ≤ -g₀/g₁ + f₁/2.
        Real r = -g0 / g1 - mid;

        // s = +1:
        if (r >= 0)
        {
            Real rsqr = r * r;
            if (discr < rsqr)
            {
                SpecialIntersection(mid + sqrtDiscr, true, result);
            }
            else if (discr == rsqr)
            {
                SpecialIntersection(mid + sqrtDiscr, false, result);
            }
        }

        // s = -1:
```

```
    if (r > 0)
    {
        SpecialIntersection(mid − sqrtDiscr, true, result);
    }
    else
    {
        Real rsqr = r * r;
        if (discr > rsqr)
        {
            SpecialIntersection(mid − sqrtDiscr, true, result);
        }
        else if (discr == rsqr)
        {
            SpecialIntersection(mid − sqrtDiscr, false, result);
        }
    }
}
else if (g1 < 0)
{
    // It is required that s√(f₁²/4 − f₀) ≥ −g₀/g₁ + f₁/2.
    Real r = −g0 / g1 − mid;

    // s = −1:
    if (r <= 0)
    {
        Real rsqr = r * r;
        if (discr < rsqr)
        {
            SpecialIntersection(mid − sqrtDiscr, true, result);
        }
        else
        {
            SpecialIntersection(mid − sqrtDiscr, false, result);
        }
    }

    // s = +1:
    if (r < 0)
    {
        SpecialIntersection(mid + sqrtDiscr, true, result);
    }
    else
    {
        Real rsqr = r * r;
        if (discr > rsqr)
        {
            SpecialIntersection(mid + sqrtDiscr, true, result);
        }
        else if (discr == rsqr)
        {
            SpecialIntersection(mid + sqrtDiscr, false, result);
        }
    }
}
else  // g1 = 0
{
    // The graphs of c(x) and f(x) are parabolas of the same shape. One is a
    // vertical translation of the other.
    if (g0 < 0)
    {
        // The graph of f(x) is above that of c(x).
        SpecialIntersection(mid − sqrtDiscr, true, result);
        SpecialIntersection(mid + sqrtDiscr, true, result);
    }
    else if (g0 == 0)
```

The required condition text: $s\sqrt{f_1^2/4 - f_0} \ge -g_0/g_1 + f_1/2$.

```
        {
            // The graphs of c(x) and f(x) are the same parabola.
            SpecialIntersection(mid - sqrtDiscr, false, result);
            SpecialIntersection(mid + sqrtDiscr, false, result);
        }
        // else graph of f(x) is below that of c(x), no intersections
    }
}
else if (discr == 0)
{
    // The theoretical root of e(x) is x = -e1/2.
    Real nchat = -(c0 + mid * (c1 + mid * c2));
    if (nchat > 0)
    {
        SpecialIntersection(mid, true, result);
    }
    else if (nchat == 0)
    {
        SpecialIntersection(mid, false, result);
    }
}

void SpecialIntersection(Real x, bool transverse, Result& result)
{
    if (transverse)
    {
        Real translate = (a2 + x * a4) / 2;
        Real nc = -(c0 + x * (c1 + x * c2));
        if (nc < 0)
        {
            // Clamp to eliminate the rounding error, but duplicate the point
            // because it is a transverse intersection.
            nc = 0;
        }

        Real w = sqrt(nc);
        Real y = w - translate;
        result.intersection[result.numPoints] = { x, y };
        result.isTransverse[result.numPoints++] = true;
        w = -w;
        y = w - translate;
        result.intersection[result.numPoints] = { x, y };
        result.isTransverse[result.numPoints++] = true;
    }
    else
    {
        // The vertical line at the root is tangent to the ellipse.
        Real y = -(a2 + x * a4) / 2;   // w = 0
        result.intersection[result.numPoints] = { x, y };
        result.isTransverse[result.numPoints++] = false;
    }
}
```

Listing 8.46: An implementation for the case $d_4 = 0$, $d_2 = 0$ and $e_2 \neq 0$.

8.7 Intersection of Ellipsoids

Given two ellipsoids defined implicitly by quadratic polynomial equations, the goal of this section is to describe the algorithms for the test-intersection and find-intersection queries for the ellipsoids. The test-intersection query considers the ellipses to be solids and determines whether or not they are overlapping, just touching or separated. The find-intersection query considers the ellipses to be hollow and estimates points of intersection if any. The construction of an exact curve of intersection is not possible with arbitrary-precision arithmetic; it is formulated as the solution to a system of ordinary differential equations that can be solved numerically.

8.7.1 Ellipsoid Representations

Given an ellipsoid in a standard form, it can be converted to a quadratic equation of three variables. The conversion in the opposite direction requires slightly more work. The quadratic equation must have solutions, and it must represent an ellipsoid rather than other quadric surfaces such as paraboloids or hyperboloids.

8.7.1.1 The Standard Form for an Ellipsoid

Let the ellipsoid center be $\mathbf{C}$. Let the ellipsoid axis directions be $\mathbf{U}_0$, $\mathbf{U}_1$ and $\mathbf{U}_2$ that form an orthonormal set. Let the ellipsoid extents along those axes be ℓ_0, ℓ_1 and ℓ_2, a triple of positive numbers, each measuring the distance from the center to an extreme point along the corresponding axis. An ellipsoid point $\mathbf{X} = (x, y, z)$ is represented in the coordinate system $\{\mathbf{C}; \mathbf{U}_0, \mathbf{U}_1, \mathbf{U}_2\}$ by $\mathbf{X} = \mathbf{C} + \sum_{i=0}^{2} \xi_i \mathbf{U}_i$, where $\sum_{i=0}^{2} (\xi_i/\ell_i)^2 = 1$. The coordinates can be computed by projection, $\xi_i = \mathbf{U}_i \cdot (\mathbf{X} - \mathbf{C})$, in which case

$$
\begin{aligned}
1 &= \sum_{i=0}^{2} (\xi_i/\ell_i)^2 \\
&= \sum_{i=0}^{2} (\mathbf{U}_i \cdot (\mathbf{X} - \mathbf{C})/\ell_i)^2 \\
&= (\mathbf{X} - \mathbf{C})^{\mathsf{T}} \left(\sum_{i=0}^{2} \mathbf{U}_i \mathbf{U}_i^{\mathsf{T}}/\ell_i^2 \right) (\mathbf{X} - \mathbf{C}) \\
&= (\mathbf{X} - \mathbf{C})^{\mathsf{T}} A (\mathbf{X} - \mathbf{C})
\end{aligned}
\tag{8.46}
$$

where the last equality defines the positive definite matrix A. By definition, such a matrix is symmetric, has positive eigenvalues and is invertible.

In practice, the axis directions might be obtained from vectors $\mathbf{V}_i$ by normalizing, $\mathbf{U}_i = \mathbf{V}_i/|\mathbf{V}_i|$. The normalization generally cannot be performed without rounding errors because of the implied square root when computing the length of $\mathbf{V}_i$. To avoid introducing this error into the inputs of the intersection query, the matrix A can be written as

$$A = \sum_{i=0}^{2} \frac{\mathbf{V}_i \mathbf{V}_i^{\mathsf{T}}}{\ell_i^2 |\mathbf{V}_i|^2} \tag{8.47}$$

The conversion from this representation to a quadratic equation in three variables involves only rational operations, so no rounding errors are introduced because of normalization.

Generally, the formulation of equation (8.46) works for n-dimensional hyperellipsoids simply by replacing the upper index of the summations by $n-1$.

8.7.1.2 Conversion to a Quadratic Equation

Equation (8.46) expands into a quadratic equation

$$k_0 + k_1 x + k_2 y + k_3 z + k_4 x^2 + k_5 xy + k_6 xz + k_7 y^2 + k_8 yz + k_9 z^2 = 0 \tag{8.48}$$

where the k_i depend on $\mathbf{C}$, $\mathbf{U}_i$ and ℓ_i for $i \in \{0, 1, 2\}$. Conversely, given the coefficients of equation (8.48), factor to the standard form of equation (8.46). The quadratic equation in vector-matrix form is

$$\mathbf{X}^{\mathsf{T}} K \mathbf{X} + \mathbf{B}^{\mathsf{T}} \mathbf{X} + k_0 =$$
$$\begin{bmatrix} x & y & z \end{bmatrix} \begin{bmatrix} k_4 & k_5/2 & k_6/2 \\ k_5/2 & k_7 & k_8/2 \\ k_6/2 & k_8/2 & k_9 \end{bmatrix} \begin{bmatrix} x \\ y \\ z \end{bmatrix} + \begin{bmatrix} k_1 & k_2 & k_3 \end{bmatrix} \begin{bmatrix} x \\ y \\ z \end{bmatrix} + k_0 = 0 \tag{8.49}$$

where K and $\mathbf{B}$ are defined by the first equality. Completing the square is shown in coordinate-free notation of equations (8.24) through (8.26), so those equations apply as well to ellipsoids.

8.7.2 Test-Intersection Query for Ellipsoids

As it turns out, the algorithm for the test-intersection query of ellipses is coordinate free in the sense of equations (8.30), (8.31) and (8.32). Of course in the ellipsoid case, the matrices are 3×3. The diagonal matrices that occur in the equations for $f(t)$, $f'(t)$ and $f''(t)$ have third components involving negative powers of $(t + d_2^2)$.

8.7.3 Find-Intersection Query for Ellipsoids

The find-intersection query for ellipsoids produces a set that consists of points or closed curves. Generally, the curves might not have closed-form representations, so the query can produce only estimates of the intersection set.

The ideas are illustrated for a sphere $x^2 + y^2 + z^2 = 1$ and an axis-aligned ellipsoid $d_0^2(x-c_0)^2 + d_1^2(y-c_1)^2 + d_2^2(z-c_2)^2 = 1$, where $0 < d_0 \le d_1 \le d_2$. The algorithm for two ellipsoids reduces to this case using affine transformations that map one ellipsoid to the unit sphere centered at the origin and the other ellipsoid to an axis-aligned ellipsoid. There are 32 cases to analyze depending on whether or not each c_i is zero (8 possibilities) and depending on the ordering of the d_i (4 possibilities). The orderings are $d_0 = d_1 = d_2$, $d_0 = d_1 < d_2$, $d_0 < d_1 = d_2$ and $d_0 < d_1 < d_2$. The case when $d_0 = d_1 = d_2$ is for two spheres. An analysis is provided separately. Representative subcases for the other considitons are provided here; the remaining ones are similar.

8.7.3.1 Two Spheres

Let the sphere equations be $|\mathbf{X} - \mathbf{C}_i|^2 = r_i^2$ for $i \in \{0,1\}$. If the spheres intersect in a circle, the plane of that circle has a point on the line segment connecting $\mathbf{C}_0$ to $\mathbf{C}_1$. Define $\mathbf{U} = \mathbf{C}_1 - \mathbf{C}_0$. The plane point is $\mathbf{C}_0 + s\mathbf{U}$. A point on the first sphere that generates the circle of intersection is of the form $\mathbf{X} = \mathbf{C}_0 + s\mathbf{U} + \mathbf{V}$, where $\mathbf{V}$ is some vector perpendicular to $\mathbf{U}$. The point on the second sphere that generates the same intersection point is of the form $\mathbf{X} = \mathbf{C}_1 + (s-1)\mathbf{V}$. Substituting these into the sphere equations produces

$$\begin{aligned} r_0^2 &= |\mathbf{X} - \mathbf{C}_0|^2 = s^2|\mathbf{U}|^2 + |\mathbf{V}|^2 \\ r_1^2 &= |\mathbf{X} - \mathbf{C}_1|^2 = (s-1)^2|\mathbf{U}|^2 + |\mathbf{V}|^2 \end{aligned} \qquad (8.50)$$

Subtracting the two equations and solving for s produces

$$s = \frac{1}{2}\left(\frac{r_0^2 - r_1^2}{|\mathbf{U}|^2} + 1\right) \qquad (8.51)$$

The squared length of $\mathbf{V}$ satisfies the equation

$$\begin{aligned} |\mathbf{V}|^2 &= r_0^2 - s^2|\mathbf{U}|^2 \\ &= r_0^2 - \left(\frac{((r_0^2 - r_1^2) + |\mathbf{U}|^2)^2}{4|\mathbf{U}|^2}\right) \\ &= \frac{-1}{4|\mathbf{U}|^2}\left(|\mathbf{U}|^2 - (r_0 - r_1)^2\right)\left(|\mathbf{U}|^2 - (r_0 + r_1)^2\right) \end{aligned} \qquad (8.52)$$

The right-hand side of the last equality must be nonnegative because $|\mathbf{V}|^2 \geq 0$, which implies

$$|r_0 - r_1| \leq |\mathbf{U}| \leq |r_0 + r_1| \qquad (8.53)$$

If $|\mathbf{U}| = |r_0 + r_1|$, each sphere is outside the other sphere but just tangent. The point of intersection is $\mathbf{C}_0 + (r_0/(r_0 + r_1))\mathbf{U}$. If $|\mathbf{U}| = |r_0 - r_1|$, the spheres are nested and just tangent. The spheres are the same when $|\mathbf{U}| = 0$ and $r_0 = r_1$; otherwise, the point of intersection is $\mathbf{C}_0 + (r_0/(r_0 - r_1))\mathbf{U}$. If $|r_0 - r_1| < |\mathbf{U}| < |r_0 + r_1|$, then the two spheres intersect in a circle which lives in the plane that contains the point $\mathbf{C} + s\mathbf{U}$, where s is given by equation (8.51), and with normal vector $\mathbf{U}$. Figure 8.17 shows the various relationships for the two spheres.

8.7.3.2 Sphere-Ellipsoid: 3-Zero Center

Let $c_0 = c_1 = c_2 = 0$, where the sphere and ellipsoid are concentric.

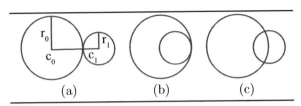

FIGURE 8.17: Relationship of two spheres, $\mathbf{U} = \mathbf{C}_1 - \mathbf{C}_0$. (a) $|\mathbf{U}| = |r_0 + r_1|$. (b) $|\mathbf{U}| = |r_0 - r_1|$. (c) $|r_0 - r_1| < |\mathbf{U}| < |r_0 + r_1|$.

Case $d_0 = d_1 < d_2$. Let $d_0 = 1$. The intersection set is the circle $x^2 + y^2 = 1$ regardless of the value of d_2. Let $d_0 < 1$. If $d_2 < 1$, the intersection set consists of two circles $x^2 + y^2 = (d_2^2 - 1)/(d_2^2 - d_0^2)$ for $z = \pm(1 - d_0^2)/(d_2^2 - d_0^2)$. If $d_2 = 1$, the intersection set consists of the points $(0, 0, \pm 1)$. If $d_2 < 1$, the intersection set is empty. Let $d_0 > 1$; then $d_2 > 1$ and the intersection set is empty.

Case $d_0 < d_1 = d_2$. The intersection sets are constructed similar to that of the case $d_0 = d_1 < d_2$ but with the roles of x and z reversed.

Case $d_0 < d_1 < d_2$. The sphere equation implies $z^2 = 1 - x^2 - y^2$. Substituting this into the ellipsoid equation leads to $(d_2^2 - d_0^2)x^2 + (d_2^2 - d_1^2)y^2 = d_2^2 - 1$. The coefficients on the left-hand side are positive. If $d_2 < 1$, the right-hand side is negative in which case the intersection set is empty. If $d_2 = 1$, the right-hand side is zero in which case the intersection set consists of the points $(0, 0, \pm 1)$. If $d_2 > 1$, the intersection set consists of two curves, each nonplanar. The (x, y) values are on the ellipse $(x/a)^2 + (y/b)^2 = 1$, where $a^2 = (d_2^2 - 1)/(d_2^2 - d_0^2)$ and $b^2 = (d_2^2 - 1)/(d_2^2 - d_1^2)$. The curve z-values are determined by $z^2 = 1 - x^2 - y^2$. A parameterization for the positive z-curve is

$$(x(t), y(t), z(t)) = \left(a\cos(t), b\sin(t), \sqrt{1 - a^2\cos^2(t) - b^2\sin^2(t)} \right) \quad (8.54)$$

for $t \in [0, 2\pi)$.

8.7.3.3 Sphere-Ellipsoid: 2-Zero Center

Let $c_0 = c_1 = 0$ and $c_2 \neq 0$, where the sphere and ellipsoid centers are on the z-axis.

Case $d_0 = d_1 < d_2$. The ellipsoid equation is $d_0^2(x^2 + y^2) + d_2^2(z - c_2)^2 = 1$. The sphere equation implies $x^2 + y^2 = 1 - z^2$. Substituting this into the ellipsoid equation leads to

$$(d_2^2 - d_0^2)z^2 - 2c_2 d_2^2 z + (d_0^2 + c_2^2 d_2^2 - 1) = 0 \quad (8.55)$$

The intersection set is empty when this quadratic equation has no real-valued roots. It is also empty when any real-valued roots satisfy $z^2 > 1$. The intersection set contains a single point when a real-valued root satisfies $z^2 = 1$.

The intersection set contains a circle for each real-valued root that satisfies $|z| < 1$.

Case $d_0 < d_1 = d_2$. The ellipsoid equation is $d_0^2 x^2 + d_1^2 y^2 + d_1^2 (z - c_2)^2 = 1$. The sphere equation implies $y^2 = 1 - x^2 - z^2$. Substituting this into the ellipsoid equation leads to

$$z = \frac{(c_2^2 d_2^2 - 1) - (d_1^2 - d_0^2) x^2}{2 c_2 d_1^2} \tag{8.56}$$

This defines a parabolic cylinder, and its projection onto the xz-plane is a parabola. The intersection set for the sphere and ellipsoid is empty when the parabola does not intersect the circle $x^2 + z^2 = 1$. The intersection set is a single point when the parabola and circle intersect in a single point. The intersection set consists of a nonplanar closed curve when the parabola and circle intersect in a parabolic arc. In this case, the x-variable can be used to parameterize the curve,

$$\begin{aligned} x(t) &= t \\ z(t) &= ((c_2^2 d_2^2 - 1) - (d_1^2 - d_0^2) t^2)/(2 c_2 d_1^2) \\ y(t) &= \pm \sqrt{1 - t^2 - z(t)^2} \end{aligned} \tag{8.57}$$

where the sign of $y(t)$ depends on the sign of c_2.

Case $d_0 < d_1 < d_2$. The ellipsoid equation is $d_0^2 x^2 + d_1^2 y^2 + d_2^2 (z - c_2)^2 = 1$. The sphere equation implies $z^2 = 1 - x^2 - y^2$. Substituting this into the ellipsoid equation leads to

$$z = \frac{((c_2^2 + 1) d_2^2 - 1) - (d_2^2 - d_0^2) x^2 - (d_2^2 - d_1^2) y^2}{2 c_2 d_2^2} \tag{8.58}$$

The graph of z is an elliptical paraboloid that opens downward. It is sufficient to analyze the case when $c_2 > 0$, because by symmetry the intersection set (when it exists) for $c_2 < 0$ is the negative of the intersection set (when it exists) for $c_2 > 0$. The vertex of the elliptical paraboloid occurs at $(x, y) = (0, 0)$ with $z_{\max} = ((c_2^2 + 1) d_2^2 - 1)/(2 c_2 d_2^2)$.

From the geometric configuration of the objects, if the ellipsoid is outside the sphere but just touching the sphere, it must be that $c_2 = 1 + 1/d_2$, where the right-hand side is the sum of the radius of the sphere (1) and the z-axis extent of the ellipsoid ($1/d_2$). This implies $z_{\max} = 1$, as expected. If the ellipsoid is inside the sphere but just touching the sphere, it must be that $c_2 + 1/d_2 = 1$. This also implies $z_{\max} = 1$.

The xy-curve along which the z-heights define an intersection curve is not a quadratic curve. Substituting equation (8.58) into the sphere equation produces

$$p(x, y) = x^2 + y^2 + \left(\frac{((c_2^2 + 1) d_2^2 - 1) - (d_2^2 - d_0^2) x^2 - (d_2^2 - d_1^2) y^2}{2 c_2 d_2^2} \right)^2 = 1 \tag{8.59}$$

The level set $p(x, y) = 1$, if not empty, can be approximated by polylines using a raster sampling algorithm such as marching squares.

8.7.3.4   Sphere-Ellipsoid: 1-Zero Center

Let $c_0 \neq 0$, $c_1 \neq 0$ and $c_2 = 0$, where the sphere and ellipsoid centers are on the xy-plane.

Case $d_0 = d_1 < d_2$. The ellipsoid equation is $d_0^2(x - c_0)^2 + d_0^2(y - c_1)^2 + d_2^2 z^2 = 1$. The sphere equation implies $z^2 = 1 - x^2 - y^2$. Substituting this into the ellipsoid equation leads to

$$(d_2^2 - d_0^2)\left(\left(x + \tfrac{c_0 d_0^2}{d_2^2 - d_0^2}\right)^2 + \left(y + \tfrac{c_1 d_0^2}{d_2^2 - d_0^2}\right)^2\right) = \tfrac{(c_0^2 + c_1^2)d_0^2(d_2^2 - 2d_0^2)}{d_2^2 - d_0^2} + d_2^2 - 1 \quad (8.60)$$

Define λ to be the right-hand side of the equation. If $\lambda < 0$, the intersection set is empty. If $\lambda = 0$, the intersection set is a point. If $\lambda > 0$, the equation defines a circle. The intersection set is a curve where the (x, y) values live on a circular arc.

Case $d_0 < d_1 = d_2$. The ellipsoid equation is $d_0^2(x - c_0)^2 + d_1^2(y - c_1)^2 + d_1^2 z^2 = 1$. The sphere equation implies $z^2 = 1 - x^2 - y^2$. Substituting this into the ellipsoid equation leads to

$$y = \frac{(c_0^2 d_0^2 + c_1^2 d_1^2 + d_1^2 - 1) - 2c_0 d_0^2 x - (d_1^2 - d_0^2)x^2}{2c_1 d_1^2} \quad (8.61)$$

The graph is a parabolic cylinder. The analysis of intersection is similar to that of the case of two zero-valued centers with $d_0 < d_1 = d_2$.

Case $d_0 < d_1 < d_2$. The ellipsoid equation is $d_0^2(x - c_0)^2 + d_1^2(y - c_1)^2 + d_2^2 z^2 = 1$. The sphere equation implies $z^2 = 1 - x^2 - y^2$. Substituting this into the ellipsoid equation leads to

$$(d_2^2 - d_0^2)\left(x + \tfrac{c_0 d_0^2}{d_2^2 - d_0^2}\right)^2 + (d_2^2 - d_1^2)\left(y + \tfrac{c_1 d_1^2}{d_2^2 - d_1^2}\right)^2 =$$
$$d_2^2\left(\tfrac{c_0^2 d_0^2}{d_2^2 - d_0^2} + \tfrac{c_1^2 d_1^2}{d_2^2 - d_1^2} + 1\right) - 1 \quad (8.62)$$

Define λ to be the right-hand side of the equation. If $\lambda < 0$, the intersection set is empty. If $\lambda = 0$, the intersection set is a point. If $\lambda > 0$, the equation defines an ellipse. The intersection set is a curve where the (x, y) values live on an elliptical arc.

8.7.3.5   Sphere-Ellipsoid: No-Zero Center

The ellipsoid equation is $d_0^2(x - c_0)^2 + d_1^2(y - c_1)^2 + d_2^2(z - c_2)^2 = 1$. The sphere equation implies $z^2 = 1 - x^2 - y^2$. Substituting this into the ellipsoid equation leads to

$$2c_2 d_2 z = d_2^2\left(\tfrac{c_0^2 d_0^2}{d_2^2 - d_0^2} + \tfrac{c_1^2 d_1^2}{d_2^2 - d_1^2} + c_2^2 + 1\right) - 1$$
$$- (d_2^2 - d_0^2)\left(x + \tfrac{c_0 d_0^2}{d_2^2 - d_0^2}\right)^2 - (d_2^2 - d_1^2)\left(y + \tfrac{c_1 d_1^2}{d_2^2 - d_1^2}\right)^2 \quad (8.63)$$

Solve for $z = z(x, y)$, the latter notation to emphasize z is a function of (x, y). The graph is an elliptical paraboloid that opens downward. The xy-curve along which the z-heights define an intersection curve is not a quadratic curve. Substitute equation (8.63) into the sphere equation to obtain

$$p(x, y) = x^2 + y^2 + z(x, y)^2 = 1 \qquad (8.64)$$

The level set $p(x, y) = 1$, if not empty, can be approximated by polylines using a raster sampling algorithm such as marching squares.

8.7.3.6   Reduction to a Sphere-Ellipsoid Query

The ellipsoid equations are $(\mathbf{Z} - \mathbf{C}_i)^\mathsf{T} A_i (\mathbf{Z} - \mathbf{C}_i) = 1$. Let the first ellipsoid have center $\mathbf{C}_0$, unit-length axis directions $\mathbf{U}_j$ and extents ℓ_j for $j \in \{0, 1, 2\}$. Define the rotation matrix $R_0 = [\mathbf{U}_0 \ \mathbf{U}_1 \ \mathbf{U}_2]$ whose columns are the axis directions. Define $L_0 = \mathrm{Diag}(\ell_0, \ell_1, \ell_2)$ so that $A_0 = R_0 L_0^{-2} R_0^\mathsf{T}$.

The first ellipsoid equation is transformed to a sphere equation $\mathbf{Y}^\mathsf{T} \mathbf{Y} = 1$ by the affine transformation $\mathbf{Y} = L_0^{-1} R_0^\mathsf{T} (\mathbf{Z} - \mathbf{C}_0)$. The inverse transformation is $\mathbf{Z} = R_0 L_0 \mathbf{Y} + \mathbf{C}_0$. Substituting this into the second ellipsoid equation produces $(\mathbf{Y} - \mathbf{K})^\mathsf{T} A (\mathbf{Y} - \mathbf{K}) = 1$, where $A = L_0 R_0^\mathsf{T} A_1 R_0 L_0$ and $\mathbf{K} = L_0^{-1} R_0^\mathsf{T} (\mathbf{C}_1 - \mathbf{C}_0)$.

The unit-length axis directions are $\mathbf{U}_j = \mathbf{V}_j / |\mathbf{V}_j|$ for $j \in \{0, 1, 2\}$, where $\mathbf{V}_j$ is not necessarily unit length. Define the matrices $Q_0 = [\mathbf{V}_0 \ \mathbf{V}_1 \ \mathbf{V}_2]$ and $N_0 = \mathrm{Diag}(|\mathbf{V}_0|, |\mathbf{V}_1|, |\mathbf{V}_2|)$. Consequently, the rotation matrix is $R_0 = Q_0 N_0^{-1}$. The parameters of the second ellipsoid equation are $A = L_0 N_0^{-1} Q_0^\mathsf{T} A_1 Q_0 N_0^{-1} L_0$ and $\mathbf{K} = L_0^{-1} N_0^{-1} Q_0^\mathsf{T} (\mathbf{C}_1 - \mathbf{C}_0)$. The presence of N_0 requires the elements of A and $\mathbf{K}$ to be quadratic-field numbers in order to support exact arithmetic.

The find-intersection queries were analyzed for a sphere and an axis-aligned ellipsoid. The matrix A is not necessarily diagonal, but it can be factored using an eigendecomposition, $A = RD^2 R^\mathsf{T}$, where R is a rotation matrix and D is a diagonal matrix with positive diagonal entries. The sphere equation $\mathbf{Y}^\mathsf{T} \mathbf{Y} = 1$ is transformed to another sphere equation $\mathbf{X}^\mathsf{T} \mathbf{X} = 1$ and the ellipsoid equation $(\mathbf{Y} - \mathbf{K})^\mathsf{T} A (\mathbf{Y} - \mathbf{K}) = 1$ is transformed to an axis-aligned ellipsoid equation $(\mathbf{X} - \mathbf{C})^\mathsf{T} D^2 (\mathbf{X} - \mathbf{C}) = 1$, where $\mathbf{X} = R^\mathsf{T} \mathbf{Y}$ and $\mathbf{C} = R^\mathsf{T} \mathbf{K}$.

The computations for the find-intersection queries used rational numbers, but to produce exact representations of eigenvalues and eigenvectors for 3×3 symmetric matrices, it is necessary to use quadratic-field numbers and algebraic numbers as presented in Section 6.3.3 in order to compute the eigendecomposition $A = RD^2 R^\mathsf{T}$.

Chapter 9

Computational Geometry Algorithms

This section describes some of the classical computational geometry algorithms involving point sets, including convex hull computation, Delaunay triangulation and computing minimum-area or minimum-volume bounding regions. All involve subproblems that require exact computation of signs, a topic that was discussed in Chapter 4.

The sign tests for convex hull and Delaunay triangulation algorithms are basically tests for the signs of determinants, although to compute the elements of the matrices involves some additional operations that are covered by the primal queries.

The minimum-area rectangle and minimum-volume box algorithms are more interesting in that they involve unit-length vectors. Because vector normalization suffers generally from floating-point rounding errors, these algorithms are designed to use unnormalized direction vectors. The final results are computed using arbitrary-precision arithmetic, but these must be converted back to floating-point results which require estimation of square roots, a topic covered in Chapter 5.

9.1 Convex Hull of Points in 2D

Consider a finite point set S. If all points in the set are collinear, the convex hull is a line segment. When at least three points are not collinear, the convex hull is a region bounded by a convex polygon. Figure 9.1 shows a point set and its convex hull. The vertices of the convex hull are necessarily a subset of the original point set. Construction of the convex hull amounts to identifying the points in S that are the vertices of the convex polygon.

Numerous algorithms have been developed for computing the convex hull of point sets. A summary of these is found in [21] and includes *gift wrapping*, *quickhull*, *Graham's algorithm*, *incremental construction* and a *divide-and-conquer method*. Another algorithm which is efficient is Andrew's algorithm [2] that uses monotone chains. These algorithms have brief descriptions at [32]. Only the incremental construction and the divide-and-conquer algorithms are

FIGURE 9.1: A point set and its convex hull. The points are drawn in dark gray, except for those points that became hull vertices which are drawn in black. The hull is shown in light gray.

discussed here; however, the other algorithms have the same type of primal queries that need to be handled properly for correct output. The divide-and-conquer method is what is implemented in the GTL. Various computational geometry books make restrictions on the point sets in order to simplify the constructions and proofs. Typical assumptions include no duplicate points, no collinear points or points with only integer coordinates to allow exact arithmetic. In practice, these restrictions are usually never satisfied, especially when using floating-point arithmetic. The discussions here pay close attention to the pathological problems that can arise in order to provide a robust implementation using arbitrary-precision arithmetic.

A heuristic is used to eliminate input points from the hull construction. It involves an idea [1], which requires $O(n)$ time to execute. A linear search is performed to locate four points. Choose the point that has minimum x-value. If two or more points attain that minimum, choose the one that has the minimum y-value. Points can be chosen similarly that attain the maximum x-value, the minimum y-value and the maximum y-value. The four points form a convex quadrilateral. A second linear pass is made over the input points, discarding any points that lie inside the quadrilateral because these points cannot be vertices of the convex polygon that is the hull. In practice, the preprocessing step can lead to a linear expected time.

9.1.1   Incremental Construction

Given a set of points V_i, $0 \le i < n$, each point is inserted into an already constructed convex hull of the previous points. The pseudocode is shown in Listing 9.1.

```
ConvexPolygon IncrementalHull(int n, Point V[])
{
    ConvexPolygon hull; hull[0] = V[0];
    for (int i = 1; i < n; ++i) { Merge(V[i], hull); }
    return hull;
}
```

Listing 9.1: Pseudocode for the incremental construction of a 2D convex hull.

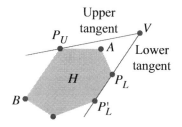

FIGURE 9.2: A convex hull H, a point $\mathbf{V}$ outside H and the two tangents from $\mathbf{V}$ to the hull. The upper and lower tangent points are labeled as $\mathbf{P}_U$ and $\mathbf{P}_L$, respectively.

The heart of the problem is how to construct the convex hull of a convex polygon H and a point $\mathbf{V}$, the operation named Merge in the pseudocode. If $\mathbf{V}$ is inside H, the merge step does nothing. But if $\mathbf{V}$ is outside H, the merge step must find rays emanating from $\mathbf{V}$ that just touch the hull. These rays are called *tangents* to the hull. Figure 9.2 illustrates.

A tangent has the property that the hull is entirely on one side of the line with at most a vertex or an edge of points on the line. In Figure 9.2, the upper tangent intersects the current hull in a single point. The lower tangent intersects along an edge of the current hull. The points of tangency are the extreme points of all the hull vertices that are visible from $\mathbf{V}$. The other hull vertices are occluded from $\mathbf{V}$ by the hull itself. In Figure 9.2, the lower tangent contains an edge with endpoints $\mathbf{P}_L$ and $\mathbf{P}'_L$, but only $\mathbf{P}_L$ is visible to $\mathbf{V}$.

The condition of visibility from $\mathbf{V}$ can be further exploited. The current hull edges inside the cone defined by the two tangents are visible to $\mathbf{V}$. These edges are inside the new hull containing H and $\mathbf{V}$. The new hull includes all the occluded edges of the current hull and new edges formed by the line segments from $\mathbf{V}$ to the tangent points. In the example of Figure 9.2, two edges are visible to $\mathbf{V}$ and can be discarded. The new edges are $\langle \mathbf{V}, \mathbf{P}_U \rangle$ and $\langle \mathbf{V}, \mathbf{P}_L \rangle$. Because the edge $\langle \mathbf{P}'_L, \mathbf{P}_L \rangle$ is entirely on the lower tangent, that edge can also be discarded and replaced by the new edge $\langle \mathbf{V}, \mathbf{P}'_L \rangle$. If this step is not performed, the final hull of the points will contain collinear edges. Such edges can be collapsed in a post-processing phase.

Determining whether or not an edge is visible is a matter of computing the order of three points, the endpoints of the directed edge and the point $\mathbf{V}$. In Figure 9.2, the directed edge $\langle \mathbf{P}_L, \mathbf{A} \rangle$ is visible to $\mathbf{V}$. The triangle $\langle \mathbf{V}, \mathbf{P}_L, \mathbf{A} \rangle$ is clockwise ordered. The directed edge $\langle \mathbf{P}_U, \mathbf{B} \rangle$ is not visible to $\mathbf{V}$. The triangle $\langle \mathbf{V}, \mathbf{P}_U, \mathbf{B} \rangle$ is counterclockwise ordered. Only $\mathbf{P}_L$ of the directed edge $\langle \mathbf{P}'_L, \mathbf{P}_L \rangle$ is visible to $\mathbf{V}$. The triangle $\langle \mathbf{V}, \mathbf{P}'_L, \mathbf{P}_L \rangle$ is degenerate (a line segment). The cases are quantified by a dot product test. Let $\langle \mathbf{Q}_0, \mathbf{Q}_1 \rangle$ be a directed hull edge and define $\mathbf{D} = \mathbf{Q}_1 - \mathbf{Q}_0$ and $\mathbf{N} = -\mathbf{D}^\perp$, an inner pointing normal to the edge. The edge is visible to $\mathbf{V}$ whenever $\mathbf{N} \cdot (\mathbf{V} - \mathbf{Q}_0) < 0$ and not visible to $\mathbf{V}$ whenever $\mathbf{N} \cdot (\mathbf{V} - \mathbf{Q}_0) > 0$. If the dot product is zero, then only the closest endpoint of the edge is visible to $\mathbf{V}$. Endpoint $\mathbf{Q}_0$ is closest if $\mathbf{D} \cdot (\mathbf{V} - \mathbf{Q}_0) < 0$; endpoint $\mathbf{Q}_1$ is closest if $\mathbf{D} \cdot (\mathbf{V} - \mathbf{Q}_0) > |\mathbf{D}|^2$.

The asymptotic order of the algorithm depends on the amount of work that must be done in the merge step. In the worst case, each input point to Merge is outside the current hull and the tangent points are found by iterating over all hull vertices and testing the dot product conditions. The order is $O(n^2)$. Because of this, one hope is that the initial points are ordered in such a way that most of the time the input point is in the current hull. This is the idea of randomized algorithms where the input points are randomly permuted in an attempt to generate a large partial hull from the first few input points. When this happens, many of the remaining points most likely will fall inside the current hull. Because the relationship between the next input point and the current hull is not known, a search over the hull vertices must be made to find the tangent points. A randomized algorithm is discussed in [7]. The same idea occurs in Section 9.4 when computing the minimum-area circle containing a point set.

A nonrandomized approach that guarantees an $O(n \log n)$ algorithm actually sorts the points so that the next input point is outside the current hull. The sort of the points dominates the algorithm time. The points are sorted using the less-than operation: $(x_0, y_0) < (x_1, y_1)$ when $x_0 < x_1$ or when $x_0 = x_1$ and $y_0 < y_1$. After the sort, duplicate points can be eliminated.

The algorithm has information about the relationship between the next input and the current hull so that the tangent construction is only $O(n)$ over the total life time of the loop in the pseudocode. In particular, the last inserted hull vertex is the starting point for the search for the points of tangency and may already be a tangent point itself. Although any single search might require visiting a significant number of points on the current hull, each such visited point will be interior to the merged hull and discarded. The average cost per discarded point is effectively constant time, so over the life time of the loop, the total time is $O(n)$.

The first point is the initial hull. As input points are processed, a flag type is maintained that indicates whether the hull is a single point (POINT), a line segment represented by two distinct points (LINEAR) or a convex polygon with positive area (PLANAR). Initially the flag is POINT because the initial point stored by the hull is the first input point. By keeping track of this flag, the convex hull algorithm can detect degeneracies in dimension and handle the inputs accordingly. The points might be collinear, which is a 1D problem. The pseudocode for this modification is shown in Listing 9.2.

```
ConvexPolygon IncrementalHull(int n, Point V[n])
{
    Sort(n,V);
    RemoveDuplicates(n,V);   // n can decrease, V has contiguous elements
    ConvexPolygon hull;
    type = POINT;
    hull[0] = V[0];
    for (int i = 1; i < n; i++)
```

```
{
    switch (type)
    {
        case POINT:
            type = LINEAR;
            hull[1] = V[i];
            break;
        case LINEAR:
            MergeLinear(V[i], hull, type);
            break;
        case PLANAR:
            MergePlanar(V[i], hull);
            break;
    }
}
    return hull;
}
```

Listing 9.2: Pseudocode for the incremental construction of a convex hull in 2D that also detects whether the points are collinear.

If the current hull has one point, the uniqueness of the points implies that V[i] is different from the one already in the hull. The point is added to the current hull to form a line segment and the type flag is changed accordingly.

If the current hull has two points (a line segment), the function MergeLinear determines whether or not the current input point is on the same line as the line segment. If it is on the same line, the current hull is updated and remains a line segment. If the input point is not on the same line, the current hull and input point form a triangle. In this case, the triangle is stored as the current hull and the type flag is changed accordingly. Moreover, the hull is stored as a set of counterclockwise ordered points. This requires the collinearity test to do slightly more than just determine whether the input point is on or off the line. If the hull is the line segment $\langle \mathbf{Q}_0, \mathbf{Q}_1 \rangle$ and the input point is $\mathbf{P}$, Figure 9.3 shows the five possibilities for the relationship of $\mathbf{P}$ to the line segment.

The collinearity test uses a normal vector to the line containing the segment $\langle \mathbf{Q}_0, \mathbf{Q}_1 \rangle$. If $\mathbf{D} = \mathbf{Q}_1 - \mathbf{Q}_0$, then $\mathbf{N} = -\mathbf{D}^{\perp}$, a normal vector that points to the left as the segment is traversed from $\mathbf{Q}_0$ to $\mathbf{Q}_1$. Define $\mathbf{A} = \mathbf{P} - \mathbf{Q}_0$. The possibilities, labeled according to Figure 9.3, are characterized by (a) $\mathbf{N} \cdot \mathbf{A} > 0$, (b) $\mathbf{N} \cdot \mathbf{A} < 0$, (c) $\mathbf{N} \cdot \mathbf{A} = 0$ and $\mathbf{D} \cdot \mathbf{A} < 0$, (d) $\mathbf{N} \cdot \mathbf{A} = 0$ and $\mathbf{D} \cdot \mathbf{A} > \mathbf{D} \cdot \mathbf{D}$ and (e) $\mathbf{N} \cdot \mathbf{A} = 0$ and $0 \le \mathbf{D} \cdot \mathbf{A} \le \mathbf{D} \cdot \mathbf{D}$. The pseudocode of Listing 9.3 uses a flag to distinguish between these cases; the values are POSITIVE, NEGATIVE, COLLINEAR_LEFT, COLLINEAR_RIGHT and COLLINEAR_CONTAIN.

```
int CollinearTest(Point P, Point Q0, Point Q1)
{
    Point D = Q1 - Q0, N = -Perp(D), A = P - Q0;
    float NdA = Dot(N,A);
    if (NdA > 0) { return POSITIVE; }
    if (NdA < 0) { return NEGATIVE; }
    float DdA = Dot(D,A);
    if (DdA < 0) { return COLLINEAR_LEFT; }
    if (DdA > Dot(D,D)) { return COLLINEAR_RIGHT; }
    return COLLINEAR_CONTAIN;
}
```

Listing 9.3: Pseudocode for testing whether three points are collinear.

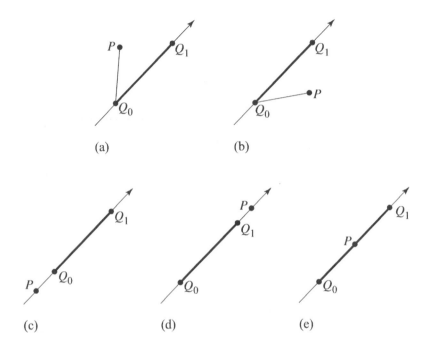

FIGURE 9.3: The five possibilities for the relationship of **P** to a line segment with endpoints $\mathbf{Q}_0$ and $\mathbf{Q}_1$. **P** is (a) to the left of the segment, (b) to the right of the segment, (c) on the line to the left of the segment, (d) on the line to the right of the segment or (e) on the line and contained by the segment.

The five possible matches are exactly those discussed for visibility of vertices and edges for the current hull from the input point **V**. The pseudocode for merging is contained in Listing 9.4. If the hull becomes a triangle, the vertices are arranged in counterclockwise order.

```
void MergeLinear(Point P, ConvexPolygon& hull, int& type)
{
    switch (CollinearTest(P,hull[0],hull[1]))
    {
        case POSITIVE:
            type = PLANAR;
            hull = {P, hull[0], hull[1]};
            break;
        case NEGATIVE:
            type = PLANAR;
            hull = {P, hull[1], hull[0]};
            break;
        case COLLINEAR_LEFT:
            // collinear order <P,Q0,Q1>
            hull = {P,Q1};
            break;
        case COLLINEAR_RIGHT:
            // collinear order <Q0,Q1,P>
            hull = {Q0,P};
            break;
        case COLLINEAR_CONTAIN:
            // collinear order <Q0,P,Q1>, hull does not change
            break;
    }
}
```

Listing 9.4: Pseudocode for the merge operation when the current hull is a line segment.

Although theoretically correct, CollinearTest suffers from the usual problems with floating point round-off error. Points can be nearly collinear, but may as well be treated as if they were collinear. An epsilon-tolerance system might be used to test whether points are nearly collinear, but even this is no guarantee that the convex hull computations are correct. It is better to use interval arithmetic or arbitrary-precision for exact collinear tests.

Once the current hull has three or more points, it is guaranteed to remain a convex polygon with positive area regardless of the values of any further input points.

The final function to discuss is MergePlanar. Once the first triangle, if any, is created by MergeLinear, the last inserted point that led to the triangle is always stored in hull[0]. This point is a good candidate for searching for the tangent points formed by the next input point and the current hull. The planar merge contains two loops, one to find the upper tangent point and one to find the lower tangent point. The loop bodies just test for visibility based on the results of CollinearTest applied to the input point and edges of the current hull. The pseudocode is shown in Listing 9.5.

```
void MergePlanar(Point P, ConvexPolygon& hull)
{
    // find upper tangent point
    for (U = 0; i = 1; U < hull.N; U = i, i = (i+1) mod hull.N)
    {
```

```
test = CollinearTest(P, hull[U], hull[i]);

if (test == NEGATIVE) // edge visible, go to next edge
{
    continue;
}

if (test == POSITIVE          // edge not visible,
|| test == COLLINEAR_LEFT )   // only edge endpoint is visible
{
    // upper tangent found
    break;
}

// test == COLLINEAR_CONTAIN || test == COLLINEAR_RIGHT
// Theoretically cannot occur when input points are distinct and sorted, but can
// occur because of floating point round-off when P is very close to the current
// hull. Assume P is on the hull polygon, so nothing to do.
return;
}

// find lower tangent point
for (L = 0; i = hull.N−1; i >= 0; L = i, i−−)
{
    test = CollinearTest(P, hull[i], hull[L]);

    if (test == NEGATIVE) // edge visible, go to next edge
    {
        continue;
    }

    if (test == POSITIVE           // edge not visible,
    || test == COLLINEAR_RIGHT)    // only edge endpoint is visible
    {
        // lower tangent found
        break;
    }

    // test == COLLINEAR_CONTAIN || test == COLLINEAR_LEFT
    // Theoretically cannot occur when input points are distinct and sorted, but can
    // occur because of floating point round-off when P is very close to the current
    // hull. Assume P is on the hull polygon, so nothing to do.
    return;
}

// Both tangent points found. Now do:
// 1. Remove visible edges from current hull.
// 2. Add new edges formed by P and tangent points.
}
```

Listing 9.5: Pseudocode for the merge operation when the current hull is a convex polygon.

The simplest algorithm for updating the hull in steps 1 and 2 indicated in the pseudocode is to create a temporary hull from the current hull and input point by iteration as shown in Listing 9.6

```
ConvexPolygon tmpHull;
tmpHull[0] = P;
for (i = 1; true; i++, U = (U+1) mod hull.N)
{
    tmpHull[i] = hull[U];
```

```
    if (U == L)
    {
        break;
    }
}
hull = tmpHull;
```

Listing 9.6: Pseudocode for removing the visible edges and adding new edges formed by the incoming point and the tangent points.

However, the iteration is $O(n)$, so the incremental algorithm becomes $O(n^2)$. To avoid this, it is important to maintain the hull as some type of linked structure so that the linked chain of visible edges can be disconnected at the tangent points, an $O(1)$ operation, *and deletion needs to be done in $O(1)$ time.* The chain should not be deleted one node at a time; otherwise the algorithm is back to $O(n)$ time. This requires an implementation that pays close attention to memory management. After the linked chain is removed, new links are added from the node representing **P** to the nodes representing the tangent points.

An important note about the architecture of the algorithm is in order. All of the problems due to floating point round-off errors are encapsulated by the function CollinearTest. Any unexpected results from an application of the incremental hull algorithm can be due only to the implementation of CollinearTest, particularly if an epsilon-threshold approach is used. The encapsulation makes it easy to debug any problems that arise in the application.

9.1.2 Divide-and-Conquer Method

A standard paradigm in computer science is *divide-and-conquer*. The idea is to take a problem, divide it into two smaller problems of the same type, solve the smaller problems and merge the results to construct the solution to the original problem. If the problem has n inputs and T_n is the time it takes to solve the problem, the division into two smaller problems, each with half the inputs, leads to the recursion formula $T_n = 2T_{n/2} + M_n$. Each smaller problem has (approximately) $n/2$ inputs and takes $T_{n/2}$ time to solve (by definition of T_k). The quantity M_n represents the time it takes to merge the solutions to the two smaller problems. If M_n takes linear time, $O(n)$, then it can be shown that the solution T_n is $O(n \log n)$. Recurrences of this form are discussed in detail in [5]. The divide-and-conquer method applied to convex hulls turns out to have a linear time merge, so the convex hull algorithm for a set of n points takes $O(n \log n)$ time.

As in the incremental construction of the convex hull, the input points are sorted according to the same scheme: $(x_0, y_0) < (x_1, y_1)$ when $x_0 < x_1$ or when $x_0 = x_1$ and $y_0 < y_1$. No assumptions are made about the structure of the point set. Just as in the incremental hull algorithm, the input points are sorted and duplicates are removed. Listing 9.7 contains the initial pseudocode.

```
ConvexPolygon DividAndConquerHull(int n, Point V[n])
{
```

```
Sort(n,V);
RemoveDuplicates(n,V);   // n can decrease, V has contiguous elements
ConvexPolygon hull;
GetHull(0,n−1,V, hull);
return hull;
}
```

Listing 9.7: Pseudocode for the divide-and-conquer construction of a convex hull in 2D.

The recursive construction occurs in GetHull. Its structure is shown in Listing 9.8. The values i0 and i1 are the first and last indices of a subset of points whose convex hull must be computed.

```
void GetHull(int i0, int i1, Point V[], ConvexPolygon& hull)
{
    int quantity = i1 − i0 + 1;
    if (quantity > 1)
    {
        // middle index of input range
        int mid = (i0+i1)/2;

        // find hull of subsets (mid-i0+1 ≥ i1-mid)
        ConvexPolygon LHull, RHull;
        GetHull(i0 , mid ,V, LHull);
        GetHull(mid+1,i1 ,V, RHull);

        // merge the convex hulls into a single convex hull
        Merge(LHull , RHull , hull);
    }
    else
    {
        // convex hull is a single point
        hull[0] = V[i0];
    }
}
```

Listing 9.8: Pseudocode for the recursive hull finding of the divide-and-conquer algorithm.

The technical problem is how Merge computes the convex hull of two convex hulls. The idea is an extension of that for computing the convex hull of a single point, a convex set itself, and a convex polygon. In the latter case, the merge depended on finding upper and lower tangents to the hull and containing the single point. Figure 9.2 shows the typical situation. For two convex polygons, the upper and lower tangents to both hulls must be computed. Figure 9.4 shows the typical situation. Unlike the incremental hull problem, one of the tangent points is not known ahead of time. An exhaustive search over pairs of points, one from each polygon, results in an $O(n^2)$ merge. An $O(n)$ merge is readily available instead if the following *walking algorithm* is performed on the left hull H_L and the right hull H_R.

The method is described for finding the lower tangent to the hulls. Find the point $\mathbf{P}_i$ on H_L with the largest x component, a linear-time process. Find the point $\mathbf{Q}_j$ on H_R with the smallest x-component, also a linear-time process. If the line containing $\mathbf{P}_i$ and $\mathbf{Q}_j$ is not tangent to H_L, traverse the vertices of H_L in the clockwise direction (decrement i) until the line is tangent to

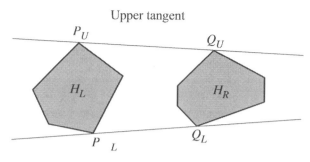

FIGURE 9.4: Two convex hulls H_0 and H_1 and their upper and lower tangents.

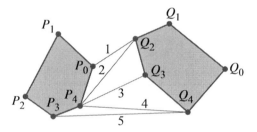

FIGURE 9.5: Two convex hulls H_0 and H_1 and the incremental search for the lower tangent.

H_L. Now switch to H_R. If the line containing the current $\mathbf{P}_i$ and $\mathbf{Q}_j$ is not tangent to H_R, traverse the vertices of H_R in the counterclockwise direction (increment j) until the line is tangent to H_R. This traversal produces a new line that might no longer be tangent to H_L. Alternately repeat the traversals until the line is tangent to both hulls. Figure 9.5 shows a typical situation. The extreme points are $\mathbf{P}_0$ and $\mathbf{Q}_2$. The initial segment, labeled 1, is $\langle \mathbf{P}_0, \mathbf{Q}_2 \rangle$. This segment is not tangent to the left hull at $\mathbf{P}_0$, so the left hull index is decremented (modulo 5) and the new segment, labeled 2, is $\langle \mathbf{P}_4, \mathbf{Q}_2 \rangle$. This segment is tangent to the left hull at $\mathbf{P}_4$, but it is not tangent to the right hull at $\mathbf{Q}_2$. The right hull index is incremented and the new segment, labeled 3, is $\langle \mathbf{P}_4, \mathbf{Q}_3 \rangle$. The segment is not tangent to the right hull, so the right hull index is incremented again and the new segment, labeled 4, is $\langle \mathbf{P}_4, \mathbf{Q}_4 \rangle$. The segment is now tangent to the right hull, but not tangent to the left hull. The left hull index is decremented and the new segment, labeled 5, is $\langle \mathbf{P}_3, \mathbf{Q}_4 \rangle$. This segment is tangent to both hulls and is the lower tangent to the hull. It is possible that a tangent is collinear with a hull edge that shares the tangent point, but rather than test for this in each merge and extend the tangent to include the collinear edge if necessary, removal of collinear edges can be done as a postprocess on the convex polygon returned by the hull construction.

Listing 9.9 contains pseudocode for the merge. The case of small sets near the leaf nodes of the implicit binary tree implied by the recursion are specially handled.

```
void Merge(ConvexPolygon LHull, ConvexPolygon RHull, ConvexPolygon& hull)
{
    if (LHull.n == 1 && RHull.n == 1)
    {
        // duplicate points were removed earlier, the hull is a line segment
        hull[0] = LHull[0];
        hull[1] = RHull[0];
        return;
    }

    if (LHull.n == 1 && RHull.n == 2)
    {
        // merge point and line segment, result in RHull
        MergeLinear(LHull[0], RHull);
        hull = RHull;
        return;
    }

    if (LHull.n == 2 && RHull.n == 1)
    {
        // merge point and line segment, result in LHull
        MergeLinear(RHull[0], LHull);
        hull = LHull;
        return;
    }

    if (LHull.n == 2 && RHull.n == 2)
    {
        // merge point and line segment, result in LHull
        MergeLinear(RHull[1], LHull);
        if (LHull.n == 2)
        {
            // RHull[1] was on line of LHull, merge next point
            MergeLinear(RHull[0], LHull);
            hull = LHull;
            return;
        }

        // RHull[1] and LHull form a triangle. Remove RHull[1] so that RHull is a single
        // point. LHull has been modified to be a triangle. Let the tangent search take
        // care of the merge.
        RHull.Remove(1);
    }

    // find indices of extreme points with respect to x
    LMax = IndexOfMaximum{LHull[i].x};
    RMin = IndexOfMinimum{RHull[i].x};

    // get lower tangent to hulls, start search at extreme points
    LLIndex = LMax;    // lower left index
    LRIndex = RMin;    // lower right index
    GetTangent(LHull, RHull, LLIndex, LRIndex);

    // get upper tangent to hulls, start search at extreme points
    ULIndex = LMax;    // upper left index
```

```
URIndex = RMin;   // upper right index
GetTangent(RHull , LHull , URIndex , ULIndex );

// construct the counterclockwise-ordered merged-hull vertices
ConvexPolygon tmpHull;
i = 0;
for (each j between LRIndex and URIndex inclusive) do
{
    tmpHull[i] = hull[j];
    i++;
}
for (each j between ULIndex and LLIndex inclusive) do
{
    tmpHull[i] = hull[j];
    i++;
}
hull = tmpHull;
}
```

Listing 9.9: Pseudocode for the divide-and-conquer merge.

The function MergeLinear has identical structure to the one used in the incremental hull construction, with the minor change in semantics that the input line segment polygon is modified to store the merged hull.

The tangent search uses the same concepts of visibility as in the incremental hull construction. As described previously, the search flip-flops between the two input hulls. The input indices L and U are the starting ones for the search. On return, the indices correspond to the tangent points on the two hulls. Listing 9.10 contains the pseudocode.

```
void GetTangent(ConvexPolygon LHull , ConvexPolygon RHull , int& L, int& R)
{
    // In theory the loop terminates in a finite number of steps, but the upper bound for
    // the loop variable is used to trap problems caused by floating-point round-off errors
    // that might lead to an infinite loop.
    for (int i = 0; i < LHull.n + RHull.n; i++)
    {
        // endpoints of potential tangent
        Point L1 = LHull[L], R0 = RHull[R];
        // walk clockwise along left hull to find tangency
        int Lm1 = (L-1) mod LHull.n;
        Point L0 = LHull[Lm1];
        int test = CollinearTest(R0,L0,L1);
        if (test == NEGATIVE || test == COLLINEAR_LEFT)
        { L = Lm1; continue; }
        // walk counterclockwise along right hull to find tangency
        int Rp1 = (R+1) mod RHull.n;
        Point R1 = RHull[Rp1];
        test = CollinearTest(L1,R0,R1);
        if (test == NEGATIVE || test == COLLINEAR_RIGHT)
        { R = Rp1; continue; }
        // tangent segment has been found
        break;
    }
    // Trap any problems due to floating-point round-off errors. Code
    // cannot reach here using arbitrary-precision arithmetic.
    assert(i < LHull.n + RHull.n);
}
```

Listing 9.10: Pseudocode for computing hull tangents in the divide-and-conquer algorithm.

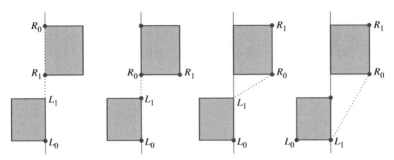

FIGURE 9.6: Extreme points used to initialize tangent search are on the same vertical line. The initial visibility tests both do not yield a NEGATIVE test, yet the initial segment connecting the extremes is not a tangent to the hulls. The sequence of changes is from left to right. The current candidate for a tangent is drawn in black.

As each vertex is visited on one hull, the current edge on the other hull is tested for visibility using CollinearTest. When visible, the returned value is usually NEGATIVE. However, care must be taken when the initial extreme points on the hulls are on the same vertical line. Figure 9.6 shows a typical scenario. The initial candidate tangent is $\langle \mathbf{L}_1, \mathbf{R}_0 \rangle$, shown in the upper left of Figure 9.6. In attempting to traverse the left hull, the output of CollinearTest(R0,L0,L1) is COLLINEAR_RIGHT. The left hull index remains unchanged and a traversal is attempted on the right hull. The output of CollinearTest(L1,R0,R1) is also COLLINEAR_RIGHT. In this case the right hull index is incremented, effectively as if $\mathbf{R}_0$ were slightly to the right of the common vertical line. The upper right of Figure 9.6 shows the current state after the increment. The traversal switches back to the left hull. The output of CollinearTest(R0,L0,L1) is once again COLLINEAR_RIGHT and the left hull index remains unchanged. The traversal switches to the right hull. The output of CollinearTest(L1,R0,R1) is COLLINEAR_RIGHT and the right hull index is incremented, again as if $\mathbf{R}_0$ were slightly to the right of the common vertical line. The lower left of Figure 9.6 shows the current state after the increment. Switching back to the left hull, the output of CollinearTest(R0,L0,L1) is NEGATIVE because the edge $\langle \mathbf{R}_0, \mathbf{R}_1 \rangle$ is fully visible. The left hull index is decremented. The lower right of Figure 9.6 shows the current state after the decrement. The loop is iterated one more time, but both calls to CollinearTest return POSITIVE and $\langle \mathbf{L}_1, \mathbf{R}_0 \rangle$ in the lower left of Figure 9.6 is tangent to the two hulls.

Once both tangents to the hulls are found, the construction of the merged hull is structured the same as for the incremental hull construction. The pseudocode shows the creation of a temporary convex polygon that contains subsets of indices from both hulls based on the tangent point locations, but just as in the incremental construction, a linked list structure can be used and the detachment, attachment and sublist deletion can all be performed in $O(1)$

time. However, the total time is still $O(n)$ because of the traversals over the two input hulls to find the extreme points.

9.2   Convex Hull of Points in 3D

The ideas in 2D for constructing convex hulls of point sets using the incremental method or the divide-and-conquer method extend naturally to 3D. The incremental method has an easily implementable extension. The divide-and-conquer method is significantly more difficult to implement. The algorithm has frequent occurrences of visibility tests, which can be formulated as testing the signs of determinants. Floating-point arithmetic can lead to misclassification of the signs, so interval arithmetic and/or arbitrary-precision arithmetic should be used instead for an error-free implementation.

9.2.1   Incremental Construction

The 3D algorithm is similar to the 2D algorithm. Each point is processed and merged with the convex hull of the previous points. The dimension of the hull is monitored to make sure that collinear points lead to a line segment hull and coplanar points lead to a planar convex polygon. The typical case is when the hull becomes a convex polyhedron.

The merge operation is slightly more complex than in the 2D case. Instead of two tangent lines, a *visibility cone* is obtained—not to be confused with the cone that is a quadric surface—whose vertex is the point to be merged and whose final edges form a closed polyline of current hull edges that separate the visible faces from the hidden ones. The closed polyline is sometimes called the *terminator*, a word used in astronomy to denote the boundary between the lit and unlit regions of an astronomical body. Figure 9.7 illustrates the typical situation. The visible faces must be removed from the current hull and the faces of the visibility cone must be added. A simple algorithm for doing this involves traversing over all current faces, finding those faces with an edge on the terminator and storing the edges in some data structure. During the traversal, visible faces are discarded and hidden faces are kept. Once all faces have been visited, the terminator is known as a closed polyline. The polyline is traversed and visibility faces formed by each edge with $\mathbf{P}$ are constructed and added to the merged hull data structure.

An algorithm for finding the terminator that is more efficient, but more complicated to implement, uses a linear search for a terminator edge. If a face lies on the plane $\mathbf{N} \cdot \mathbf{X} + d = 0$ where $\mathbf{N}$ is a unit length normal, the signed distance from $\mathbf{P}$ to the plane is $\delta = \mathbf{N} \cdot \mathbf{P} + d$. If $\delta > 0$, the plane is visible to $\mathbf{P}$ (and so is the corresponding face). If $\delta <= 0$, the plane is hidden, as is the corresponding face. In the case $\delta = 0$, the closest edge of the face

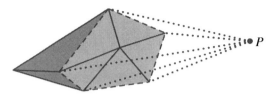

Current hull

FIGURE 9.7: The current hull and point to be merged. The visible faces are drawn in light gray. The hidden faces are drawn in dark gray. The polyline separating the two sets is drawn as a sequence of dashed lines. The other edges of the visibility cone are drawn as dotted lines.

is potentially visible to **P**, but that edge is part of another face for which $\delta \geq 0$. The face mesh for the current convex hull has a dual graph whose nodes represent the faces and whose arcs represent the edges of the faces. In particular, an arc between two nodes indicates that the corresponding faces are adjacent. Each node is assigned the signed distance from **P** to the face. Starting at a node in the graph with positive signed distance, a search is made to find a path of nodes whose distances are decreasing (more accurately, nonincreasing). The next node visited from the current node is the one whose signed distance is the smallest positive value of all adjacent nodes. Because the hull is convex, eventually a node must be reached that has at least one adjacent node with a nonpositive signed distance. The shared edge is on the terminator by definition. Once a first terminator edge is found, and assuming a data structure that maintains a list of adjacent edges for each vertex, the terminator can be traversed.

Observe that this approach is closely related to finding a zero level curve of an image (the signed distances) defined on a graph of pixels. The intuition on the order of the algorithm follows from this. If the image were square with n pixels (number of faces in the problem), the linear search for the first point on the zero level curve is $O(\sqrt{n})$. The traversal along the zero level curve (the terminator in the problem) is also a linear search, again taking $O(\sqrt{n})$ time. The simple algorithm mentioned earlier visits all triangles, taking $O(n)$ time, an asymptotically slower method.

Listing 9.11 contains the pseudocode for the top-level call.

```
ConvexPolyhedron IncrementalHull(int n, Point V[n])
{
    Sort(n,V);
    RemoveDuplicates(n,V);
    ConvexPolyhedron hull;
    type = POINT;
    hull[0] = V[0];
    for (i = 1; i < n; ++i)
    {
        switch (type)
        {
```

```
        case POINT:
            type = LINEAR;
            hull[1] = V[i];
            break;
        case LINEAR:
            MergeLinear(V[i], hull, type);
            break;
        case PLANAR:
            MergePlanar(V[i], hull, type);
            break;
        case SPATIAL:
            MergeSpatial(V[i], hull);
            break;
        }
    }
    return hull;
}
```

Listing 9.11: Pseudocode for the incremental construction of a convex hull in 3D.

The data structure for the convex polyhedron is most likely different for the spatial case than for the other cases. The natural storage for a linear hull is an array of two points, the endpoints of the line segment that is the hull. The natural storage for a planar hull is an array or list of ordered points. The natural storage for a spatial hull is more complicated. In its most abstract form, the data structure is a vertex-edge-face table that allows adding and removing each of the primitive components. In a triangle-based application, the faces are stored as triangle fans. For 2D convex polygons, support can be added for collapsing collinear edges to a single edge. In 3D, the triangle fans can be collapsed into convex polygons and the collinear edges of those convex polygons can be collapsed into single edges.

The function MergeLinear is nearly identical to the one for the 2D incremental hull. However, if the three input points (the next point to be merged and the endpoints of the current line segment hull) are not collinear, they lie on a plane and have no specific ordering (*i.e.* positive or negative as in the 2D case) until a normal vector is chosen for that plane. A normal vector should be chosen so that if the hull eventually becomes spatial, the first face is a convex polygon and the normal can be used to reorder the vertices (if necessary) so that the polygon is counterclockwise ordered when viewed from outside the hull.

The function MergePlanar is slightly different from that of the 2D case. If the next input point is on the current plane, then the 2D merge algorithm is applied to update the current hull, a convex planar polygon, to another convex planar polygon. The merge is, of course, applied to points as 3D entities. If the next input point is not on the current plane, the hull becomes spatial and MergeSpatial takes over for subsequent merges. If the data structure used to represent convex polyhedrons is a triangle mesh stored as a vertex-edge-triangle table, then the current hull, a convex planar polygon, must be fanned into triangles that are added to the table. The additional triangles formed by the next input point and the edges of the convex polygon are also added. The normal vector calculated earlier can be used at this time to make sure the triangles are added to be counterclockwise ordered when viewed from the outside of the spatial hull.

The function MergeSpatial performs the duties described earlier. By whatever means, the visible faces of the current hull are removed and the new faces formed by the terminator and the next input point are added.

9.2.2   Divide-and-Conquer Method

The basic construction is similar to that in 2D. The input points are sorted along some axis. The set of points is divided into two sets and the hulls are computed recursively on those sets. The resulting hulls are merged into a single hull with an algorithm that is $O(n)$ in time.

The idea is to wrap a plane about the two input hulls. The end result is a strip consisting of triangles and/or quadrilaterals that become the new faces of the merged hull. Figure 9.8 illustrates with two icosahedrons that are merged into a single convex polyhedron. The wrapping begins by finding a supporting plane for the two input hulls, a plane that is tangent to both hulls. For each hull the set of tangency is either a vertex, an edge or a face. If the set is a face, consider only a single edge of the face, one visible to the other supporting set, to start the wrapping process. Because only vertices and edges need to be considered, the new faces on the merged hull are either triangles or quadrilaterals.

Regardless of the type of supporting sets for the hulls, there must be vertices $\mathbf{P}_0$ and $\mathbf{Q}_0$, one from each hull, so that the line segment $\langle \mathbf{P}_0, \mathbf{Q}_0 \rangle$ is an edge of the merged hull. One half of the supporting plane containing that edge is folded along the line containing the edge until another hull vertex is encountered. If this vertex is on the first hull, call it $\mathbf{P}_1$, then it must be adjacent to $\mathbf{P}_0$. The triangle $\langle \mathbf{P}_0, \mathbf{P}_1, \mathbf{Q}_0 \rangle$ is a face of the merged hull. Similarly, if the vertex is on the second hull, call it $\mathbf{Q}_1$, then it must be adjacent to $\mathbf{Q}_0$. The triangle $\langle \mathbf{Q}_0, \mathbf{Q}_1, \mathbf{P} \rangle$ is a face of the merged hull. It is possible that both $\mathbf{P}_1$ and $\mathbf{Q}_1$ are encountered simultaneously in which case the quadrilateral formed by the four points is a face of the merged hull. The plane is folded again on the line containing the next leading edge of the last found face. The process is repeated until the original folding edge is revisited. As described in [21], the asymptotical analysis shows that the amortized cost for this search is $O(n)$.

Once the merged hull faces are constructed by the plane wrapping, the old faces that are no longer visible must be removed. In the 3D incremental hull construction, the merge is applied to a single point and a convex polyhedron. Recall that the terminator is the closed polyline of edges on the convex polyhedron that separates the visible faces from the hidden ones relative to the single point. As a graph whose nodes are the terminator vertices and whose arcs are the edges connecting consecutive vertices, the terminator is a simple cycle. The merge step in the incremental hull involved finding the terminator. The most efficient algorithm was to find an edge of the terminator and

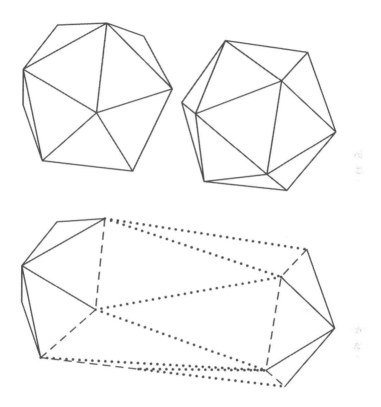

FIGURE 9.8: The top image shows two icosahedrons. The bottom image shows the merged hull. The dotted lines indicate those edges that are part of faces of the original hulls. The dashed lines indicate those edges that are part of the newly added faces.

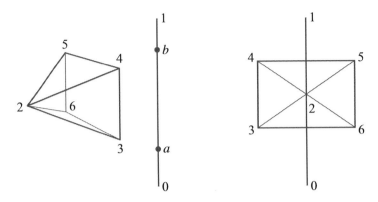

FIGURE 9.9: The left image is a side view of the pyramid and line segment. The right image is a view from behind the line segment. The line segment $\langle 0, a \rangle$ can see only triangle $\langle 2, 3, 6 \rangle$ and quadrilateral $\langle 3, 4, 5, 6 \rangle$. The line segment $\langle a, b \rangle$ can see only the quadrilateral. The line segment $\langle b, 1 \rangle$ can see only triangle $\langle 2, 4, 5 \rangle$ and the quadrilateral. The faces that are hidden in all cases are the triangles $\langle 2, 3, 4 \rangle$ and $\langle 2, 5, 6 \rangle$. The terminator consists of the boundaries of these triangles, a sequence of line segments forming two cycles, not a simple cycle.

then traverse adjacent edges of the terminator that separate two faces, one of positive signed distance and one of nonpositive signed distance. This traversal succeeds because the terminator is a simple cycle. Figure 9.8 might lead one to believe that the terminators for the two input hulls are both simple cycles. As it turns out, this is not necessarily the case. A simple example to illustrate this involves merging a convex polyhedron and a line segment. The faces that are kept in the merged hull are those that are hidden to *all* points on the line segment. Equivalently, the discarded faces are those that are visible to *some* point on the line segment. Figure 9.9 shows an example where the convex polyhedron is a pyramid. The terminator for the pyramid consists of two triangles that share a single vertex. Because of this possibility, one should be careful not to assume that the terminators are simple cycles when attempting to delete the visible faces of each input hull. A correct method is to traverse all edges of the terminator and detach the visible faces from the hidden ones. It is true that the visible faces on an input hull are in the same connected component, so a depth-first search may be used to delete them one at a time. However, with extra work, an $O(1)$ delete algorithm can be used as long as the application provides a sophisticated memory manager along the lines that were mentioned for incremental hull construction in 2D. The idea is to detach the visible faces from the hidden ones, but allow the component of visible faces to exist until the full hull is constructed. At that time, an iteration is made over the hull to construct a copy of it. The previous copy and all the dangling

FIGURE 9.10: Triangulations of finite point sets.

components are part of temporary workspace in memory that is deleted all at once.

9.3 Delaunay Triangulation

A *triangulation* of a finite set of points $S \subset \mathbb{R}^2$ is a set of triangles whose vertices are the points in S and whose edges connect pairs of points in S. Each point of S is required to occur in at least one triangle. The edges are only allowed to intersect at the vertices. An optional requirement is that the union of the triangles is the convex hull of S. Figure 9.10 shows triangulations of two point sets. The triangulation on the left includes the optional requirement, but the triangulation on the right does not. Similar terminology is used for constructing tetrahedra whose vertices are points in a finite set $S \subset \mathbb{R}^3$. The computational geometry researchers also refer to this as a triangulation, but some practitioners call this a *tetrahedralization*. For $S \subset \mathbb{R}^d$, an object whose vertices are in S is called a *simplex* (plural *simplicies*), the generalization of triangle and tetrahedron to higher dimensions. Perhaps *simplexification* is as good a term as any for constructing the simplices whose vertices are in S.

In 2D, a common desire in a triangulation is that there not be long, thin triangles. Consider the case of four points forming a convex quadrilateral. Figure 9.11 shows the two different choices for triangulation where the vertices are $(\pm 2, 0)$ and $(0, \pm 1)$. The goal is to select the triangulation that maximizes the minimum angle. The triangulation of Figure 9.11(b) has this property. The concept of maximizing the minimum angle produces a *Delaunay triangulation*. A better formal development is presented in computational geometry books and is based on understanding *Voronoi diagrams* for finite point sets and constructing the Delaunay triangulation from it. An important concept is that of a *circumcircle* of a triangle, which is the circle containing the three vertices of the triangle. Although the angles of the triangles can be computed explicitly, the choice of one of the two triangulations is equivalently determined by containment of one point within the circumcircle of the other three points. In Figure 9.12, $(0, -1)$ is inside the circumcircle of triangle $\langle (2,0), (0,1), (-2,0) \rangle$,

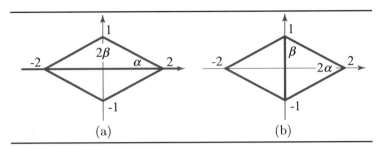

FIGURE 9.11: The two triangulations for a convex quadrilateral. The angle $\alpha \doteq 0.46$ radians and the angle $\beta \doteq 1.11$ radians. (a) The minimum angle of the top triangle is α, which is smaller than β. (b) The minimum angle is 2α radians, which is smaller than β. The triangles on the right maximize the minimum angle.

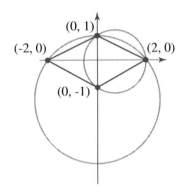

FIGURE 9.12: Two circumcircles for the triangles of Figure 9.11.

but $(-2,0)$ is outside the circumcircle of triangle $\langle(2,0),(0,1),(0,-1)\rangle$. The Delaunay triangulation has the property that the circumcircle of each triangle contains no other points of the input set. This property is used for incremental construction of the triangulation, the topic discussed next. The original ideas of constructing the triangulation incrementally are found in [4, 29]. This section describes approach [29]. A good description of the practical problems that occur with implementing the algorithm in 3D is presented in [10].

9.3.1   Incremental Construction

Begin with a given finite set of points $S \subset \mathbb{R}^d$ whose convex hull has a positive volume; that is, the intrinsic dimensional of the hull is d and so it is not degenerate. To illustrate, consider a finite set of points in $\mathbb{R}^2$. The hull has intrinsic dimension 2 when it is a convex polygon, 1 when it is a line segment or 0 when all points are the same. In $\mathbb{R}^3$, the hull has intrinsic dimension 3 when it is a convex polyhedron, 2 when it is a convex polygon in some plane, 1 when it is a line segment or 0 when all points are the same.

9.3.1.1 Inserting Points

For each step, there is a mesh of simplices generated from the points already processed and a pending point that is to be inserted into the mesh. The invariant is that each simplex has a *circumscribed hypersphere* that contains no mesh points other than the vertices of that simplex. The initial phase of the insertion is to determine which simplex contains the pending point. The recommended approach is to attempt a *linear walk* through the simplices.

The idea is illustrated in 2D. The current set of Delaunay triangles is represented as an *edge-triangle manifold mesh*. Each edge is shared by at most two triangles. An edge that is shared by only one triangle is part of the convex hull that forms the boundary of the union of the Delaunay triangles. Let $\mathbf{P}$ be the pending point. An initial triangle $T = \langle \mathbf{V}_0, \mathbf{V}_1, \mathbf{V}_2 \rangle$ is selected for the search. If $\mathbf{P}$ is in the triangle, the search is finished. If it is not in the triangle, the line segment connecting the triangle centroid $\mathbf{C} = (\mathbf{V}_0 + \mathbf{V}_1 + \mathbf{V}_2)/3$ to $\mathbf{P}$ must intersect one of the triangle edges. If the intersection point is strictly in the interior of the edge, the triangle A adjacent to that edge is selected as the next one to visit. If the intersection point is a vertex of T, then either edge can be selected. It is possible that the intersected edge of T has no adjacent triangle, in which case $\mathbf{P}$ is outside the current triangulation and the search is terminated. Figure 9.13 illustrates the linear walk.

When $\mathbf{P}$ is inside a Delaunay triangle, subdividing that triangle into three triangles using $\mathbf{P}$ and the Delaunay triangle vertices does not generally produce (sub)triangles that satisfy the empty circumcircle condition. A local re-triangulation of the mesh is required that involves computing an *insertion polygon*, which is described later. When $\mathbf{P}$ is outside the mesh of Delaunay triangles, the insertion polygon is slightly more complicated to compute.

9.3.1.2 Linear Walks and Intrinsic Dimension

The linear walk algorithm is well defined when there exists at least one Delaunay triangle in the mesh. However, a first triangle must be computed. Assuming an *intrinsic dimension* 2, there must be at least one triangle, so an algorithm is needed to compute it. If the intrinsic dimension is 1, there is no such triangle. The approach of [29] is to compute a *supertriangle* that contains the input points. This triangle is used as the first triangle. The input points are inserted one-at-a-time to construct the Delaunay triangulation. After all input points are processed, triangles in the mesh that contain edges of the supertriangle are removed and the remaining triangles form the Delaunay triangulation of the input points. As it turns out, this approach is not guaranteed to work. The final triangulation might not be the convex hull of the

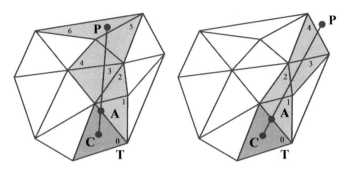

FIGURE 9.13: Two linear walks are shown with the order of visited triangles numbered accordingly. The left image shows a triangle mesh where the dark-gray triangle is the initial selection T. The point $\mathbf{P}$ is not inside T, and the line segment connecting the centroid $\mathbf{C}$ to $\mathbf{P}$ intersects an edge for which triangle A is adjacent. The search continues using $T \leftarrow A$. The right image shows an example where $\mathbf{P}$ is outside the current mesh. The search terminates once it is determined that the triangle edge is a hull edge (no adjacent triangle).

input points. My original 2D Delaunay triangulation code used the supertriangle approach. A user filed a bug report; it turned out to be a case where the final triangulation was not the convex hull of the input points. I posted to comp. graphics. algorithms (a long time ago) asking about supertriangles, and Jeff Erickson (Computational Geometer/Topologist and Professor of Computer Science at University of Illinois at Urbana–Champaign) responded and agreed that this will not always work, indicating it becomes a point-visibility problem where the supertriangle might have to be made arbitrarily larger for the algorithm to work.

Instead, the determination of intrinsic dimension and the selection of the first triangle should be combined into a single process. The computation of dimension can be done with either floating-point arithmetic or arbitrary-precision arithmetic. The former might be preferred when application-specific knowledge is available about error tolerances of the input points; that is, a user-provided tolerance $\varepsilon \geq 0$ can be used to give a fuzzy measure of intrinsic dimension.

The determination starts with computing the axis-aligned bounding box of the input points, represented as two diagonally opposite corners $\mathbf{V}_{\min}$ and $\mathbf{V}_{\max}$ which are points from the input set. Let $r_{\max}$ be the largest length of an edge of the bounding box. If $r_{\max} \leq \varepsilon$, the intrinsic dimension is selected to be 0. If $\varepsilon = 0$, this implies that all the input points are exactly the same point. If $\varepsilon > 0$ but small, this implies that all the input points are clustered tightly together.

When $r_{\max} > \varepsilon$, the intrinsic dimension is at least 1. Define $\mathbf{\Delta} = \mathbf{V}_{\max} - \mathbf{V}_{\min}$ whose length $|\mathbf{\Delta}|$ is an approximate measure of the maximum distance between points in the input set. Define $\mathbf{D}_0 = \boldsymbol{\Delta}/|\boldsymbol{\Delta}|$ and $\mathbf{D}_1 = -\mathbf{D}_0^\perp$, so that the affine coordinate system with origin $\mathbf{V}_{\min}$ and unit-length directions $\mathbf{D}_0$ and $\mathbf{D}_1$ is right-handed. For a point $\mathbf{P}$, the signed distance to the line $\mathbf{V}_{\min} + t\mathbf{D}_0$ is $d = \mathbf{D}_1 \cdot (\mathbf{P} - \mathbf{V}_{\min})$. Compute the signed maximum distance $d_{\max}$ from input points to the line. Let $\mathbf{V}_{\text{far}}$ be the input point that attains that value. If $|d_{\max}| \leq \varepsilon r_{\max}$, the maximum distance to the line from the input points is small relative to the length of $\boldsymbol{\Delta}$. In this case, the intrinsic dimension is selected to be 1. Otherwise, the intrinsic dimension is selected to be 2. The sign of $d_{\max}$ is used to determine whether $\langle \mathbf{V}_{\min}, \mathbf{V}_{\max}, \mathbf{V}_{\text{far}} \rangle$ is clockwise or counterclockwise ordered.

If the intrinsic dimension is 0, the output of the Delaunay triangulation is a single point (degenerate triangulation), perhaps chosen to be the average of the input points when a positive ε was used. If the intrinsic dimension is 1, the output of the Delaunay triangulation is a line segment (degenerate triangulation). When a positive ε is used, the segment is computed by projecting the input points $\mathbf{P}_i$ onto the line $t_i = \mathbf{D}_0 \cdot (\mathbf{P}_i - \mathbf{V}_{\min})$ and computing the indices i_0 and i_1 that produce the extremes $t_{\min}$ and $t_{\max}$. The segment endpoints are $\mathbf{P}_{i_0}$ and $\mathbf{P}_{i_1}$. If the intrinsic dimension is 2, the first triangle of the Delaunay triangulation is either $\langle \mathbf{V}_{\min}, \mathbf{V}_{\max}, \mathbf{V}_{\text{far}} \rangle$ or $\langle \mathbf{V}_{\min}, \mathbf{V}_{\text{far}}, \mathbf{V}_{\max} \rangle$, whichever is counterclockwise ordered. The three vertices are discarded from the input set and the remaining input points are inserted one-at-a-time to create the triangulation.

The linear walk for n^2 triangles is $O(n)$. Unfortunately, the asymptotic order does not extend to the same concept in higher dimensions. The mechanics are the same. Given a point $\mathbf{P}$, an initial tetrahedron is selected. If $\mathbf{P}$ is inside the tetrahedron, the search is complete. If it is not inside the tetrahedron, the centroid $\mathbf{C}$ of the tetrahedron is computed and the line segment connecting $\mathbf{C}$ to $\mathbf{P}$ is processed to determine which face of the tetrahedron is intersected. The tetrahedron adjacent to that face becomes the next search tetrahedron, if it exists. The search is repeated until a tetrahedron is found that contains $\mathbf{P}$ or none is found because $\mathbf{P}$ is outside the current mesh of tetrahedra. As it turns out, there are pathological data sets for which the walk can be quite long [26]. A 3D Delaunay triangulation can have $O(n^2)$ tetrahedra. In the cited paper, it is shown that a line can stab $O(n^2)$ tetrahedra. In fact, for d dimensions, a line can stab on the order of $n^{\lceil d/2 \rceil}$ simplices.

9.3.1.3 The Insertion Step

Now consider the insertion of a point in general dimensions. The circumscribing hypersphere of a simplex is called a circumhypersphere. The condition for a Delaunay triangulation is that the circumhypersphere of a simplex does not contain any input points other than the vertices of that simplex; this is called the *empty circumhypersphere constraint*. The algorithm is described in steps. The presentation is from [10], but the flawed supertriangle/supersim-

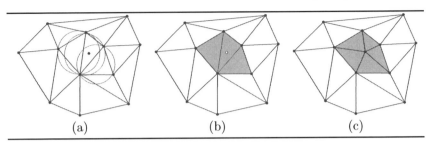

FIGURE 9.14: (a) Circumcircles containing the next point to be inserted. (b) The insertion polygon for the next point to be inserted. (c) The modified insertion polygon that restores the empty circumcircle condition for the total mesh.

plex approach is skipped, using instead the algorithm described previously for simultaneously computing the intrinsic dimension and first triangle.

1. Compute the intrinsic dimension of the input points and an initial simplex as described previously in Section 9.3.1.2. The remaining steps are computed for the intrinsic dimension, projecting the input points accordingly to the proper space for insertion.

2. The initial simplex is added as the first simplex in a mesh of simplices. The mesh maintains the vertices and all the necessary among connectivity simplices. Moreover, the circumhypersphere for each simplex is stored to avoid having to recalculate centers and radii during the incremental updates. Now insert the points one-at-a-time.

3. If the pending point is contained in a simplex of the current mesh, then apply the following steps.

   (a) Determine which circumhyperspheres contain the given point. Here is where the direct appeal is made to satisfying the empty circumhypersphere condition. Before insertion, the empty condition is satisfied for all simplices. When the point is inserted, the simplices corresponding to the circumhyperspheres that violate the empty condition must be modified. The search for the containing hyperspheres is implemented as a search over simplices using the (attempted) linear walk described previously. Once the containing simplex or (simplices if the input point is on a shared boundary component) is found, a depth-first search can be performed to find other simplices whose circumhyperspheres contain the input point. Figure 9.14(a) illustrates in 2D circumcircles that contain the to-be-inserted point.

   (b) The union of the simplices whose circumhyperspheres contain the input point form a *d*-dimensional polyhedron called the *insertion polyhedron*. Locate the boundary faces of that polyhedron. Figure 9.14(b) illustrates in 2D the boundary edges of the polygons.

(c) Create new simplices by connecting the input point to the boundary faces and then remove the old simplices whose union was the insertion polyhedron. Figure 9.14(c) illustrates the retriangulation in 2D.

4. If the input point is outside the current mesh, then apply the following steps.

   (a) Determine which faces of the convex hull of the current mesh are visible to the input point.

   (b) Determine those faces whose corresponding simplices have circumhyperspheres containing the input point.

   (c) The union of the simplices from the previous step is a *subset* of the insertion polyhedron. The full insertion polyhedron also contains additional simplices. Each one of these has the input point as vertex and a visible hull face that is from a Delaunay simplex whose circumhypersphere does *not* contain the pending point.

   (d) Create new simplices by connecting the input point to the back-facing boundary faces of the insertion polyhedron and then remove the old simplices whose union was a subset of the insertion polyhedron. Figure 9.15 illustrates the retriangulation in 2D.

9.3.2   Construction by Convex Hull

The Delaunay triangulation of a finite point set $S \subset \mathbb{R}^d$ for any dimension d is obtainable from the convex hull of $S' = \{(\mathbf{X}, |\mathbf{X}|^2) : \mathbf{X} \in S\} \subset \mathbb{R}^d \times \mathbb{R} = \mathbb{R}d + 1$, as shown in [9]. In particular, let the convex hull be constructed so that its hyperfaces are $d+1$-dimensional simplices. Each simplex has a normal vector in $\mathbb{R}^d \times \mathbb{R}$, say $(\mathbf{N}, \lambda)$. The simplices for which $\lambda < 0$ form what is called the *lower hull*. The other simplices form the *upper hull*. The projections of the simplices of the lower hull onto $\mathbb{R}^d$ are themselves simplices (of dimension d) and are the Delaunay triangulation of S.

A simple illustration is shown in Figure 9.16 for a 2D triangulation obtained from a 3D convex hull. The five input points are $(0,0)$, $(0, \pm 1)$ and $(1, \pm 1)$. Figure 9.16(b) shows the Delaunay triangulation. Figure 9.16(a) shows the convex hull of the lifted points $(0,0,0)$, $(0, \pm 1, 1)$ and $(1, \pm 1, 2)$. The lower hull consists of three triangles. The counterclockwise ordered triangle $\langle (0,0,0), (0,1,1), (1,1,2) \rangle$ has normal vector $(1,1,-1)$. The third component is negative, so this triangle is on the lower hull and is projected onto the xy-plane to obtain the counterclockwise ordered Delaunay triangle $\langle (0,0), (1,1), (0,1) \rangle$. Similarly, the triangles $\langle (0,0,0), (1,-1,2), (0,-1,1) \rangle$ and

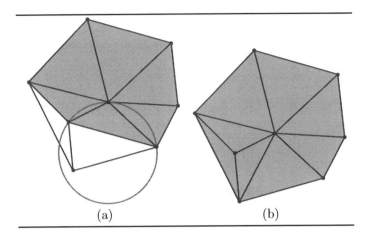

(a)   (b)

FIGURE 9.15: (a) A circumcircle containing the next point to be inserted. That point is outside the current triangulation. Two edges of the triangulation are visible to the point. The insertion polygon consists of the triangle whose circumcircle contains the point and the two triangles formed by the point and the visible edges. (b) The modified insertion polygon that restores the empty circumcircle condition for the total mesh.

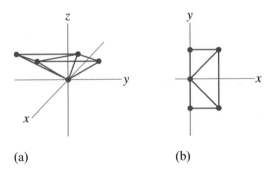

(a)   (b)

FIGURE 9.16: (a) Convex hull of 2D points lifted onto a paraboloid in 3D. (b) The corresponding Delaunay triangulation, the projection of the lower hull onto the xy-plane.

$\langle (0,0,0), (1,1,2), (1,-1,2) \rangle$ have normals with negative third component, so the xy-projections of these are part of the triangulation. The counterclockwise ordered triangle $\langle (0,1,1), (0,0,0), (0,-1,1) \rangle$ has normal vector $(-2,0,0)$. The third component is zero, so it is not part of the lower hull. The projection is a degenerate triangle and does not contribute to the triangulation. The upper hull consists of two triangles that are discarded.

This result is particularly useful in that implementing an incremental convex hull algorithm is less complicated than implementing a Delaunay triangulation in large dimensions.

9.4   Minimum-Area Circle of Points

An $O(n)$ method for finding *some* bounding circle is to compute the minimum-area axis-aligned rectangle that contains the points, then choose a circle that circumscribes the rectangle. In most cases this circle is not the minimum-area circle containing the points. In fact, sometimes the input points are all strictly interior to the circle. For example, this situation occurs for the points $\{(\pm 2, 0), (0, \pm 1)\}$. The bounding circle is centered at $(0,0)$ and has radius $\sqrt{5}$. The maximum distance from the origin to an input point is 2. Many applications require a better fit than this.

A *support point* for a bounding circle is an input point that lies exactly on the circle. The minimum-area circle containing the points clearly must be supported by at least two input points; otherwise the purported circle could be shrunk in size until it does touch another input point. Even though the point set could have more than two input points, the minimum-area circle might only have two supporting points. For example, the points $\{(-1,0), (0,0), (1,0)\}$ are collinear. The minimum-area circle containing them has center $(0,0)$ and radius 1. The supporting points are $(\pm 1, 0)$. In other examples, the number of supporting points is three. It is possible for the number of input points exactly on the minimum-area circle to be four or more, but only three are necessary because three noncollinear points uniquely determine the circle.

At least two input points must be on the circle, so it is tempting to assume that those two points must be the ones farthest apart. This is not the case based on the following counterexample. Let the input points be $\{(1,0), (-1/2, \sqrt{3}/2), (-1/2, -\sqrt{3}/2), (-3/4, 0)\}$. The points form a convex quadrilateral. The first three points form an equilateral triangle, the common length of the sides being $\sqrt{3}$. The distance from $(1,0)$ to $(-3/4, 0)$ is $7/4 > \sqrt{3}$. Therefore, $(1,0)$ and $(-3/4, 0)$ form the most separated pair of input points. The minimum-area bounding circle is the one containing the equilateral triangle and has center $(0,0)$ and radius 1. The circle containing $(1,0)$, $(-1/2, \sqrt{3}/2)$, and $(-3/4, 0)$ has center $(1/8, \sqrt{3}/8)$ and radius $\sqrt{13}/4 < 1$, but $(-1/2, -\sqrt{3}/2)$ is not in that circle. The circle with antipodal points

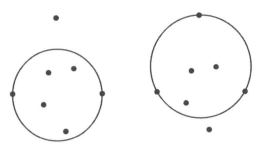

FIGURE 9.17: Left: Current bounding circle and a point that is outside the circle, causing the circle to grow. Right: The new bounding circle, but a point inside the old circle is now outside the new circle, causing a restart of the algorithm.

$(-3/4, 0)$ and $(1, 0)$ has center $(1/8, 0)$ and radius $7/8$, but $(-1/2, \pm\sqrt{3}/2)$ are not in that circle because the distance from those points to the circle center is approximately $1.068 > 7/8$.

An exhaustive approach will produce the answer, but is slow. All triples of points are analyzed. The minimum-area circle containing the three points is either the circumscribed circle or a circle for which two of the three points are antipodal. This is particularly the case when the three points are collinear. The bounding circle of minimum radius in this process is tracked during the analysis. The final circle is the minimum-area circle for the input set. The algorithm is $O(n^3)$.

A more efficient approach is to *grow* a circle to contain the points. The initial circle is the one that contains the first two input points. Each additional point is tested for inclusion in that circle. If all are contained, with some possibly on the circle itself, the initial circle is the one of minimum area. More likely is that one of the remaining points $\mathbf{Q}$ is outside the initial circle. If this happens, the initial circle was not large enough and must be grown to include $\mathbf{Q}$. In fact, $\mathbf{Q}$ will be used as a supporting point for this new circle. A problem, as illustrated by Figure 9.17, is that many point-in-circle tests were performed before $\mathbf{Q}$ was encountered. When the initial circle is modified to a new circle, points in the initial circle might not be in the modified one. Effectively, the algorithm must start over and all the points have to be tested for containment in the new circle.

If the initial circle is the minimum-area circle, that was determined by testing $n - 2 = O(n)$ points. If only m restarts are needed and m is effectively a small constant compared to n, then the algorithm is $O(n)$. However, if m is comparable in size to n, the asymptotic behavior is worse than $O(n)$. To see this, consider the points on a semicircle, $\mathbf{P}_i = (\cos\theta_i, \sin\theta_i)$ where $\theta_i = \pi i/(n-1)$ for $0 \le i < n$. The initial bounding circle is supported by $\mathbf{P}_0$ and $\mathbf{P}_1$. The next point $\mathbf{P}_2$ is outside that circle, so the algorithm is restarted. The new circle is supported by $\mathbf{P}_0$ and $\mathbf{P}_2$. The point $\mathbf{P}_1$ is inside this circle, but $\mathbf{P}_3$ is not. At the i-th iteration, the current bounding circle is supported by $\mathbf{P}_0$ and $\mathbf{P}_i$, points $\mathbf{P}_j$ for $0 < j < i$ are inside the circle, but $\mathbf{P}_{i+1}$ is not; that is, the algorithm must restart each time. The i-th iteration requires i point-in-circle tests. The minimum-area circle is only known once the point $\mathbf{P}_{n-1}$ is reached, and in fact all input points are on the circle. The total number of point-in-circle tests is $\sum_{i=1}^{n-1} = n(n-1)/2 = O(n^2)$. More complicated examples of this type even lead to $O(n^3)$ behavior, just like the exhaustive approach.

Taking a closer look at the semicircle example, suppose that instead of processing the points in the order given, the points are randomly permuted and then processed. For the sake of argument, let $\mathbf{P}_0$ always be a supporting point. If the second point in the permuted set is $\mathbf{P}_j$ where j is nearly $n-1$, the initial circle is quite large. In the ordered case, it took j iterations to get to this circle. In the permuted case, a lot of time was saved. Another point $\mathbf{P}_k$, processed in the permuted case that causes a restart, hopefully will have index k that is larger than $j+1$, again skipping a couple of iterations that were performed in the ordered case. The hope is that the number of restarts, m, is effectively a small constant compared to n, in which case the algorithm is $O(n)$.

The formalization of this approach by E. Welzl is found in [30] and is one of a class of algorithms called *randomized linear algorithms*. The permutation of the input data has *expected time* behavior of $O(n)$. This does not mean that all input data sets will run in this time. It is possible, though not highly probable, that the permutation of the input points leads to an ordering that does cause superlinear behavior. For example, the permutation for the semicircle problem might turn out to be the identity, in which case that example runs in $O(n^2)$ time. Assuming uniform distribution of the permutations, the probability that the permutation is the identity in that example is $1/n!$, a very small number for large n. Of course, other permutations that result in only a couple of transpositions will cause similar slow construction of the circle, but as noted, the expected time is $O(n)$. The concept applies to higher dimensions, of which the 3D problem is discussed next. In d-dimensional space, the expected number of point-in-circle tests is $n(d+1)!$; that is, the asymptotic constant is approximately $(d+1)!$.

The recursive formulation of the algorithm is shown in Listing 9.12.

```
Circle2 MinimumAreaCircle(PointSet input, PointSet support)
{
    if (input is not empty)
    {
        Vector2 P = GetRandomElementOf(input);
        PointSet input' = input - {P};   // Remove P from the input.
        Circle2 C = MinimumAreaCircle(input', support);
        if (P is inside C)
        {
            return C;
        }
        else
        {
```

```
            support' = support + {P}';   // Add P to the support.
            return MinimumAreaCircle(input', support');
        }
    }
    else
    {
        return CircleOf(support);
    }
}
```

Listing 9.12: Pseudocode for a recursive algorithm that computes the minimum-area circle containing points.

A nonrecursive formulation of the algorithm is shown in Listing 9.13.

```
Circle2 MinimumAreaCircle(int N, Point P[N])
{
    randomly permute P[0] through P[N−1];
    Circle2 C = ExactCircle1(P[0]);   // center P[0], radius 0
    support = { P[0] };
    for (int i = 1; i < N; /**/)
    {
        if (P[i] is not an element of support)
        {
            if (P[i] is not contained by C)
            {
                C = Update(P[i], support);
                i = 0;   // Restart the algorithm for the new circle.
                continue;
            }
        }
        ++i;
    }
    return C;
}
```

Listing 9.13: Pseudocode for a nonrecursive algorithm that computes the minimum-area circle containing points.

The Update function has the job of adding P[i] to the support set Support and removing other elements of Support that are no longer supporting points because of the addition of P. Beware that this function must be implemented with care when using floating-point arithmetic. The problem is that old supporting points are tested for containment in various combinations of the supporting points and P[i]. One of those combinations must theoretically contain all the old supporting points. However, numerical rounding errors can cause a situation where none of the combinations appears to contain all the points. Even with the introduction of a numerical epsilon for point-in-circle tests, problems can still occur. One solution is to trap the case when no circle appears to contain all the support points and use the circle for which the offending point outside the circle is closest to that circle, compared to the same offending points for the other circles. The construction of the circles for the various combinations relies on the existence of functions that calculate the minimum-area circle of two points and of three points. An implementation must, of course, provide these.

Another potential problem with floating-point arithmetic is that the update call always assigns a new circle to the current minimum-area circle C. It is possible to encounter a situation where the loop becomes infinite because of a cycle of two points in the support set that are alternately swapped out. The problem is that, in theory, the circle returned by the update has larger radius than the current circle C. However, numerical rounding errors cause the radius of the returned circle to be smaller, which causes the infinite loop. The solution is to replace the innermost block of Listing 9.13 starting with the Update call as shown in Listing 9.14.

```
Circle tmp = Update(P[i],support);
if (tmp.radius > C.radius)
{
    C = tmp;
    i = 0;
    continue;
}
```

Listing 9.14: A modification to make the support update more robust.

Other concerns that an implementation must address include handling duplicate input points and points that are distinct but numerically nearly identical. The construction of circles containing three noncollinear points shows up in an implementation. When computing the circumscribed circle collinear points, the linear system that determines the center and radius is singular. The determinant is zero. When using floating-point arithmetic, points that are nearly collinear can produce a determinant nearly zero, so the implementation should handle this properly instead by discarding the middle point from the three nearly noncollinear and then computing the minimum-area circle containing the remaining two points.

To avoid the rounding problems, the algorithm can be implemented using arbitrary-precision arithmetic. The GTL provides an implementation in class MinimumAreaCircle2. The circle construction uses linear system solvers, so division must be supported. BSRational is the class used for exact computation. Although Listing 9.13 appears to be simple, a lot of details are hidden by the Update call. Functions ExactCircle2 and ExactCircle3 are required to compute the minimum-area circles for 2 or 3 points. Functions UpdateSupport1, Update-Support2 and UpdateSupport3 encapsulate the management of the support set depending on whether the current set has 1, 2 or 3 points. As is true of many geometric algorithms, the devil is in the details when implementing them.

9.5   Minimum-Volume Sphere of Points

The problem of constructing the minimum-volume sphere that contains a set of input points is handled in the same manner as the 2D problem of finding a minimum-area circle containing a set of points discussed in Section 9.4. That section should be read first to understand the intuition and ideas.

To obtain a bounding sphere, the average of the input points can be used as the center of the sphere. The radius is determined by the largest distance from the center to any of the input points. This algorithm is easy to implement but generally does not produce the minimum-volume sphere containing the points.

The randomized algorithm in [30] applies in general dimensions, so it applies to 3D in particular. The recursive formulation is identical to the 2D formulation, but the function computes spheres instead of circles. Listing 9.15 contains the pseudocode.

```
Sphere MinimumVolumeSphere(PointSet input, PointSet support)
{
    if (input is not empty)
    {
        Vector3 P = GetRandomElementOf(input);
        PointSet input' = input - {P};    // Remove P from the input.
        Sphere3 S = MinimumVolumeSphere(input', support);
        if (P is inside S)
        {
            return S;
        }
        else
        {
            support' = support + {P}';    // Add P to the support.
            return MinimumVolumeSphere(input', support');
        }
    }
    else
    {
        return SphereOf(support);
    }
}
```

Listing 9.15: Pseudocode for a recursive algorithm that computes the minimum-volume sphere containing points.

The nonrecursive formulation is also similar to the one in two dimensions. Listing 9.16 contains the pseudocode.

```
Sphere3 MinimumVolumeSphere(int N, Point P[N])
{
    randomly permute P[0] through P[N-1];
    Sphere3 S = ExactSphere1(P[0]);    // center P[0], radius 0
    support = { P[0] };
    for (int i = 1; i < N; /**/)
    {
        if (P[i] is not an element of support)
        {
            if (P[i] is not contained by S)
            {
                S = Update(P[i], upport);
                i = 0;    // Restart the algorithm for the new sphere.
                continue;
            }
        }
        ++i;
    }
    return S;
}
```

Listing 9.16: Pseudocode for a nonrecursive algorithm that computes the minimum-volume sphere containing points.

The same numerical concerns that arise in the 2D problem must be addressed in the 3D problem. See the end of Section 9.4 for those concerns and how to deal with them in an implementation.

To avoid the rounding problems, the algorithm can be implemented using arbitrary-precision arithmetic. The GTL provides an implementation in the class MinimumVolumeSphere3. The sphere construction uses linear system solvers, so division must be supported. BSRational is the class used for exact computation. Although Listing 9.16 appears to be simple, a lot of details are hidden by the Update call. Functions ExactSphere2, ExactSphere3 and Exact-Sphere4 are required to compute the minimum-volume spheres for 2, 3 or 4 points. Functions UpdateSupport1, UpdateSupport2, UpdateSupport3 and Update-Support4 encapsulate the management of the support set depending on whether the current set has 1, 2, 3 or 4 points. As true of many geometric algorithms, the devil is in the details when implementing them.

9.6 Minimum-Area Rectangle of Points

Given a finite set of 2D points, the goal is to compute the minimum-area rectangle that contains the points. The rectangle is not required to be axis aligned, and generally it will not be. It is intuitive that the minimum-area rectangle for the points is supported by the convex hull of the points. The hull is a convex polygon, so any points strictly interior to the polygon have no influence on the bounding rectangle.

Let the convex polygon have counterclockwise-ordered vertices $\mathbf{V}_i$ for $0 \leq i < n$. It is essential to require that the polygon have no triple of collinear vertices. The implementation is simpler with this constraint. An edge of the minimum-area bounding rectangle must be coincident with some edge of the polygon [12]; in some cases, multiple edges of the rectangle can coincide with polygon edges.

In the discussion, the *perp* operator is $\text{Perp}(x, y) = (y, -x)$. If (x, y) is unit length, then the set of vectors $\{(x, y), -\text{Perp}(x, y)\}$ is right-handed and orthonormal.

9.6.1 The Exhaustive Search Algorithm

The input is a set of m points. The convex hull must be computed first, and the output is a set of n points which form a convex polygon. The asymptotic behavior of the convex hull algorithm depends on m, where potentially m is much larger than n. Once the convex polygon is computed, the minimum-area rectangle can be constructed from it.

The simplest algorithm to implement involves iterating over the edges of the convex polygon. For each edge, compute the smallest bounding rectangle that has an edge coincident with the polygon edge. Of all n rectangles, choose the one with the minimum area. To compute the bounding rectangle for an edge, project the polygon vertices onto the line of the edge. The maximum distance between the projected vertices is the width of the rectangle. Now project the polygon vertices onto the line perpendicular to the polygon edge. The maximum distance between the projected vertices is the height of the rectangle. For the specified polygon edge, compute the rectangle axis directions and the extents along those directions. Pseudocode for the algorithm is provided in Listing 9.17.

```
struct Rectangle
{
    Vector2<Real> center, axis[2];
    Real extent[2], area;   // area = 4 * extent[0] * extent[1]
};

Rectangle MinAreaRectangleOfHull(std::<Vector2<Real>> const& polygon)
{
    Rectangle minRect;
    minRect.area = maxReal;   // largest finite floating-point number
    size_t size = polygon.size();
    for (size_t i0 = size - 1, i1 = 0; i1 < size; i0 = i1++)
    {
        Vector2<Real> origin = polygon[i0];
        Vector2<Real> U0 = polygon[i1] - origin;
        Normalize(U0);   // length of U0 is 1
        Vector2<Real> U1 = -Perp(U0);   // length of U1 is 1
        // The projection onto the U0-axis is [min0,max0]. The projection onto
        // the U1-axis is [0,max1]. The extreme min1 = 0 is guaranteed.
        Real min0 = 0, max0 = 0, max1 = 0;
        for (size_t j = 0; j < size; ++j)
        {
            Vector2<Real> D = polygon[j] - origin;
            Real dot = Dot(U0, D);
            if (dot < min0)
            {
                min0 = dot;
            }
            else if (dot > max0)
            {
                max0 = dot;
            }
            dot = Dot(U1,D);
            if (dot > max1)
            {
                max1 = dot;
            }
        }
        Real range0 = max0 - min0;
        Real area = range0 * max1;
        if (area < minRect.area)
        {
            Real average0 = (min0 + max0) / 2, halfMax1 = max1 / 2;
            minRect.center = origin + average0 * U0 + halfMax1 * U1;
            minRect.axis[0] = U0;
            minRect.axis[1] = U1;
            minRect.extent[0] = range0 / 2;
            minRect.extent[1] = max1 / 2;
            minRect.area = area;
        }
    }
    return minRect;
}
```

```
Rectangle MinAreaRectangleOfPoints(
    std::vector<Vector2<Real>> const& points)
{
    // Assumptions for input: points.size() ≥ 3, points[] are not collinear.
    // Assumptions for output: polygon.size() ≥ 3, polygon[] are counterclockwise ordered,
    // no triple of polygon[] is collinear.
    std::vector<Vector2<Real>> polygon;
    ComputeConvexHull(points, polygon);
    return MinAreaRectangleOfHull(polygon);
}
```

Listing 9.17: The $O(n^2)$ algorithm for computing the minimum-area rectangle containing a convex polygon.

The two loops make it clear why the algorithm is $O(n^2)$. If the number of vertices n is small, this is a viable algorithm to use in practice. However, the challenging part of implementing the algorithm using floating-point arithmetic is to compute the convex hull of the points robustly. The minimum-area rectangle construction for a convex polygon is a subproblem for computing the minimum-volume box containing a convex polyhedron [20]. In this context, the $O(n^2)$ behavior can be noticeable, so it is worthwhile to have a faster algorithm available for the 3D setting.

9.6.2 The Rotating Calipers Algorithm

The rotating calipers algorithm is credited to [25]—although that name was not used—for locating antipodal points of a convex polygon when computing the diameter. The algorithm may be found in a source more readily available [22, Theorem 4.18]. The name of the algorithm is due to G. T. Toussaint [27], an article that describes many uses for the rotating calipers.

Applied to the minimum-area rectangle problem, the rotating calipers algorithm starts with a bounding rectangle having an edge coincident with a polygon edge and a supporting set of polygon vertices for the other polygon edges. The rectangle axes are rotated counterclockwise by the smallest angle that leads to the rectangle being coincident with another polygon edge. The new supporting set of vertices is built from the previous set and from the new polygon edge vertices.

In the remainder of this section, a polygon edge $\langle \mathbf{V}_i, \mathbf{V}_{i+1} \rangle$ will be referenced by its indices $\langle i, i+1 \rangle$, the latter still called a polygon edge. The index addition is computed modulo n, the number of vertices of the polygon. The *supporting vertices* for a rectangle form a multiset $S = \{\mathbf{V}_{i_0}, \mathbf{V}_{i_1}, \mathbf{V}_{i_2}, \mathbf{V}_{i_3}\}$, each vertex supporting an edge of the rectangle. They are listed in the order: bottom, right, top and left. One vertex can support two edges, which is why S can be a multiset (duplicate elements). The *supporting indices* are $I = \{i_0, i_1, i_2, i_3\}$.

Figure 9.18 shows the typical configuration for a bounding rectangle with edge coincident to a polygon edge and with three additional supporting vertices. In Figure 9.18, the initial rectangle has its bottom edge supported by

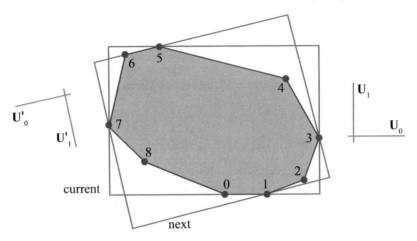

FIGURE 9.18: The typical configuration of a bounding rectangle corresponding to a polygon edge. The polygon vertices are $\mathbf{V}_i$ for $0 \leq i \leq 8$; they are labeled in the figure only with the subscript. The current rectangle has axis directions $\mathbf{U}_0$ and $\mathbf{U}_1$ and is supported by edge $\langle 0, 1 \rangle$. The minimum rotation is determined by edge $\langle 5, 6 \rangle$, which makes it the next edge to process. The next rectangle has axis directions $\mathbf{U}_0'$ and $\mathbf{U}_1'$.

polygon edge $\langle 0, 1 \rangle$; consider the counterclockwise-most vertex $\mathbf{V}_1$ to be the supporting vertex. The right edge of the rectangle is supported by $\mathbf{V}_3$, the top edge of the rectangle is supported by $\mathbf{V}_5$, and the left edge of the rectangle is supported by $\mathbf{V}_7$. The supporting indices for the axis directions $\{\mathbf{U}_0, \mathbf{U}_1\}$ are $I = \{1, 3, 5, 7\}$.

The candidate rotation angles are those formed by $\langle 1, 2 \rangle$ with the bottom edge, $\langle 3, 4 \rangle$ with the right edge, $\langle 5, 6 \rangle$ with the top edge and $\langle 7, 8 \rangle$ with the left edge. The minimum angle between the polygon edges and the rectangle edges is attained by $\langle 5, 6 \rangle$. Rotate the current rectangle to the next rectangle by the angle between the top edge of the current rectangle and $\langle 5, 6 \rangle$. Figure 9.18 shows that the next rectangle has edge coincident with $\langle 5, 6 \rangle$, but the other polygon edges were not reached by this rotation because their angles are larger than the minimum angle. The naming of the next rectangle edge directions is designed to provide the configuration given for the initial rectangle. The new bottom edge is $\langle 5, 6 \rangle$, and its counterclockwise-most vertex $\mathbf{V}_6$ is chosen as the support point for the bottom edge. The new axis directions are $\mathbf{U}_0' = (\mathbf{V}_6 - \mathbf{V}_5)/|\mathbf{V}_6 - \mathbf{V}_5|$ and $\mathbf{U}_1' = -\operatorname{Perp}(\mathbf{U}_0')$. The supporting indices for the axis directions $\{\mathbf{U}_0', \mathbf{U}_1'\}$ are $I' = \{6, 7, 1, 3\}$.

A single loop is used to visit the minimum-area candidate rectangles. The loop invariant is that the axis directions $\{\mathbf{U}_0, \mathbf{U}_1\}$ and supporting indices $I = \{b, r, t, \ell\}$ are ordered by the edges they support: bottom (b), right (r), top (t) and left (ℓ). The polygon edge $\langle b - 1, b \rangle$ is coincident with the rectangle's bottom edge. $\mathbf{V}_b$ is required to be the counterclockwise-most vertex on the bottom edge. In the previous example, $5 \in I$ is selected because of the minimum-angle constraint. The remaining elements of I support the rotated rectangle, so they become elements of I'. The successor of $\mathbf{V}_5$ is $\mathbf{V}_6$, so 6 becomes an element of I'.

9.6.2.1 Computing the Initial Rectangle

Let the polygon vertices be $\mathbf{V}_i$ for $0 \le i < n$. The initial rectangle has its bottom edge coincident with the polygon edge $\langle n-1, 0 \rangle$. By starting with this edge, the modulus argument in the loop indexing is avoided. The initial axis directions are $\mathbf{U}_0 = (\mathbf{V}_0 - \mathbf{V}_{n-1})/|\mathbf{V}_0 - \mathbf{V}_{n-1}|$ and $\mathbf{U}_1 = -\operatorname{Perp}(\mathbf{U}_0)$.

The polygon vertices are converted to the coordinate system with origin $\mathbf{V}_0$ and axis directions $\mathbf{U}_0$ and $\mathbf{U}_1$. A search must be used to find the extreme values of the converted points. An extreme value is typically generated by one vertex, but it is possible that it can be generated by two vertices. In particular, this happens when a polygon edge is parallel to one of the axis directions. Because the assumption is that no triple of vertices is collinear, it is not possible to have three or more vertices attain the extreme value in an axis direction.

When an extreme value occurs twice because a polygon edge is parallel to an axis direction, the supporting point for the corresponding edge of the rectangle is chosen to be the counterclockwise-most vertex of the edge. This is required because the update step computes rotation angles for edges emanating from the supporting vertex, and those edges must have direction pointing to the interior of the rectangle. For example, Figure 9.18 shows that $\langle 0, 1 \rangle$ is parallel to $\mathbf{U}_0$. Choose $\mathbf{V}_1$ as the support vertex and then the emanating edge used in determining the minimal rotation angle is $\langle 1, 2 \rangle$.

Listing 9.18 shows how to compute the smallest rectangle that has an edge coincident with a specified polygon edge. The Rectangle structure stores the axis directions and the supporting indices. The area of the rectangle is also stored for use in the rectangle update when applying the rotating calipers algorithm. This function is used to compute the initial rectangle for the rotating calipers method, but in the implementation it is also used for the exhaustive algorithm.

```
struct Rectangle
{
    Vector2<Real> U[2];
    int index[4];    // order: bottom, right, top, left
    Real area;
};

Rectangle SmallestRectangle(int j0, int j1,
    std::vector<Vector2<Real>> const& vertices)
{
    Rectangle rect;
    rect.U[0] = vertices[j1] - vertices[j0];
    Normalize(rect.U[0]);    // length of rect.U[0] is 1
    rect.U[1] = -Perp(rect.U[0]);
    rect.index = { j1, j1, j1, j1 };
```

```
Vector2<Real> origin = vertices[j1];
Vector2<Real> zero(0, 0);
Vector2<Real> support[4] = { zero, zero, zero, zero };

for (size_t i = 0; i < vertices.size(); ++i)
{
    // Convert vertices[i] to coordinate system with origin vertices[j1] and axis
    // directions rect.U[0] and rect.U[1]. The converted point is v.
    Vector2<Real> diff = vertices[i] - origin;
    Vector2<Real> v = { Dot(rect.U[0], diff), Dot(rect.U[1], diff) };

    // The right-most vertex of the bottom edge is vertices[i1]. The assumption of
    // no triple of collinear vertices guarantees that rect.index[0] is i1, which is the
    // initial value assigned at the beginning of this function. Therefore, there is no
    // need to test for other vertices farther to the right than vertices[i1].

    if (v[0] > support[1][0] ||
        (v[0] == support[1][0] && v[1] > support[1][1]))
    {
        // new right maximum OR same right maximum but closer to top
        rect.index[1] = i;
        support[1] = v;
    }

    if (v[1] > support[2][1] ||
        (v[1] == support[2][1] && v[0] < support[2][0]))
    {
        // new top maximum OR same top maximum but closer to left
        rect.index[2] = i;
        support[2] = v;
    }

    if (v[0] < support[3][0] ||
        (v[0] == support[3][0] && v[1] < support[3][1]))
    {
        // new left minimum OR same left minimum but closer to bottom
        rect.index[3] = i;
        support[3] = v;
    }
}

// The comment in the loop has the implication that support[0] == zero, so the
// height (support[2][1] - support[0][1]) is support[2][1].
Real width = support[1][0] - support[3][0], height = support[2][1];
rect.area = width * height;
}
```

Listing 9.18: Pseudocode for computing the smallest rectangle that has an edge coincident with a specified a polygon edge $\langle i_0, i_1 \rangle$.

Figure 9.19 shows a configuration where two polygon edges are parallel to rectangle edges, in which case two extreme values occur twice.

9.6.2.2   Updating the Rectangle

After computing the initial rectangle, the rotation angle must be determined to obtain the next polygon edge and its corresponding rectangle. The typical configuration of one coincident edge and three other supporting vertices has the essence of the idea for the rectangle update, but other configurations can arise that require special handling. In the discussion, arithmetic

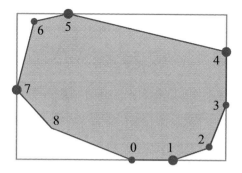

FIGURE 9.19: The supporting vertices of the polygon are drawn as large solid boxes. The edge $\langle 0, 1 \rangle$ supports the bottom edge of the rectangle and $\mathbf{V}_1$ is a supporting vertex. The edge $\langle 3, 4 \rangle$ supports the right edge of the rectangle and $\mathbf{V}_4$ is a supporting vertex.

on the indices into the polygon vertices is performed modulo the number of vertices: the indices $i + j$, $i + j + n$ and $i + j - n$ all refer to the same vertex.

9.6.2.3 Distinct Supporting Vertices

The typical configuration of Figure 9.18 is the simplest to update. A single polygon edge is coincident with the rectangle and has unique vertices supporting the other three edges. The supporting indices are $I = \{i_0, i_1, i_2, i_3\}$. Let $\langle i_j, i_j + 1 \rangle$ be the unique edge that forms the minimum angle with the rectangle edge it emanates from, where $j \in \{0, 1, 2, 3\}$. In Figure 9.18, the vertex from which the edge emanates is $\mathbf{V}_5$ ($j = 2$).

The new coincident edge is $\langle i_j, i_j + 1 \rangle$. The new supporting indices I' are obtained from I by replacing i_j with $i_j + 1$ and by permuting so that i_j is the first (bottom-supporting) vertex: $I' = \{i_j + 1, i_{j+1}, i_{j+2}, i_{j+3}\}$. The additions in the j-subscripts are computed modulo 4.

9.6.2.4 Duplicate Supporting Vertices

It is possible that one polygon vertex supports two rectangle edges, in which case the vertex is a corner of the rectangle. Figure 9.20 shows such a configuration. The current rectangles are the darker of the two and the next rectangles are the lighter of the two.

The selection of the new coincident edge and the update of the supporting indices are performed just as in the case of distinct supporting indices, except there is no minimum-angle candidate edge emanating from the first of the duplicate vertices. In the example of Figure 9.20(a), $I = \{1, 3, 3, 5\}$. $\langle 1, 2 \rangle$ is a candidate edge. There is no edge emanating from the first occurrence of $\mathbf{V}_3$; think of the edge as $\langle 3, 3 \rangle$, which is degenerate. In either case, that supporting vertex is skipped. The edge emanating from the second occurrence

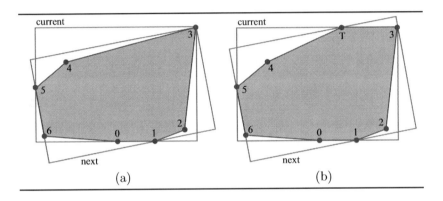

FIGURE 9.20: (a) A configuration where a polygon vertex supports two rectangle edges. $\mathbf{V}_3$ supports the right edge and the top edge. The supporting indices for the current rectangle are $I = \{1,3,3,5\}$. The supporting indices for the next rectangle are $I' = \{6,1,3,3\}$. (b) The duplicate-vertex configuration can be thought of as the limiting case of a distinct-vertex configuration, where $\mathbf{V}_T \to \mathbf{V}_3$. The supporting indices for the current rectangle are $I = \{1,3,T,5\}$. The supporting indices for the next rectangle are $I' = \{6,1,3,T\}$. Now move $\mathbf{V}_T$ to the right so that it coincides with $\mathbf{V}_3$. The current rectangles do not change during this process, but the top edge of the next rectangle of the distinct-vertex case becomes the top edge of the next rectangle of the duplicate-vertex case.

of $\mathbf{V}_3$, namely, $\langle 3,4\rangle$, is a candidate edge. Finally, $\langle 5,6\rangle$ is a candidate edge. As illustrated, the minimum-angle edge is $\langle 5,6\rangle$. I' is generated from I by replacing $\mathbf{V}_5$ by $\mathbf{V}_6$, the counterclockwise-most vertex of the edge, and the vertices are cycled so that $\mathbf{V}_6$ occurs first: $I' = \{6,1,3,3\}$.

9.6.2.5 Multiple Polygon Edges of Minimum Angle

It is possible that the minimum angle is attained by two or more polygon edges. Figure 9.21 illustrates several possibilities.

In Figure 9.21(a), the supporting indices for the current rectangle are $I = \{1,3,4,6\}$. Two polygon edges attain the minimum rotation angle: $\langle 1,2\rangle$ and $\langle 4,5\rangle$. Choosing $\langle 1,2\rangle$ as the new bottom edge, the corresponding support is $\mathbf{V}_2$. Edge $\langle 4,5\rangle$ supports the new top edge and the support is $\mathbf{V}_5$. The new supporting indices are $I' = \{2,3,5,6\}$. To obtain I' from I, the old support $\mathbf{V}_1$ is replaced by the other endpoint $\mathbf{V}_2$ and the old support $\mathbf{V}_4$ is replaced by the other endpoint $\mathbf{V}_5$. No cycling is necessary, because $\mathbf{V}_2$ is the bottom support and 2 is already the first element in I'.

In Figure 9.21(b), the supporting indices for the current rectangle are $I = \{1,2,3,5\}$. Two polygon edges attain the minimum rotation angle: $\langle 1,2\rangle$ and $\langle 3,4\rangle$. Choosing $\langle 1,2\rangle$ as the new bottom edge, the corresponding support is $\mathbf{V}_2$. Edge $\langle 3,4\rangle$ supports the new top edge and the support is $\mathbf{V}_4$. The new supporting indices are $I' = \{2,2,4,5\}$. Observe that $\mathbf{V}_2$ is a duplicate that supports two edges of the rectangle. To obtain I' from I, the old support $\mathbf{V}_1$ is replaced by the other endpoint $\mathbf{V}_2$ and the old support $\mathbf{V}_3$ is replaced by the other endpoint $\mathbf{V}_4$. No cycling is necessary, because $\mathbf{V}_2$ is the bottom support and 2 is already the first element in I'.

In Figure 9.21(c), the supporting indices for the current rectangle are $I = \{1,2,3,4\}$. Two polygon edges attain the minimum rotation angle: $\langle 1,2\rangle$ and $\langle 3,4\rangle$. Choosing $\langle 1,2\rangle$ as the new bottom edge, the corresponding support is $\mathbf{V}_2$. Edge $\langle 3,4\rangle$ supports the new top edge and the support is $\mathbf{V}_4$. The new supporting indices are $I' = \{2,2,4,4\}$. The point $\mathbf{V}_2$ is a duplicate that supports two edges of the rectangle and $\mathbf{V}_4$ is a duplicate that supports the other two edges. To obtain I' from I, the old support $\mathbf{V}_1$ is replaced by the other endpoint $\mathbf{V}_2$ and the old support $\mathbf{V}_3$ is replaced by the other endpoint $\mathbf{V}_4$. No cycling is necessary, because $\mathbf{V}_2$ is the bottom support and 2 is already the first element in I'.

In Figure 9.21(d), the supporting indices for the current rectangle are $I = \{1,3,4,6\}$. Three polygon edges attain the minimum rotation angle; $\langle 1,2\rangle$, $\langle 4,5\rangle$ and $\langle 6,0\rangle$. Choosing $\langle 1,2\rangle$ as the new bottom edge, the corresponding support is $\mathbf{V}_2$. $\langle 4,5\rangle$ supports the new top edge and the support is $\mathbf{V}_5$. $\langle 6,0\rangle$ supports the new left edge and the support is $\mathbf{V}_0$. The new supporting indices are $I' = \{2,3,5,0\}$. To obtain I' from I, the old support $\mathbf{V}_1$ is replaced by the other endpoint $\mathbf{V}_2$, the old support $\mathbf{V}_4$ is replaced by the other endpoint $\mathbf{V}_5$, and the old support $\mathbf{V}_6$ is replaced by the other endpoint $\mathbf{V}_0$.

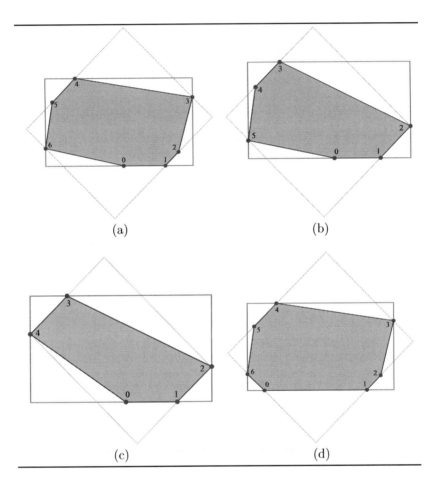

(a)   (b)

(c)   (d)

FIGURE 9.21: (a), (b) and (c) are configurations where two polygon edges attain the minimum angle. (d) is a configuration where three polygon edges attain the minimum angle.

9.6.2.6 The General Update Step

The current rectangle has bottom edge coincident with the polygon edge $\langle \mathbf{V}_{i_0-1}, \mathbf{V}_{i_0} \rangle$. The corresponding axis direction is $\mathbf{U}_0 = (\mathbf{V}_{i_0} - \mathbf{V}_{i_0-1})/|\mathbf{V}_{i_0} - \mathbf{V}_{i_0-1}|$. The perpendicular axis has direction $\mathbf{U}_1 = -\mathrm{Perp}(\mathbf{U}_0)$. The supporting indices are $I = \{i_0, i_1, i_2, i_3\}$. The next rectangle has bottom edge coincident with the polygon edge $\langle i_0' - 1, i_0' \rangle$. The corresponding axis direction is $\mathbf{U}_0' = (\mathbf{V}_{i_0'} - \mathbf{V}_{i_0'-1})/|\mathbf{V}_{i_0'} - \mathbf{V}_{i_0'-1}|$. The perpendicular axis has direction $\mathbf{U}_1' = -\mathrm{Perp}(\mathbf{U}_0')$. The supporting indices are $I' = \{i_0', i_1', i_2', i_3'\}$. It remains to determine I' from I.

Define the set $M \subseteq \{0, 1, 2, 3\}$ as follows: if $m \in M$, then $i_m \in I$ and the polygon edge $\langle i_m, i_m + 1 \rangle$ forms the minimum angle with the rectangle edge supported by $\mathbf{V}_{i_m}$. The index addition $i_m + 1$ is computed modulo n. When M has multiple elements, the minimum angle is attained multiple times. In the example of Figure 9.18, $I = \{1, 3, 5, 7\}$ and $\langle 5, 6 \rangle$ attains the minimum angle, so $M = \{2\}$. In the example of Figure 9.20(a), $I = \{1, 3, 3, 5\}$ and $\langle 5, 6 \rangle$ attains the minimum angle, so $M = \{3\}$. In the examples of Figure 9.21(a-c), $M = \{0, 2\}$. In the example of Figure 9.21(d), $M = \{0, 2, 3\}$.

Start with an empty M. Process each $i_k \in I$ for which $i_{k+1} \neq i_k$, where the index addition $k + 1$ is computed modulo 4. Compute the angle θ_k formed by $\langle i_k, i_k + 1 \rangle$ and the supported rectangle edge, where the index addition $i_k + 1$ is computed modulo n. It is necessary that $\theta_k \geq 0$. If $\theta_k > 0$, store the pair (θ_k, k) in a set A sorted on the angle component. After processing all elements of I, if A is nonempty, then its first element is $(\theta_{k_{\min}}, k_{\min})$. Iterate over A and insert all the index components k into M for which $\theta_k = \theta_{k_{\min}}$. It is possible that A is empty, in which case the original polygon must already be a rectangle.

To generate I' from I, for each $m \in M$ replace i_m by $i_m + 1$, where the index addition is computed modulo n. The resulting multiset of four elements is J. Let m_0 be the smallest element of M. The next rectangle is selected so that its bottom edge is supported by $\langle i_{m_0} - 1, i_{m_0} \rangle$; that is, $i_0' = i_{m_0}$. Cycle the elements of J so that i_{m_0} occurs first, which produces the multiset I'.

9.6.3 A Robust Implementation

The correctness of the algorithm depends first on the input polygon being convex, even when the vertices have floating-point components. Experiments have shown that for moderately large n, generating n random angles in $[0, 2\pi)$, sorting them and then generating vertices $(a \cos \theta, b \sin \theta)$ on an ellipse $(x/a)^2 + (y/b)^2 = 1$ can lead to a vertex set for which not all the generated vertices are part of the convex hull. Of course, this is a consequence of numerical rounding errors when computing the sine and cosine functions and the products by the ellipse extents. If a convex hull algorithm is not applied to these points, the exhaustive algorithm and the rotating calipers algorithm can produce slightly different results.

The correctness of the algorithm is also thwarted by the rounding errors that occur when normalizing the edges to obtain unit-length vectors. These errors are further propagated in the various algebraic operations used to compute the angles and areas.

To obtain a correct result, it is sufficient to use exact rational arithmetic in the implementation. However, normalizing a vector generally cannot be done exactly using rational arithmetic. The normalization can actually be omitted by making some algebraic observations. The minimum-area box can be computed exactly. If an oriented-box representation is needed with unit-length axis directions, this can be achieved at the very end of the process, incurring floating-point rounding errors only in the conversion of rational values to floating-point values. These occur when computing the extents in the axis directions and when normalizing vectors to obtain unit-length directions.

9.6.3.1   Avoiding Normalization

Consider the computation of the smallest rectangle for a specified polygon edge $\langle j_0, j_1 \rangle$. Let $\mathbf{W}_0 = \mathbf{V}_{j_1} - \mathbf{V}_{j_0}$ and $\mathbf{W}_1 = -\operatorname{Perp}(\mathbf{W}_0)$, which are the unnormalized axis directions with $|\mathbf{W}_1| = |\mathbf{W}_0|$. The unit-length axis directions are $\mathbf{U}_i = \mathbf{W}_i / |\mathbf{W}_0|$ for $i = 0, 1$. Let the support vertices be $\mathbf{V}_b$, $\mathbf{V}_r$, $\mathbf{V}_t$ and $\mathbf{V}_\ell$ whose subscripts indicate the edges they support: bottom (b), right (r), top (t) and left (ℓ). The width w and height h of the rectangle are

$$w = \mathbf{U}_0 \cdot (\mathbf{V}_r - \mathbf{V}_\ell), \quad h = \mathbf{U}_1 \cdot (\mathbf{V}_t - \mathbf{V}_b) \tag{9.1}$$

and the area a is

$$a = wh = \frac{(\mathbf{W}_0 \cdot (\mathbf{V}_r - \mathbf{V}_\ell))(\mathbf{W}_1 \cdot (\mathbf{V}_t - \mathbf{V}_b))}{|\mathbf{W}_0|^2} \tag{9.2}$$

Both the numerator and denominator of the fraction for the area can be computed exactly using rational arithmetic when the input vertices have rational components.

The construction of the support vertices uses comparisons of dot products. For example, Listing 9.18 has a loop with comparisons for the current right-edge support. The comparison v[0] > support[1][0] is an implementation of

$$\mathbf{U}_0 \cdot (\mathbf{V}_i - \mathbf{V}_{i_1}) > \mathbf{U}_0 \cdot (\mathbf{V}_{r'} - \mathbf{V}_{i_1}) \tag{9.3}$$

where $\mathbf{V}_{i_1}$ is the origin of the coordinate system, r' is the index into the vertex array that corresponds to the current support vertex and i is the index of the vertex under consideration. The Boolean value of the comparison is equivalent to the one obtained by using unnormalized vectors,

$$\mathbf{W}_0 \cdot (\mathbf{V}_i - \mathbf{V}_{i_1}) > \mathbf{W}_0 \cdot (\mathbf{V}_{r'} - \mathbf{V}_{i_1}) \tag{9.4}$$

The expressions in the comparison can be computed exactly using rational arithmetic.

9.6.3.2 Indirect Comparisons of Angles

The edge must be located that emanates from a support vertex that points inside the rectangle and, of all such edges, forms the minimum angle with the rectangle edge corresponding to the support vertex. Let $\mathbf{D}$ be the unit-length rectangle edge direction using counterclockwise ordering. That direction is $\mathbf{U}_0$ for the bottom edge, $\mathbf{U}_1$ for the right edge, $-\mathbf{U}_0$ for the top edge and $-\mathbf{U}_1$ for the left edge. For an emanating edge originating at support vertex $\mathbf{V}_s$ and terminating at $\mathbf{V}_f$ inside the rectangle, the vector formed by the vertices is $\mathbf{E} = \mathbf{V}_f - \mathbf{V}_s$. The angle θ between $\mathbf{D}$ and $\mathbf{E}$ is determined by

$$\cos\theta = \frac{\mathbf{D} \cdot \mathbf{E}}{|\mathbf{E}|} \tag{9.5}$$

Apply the inverse cosine function (acos) to extract the angle itself. The vector $\mathbf{D}$ is obtained by normalizing one of $\mathbf{U}_0$ or $\mathbf{U}_1$, which cannot generally be done exactly with rational arithmetic. Similarly, the length of $\mathbf{E}$ must be computed, which is effectively another normalization. The inverse cosine function cannot be computed exactly.

Observe that $\theta \in (0, \pi/2]$. The angle must be positive because the edge is directed toward the rectangle interior. If the angle attains the maximum $\pi/2$, then the support vertex must be a corner of the rectangle. Unless the polygon is already a rectangle, there must be at least one other bounding rectangle edge that has an emanating edge with angle smaller than $\pi/2$.

To avoid the inexact computations to obtain θ, instead compute the quantity $|\mathbf{U}_0|^2 \sin^2\theta$, which is a positive and increasing function of θ. Sorting of θ and $|\mathbf{U}_0|^2 \sin^2\theta$ lead to the same ordering. Using some algebra and trigonometry, it can be shown that

$$|\mathbf{U}_0|^2 \sin^2\theta = \frac{(\mathbf{W}_i \cdot \mathrm{Perp}(\mathbf{E}))^2}{|\mathbf{E}|^2} \tag{9.6}$$

where $\mathbf{D} = \pm\mathbf{U}_i$ for some choice of sign and of index i. The fraction on the right-hand side of the equation can be computed exactly using rational arithmetic.

The quantities of equation (9.6) are computed for all emanating edges and stored in an array as they are encountered. The values must be sorted to identify those that attain the minimum value. Although any comparison-based sort will work, swapping of array elements has an associated cost when the values are arbitrary precision rational numbers. The GTL implementation uses an indirect sort by maintaining an array of integer indices into the array of values. The integer indices are swapped as needed to produce a final integer array that represents the sorted values.

9.6.3.3 Updating the Support Information

This is a straightforward implementation of the ideas presented in the general update. The only issue not mentioned yet is that as the rotating calipers algorithm progresses, the polygon edges are not visited sequentially in-order. Moreover, if the polygon has pairs of parallel edge, it is possible that the minimum-area rectangle is computed without visiting all polygon edges.

In the GTL implementation, an array of n Boolean values is maintained, one for each counterclockwise-most vertex of a polygon edge. The Boolean values are all initially false. After the smallest rectangle is computed for a polygon edge $\langle i_0, i_1 \rangle$, the Boolean value at index i_1 is set to true. When the support information is updated during each pass of the algorithm, the Boolean value is tested to see whether the edge has been visited a second time. If it has been visited before, the algorithm terminates; otherwise, there will be an infinite loop.

9.6.3.4   Conversion to a Floating-Point Rectangle

The GTL implementation of the rotating calipers algorithm tracks the minimum-area rectangle via the data structure shown in Listing 9.19.

```
struct Rectangle
{
    Vector2<ComputeType> U[2];
    std::array<int, 4> index;   // order: bottom, right, top, left
    Real sqrLenU0;   // squared length of U[0]
    Real area;
};
```

Listing 9.19: The rectangle data structure for the minimum-area rectangle implementation.

This is slightly modified from that of Listing 9.18; the squared length of $\mathbf{U}_0$ is stored for use throughout the code. The ComputeType is a rational type.

The rectangle center and squared extents can be computed exactly from the minimum-area rectangle minRect as shown in Listing 9.20.

```
Vector2<ComputeType> sum[2] =
{
    rvertices[minRect.index[1]] + rvertices[minRect.index[3]],
    rvertices[minRect.index[2]] + rvertices[minRect.index[0]]
};
Vector2<ComputeType> difference[2] =
{
    rvertices[minRect.index[1]] - rvertices[minRect.index[3]],
    rvertices[minRect.index[2]] - rvertices[minRect.index[0]]
};
Vector2<ComputeType> center = mHalf * (
    Dot(minRect.U[0], sum[0]) * minRect.U[0] +
    Dot(minRect.U[1], sum[1]) * minRect.U[1]) / minRect.sqrLenU0;
Vector2<ComputeType> sqrExtent;
for (int i = 0; i < 2; ++i)
{
    sqrExtent[i] = mHalf * Dot(minRect.U[i], difference[i]);
    sqrExtent[i] *= sqrExtent[i];
    sqrExtent[i] /= minRect.sqrLenU0;
}
```

Listing 9.20: Computations for the rectangle center and squared extents in the minimum-area rectangle implementation.

The array name rvertices stores the rational representation of the floating-point vertices reference in previous parts of this section.

The conversion to the floating-point representation of the box has some loss of precision, but this occurs at the very end, as shown in Listing 9.21.

```
OrientedBox2<Real> itMinRect;    // input-type minimum-area rectangle
for (int i = 0; i < 2; ++i)
{
    itMinRect.center[i] = (Real)center[i];
    itMinRect.extent[i] = sqrt((Real)sqrExtent[i]);

    // Before converting to floating-point, factor out the maximum component using
    // ComputeType to generate rational numbers in a range that avoids loss of
    // precision during the conversion and normalization.
    Vector2<ComputeType> axis = minRect.U[i];
    ComputeType cmax = max(abs(axis[0]), abs(axis[1]));
    ComputeType invCMax = 1 / cmax;
    for (int j = 0; j < 2; ++j)
    {
        itMinRect.axis[i][j] = (Real)(axis[j] * invCMax);
    }
    Normalize(itMinRect.axis[i]);
}

// Quantities accessible through get-accessors in the public interface.
supportIndices = minRect.index;
area = (Real)minRect.area;
```

Listing 9.21: Conversion of the arbitrary-precision rectangle to a floating-point rectangle in the minimum-area rectangle implementation.

If there is a need to continue working with the exact rational data generated by the rotating calipers algorithm rather than the floating-point rectangle, the GTL implementation allows access to it. The GTL implementation is the class MinimumAreaBox2.

9.7 Minimum-Volume Box of Points

Given a finite set of 3D points, the goal is to compute the minimum-volume box that contains the points. The box is not required to be axis aligned, and generally it will not be. It is intuitive that the minimum-volume box for the points is supported by the convex hull of the points. The hull is a convex polyhedron, so any points interior to the polyhedron have no influence on the bounding box. Therefore, the first step of the algorithm is to compute the convex hull of the 3D points.

The minimum-volume box has a face coincident with a hull face or has three mutually orthogonal edges coincident with three hull edges that are mutually orthogonal; see O'Rourke [20]. The implementation consists of two parts. The first part processes all the hull faces and the second part processes all triples of mutually orthogonal edges. As each candidate box is computed, the minimum-volume box is updated to that candidate when the candidate's volume is smaller.

9.7.1 Processing Hull Faces

For a specified hull face, the minimum-volume box with a face coincident to the hull face can be computed by projecting the hull vertices to the plane of the hull face and to a normal line of that plane. Let the normal line have unit-length normal $\mathbf{N}$ which points to the side of the plane on which the hull lies.

Not all hull vertices have to be projected onto the plane. The projection onto the plane is necessary only for an extreme polyline of hull edges. Each edge of this polyline is shared by two hull faces. Let the face normals be $\mathbf{N}_0$ and $\mathbf{N}_1$, both pointing inside the hull, where $\mathbf{N} \cdot \mathbf{N}_0 < 0 \leq \mathbf{N} \cdot \mathbf{N}_1$ or $\mathbf{N} \cdot \mathbf{N}_1 < 0 \leq \mathbf{N} \cdot \mathbf{N}_0$. The extreme polyline is the terminator for the convex hull faces whose inner-pointing normals form an obtuse angle with the plane normal $\mathbf{N}$. The projection of the extreme polyline onto the plane is a convex polygon $\mathcal{P}$.

The projection of the hull vertices onto the normal line is a line segment of length h. This measurement is the height of the bounding box of the hull. The base of the bounding box has area A which must be minimized to obtain the minimum volume $V_{\min} = hA_{\min}$. To accomplish this, the algorithm for computing the minimum-area rectangle of a convex polygon living in a plane can be used. The algorithm uses the method of rotating calipers, which is described in Section 9.6.

The rotating calipers algorithm is typically described as if real-valued arithmetic is used; all computations involved are exact. When using floating-point arithmetic, numerical rounding errors can lead to incorrect results. In the algorithm for computing the minimum-area rectangle containing points, arbitrary-precision arithmetic was used to compute the minimum-area rectangle exactly. However, the algorithm depends on selecting an edge with (not necessarily unit-length) direction $\mathbf{U} = (u_0, u_1)$ and using an orthogonal vector of the same length, $\mathbf{U}^\perp = (-u_1, u_0)$, to avoid normalization of vectors by an inverse square root operation. The fact that $|\mathbf{U}| = |\mathbf{U}^\perp|$ was sufficient to allow the use of exact arithmetic.

In the 3D case, the projection of a point onto a plane can use exact arithmetic. If $\mathbf{P}_0$ is a point in the plane and $\mathbf{P}_1$ is a point off the plane, and if $\mathbf{N}$ is a (not necessarily unit length) normal vector for the plane, the projection of $\mathbf{P}_1$ is

$$\mathbf{Q}_1 = \mathbf{P}_1 - \frac{\mathbf{N}}{|\mathbf{N}|} \cdot (\mathbf{P}_1 - \mathbf{P}_0)\frac{\mathbf{N}}{|\mathbf{N}|} = \mathbf{P}_1 - \frac{\mathbf{N} \cdot (\mathbf{P}_1 - \mathbf{P}_0)\mathbf{N}}{|\mathbf{N}|^2} \tag{9.7}$$

The right-hand side can be computed exactly using arbitrary-precision arithmetic. To apply the 2D rotating calipers algorithm, the direction of an edge of the convex polygon $\mathcal{P}$ (the projection of the extreme polyline) is $\mathbf{U}$, which is not necessarily unit length and is in the plane, so $\mathbf{N} \cdot \mathbf{U} = 0$. To obtain a vector in the plane perpendicular to $\mathbf{U}$, use $\mathbf{U}^{\perp} = \mathbf{N} \times \mathbf{U}$. However, $|\mathbf{U}^{\perp}| = |\mathbf{N}||\mathbf{U}|$, which is not equal to $|\mathbf{U}|$ when $|\mathbf{N}| \neq 1$. In the attempt to use exact arithmetic, one can only build normals $\mathbf{N}$ using cross products of two linearly independent edge directions, but such vectors are generally not unit length.

9.7.1.1 Comparing Areas

The rotating calipers algorithm must be modified for 3D different from what was done for 2D. In fact, the extreme polyline does not have to be projected explicitly to $\mathcal{P}$. The polyline can be worked with directly to generate for each edge a set of vectors, not necessarily unit length. The edge direction is the difference of endpoints, say, $\mathbf{E}$. Compute $\mathbf{U}_1 = \mathbf{N} \times \mathbf{E}$ and $\mathbf{U}_0 = \mathbf{U}_1 \times \mathbf{N}$. The vectors $\mathbf{N}$, $\mathbf{U}_0$, and $\mathbf{U}_1$ are mutually perpendicular. The lengths are $|\mathbf{N}|$, $|\mathbf{N}||\mathbf{E}|$ and $|\mathbf{N}|^2|\mathbf{E}|$, respectively. $\mathbf{U}_0$ acts as the convex polygon edge direction and $\mathbf{U}_1$ acts as a direction perpendicular to $\mathbf{U}_0$ that is also in the plane of the convex polygon. The difference of the extreme points of the extreme polyline in the direction $\mathbf{U}_0$ is named $\boldsymbol{\Delta}_0$. The difference of the extreme points of the extreme polyline in the direction $\mathbf{U}_1$ is named $\boldsymbol{\Delta}_1$. The area of the rectangle that has an edge of $\mathcal{P}$ coincident with $\mathbf{E}$ is

$$A = \left(\frac{\mathbf{U}_0}{|\mathbf{U}_0|} \boldsymbol{\Delta}_0 \right) \left(\frac{\mathbf{U}_1}{|\mathbf{U}_1|} \boldsymbol{\Delta}_1 \right) = \frac{(\mathbf{U}_0 \cdot \boldsymbol{\Delta}_0)(\mathbf{U}_1 \cdot \boldsymbol{\Delta}_1)}{|\mathbf{N}|^3 |\mathbf{E}|^2} \qquad (9.8)$$

The numerator can be computed exactly using arbitrary precision arithmetic. The denominator has an odd power of the length of $|\mathbf{N}|$, which requires a square root operation that leads to approximation error. But $|\mathbf{N}|$ is a constant regardless of the edge of $\mathcal{P}$ being processed. Rather than comparing areas as the calipers are rotated for $\mathcal{P}$, instead compare the values of

$$A' = \frac{(\mathbf{U}_0 \cdot \boldsymbol{\Delta}_0)(\mathbf{U}_1 \cdot \boldsymbol{\Delta}_1)}{|\mathbf{N}|^2 |\mathbf{E}|^2} \qquad (9.9)$$

The denominator of this fraction can be computed exactly. Effectively, values of $|\mathbf{N}|A$ are compared without ever having to compute $|\mathbf{N}|$ directly.

9.7.1.2 Comparing Volumes

Once the minimum-area rectangle for $\mathcal{P}$ is selected, the volume of the bounding box must be computed in order to update the current minimum-volume box. Let the difference of the extreme points in the direction $\mathbf{N}$ be named $\boldsymbol{\Delta}$. The volume of the bounding box is

$$V = A \left(\frac{\mathbf{N}}{|\mathbf{N}|} \cdot \boldsymbol{\Delta} \right) = \frac{(\mathbf{U}_0 \cdot \boldsymbol{\Delta}_0)(\mathbf{U}_1 \cdot \boldsymbol{\Delta}_1)(\mathbf{N} \cdot \boldsymbol{\Delta})}{|\mathbf{N}|^4 |\mathbf{E}|^2} \qquad (9.10)$$

The numerator and denominator can be computed exactly using arbitrary precision arithmetic; therefore, the minimum-volume box is updated as each face of the hull is processed without any approximation or rounding errors.

9.7.1.3 Comparing Angles

In the 2D rotating calipers algorithms, the minimum angle had to be computed between a convex polygon edge and the bounding rectangle edge from which the polygon edge emanated. The search for the minimum angle was performed without computing the angles explicitly, instead using quantities that are equivalently ordered with the angles. The same is true in the 3D setting. In this case $0 \geq \theta_0 < \theta_1 \leq \pi/2$ if and only if $\sin^2 \theta_0 < \sin^2 \theta_1$. If $\mathbf{D}$ is the direction for a rectangle edge, $\mathbf{E}$ is the direction for a convex polygon edge, and $\mathbf{U}_0 = (\mathbf{N} \times \mathbf{E}) \times \mathbf{N}$, all not necessarily unit length vectors, then $\mathbf{D}$ and $\mathbf{U}_0$ are in the projection plane and have an angle θ between them. From basic geometry,

$$|\mathbf{D} \times \mathbf{U}_0| = |\mathbf{D}||\mathbf{U}_0| \sin \theta \tag{9.11}$$

which can be solved for

$$\sin^2 \theta = \frac{|\mathbf{D} \times \mathbf{U}_0|^2}{|\mathbf{D}|^2 |\mathbf{U}_0|^2} \tag{9.12}$$

The numerator and denominator can be computed exactly using arbitrary precision arithmetic.

9.7.2 Processing Hull Edges

For n edges, the algorithm is theoretically $O(n^3)$ because there are three nested loops when searching for three mutually orthogonal edges. This sounds expensive, but in practice the constant of the asymptotic order analysis is small because in most cases, a dot product is computed between two edge directions, the edges are deemed not orthogonal and then the innermost loop is skipped. The pseudocode is shown in Listing 9.22.

```
array<Vertices> vertices(m);   // m vertices in the hull
array<Edges> edges(n);   // n edges in the hull
Vector3 U[3], sqrlen;
for (int i2 = 0; i2 < n; ++i2)
{
    U[2] = vertices[edges[i2].V[1]] − vertices[edges[i2].V[0]];
    for (int i1 = i2 + 1; i1 < n; ++i1)
    {
        U[1] = vertices[edges[i1].V[1]] − vertices[edges[i1].V[0]];
        if (Dot(U[1], U[2]) != 0)
        {
            continue;
        }
        sqrlen[1] = Dot(U[1], U[1]);

        for (int i0 = i1 + 1; i0 < n; ++i0)
        {
            U[0] = vertices[edges[i0].V[1]] − vertices[edges[i0].V[0]];
            if (Dot(U[0], U[1]) != 0)
            {
                continue;
            }
            sqrlen[0] = Dot(U[0], U[0]);

            // The three edges are mutually orthogonal. To support exact arithmetic
            // for volume computation, replace U[2] by a parallel vector.
```

```
U[2] = Cross(U[0], U[1]);
sqrlen[2] = sqrlen[0] * sqrlen[1];

// Compute the extremes of the scaled projections onto the axes using
// vertices(0) as the origin. The vectors umin and umax store the
// componentwise extremes in the U[] directions.
Vector3 umin(0,0,0), umax(0,0,0);
for (int j = 0; j < m; ++j)
{
    Vector3 diff = vertices[j] - vertices[0];
    for (int k = 0; k < 3; ++k)
    {
        Numeric dot = Dot(diff, U[k]);
        if (dot < umin[k])
        {
            umin[k] = dot;
        }
        else if (dot > umax[k])
        {
            umax[k] = dot;
        }
    }
}

// Compute the volume of the box.
Vector3 delta = umax - umin;
Numeric ratio0 = delta[0] / sqrlen[0];
Numeric ratio1 = delta[1] / sqrlen[1];
Numeric volume = ratio0 * ratio1 * delta[2];

// Compare the volume to the current candidate's volume for the
// minimum-volume box and update if necessary.
<code goes here>;
        }
    }
}
```

Listing 9.22: Pseudocode for finding three mutually orthogonal edges and computing the volume of the enclosing box supported by those edges.

9.7.3 Conversion to a Floating-Point Box

The GTL implementation of the rotating calipers algorithm tracks the minimum-volume box via the data structure shown in Listing 9.23.

```
struct Box
{
    Vector3<ComputeType> P, U[3];
    ComputeType sqrLenU[3], range[3][2], volume;
};
```

Listing 9.23: The box data structure for the minimum-volume box implementation.

The ComputeType is a rational type. The point P acts as an origin and the box axis directions (not necessarily unit length) are U[]. The squared lengths of the axis directions are sqrLenU[]. The range member stores the extreme values for the three directions, the minimum stored in range[][0] and the maximum stored in range[][1].

The conversion to the floating-point representation of the box has some loss of precision, but this occurs at the very end, as shown in Listing 9.24.

```
OrientedBox3<Real> itMinBox;   // input-type minimum-volume box
ComputeType half(0.5), one(1);

// Compute the box center exactly.
for (int i = 0; i < 3 ++i)
{
    ComputeType average =
        half * (minBox.range[i][0] + minBox.range[i][1]);
    center += (average / minBox.sqrLenU[i]) * minBox.U[i];
}

// Compute the squared extents exactly.
Vector3<ComputeType> sqrExtent;
for (int i = 0; i < 3; ++i)
{
    sqrExtent[i] = half * (minBox.range[i][1] - minBox.range[i][0]);
    sqrExtent[i] *= sqrExtent[i];
    sqrExtent[i] /= minBox.sqrLenU[i];
}

for (int i = 0; i < 3; ++i)
{
    itMinBox.center[i] = (InputType)center[i];
    itMinBox.extent[i] = sqrt((InputType)sqrExtent[i]);

    // Before converting to floating-point, factor out the maximum component
    // using ComputeType to generate rational numbers in a range that avoids
    // loss of precision during the conversion and normalization.
    Vector3<ComputeType> const& axis = minBox.U[i];
    ComputeType cmax = std::max(std::abs(axis[0]), std::abs(axis[1]));
    cmax = std::max(cmax, std::abs(axis[2]));
    ComputeType invCMax = one / cmax;
    for (int j = 0; j < 3; ++j)
    {
        itMinBox.axis[i][j] = (InputType)(axis[j] * invCMax);
    }
    Normalize(itMinBox.axis[i]);
}

// Quantity accessible through the get-accessor in the public interface.
volume = (Real)minBox.volume;
```

Listing 9.24: Conversion of the arbitrary-precision box to a floating-point box in the minimum-volume box implementation.

If there is a need to continue working with the exact rational data generated by the algorithm rather than the floating-point rectangle, the GTL implementation allows access to it. The GTL implementation is the class MinimumVolumeBox3.

Bibliography

[1] Selim G. Akl and Godfried T. Toussaint. Efficient convex hull algorithms for pattern recognition applications. In *Proc. 4th Int'l Joint Conf. on Pattern Recognition*, pages 483–487, Kyoto, Japan, 1978.

[2] A.M. Andrew. Another efficient algorithm for convex hulls in two dimensions. *Info. Proc. Letters*, 9:216–219, 1979.

[3] IEEE Standards Association. "IEEE 754-2008 - IEEE Standard for Floating-Point Arithmetic". https://standards.ieee.org/standard/754-2008.html. Accessed September 5, 2019.

[4] A. Bowyer. Computing dirichlet tessellations. *The Computer Journal*, 24(2):162–166, 1981.

[5] Thomas H. Cormen, Charles E. Leiserson, and Ronald L. Rivest. *Introduction to Algorithms*. The MIT Press, Cambridge MA, 1990.

[6] Richard W. Cottle, Jong-Shi Pang, and Richard E. Stone. *The Linear Complementarity Problem*. Academic Press, San Diego, CA, 1992.

[7] Mark de Berg (editor), Otfried Cheong, Marc van Kreveld, and Mark Overmars. *Computational Geometry: Algorithms and Applications (2nd edition)*. Springer, Berlin, 3rd edition, April 2018.

[8] David Eberly. "The Laplace Expansion Theorem: Computing the Determinants and Inverses of Matrices". https://www.geometrictools.com/Documentation/LaplaceExpansionTheorem.pdf, August 2008.

[9] H. Edelsbrunner and R. Seidel. Voronoi diagrams and arrangements. *Disc. Comp. Geom.*, 1:25–44, 1986.

[10] D. A. Field. Implementing Watson's algorithm in three dimensions. In *Proceedings of the Second Annual Symposium on Computational Geometry*, pages 246–259, New York, NY, USA, 1986. Association for Computing Machinery.

[11] James D. Foley, Andries van Dam, Steven K. Feiner, and John F. Hughes. *Computer Graphics: Principles and Practice*. Addison–Wesley, Reading, MA, 1990.

[12] H. Freeman and R. Shapira. Determining the minimum-area encasing rectangle for an arbitrary closed curve. In *Communications of the ACM*, volume 18, pages 409–413, New York, NY, July 1975.

[13] Joel Friedman. "Linear Complementarity and Mathematical (Non-linear) Programming". http://www.math.ubc.ca/~jf/courses/340/pap. pdf, April 1998.

[14] Gene H. Golub and Charles F. Van Loan. *Matrix Computations*. Johns Hopkins University Press, 3rd edition, October 1996.

[15] Roger A. Horn and Charles R. Johnson. *Matrix Analysis*. Cambridge University Press, Cambridge, England, 1985.

[16] Donald E. Knuth. *The Art of Computer Programming: Seminumerical Algorithms*, volume 2. Addison–Wesley, Reading, Massachusetts, 3rd edition, 1997.

[17] Ron Levine. "Collision of Moving Objects". On the game developer algorithms list at http://www.sourceforce.net, November 2000.

[18] Y-D. Liang and B. A. Barsky. A new concept and method for line clipping. *ACM Transactions on Graphics*, 3(1):1–22, 1984.

[19] Wolfram MathWorld and Eric Weisstein. "Vieta's Substitution". http:// mathworld.wolfram.com/VietasSubstitution.html. Accessed September 7, 2019.

[20] Joseph O'Rourke. Finding minimal enclosing boxes. *International Journal of Computer & Information Sciences*, 14(3):183–199, 1985.

[21] Joseph O'Rourke. *Computational Geometry in C*. Cambridge University Press, Cambridge, England, 2nd edition edition, 1994.

[22] Franco P. Preparata and Michael Ian Shamos. *Computational Geometry: An Introduction*. Springer–Verlag, New York, 1985.

[23] E. L. Rees. Graphical discussion of the roots of a quartic equation. *The American Mathematical Monthly*, 29(2):51–55, February 1922.

[24] C++ Reference. "Floating-Point Environment". https://en.cppreference. com/w/cpp/numeric/fenv. Accessed August 20, 2019.

[25] Michael Ian Shamos. "Computational Geometry". PhD thesis, Yale University, 1978.

[26] Jonathan Richard Shewchuk. "Stabbing Delaunay Tetrahedralizations". http://www.cs.cmu.edu/~jrs/papers/stab.ps, 2000.

[27] Godfried Toussaint. Solving geometric problems with the rotating calipers. In *Proceedings of the IEEE*, Athens, Greece, 1983.

[28] Robert J. Vanderbei. "Linear Programming: Chapter 3 - Degeneracy". http://www.princeton.edu/~rvdb/522/Fall13/lectures/lec3.pdf, September 2013.

[29] D. Watson. Computing the n-dimensional Delaunay tessellation with applications to Voronoi polytopes. *The Computer Journal*, 24(2):167–172, 1981.

[30] Emo Welzl. Smallest enclosing disks (balls and ellipsoids). *Lecture Notes in Computer Science, New Results and New Trends in Computer Science*, 555:359–370, 1991.

[31] Wikipedia. "Abel–Ruffini Theorem". https://en.wikipedia.org/wiki/Abel-Ruffini_theorem. Accessed September 7, 2019.

[32] Wikipedia. "Convex Hull Algorithms". https://en.wikipedia.org/wiki/Convex_hull_algorithms. Accessed September 7, 2019.

[33] Wikipedia. "Cubic Equation". https://en.wikipedia.org/wiki/Cubic_equation. Accessed September 7, 2019.

[34] Wikipedia. "Descartes' Rule of Signs". https://en.wikipedia.org/wiki/Descartes%27_rule_of_signs. Accessed September 7, 2019.

[35] Wikipedia. "Discriminant". https://en.wikipedia.org/wiki/Discriminant. Accessed September 7, 2019.

[36] Wikipedia. "Eigenvalue Algorithm". https://en.wikipedia.org/wiki/Eigenvalue_algorithm. Accessed September 7, 2019.

[37] Wikipedia. "Geometrical Properties of Polynomial Roots". https://en.wikipedia.org/wiki/Geometrical_properties_of_polynomial_roots. Accessed September 7, 2019.

[38] Wikipedia. "Methods of Computing Square Roots". https://en.wikipedia.org/wiki/Methods_of_computing_square_roots#Babylonian_method. Accessed September 7, 2019.

[39] Wikipedia. "Quadratic Fields". https://en.wikipedia.org/wiki/Quadratic_field. Accessed September 7, 2019.

[40] Wikipedia. "Quartic function". https://en.wikipedia.org/wiki/Quartic_function. Accessed September 7, 2019.

[41] Wikipedia. "Quartic Roots: Ferrari's Solution". https://en.wikipedia.org/wiki/Quartic_function#Ferrari's_solution. Accessed September 7, 2019.

[42] Wikipedia. "Real-root Isolation". https://en.wikipedia.org/wiki/Quadratic_field. Accessed September 7, 2019.

[43] Wikipedia. "Sturm's Theorem". https://en.wikipedia.org/wiki/Sturm%27s_theorem. Accessed September 7, 2019.

[44] Wolfram Research, Inc. *Mathematica 12.0.* Wolfram Research, Inc., Champaign, Illinois, 2019.

Index

2-point compactification of real numbers, 261

algebraic number, 5, 6, 170, 210
aligned box, 239

binary scientific conversions, 52–62
    BSNumber to BSNumber, 60–62
    BSNumber to floating-point, 54–57
    BSRational to BSNumber, 57–60
    floating-point to BSNumber, 53–54
binary scientific notation, 47
binary scientific number, 48–51
    addition, 49
    multiplication, 50–51
    subtraction, 50
binary scientific performance, 62–69
binary scientific rational, 51–52
    addition and subtraction, 52
    multiplication and division, 52

C++ comparison operators, 98
cone definitions, 259–260
convex hull of 2D points, 301–315
    Akl and Toussaint heuristic, 302
    divide-and-conquer method, 301, 309–315
    gift wrapping, 301
    Graham's algorithm, 301
    incremental construction, 301–309
    quick hull, 301
convex hull of 3D points, 315–321
    divide-and-conquer method, 318–321

    incremental construction, 315–318
    terminator, 315–316
    visibility cone, 315–316
convex quadratic programming problem, 177
    eliminate unconstrained variables, 177–178
    reduce dimension for equality constraints, 178–179

Delaunay empty circumhypersphere constraint, 325
Delaunay triangulation, 321
    circumcircle, 321
    circumscribed hypersphere, 323
    edge-triangle manifold mesh, 323
    incremental construction, 322–327
    insertion polygon, 323
    intrinsic dimension, 323
    linear walk, 323
    supersimplex, 326
    supertriangle, 323
distance query
    box-box, 190–191, 195–197

eigendecomposition
    2×2 symmetric matrix, 169–170, 279–281
    3×3 symmetric matrix, 6–22, 170–172, 299
elimination theory, 170
ellipse
    conversion to quadratic equation, 278–279
    rational form, 278

standard form, 278
ellipsoid
    conversion to quadratic equation,
        294
    rational form, 294
    standard form, 293
error-free implementation
    defined, 1
estimate rational, 103–104
estimate square root of rational, 104–
        107
expression tree, 74–76, 78
extended real numbers, 71

fast Fourier transform, 127, 166
find-intersection
    ellipse-ellipse, 282–292
    ellipsoid-ellipsoid, 294–299
    interval-interval, 265–266
    line-box, 254–255
    line-cone, 262–264
    line-sphere, 237
    ray-box, 255–257
    ray-cone, 273–274
    ray-sphere, 237–238
    segment-box, 257–259
    segment-cone, 274–276
    segment-sphere, 238–239
find-intersection query, 209
floating-point, 1, 35–46
    biased exponent, 36, 39
    binary encoding, 35–41
        double, 39–41
        float, 36–39
    exponent, 36, 39
    flush-to-zero semantics, 35
    fused multiply-add, 167
    normal, 37, 39
    not-a-number (NaN), 35, 36, 129
        quiet, 35, 36
        signaling, 35, 36
    overflow, 21, 35
    payload, 35, 36
    rounding modes, 35, 41–46

round-to-nearest-ties-to-away, 41–
        43
round-to-nearest-ties-to-even, 41–
        42, 58, 73, 74
round-toward-negative, 41, 44,
        58, 73, 74
round-toward-positive, 41, 44,
        58, 73, 74, 104
round-toward-zero, 41, 43, 58
rounding support in C++, 44–46
signed infinities, 35, 36, 38, 40
signed zeros, 36, 38, 40
subnormal, 37, 39, 129
trailing significand, 37, 39
underflow, 21, 35
function
    C^1-continuity, 135
    convex, 110, 138
    domain, 71
    evaluation, 128–131
    range, 71
    removable singularity, 128
    Taylor series, 128

Gauss-Seidel method, 166–168
Gaussian elimination, 165
GTL
    APInterval, 73
    BSNumber, 49–52
    BSPrecision, 65
    BSRational, 52
    Cone, 261
    FPInterval, 73, 78
    IEEEBinary, 53
    IEEEBinary32, 38, 46
    IEEEBinary64, 40, 46
    LCPSolver, 187
    MinimumAreaBox2, 349
    MinimumAreaCircle2, 333
    MinimumVolumeBox3, 354
    MinimumVolumeSphere3, 335
    QFNumber, 103
    SolveQuadratic, 286, 288
    SolveQuartic, 285, 287
    SymmetricEigensolver3x3, 11

UIntegerAP32, 62
UIntegerFP32<N>, 62

intersection
 tangential, 283
 transverse, 283
interval
 closed, 71
 half-closed, 71
 half-open, 71
 open, 71
interval arithmetic, 71–88
 operations, 72–79
 primal queries, 81–88
  abstraction, 81
  ToCircumcircle, 84
  ToCircumsphere, 87
  ToLine, 82
  ToPlane, 85
  ToTetrahedron, 86
  ToTriangle, 82
 signs of determinants, 79–80

Lagrange multipliers, 209, 280
Lemke's method, 175–177, 179–189
 avoid cycles by perturbations, 187–189
 dictionary, 180
  balanced, 180
  feasible, 180
  terminal, 180
 minimum-ratio rule, 182, 186
 variable
  basic, 180
  complementary, 180
  nonbasic, 180
Liang–Barsky clipping, 250–254
linear complementarity problem, 176, 179
linear programming problem, 177, 179

marching squares, 297, 299
matrix
 characteristic polynomial, 6, 17, 162
 determinant

 2 × 2, 67, 80
 3 × 3, 67, 80
 4 × 4, 67, 80
 Laplace expansion theorem, 67
 norm, 161
 skew-symmetric, 128
 spectral radius, 161
method of separating axes, 209–222
 2D convex polygon, 213
 3D convex polygon, 217
 3D convex polyhedron, 215
 contact of moving 2D triangles, 223–229
 contact of moving 3D triangles, 229–233
 contact set, 222
 moving convex objects, 218–222
minimum-area circle of points, 329–333
 randomized algorithm, 331
 support point, 329
 Welzl's algorithm, 331
minimum-area rectangle of points, 335–349
 exhaustive search, 335–337
 rotating calipers, 337–345
  supporting indices, 337
  supporting vertices, 337
minimum-volume box of points, 349–354
 O'Rourke's algorithm, 349
minimum-volume sphere of points, 333–335
Minkowski sum, 240, 243, 244, 246, 247

oriented box, 239

perp operator, 335
polynomial
 Abel–Ruffini theorem, 142, 160
 bounding interval for root, 160
 Carmichael and Mason bound, 162
 Cauchy's bound, 162

cubic roots, 147–151
depressed, 144
discriminant, 142–144
elementary symmetric, 145
fundamental theorem of algebra,
        141
maximization, 112–113, 121–125
minimax, 131
modular operation, 5, 170, 210
monic, 144
multiple root, 141
multiplicity of root, 141
pair of complex conjugate roots,
        142
quadratic roots, 145–147
quartic
    biquadratic, 153
    Ferrari's solution, 153
    Vieta's substitution, 153
quartic roots, 152–160
resultant, 121–123, 143, 161
root bounding by derivatives,
        161–162
root bounding by Sturm se-
        quences, 162–163
root counting, 160
root counting by Descartes' rule
        of signs, 164
root isolation, 164
    Akritas and Collins bisection,
        164
    Budan's theorem, 164
    Obreschkoff and Ostrowski the-
        orem, 164
    Uspensky's theorem, 164
    Vincent's theorem, 164
simple root, 141
Sylvester matrix, 143
Taylor, 131

quadratic field
    arithmetic operations, 95–96, 101–
        102
    1-root addition, 95
    1-root division, 95

1-root multiplication, 95
1-root subtraction, 95
2-root addition, 102
2-root division, 102
2-root multiplication, 102
2-root subtraction, 102
composition, 102–103
defined, 95
estimate 1-root, 107–110
estimate 2-root, 110–125
estimate square root d, 96
estimation, 103–125
multiple square roots, 101–103
non-square-free d, 96–97
number, 95
    1-root, 107, 109
    2-root, 5, 110, 111, 209, 242,
        246, 248
    comparison, 98–101
rational d, 97
square-free d, 95
square-free vector length, 97
used for eigendecomposition, 170
quadratic programming problem, 176

randomized algorithm, 304
robust implementation
    defined, 1
root finding
    bisection, 104, 114–115, 131–135
        arbitrary-precision, 133, 134
    Hybrid Newton-Bisection, 138–
        139
    Newton's method, 104, 108, 111–
        115, 135–138
        arbitrary-precision, 139
    polynomial, 141–164

simplex algorithm, 179
simplexification, 321
stack
    SignDeterminant size, 80
    ToCircumcircle size, 84
    ToCircumsphere size, 88
    ToLine size, 82

ToPlane size, 85
ToTetrahedron size, 87
ToTriangle size, 83
set size via compiler, 69

tableau method, 179
test-intersection
ellipse-ellipse, 279–282
ellipsoid-ellipsoid, 294
line-box, 240–243
line-sphere, 234–235
ray-box, 243–246
ray-sphere, 235
segment-box, 246–249
segment-sphere, 236
test-intersection query, 209
triangle-box, 199–201
triangle-cylinder, 191–192, 197–199, 201–208
tetrahedralization, 321
triangulation, 321

variable
auxiliary, 180
Voronoi diagrams, 321